Transfer of Movables in Europe

National Reports on the Transfer of Movables in Europe

Volume 2:
England and Wales, Ireland, Scotland, Cyprus

edited by

Wolfgang Faber / Brigitta Lurger

Schriften zur Europäischen Rechtswissenschaft /
European Legal Studies / Etudes juridiques européennes

Band II / Volume II / Volume II

European Legal Studies Institute, Osnabrück
Molengraaff Institute for Private Law, Utrecht
Amsterdam Institute for Private Law
Institute of European and Comparative Law, Oxford
Institut für Zivilrecht, Ausländisches und Internationales Privatrecht, Graz

sellier.

**european law
publishers**

Schriften zur Europäischen Rechtswissenschaft /
European Legal Studies / Etudes juridiques européennes

herausgegeben

im European Legal Studies Institute, Osnabrück
von Christian von Bar

im Molengraaff Institute for Private Law, Utrecht
von Ewoud Hondius

im Amsterdam Institute for Private Law
von Martijn W. Hesselink

im Institute of European and Comparative Law, Oxford
von Stefan Vogenauer

im Institut für Zivilrecht, Ausländisches und Internationales Privatrecht, Graz
von Brigitta Lurger

This series of national reports is published with the financial support of:
Bundesministerium für Wissenschaft und Forschung (Vienna);
Swiss Institute of Comparative Law (Lausanne);
Land Salzburg;
Evers-Marcic-Stiftung an der Rechtswissenschaftlichen Fakultät Salzburg.

ISBN 978-3-86653-096-6

The Deutsche Nationalbibliothek lists this publication in the Deutsche Nationalbiblio-
grafie; detailed bibliographic data are available in the Internet at http://dnb.d-nb.de.

© 2009 by sellier. european law publishers GmbH, Munich.

Design: Sandra Sellier, Munich. Production: Karina Hack, Munich. Typeface:
Goudy Old Style and Goudy Sans from Linotype. Printing and binding: AZ Druck
und Datentechnik GmbH, Kempten. Printed on acid-free, non-ageing paper.
Printed in Germany.

Preface

This is the second volume of a series of national reports on basic issues concerning the acquisition and loss of ownership of movable assets. The series is planned to cover 27 European legal systems, distributed over six volumes, and appears as a by-product of the research activities of the Graz & Salzburg working group 'Transfer of Movables' within the 'Study Group on a European Civil Code'.[1] Starting with general property law issues like the concepts of ownership and possession employed in the respective legal systems, and the related means of protection, the reports primarily deal with the 'derivative' transfer of ownership, but extend to good faith acquisition from a non-owner, acquisitive prescription, processing and commingling, and further related issues. Corresponding to the working group's task within the Study Group, the reports are generally restricted to movable assets and basically leave aside fiduciary transfers, such as transfers for security purposes. After all, they do, however, not only cover mere property law issues, but also much of the related law of obligations, enforcement law and insolvency law – in a generally accessible language, *i.e.* English.[2]

This second volume covers European common law countries and mixed legal systems, reflecting the numerous interactions between the legal developments in these countries. Literature and abbreviations are listed in common tables at the end of this volume. The texts of statutory provisions discussed in this book can largely be obtained via internet.[3]

Publishing the whole series of national reports would not be possible without generous support by a number of institutions. Financial support has been given by the Austrian Ministry of Science and Research (Bun-

---

1   For further information on this project, see *Lurger*, Introduction to the Project 'Transfer of Movables': Organisational Framework, Basic Issues and Goals, in: Faber/Lurger (eds.), Rules for the Transfer of Movables – A Candidate for European Harmonisation or National Reforms? (2008), 1.

2   The concept of these reports is further described in the preface to the first volume of that series: Faber/Lurger (eds.), National Reports on the Transfer of Movables in Europe – Volume I: Austria, Estonia, Italy, Slovenia (2008).

3   For England/Wales and Scotland, see http://www.statutelaw.gov.uk; for Ireland, see *e.g.* http://www.irishstatutebook.ie. For Cyprus, no full translations of statutes into English have been available, but the wording of important statutory provisions is usually reflected in the report.

desministerium für Wissenschaft und Forschung), the Swiss Institute of Comparative Law (Lausanne), the Land Salzburg and the Evers-Marcic-Stiftung an der Rechtswissenschaftlichen Fakultät der Universität Salzburg. The editors wish to express their gratitude to all these institutions. We also wish to thank Mrs Monika Lammer for formatting the manuscripts and, in particular, our colleague Ernest Weiker, LLB, for all the editorial work he has carried out.

September 2008
Salzburg and Graz   *Wolfgang Faber*
                                                           Brigitta Lurger

List of Contributors

Karolina Anastasiou
Advocate

David L Carey Miller
Professor Emeritus of Property Law, University of Aberdeen;
Visiting Senior Research Fellow, Institute for Advanced Legal Studies
(IALS), London

Malcolm M Combe
Solicitor, Tods Murray LLP, Edinburgh

Sandra Frisby
Baker & McKenzie Associate Professor and Reader in Company and
Commercial Law at the University of Nottingham

Caterina Gardiner
Lecturer in Law, National University of Ireland, Galway

Michael Jones
Barrister, Gray's Inn Tax Chambers, London

Stephanie Laulhé Shaelou
Assistant professor, Law Department, University of Nicosia, Cyprus

Andrew J M Steven
Lecturer in Law, University of Edinburgh

Stelia Stylianou
Advocate

Scott Wortley
Lecturer in Law, University of Edinburgh

Contents

National Report on the Transfer of Movables in England and Wales

Sandra Frisby
Michael Jones

Table of Contents

Part II:
Derivative acquisition

5. Which system of transfer is used?

6. Transfer or acquisition by means of indirect representation

Part I:
Basic information on English property law

I. Basic information on property law

1.1. General basics

The English law of property can be found in a combination of statute law and case law (also termed 'common law'). The full text of the various statutory provisions in the following text can be found on the Website of the Office of Public Sector Information: see http://www.opsi.gov.uk/acts.htm. The term 'common law' habitually embraces three meanings, all three of which are used in this report.[1] The first describes a system that is contrasted with a civilian jurisdiction. The second meaning of the term is used as a synonym for judge-made law or case law as opposed to statute law. The third, and perhaps the most complicated, describes one half of a fundamental division between two distinct bodies of rules that underlies English law: the common law and equity.[2] This division developed in the mediaeval period of English history and continues to this day.[3]

The potential for injustice in the early common law system lead to petitions being made by unhappy litigants to the King in council for relief; in time it became customary for these petitions to be heard by the Chancellor in a Court of Chancery. From the 17th century onwards this initially extraordinary jurisdiction was transformed, under a succession of chancellors, into a more systemised and rigid corpus of rules. Under the Judicature Acts of 1873 and 1875 the procedural, but not substantive, rules of the two jurisdictions were fused into one Supreme Court of Judicature, which could administer both law and equity. The same basic court structure persists today.

---

[1] It is hoped that the context will make clear which meaning is intended.

[2] What follows is an extremely simplified and contracted summary. Reference should be made to leading texts in this area. See, for example, Maitland, *Equity: A Course of Lectures* (1969); Meagher, Heydon and Leeming, *Meagher, Gummow and Lehane's Equity: Doctrines and Remedies* (2002); McGhee, *Snell's Equity* (2005).

[3] This is in spite of some *dicta* to the contrary; see, for example, *United Scientific Holdings Ltd v Burnley Borough Council* [1978] AC 904 *per* Lord Diplock, and Hanbury 'The Future of Equity' (1987) 93 LQR 529.

Equity has intervened variously across the legal landscape, but has had perhaps its most profound influence in the field of property law, particularly with the trust. There appears to be a *numerus clausus* of proprietary rights,[4] although such a restriction emerges from case law rather than from any statute; accordingly, as a judge-made principle, it is theoretically open to the courts to vary it.

The distinction between rights *in rem* and those that are merely *in personam* is one upheld in English law and focuses upon against whom rights are exigible.[5] The contrast between the two classes is never sharper than upon insolvency,[6] a point at which point 'property' rights are tested, and so it is no surprise that several cases exploring the *in rem/in personam* boundary are set in an insolvency context.[7]

1.2.   The notion of ownership

In contrast to the Roman idea of *dominium*, English common law does not recognise 'ownership' as absolute entitlement. The modern view of the content of the concept is that formed by Professor Honoré in his essay 'Ownership', and is broadly regarded as 'the greatest possible interest in a thing which a mature legal system of law recognises'.[8]

The concept consists of a bundle of various 'incidents'. None of the incidents are individually necessary, although they may be together sufficient, for a person to be designated 'owner' of a given thing and they may be listed as follows: the right to possess, the right to use, the right to manage, the right to the income of the thing, the right to the capital (including the right to destroy), the right to security, the rights or incidents of transmissibility and absence of term, the prohibition of harmful use, liability to execution, and the incident of residuarity.[9] The thesis en-

---

4   Swadling, 'The Proprietary Effect of a Hire of Goods', in *Interests in Goods* (1998), citing in support, *inter alia*, *Hill v Tupper* (1863) 2 H & C 121. See also, Nolan, 'Equitable Property', (2006) 122 LQR 232 at p 260 *et seq.*

5   See Pretto-Sakmann, *The Boundaries of Personal Property: Shares and Sub-shares* (2005).

6   See generally, Goode, 'Ownership and Obligation in Commercial Transactions', [1987] LQR 433.

7   For an argument advocating a re-drawing of this conceptual boundary see Pretto-Sakmann above, n 5; for a discussion about whether the boundary actually exists see Rotherham, *Proprietary Remedies in Context* (2002) at pp 54-55.

8   Honoré, 'Ownership', in Guest (ed), *Oxford Essays in Jurisprudence* (1961), at p 108.

9   *Ibid* at p 113. It is important to note that Honoré is concerned here with the incidents necessary in a system that recognises a 'liberal notion of ownership', (*i.e.* private ownership); he identifies that a system that did not admit these incidents might still have a version of ownership, albeit modified in respect of the 'liberal notion'.

visages that the individual incidents of ownership can be transferred from the bundle to other parties without the transferee becoming the 'owner': Hence the idea that ownership equates with having the residue of rights in the thing,[10] the incidents vesting in the 'owner' once any lesser interests granted in respect of the thing terminate.

1.3. The relativity of ownership

One constraint, or, arguably, benefit, of the adversarial system of English law is that since questions of proprietary entitlement fall to be determined only between the litigants in the case title is viewed as a relative, rather than absolute, matter.[11] This has the advantage of avoiding the evidential difficulties of essentially proving a negative, *i.e.* that no one else has a better title to the asset.[12]

A further feature of the relative system is the concept of 'possessory title',[13] a form of entitlement that flows from a presumption that the person in possession is the owner.[14] The finder of a thing, for example, acquires a title that is good against the whole world, save the person who lost the chattel. In terms of relativity, it is submitted that the finder is the 'owner' as regards everyone but the person whose thing he found.[15] It has been suggested that where, for example, the finder (P2) is dispossessed by another (P3), who in turn is dispossessed by someone else (P4), who does not derive his title through P3's original wrong, the finder (P2) is not able to maintain an action against P4 because when the finder loses possession he also loses title.[16] It is submitted that this conclusion is not, however, inescapable. Possession is only *prima facie* evidence of ownership. Where some other explanation for it is presented (subject to *ius tertii* rules, as to which see below) that presumption is rebutted. Unless and until that occurs the possessor of a thing looks to all the world like its owner, and should therefore enjoy all the incidents of ownership, includ-

---

[10] Goode, above n 6, p 31.

[11] See *Waverley Borough Council v Fletcher* [1996] QB 334 at p 345 *per* Auld LJ; also, *Armory v Delamirie* (1722) 1 Str 505; *Costello v Chief Constable of Derbyshire Constabulary* [2001] 1 WLR 1437; *Jaroo v A-G of Trinidad and Tobago* [2002] 1 AC 871.

[12] See further, Fox, 'Relativity of Title at Law and Equity', [2006] CLJ 330 at p 339.

[13] *Costello v Chief Constable of Derbyshire Constabulary* [2001] 1 WLR 1437; *Jaroo v A-G of Trinidad and Tobago* [2002] 1 AC 871 at p 881 *per* Lord Hope.

[14] See, Pollock and Wright, *An Essay in Possession in the Common Law* (1888) at p 25.

[15] See, for example, *Parker v British Airways Board* [1982] at p 1017 *per* Donaldson LJ.

[16] Goode, *Commercial Law* (2004) at pp 32-33. Fox, above n 12, pp 344-351. This is said to be based on the principle that possession, like ownership, is indivisible, and so no more than two legal titles can exist in goods at the same time.

ing the right to immediate possession. This conclusion is not inconsistent with the principle that ownership is indivisible: The *prima facie* nature of the finder's ownership is predicated on there being none able to prove a better title, *i.e.* there is only one 'owner' recognised by the law. Alternatively, if a litigant, who can prove a superior title, successfully challenges the finder, there will again be recognised only one owner. Thus, ownership enjoys, if that is the correct term, an involved and complicated relationship with possession. On the one hand ownership is said to carry with it the 'right to possess' the thing owned. On the other possession might be described as, *prima facie*, a root of title.[17]

1.4. Protection of property rights

English law protects property rights using torts rather than property law. Two such torts now cover a field that was once occupied by several actions.[18] They are trespass to goods and conversion, with the latter of the two occupying the most ground. The vindication of rights of 'ownership' is achieved by means of the tort of conversion, with the claimant's right to sue being based on his right to possess. This perhaps helps to explain why, in the absence of a need to do so, English law has never really worked out a legal definition of ownership, concentrating instead on possession.

1.4.1. Conversion

(a) General

The ambit of the tort is such that provision of comprehensive definition is commonly recognised to be impossible, but a description often cited is from *Lancashire v Yorkshire Railway Co v MacNicoll*:[19]

> 'Dealing with goods in a manner inconsistent with the right of the true owner amounts to a conversion, provided that it is also established that there is also an intention on the part of the defendant in so doing to deny the owner's right or to assert a right which is inconsistent with the owner's right.'

---

[17] See *Crossley Vaines on Personal Property* (1973) at p 45.
[18] For details see Rogers, *Winfield & Jolowicz on Tort* (2002), chapter 17.
[19] (1918) 88 LJ (KB) 601 at p 605 *per* Atkin J.

Another, more recent explanation was along the following lines:[20]

> 'Conversion of goods can occur in so many different circumstances that framing a precise definition of universal application is well nigh impossible. In general, the basic features of the tort are threefold. First, the defendant's conduct was inconsistent with the rights of the owner (or other person entitled to possession). Second, the conduct was deliberate, not accidental. Third, the conduct was so extensive an encroachment on the rights of the owner as to exclude him from use and possession of the goods. The contrast is with lesser acts of interference. If these cause damage they may give rise to claims for trespass or in negligence, but they do not constitute conversion.'

A close reading of these quotations reveals that conversion is a tort of strict liability and that the necessary 'intention' refers only to *the act* that amounts to a denial of the true owner's rights, not to the denial itself. It is enough that a defendant wilfully does an act inconsistent with the rights of the owner: There is no need for him to even know of any 'better' rights to the chattel. It has been said that the tort of conversion, with its strict liability, performs a similar function to the action of *vindicatio*, which is absent from English common law.[21] Only tangible movable property can be converted, including coins and notes although their currency makes conversion actions difficult to maintain (see below). The allegedly tortious act must be seriously inconsistent with the owner's rights, so that not every kind of interference will generate liability in conversion. The following types of activity have grounded actions in conversion:

(a) Disposition – The clearest example of the tort comes in the form of some kind of disposition of the chattel, either in the form of sale or gift. Both the disponor and the disponee attract potential liability since both act in a manner inconsistent with the owner's rights, although in this situation the so-called exceptions to *nemo dat* may become an important shield for the disponee.[22] The mere entry into a contract of sale without delivery of the chattel will not amount to a tort,[23] unless a *nemo dat* ex-

---

[20] *Kuwait Airways Corp v Iraqi Airways Co (No 3)* [2002] 2 AC 883 at p 1084 *per* Lord Nicholls.

[21] 'Common law' here is used here in its narrow sense, *i.e.* as opposed to equity, where an action akin to the *vindicatio* does exist. See Birks (ed), *Laundering and Tracing* (1995).

[22] See below at section 10: The exceptions act not as a defence in the strict sense, but instead provide the disponee with superior title to that of the claimant. In a similar way a *bona fide* purchaser of the legal title for value without notice will be protected from conversion claims made by equitable owners (see below at section 5.2.2).

[23] *Lancashire Wagon Co v Fitzhugh* (1861) 6 H & N 502; and now s. 11(3) of the Torts (Interference with Goods) Act 1977.

ception applies, and thus a transfer of title in the asset, occurs even before delivery.[24]

(b) Asportation – A taking of the chattel will usually amount to a trespass but there must be an intention to exercise permanent or temporary dominion for it to amount to a conversion. In *Fouldes v Willoughby*[25] the defendant removed the claimant's horses from a ferry and led them ashore, but a lack of any intention to exercise any dominion over the horses meant that there could be no liability in conversion. It has been held that even a temporary taking can amount to a conversion.[26]

(c) Damage, destruction or loss – A minor act of damage is said not to amount to a conversion, it may however be a trespass. On the other hand, destruction of the goods, or perhaps more accurately, destruction of title to goods (*i.e.* through mixing, *etc.*), will amount to a conversion.[27] The act must of course be deliberate and it is clear that negligent loss or destruction does not generate liability in conversion at common law.[28] One case that stands out from the general position is *Moorgate Mercantile Credit v Finch*,[29] in which the defendant smuggled watches using a hired car, which was accordingly confiscated. The Court of Appeal held that the defendant must be taken to have intended the forfeiture of the car, which was the natural and probable consequence of his conduct, and that, therefore, his act amounted to conversion.

(d) Detention – Mere possession of another's chattel is not a sufficient assertion of dominion to amount to a conversion, nor, without more, is a refusal by the possessor of a chattel to meet a demand for its return made by anyone with superior title. In the latter situation an action in detinue would be available but for its abolition by the 1977 Act, which did not bring this instance of liability within the scope of conversion. Absence of liability in this case might therefore be regarded as a very small chink in the protection of proprietary rights. However, repeated refusals to return the item when asked by someone with a bet-

---

[24] *Lancashire Wagon Co v Fitzhugh.*

[25] (1841) 8 M & W 540.

[26] *The Playa Larga* [1983] 2 Lloyd's Rep 171 at p 181 *per* Ackner LJ.

[27] For example, *Lancashire and Yorkshire Railway Co v MacNicoll* (1918) 88 LJ KB 601, where the defendant poured the claimant's carbolic acid into a tank, mistakenly believing it to be the creosote that he had ordered. The identity of the acid was lost in the resultant mixture, and therefore so too was the claimant's title to it.

[28] *Williams v Gesse* (1837) 3 Bing NC 849. However, a negligent bailee could be liable in detinue at common law. Section 2 of TIGA 1977 abolished that tort and expressly extended the range of conversion to cover such a situation (s. 2(2)).

[29] [1962] 1 QB 701.

ter right to possession could amount to a sufficient assertion of entitlement to give rise to liability in conversion.[30]

(e) Misdelivery – A bailee who loses a chattel through negligence will be liable in conversion under s. 2(2) of the 1977 Act, and a bailee who delivers to the wrong recipient will also be liable even if that occurs by mistake.[31]

(b)   Who is liable?

Since one chattel can be subject to several dispositions there may be several defendants to an action in conversion. The position is complicated further if one of those dealing with the asset is an agent or intermediary acting on another's behalf. To assert the title of another may still be a conversion: All the tort requires is the assertion of a title other than that of the true owner. There are however exceptions to the rule that a lack of knowledge of a superior title is no defence. One exception stems from the case of *Hollins v Fowler*,[32] in which it was said that:

> 'On principle, one who deals with goods at the request of the person who has the actual custody of them, in the bona fide belief that the custodier is the true owner, or has the authority of the true owner, should be excused for what he does if the act is of such a nature as would be excused if done by the authority of the person in possession, if he was a finder of the goods, or entrusted with their custody.'

The effect of the exception and the authorities from which it springs is difficult to define precisely, but one interpretation[33] is that if the agent or intermediary simply returns the goods to the apparent owner in good faith or delivers the goods on the apparent owner's instructions without knowledge that a transfer of title is involved then he is safe from liability in conversion. However, if the agent knows that a question of title transfer is involved, as were he to effect a sale of the asset, then the role that

---

[30] See *Kuwait Airways Corp v Iraqi Airways Co* [2002] 2 AC 883 at pp 1084-1085 *per* Lord Nicholls. An intention to keep the goods is required, which can be demonstrated by a refusal to deliver up the chattel when asked. This is not, however, the only way of showing such an intention. Wilful detention and an intention to deny the true owner might also suffice: *Clayton v Le Roy* [1911] 2 KB 1031.

[31] *Devereux v Barclay* (1819) 2 B & Ald 702.

[32] (1875) LR 7 HL 757 at pp 766-767 *per* Blackburn J.

[33] *Marcq v Christie, Manson & Woods Ltd* [2003] 3 All ER 561.

the agent plays in the disposition will be important.[34] This test is extremely artificial but the persons it attempts to shield from liability, *i.e.* those carrying out purely ministerial tasks with the goods, seem deserving of protection.

Another category of defendant entitled to protection is the 'involuntary bailee' who is the victim of fraud.[35] He will be protected where he has acted reasonably and without negligence in handing the goods received over to the fraudster.[36]

1.4.2. Entitlement to sue

Deep down conversion is concerned with protecting ownership and so entitlement to sue in conversion is grounded not just in possession but also in the right to immediate possession.[37] An equitable owner who has neither possession of the chattel nor a right to immediate possession of it cannot sue in conversion.[38] Nor can such an owner whose interest has been extinguished by the acquisition of the chattel by a *bona fide* purchaser of the legal title for value without notice.[39]

An owner will be unable to maintain an action in conversion if he has bailed a chattel for a term.[40] In this situation he is out of actual possession and has no right to immediate possession. The bailee, however, may sue.[41] Moreover, an owner without standing to sue in conversion may have a special action on the case for damage done to his reversionary interest in bailed goods.[42] It should be noted however that if the bailee has already recovered from the defendant then the bailor's action for damage to his reversionary interest is barred.[43]

---

[34] *Barker v Furlong* [1891] 2 Ch 172; *R H Willis & Sons v British Car Auctions Ltd* [1978] 1 WLR 438.

[35] *Elvin and Powell Ltd v Plummer Roddis Ltd* (1933) 50 TLR 158.

[36] *Ibid.* However, where the defendant assumes control of the item he runs the risk of liability: see *Hiort v Bott* (1874) LR 9 Ex 86.

[37] *Gordon v Harper* (1796) 7 TR 9.

[38] *MCC Proceeds Inc v Lehman Brothers International (Europe)* [1998] 4 All ER 675.

[39] *Ibid.* See below at section 10 on good faith acquisitions.

[40] On bailment see below at section 2.3.

[41] *The Winkfield* [1902] P 42, (an action in negligence, but the rules are the same as for conversion), in which it was held that the bailee could recover in full but had a duty to account to his bailor for the amount recovered over and above the value of the his interest.

[42] *Mears v London & South Western Railway Co* (1862) 22 CB(NS) 850; see also s. 1(1)(d) of TIGA 1977.

[43] *Nicolls v Bastard* (1835) 2 Cr M & R 659.

A bailor for a term may reacquire the right to immediate possession where his bailor commits an act that amounts to a repudiation of the bailment, for example a wrongful sale of goods.[44] A bailor at will does have the right to immediate possession since he can recall the asset at any time, and because his bailee has possession he too has standing to sue. Should either of the two recover damages from the defendant then the other's action is barred.[45] Just as a bailee must account to his bailor for the damages recovered minus the value of the bailee's interest, if any, in the goods converted, so too must a bailor, who has recovered damages, account for any interest his bailee had in the goods.[46]

(a)   Jus tertii

At common law the general rule was that it was no defence to point to another who had a better right to possession than the claimant. An exception was where the claimant was relying on a right to immediate possession,[47] in which case the *jus tertii* could be pleaded. However, as an exception to the exception, a defendant bailee was estopped from setting up a *jus tertii* defence against a claim by his bailor,[48] unless evicted by someone with title superior to that of the bailor. One of the consequences of this rule and the relative nature of title under English law is that someone who had dishonestly acquired an asset was able to maintain an action in conversion, with the defendant unable to object.[49]

Fortunately these rules were altered by s. 8 of the 1977 Torts (Interference With Goods) Act, which attempted to ameliorate many of the procedural difficulties that can arise in a convoluted conversion action. That section abolished the general rule that *jus tertii* could not be pleaded, (s. 8(1)), and goes on to require that the claimant give particulars of his

---

[44]   *Fenn v Bittleston* (1851) 7 Ex 152; *North Central Wagon & Finance Co v Graham* [1950] 2 KB 7.

[45]   *Nicolls v Bastard* (1835) 2 Cr M & R 659; *O'Sullivan v] Williams* [1992] 3 All ER 385.

[46]   *O'Sullivan v Williams* [1992] 3 All ER 385.

[47]   *Leake v Loveday* (1842) 4 M & G 972. One explanation of the rule relies upon the concept of peaceful possession and aim of deterring potential breaches of the peace, which might arise from defendants dispossessing others on the basis of a *jus tertii*. However, where the claimant is out of possession this policy does not apply; since conversion is a denial of title the defendant is permitted to attack the basis upon which a claimant makes his claim (*i.e.* right to immediate possession); see, Rogers, above n 18, at p 607, n 42.

[48]   *Biddle v Bond* (1865) 6 B & S 225.

[49]   See for example, *Armory v Delamirie* (1722) 1 Stra 505.

title and to identify others who claim an interest in the goods in question (s. 8(1)(a) and (b)). In addition, it allows a defendant to apply to join other parties to the action for the purpose of establishing whether there exists another who has either a better title than the claimant or a claim against the defendant, making him doubly liable (s. 8(2)(c)); if a party fails to appear on an application within 8(2)(c) the court may deprive him of any right of action against the defendant on any terms. These rules are designed to group all potential players into one action.

Further procedural rules in s. 7 of the Act attempt to avoid double liability: where there are two or more claimants, relief shall be such as to avoid double liability (s. 7(2)); where a single claimant recovers from a defendant, the claimant is liable to account over to another person having a right to claim to such an extent as will avoid double liability (s. 7(3)). If the claimant has accounted to the other right holder then the defendant has a complete defence to any action brought by further claimants in respect of the same conversion (s. 5(4)). Moreover, where a claimant has been fully compensated then his title is extinguished (s. 5(1)), which means that he is prevented from subsequently suing other defendants for converting the same chattel. As further protection, where a defendant has been the subject of a double claim, any claimant who is accordingly unjustly enriched is required by s. 7(4) to make restitution to the defendant.

(b)   Remedies

The measure of damages in a successful claim is generally the market value of the chattel at the time it was converted.[50] For this reason the action has been described as the 'forced judicial sale of the chattel to the defendant'.[51] In addition to this, damages for consequential losses, if not too remote, will also be available.[52] Such losses might include post-conversion increases in value of the chattel,[53] which in effect shifts the date on which the chattel is valued from date of conversion to date of judgment. If the defendant returns the undamaged chattel to the claim-

---

[50] *General and Finance Facilities v Cooks Cars (Romford) Ltd* [1963] 1 WLR 644 at p 649 *per* Diplock LJ. In addition, any doubt caused by the defendant about the value of the chattel will be resolved in the claimant's favour.

[51] Prosser (1957) Cornell LR 168.

[52] For the appropriate remoteness test to be applied see *Kuwait Airways Corpn v Iraqi Airways Co* [2002] 2 AC 883 at 1096 *per* Lord Nicholls, in which a distinction is made according to the behaviour of the defendant.

[53] *The Playa Larga* [1983] 2 Lloyd's Rep 171.

ant before judgment then nominal damages only will be appropriate,[54] and the principle ought to be the same where the chattel would have been lost in any event.[55] Special rules of quantification of damages appear to apply to hire-purchase cases: see *Wickham Holdings Ltd v Brook House Motors Ltd*.[56]

There is also a hint that in the appropriate situation the claimant may be able to recover on a restitutionary basis any gain the defendant enjoyed from the chattel, although this possibility is yet to be fully explored.[57] Where the defendant is in possession or control of the chattel three possible forms of judgment are available (s. 3). They are (a) an order for delivery of the goods and for payment of any consequential damages; (b) an order for delivery of the goods with the alternative of paying damages for the goods together in either case with consequential losses; or (c) damages (s. 3(2)). Relief under s. 3(2)(a) is at the discretion of the court and the claimant may choose between the other two (s. 3(3)(b)). No guidance is given on how to exercise this discretion but resort to old case law on the topic reveals that specific restitution of goods would not be ordered where damages would be an adequate remedy.[58]

(c)   Improvements to the chattel

Where a person who has converted a chattel has improved it and in doing so has increased the value of the chattel the 1977 Act will prevent the claimant from being unjustly enriched. By s. 6(1), if the defendant/improver acted in the mistaken but honest belief that he had a good title to them then an allowance shall be made for the increase in value attributable to him when damages are being assessed.[59] Similarly, where the defendant is not the improver but an direct or indirect disponee from him then s. 6(2) permits a reduction in damages on the same basis as in subsection (1); this is done on the basis that the price paid by the purchaser will reflect the value of improvements made to the chattel. Again the purchaser here must have acted in good faith. Furthermore, under s. 3(7),

---

54 *Roberts v Wyatt* (1810) 2 Taunt 268.

55 *Kuwait Airways*, above n 52 at p 1090 *per* Lord Nicholls.

56 [1967] 1 WLR 295.

57 *Kuwait Airways*, above n 52 at p 1093 *per* Lord Nicholls.

58 *Cohen v Roche* [1927] 1 KB 169: Antique chairs held to be ordinary items of commerce in the hands of claimant dealer, therefore recovery *in specie* not available.

59 It has been suggested that where an improver has not acted in good faith he may still benefit from an allowance by application of the common law on the presumption that the Act did not change the common law areas it left untouched: see *Clerk and Lindsell* on *Torts* (2006), para 17-97 and *Munro v Willmott* [1949] 1 KB 295.

where an order is made for the return of the chattel it may be a condition of the order that any allowance available in respect of ss. 6(1) or (2) is paid to the defendant before the chattel is delivered up.

(d)   Limitation periods

In theory, where a chattel is not destroyed its owner would never want for a defendant to sue if a new time limit ran from every converting act. In order to prevent this from occurring s. 3(1) of the Limitation Act 1980 provides that a six year time limit will begin to run from the first act of conversion, provided the 'owner' does not regain possession in the meantime. In addition there is a form of acquisition of absolute title by virtue of s. 3(2) that is akin to the doctrine of adverse possession found in the law of real property.

There is an exception to this position where the owner has been dispossessed by a thief. In this case the time limit only runs from the time of the first good faith purchase of the chattel (s. 4). There does not appear to be a time limit on the bringing of an action in respect of the theft or in respect of any conversion related to the theft.

(e)   Self-help

For obvious reasons, use of self-help is not encouraged, as is arguably reflected by the lack of clear guidelines on the topic in either case law or statute. Recaption, *i.e.* the extra-judicial re-taking of a chattel, is possible but must be carried out using only reasonable means. It seems that reasonable force may be used even where the wrongful possessor has not committed trespass against the recaptor. Moreover, it appears that an owner might be permitted to enter onto the land occupied by another in order to re-take the chattel, not only where the occupier of the land has committed a trespassory taking as against the recaptor, but also perhaps in other cases.[60] In addition, English criminal law permits a person to defend his property. Reference should be made to specialist texts on criminal law for detail.

---

[60]   See Bridge, *Personal Property* Law (2002) at pp 77-78.

2. Possession

2.1. Notion of possession

Although the right to possession is merely one of the rights that make up the concept of 'ownership', and so in this sense is subordinate to it, in everyday practice possession is far more important than 'ownership'.[61] Since the owner of the thing is said to have the *best* right to possession of it (unless he has transferred it, as to which see below), this approach indirectly protects ownership, as we have seen in the case of conversion.

2.2. Elements of possession

The legal concept of possession has two limbs: there must be factual control exercised over the chattel, coupled with an intention to exclude all others from such control (the *animus possidendi*). Since the extent to which factual control can be exercised over an asset depends upon the type of chattel in question, what is necessary in order to satisfy the first limb will vary according to the circumstances of any given case. An example often given to illustrate this is *Young v Hitchens*,[62] in which the claimant had encompassed a shoal of fish almost entirely with his net. All that remained was for a 'stop net' to be lowered onto the only gap in the net from which the fish might escape. Before this could be done the defendant rowed his boat into a position that rendered the operation impossible. To the question whether the claimant was in possession of the fish, the court held that the very strong possibility that the claimant would completely capture the fish was not sufficient to create a right of possession against the defendant; complete capture was necessary.

This can be compared with a very different type of chattel: a sunken freighter in *The Tubantia*.[63] The claimants worked on the wreck whenever the elements allowed for a time totalling a matter of days. During that time they had carried out some work buoying the wreck and had also extracted a small amount of cargo from it at disproportionate expense. When the defendants attempted to interfere with this work and to claim possession of the wreck the claimants brought a claim alleging that the defendants' acts amounted to a trespass and/or an unlawful interference with the wreck. In deciding that the defendants had indeed wrongfully

---

61 This is because, as well as being a matter of law, possession, unlike ownership, is a matter of fact that can be proved with appropriate evidence. This lends itself to resolving disputes in practice.

62 (1884) 6 QB 606.

63 [1924] P 78.

interfered with the wreck, Sir Henry Duke agreed that the claimants had possession of it. The nature and location of the chattel were factors that the judge clearly took into account, holding that 'there was the use and occupation of which the subject matter was capable' and that 'unwieldy as the wreck was, they were dealing with it as a whole'.[64] Thus the amount and type of control necessary to demonstrate *de facto* possession is an elastic requirement that varies according to the subject matter of the action.

It is said that possession can be enjoyed through another where that other has factual control of an item that does not amount to possession, for example where an employee has control of his employer's property or where a guest has control of his host's cutlery.[65] The name given to this concept is 'custody', although its distinction from that of possession is not as important as it was before the offence of larceny was replaced by theft. In addition it has been held that control of a larger asset containing a smaller one, or of land on or under which an asset is located, can amount to possession of the items in or on the containing property.[66]

It may be possible for possession to be abandoned,[67] but until such time as that occurs or until possession of the thing is taken up by another, it seems that the owner will have legal possession even if he is temporarily lacking the factual control of the item that was sufficient for this original acquisition in the first place.[68]

---

[64] *Ibid* at p 90.

[65] Harris 'The Concept of Possession in English Law', in Guest (ed), *Oxford Essays in Jurisprudence*, (1961), at p 78. See also *Parker v British Airways Board* [1982] QB 1004 at p 1017 *per* Donaldson LJ: 'Unless otherwise agreed, any servant or agent who finds a chattel in the course of his employment or agency and not wholly incidentally or collaterally thereto and who takes it into his care and control does so on behalf of his employer or principal who acquires a finder's rights to the exclusion of those of the actual finder'.

[66] *Parker v British Airways* (above) and *South Staffordshire Water Co v Sharman* [1896] 2 QB 44.

[67] See below at section 13.

[68] A *dictum* to this effect lies in the judgment in *The Tubantia*, above n 63, at p 89: 'I cannot doubt that if the owners of the *Tubantia* in 1916 had put themselves, in 1923, in the position in which the plaintiffs put themselves they would be held to have been in actual possession. It would not be safe, though, to rely on this, for there is a presumption in law which aids the operative effect of the possessory acts of an owner.'

2.3.   Bailment

2.3.1.   General

A bailment is a relationship in which one party (the bailee) is voluntarily
in possession of assets to which another party (the bailor) has better title.[69] Possession is key to the concept, as is demonstrated by *Ashby v Tolhurst*.[70] The relationship can be based on agreement (contract) but need
not necessarily be so and gratuitous bailments, for example the deposit of
luggage with a coach driver during travel on his coach,[71] are common. It
seems that the obligations created by the bailment are in part contractual
(where appropriate) and in part tortious; whether or not bailment is an
independent source of obligations is a matter of debate.[72]

It is recognised that such a relationship can be of two main types: 'at
will', meaning that the bailor can call for possession to be returned at any
time; or 'for a term', meaning that the bailor only has a right to the return
of the asset upon expiration of the certain period (save where the bailment has been repudiated: see below). Unless the bailor has made a binding promise to allow the bailee to retain possession for a fixed term, the
bailment is at will. The bailment concept (either at will or for a term)
was traditionally divided into six categories taken from one of the leading
cases:[73]

1. A deposit for the bailor's purpose without reward for the bailee.
2. A gratuitous loan for the bailee's purposes.
3. Hire for the bailee's purpose.
4. A pledge (a form of possessory security).
5. A deposit of the goods in order that the bailee perform
   some service on them for reward.
6. As with 5. but without reward.

The degree of care required of the bailee until recently depended upon
how the bailment in question was characterised. The modern approach to

---

69 *Halsbury's Laws*, (4ᵗʰ ed reissue), vol 3(1), para 1. See generally Palmer, *Bailment*
    (1991).
70 [1937] 2 KB 242.
71 See *Houghland v R R Low (Luxury Coaches) Ltd* [1962] 1 QB 694.
72 See, for example, Bell, 'The Place of Bailment in the Modern Law of Obligations',
    in Palmer and McKendrick (eds), *Interests in Goods* (1998) at p 471 *et seq*; McMeel,
    'The Redundancy of Bailment', [2003] LMCLQ 169.
73 *Coggs v Bernard* (1703) 2 Ld Raym 909 *per* Holt CJ. This classification has been
    rearranged from six into five parts in some works: see *Halsbury's Laws*, (4ᵗʰ ed reis-
    sue), vol 3(1), para 2.

liability, however, imposes a common duty on bailees of all types to take reasonable care of their bailor's goods and the standard required will depend on the circumstances of each case.[74] Since bailments can, and frequently do, arise as a matter of contract it is of course open to the parties to vary the type and level of duties owed from this starting point, and the position is further modified by various statutes that extend or restrict the exclusion or reduction of liability in given contexts.[75] It also appears that the standard of care expected of the bailee is tightened up where he deviates in some regard from the terms of the bailment, for example by storing the chattel with another without authority,[76] or by failing to return it upon demand.[77] In this situation liability becomes strict and the errant bailee is liable for all losses flowing from the breach.

Besides the common duty to take reasonable care of the goods, the bailee's principal duty is to return the goods at the end of the bailment.[78] There is also a duty not to deviate and a duty not to convert the goods. Moreover, because all that is necessary for a bailment to arise is for someone voluntarily to take possession of the goods of another it appears that such a relationship arises where a finder or thief take possession of an item. In such cases there is also a positive duty on the bailee to take reasonable steps to seek out the person with better title to the goods,[79] and it is therefore argued that a thief or a finder who makes no effort to locate the owner are both strictly liable for loss or damage to the goods under their control.[80]

Despite the infiltration of the general law of negligence, one aspect of the question of a bailee's liability is unusual: The burden of proof is reversed so that it is not for the bailor to show a breach of duty by the bailee, but instead for the latter to show that any loss or damage to the former's goods occurred in spite of reasonable steps being taken. It is submitted that this is merely an example of a situation where the law of

---

[74] *Houghland v R R Low (Luxury Coaches) Ltd* [1962] 1 QB 694 *per* Ormerod LJ at p 698. It should be noted that the reasoning behind the imposition of this common but variable duty is the acknowledgment that any given bailment will not necessarily fit into the traditional 'watertight compartments' and that there is a spectrum of models. It is submitted that for this reason the traditional classification is now only of assistance as a framework.

[75] For example, the Carriers Act 1830, Carriage of Goods by Sea Act 1971, Carriage by Air Act 1961.

[76] *Edwards v Newland & Co* [1950] 2 KB 534 at p 540 *per* Tucker LJ and p 542 *per* Lord Denning.

[77] *Mitchell v Ealing London Borough Council* [1979] 1 QB 1 at p 6.

[78] *Ibid* at p 6.

[79] *Parker v British Airways Board* [1982] QB 1004 at p 1017 *per* Donaldson LJ.

[80] Clarke & Kohler, 'Property Law' (2005) at p 651.

evidence switches the location of the burden for practical reasons: The bailee was, by definition, in possession of the goods and so is the best placed of the two parties to provide evidence of what happened to them.

2.3.2. Sub-bailment

A sub-bailment occurs where a bailee, with the consent of his bailor, transfers possession to another party, who is then the sub-bailee in relation to the bailor (or head-bailor). The relationship between the bailor and sub-bailee is still not very clear. The concept has been used to evade difficulties with privity of contract, for example in *Morris v C W Martin & Sons*,[81] in which the claimant bailed her fur stole for cleaning with a furrier. The furrier did not do any cleaning himself and so, with the claimant's consent, he sub-bailed the stole to the defendant for the purpose of cleaning it and did so on contractual terms, one of which was a liability exclusion clause. While the item was being cleaned it was stolen by one of the defendant's employees and never recovered; the claimant sued the defendant as sub-bailee for breach of duty to take reasonable care of the fur. It was held by the Court of Appeal that, as her sub-bailee, the defendant owed to the claimant a duty to take reasonable care and a duty not to convert the stole, and, since the exclusion clause did not cover the circumstances, that the defendant was liable to the owner for the loss of the fur. According to Lord Denning MR, *obiter*, had the exclusion clause been worded so as to cover the situation at hand then the defendant would have been able to rely upon it against the claimant but only if the claimant had expressly or impliedly consented to the head-bailee sub-bailing on those terms.

More recently, the Privy Council considered sub-bailment on terms in *The Pioneer Container*.[82] The bailors were cargo owners who bailed their goods to shippers on agreement that the bailees could sub-bail 'on any terms'. This was done and the goods were handed over to the defendant ship owners for part of the journey, during which the vessel in question sank with all of her cargo. The terms on which the bailee sub-bailed to the defendant included an exclusive jurisdiction clause. The advice of the Privy Council was that the owner could proceed directly against the sub-bailee under the law of bailment without having to rely on the contract of sub-bailment between the bailee and the sub-bailee; that the sub-bailee could only rely on terms affecting his relationship with the owner/head-bailor if the latter had expressly, impliedly or apparently authorised them,

---

[81] [1966] 1 QB 716.
[82] [1994] 2 AC 324.

and that accordingly, given the consent to 'any terms', the owners were bound by the jurisdiction clause.

2.4.   Acquisition of possession

2.4.1.   Actual delivery

Delivery can be effected in a number of ways. The first method, actual delivery, accords with the everyday meaning of the word. 'Delivery' under section 61(1) of the Sale of Goods Act 1979 'means voluntary transfer of possession from one person to another'. It is a bi-lateral process involving the seller surrendering factual control of the chattel to the buyer who simultaneously demonstrates an intention to possess, as described above.

2.4.2.   Constructive delivery

A second form of transfer is constructive delivery, which transfers control of the chattel without giving the transferee actual possession of it. Constructive delivery of a chattel can occur in several ways, one of which is the actual delivery of the effective means of securing actual possession of the item in question: *Wrightson v McArthur and Hutchinsons (1919) Ltd.*[83] Here the claimant was given possession of the keys to two locked rooms in the defendant's premises, (but not to the outer door), by the defendant as a form of security; inside the rooms were certain specified goods that the claimant was entitled to remove. When the defendant went into liquidation the liquidator sought to treat the transaction as void and so the claimant sought a declaration that the goods were in his possession and that he was entitled to remove them. Rowlett J. held that the delivery of the keys coupled with an irrevocable licence to enter the premises gave the claimant possession of the goods in the rooms and an entitlement to remove them. It was said that had the keys to the outer door of the premises been handed to the claimant or had the goods been contained in an apartment on the land of a third party then the issue would have been more easily resolved in the claimant's favour. The delivery was said not to be symbolic nor constructive but actual.[84] This was said to

---

[83] [1921] KB 807. Whether or not the delivery of a key in this circumstance is a form of actual or constructive delivery is not clear. The weight of the *dicta* and of commentary falls on the side of the former, although it is submitted that little rests upon such a categorisation.

[84] *Ibid* at p 816.

have been based on a *dictum* of Lord Hardwicke in *Ward v Turner*[85] to the effect that 'the key is the means of coming at the possession'. This interpretation is supported by Pollock and Wright in their important treatise on possession.[86]

Where the deliveror retains a duplicate key then there is *obiter dicta* to the effect that possession will not have been transferred to the deliveree because the deliveror retains control over the property,[87] that is unless the deliveree consents to retention of the second key, which is kept for a purpose other than taking the possession of the goods.[88] However, it has been said that delivery of all of the keys would not make commercial sense.[89] Moreover, Pollock and Wright suggest that:

> 'If a vendor has delivered the key to the purchaser with the expressed intent that the purchaser may at any time get at the goods, the purchaser will have possession although the vendor really intends himself to get at the goods by means of another key. The vendor would clearly be estopped from denying that he intended the possession to pass; and the effect of his overt act as regards third parties cannot be altered by his secret intent.'

Delivery can also be made to a party without him receiving physical control of the goods where his agent assumes possession of them on account of his principal. Where the goods are received by an employee then, as mentioned above, the employer enjoys possession through the employee, who has mere custody of the goods.[90] In this way actual, rather than constructive delivery is achieved, although it is submitted that the distinction appears artificial.

Symbolic delivery entails the physical transfer of a small quantity of the goods in question from a larger amount or quantity of the same coupled with an intention present in both parties to the transaction that delivery of part is delivery of the whole.[91] Should either party dissent or not

---

[85] (1752) 2 Ves Sen 431.

[86] Pollock and Wright *An Essay on the Law of Possession.*

[87] *Re Craven's Estate* [1937] Ch 423.

[88] *Hilton v Tucker* (1888) 39 Ch D 669, in which the deliveree was deemed to have exclusive control because the deliveror's access was acknowledged to be subject to the creditor's superior control.

[89] *Sanders v Maclean* 1883 (11 QBD 343), *per* Bowen LJ. It might be that the distinction here stems from understandably differing judicial attitudes in two diverse contexts: commerce on the one hand and death-bed gifts on the other.

[90] Bridge, above n 60 at p 44.

[91] *Kemp v Falk* (1882) 7 App Cas 573 at p 586 *per* Lord Blackburn.

so intend then it stands for delivery only of that part physically transferred.[92]

A further form of constructive delivery is attornment. In this situation
there will be a third party acting as the seller's bailee who will retain
physical control of the assets in question throughout the process. Upon
instruction by the seller, the third party bailee will attorn to the buyer,
i.e. acknowledge to the buyer that he holds the goods on his behalf; this
last part seems vital. Various acts have been described as amounting to
attornments, all of which have in common a communication of some
form to the buyer:[93]

> 'If the warehouseman writes on the order in the presence of the messenger the
> word "accepted," so that he sees it; if he makes delivery of part of the goods, as
> in the case of Gillett v. Hill 2 Cr. & M. 530, where a delivery of five sacks of
> flour in compliance with an order to deliver 5 sacks ex 20," was held to be an
> admission of the possession of twenty sacks; if he makes a claim for charges on
> the person presenting the delivery order; or if he tells him that he has entered
> his right to the goods in his books. In each of those cases I think it ought to be
> found that the warehouseman had attorned. But I do not see how it is possible
> to get an attornment or recognition of the title of the person named in the or-
> der out of the mere fact that an order is brought by a messenger and given to a
> clerk, where nothing is done which is communicated to the other party.'

2.5.   Protection of possession: trespass to goods

Like ownership, the protection of possession under English law is
achieved not through the law of property but the law of torts. The work
in this area is carried out by the tort of trespass to goods.

This tort undoubtedly protects possessory interests, but whether 'possession' here includes not only actual possession but also the right to
immediate possession is unclear. There is some limited support for the
view that the expression covers both concepts in the case of *Wilson v
Lombank Ltd*,[94] albeit this stems from a concession by one of the parties to
the case. It has been argued however that this is not an appropriate
course for the law to take and that only actual possession should be capable of grounding a claim in trespass.[95]

---

[92] *Ibid.*

[93] *Laurie and Morewood v Dudin and Sons* [1926] 1 KB 223 at p 237 *per* Scrutton LJ. In
       this case an entry had been made in the defendants' books, but this entry was not
       communicated to the claimants. It was held that there was no attornment.

[94] [1963] 1 WLR 1294.

[95] See Bridge, above n 60 at p 52, and Rogers, above n 18 at p 594.

The tort itself requires direct and wrongful physical interference with the goods by the alleged tortfeasor.[96] An example of trespass would be the scratching of a car door.[97] The action formerly covered the taking of property but other examples of the now expanded form include the mere use of chattels where no damage is inflicted. The tort is said to be actionable *per se* so that a technical trespass that occasions no loss or damage will still be capable of generating liability although damages recovered will be nominal;[98] this position mirrors that encountered in the law of real property and arguably acts as a useful method of protecting title in the absence of a form of *vindicatio* in English law. It is submitted however that if trespass is to act as a form of *de facto vindicatio*, as Bridge suggests it ought, then the right to possess must provide a claimant with sufficient standing to sue for otherwise his title is meaningless when he is out of actual possession. Conversion, as discussed above at section 1.4, is still open to him but the two torts do not cover precisely the same ground.

In addition to showing a direct and voluntary trespassory act, there also appears to be a mental element that a claimant must prove in order to succeed. Intentional acts of trespass clearly fall within the ambit of the tort but the position is less clear with regard to unintentional trespass to goods. There is authority to the effect that negligence on the part of the defendant would have to be shown before he could be fixed with liability,[99] but the traditional view is said to be that once direct injury has been shown the burden of proof switches to the defendant to establish the defence of 'inevitable accident'.[100] However, by analogy with more modern decisions in the related field of unintentional trespass to the person it is strongly arguable that the claimant must show negligence (and perhaps also actual loss) in order to establish liability.[101]

If the interference is proved to be intentionally inflicted then motive and mistake do not appear to assist the tortfeasor with a defence to liability, but such factors may affect the question of quantum of damages awarded.[102] The commonest remedies available will be damages and/or an

---

96 Rogers, above n 18 at p 593.

97 By analogy with *Fouldes v Willoughby* (1841) 8 M & W 540 *per* Alderson B.

98 See *The Mediana* [1900] AC 113 at p 117 *per* Lord Halsbury: 'Supposing a person took away a chair out of my room and kept it for 12 months, could anybody say you had a right to diminish the damages by showing that I did not usually sit in that chair, or that there were plenty of other chairs in the room? The proposition so nakedly stated appears to me to be absurd'.

99 *National Coal Board v Evans* [1951] 2 KB 861.

100 See Rogers, above n 18 at p 594.

101 *Ibid*, citing *Fowler v Lanning* [1959] 1 QB 426; see also Bridge, above n 60 at p 50.

102 Bridge, above n 60 at p 50, citing *Kirk v Gregory* (1876) 1 Ex D 55 and *Wilson v Lombank Ltd* [1963] 1 WLR 1294.

injunction, however there are instances of a successful claimant being awarded damages not for any physical loss to the asset but for the use value the defendant received.[103] This might be explained as a form of restitutionary remedy that strips the defendant of the benefit of using the chattel without paying hire.[104] Moreover, the procedural provisions applied to conversion by the 1977 Act apply equally to trespass.[105]

3.   The proprietary status of rights to hold, use or acquire movables

3.1.   Introduction

This section considers whether, in English law, rights to hold, use or acquire movables are properly characterised as rights *in rem* (*i.e.*, proprietary rights) or rights *in personam* (*i.e.*, personal or purely contractual rights). This seemingly straightforward enquiry is complicated by a number of factors, amongst which may be numbered the elusiveness of a clear exposition of what is meant by the term 'proprietary right', the resort to equity[106] sometimes notable amongst the judiciary as a means of achieving a 'fair' outcome, and the variety of transactions, arrangements and circumstances out of which rights to hold, use or acquire arise. Equally, rights such as these may be protected by recourse to legal rules and principles that do not, of themselves, *require* the right in question to be characterised as a proprietary right but, if successfully invoked, result in a remedy or form of protection commonly associated with proprietary rights.

In considering the precise nature of such rights it is necessary to acknowledge that English law has never attempted to develop in relation to movables (or personalty, as they are more commonly referred to in the English parlance) anything like as precise a system of legal regulation as that which exists in the realm of immovable property (or land/real property). This is to some extent as a result of the historical perspective of the relative values of land and personalty, with the latter subjected to a somewhat *ad hoc* system of development precisely because of its lesser status in this regard. This much was remarked upon by Blackstone in 1766, but it is also worth noting his observation that the then recent escalation in commercial activity, and its focus on personalty, had alerted

---

[103] For example, *Strand Electric and Engineering Co v Brisford Entertainments* [1952] 2 QB 246.

[104] See Burrows, *The Law of Restitution* (2002) at p 468 *et seq*.

[105] See above at section 1.4.

[106] See section 1.1 above.

the courts to the fact that that species of property should be taken seriously as a store of value.[107]

A further explanation for the arguably unstructured nature of personal property law in England is simply that that category of property is so broad,[108] and encompasses such a variety of forms, that no single system of governance could possibly be devised that would be appropriate to every element. Thus, in the common law tradition, developments have been largely incremental and respond to a particular set of facts before the court in question, although certain aspects of the law governing the transfer of movables have been enshrined in various statutes.[109] This is not to suggest that there are *no* general principles of law underpinning the various developments, but rather that no thought has ever been given to attempting to devise a universal approach applicable to all forms of personalty and all questions relating to it.

3.1.1. What is meant by a proprietary right?

This simple enquiry might perhaps seem eccentric to those from a civil law background. Sjef van Erp, in discussing the *numerus clausus* doctrine, describes 'real rights' (or proprietary rights for these purposes) as 'rights against the world, distinguished from merely personal rights'[110] without further exposition. This minimalism is no doubt achieved by reference to the effects of the *numerus clausus* doctrine itself, which segregates proprietary rights from personal rights by confining their number in a 'listing' exercise.

The idea that the doctrine is exclusive to the civil law jurisdictions and unknown in common law jurisdictions is misleading.[111] At least two

---

[107] See Blackstone, W, *Commentaries on the Laws of England: Volume II: Of the Rights of Things* (1766), p 385.

[108] Comprising all 'items', whether tangible or intangible, which have been recognised as 'property', with the exception of land.

[109] But not necessarily to the exclusion of a concurrent common law or equitable jurisdiction. For example, s. 136 of the Law of Property Act 1925 deals with the requirements for an assignment of a chose in action, one of which is that notice of the assignment be given to the account debtor. The failure to give notice does not prevent an equitable assignment occurring: *Gorringe v Irwell India Rubber Works* (1886) 34 Ch D 128.

[110] Sjef van Erp, 'A Numerus Quasi-Clausus of Property Rights as a Constitutive Element of a Future European Property Law?', vol 7.2 EJCL (June 2003), http://www.ejcl.org/72/art72-2.html, p 1.

[111] As van Erp himself states, the doctrine 'is not unknown in literature on the common law.': *ibid*.

major commentaries refer to its application in the English property law regimes, Clarke and Kohler observing that:

> '… it is necessary here to note that the traditional approach of property law to the problem … has been to limit the number of different types of property interest that might exist.'[112]

Swadling also explores this idea.[113] Whilst he adheres to the basic notion that a closed list of rights that can be described as proprietary exists in English law, he acknowledges, but ultimately refutes, the notion that a different taxonomy could be based on the one House of Lords authority that explores head-on the question of what is meant by a proprietary right. In *National Provincial Bank Ltd v Ainsworth*[114] their Lordships were asked to consider whether, if a husband was subject to an obligation to provide a home for his wife, the right of the wife[115] as against the husband could be enforced against a mortgagee of the property (*i.e.*, to use van Erp's terminology, did this right constitute a right against the world?). The House of Lords held that it could not. However, as Swadling points out,[116] the reasoning was based not on the fact that the 'deserted wife's equity' fell outside a recognised list of rights but rather that the right did not satisfy the necessary criteria of a property right. Lord Wilberforce put the matter thus:

> 'Before a right or an interest can be admitted into the category of property, or of a right affecting property, it must be definable, identifiable by third parties, capable in its nature of assumption by third parties, and have some degree of permanence, or stability.'[117]

In other words, the inventory of proprietary rights already recognised by English law is not a closed one, and any right possessing the characteristics enumerated by Lord Wilberforce may be admitted.

There is, of course, an inherent circularity which bedevils this method of identifying property rights, as cogently noted by Gray, whose observations are worth citing at length:

> 'This preoccupation with assignability of benefit and enforceability of burden doubtless owes much to the fact that the formative phases of the common law

---

[112] Clarke, A, and Kohler, P, *Property Law: Cases and Materials* (2005), para 9.1.2.
[113] See, generally, *English Private Law* (2000), Chapter 4.
[114] [1965] AC 1175.
[115] Generally termed 'the deserted wife's equity'.
[116] Above n 114, para 4.14.
[117] [1965] AC 1175, 1247-1248.

concept of property coincided with a remarkable culture of bargain and exchange. Non-transferrable rights, or rights which failed on transfer were simply not 'property'. Within the crucible of transfer lawyers affected to demarcate rights of 'property' from rights founded in contract and tort ... only brief reflection is required in order to perceive the horrible circularity of such hallmarks of 'property'. If naively we ask which rights are proprietary, we are told that they are those rights which are assignable to and enforceable against third parties. When we then ask what rights these may be, we are told that they comprise, of course, the rights which are traditionally identified as 'proprietary'. 'Property' is 'property' because it is 'property: Property status and proprietary consequence confuse each other in a deadening embrace of cause and effect.'[118]

To the extent that the *Ainsworth* case represents English law, it is possible to suggest that proprietary rights have certain characteristics the most notable of which, again returning to van Erp's definition, is that they can be asserted against 'the world'. Even here, however, some caution should be exercised. Bridge notes:

'The touchstone of a property right is its universality: it can be asserted against the world at large and not, for example, only against another individual such as a contracting partner. *This is not to say, however, that universal rights are invincible ...*'[119]

Bridge is by no means alone in identifying universal enforceability as the acid test of a property right.[120] Swadling writes in terms of such a right's 'exigiblity against persons other than the grantor',[121] and Worthington notes that proprietary interests 'are effective against third parties, not simply between the contracting parties.'[122] But, as Gray points out, the identification of a characteristic of a right does not, of itself, assist in the question of which rights can claim that characteristic. This is important to the current discussion because as yet rights to hold, use or acquire personalty have not authoritatively been categorised as proprietary rights,[123] and the question as to whether they may satisfy the universal

---

[118] Gray, 'Property in Thin Air', [1991] CLJ 252, 293.

[119] Bridge, M, *Personal Property Law* (2002), p 28 (italics added).

[120] Subject to certain qualifications: The manner in which admitted property rights can be overridden are examined elsewhere in this Report – see section 10.

[121] *English Private Law*, above n 114 para 4.5. See also Pretto-Sakmann, A, *Boundaries of Personal Property* (2005), p 88.

[122] Worthington, S, *Proprietary Interests in Commercial Transactions* (1996), p 101.

[123] To be explained below.

enforceability test is probably critical to a determination of their status. It will be addressed below in some detail.[124]

3.2.   Rights to hold and to use

This section focuses largely on the rights to hold and to use *tangible movables*. This is largely because by far the majority of the authority and academic commentary in this area concerns tangibles, but it should be acknowledged that rights to hold and to use intangibles, and particularly items of intellectual property, may be the subject of similar agreements, often termed licences. A further focus of this section is on rights to hold and to use movables arising *consensually*, and so effectively involving a transfer of *possession* of the movable on the understanding that the transferee may hold and use it.[125] Rights such as these arising non-consensually (such as the rights of one who finds) are addressed separately in a later section.[126]

3.2.1.   The concept of bailment

(a)   General

The term used to describe a transfer of possession is 'bailment', a concept of some considerable vintage and described by Pollock and Wright in the following terms:

> '... any person is to be considered as a bailee who otherwise than as a servant either receives possession of a thing from another or consents to receive or hold possession of a thing for another upon an undertaking with the other person either to keep or return or deliver to him the specific thing according to the directions antecedent or future of the other person.'[127]

The generality of the above statement emphasises that bailment may encompass any number of circumstances, and that it's central feature is an *impermanent* transfer of possession from one party to another. In his classic judgment in *Coggs v Bernard*[128] Lord Holt CJ categorised bailments into 'types' in order to determine the standard of care required of the

---

[124] See the following discussion in this section.

[125] On the requirements for such a transfer see above at section 2.5.

[126] See below, section 11.

[127] Pollock and Wright, *An Essay on Possession in the Common Law* (1888), p 163.

[128] (1703) 2 Ld Raym 909.

bailee, these being: a deposit for the bailor's purpose; a gratuitous loan for the bailee's purpose; a hire for the bailee's purpose; a pledge (the deposit of personalty as security); a deposit in order that the bailee perform a paid service, and; a deposit in order that the bailee perform a gratuitous service. Of this catalogue, it is well established that a pledge, whereby the pledgor, in return for an advance of (usually) money, deposits personalty with the pledgee, confers upon the pledgee a proprietary right in the personalty which can be asserted 'against the world'.[129] In relation to the other categories of bailment, English law as yet appears undecided upon the central question of whether the bailee has any property right in the movable in question.

(b)   Chattel leases and hire purchase agreements

Chattel leases (*i.e.*, a lease of a movable) and hire purchase agreements are both transactions which fall under the umbrella of bailment and are both of considerable commercial significance. The Court of Appeal has made the following observation:

> 'Leases and hire purchase contracts are means by which companies obtain the right to use or purchase assets. In the UK there is normally no provision in a lease contract for legal title to the leased asset to pass to the lessee ... A hire purchase contract has similar features to a lease except that under a hire purchase contract the hirer may acquire legal title by exercising an option to purchase the asset upon fulfilment of certain conditions (normally the payment of an agreed number of instalments).'[130]

Two points may usefully be made here, the first being that although the learned Lord Justice refers to *companies* obtaining the right to use or purchase assets both chattel leases and hire purchase agreements are commonly used also in the consumer field, and usually in relation to movables of relatively high value.[131] In structure, these two transactions differ, and a brief explanation of their respective basic elements is necessary. The second point is that, structurally, a hire purchase agreement differs from a chattel lease, in that under the former it is routine for the 'lessee',[132] as part of the contract of hire, to be given the opportunity to exercise an

---

[129] *Carter v Wake* (1877) 4 Ch D 605; *Sewell v Burdick* (1884) 10 App Cas 74. It is said that the pledgee has a 'special property' in the subject matter of the pledge.

[130] *On Demand Information Plc v Michael Gerson (Finance) Plc* [2000] 4 All ER 734, at p 737, *per* Robert Walker LJ.

[131] The most obvious example being motor vehicles.

[132] For want of a better description.

option to purchase the movable, usually for a nominal payment, once all the hire instalments have been met. This feature is invariably absent in chattel leasing agreements, although, functionally, the two transactions appear to perform a similar dominant purpose, which is to give the lessee a right to possess and to use the movable. Whether these rights are con-ferred by way of lease or hire purchase, however, they clearly originate in contract and may therefore be asserted against the 'lessor'. This much, though, simply begs the question as to whether they are purely personal rights. Swadling puts the enquiry:

> 'If A hires goods from B for a fixed period, possession of the goods being given to A, and before the end of the fixed period B sells the goods to C, is C bound by the contract of hire entered into between A and B?'[133]

He goes on to note that personal rights arising from a contract between A and B would have no effect on C because of the doctrine of privity of contract, whereas if the contract in question gives rise to either legal or equitable proprietary rights then A will be able to assert those rights against C. Before considering the various contentions put forward in favour of one or the other positions, it is worth a slight diversion into the area of real property, as this may inform the discussion and may also sug-gest the course of future developments.

3.2.2.   The status of a lease of land and the lease/licence dichotomy

(a)   The proprietary effect of a lease of land

The doctrine of estates allows for rights in and over land to exist and to be divided up along a time line,[134] so that several estates (and interests) can co-exist in relation to the same piece of land. One such estate is the leasehold estate, or term of years absolute.[135] There is absolutely no ques-tion that the grant of a leasehold estate confers upon the lessee a proprie-tary right, which may be legal or equitable. Three elements of this state-ment should be examined.

---

[133] Swadling, W, *The Proprietary Effect of a Hire of Goods*, in *Interests in Goods* (1998), p 49.

[134] For detailed expositions on the doctrine see: Gravells, N P, *Land Law: Text and Materials* (2004); Burn, E H, *Cheshire & Burn's Modern Law of Real Property* (2000), pp 25-37; Thompson, M, *Modern Land Law* (2006), pp 23-34.

[135] Law of Property Act 1925, s. 1(1)(b).

The first is that there are certain essential characteristics of a lease which must be present if the grant is to constitute a lease at all.[136] These are, briefly, that the lessee must be granted exclusive possession of the land and that the grant must be for a term certain. This latter require-ment means that the point at which the lease is to commence and its *maximum* duration must be ascertainable from the outset.[137] Thus, an agreement that gives one party exclusive possession of land until the hap-pening of a certain event[138] will not create a lease, whereas an agreement to grant exclusive possession for, say, ten years, subject to the happening of a certain event at some earlier point will be an effective grant of a lease. In the latter example the maximum duration is ascertainable, not so in the former. A failure to specify a maximum duration is therefore fatal to the grant of a *lease*, but may nevertheless confer upon the grantee rights under a contractual licence.[139]

The second point worth noting is that English land law may require admittedly proprietary rights to be *perfected* via a system of registration if they are to remain enforceable against the world. As far as leases are concerned, if they are created for a term exceeding seven years they con-stitute a 'registrable disposition'[140] and will lose priority to a subsequent registered disposition for valuable consideration if not duly registered.[141] Leases granted for a term of less than seven years constitute an 'unregis-tered interest which overrides a registered disposition'.[142] In other words the grant of a lease for a period less than seven years has full proprietary effect, in that it may be asserted against 'the world' notwithstanding a lack of registration.

The use of the term 'grant' here should be properly understood, and reflects one fundamental distinction between the operation of the com-mon law and equity (the third of the points referred to above). A *legal* estate in land may only be created by the use of a deed,[143] *unless*, for pre-sent purposes, the conveyance amounts to a lease or tenancy 'not required by law to be made in writing.'[144] According to s. 54(2) Law of Property Act 1925, leases taking effect in possession for a term of less than *three*

---

[136] Law of Property Act 1925, s. 205(xxvii), and see *Street v Mountford* [1985] AC 809.

[137] *Prudential Assurance Co Ltd v London Residuary Body* [1992] 2 AC 386.

[138] See, *e.g.*, *Lace v Chantler* [1944] KB 368 (lease for the duration of the war).

[139] Which would require consideration. Interestingly, consideration is not a require-ment for the creation of a lease; see Law of Property Act 1925, s. 205(xxvii) – ('whether or not at a rent').

[140] Land Registration Act 2002, s. 27(2)(b).

[141] *Ibid*, s. 29(1).

[142] *Ibid*, Schedule 3, para 1.

[143] Law of Property Act 1925, s. 52(1).

[144] *Ibid*, s. 52(1)(d).

years need not be created by deed to be recognised at law. Thus leases created for a term exceeding three years but not exceeding seven years require a deed to take advantage of the protective effect of Schedule 3, para (1), but any lease not exceeding three years will automatically fall within the paragraph, whether granted by deed or not.

Leases which do not comply with the deed requirement and which do not fall within the category of leases that may be created without the use of a deed may nevertheless be recognised in equity.[145] In summary, for equity to recognise and give effect to an agreement to grant a lease made other than by deed the contract of grant must be written and signed by both parties to it and contain the terms of the lease,[146] and must be for valuable consideration. The agreement must also be one in relation to which a court would grant specific performance, which, being an equitable remedy, is discretionary: In the present context, the issue is whether or not the claimant has conducted himself in such a way as to cause the court to exercise its discretion against him.[147] If these conditions are satisfied the lessee has a valid equitable lease which confers a proprietary right upon him. For it to be perfected it should be registered, but, in the absence of registration, it may be protected under Schedule 3, para 2 of the Land Registration Act 2002. As noted above, only legal leases are subject to the protection of para 1 of that Schedule. Paragraph 2, however, protects the interest of persons in actual occupation of the land in question against a subsequent registered disponee, *provided* that the lessee's occupation would be obvious on a reasonably careful inspection of the land,[148] *and* that a lessee of whom inquiry is made does not fail to disclose the interest when he could reasonably be expected to do so.[149]

What does all of the above tell us about the proprietary status of leases of land? The most salient point to note is that whilst an agreement made by deed or in writing will give rise to a proprietary right over the land which is capable of binding third parties (strangers to the original agreement), for it to have that effect it must either be perfected by registration *unless* it takes effect in possession and is for a term not exceeding seven years *or* the lessee is in actual and obvious occupation of the land. A moment's thought leads to the conclusion that the legislation attempts to strike a balance between the interests of the lessee and those of potential purchasers of the land in order to achieve the dual aims of protecting

---

[145] Under the doctrine in *Walsh v Lonsdale* (1882) 21 Ch D 9.

[146] Law of Property (Miscellaneous Provisions) Act 1989, s. 2.

[147] For examples, see *Coatsworth v Johnson* (1886) 55 LJQB 220 (lessee in breach of obligations under the lease); *Cornish v Brook Green Laundry Ltd* [1959] 1 QB 394 (failure to comply with a condition precedent to the grant of a lease).

[148] Land Registration Act 2002, Sch 3, para 2(c)(i).

[149] *Ibid*, para 2(b).

property rights whilst ensuring that the marketability of a valuable asset is not impeded by the possibility that one's acquisition of and right over that asset will be subject to undiscovered and undiscoverable property rights. Thus, pre-existing property rights may be defeated if they are not registered *or* if they are not obvious. As a corollary, a potential purchaser of land is protected by his ability to check a register in the first instance and, in the second instance, by the fact that his ownership rights (if themselves registered) will override an unregistered lease where the lessee's occupation of the land was not obvious.

This system offers, or at least attempts to offer, a workable solution to the perennial conflict between holders of a wide variety of property rights and those who seek to acquire ownership rights (or, indeed, some other form of right) in the same item of property. It qualifies the universality of the proposition that proprietary rights may be enforced against the world so as to ensure that the very existence of such rights does not militate against the free alienability of valuable resources unless certain conditions are satisfied. In the case of land, and in the context of leases, property rights lose their universally enforceable character in the event of non-registration or, critically, where *the lessee is not in actual and obvious occupation of the land*. Further reflection demonstrates the role played by *de facto possession* here: It serves to *alert* a prospective purchaser of the land of a pre-existing right which, potentially, may be enforceable against him. This may be an important point of comparison when it comes to considering whether a lessee *in possession of personalty* might claim similar protection.

(b)   The contractual licence: merely a right *in personam*?

The grant of a right to occupy land may not amount to a lease, either because exclusive possession is not granted[150] or because the maximum duration of the grant is not ascertainable.[151] To the extent that the grantee enters into possession of the land he will occupy it under some form of licence.[152] Where consideration is provided in return for the grant the arrangement is commonly termed a contractual licence. In the question of whether the grant of a contractual licence amounts to the grant of a proprietary interest in the land the subject matter of the grant has been the subject of some debate in the English courts. In short, the orthodox position

---

150 See, for a fuller exposition, A G *Securities v Vaughan, Antoniades v Villiers* [1990] 1 AC 417.

151 See above at section 3.2.2.(a).

152 Detailed treatment of the subject of licences over land can be found in the leading texts, some of which are mentioned above at n 135.

is that stated in the House of Lords in *King v David Allen and Sons (Billposting) Ltd*.[153] That case concerned the right, granted by contract, to post advertisements on the walls of a theatre, this right being held to be unenforceable against a successor in title of the original grantor on the ground that a licence of this nature created only personal rights.

Notwithstanding the efforts of, in particular, Lord Denning in subsequent cases[154] to clothe contractual licences with proprietary status, it now appears reasonably well settled that they confer upon the licensee rights enforceable only against the original grantor. This was the conclusion of the Court of Appeal in *Ashburn Anstalt v Arnold*,[155] but it should be noted here that the learned Lord Justices expressly contemplated that a successor in title of the original grantor might yet be compelled to give effect to the rights of the licensee via the imposition of a constructive trust. As to when a constructive trust might be imposed, the Court of Appeal in *Lloyd v Dugdale*[156] was adamant that the successor's notice of the licence was insufficient and that the court must be satisfied that 'the conscience of the estate owner is affected so that it would be inequitable to allow him to deny the claimant an interest in the property ...'[157] The critical question for the court in *Lloyd v Dugdale* was whether the successor in title of the original licensor had, in the course of acquiring the estate, undertaken, expressly or impliedly, to give effect to the rights of the licensee. Such an undertaking might be inferred from the fact that the successor in title had paid a reduced price, but should not be inferred lightly.

Therefore, whilst rights under a contractual licence might turn out to be exigible against successors in title of the licensor if the kinds of circumstances described in *Lloyd v Dugdale* are present, this of itself does not necessarily point to their proprietary status: They may be asserted against *the successor* precisely because he has undertaken to give effect to them, and therefore assumed what can only be described as a *personal* obligation towards the licensee. This obligation will be enforced in equity, usually by the imposition of a constructive trust, but its existence does not mean that the right itself has suddenly become one enforceable against *the world*.

This dichotomy between the lease and the contractual licence raises some interesting points which may be enlightening in relation to the question of similar rights to possess over personalty. It may well seem excessively technical, given that both lease and contractual licence have

---

[153] [1916] 2 AC 54. See also *Clore v Theatrical Properties Ltd* [1936] 3 All ER 483.
[154] See *Errington v Errington & Woods* [1952] 1 KB 290 (and the critique of Wade, (1952) 68 LQR 337); *Binions v Evans* [1972] Ch 359.
[155] [1989] Ch 1.
[156] [2001] EWCA Civ 1754.
[157] *Ibid*, at para 52.

their origin in contract but only the former seems capable of being described as proprietary. The distinguishing factor between the two agreements, whether it be the lack of exclusive possession or of a certain duration, might well be thought inadequate to justify the difference in result in this regard. To the extent that English land law has, at its heart, the objective of balancing the rights of different types of 'claimants' over land there would seem in principle to be no objection to recognising the proprietary status of a contractual licence, and at the same time subjecting it to the same 'perfection' regime as a lease, whether perfection takes the form of registration or obvious occupation.[158] Be that as it may, Swadling cites the treatment of contractual licences of land in support of an argument that English law follows a *numerus clausus* approach to property rights.[159] If that is correct, the question of whether leases (or similar rights of possession) over personalty can now be examined from a comparative perspective.

3.3. Proprietary status of leases and other bailments of movables

3.3.1. Transmissibilty of possessory rights

If transmissibility is a feature of a proprietary right then there is no doubt that the right to possess personalty may be transferred in certain circumstances. However, the right to transfer possession will often arise contractually, and so involve the consent of the bailor. Such consent may be express or implied.[160] In practice, much will depend on the type and purpose of the bailment in question, so that, for example, where the bailment in question is to allow the bailee to transport the bailor's good the bailee may well be expressly or impliedly authorised to 'sub-bail' the goods for a part of the journey,[161] which would give rise to a possessory right in the sub-bailee. In the specific context of a chattel lease it is not uncommon for express authority to sub-lease to be granted,[162] and, indeed, if the approach of the Privy

---

158 One possible objection of a logistical nature would be that the concept of a contractual licence covers such a wide variety of claims that it would be bizarre to suggest that they all have proprietary status (for example, the right to attend and view a football match is conferred by way of a contractual licence). The mere fact that such a licence is of a transient nature does not, however, distinguish it from a lease in substance, for there is no doubt that periodic tenancies as short as one week are recognised at law.

159 *English Private Law*, above n 114, para 4.13.

160 See *The Pioneer Container* [1994] AC 324.

161 *Ibid.*

162 See, for example, *Re Atlantic Computer Systems Plc* [1992] Ch 505.

Council in *The Pioneer Container*[163] is correct it may be sufficient that the bailee has *apparent authority* to sub-bail.

This is of some interest in that it shifts the transmissibility of a right to possess somewhat beyond the purely contractual, as a sub-bailee may be able to assert his possession against a bailor who has not actually or impliedly consented to sub-bailment in the first instance. A case in point is *Whiteley v Hilt*,[164] where the bailee of a piano under a hire purchase agreement sold the piano at a time when she had not fallen into arrears with the instalment payments. The Court of Appeal held that she was competent to assign, not the piano itself, but her rights under the transaction of hire, Warrington LJ noting:

> 'The general property in the chattel no doubt remained in the plaintiffs, but that general property in it was qualified and limited by the contractual interest conferred by the agreement upon the hirer ... Now, was that interest assignable? In my opinion it clearly was.'[165]

Of course, it is perfectly possible to avoid the above outcome simply by contractually prohibiting the bailee from transferring his rights, but it would appear that without such a prohibition, or some term which automatically terminates the contract of hire on any attempt at alienation, the bailor either impliedly consents to a transfer of possessory rights *or* can be said to have apparently authorised the same.

One further point worth mentioning here is that a bailee might be competent to transfer *greater rights than he himself possesses* under the exceptions to the rule of *nemo dat quod non habet* contained in the Sale of Goods Act 1979, the Factors Act 1889 and the Hire Purchase Act 1964.[166] However, although it is certainly the case that possessory rights may be transmitted it is equally clear that the *right or ability to transmit* emanates not from the fact of possession itself but from some conduct of the bailor or from statute. Transmissibility, it might therefore be contended, is not a universal or unqualified feature of a possessory right.[167]

---

[163] Above n 61.

[164] [1918] 2 KB 808.

[165] *Ibid*, p 820.

[166] See below at section 10. Essentially, a transferee from a bailor might acquire 'ownership' rights over the item in question.

[167] The same can be said with regard to leases of land, where the right to exclusive possession may be transferred if sub-leasing is authorised by the lessor.

3.3.2. Protection conferred by virtue of possession

One starting point is that English law offers *protection* to any party in possession of a movable purely by virtue of that possession through the tort of conversion. A party in possession, if wrongfully dispossessed, may bring an action in conversion notwithstanding that he has only limited rights (*i.e.*, rights other than ownership) in the item in question. This is the case even where the possession of the claimant has not been authorised by the owner of the item, and will protect even wrongful possession (of, for example, a thief). This rule is of ancient origin. In *Armory v Delamirie*[168] a chimney sweep's 'boy' 'found' a ring set with stones, which he took for valuation to a goldsmith. The goldsmith's apprentice removed the stones. The sweep's boy was held competent to bring an action in trover (the predecessor of a conversion action) to recover the stones. A much more modern, and perhaps even more graphic illustration of this principle is *Costello v Chief Constable of Derbyshire*.[169] Mr Costello was in possession of a stolen car, the judge finding as a fact that he knew it was stolen. The car was confiscated by police under statutory powers, which later expired. They refused to comply with Mr Costello's requests to return the car. In the Court of Appeal, confirming the claimant's right to bring an action in conversion, Lightman J stated:

> 'The fact of possession of a chattel of itself gives to the possessor a possessory title and the possessor is entitled to rely on such title without reference to the circumstances in which such possession was obtained: his entitlement to do so is not prejudiced by the fact that he obtained such possession unlawfully or under an illegal transaction. *His claim can only be defeated by proof of a title superior to his possessory title*.'[170]

This final sentence is illuminating in that it illustrates that, at least for the purposes of the tort of conversion, a possessory right (or title, to use the learned judge's terminology) is not good against the world *per se*, and may be defeated by proof of a superior right. This will be the case whether the right of possession arises out of a consensual bailment or otherwise. Defensive rights such as this, therefore, are not necessarily indicative of proprietary status in the sense that they may not be asserted against the whole world.

Returning to Swadling's basic enquiry as to the nature of the rights of a chattel lessee,[171] the fact that a lessee in possession of personalty may

---

[168] (1722) All ER Rep 121.
[169] [2001] EWCA Civ 381.
[170] *Ibid*, para 14 (italics added).
[171] Above at section 3.2.1.

bring an action in conversion for interference with that possession tells us nothing about the *proprietary* nature of his *possessory* rights. Were such a lessee to be dispossessed by a successor in title of the lessor it is unclear as to whether the lessee could possibly succeed in a conversion claim against the successor in title,[172] who might simply argue that his ownership rights trump the claimant's 'mere' possessory rights. The basic point here would be that the tort of conversion protects 'possession' rather than 'ownership' *per se*, but has nothing to say about the general nature of possessory rights.

On the other hand, there is authority to the effect that a successor in title *could not* bring an action in conversion against the lessee. In *Rich v Aldred*[173] Holt CJ noted:

> 'If A bail goods to C, and after give his whole right in them to B, B cannot maintain detinue for them against C because the special property that C acquires by the bailment, is not thereby transferred to B.'

Richard Calnan, in an illuminating piece, uses this case to argue cogently that rights under leases of movables are unarguably proprietary.[174] This supports an argument suggested by Goode to the effect that the rule *nemo dat non quod habet* would apply so as to make the lessee's rights enforceable against a successor in title of the lessor:

> 'A further aspect of the nemo dat rule is that any transfer by the owner himself takes subject to existing real rights, so that if the asset is subject to a security interest the purchaser's rights are qualified by that interest, and if the goods are in the possession of a lessee the purchaser takes them subject to the rights enjoyed by the lessee by virtue of his possession under the lease.'[175]

Swadling, however, counters that this assumes that the possessory right the lessor purports to transfer is proprietary, and therefore begs the question of the rule's application at all. In other words, this contention runs counter to the *numerus clausus* principle.[176]

At this juncture, therefore, the best that can be said is that there is no consensus on the question as to whether the fact of possession is protected in such a way as to clothe it with proprietary status at law.

---

[172] No case has yet considered this scenario.

[173] (1705) 6 Mod 216.

[174] Calnan, R, *Property, Security and Possession in Insolvency Law*, (1997) 11 JIBFL 530.

[175] Goode, R, *Commercial Law* (2004), p 55.

[176] See *The Proprietary Effect of a Hire of Goods*, above n 134, pp 515-516.

3.3.3.   Proprietary status in equity?

(a)   Resort to equity

An interesting question is whether, if rights under bailments of personalty are proprietary in nature, they confer legal or equitable proprietary rights. One difficulty with the former is that, in relation to personal property, the doctrine of estates has never applied as it does in land which, as noted above, allows concurrent legal titles to exist in the same land. It is worth noting, however, that the fact that a *leasehold* estate in land exists at all under that doctrine is something of a historical anomaly and there appears to be no *doctrinal* reason why a similar approach could not be taken to leases of personalty. Indeed, this much has been asserted by Palmer, who observes:

> 'A bailment gives rise to a form of property because it creates a division of interests in rem within the compass of a single chattel. The division is chronological rather than geographical; as in the case of leaseholds, a bailment divides the ownership of the res "on a plane of time". The bailee obtains a legal interest in the form of possession, which is in many respects equivalent to an estate in land ...'[177]

There is certainly much to be said in favour of the direct comparison of the treatment of leases in land law and in the law of personal property. On the other hand, one might argue that, as noted above,[178] leases of land are subject to a regime which requires their *notification* (whether by registration or obvious occupation), and the same cannot be said in relation to the vast majority of species of personal property. This point is further developed below.[179] For present purposes it is sufficient to note that arguments that bailments of property confer proprietary rights have often focused on the equitable dimension.

(b)   Restraining legal rights in equity: *De Mattos v Gibson*

This is the area in which much of the debate concerning the proprietary character of a possessory right conferred by contract has taken place. Much of this debate takes as its starting point the case of *De Mattos v Gibson*.[180] The claimant in this case entered into a charterparty agree-

---

[177] *Palmer on Bailment* (1979), p 65.
[178] See section 3.2.2.(a).
[179] See section 3.3.4.
[180] (1858) 4 De G & J 276.

ment with the prospective owner of a ship, who subsequently mortgaged the ship to the defendant, the mortgage advance being used to acquire the ship. The defendant had, at all times, knowledge of the pre-existing charterparty, the consideration for which was paid by the claimant and transferred to the defendant in partial discharge of the mortgage debt. The ship, in the course of the charterparty and before it had reached its destination, was repaired in port and the repairer claimed a lien over it for his fees. At this point the defendant claimed to be able to exercise his power of sale over the ship and instructed the repairer to complete the repairs and return the ship to its port of origin. The claimant sought an order for specific performance of the charterparty and an injunction against using the ship other than in accordance with the terms of the charterparty, both being equitable remedies. The Court of Appeal granted the injunction, Knight-Bruce LJ reasoning thus:

> 'Reason and justice seem to prescribe that, at least as a general rule, where a man, by gift or purchase, acquires property from another, with knowledge of a previous contract, lawfully and for valuable consideration made by him with a third person, to use and employ the property for a particular purpose in a specified manner, the acquirer shall not, to the material damage of the third person, in opposition to the contract and inconsistently with it, use and employ the property in a manner not allowable to the giver or the seller.'[181]

A preliminary observation to make is that the Court of Appeal in *De Mattos v Gibson* was not concerned as to the proprietary effect or otherwise of the claimant's rights, and, further, the nature of the charterparty in question was such that the claimant was not actually in possession of the ship. Nevertheless, the case has been cited as authority for the proposition that rights arising under a contract may effectively 'run with the chattel' and that any attempt to interfere with them will attract the protective jurisdiction of equity in the form of an injunction.

There is a clear parallel between the reasoning of Knight-Bruce LJ in relation to personalty and that of Lord Cottenham LC in *Tulk v Moxhay*[182] in relation to land. In that case a plot of land was sold subject to a covenant entered into by the purchaser to maintain the land as an open space and to keep it in good order. The land was subsequently conveyed to a purchaser without the insertion of a similar covenant, although the purchaser knew of it. When he proposed to build on the land in question Lord Cottenham granted an injunction to prevent such action and stated:

---

[181] *Ibid*, p 282.
[182] (1848) 2 PH 774.

'It is said that, the covenant being one which does not run with the land, this court cannot enforce it, but the question is not whether the covenant runs with the land, but whether a party shall be permitted to use the land in a manner inconsistent with the contract entered into by his vendor, with notice of which he purchased. Of course, the price would be affected by the covenant, and nothing could be more inequitable than that the original purchaser should be able to sell the property the next day for a greater price, in consideration of the assignee being allowed to escape from the liability which he had himself undertaken.'[183]

It may be argued, therefore, that *De Mattos v Gibson* is simply a logical extension of a development of land law into the law of personalty. However, as Swadling points out, the doctrine in *Tulk v Moxhay* has itself undergone considerable development since its inception and seen considerable restrictions placed on its scope.[184] Notwithstanding Lord Cottenham's assertion that the question was not as to whether a covenant may run with the land, it is now clear that a successful invocation of the doctrine produces precisely that effect.[185] Moreover, the central pre-occupation of *Tulk v Moxhay* is the fact that the purchaser of the land was aware of the covenant in question,[186] so that notice was the major determinant in the case. Modern land law has largely replaced the relevance of notice with a registration regime, so that covenants over land, to be successfully enforced against a purchaser of the land, have to be registered.

De Mattos v Gibson was approved by the Privy Council in *Lord Strathcona Steamship Co Ltd v Dominion Coal Co Ltd*,[187] which again concerned a charterparty and a change in ownership of the vessel during its course. However, subsequent cases have doubted the authority of both *De Mattos* and *Lord Strathcona*, Halsbury's Laws noting:

'It therefore seems clear that, at very least, the authority of the decision in Lord Strathcona Steamship Co Ltd v Dominion Coal Co Ltd … has been severely shaken; that the generality of the dictum by Knight Bruce LJ has been denied; and that the principle is unlikely to be applied outside the limited field of ships and their charters, unless, perhaps, it can be supported under the good faith doctrine …'[188]

---

[183] *Ibid.*

[184] *The Proprietary Effect of a Hire of Goods*, above n 134, p 495.

[185] On covenants in land law generally, see the works listed at n 135 above.

[186] Emphasising the doctrine's equitable origins. A restrictive covenant is now recognised as an equitable proprietary interest in land.

[187] [1926] AC 108.

[188] *Halsbury's Laws of England*, para 750, n 15.

Nevertheless, *De Mattos v Gibson* has never been overruled and so, for the present, remains authority, albeit uncertain, for the proposition that a successor in title may be injuncted against using personal property other than in accordance with rights of which he has notice. It should be noted, however, that there seems to have been no suggestion that the case imports wholesale into the area of personalty any regime resembling that in the area of land law relating to restrictive covenants. As noted above, covenants concerning freehold land are now recognised as proprietary interests in equity and so, potentially, can 'run with the land'[189] and be asserted against successors in title of the covenator. It is virtually unthinkable that *De Mattos v Gibson* supports a similar analysis in relation to movables.

In fact, the reasoning in *De Mattos* and, more tellingly, in *Lord Strathcona*, appears to resemble more closely the approach of the courts in relation to those claiming to be able to enforce contractual licences against successors in title of the licensor. Both Worthington, indirectly, and McFarlane, directly, make this point. Worthington notes:

> '[The aim of the courts] seems to be to deny the defendant an unjust enrichment, not to protect the commercial interests of the primary contracting parties. The courts presume that the asset (or any interest in it) was acquired by the defendant for a price which reflects the restrictions on its use; given that, they find it inequitable that the defendant should make a profit by dealing with the asset free of the restrictions.'[190]

She goes on the to draw a parallel between *De Mattos* and *Lord Strathcona* and the position of trustees who assume an obligation to hold and deal with property for the benefit of another (or at least not to his detriment).[191] MacFarlane explicitly refers to the contractual licence cases as comparable with the approach in *De Mattos* and *Lord Strathcona*.[192]

The correspondence of the *De Mattos* approach with that of the courts in the area of contractual licences is, it is submitted, a realistic one, and it leads to the conclusion that whilst possessory rights may be asserted against successors in title, such enforcement is available *only* where the successor in question not only has notice of the possessory right but has also agreed, expressly or impliedly, to give effect to it, as in *Lloyd v Dug-*

---

[189] Notwithstanding Lord Cottenham's assertion in *Tulk v Moxhay* that the issue was not whether the covenant ran with the land.

[190] Worthington, S, *Proprietary Interests in Commercial Transactions* (1996), p 103.

[191] *Ibid*, p 109.

[192] MacFarlane, B, 'Identifying Property Rights: A Reply to Mr Watt', [2003] Conveyancer and Property Lawyer 473, 477.

dale.[193] If this is correct, the right in question is *not* proprietary in the sense that it can be enforced against the world, and, in fact, remains a purely personal right against the successor in title who has agreed to give effect to it. The fact that enforcement of the right is effected by means of a constructive trust does not, of itself, confer proprietary status on it.

(c) Calculating damages for conversion

In *Wickham Holdings Ltd v Brooke House Motors Ltd*[194] the Court of Appeal was asked to consider the correct measure of damages for the conversion of a car bailed on hire purchase terms. The hire purchase agreement stated that the hirer was not to dispose of the vehicle and that any such disposition would entitle the claimant owner to repossess it. The hirer, having paid roughly three quarters of the contract value of the car, sold it to the defendant, who had contacted the claimant for a settlement price. A price was agreed but, due to an administrative error, the defendant did not pay it within the time allowed. The claimant then sued in conversion, claiming that the measure of damages was the value of the car at the time of the conversion, which was around £100 more than the settlement figure quoted.

All three judges in the Court of Appeal agreed that the claimant was only entitled to recover what it had lost by the wrongful act of the defendant, this being the balance outstanding on the hire-purchase price and not the value of the car at the date of the conversion. Lord Denning, going further than was necessary for the decision, asserted:

'In a hire-purchase transaction there are two proprietary interests: the finance company's interest and the hirer's interest.'[195]

Whilst this *dicta* in unquestionable in its recognition of the proprietary status of a hirer's possessory rights it is worth noting that the two other judges, whilst agreeing with the outcome, did not adopt Lord Denning's analysis. This reasoning has never been followed and was not even referred to in three more recent judgments, to be considered in the next section. Therefore its authority is somewhat less than established.

---

[193] [2001] EWCA Civ 1754, and see the discussion at section 3.2.2.(b) above.
[194] [1967] 1 WLR 295.
[195] *Ibid*, pp 299H – 300A.

(d)   Equitable relief against forfeiture: recognition of the proprietary status of possessory rights?

By virtue of s. 146 Law of Property Act 1925 a lessee of land may apply to the court for relief against forfeiture of the lease in the event of a breach of a leasehold covenant. Alongside the statutory regime the court retains an inherent equitable jurisdiction to relieve against forfeiture which has recently been pressed into service in the case of personalty.

In *Re Piggin: Dicker v Lombank*[196] a van held on hire purchase terms was repossessed by the defendant owner when the hirer became bankrupt and defaulted on the hire payments. The hirer's trustee in bankruptcy offered to pay the remainder of the instalments in return for the return of the van, but the defendant refused. The county court judge held that it would be inequitable for the defendant to retain both the van and the instalments already paid and ordered the defendant to pay to the trustee a sum representing the difference between the latter and the van's value.[197] The fact of the hirer's bankruptcy may well have influenced this decision, as his creditors would be the beneficiaries and it might be seen, in such circumstances, as unfair that the defendant/owner would receive a 'windfall' by virtue of the exercise of his contractual right to repossess.

This theme was revisited in *Transag Haulage Ltd (IAR) v Leyland DAF Finance Plc*,[198] a case of corporate insolvency involving a hire purchase agreement. It is worth noting at this stage that in *Helby v Matthews*[199] the House of Lords had held that the hirer of a piano on hire purchase terms was not a person who had 'bought or agreed to buy' the piano and so was not a buyer in possession for the purposes of what is now s. 25 Sale of Goods Act 1979.[200] Lord MacNaghten said this of the nature of the hirer's rights:

'... no one of those monthly payments until the very last in the series was reached, nor all of them put together without the last, should confer upon the customer any proprietary right in the piano or any interest in the nature of a lien or any interest of any sort or kind beyond the right to keep the instrument and use it for a month to come.'[201]

---

[196] (1962) 112 LJ 424.

[197] See Pawlowski, M, 'The Forfeiture of Possessory Rights in Land and Chattels', (1999) 21 Liverpool Law Review, 77.

[198] [1994] BCC 356.

[199] [1895] AC 471.

[200] See below, section 10.

[201] [1895] AC 471, p 481.

This appears to fix the hirer's rights very firmly in the law of obligations rather than the law of property. In *Transag*, a rather different approach to a very different question was taken. Transag was in possession of lorries under a hire purchase agreement with Leyland DAF. The agreement contained a list of events of default entitling the hirer to terminate the agreement and repossess the lorries. These included a failure to meet instalments and the appointment of a receiver in relation to the company. A receiver was appointed over Transag's assets and Leyland DAF terminated the agreement and demanded possession of the lorries. At the time, Transag had not defaulted on instalment obligations, but £14,000 remained to be paid in future instalments. The lorries were worth around £22,000 each and the receiver, anxious to continue to use them in Transag's business, offered to pay the outstanding instalments. Leyland DAF refused this offer and called for the delivery up of the lorries. The receiver applied to the court for equitable relief against forfeiture.

Knox J noted that there was Court of Appeal authority for the proposition that the court's inherent equitable jurisdiction to grant relief against forfeiture was available in the case of personalty.[202] However, the doctrine was restricted in application to contracts transferring proprietary or possessory rights. The learned judge then held that the *option to purchase* conferred by the agreement was a proprietary right,[203] and that therefore the court had jurisdiction to grant relief. No mention was made as to whether the right to possess of itself was sufficient to trigger the jurisdiction, or indeed, given the termination of the hire contract on the appointment of a receiver, that right subsisted at all. On the facts, it was appropriate to exercise discretion in favour of granting relief.

This of itself suggests a typical hire purchase agreement, conferring as it does an option to purchase the subject matter of the contract, gives the hirer a proprietary right in the movable consisting of the option to purchase it. In some respects this is in accordance with principles of the law of real property, where an option to purchase land has long been recognised as an equitable property right in the land itself.[204] Such an option must, however, be protected by registration if it is to be enforceable against a successor in title of the grantor, unless the option holder is in actual and obvious occupation of the land.[205] Given that there is no such

---

[202] See *BICC plc v Burndy Corporation* [1985] Ch 232.

[203] This point is discussed below at section 3.4.2.(b).

[204] See *London and South Western Railway Co v Gomm* (1882) 20 Ch D 562. This can be contrasted with a right of pre-emption which, because the grantor reserves to himself the decision as to whether to dispose of the land itself, does not confer property rights over the land on the grantee unless and until the grantor indicates a willingness to sell: *Pritchard v Briggs* [1980] Ch 338.

[205] See Land Registration Act 2002, Sch 3, para 2.

registration regime as concerns personalty, the comparison is an imperfect one.

A chattel lease does not usually confer an option to purchase on the lessee, so the question remained as to whether the possession enjoyed by the lessee could be protected from forfeiture under the equitable jurisdiction of the court. This question was answered in the affirmative by the Court of Appeal in *On Demand Information Plc v Michael Gerson (Finance) Plc*.[206] The lease in question was of video equipment, and the agreement, like that in *Transag Haulage*, gave the owner the right to terminate and repossess if the company entered receivership, as it subsequently did. On an application by the receiver for relief against forfeiture, Robert Walker LJ stated:

> 'I think that Knox J [in *Transag Haulage*] could have based his decision on Transag's possessory rights during the currency of each of the hire-purchase agreements, as well as on its option to purchase ... Those possessory rights arose under contracts but I cannot accept the submission that those rights, or the rights of On Demand under the finance leases, were purely contractual rights if that intensitive implies that they had insufficient possessory character to meet the principles which emerge from the authorities considered above ... Contractual rights which entitle the hirer to indefinite possession of chattels so long as the hire payments are duly made, and which qualify and limit the owner's general property in the chattels, cannot aptly be described as purely contractual rights.'[207]

In the House of Lords, the Law Lords affirmed the reasoning of the Court of Appeal on this point, Lord Millett observing:

> '[The Court of Appeal] rejected the lessor's objection that the leases were purely contractual in nature, and that the jurisdiction to grant relief from forfeiture was restricted to cases where the forfeiture of proprietary rights strictly so-called was in question. As Robert Walker LJ put it, contractual rights which entitle the hirer to indefinite possession of chattels so long as the hire payments are duly made, and which qualify and limit the owner's general property in the chattels, cannot aptly be described as purely contractual rights. For my own part, I regard this conclusion as in accordance with principle; any other would restrict the exercise of a beneficent jurisdiction without any rational justification.'[208]

---

[206] [2000] 4 All ER 734.
[207] *Ibid.*
[208] [2002] UKHL 13.

What can be made of these remarks? In particular, are these cases authority for the proposition that the rights of a lessee of movables are proprietary rather than contractual? A number of points may be made here, the most obvious of which is that neither Robert Walker LJ nor Lord Millet expressed that conclusion in those precise terms. Indeed, the former appears to distinguish between 'proprietary' rights and 'possessory' rights, rather than conflating the two. Equally, the fact that the case was concerned with relief against forfeiture[209] may be important for two reasons. Firstly, the relief granted is, by definition, against the *lessor* of the movable and so might be said to lack the universally enforceable character of proprietary rights proper. Secondly, it may well be that the exigencies of insolvency were a considerable impetus in the outcome: Were relief not granted the lessor (both in *Transag Haulage* and *Michael Gerson*) would arguably receive a windfall at the expense of the creditors of the insolvent lessee. Whether these cases genuinely establish the proprietary character of the rights of a 'lessee' under either a hire purchase agreement or a chattel lease perhaps remains an open question, although Bridge is convinced:

'*On Demand* establishes beyond any doubt that a hirer's right to possession is proprietary and not merely contractual.'[210]

However, it is submitted that unless and until a court is faced with the explicit question as to whether a lessee can *directly* assert his right to possess against a successor in title of the lessor,[211] which, of course, was not in issue in either *Transag* or *Michael Gerson*, there remains some room for doubt.

3.3.4.   Conclusion

As yet, no case has categorically decided the question of whether a right to possess a movable, granted by way of lease or hire purchase agreement, confers upon the possessor a proprietary right in the movable or remains a

---

[209] Which was granted in relation to the proceeds of sale of the leased equipment in the House of Lords.

[210] Bridge, M, *Personal Property Law* (2002), p 28.

[211] Where the successor in title acquires the leased item with knowledge of the lessee's rights there remains the possibility that the lessee may be awarded damages for the tort of interference with contractual relations. Indeed, *De Mattos v Gibson* has been explained as establishing an equitable counterpart to this tort: see *Swiss Bank Corp. v Lloyds Bank Ltd* [1982] AC 584, but see also Worthington, S, n 191 above, for criticism of this analysis.

contractual right enforceable only against the lessor. In policy and commercial terms, the acknowledgement that such an interest is proprietary would arguably be beneficial,[212] and Watt argues strongly in favour of such a position, but also concedes that:

> 'The recognition of the lessee's right might be said to tie up commerce with a range of hidden interests which will make the purchaser more wary and restrict the free marketability of chattels.'[213]

In response to this, he points out that if the right conferred by a lease is *equitable*, then the danger is illusory as that right is vulnerable to the purchaser of the legal estate for value and without notice of the lessee's rights.[214] This idea is worthy of examination, not least because the question of what would constitute 'notice'. As noted above, the relevance of notice in the context of land has largely been replaced with a registration regime, although the rights of those in actual and obvious occupation may be protected even when the right has not been registered. In the case of a lease of a movable, a parallel between actual and obvious occupation of land might be drawn with the lessee's possession of the movable. In the absence of a registration regime for chattel leases and hire purchase agreements[215] the fact that the movable in question is in the possession of a lessee (or indeed, not in the possession of the 'owner') might be thought an adequate form of notice to any prospective successor in title. Alternatively, it might be possible to simply require actual *knowledge* of the lessee's rights before allowing them to be asserted against a purchaser. This would conform with the position in relation to leases of land[216] and should not prove unduly burdensome to commerce and the free alienability of valuable assets.

---

[212] See, *e.g.*, Worthington, S, above n 191, p 101.

[213] Watt, G, 'The Proprietary Effect of a Chattel Lease', [2003] Conveyancer and Property Lawyer 61, at p 79.

[214] *Ibid.*

[215] The Law Commission considered the adoption of a register for such interests where the lessee was a corporation, but their recommendations in this regard have not been implemented: see Law Commission Consultation Paper 164: 'Registration of Security Interests: Company Charges and Property Other than Land' (2002), Part VII.

[216] But not contractual licences, where both occupation and knowledge of the right are insufficient to bind a successor in title of the licensor: see above at section 3.2.2.(b).

3.4. Rights to acquire personalty

3.4.1. Contracts to acquire land: the doctrine of conversion

It is again worth briefly considering the position where one party has entered into an agreement to acquire land, whether the acquisition is of the freehold (*i.e.* ownership) of the land or of a lease of land. In such circumstances, as noted above,[217] the doctrine in *Walsh v Lonsdale*[218] may operate so that an equitable version of the estate in question is created by virtue of the agreement which, if duly registered or protected by actual and obvious occupation, may be enforced against a subsequent and different purchaser of the estate.[219] The effect of this doctrine is therefore *anticipatory*: Equity simply anticipates proper performance of the agreement to create a *legal* estate.

3.4.2. Contracts to acquire personalty

(a) The availability of specific performance

The extent to which the doctrine of conversion applies in cases of personalty is unclear. There is certainly authority to the effect that the agreement to lease an aircraft would give rise to an immediate equitable proprietary right in the aircraft in favour of the lessee, but there are certain difficulties with this conclusion. The case which establishes the proposition is *Bristol Airport plc v Powdrill*.[220] It involved an aircraft which had been leased to a company, that company then falling into financial distress and being made the subject of insolvency proceedings, specifically an administration order. The airport was seeking to exercise a statutory lien over the aircraft for unpaid airport charges. Under what was then s. 11 Insolvency Act 1986[221] any steps to enforce security over the 'property of the company' required either the consent of the administrator or the leave of the court. The airport's argument was that the leased aircraft was not the company's property, and therefore no leave was necessary. Browne-Wilkinson V-C, rejecting that contention, observed:

---

[217] See section 3.2.2.(a).

[218] (1882) 21 Ch D 9.

[219] In other words, the first contracting party has a proprietary interest in the land in question and, should the owner purport to dispose of it in breach of the agreement, is able to assert that interest against the disponee.

[220] [1990] Ch 744.

[221] See now Insolvency Act 1986, Schedule B1, para 43.

'Although a chattel lease is a contract, it does not follow that no property interest is created in the chattel. The basic equitable principle is that if, under a
contract, A has certain rights over property as against the legal owner, which
rights are specifically enforceable in equity, A has an equitable interest in such
property. I have no doubt that a court would order specific performance of a
contract to lease an aircraft, since each aircraft has unique features peculiar to
itself.'[222]

Thus, this case might also support the argument, explored above, that
rights under a chattel lease are proprietary in nature. It also explicitly
espouses the application of the doctrine of conversion to personalty.
However, the reasoning has been criticised on the basis that it assumes
the availability of specific performance *of itself* creates equitable proprietary rights. MacFarlane puts the matter thus:

'This doctrine is irrelevant when it comes to determining the proprietary
status of a particular right, as it depends for its operation on A's being under a
binding obligation to confer on B a right which is independently recognised as
proprietary. Indeed, the doctrine of anticipation is concerned only with the
methods by which property rights can be acquired: it allows such a right to be
claimed without A's completing the planned transaction. The doctrine thus
extends the list of means by which property rights can be acquired, not the list
of rights which have proprietary status.'[223]

Browne-Wilkinson V-C might therefore be accused of putting the cart
before the horse in this regard, and it seems reasonably clear that the fact
that specific performance of a contract to acquire personalty might well
be ordered does not necessarily mean that, without such an order being
made, the prospective acquirer has any equitable property right in the
movable itself. As Meagher, Gummow and Lehane put it:

'... the hard fact is that a large part of equitable doctrine operates by reference
to a system of interests, some of which are "proprietary" in character whilst
others are not.'[224]

This has to be correct in this context. To begin with, the Sale of Goods
Act 1979, s. 52(1) entrenches the court's equitable jurisdiction in this
regard as follows:

---

[222] [1990] Ch 744, 759.

[223] 'Identifying Property Rights: A Reply to Mr Watt', above n 193. See also Swadling,
    W, 'The Proprietary Effect of a Hire of Goods', above n 134, pp 504-508.

[224] Meagher, Gummow & Lehane, *Equity: Doctrines and Remedies* (2003), para 4-015.

'In any action for breach of contract to deliver specific or ascertained goods the court may, if it thinks fit, on the plaintiff's application, by its judgment or decree direct that the contract shall be performed specifically, without giving the defendant the option of retaining the goods on payment of damages.'

Nevertheless, it has always been the case that the court's jurisdiction in this regard is discretionary, and in a contract for the sale of personalty has generally only been exercised where the contract in question is for the sale of unique items of 'unusual rarity or beauty.'[225] This reflects the nature of specific performance as a remedy, *i.e.*, that it will be available where damages for breach of a contractual obligation are inadequate, and explains why, in the case of contracts to grant rights over land, the courts have accepted without question the applicability of the equitable doctrine of conversion: Land, of itself, is unique, and damages for breach of contract would therefore be an inadequate remedy.[226] It is nowhere suggested in the Act or the authorities preceding it that the availability of specific performance, even in the case of unique movables, gives the prospective acquirer an immediate equitable interest on the conclusion of a contract for its acquisition.

Bristol Airport v Powdrill is arguably, then, of doubtful authority on the question of whether a contract to acquire a movable creates an immediate equitable interest in that movable. It should again be noted that the decision was not concerned with that specific point, but rather with the question of whether the possessory rights of the insolvent corporation over the aircraft could be construed as 'property rights' for the purposes of s. 436 Insolvency Act 1986 and there were very strong policy reasons for straining the language of the section to accommodate that conclusion.[227]

(b)   The option to purchase as a proprietary right

As noted above, in *Transag Haulage Ltd (IAR) v Leyland DAF Finance Plc*[228] Knox J held that the option to purchase conferred upon a hirer under a hire purchase agreement was proprietary in character and so

---

[225] See McGhee, J, *Snell's Equity* (2005), para 15-16.

[226] It is also worth noting that contracts for the grant of a *security interest*, such as a mortgage or charge, over personalty yet to be acquired by the grantor attract the application of the doctrine of conversion: see *Holroyd v Marshall* (1862) 10 HLC 191, *Tailby v Official Receiver* (1888) LR 13 App Cas 523.

[227] Essentially, to preserve the insolvent estate for the benefit of the general creditors of the company and to allow the administrators to continue its trading activities so as to maximise value.

[228] Above n 199.

triggered the equitable jurisdiction of the court to grant relief against forfeiture. The generality of the proposition is, it is suggested, open to some doubt. Whilstever the option holder is in possession of the movable in question under the terms of such an agreement there may be no difficulty in acknowledging that there are good commercial reasons for allowing its assertion against a successor in title of the lessor. The same cannot be said where the option to purchase is conferred without any such transfer of possession and it is tentatively suggested that in such a case a court would be slow indeed to conclude that rights under an option to purchase are enforceable against the world.[229]

This analysis is perhaps supported by reference to the equivalent position in land law, where options to purchase land are regarded as proprietary in nature[230] but rely upon registration for the universal enforceability.

4.   Field of application and definitions

4.1.   Legal rules on transfer and categories of movables

4.1.1.   Tangible movables

English personal property law draws clear distinctions between tangible and intangible property. Tangible (or corporeal) movables are generally known as *choses in possession*, reflecting the fact that rights over them are often vindicated by possession of the item in question. A further term used in this area is 'chattels', which can apply to land (chattels real) or personalty (chattels personal). In short, any item, other than land, which has a physical presence falls into the category of choses in possession. As Bridge puts it:

> 'The size of a thing is no obstacle to it being a chose in possession: microdots and ships both fall into the category.'[231]

Where the movable in question is subject to a consensual transfer (*i.e.*, derivative acquisition) for consideration[232] the transaction falls under the category of sale and for the most part will be governed by rules contained

---

[229] Although if rights under an option were to be classified as equitable, they would be vulnerable to the *bona fide* purchaser without notice of the legal estate in the movable, as Watt points out in relation to rights under chattel leases: see above, n 214.

[230] See above, section 3.3.3.(d).

[231] Bridge, M, *Personal Property Law* (2002), p 3.

[232] For the rules on gifts of movables see below, section 5.3.1.(a).

in the Sale of Goods Act 1979. Section 2 of that Act defines the contracts to which it applies:

> 'A contract of sale of goods is a contract by which the seller transfers or agrees to transfer the property in goods to the buyer for a money consideration, called the price.'

Section 2 of the Act goes on to amplify upon contracts for the sale of goods, and includes contracts of sale between one part owner and another,[233] and contracts which are absolute or conditional.[234] The critical question of what amounts to 'goods' for the purposes of the Act is answered by s. 61 in the following terms:

> '"[G]oods" includes all personal chattels other than things in action and money, and in Scotland all corporeal moveables except money; and in particular "goods" includes emblements, industrial growing crops, and things attached to or forming part of the land which are agreed to be severed before sale or under the contract of sale and includes an undivided share in goods.'

Thus, money is excluded from the operation of the Act,[235] as are 'things in action' which, for present purposes, can be described as all intangible movables.[236] The reference to 'personal' chattels excludes land, but it should be noted that it does include 'emblements, industrial growing crops and things attached to or forming part of the land which are agreed to be severed before or under the contract of sale.' A distinction has to be drawn between *fructus naturales* and *fructus industriales*, the former encompassing the natural produce of the land and the latter crops which are produced by labour.[237] Therefore, natural produce will only amount to 'goods' for the purposes of the Act if the parties to a contract for their transfer have provided in that contract for their severance.[238] In the ab-

---

[233] S. 2(2).

[234] S. 2(3).

[235] Although, as Bridge notes, where coins or notes are sought as items in their own right rather than as a medium of exchange (because, for example, of their rarity value) they may be considered as goods for the purposes of the Act: Bridge, M, *Sale of Goods* (1997), p 30.

[236] See below.

[237] The term 'emblements' applies to *fructus industriales*, and can be equated with the term 'industrial growing crops', which was added to the definition when the Sale of Goods Act was extended to cover Scotland.

[238] For more detail, see Bridge, M, *Sale of Goods* (1997), pp 22-26; Miles, R, *Blackstone's Sale & Supply of Goods & Services* (2001), paras 1.3.1-1.3.4.; Atiyah, P S, *Sale of Goods* (2005), p 77.

sence of any such provision, it may well be that the grantee has been
granted a *profit a prendre*, which is recognised as an interest in the land
itself.[239]

4.1.2. Particular 'items' as goods

(a)   Electricity, gas and liquids

There is no difficulty in applying the Sale of Goods Act to liquids, nor, it
seems, to bottled gases,[240] or gas to be supplied through a pipeline.[241] The
question of whether electricity amounts to goods for the purposes of the
Sale of Goods Act has never been directly addressed by the courts. In
Low v Blease[242] it was held that electricity was not property for the purposes of s. 4 of the Theft Act 1968 and so could not be stolen. On the
other hand, in *Bentley Bros v Metcalfe*[243] it was held that an obligation to
supply electricity to power certain machines was subject to an implied
term that the power supplied should be fit for the purpose of the supply,
and in *County of Durham Electrical Power Distribution Co v IRC*[244] a supply
of electricity was accepted as an agreement 'relating to the sale of any
goods, wares or merchandise' for the purposes of the Stamp Act 1891.
Further, Chapter 23 of the Value Added Tax Act 1994 treats a supply of
gas or electricity as a supply of goods or services, but that takes the matter
no further. Bridge suggests that private contracts involving a supply of
energy should be treated as a sale of goods contract,[245] whereas Miles
considers that electricity, having no tangible presence, cannot be considered as 'personal chattels' for the purposes of the Act.[246] In the absence of
authority directly in point, the question remains undecided.

(b)   Ships and aircraft

Both ships and aircraft are clearly personal chattels. However, as far as
ships are concerned specialist regimes may prescribe additional requirements for their transfer. The Merchant Shipping Act 1995 allows for the

---

[239] Law of Property Act 1925, s. 1(2)(a).

[240] *Marleau v People's Gas Supply Co Ltd* [1940] DLR 433.

[241] See *Erie County Natural Gas & Fuel Co Ltd v Carrol* [1911] AC 105.

[242] (1975) 119 SJ 695.

[243] [1906] 2 KB 548.

[244] [1909] 2 KB 604.

[245] Bridge, M, *Sale of Goods* (1997), p 28.

[246] Miles, R, *Blackstone's Sale & Supply of Goods & Services* (2001).

registration of 'British ships'[247] and Schedule 1 of that Act requires the transfer of a registered ship to be effected by 'a bill of sale satisfying the prescribed requirements'[248] unless the transfer will result in the ship ceasing to have a British connection. The transferee must then make an application in the prescribed form to the registrar before he will be registered as owner of the ship.[249] Transfers of aircraft, on the other hand, are *prima facie* governed by the Sale of Goods Act so that no particular requirements as to the *mode* of transfer are imposed. However, the Civil Aviation Authority is responsible for the maintenance of a register of aircraft in the UK, and the transferee of any aircraft registered with the Civil Aviation Authority must inform it in writing within 28 days of the transfer.[250]

4.1.3. Intangible movables

This category of personal property, generally termed *choses in action* in English law comprises 'items' the right to which can only be vindicated by application to court by virtue of the fact that the item is incorporeal and so cannot be physically possessed. Examples of *choses in action*, which in commercial terms is a highly valuable category of property, include debts, rights under insurance policies, company shares and all types of intellectual property including patents, licences and trademarks. *Choses in action*, under the English law taxonomy, are divided into pure intangibles and documentary intangibles. The former comprise such items as debts, company shares and goodwill, as well as intellectual property rights.[251] There is absolutely no question that, in general terms, such rights can be sold (or, more accurately, assigned) but they are excluded from the operation of the Sale of Goods Act. Many categories of intangibles are subject to special rules in relation to their transfer,[252] all of which are outside the scope of this Report.

---

[247] Merchant Shipping Act 1995, s. 8(1).

[248] *Ibid*, Sch 1, para 2(1). The prescribed requirements are those prescribed by regulations: para 14.

[249] *Ibid*, para 3.

[250] See Air Navigation Order 2005 (SI 2005/1970, art 4(12)).

[251] For recent recognition of 'novel' forms of property see *Re Celtic Extraction Ltd* [1999] 4 All ER 684 (waste management licence) and *Swift v Dairywise Farms Ltd* [2001] ECWA Civ 145 (EC milk quota).

[252] For example, in relation to company shares the basic rule is that the purported transferee does not become the 'owner' of the shares in question until the transfer is recorded in the company's register of shareholders (but see *Pennington v Waite* [2002] EWCA Civ 227).

Documentary intangibles are documents that can be said to represent underlying tangible movables. Worthington describes documentary intangibles as follows:

> 'Documentary intangibles are documents that the law regards as able to stand for the property itself: they represent the underlying right to money, goods or securities, and, importantly, they allow that right (the 'property') to be transferred by delivery of the document, supported by any necessary indorsements.'[253]

Notwithstanding that the document itself has a physical presence, documentary intangibles fall outside of the Sale of Goods Act. As Worthington points out, the rights represented by the document may be transferred by delivery and indorsement of the document itself.

---

[253] Worthington, *Personal Property Law: Text and Materials* (2000), p 5.

Part II:
Derivative acquisition

5. Which system of transfer is used?

5.1. Overview

5.1.1. The unitary system of transfer

In very general terms, a transfer of a movable will operate to transfer all rights associated with ownership from transferor to transferee at one single moment. However, as will be seen, English law for the most part allows the parties to an agreement to transfer ownership of a movable to make whatever bargain they see fit, so that the terms of their agreement may provide that, for example, possession of the movable is to remain with the transferor. A specific example of such an agreement would be a chattel mortgage, which, although in substance is a security agreement, takes the form of an outright transfer of ownership rights to the mortgagee subject to a provision for retransfer on discharge of the mortgagor's indebtedness. Thus, whilst the agreement provides for the mortgagee to 'own' the movable, it is contemplated that the right to possess it will remain with the mortgagor.

Equally, mention should be made of the possibility that a transfer of a movable to the transferee to be held *on trust* for another party will specifically provide that that other party may have rights of possession, but not ownership, of the movable in question. However, both of the above examples are departures from the general rule that, unless the parties provide otherwise, transfer of all rights associated with ownership will occur simultaneously.

5.1.2. The applicable rules

The legal rules relating to a transfer of movables differ according to the *type* of transfer in question. The specific rules will be examined in detail below,[254] but for present purposes it is useful to note that the paradigm

---

[254] See para 5.4.

example of derivative acquisition, *i.e.*, through a sale of a movable from one party to another, will be governed by the provisions of the Sale of Goods Act 1979. It will be recalled from Part 4 above that any contract by which 'the seller transfers or agrees to transfer the property in the goods for a money consideration called the price'[255] will be governed by the Act, whereas, and as a corollary, any agreement from which any of the vital elements in s. 2(1) are missing will not.

An example of such an agreement is a transfer by way of gift, as no consideration, let alone a money consideration, will flow from the transferee in such a case.[256] Equally, where consideration other than a money consideration is envisaged, such as an exchange of one movable for another, or in return for the provision of services, the Act will not apply. This is important, given the emphasis of the Sale of Goods Act on party autonomy: As will be seen, it is largely open to the parties to the contract to determine at what point property (or, to put it another way, ownership) in the movable is transferred from seller to buyer.[257]

It is also important to appreciate that the English system, whilst recognising that entry into a valid contract for the sale of a movable gives rise to an *obligation* to transfer, does not automatically translate that obligation into a property right in the buyer. A failure on the part of the seller to *actually deliver* the movable will almost invariably constitute a breach of contract, but the buyer's remedy may sound in damages rather than a court order for specific performance.[258] Whilst the Sale of Goods Act explicitly entrenches the equitable remedy of specific performance,[259] the general equitable jurisdiction proceeds on the basis that such an award will be made only when an award of damages would be inadequate.

5.1.3. The basic requirements

As will be seen,[260] the English system proceeds from the contract or agreement giving rise to the obligation to transfer ownership, and does not require any further 'real agreement' beyond that contract. There is no requirement that the movable be delivered for ownership rights in it to pass under a sale of goods agreement, as the question of precisely *when*

---

[255] Section 2(1) Sale of Goods Act 1979.

[256] See below at section 5.3.

[257] This general proposition is subject to an important qualification where the movables in question are 'generic' rather than specific: see below at sections 5.2. and 5.3.

[258] *I.e.*, an order for delivery up of the movable.

[259] In s. 52. See above at section 3.4.2.(a).

[260] Below, section 5.4.

that occurs is left to the parties.[261] Nor, unless the parties specifically require payment to be made before the transferee acquires ownership of the movable, is there any requirement in law for such payment.[262] Delivery of the movable, which may include constructive delivery in the case of very large or bulky items, or some communication of the means of acquiring possession of it, will be necessary to transfer ownership in a transaction of gift, unless a valid declaration of trust is made by the transferor in favour of the transferee.[263] A transfer by way of gift by definition requires no consideration, and, although a transfer by way of sale requires there to be a money consideration, payment of that consideration is not a necessary pre-condition of the passing of property rights from seller to buyer.[264]

5.2. General issues

5.2.1. Specific and generic Goods

The detailed rules for the passing of property rights in specific and generic goods are dealt with later in this report,[265] but the distinction between the two is of some considerable practical importance in the context of a contract of sale, so some preliminary observations are warranted here. The fundamental implication of whether a movable is specific or generic is that *only* a contract for the sale of the former is capable of passing property rights in its subject matter. In other words, subject to one important qualification, a buyer of generic goods (or, to use the English terminology, 'unascertained goods') does not and cannot acquire property rights in those goods unless and until they become 'ascertained', usually by a process known as 'unconditional appropriation to the contract'. This is as a result of s. 16 Sale of Goods Act 1979, which provides:

> 'Subject to section 20A below, where there is a contract for the sale of unascertained goods no property in the goods is transferred to the buyer unless and until the goods are ascertained.'

---

[261] *Ibid.*

[262] It is not uncommon to find that the parties specify payment as a condition of the passing of the seller's ownership rights to the buyer: see below, in relation to retention of title at section 12.

[263] See below, section 5.4.

[264] See ss. 17 and 19 Sale of Goods Act 1979.

[265] See below at 5.4.2.

This is a mandatory rule of law, of which the parties to the contract cannot contract out. Its significance lies in two main areas, the first being the insolvency of the seller of unascertained goods, which will consign the buyer who has paid in advance of delivery to an inevitably worthless claim in damages for breach of contract if the seller's trustee in bankruptcy[266] or liquidator[267] refuses to perform the seller's delivery obligations.[268] The second is where the goods are destroyed or damaged, as, as will be seen below,[269] the general rule is that risk passes with property, so that a seller of unascertained goods will bear the risk of damage or destruction of the goods.[270] Therefore the question of whether movables which are the subject of a contract of sale are specific or unascertained is of importance.

(a)   The 'specific'/'unascertained' dichotomy

Specific goods are defined in the Sale of Goods Act as any goods which are 'identified and agreed upon at the time a contract of sale is made ...'[271] Specific goods also include 'an undivided share, specified as a fraction or percentage, of goods identified and agreed on as aforesaid'.[272] Unascertained goods are nowhere defined in the Act so that, by default, they will comprise any goods that are not specific. As noted above, the mandatory rule of law stated in s. 16 Sale of Goods Act provides that property in unascertained goods cannot pass to the buyer, and this rule is supplemented by s. 18, rule 5 of the same Act. It provides that property in unascertained goods will presumptively[273] pass when they are:

---

[266] In the case of personal bankruptcy.

[267] In the case of corporate insolvency.

[268] Which he invariably will. On the insolvency of the seller and the buyer, see below at section 7.

[269] See below at section 8.

[270] In practice, this is probably not significant as in many cases delivery of the goods to the buyer, or even to a carrier, will amount to an 'unconditional appropriation' sufficient to pass property: see below.

[271] Sale of Goods Act 1979, s. 61. See Bridge, *The Sale of Goods* (1997), p 40; Atiyah, Adams & MacQueen, *The Sale of Goods* (2005), p 323.

[272] *Ibid.* These words were inserted into the 1979 Act by s. 2(d) Sale of Goods (Amendment) Act 1995 in order to reflect the insertion of the new s. 20A into the 1979 Act: see below.

[273] This rule, as all the presumptive rules in s. 18, is subject to contrary intention, so that, for example, where a seller of unascertained goods retains title to them until the buyer meets his payment obligations, unconditional appropriation will not operate to pass property to the buyer.

'... unconditionally appropriated to the contract, either by the seller with the assent of the buyer or by the buyer with the assent of the seller, the property in the goods then passes to the buyer; and the assent may be express or implied, and may be given either before or after the appropriation is made.'

The process of unconditional appropriation is dealt with at paragraph 5.4.2.2. of this report. It is, however, pertinent to note here that where unconditional appropriation has not taken place, the courts have been consistently unsympathetic towards arguments aimed at avoiding what appears to be a clear statutory scheme.

(b) Equitable proprietary rights in unascertained goods

'Whatever the intentions of the parties, where there is a contract for the sale of unascertained goods, no property can pass until the goods are ascertained ...'[274]

This straightforward proposition might be subject to qualification if it were possible to assert that, notwithstanding the fact that no unconditional appropriation of unascertained goods has occurred, nevertheless their buyer, having paid the price for them, can assert that he has acquired full beneficial ownership of them. This would require the courts to accept that it is open to the parties to create equitable property rights in unascertained goods by virtue of an equitable assignment of the goods, or that specific performance of a contract for the sale of unascertained goods may be ordered, or, indeed, that the equitable doctrine of conversion can apply in the context of a contract for the sale of unascertained goods.

The equitable doctrine, if applicable, would consider that, as equity looks upon done that which ought to be done, a seller who has been paid[275] for unascertained goods comes under an obligation to ensure that the buyer acquires the property rights in those goods for which he has contracted, presumably by unconditionally appropriating those goods to the contract. Having regard to this obligation, equity goes one stage further and recognises an immediate *equitable* interest in the property in question, which would be enforceable against all but the *bona fide* purchaser for value of the legal estate. That this doctrine could apply in the context of movables[276] was

---

[274] *Karlshamns Oljefabriker v Eastport Navigation Corp* [1982] 1 All ER 208, 212 *per* Mustill J. – See Bridge, above n 271, pp 77-83. See also the very clear and thoughtful treatment of this matter by McKendrick, 'The Passing of Property in Part of a Bulk', in: Palmer & McKendrick (ed), *Interests in Goods* (1998), Chapter 19.

[275] But not a seller who has yet to be paid: equity will not assist a volunteer.

[276] It is a well recognised feature of contracts for the disposition of an interest in land: see *Walsh v Lonsdale* (1882) 21 Ch D 9.

confirmed by the House of Lords in *Holroyd v Marshall*,[277] although in relation to an agreement to grant a mortgage over property to be acquired by the debtor at a later date, rather than in relation to a contract for the sale. However, in *Re Wait*[278] the majority of the Court of Appeal considered that this approach could not be taken in relation to a contract for the sale of unascertained goods as the Sale of Goods Act represented a definitive and comprehensive statement of how property rights could arise under a contract of sale. Atkin LJ put the matter thus:

'The total sum of legal relations (meaning by the word "legal" existing in equity as well as in common law) arising out of the contract for the sale of goods may well be regarded as defined by the Code. It would have been futile in a code intended for commercial men to have created an elaborate structure of rules dealing with rights at law, if at the same time it was intended to leave, subsisting with the legal rights, equitable rights inconsistent with, more extensive, and coming into existence earlier than the rights so carefully set out in the various sections of the Code. The rules for transfer of property as between seller and buyer, performance of the contract, rights of the unpaid seller against the goods, unpaid sellers' lien, remedies of the seller, remedies of the buyer, appear to be complete and exclusive statements of the legal relations both in law and equity.'[279]

Thus, an interpretation of the scheme of the Sale of Goods Act leads, according to Atkin LJ, to the conclusion that equitable rights in property being the subject of a contract of sale should not be imported where it is statutorily provided that legal title cannot pass until ascertainment has taken place. Bridge notes that the learned Lord Justice did concede that a seller of goods could explicitly provide for an 'equity' arising by way of charge, assignment or other disposition, but considered that no such provision had been made by the terms of the agreement before him.[280] However, he also notes that, given that the creation of such rights would almost certainly inhibit the seller's trading operations, the courts would be slow to reach the conclusion that this was the actual intention of the parties.[281]

---

[277] (1862) 10 HLC 191.

[278] [1927] 1 Ch 606.

[279] *Ibid.* For cogent criticism of this approach, see Sir Frederick Pollock, (1927) 43 LQR 293.

[280] See Bridge, M, *The Sale of Goods* (1997), p 83.

[281] *Ibid*, p 83. This is entirely consonant with the approach of the courts to the construction of retention of title clauses which purport to extend to the proceeds of a resale of the goods or to products manufactured with them: see below at section 12.

This approach was confirmed by the Privy Council in *Re Goldcorp Exchange Ltd.*[282] The case concerned a company which dealt in gold and other precious metals. The company sent brochures inviting investment in these items, and investors were promised that the company would retain a sufficient stock of metal to fulfil all its obligations and that the investors could call for delivery of 'their' metal, for which they were presented with a certificate of ownership, on payment of a nominal fee and delivery costs. In fact, no adequate store of metals was acquired and, when the company entered insolvency proceedings, its bank claimed priority under its security interest over what metals *were* held by the company. The pre-paying investors argued that, whilst the metals in question had at all times remained unascertained, so that title could not have passed to them under the New Zealand equivalent of s. 16 Sale of Goods Act 1979, the terms of the contract gave rise to a trust of the company's stocks of metals, with those customers as the beneficiaries. Lord Mustill dealt with that argument by cogently demonstrating that no intention to create such a trust could be inferred from the terms of the contract:

> 'The company cannot have intended to create an interest in its general stock of gold which would have inhibited any dealings with it otherwise than for the purpose of delivery under the non-allocated sale contracts.'[283]

Attempts in the same case to persuade the court that other equitable rights, such as those under a Quistclose or constructive trust, or based on estoppel, arose out of the contractual nexus between the parties were rejected.

The overall conclusions to be drawn from this analysis must be that it will be a very unusual case indeed where a court is persuaded that equitable proprietary rights in unascertained goods will arise out of a contract for their sale. Therefore, the perceived integrity of the Sale of Goods Act scheme for the passing of property has, and no doubt will continue to be, jealously guarded from equitable intervention. The harshness of cases like *Re Wait* has been somewhat tempered by the enactment of s. 20A of the Sale of Goods Act, which now allows for the transfer of property rights to goods which form part of a bulk.[284]

---

[282] [1995] 1 AC 74.
[283] *Ibid*, p 91.
[284] See below at section 5.4.2.(b).

5.2.2. Party autonomy

Party autonomy plays a central role in the rules governing the transfer of
movable property in English law. Indeed, what might be described as the
paradigm vehicle for the transfer of movable property, the sale of goods,
proceeds upon the basis that the precise moment at which property passes
falls to be determined by the parties to the contract of sale.[285] There is
one notable exception to this general rule, dealt with immediately above,
where the subject matter of the contract is unascertained goods, although
even in that context it has been conceded that the parties may, by explicitly so providing, confer upon the buyer *equitable proprietary rights* in unascertained goods.[286] Moreover, s. 20A of the Sale of Goods Act 1979 tem-
pers the perceived harshness of this rule by allowing parties to a contract
for the sale of unascertained goods to provide that property rights in a
proportion of an identified bulk shall pass from seller to pre-paying
buyer.[287]

    In terms of transactions other than sale, party autonomy is arguably
more restricted, in the sense that a gift of property must be perfected by
delivery, or a delivery equivalent, to be valid and enforceable.[288] However, an alternative to delivery is a declaration of trust over the property
in question, conferring equitable proprietary rights on the donee. Indeed,
the superimposition of equitable property rights onto the legal map affords English law considerable (but not unlimited) flexibility in terms of
the creation of property rights. It might be argued that equitable proprietary rights are unacceptably prejudicial to third parties, in that they do
not require registration,[289] or, indeed, any form of physical possession or
control on the part of the beneficiary to alert a third party to his equitable rights in the property. However, it is a well established principle that
the *bona fide* purchaser of a legal estate in property without notice of the
pre-existing equitable rights in that same property takes it unencumbered
by those rights.[290] Moreover, in the context of the law of personal property, the courts have been reluctant to allow the doctrine of *constructive*

---

[285] See below at section 5.4.

[286] *Re Wait* [1927] 1 Ch 606, and see the discussion in section 5.2.1. above.

[287] See below at section 5.4.2.(b).

[288] See below at section 5.4.1.

[289] With the exception of equitable charges, which depend for their validity in the
      event of the insolvency of the chargor on registration within 21 days of creation
      under the scheme in the Companies Act 1985, ss. 395, 396.

[290] *Pilcher v Rawlins* (1872) 7 Ch App 259.

notice[291] to infiltrate commercial transactions. In *Manchester Trust v Furness*[292] it was asserted that:

> '... as regards the extension of the equitable doctrines of constructive notice to commercial transactions, the Courts have always set their faces resolutely against it. The equitable doctrines of constructive notice are common enough in dealing with land and estates, with which the Court is familiar; but there have been repeated protests against the introduction into commercial transactions of anything like an extension of those doctrines, and the protest is founded on perfect good sense. In dealing with estates in land title is everything, and it can be leisurely investigated; in commercial transactions possession is everything, and there is no time to investigate title; and if we were to extend the doctrine of constructive notice to commercial transactions we should be doing infinite mischief and paralysing the trade of the country.'[293]

It might also be argued, aside from the creation of equitable proprietary rights, the English law deference to party autonomy prejudices third parties in other respects. Because a transfer of ownership rights can be effected without any contemporaneous transfer of possession,[294] the possibility that the same movable could be the subject of several purported transfers arises. This is addressed by the rules on overriding legal rights as detailed below.[295]

5.3. Requirement of a valid obligation to transfer ownership

5.3.1. Types of obligation

(a) Gift

The English doctrine of consideration ensures that a gift and a contract are conceptually distinct while executory; once the transaction is executed, however, that distinction lessens somewhat. A promise to make a gift is not one enforceable by the intended donee unless it is made by

---

[291] The knowledge that a party *would have acquired* had he made all those reasonable enquiries that a prudent party in his position would have made.

[292] [1895] 2 QB 539.

[293] *Per* Lindley LJ at 545.

[294] See below at section 5.4.

[295] At section 10.

deed,[296] but once the subject matter of the gift has been transferred to the donee the gift becomes legally binding (provided that that disposition is coupled with a present intention in the donor to transfer an immediate benefit to the donee).[297] Perhaps the best justification for this rule is that it preserves the right of the potential donor to change his mind. There are three ways in which the gratuitous disposition might take effect: by execution and delivery of a deed;[298] by the physical delivery of the object; or by the institution of a trust in favour of the donee.[299]

(b)   Contract

Certainly the most common method used to effect a transfer of ownership in a sale of goods is a contract of sale, but it has been cogently argued that this is not the only method.[300] Before the enactment of the Sale of Goods Act 1893 (the pre-cursor of the 1979 Act) property could be passed by means of delivery and deed as well as by contract. However, the Act is silent as to the other two methods, speaking only of contract, and its description as a 'Code' of the law in this area points to the conclusion that delivery and deed were impliedly abolished as means of passing title in sales transactions. Where the contract is void, however, it might be that title may pass by other means.

(c)   Unjust enrichment

Whether or not proprietary rights, including ownership, can be created as a result of unjust enrichment is a matter of intense debate and reference should be made to standard works on restitution for details. As the law currently stands there is authority, albeit now heavily criticised,[301] that money paid as on a mistaken basis is held on trust by the payee for the payer: *Chase Manhattan Bank v Israel-British Bank*.[302] Moreover, the law of

---

[296] This position is maintained in equity, which 'will not assist a volunteer', although authorities such as *Re Rose* [1949] Ch 78 and *Pennington v Waine* [2002] 1 WLR 2075 arguably blur the edges of the theoretical distinction.

[297] *Cochrane v Moore* (1890) 25 QBD 57.

[298] See The Law of Property (Miscellaneous Provisions) Act 1989, s. 1(2) for requirements.

[299] Reference should be made to standard texts on equity for details.

[300] See, Swadling, 'Rescission, Property and the Common Law', [2005] 121 LQR 123.

[301] *Westdeutsche Landesbank Zentrale v Islington London Borough Council* [1996] AC 669 at p 715 *per* Lord Browne-Wilkinson.

[302] [1981] 1 Ch 105.

rescission arguably operates to reverse unjust enrichment and so might be regarded as a proprietary response, since it operates to revest title, but even this is subject to doubt.[303]

(d)   Wrongs

Again, whether a wrong can generate property rights is a controversial question. There is one case in which that occurred (*Attorney-General of Hong Kong v Reid*),[304] but this has been the subject of academic criticism.[305]

5.3.2.   Defective obligations

(a)   Capacity

Under a sale of goods contract 'capacity to buy and sell is regulated by the general law concerning capacity to contract and to transfer and acquire property'.[306] A minor, *i.e.* one aged under 18,[307] or one who by reason of mental incapacity or drunkenness is incompetent to contract, must pay a reasonable price for 'necessaries'[308] that have been sold and delivered to them.[309]

Minors are bound by contracts for necessaries, but only if the contract is on the whole for their benefit. Where a contract is incapable of being divided and pertains to both necessaries and non-necessaries the minor is not bound. It is submitted that a minor is bound by both executory and executed contracts for the sale of goods.[310] Secondly, a minor's contract is voidable at his option in four cases: contracts concerning land; shares in companies; partnership; marriage settlements.[311] Where the contract falls into neither of the two preceding categories it will not bind the minor but does have legal effects.

---

[303] Swadling, above n 300.

[304] [1994] 1 AC 324.

[305] See, for example, Crilley, 'A Case of Proprietary Overkill', [1994] RLR 57.

[306] Sale of Goods Act 1979, s. 3(1).

[307] Family Law Reform Act 1969, s. 1.

[308] Defined as 'goods suitable to the condition in life of the minor or other person concerned and to his actual requirements at the time of the sale and delivery': SGA 1979, s. 3(3).

[309] Sale of Goods Act 1979, s. 3(2).

[310] See, Treitel, *The Law of Contract* (2003), at p 542.

[311] *Ibid* at pp 545-547.

First, the other party is bound.[312] Secondly, it can be ratified by a minor upon reaching majority, at which point he will be fully bound. Thirdly, once the contract has been executed the fact that it did not bind him by reason of his majority will not permit him to recover the money paid or property transferred;[313] he has at his disposal only those remedies available to an adult in the same situation. It seems that property may pass to a minor, in spite of the contract not binding him, if the property is delivered to him.[314] This seems to add force to the argument above at 5.3.1.2, that property can pass by delivery in spite of a void contract.[315] Moreover, property can also pass from a minor under a contract that does not bind him,[316] although it is perhaps arguable that if he lacks the capacity to contract he might also lack the capacity to transfer property.

Generally contracts made with a person under a mental incapacity[317] are valid, but if at the time of contracting the counterparty knows of the other's disability then the contract is voidable at the option of the *incapax*.[318] However, the person becomes bound if, having been cured of his disability, he ratifies the contract. Where the counterparty is unaware of the disability then the contract binds the *incapax* and he may not escape the bargain merely on the grounds that it is more favourable in its terms to the counterparty.[319]

If a person under a disability has his property subject to the control of the court then an attempt to dispose of it will not bind him.[320] It is said that where a contract for necessaries is made by an *incapax* in a situation where it binds him then s. 3(2) Sale of Goods Act 1979 does not affect the contract and the counterparty can enforce it.[321] This is to be compared with the situation in which the counterparty knows of the disability. Here the other party is limited to recovery of a reasonable price.

Similar rules apply to a contracting party whose understanding of the transaction is fundamentally impaired by reason of drink and the counterparty knows this.[322] If he ratifies when sober the contract binds as

---

[312] *Farnham v Atkins* (1670) 1 Sid 446.

[313] *Wilson v Kearse* (1800) Peake Add Cas 196.

[314] *Stocks v Wilson* [1913] 2 KB 235.

[315] See, Swadling, above n 300 at p 141.

[316] *Chaplin v Leslie Frewin (Publishers) Ltd* [1966] Ch 71.

[317] I.e. a person suffering from a mental disorder within the Mental Health Act 1983.

[318] *Imperial Loan Co v Stone* [1892] 1 QB 599.

[319] *Hart v O'Connor* [1985] AC 1000. This rule does not prevent the disabled party from invoking the standard rules on unconscionable bargains and undue influence.

[320] *Re Walker* [1905] 1 Ch 160.

[321] Treitel, above n 310 at p 558.

[322] *Gore v Gibson* (1843) 13 M & W 623.

normal. Moreover, he is liable for necessaries in the same way as an *incapax*.[323]

Reforms in the area of company law have meant that in the majority of cases a company's lack of capacity by reason of anything in its memorandum is not a matter that can call the validity of a transaction into question.[324] Moreover, where a person deals in good faith with a company, the power of the board of directors to bind the company, or authorise others to do so, shall be deemed free of any limitations under the company's constitution (s. 35A).

(b)   Void contract

The classic case here is *Cundy v Lindsay*.[325] In that case it was held that no contract was formed between the two would-be parties, with the result that title to the goods in question never moved from their original owner. Thus, it seems that a void contract leads to a void title. This approach, which has been followed without question by subsequent cases,[326] appears to overlook the possibility of passing title to chattels by other means.[327] Accordingly, there is something of an inconsistency between *Cundy v Lindsay* and the cases that follow it, and authorities on incapacity and illegality, in which property was held to pass independently of any contract.[328]

(c)   Voidable contract

The traditional view is that where a contract that is capable of being avoided is rescinded it revests title to any goods transferred under it.[329] The proprietary consequences of this and its relation to the *nemo dat* rule are discussed below at 10.1.5. *et seq*. It has also been argued that cases in this category do not consider other potential methods by which title might be passed.[330]

---

[323] *Ibid.*

[324] Companies Act 1985, s. 35(1). For more detail on this area see Davies, *Gower and Davies' Principles of Modern Company Law* (2003), chapter 7.

[325] (1878) 3 App Cas 459.

[326] See, for example, *Shogun Finance Ltd v Hudson* [2004] 1 AC 919.

[327] See above at 5.3.2.(a).

[328] *Stocks v Wilson* [1913] 2 KB 235; *Singh v Ali* [1960] AC 167. See, Swadling, above n 300, at pp 142.

[329] For example, *Lewis v Avery* [1972] 1 QB 198; *Car & Universal Finance Co Ltd v Caldwell* [1965] 1 QB 525.

[330] Swadling, above n 300.

(d)   Breach

A breach of the contract by one party may entitle the other to a number
of remedies, but does not automatically terminate the agreement. The
'innocent' party, *i.e.* the party not in breach, is given the choice of terminating or affirming the contract.[331] The injured party is entitled as of
right to compensation in damages.[332] In a sale of goods context the seller
may maintain an action for the price of the goods where property in them
has passed to a buyer that wrongfully neglects or refuses to pay for them
(s. 49 SGA 1979). Equally, a buyer may maintain an action for damages
for non-delivery (s. 51 SGA 1979). The injured party may also seek specific performance of the defaulting party's obligation. This might entail the
transfer of specific or ascertained property by the seller to the buyer where
'the court thinks fit' (s. 52 Sale of Goods Act 1979). The remedy is discretionary, and will only be granted where the goods in question are
'unique' in the sense that damages would not be an adequate remedy for
the buyer; several factors can affect the exercise of the discretion, for
example, the conduct of the claimant.[333]

5.4.   Delivery and delivery equivalents

5.4.1.   Gifts

As mentioned above, delivery is used as one of the methods by which a
gift of a chattel can be perfected. In order to qualify the act must amount
to a clear, unequivocal transfer of possession.[334] An actual delivery will
clearly suffice, however, this can be difficult to achieve in the case of
some chattels, for example, a church organ, which was the subject of the
gift in *Rawlinson v Mort*.[335] The organ was on loan to the church in which
it was situated but the owner sought to give it to the church organist and
so he gave him a letter from the vicar evidencing the loan and the receipts from the organ's purchase. In addition he placed his hand on the
organ and announced in front of the organist and another party that he
was giving it to the organist. It was held that the gift was complete, if not

---

[331] See Treitel, above n 310, at pp 844.

[332] *Ibid* at p 926.

[333] *Ibid* at pp 1026-1029.

[334] *Re Cole* [1964] Ch 175. In this case a husband took his wife on a tour of their new
home, after which he told her, 'it's all yours'. It was held that this was not a sufficient act of delivery, with the result that contents of the house fell into the husband's estate on his bankruptcy.

[335] (1905) 93 LT 555.

when the *indicia* of title were actually delivered to the organist then when the owner performed the later act.

Another form of delivery that diverged from the standard model occurred in *Thomas v Times Book Co*,[336] in which Dylan Thomas, having lost the original manuscript for his play 'Under Milk Wood', told the donee that if he found it he could keep it and then suggested a number of locations he might try. It was held that there was both a donative intent and sufficient act of delivery to perfect a gift. Although not mentioned in the reasoning, it is submitted that this might be categorised as a form of delivery that fits the definition of constructive delivery: What the donor gave was not the chattel itself but the means by which effective control of it might be obtained. The delivery can precede the words of gift,[337] so that if the intended donee is in possession of the chattel only the requirement of donative intent need be fulfilled.[338]

5.4.2. Sale

Delivery, either actual or constructive, is not necessary in order that property in goods can pass from a seller to a buyer, since property can pass under a contract of sale;[339] for this reason delivery does not assume the same legal significance as it does in other areas, although, of course, it is practically important. Delivery terminates the seller's possession of the goods and with it any lien he may have enjoyed. The passing of property can occur before, at the time of or after delivery, and it is the duty of the seller to deliver the goods and of the buyer to accept and pay for them, in accordance with the terms of the contract (s. 27 Sale of Goods Act 1979). This subject is governed by the Sale of Goods Act 1979,[340] the central tenet of which is the intention of the parties to the contract of sale.

(a)   Specific goods

Section 17 of the Act states that property in specific goods will pass when the parties intend it to, and in ascertaining that intention the court is directed to have regard to the terms of the contract, the conduct of the parties and the circumstances of the case (s. 17(2)). The Act does not

---

[336] [1966] 2 All ER 241.

[337] *Re Cole* [1964] Ch 175 at p 191 *per* Pearson LJ.

[338] *Re Stoneham* [1919] 1 Ch 149.

[339] The question of the precise role of delivery in the context of sale is, however, yet to be resolved.

[340] Following the Sale of Goods Act 1893, which first codified the area.

just leave the courts with this 'vague'[341] provision; it goes on to provide in s. 18 a set of presumptive rules for use in ascertaining intention, which, being presumption, can of course be rebutted by contrary intention expressed by the parties.

Rule 1 provides that 'where there is an unconditional contract for the sale of specific goods in a deliverable state the property in the goods passes to the buyer when the contract is made, and it is immaterial whether the time of payment or the time of delivery, or both, be postponed'. The term 'unconditional contract' refers to one not subject to any condition upon the fulfilment of which the transfer of property depends.[342] Goods are in a 'deliverable state' 'when they are in such a state that the buyer would under the contract be bound to take delivery of them' (s. 61(5)), and it has been said that 'deliverable state' does not 'depend upon the mere completeness of the subject matter in all its parts. It depends on the actual state of the goods at the date of the contract and the state in which they are to be delivered by the terms of the contract'.[343] The rule has been criticised as being commercially unrealistic, for example in that it leaves the seller to risk the buyer's insolvency as soon as the contract is made, and for this reason it seems to take very little to persuade a court that there is somewhere demonstrated a contrary intention that rebuts the rule.

Rule 2 deals with the situation in which there is a contract for the sale of specific goods and the seller is bound to do something to the goods for the purpose of putting them into a deliverable state. Where this is the case, the property does not pass until the thing is done and the buyer has notice of that is has been done. Accordingly, rule 2 fits with the 'deliverable state' requirement in the first rule. It is submitted that the 'notice' element requires actual knowledge and not constructive knowledge in line with the general rule that there is no room for the latter form in commercial transactions.[344]

Rule 3 similarly fits with the principle of the first rule. Under rule 3, where there is a contract for the sale of specific goods in a deliverable state but the seller is bound to weigh, measure, test or do some other act or thing with reference to the goods for the purpose of ascertaining the price, the property does not pass until the act or thing is done and the buyer has notice that it has been done.

Rule 4 covers sales on approval and sale and return, and states that:

---

[341] See *Varley v Whipp* [1900] 1 QB 513 at p 517 *per* Channell J.

[342] See *Benjamin's* at 5-019.

[343] *Underwood Ltd v Burgh Castle Brick and Cement Syndicate* [1922] 1 KB 343 at p 345 *per* Bankes LJ.

[344] See *Benjamin's*, at 5-034.

'When goods are delivered to the buyer on approval or on sale or return or other similar terms the property in the goods passes to the buyer:

(a) when he signifies his approval or acceptance to the seller or does any other act adopting the transaction;

(b) if he does not signify his approval or acceptance to the seller but retains the goods without giving notice of the rejection, then, if a time has been fixed for the return of the goods, on the expiration of that time, and, if no time has been fixed, or the expiration of a reasonable time.'

The sale or return transaction is operated with a view to resell to a sub-buyer and involves an offer to sell made by the seller to the buyer. A sale made on an approval basis is similar, save that no resale is contemplated. The question of what amounts to a reasonable time is, it submitted, a question to be answered on a case by case basis.[345]

The buyer is able to reject the goods before the time expires or the events deemed to be acceptance occur: *Atari Corp (UK) Ltd v Electronic Boutique Stores Ltd*.[346] In that case a statement of rejection was made, giving a generic description of the goods, which was held to be sufficient. The 'buyer' did not need to assemble the goods in one place ready for return, nor did the buyer have to return all or nothing. It was possible for the extent of the acceptance of the seller's offer to be referenced to the quantity of goods sold on to sub-buyers.

(b)   Unascertained goods

Section 16 of the Act states that, subject to section 20A (see below), where there is a contract for the sale of unascertained goods no property in the goods is transferred to the buyer unless and until the goods are ascertained. Ascertainment means the identification by the seller of the particular goods that are to form the subject matter of the contract,[347] and while ascertainment does not in itself pass property, it does remove the impediment to transfer occurring. The harshness of s. 16 is demonstrated by cases in which the buyer of part of a bulk has paid the purchase price

---

[345] See, for example, *Poole v Smith's Cars (Balham) Ltd* [1962] 2 All ER 482, in which the court held that after two months a reasonable time had expired, taking into account the circumstances of the case, including that the buyer had failed to respond to the seller's demands for the return of the car.

[346] [1998] QB 539.

[347] This can occur fortuitously, for example, where, after a number of contracts had been satisfied from a bulk, an amount remained which constituted the amount sold to a buyer: *The Elafi* [1982] 1 All ER 208. This is now placed on a statutory footing, see rules 5(3) and 5(4) SGA 1979.

to the seller, who has then become insolvent before property in the goods has passed.[348]

As a response to this the Sale of Goods (Amendment) Act 1995 was passed. Consequently a buyer who has paid for a specified quantity of unascertained goods that form part of an identified bulk can obtain property in an undivided and proportionate share of the bulk and thereby become an owner in common of the bulk (s. 20A).

Rule 5 in s. 18 concerns unascertained goods. Sub-rule (1) presumptively operates to pass property where goods 'in a deliverable state are unconditionally appropriated to the contract, either by the seller with the assent of the buyer or by the buyer with the assent of the seller'. Sub-rule (2) deals, *inter alia*, with the situation in which a carrier is used to transport the goods. The phrase 'unconditional appropriation' appears to set a high hurdle, having been held to require 'an intention to attach the contract irrevocably to the goods so that those goods and no others are the subject of the sale and become the property of the buyer'.[349] Usually, but not necessarily, the appropriating act will be the final act to be performed by the seller.[350]

5.5.   Right to dispose

Ownership of property in English law can be validly transferred by someone other than its owner. An obvious example arises where the property of a company is disposed of in some manner by its agents. An agent with express or implied authority to do so may validly transfer the property of his principal, see section 6 below. A different situation arises where the agent is not expressly authorised but appears to be because of a representation made by the true owner. Here ownership can pass to a third party but for different reasons, and this is considered in more detail below in section 12. It is possible for a principal to ratify an unauthorised act, provided the requirements for effective ratification are met.[351] The effect of a successful ratification by the principal is retrospectively to validate the acts of the agent.

Another similar method by which equitable ownership can be transferred by a non-owner is through the use of an equitable power, the exercise of which serves to transfer only an equitable interest in the property in question. This is a complex and involved topic that shades into the

---

[348] See *Re Wait* [1927] 1 Ch 606.

[349] *Carlos Federspiel & Co v Chalres Twigg & Co* [1957] 1 Lloyd's Rep 240 at p 255 *per* Pearson J. See further *Benjamin's*, at 5-071.

[350] *Ibid.*

[351] See, generally, *Bowstead & Reynolds on Agency* (2001).

law of trusts and reference should be made to specific works on the subject for more information.

6. Transfer or acquisition by means of indirect representation

6.1. Indirect representation in English Law

'[The] dichotomy between direct and indirect representation is unlikely to be attractive to common law systems, which tend to reach the result of direct representation with more facility than the civil law.'[352]

Whilst Bowstead continues that there is no *doctrinal* objection to a concept of indirect representation at common law,[353] that system has developed to distinguish starkly between *disclosed and undisclosed agency*, and to treat the two circumstances differently when it comes to questions of privity of contract between the principal and the third party to an agreement made for that principal by an agent. In the current context, the question would, under English law, tend to be framed as to whether a principal for whom property is acquired by an agent obtains rights directly in that property, or whether the agent acquires those rights and is then under some kind of obligation to hold them for or transfer them to the principal. The answer to this question may depend upon whether the principal is disclosed or undisclosed, as will the perhaps more important question of whether the principal can assert rights directly against the third party.[354]

6.1.1. Direct representation/disclosed principal

In very general terms, no difficulties arise in a case where an agent acting for a disclosed principal contracts with a third party to transfer the principal's property to the third party or to acquire the third party's property for the principal. In such circumstances, and this would appear to include

---

[352] *Bowstead & Reynolds on Agency* (2001), para 1-021.

[353] *Ibid*, and see, in support of this proposition, several 19th century cases on 'commission agents', who appear in many respects, to operate in a manner which would be understood as indirect representation in a civil law system. Such cases include *Ireland v Livingstone* (1872) LR 5 HL 396; *Armstrong v Stokes* (1872) LR 7 QB 598.

[354] For a lucid discussion of the difficulties surrounding English law's acceptance of the undisclosed principal doctrine, see Reynolds, 'Practical Problems of the Undisclosed Principal Doctrine', [1983] CLP 119.

circumstances where the principal is unnamed, there is privity of contract between principal and third party and all the implications of that privity arise, including the principal's ability to sue the third party directly for specific performance of the contract. Where the subject matter of the contract is real property (*i.e.*, land), the contract itself will generate an immediate equitable interest in its subject matter in favour of the principal. Where it is goods, and so subject to the Sale of Goods Act 1979, the normal rules as to passing of property will apply to pass title to the principal or to the third party as the case may be.[355]

6.1.2.   Undisclosed principal

The undisclosed principal is arguably the nearest common law equivalent to indirect representation as that term is understood in civil law jurisdictions.[356] The undisclosed principal (as opposed to the *unnamed* principal) is one of whose existence the third party is entirely unaware when he enters into agreement with an agent acting on behalf of such a principal. In other words, the third party believes a person who is actually acting as agent to be the principal. Thus, in the current context, where the principal is undisclosed the third party believes either that he is buying the agent's property or that he is selling his property to the agent. The question then arises as to the nature of any interest of the principal in property purchased by the agent on his behalf.

In this regard, English law has not developed a clear and settled position. It is certainly true that an undisclosed principal can sue, and be sued, on a contract made on his behalf by his agent, but this does not necessarily amount to the proposition that he is a full party to that contract. Two possibilities appear to have been canvassed by the courts and commentators, the first being that the undisclosed principal is a party to any contract made by an agent on his behalf,[357] but that his rights to intervene on such a contract are qualified by rules designed to protect the third party who knew nothing of his existence at the time of contracting. A second is that the contract is that of the agent and that the undisclosed principal, whilst not a party to it, may nevertheless intervene on it.[358] An

---

[355] See above at paragraph 5.4.

[356] See, for example, Hamel, *Le Contrat de Commission* (1942), pp 310-327. See also, on undisclosed principals in general, *Bowstead & Reynolds on Agency*, above, n 355, paras 8.071 *et seq*; Markesinis & Munday, *An Outline of the Law of Agency* (1998), pp 153 *et seq*; Stone, *Law of Agency*, (1997) pp 93-98, 130. See also Goodhart and Hamson 'Undisclosed principles in contracts', (1932) 4 CLJ 320.

[357] See, for example, *Keighley, Maxsted & Co v Durant* [1901] AC 240, 261.

[358] See *Welsh Development Agency v Export Finance Co Ltd* [1992] BCLC 148, 173.

analogy between the position of an undisclosed principal and an assignee of a chose in action in this regard was considered, and rejected, by the Privy Council in the case of *Siu Yin Kwan v Eastern Insurance Co Ltd*.[359]

However, whichever of these positions is correct, neither offers any definitive answer to the question posed above as to the rights of an undisclosed principal in property acquired on his behalf by his agent. None of the decided cases address directly the issue of whether, where goods are acquired on behalf of an undisclosed principal, that undisclosed principal can claim that property in the goods passes to him. Rather they are concerned with the question of whether a third party can assert against an undisclosed principal rights which he could have asserted against the agent,[360] or, indeed, whether the undisclosed principal can intervene on the contract at all.[361]

Given the unsettled authorities in this area, it is therefore difficult to state with certainty when an undisclosed principal obtains *full* property in movables acquired by an agent on his behalf. However, there is room to argue that this question can be addressed by regard to the *internal consequences* of the agency relationship, which English law treats as a status based fiduciary relationship.[362] The distinguishing feature of a relationship defined as fiduciary is that, *by operation of law*, and entirely apart from any contract between the parties, duties are imposed on the fiduciary, the overarching duty being to act at all times in the interest of the beneficiary, in this case the principal.[363] Thus, it might be argued that where an agent acquires property for an undisclosed principal he falls under an immediate obligation in equity to deliver that property to the principal, or at least to hold it to the order of the principal.

Whether such an obligation confers upon the principal property rights is a difficult question. It seems almost certain that if the agent is treated as the *only* party to the contract where the principal is undisclosed, then only the agent acquires *legal* property rights in the subject matter of the contract.[364] It might be argued, however, that from the moment the agent acquires the legal property in the movable then he holds it on trust for the undisclosed principal. Where the movable is acquired with the prin-

---

[359] [1994] 2 AC 199.

[360] *Browning v Provincial Insurance Co of Canada* (1873) LR 5 PC 267; *Rabone v Williams* (1785) 7 TR 360; *Cooke & Sons v Eshelby* (1887) 12 App Cas 271.

[361] *Said v Butt* [1920] 3 KB 497; *Greer v Downs Supply Co* [1927] 2 KB 28; *Dyster v Randall* [1926] Ch 932.

[362] See, for example, *De Bussche v Alt* (1878) 8 Ch D 286.

[363] For an explanation of the distinction between contractual and fiduciary duties see *Bristol & West Building Society v Mothew* [1998] Ch 1.

[364] When this occurs will depend upon the rules for the passing of property in goods under the Sale of Goods Act 1979: see above at 5.4.

cipal's money, or the principal has provided consideration in relation to the acquisition of the movable, this seems a particularly strong contention, perhaps by analogy with the case of *Cook v Deeks*.[365] In that case company directors (who, in English law, are analogous to agents of the company) negotiated a contract on behalf of the corporate principal, only to later sign it for themselves in clear breach of their fiduciary duties to the company. The benefit of the contract was treated as belonging in equity to the company and the directors were required to account to the company for any profits they had personally gained out of it. Thus, it might be said that where property is acquired through the use of the principal's money or property the acquiring agent, although holding the bare legal title to it, has no *beneficial* interest in it and holds it on trust for the principal. The fact that that principal was undisclosed at the time of the acquisition should not make any difference to a question which proceeds entirely on the basis of the nature of the agent/principal relationship.

A more difficult question arises where the agent uses his own funds to acquire the movable for an undisclosed principal. In circumstances where it is clearly contemplated, as between agent and undisclosed principal, that the acquisition is on behalf of the principal, can the analysis above be extended to confer upon the principal an immediate equitable proprietary right in the movable? Given that the agent is a fiduciary, and again proceeding by analogy with decided cases, there may be an argument that the agent holds the movable on trust for the principal. In *A-G for Hong Kong v Reid*[366] the agent in question was a Crown prosecutor who accepted bribes from potential defendants in return for ensuring that they were not prosecuted. The Privy Council considered that, as the taking of a bribe in this way amounted to a clear breach of fiduciary duty to the principal (the Crown), the agent came under an immediate duty to account for the value of the bribe so as to disgorge the unauthorised profit he had made. The next stage of the analysis was the application of the equitable doctrine of conversion:[367] Given that the agent comes under such a duty, in equity he is taken to have complied with it and thereafter holds the bribe, and, indeed any fruits of it, on trust for the principal.

There is, however, Court of Appeal authority in direct contrast to *Reid*. In *Lister & Co v Stubbs*,[368] a principal was held to have no *proprietary* interest in a bribe taken by his employee. Whilst accepting the proposition that an agent in these circumstances was under a duty to account for the bribe, this remedy was characterised as *in personam* only, and the relationship between principal and agent that of creditor and debtor. The

---

[365] [1916] 1 AC 554.

[366] [1994] 1 AC 324.

[367] See above, paras 3.4.1, 5.2.2.(b).

[368] (1890) 45 Ch D 1.

principal distinctions between *Reid* and *Lister* are, firstly, that the former clearly allows the principal to claim any 'fruits' of the original unauthorised profit, a position which the latter does not appear to contemplate.[369] Secondly, if *Reid* is correct, the principal has a priority claim to both the amount of the unauthorised profit *and* any fruits in the event of the agent's insolvency,[370] whereas if the *Lister* approach is followed the principal ranks *pari passu* with the agent's other unsecured creditors. As a decision of the Court of Appeal, it is submitted that *Lister v Stubbs* represents English law, and, further, that in the context of unauthorised profits, is the better solution.[371]

It may well be objected, however, that the above analysis is based on an imperfect analogy. There is a fundamental difference between the cases where an agent acquires a benefit in breach of his duty and where he acquires property for an undisclosed principal, and to focus on the internal aspects of the agent/principal relationship to clothe the principal with proprietary rights ignores the position of the transferee. Indeed, in cases regarding the rights of an undisclosed principal to intervene on a contract made by his agent, the courts have developed rules to prevent such intervention where the identity of the agent is material to the third party or the contract in question is of an intensely personal nature.[372] With this is mind, it might perhaps be more instructive to compare the undisclosed principal position with that arising in the context of corporate law where a company promoter purports to contract on behalf of a company which has yet to be formed and registered (*i.e.*, a *non-existent* principal).

In these circumstances, section 36A Companies Act 1985 provides as follows:

'A contract which purports to be made by or on behalf of a company at a time when the company has not been formed has effect, subject to any agreement to the contrary, as one made with the person purporting to act for the company or as agent for it, and he is personally liable on the contract accordingly.'

The scope of this section was considered by the Court of Appeal in *Braymist v Wise Finance Co Ltd*.[373] The question arising for the court was whether s. 36C, which clearly allows a third party to hold an 'agent' pur-

---

[369] But see Virgo, *The Principles of the Law of Restitution* (1999), pp 518-544.

[370] As is often the case, insolvency turns out to be the testing ground for proprietary rights.

[371] Any argument that a proprietary analysis is necessary to require the agent to disgorge *the entirety* of his gain may be countered by reference to remoteness of gain principles.

[372] *Said v Butt* [1920] 3 KB 497, but see also *Dyster v Randall* [1926] Ch 932.

[373] [2002] EWCA Civ 127.

porting to act for an unformed company personally liable on such a contract, could also be used by the 'agent' to enforce the contract.[374] Arden
LJ considered that whilst the section itself made no such provision, the
common law would allow enforcement by the agent, but subject to a
qualification:

> '… in determining such rules the law has to have regard among other consid-
> erations to the position of third parties who claim that they would not have
> entered into a contract if they had known the other party was not the princi-
> pal whom they thought they were contracting for some other party. It may be
> that they rely on the skill of that other party or on his solvency or on some
> other quality altogether.'[375]

This seems resonant of those authorities which appear to hold that where
the identity of the agent is material an undisclosed principal may not
intervene on a contract made by the agent, although, of course, the *Braymist* analysis focuses on the identity of the purported *principal*. It might,
therefore, be argued that this approach might be appropriately adopted to
deal with questions as to whether an undisclosed principal can claim
proprietary rights enforceable against his agent where the third party who
transferred those rights in the first instance can raise an objection based
on the identity of either the agent or the undisclosed principal.

In the event, the preceding discussion is speculative in the extreme.
Given the want of any direct, or even indirect, authority on the question
of whether an undisclosed principal acquires property rights in the subject
matter of a contract entered into on his behalf by an agent, the best that
can be said is that there remains the possibility that the courts would consider that an agent holds the property acquired on trust for the principal,
but that this position may well be subject to considerable qualification.

7.   The impact of insolvency of the transferor or of the transferee

7.1.   Insolvency procedures in English Law

Before considering the particular consequences of the insolvency of either
the transferor or the transferee of a movable, it is worth briefly examining
the main insolvency procedures to which the transferor or transferee
might be subject in the event of insolvency. Individual insolvency is gen-

---

[374] English law does not allow the company, once formed, to ratify the agreement,
requiring instead a novation between company and third party.
[375] [2002] EWCA Civ 127, para 63.

erally referred to as 'bankruptcy' under the English system, with the term 'insolvency' tending to apply to companies and, in certain cases, partnerships.

In the corporate context, the predominant insolvency procedure is liquidation, which may be voluntary, in the sense that it is prompted by a resolution of the company to the effect that it should be wound up. In such circumstances, the winding up of a solvent company is known as a members' voluntary winding up and an insolvent company as a creditors' voluntary winding up (a CVL). Where, for whatever reason, no resolution is passed the company's creditors may petition the court for an order that the company be wound up. The court is afforded power to make a winding up order in the circumstances described in section 122 of the Insolvency Act 1986, those circumstances including that the company is unable to pay its debts.[376] In outline, in the event of either a voluntary or a court-ordered winding up the company's assets fall under the control of an insolvency official known as a liquidator, who will deal with those assets with a view to eventually making a distribution of their proceeds to parties eligible to claim in the liquidation.

Personal bankruptcy is dealt with by Part IX of the Insolvency Act 1986. A bankruptcy petition may be presented to the court by the bankrupt himself or by one or more of his creditors.[377] The court must be satisfied, in either event, that the debtor is unable to pay his debts.[378] On the making of a bankruptcy order the bankrupt's creditors have power to appoint a trustee in bankruptcy[379] whose main functions are to get in, realise and distribute the bankrupt's estate'[380] in accordance with the scheme of the insolvency legislation. In this respect there is a considerable similarity between a liquidator of a company and a trustee in bankruptcy of an individual.

Two further procedures in relation to corporate insolvency should be mentioned, and these are administrative receivership and administration. The former is a procedure which may be invoked by the holder of a floating charge[381] which extends, along with any other security interest or interests, to the whole or substantially the whole of a company's property.[382] Administrative receivership might almost be described as a 'privatised' insolvency procedure, in that the receiver is appointed by a single credi-

---

[376] Insolvency Act 1986, s. 122(1)(f). Section 123 goes on to define the concept of inability to pay debts.

[377] Insolvency Act 1986, s. 264.

[378] Insolvency Act 1986, ss. 267(2), 272.

[379] See Chapter 3 of Part IX Insolvency Act 1986 on trustees in bankruptcy.

[380] Insolvency Act 1986, s. 305(2).

[381] On floating charges generally see below at section 15.

[382] Insolvency Act 1986 s. 29(2).

tor (the charge holder) and is responsible for dealing with property subject to that charge holder's security in order to discharge the secured debt.[383] Given the perception that this procedure is excessively partisan, the Enterprise Act 2002 sought to limit its availability in favour of the administration procedure. This was achieved by restricting, prospectively, the ability of a floating charge holder to appoint an administrative receiver unless the appointment fell within a number of specified exceptions. The basic prohibition is now contained in s. 72A Insolvency Act 1986, but applies only where the floating charge in question was granted on or after 15 September 2003. The specific exceptions to the prohibition are contained in ss. 72B-72GA Insolvency Act 1986.

The administration procedure was first introduced into English law in the Insolvency Act 1986, following recommendations made by the Cork Report.[384] The Enterprise Act of 2002 made a number of changes to the law of administration, both substantive and procedural, which is now largely contained in Schedule B1 to the Insolvency Act 1986. An administrator may be appointed by order of the court,[385] by a qualifying floating charge holder,[386] or by the company or its directors.[387] An administrator, once appointed, is under a duty to attempt to rescue the company as a going concern *unless* he thinks that this is not reasonably practicable *or* that the company's creditors as a whole would be better served by the pursuit of some other strategy.[388]

7.1.1. Rights of avoidance ex ante in English insolvency Law

Where a contract for the transfer of a movable has been entered into but remains executory (in the sense that the property in the movable has yet to be transferred) what is the effect of the insolvency of the transferor or the transferee? The first point to make is that the fact of insolvency, or entry into a formal insolvency procedure, does not of itself have any effect on such a contract. However, it may be open to a liquidator, administrator, administrative receiver or trustee in bankruptcy to refuse to perform the outstanding obligations under it, which would, for present pur-

---

[383] There is a whole body of literature dealing with both the law of administrative receivership and administration. For an overview the reader is directed to Goode, *Principles of Corporate Insolvency Law* (2004), Chapters 9 and 10.

[384] 'Insolvency Law and Practice: Report of the Review Committee' (1982).

[385] Para 12, Schedule B1 Insolvency Act 1986.

[386] Para 14, Schedule B1 Insolvency Act 1986. This was the *quid pro quo* for such a charge holder's loss of the power to appoint and administrative receiver: see above.

[387] Para 22, Schedule B1 Insolvency Act 1986.

[388] Para 3(1), (3), Schedule B1 Insolvency Act 1986.

poses, include the obligation to deliver the movable (where the transferor is insolvent and subject to formal insolvency proceedings). Such a refusal would amount to a breach of contract, the traditional remedy for which is damages. However, any damages award would be payable in insolvency currency, leaving the transferee with what is arguably a worthless remedy.

The question arises as to whether an insolvency officer of the type described above may be compelled to perform the insolvent's obligations to transfer property rights in the movable. A liquidator is given a statutory power, under s. 178 Insolvency Act 1986, to 'disclaim' onerous property, which is defined as including 'an unprofitable contract'.[389] However, in the current context, a contract will not be unprofitable merely because the company could have made, or, indeed, could make, a better bargain.[390] Similar provisions apply to the trustee in bankruptcy of an individual insolvent.[391]

As far as administrative receivers are concerned, it has been held that such a receiver may cause the company to fail to perform its pre-receivership contractual obligation to transfer property in *Lathia v Dronsfield Bros*.[392] However, injunctive relief to prevent the breach, or an order of specific performance in relation to the contract *may* be available, but only where the counter-party to the agreement has, by virtue of it, acquired proprietary rights in its subject matter which would take priority to those of the charge holder who appointed the receiver. This much is established by the case of *Astor Chemicals Ltd v Synthetic Technology Ltd*,[393] although it should be noted that, in general, only contracts to transfer an estate or interest in land would generate such priority rights.[394] The position as regards administrators is not at all clear. The position of administrative receivers is based on their appointors' priority claim (or otherwise) over the subject matter of the contract, but an administrator may be appointed by the court or by the company or its directors itself. Even where appointed by a qualifying floating charge holder, the administrator owes duties to the general body of creditors, and, as an officer of the court,[395] is under a duty to act honourably.[396]

---

[389] Section 178(3)(a).

[390] See *Squires v AIG Europe (UK) Ltd* [2006] EWCA Civ 7, where Chadwick LJ adopted five principles summed up by Chesterman J in the Australian case of *Transmetro Corporation Ltd v Real Investments Pty Ltd* (1999) 17 ACLC 1314 at p 1329.

[391] See ss. 315-321 Insolvency Act 1986.

[392] [1987] BCLC 321.

[393] [1990] BCLC 1.

[394] See, *e.g.*, *Freevale Ltd v Metrostore Holdings Ltd* [1984] Ch 199.

[395] Insolvency Act 1986, Schedule B1 para 5.

[396] *Ex Parte James* [1803-1813] All ER Rep 78: the precise parameters of this duty have never been fully established.

One possibility, perhaps remote, is that administrators refusing to perform a contract to transfer movables could be held *personally liable* in tort
for interfering in the contractual relations between the company and
counter-party. Such an analysis was rejected in relation to administrative
receivers in *Lathia v Dronsfield*, above, and confirmed by the Court of
Appeal in *Welsh Development Agency v Export Finance Co Ltd*[397] on the
basis that a receiver is a statutory agent of the company and the case of
Said v Butt[398] establishes that an agent can never be liable for interference
with contractual relations between his principal and a third party. This
decision was based on the conceptual difficulty caused by the fact that an
agent is his principal's *alter ego*, and a principal cannot be made liable for
inducing or procuring *his own breach of contract*. The reasoning has been
criticised and seems almost certainly misconceived, but nevertheless the
Court of Appeal in *Welsh Development Agency* felt that the case had
'stood for so long and been so widely accepted that it is not for this court,
in my judgment, to interfere with that'. This might therefore suggest that
the statutory agency, which also applies to an administrator,[399] would
protect against personal liability in this respect. However, in *SCI Games
Limited v Argonaut Games Plc*,[400] an argument that administrators could be
liable in the tort of interference with contractual relations was not struck
out as disclosing no reasonable prospect of success at a full trial of the
action. The matter, therefore, remains unclear.

7.1.2. Rights of avoidance ex post

Where a movable has been transferred to or from a party (whether corporate or individual) under an executed contract it remains possible that
the transfer might be subject to an attack, and possibly reversed, in the
event of that party's insolvency. The basis for this is a raft of provisions
contained in the Insolvency Act 1986 which allow an insolvency office
holder[401] to effectively unravel executed transactions of all kinds, including transfers of the insolvent's property, or transfers *to* the insolvent of
property.

The basis of these provisions is that, whilst in general terms English
insolvency will not interfere with entitlements arising prior to insolvency,
certain transactions may be held vulnerable in circumstances where their

---

[397] [1992] BCC 270.

[398] [1920] 2 KB 497.

[399] Insolvency Act 1986, Schedule B1 para 69.

[400] [2005] EWHC 1403.

[401] A liquidator, administrator or trustee in bankruptcy, but *not* an administrative
receiver.

effect is to contravene, albeit prospectively, the principle of equality that underpins English insolvency law. As Roy Goode puts it:

'However, the principle of equity among creditors which underlies the *pari passu* rule of insolvency law will in certain conditions require the adjustment of concluded transactions which but for the winding up of the company would have remained binding on the company, and the return to the company of payments made or property transferred under the transactions or the reversal of their effect.'[402]

(a)   Transactions at an undervalue

Section 238(2) Insolvency Act 1986 provides as follows:

'Where the company has at a relevant time (defined in section 240) entered into a transaction with any person at an undervalue, the office-holder may apply to the court for an order under this section.'

A number of points should be made about this provision. Firstly, it may only be invoked by an 'office-holder', defined in s. 238(1) as a liquidator or an administrator, depending upon whether the company in question has entered into liquidation or administration. Secondly, the transaction in question must have been entered into at 'a relevant time'. This concept is defined in s. 240(1)(a) Insolvency Act as '... at a time in the period of 2 years ending with the onset of insolvency'. The onset of insolvency is the commencement of the procedure in question, so that any transactions entered into in the two year period immediately preceding that commencement are potentially vulnerable. Thirdly, this provision applies only to *corporate* insolvencies, but its effect is virtually mirrored in relation to personal bankruptcy by s. 339 Insolvency Act 1986. Fourthly, for the section to apply, the company must have been insolvent at the time the transaction was entered into, or must have become insolvent as a result of that transaction.[403] Where the transaction is entered into with a person connected with the company, it is presumed that the company was insolvent at that time, or became insolvent by virtue of entry into the transaction.[404]

The substantive question arising is what is meant by a transaction at an undervalue? Section 238(4) Insolvency Act 1986 provides:

---

[402] Goode, *Principles of Corporate Insolvency Law* (2004), p 410.

[403] Insolvency Act 1986, s. 240(2)(a), (b).

[404] *Ibid.* For the meaning of 'connected' in this context, see ss. 249 and 435 Insolvency Act 1986.

'For the purposes of this section and section 241, a company enters into a transaction with a person at an undervalue if –

(a) the company makes a gift to that person or otherwise enters into a transaction with that person on terms that provide for the company to receive no consideration, or

(b) the company enters into a transaction with that person for a consideration the value of which, in money or money's worth, is significantly less than the value, in money or money's worth, of the consideration provided by the company.'

Thus, where a company transfers property and receives no consideration in return the case will fall under s. 238(4)(a). Section 238(4)(b) is slightly less straightforward. According to Millett J, delivering judgment in the leading case on the section:

'To come within [s. 238(4)(b)] the transaction must be:

(1) entered into by the company;

(2) for a consideration;

(3) the value of which measured in money or money's worth;

(4) is significantly less than the value;

(5) also measured in money or money's worth;

(6) of the consideration provided by the company.

It requires a comparison to be made between the value obtained by the company for the transaction and the value of consideration provided by the company. Both values must be measurable in money or money's worth and both must be considered from the company's point of view.'[405]

Clearly, where the transaction in question involves the company transferring its property at demonstrably less than market value, it will fall squarely within the provision.[406] The courts have, however, been prepared to cast the net somewhat wider than only the obvious cases. For example, it has been held that, in determining the equivalence of otherwise of the consideration provided by transferor and transferee, *incidental benefits* to the transferee may be taken into account. Thus, where the transferor granted a tenancy of agricultural land to the transferee at the then market rental, the fact that the transferee, by virtue of the grant was able to negotiate a high surrender value for the tenancy, brought the case within the section: That surrender value represented an incidental benefit which

---

[405] *Re M C Bacon* [1990] BCC 78, p 92.

[406] See, for example, *National Westminster Bank plc v Jones* [2001] 1 BCLC 98, [2001] EWCA Civ 1541 (sale of farm to shell company at 15.5% below market value).

meant that the transferor received significantly less than he had parted with.[407]

Moreover, in *Phillips v Brewin Dolphin Bell Lawrie Ltd*,[408] the House of Lords considered that it was perfectly justifiable to have regard to events occurring *after* the transaction which had the effect of rendering the bargain less 'equal' than might have been thought. In that case, the sale of a stockbroking business to the defendant was agreed, the business being valued at £1.25 million. In return, the defendant agreed to discharge the vendor's liability to its employees (of approximately £125,000), and the defendant's parent company covenanted to sub-lease the vendor's computer equipment for four years, at a consideration of £312,500 per year, payable in arrears. This equipment was to be used by the defendant. Thus, the total value of the consideration provided by the defendant and its parent notionally amounted to some £1,375,000, which was more than equivalent to the value attributed to the transferred business.

After the transfer, the vendor company entered liquidation and its liquidator challenged this transaction as a transaction at an undervalue. It was pointed out in court that, whilst the bargain seemed *prima facie* an equivalent one, on the facts, it was not. The terms of the vendor's lease of its computer equipment did not permit sub-leasing, and, in any event, the defendant had already made arrangements to purchase its own computer equipment. When the vendor subsequently failed to meet instalments on its head lease of the equipment and the lessor terminated the lease the defendant's parent informed the vendor that this was a repudiatory breach and that they had elected to terminate the sub-leasing agreement. Thus, a substantial proportion of what *would* have been paid had the agreement run its course was no longer payable because of the termination of that agreement. In such circumstance, according to Lord Scott:

'In valuing the covenant ... the critical uncertainty is whether the sub-lease would survive for the four years necessary to enable all four £312,500 payments to fall due, or would survive long enough to enable some of them to fall due, or would come to an end before any had fallen due. Where the events, or some of them, on which the uncertainties depend have actually happened, it seems to me unsatisfactory and unnecessary for the court to wear blinkers and pretend that it does not know what has happened. Problems of a comparable sort may arise for judicial determination in many different areas of the law. The answers may not be uniform but may depend upon the particular context in which the

---

407 *Agricultural Mortgage Corporation v Woodward* [1995] 1 BCLC 1. The same case contemplates the possibility that an *incidental detriment to the transferor* could also be relevant to the valuation exercise to be carried out in relation to s. 238(4), although that point was left open.

408 [2001] 1 All ER 673.

problem arises. For the purposes of section 238(4) however, and the valuation of the consideration for which a company has entered into a transaction, reality should, in my opinion, be given precedence over speculation. I would hold, taking account of the events that took place in the early months of 1990, that the value of PCG's covenant in the sublease of 10 November 1989 was nil ... Where the value of the consideration for which a company enters into a section 238 transaction is as speculative as is the case here, it is, in my judgment, for the party who relies on that consideration to establish its value. PCG and Brewin Dolphin are, in the present case, unable to do so.'[409]

The above therefore represents a very strong power conferred upon insolvency office-holders to revisit transactions where it appears that the insolvent company or individual has received less than it/he has given (or given more than it/he has received! There is absolutely no reason why a transaction which involves the company or individual *acquiring* property and paying more than it is worth should not fall within the section). However, there is something approaching a 'reasonable business purpose defence' to an undervalue action, contained in s. 238(5) Insolvency Act 1986, which provides:

> 'The court shall not make an order under this section in respect of a transaction at an undervalue if it is satisfied –
> (a) that the company which entered into the transaction did so in good faith and for the purpose of carrying on its business, and
> (b) that at the time it did so there were reasonable grounds for believing that the transaction would benefit the company.'

Moreover, where the subject matter of the undervalue transaction has since been acquired by a third party, the court may not make an ordering prejudicing the interests of that third party as long as it is satisfied that that third party acquired the property without notice of the original undervalue.[410] Subject to this, the court may, if satisfied that the transaction in question falls within the section, make any order it thinks fit, including, but not restricted to, the catalogue in s. 241(1) Insolvency Act 1986, which provides:

> 'Without prejudice to the generality of sections 238(3) and 239(3), an order under either of those sections with respect to a transaction or preference entered into or given by a company may (subject to the next subsection) –
> (a) require any property transferred as part of the transaction, or in connection with the giving of the preference, to be vested in the company,

---

[409] *Ibid*, paras 26, 27.
[410] Insolvency Act 1986 s. 241(2), (2A), (3).

(b) require any property to be so vested if it represents in any person's hands the application either of the proceeds of sale of property so transferred or of money so transferred,

(c) release or discharge (in whole or in part) any security given by the company,

(d) require any person to pay, in respect of benefits received by him from the company, such sums to the office-holder as the court may direct,

(e) provide for any surety or guarantor whose obligations to any person were released or discharged (in whole or in part) under the transaction, or by the giving of the preference, to be under such new or revived obligations to that person as the court thinks appropriate,

(f) provide for security to be provided for the discharge of any obligation imposed by or arising under the order, for such an obligation to be charged on any property and for the security or charge to have the same priority as a security or charge released or discharged (in whole or in part) under the transaction or by the giving of the preference, and

(g) provide for the extent to which any person whose property is vested by the order in the company, or on whom obligations are imposed by the order, is to be able to prove in the winding up of the company for debts or other liabilities which arose from, or were released or discharged (in whole or in part) under or by, the transaction or the giving of the preference.'

It is clear, therefore, that a transfer of a movable may be effectively reversed under s. 241(1)(a) by a court order requiring the movable to be vested in the transferor.

(b)   Voidable preferences

Section 239(2)[411] Insolvency Act 1986 provides as follows:

'Where the company has at a relevant time (defined in the next section), given a preference to any person, the office-holder may apply to the court for an order under this section.'

As with transactions at an undervalue, the section only applies in cases of liquidation or administration, and where the company is insolvent at the time of the preference or becomes insolvent as a result of it.[412] Again there is a time period within which the preferential transaction must

---

[411] The equivalent provision in personal bankruptcy is s. 340.

[412] Insolvency Act 1986, s. 240(2)(a),(b). This state of affairs is *not* presumed where the preference in question is given to a connected party: cf. transactions at an undervalue.

have taken place, but it differs to that relating to transactions at an undervalue, which, it was recalled, was two years before the date of the
commencement of the insolvency. In the case of a preference, the time
limit remains at two years for transactions with connected parties, but
shrinks to six months prior to the onset of insolvency for unconnected
parties.[413]

The meaning of a 'preference' can be found in s. 239(4) Insolvency
Act 1986, which provides:

'... a company gives a preference to a person if –
(a) that person is one of the company's creditors or a surety or guarantor for
any of the company's debts or other liabilities, and
(b) the company does anything or suffers anything to be done which (in either case) has the effect of putting that person into a position which, in
the event of the company going into insolvent liquidation, will be better
than the position he would have been in if that thing had not been done.'

The first point that should be made is that the 'preferred' party must be
an existing creditor of the company at the time the preference is given, or
a surety or guarantor of its debts or other liabilities. The most obvious
example of a preference is the payment of an unsecured debt, for, as Wal-
ters puts it:

'To take an example, let us say that A Ltd has two unsecured creditors X and Y
owed £100 each and total assets of £100. On liquidation the £100 worth of assets would be distributed *pari passu* between X and Y with the result that each
would receive £50 representing a dividend on their claims of 50 pence in the
pound. If, however, on the eve of liquidation A Ltd pays X £100 exhausting its
remaining assets, X is repaid in full and Y will receive nothing. The payment to
X is technically a preference because it improves X's position relative to other
creditors: X is repaid in full rather than ranking alongside Y for dividend in A
Ltd's liquidation.'[414]

However, there is no reason to consider that the operation of the section
is confined to payments. Where, for example, a company has received
goods but not yet paid for them, and then returns the goods to the transferor, the return could certainly amount to a preference.[415] In *Weisgard v*

---

[413] Insolvency Act 1986, s. 240(1)(b).

[414] 'Preferences', in: Bennett and Armour (eds), *Vulnerable Transactions in Corporate
Insolvency* (2002).

[415] Indeed, the Cork Committee gave this as an example of a preference. See 'Insolvency Law and Practice: Report of the Review Committee' (1982), para 1208.

Pilkington[416] the company, which carried on the business of property developing, granted 999 year leases over six of its properties to its directors in return for the discharge of the debts owed to them by the company. Again, this clearly falls within the section, and demonstrates that the transfer of a movable to a creditor, as long as it relates to the discharge of a debt owed to that creditor, will be caught by the provision just as much as the straightforward payment of that debt.

It is not sufficient, however, that the transaction in question has the effect of putting the creditor into a better position than he would have been had the transaction not been entered into. That amounts to the *actus reus* of the section, but a liquidator or administrator must still establish a corporate *mens rea*. According to s. 239(5):

> 'The court shall not make an order under this section in respect of a preference given to any person *unless the company which gave the preference was influenced in deciding to give it by a desire to produce in relation to that person the effect mentioned in subsection (4)(b).*' (Italics added)

It has been stated, in relation to this subsection, that:

> 'A man is not to be taken as desiring all the necessary consequences of his actions. Some consequences may be of advantage to him and be desired by him; others may not affect him and be matters of indifference to him; while still others may be positively disadvantageous to him and not be desired by him, but be regarded by him as the unavoidable price of obtaining the desired advantages. It will still be possible to provide assistance to a company in financial difficulties provided that the company is actuated only by proper commercial considerations. Under the new regime a transaction will not be set aside as a voidable preference unless the company *positively wished to improve the creditor's position* in the event of its own insolvent liquidation. ... There is, of course, no need for there to be direct evidence of the requisite desire. Its existence may be inferred from the circumstances of the case just as the dominant intention could be inferred under the old law.'[417]

The case in question concerned the grant of security by a company in relation to a pre-existing, and unsecured, debt. Millett J considered that the company, in granting the security interest, was motivated by a desire to avoid the creditor calling in its overdraft, rather than by a positive desire to prefer that creditor, and therefore the grant did not amount to a preference under s. 239. This would seem to suggest that where any given creditor is in a position to bring pressure to bear on the company in ques-

---

[416] [1995] BCC 514.
[417] *Re MC Bacon* [1990] BCC 78, *per* Millett J, at pp 86-87.

tion, that very pressure may of itself neutralise any inference of a desire to prefer on the part of the company, and the law has been criticised in this respect.[418] It is worth noting, however, that in jurisdictions which do not require any element of desire to prefer, nevertheless a transaction will escape the preference label if it can be shown that the transaction was given in order to facilitate the continued supply of goods or services to the company in question. In *Airservices Australia v Ferrier*[419] an airline made a series of payments to Airservices (of around $10.3 million) in the period of 6 months prior to its winding up, all of these payments being in respect of existing indebtedness. It was clear that Airservices had continued to provide navigation services to the company, each provision of service giving rise to a new debt which was then discharged. The Australian High Court refused to characterise these payments as preferences:

> 'If the purpose of a payment is to secure an asset or assets of equal or greater value, the payee receives no advantage over other creditors. The other creditors are no worse off and, where the value of the assets has increased, they are actually better off. Thus, a debtor does not prefer a creditor to the other creditors if he or she pays a debt, or part of it, to induce the creditor to supply goods of equal or greater value than the amount of the payment. In that situation, it is of no relevance that the debt that is discharged happens to be a stale one. If the present value of the goods supplied is equal to or greater than the payment, the other creditors are no worse off. They are in the same position that they would have been in if the parties had so structured the transaction that the debtor paid for the new supply of goods instead of discharging the old debt ... A court ... does not allow itself to be unsighted by the shadow of the legal form when it can see that the economic effect of the transaction does not give the creditor any preference, priority or advantage over the general body of creditors.'[420]

It is possible to extrapolate from this that where a company which is in a supplier relationship with another party continues to make supplies in the hope of securing further orders, such supplies will fall outside the section, but in the absence of authority directly in point this is not altogether certain. Where, however, the transaction in question is with a connected party, the desire to prefer is presumed, and it falls to the connected party to rebut that presumption, rather than to the liquidator to demonstrate the desire.[421]

---

[418] Keay, 'Preferences in Liquidation Law: Time for a Change', [1998] Company Financial and Insolvency Law Review 198.

[419] (1996) 137 ALR 609.

[420] *Ibid*, at p 623.

[421] Insolvency Act 1986, s. 239(6). For an example of a connected party successfully rebutting the presumption see *Re Fairway Magazines Ltd* [1992] BCC 924.

Where a successful challenge to a transaction as a preference is made, the court may again make any order it thinks fit to remedy the preference, including those listed in s. 241(1) Insolvency Act 1986,[422] subject to the protection of third parties acquiring rights in good faith and without notice of the underlying preference.[423]

(c)   Transactions defrauding creditors

One further avoidance provision in the insolvency legislation is s. 423 Insolvency Act 1986, which relates to transactions defrauding creditors and which provides as follows:

'(1) This section relates to transactions entered into at an undervalue; and a person enters into such a transaction with another person if –

(a)   he makes a gift to the other person or he otherwise enters into a transaction with the other on terms that provide for him to receive no consideration;

(b)   he enters into a transaction with the other in consideration of marriage or the formation of a civil partnership; or

(c)   he enters into a transaction with the other for a consideration the value of which, in money or money's worth, is significantly less than the value, in money or money's worth, of the consideration provided by himself.

(2) Where a person has entered into such a transaction, the court may, if satisfied under the next subsection, make such order as it thinks fit for –

(a)   restoring the position to what it would have been if the transaction had not been entered into, and

(b)   protecting the interests of persons who are victims of the transaction.

(3) In the case of a person entering into such a transaction, an order shall only be made if the court is satisfied that it was entered into by him for the purpose –

(a)   of putting assets beyond the reach of a person who is making, or may at some time make, a claim against him, or

(b)   of otherwise prejudicing the interests of such a person in relation to the claim which he is making or may make.'

This is a provision of ancient vintage, Sealy and Milman noting that its antecedents date back to 1571 and that it has its origins in the Paulian

---

[422] See above at section 7.1.2.(a).

[423] Insolvency Act 1986 s. 241(2). In a case where the third party in question *must have realised* that a payment made to it constituted a preference to a director of the payee company, or must have wilfully closed its eyes to that possibility, the defence in s. 241(2) was held unavailable: see *Re Sonatacus Ltd* [2007] EWCA Civ 31.

action of Roman law.[424] There are obvious parallels with ss. 238 and 339 Insolvency Act 1986,[425] in that the section attacks transactions entered into at an undervalue, the definition of which is almost identical to that in those two sections, but s. 423 is both broader in its application than ss. 238 and 339 and, at the same time, narrower in one important respect.

Section 423 applies to transactions entered into by companies and individuals alike, and, unlike both ss. 238 and 339, is potentially open-ended in its application in that it is not limited in time. However, there may be a certain reluctance on the part of the courts to investigate transactions which are many years old.[426] Moreover, the section may be invoked not just by a liquidator, administrator or trustee in bankruptcy but also by any victim of the transaction in question.[427] However, the court may only make an order where it is satisfied that the transaction was entered into with the intention of putting assets beyond the reach of any actual or potential claimant or of otherwise prejudicing that person's interests.[428] It appears that the courts will accept that this requirement is satisfied where it is demonstrated that a substantial purpose (rather than a dominant purpose) behind the transaction is to put the assets in question beyond the reach of creditors.[429]

In the current context, therefore, the transfer of a movable at an undervalue could clearly fall within s. 423, as long as the transfer was effected for the purpose of putting it beyond the reach of any actual or potential claimants against the transferor. In the event of a successful claim, the court may make any order it thinks fit, including any of those mentioned in s. 425(1), which correspond roughly to the s. 241 catalogue noted above in relation to ss. 238 and 239 Insolvency Act 1986. Again, there is a 'saving' provision to protect third parties acquiring the property in question in good faith and without notice of the relevant circumstances.[430]

---

[424] *Annotated Guide to the Insolvency Legislation 2006/2007* (2006).

[425] Indeed, the sections may overlap on any given set of facts.

[426] See, *e.g.*, *The Law Society v Southall* [2001] EWCA Civ 2001.

[427] Insolvency Act 1986, s. 424(1)(c). Any application under s. 423 is treated as though made on behalf of every victim of the transaction: s. 424(2)).

[428] Insolvency Act 1986, s. 423(3).

[429] See *Hashmi v IRC* [2002] EWCA Civ 981; *Kubiangha v Ekpenyong* [2002] EWHC 1567.

[430] Insolvency Act 1986, s. 425(2).

7.2.   The insolvency of the transferor

7.2.1.   General

In general terms, the transferee is relatively unprotected by English law against the insolvency of the transferor. As noted above, in the case of an executory contract, it may be open to the insolvency office holder of the transferor to cause it to refuse to perform its obligations under the contract, leaving the transferee with a probably worthless damages remedy. The position is even more fraught for the pre-paying transferee. If property rights in the subject matter of the contract have not passed to him in accordance with the intentions of transferor and transferee under the contract, then he will be consigned to proving in the liquidation or bankruptcy of the transferor. Whether or not property rights have passed will, as described in section 5.4 above, depend upon the intention of the parties or, if no such intention can be discerned, on the presumptive rules contained in section 18 Sale of Goods Act 1979. Section 20A of that Act has now tempered the potential harshness of the rule in s. 16 that property in unascertained goods may not pass by providing that the pre-paying buyer of such goods may, if the conditions in s. 20A are satisfied, become part-owner of an identifiable bulk.

7.2.2.   The possibility of a constructive trust?

Whilst the pre-paying buyer will generally only be protected if he can claim that the property in the subject matter of the contract of sale has passed to him, this proposition does not take into account the possibility of equitable intervention. Whilst this possibility was canvassed, and rejected, in cases relating to contracts for the sale of unascertained goods,[431] it has re-emerged in a different context very recently. In *Neste Oy v Lloyds Bank Plc (The Tiiskeri, The Nestegas and The Enskeri)*[432] payments were made by a principal to its agent for services to be provided by the agent. One such payment was made, and accepted by the agent, at a time when it had already resolved to cease trading. It was contended that that payment at least was held on constructive trust by the agent for the principal, and so unavailable to the agent's general creditors. Bingham J accepted that contention. He noted that:

'I start from a general disinclination, shared with Lord Justice Bramwell and Mr. Justice Channell, to see the intricacies and doctrines connected with

---

431 See the discussion at section 5.2.2.(b) above.
432 [1983] 2 Lloyd's Rep 658.

trusts introduced into everyday commercial transactions ... [However] given the situation of PSL when the last payment was received, any reasonable and honest directors of that company (or the actual directors had they known of it) would, I feel sure, have arranged for the repayment of that sum to the plaintiffs without hesitation or delay. It would have seemed little short of sharp practice for PSL to take any benefit from the payment, and it would have seemed contrary to any ordinary notion of fairness that the general body of creditors should profit from the accident of a payment made at a time when there was bound to be a total failure of consideration. Of course it is true that insolvency always causes loss and perfect fairness is unattainable. The bank, and other creditors, have their legitimate claims. It nonetheless seems to me that at the time of its receipt PSL could not in good conscience retain this payment and that accordingly a constructive trust is to be inferred.'[433]

This reasoning has been somewhat open to criticism on the ground that it appears to contemplate what amounts to a *remedial constructive trust*, a device generally thought not to be recognised by English law. As Lord Browne-Wilkinson has remarked:

'... the New York law of constructive trusts has for a long time been influenced by the concept of a *remedial* constructive trust, whereas hitherto English law has for the most part only recognised an institutional constructive trust ... Under an institutional constructive trust, the trust arises by operation of law as from the date of the circumstances which give rise to it: the function of the court is merely to declare that such trust has arisen in the past. The consequences that flow from such trust having arisen (including the possibly unfair consequences to third parties who in the interim have received the trust property) are also determined by rules of law, not under a discretion. A remedial constructive trust, as I understand it, is different. It is a judicial remedy giving rise to an enforceable equitable obligation: the extent to which it operates retrospectively to the prejudice of third parties lies in the discretion of the court.'[434]

However, the reasoning of Bingham J in *Neste Oy* was accepted, with some qualification, in *Re Farepak Food and Gifts Ltd*,[435] the facts of which are so compelling of equitable intervention it is probably little wonder that the judge found as he did! Farepak was a company which operated a Christmas savings scheme, whereby its customers would pay amounts to Farepak's agents (who themselves were often customers) who then remitted the money to Farepak. The customers then became entitled to redeem

---

[433] *Ibid*, p 666.
[434] *Westdeutsche Landesbank Girozentrale Respondent v Islington London Borough Council* [1996] AC 669, at pp 714-715.
[435] [2006] EWHC 3272.

their savings against Christmas hampers or vouchers for retailers. The customers in question had often used this type of scheme in order to spread the cost of Christmas over the entire year, rather than running up large credit card debts over November and December.

As it turned out, Farepak was, by the Autumn of 2006, hopelessly insolvent. It had paid customer receipts into its bank account, and was heavily indebted to the bank. On October 11 2006, Farepak's directors resolved to place the company in insolvency proceedings and for the three days prior to that had attempted to ring fence customer money received during that period by executing, with the consent of the bank, a deed of trust in relation to money paid into a bank account. The company's administrators sought a declaration that this money could be returned to the payor customers on the basis that it was held on trust. Mann J accepted a contention, based on the *Neste Oy* reasoning, that a constructive trust of certain of the customer receipts could in principle have arisen. He noted:

'I think I can accept that the criticisms of *Neste Oy* mean that the position in a case like that one, where moneys are paid in the nature of an advance payment to be applied in acquiring goods or services which the company has already decided will not be provided, is not as clear as one would wish, but despite that I think that the decision in that case is clear enough and can be reconciled with principle. If and insofar as it could be established that moneys were paid to Farepak by customers at a time when Farepak had decided that it had ceased trading, and indeed at a time when it had indicated that payments should not be received, then there is a strong argument for saying that those moneys would be held by the company as constructive trustee from the moment they were received. As I have said, it may well be possible to justify this conclusion on the basis of a mistake, to bring it into line with Lord Browne-Wilkinson's views. So I would be minded to follow the result in Neste Oy, with modified reasoning.'[436]

On the facts of the case, there was insufficient information as to the time at which certain of the receipts were paid to the agents of Farepak, and Mann J therefore gave leave to the administrators of Farepak to adduce evidence if it was available.[437] He also considered that it might be possible, in relation to the particular bank account into which receipts had been paid, to determine that monies in that account were held on an *express* trust in favour of paying customers. However, further evidence of the date of the receipts was once again necessary, as, if the trust was es-

---

[436] *Ibid*, para 40.

[437] It appears that it was not so available in time to be brought before the judge so as to allow him to make an order. The case was expedited in order that some decision might be reached in time for Christmas, but this turned out to be impossible.

tablished at a time when those customers were *already* creditors of the company it might amount to a voidable preference under s. 239 Insolvency Act 1986.[438]

This decision is interesting in that it may represent a means of protecting pre-paying buyers from the effects of the seller's insolvency, albeit in a narrow set of circumstances. It does so not by affording them any form of property in the subject matter of the contract, but rather by ring-fencing the actual *payment* made so that it will not be available to general creditors, whether secured or unsecured, of the seller. However, the general proposition, particularly in relation to the constructive trust analysis, remains to be tested in the appellate courts.

7.3.   The insolvency of the transferee

7.3.1.   Introduction

The transferee's insolvency will only affect the transferor where property in the subject matter of the contract has been transferred but not yet paid for. As will be seen below,[439] as the trigger for the passing of property will usually be the intention of the parties, it is open to the parties to agree that the buyer will not acquire property rights in the goods until he has paid for them, a tactic which has been held to be effective in English law. However, this is a matter for the parties to provide for expressly, and there is no rule of law *implying* retention of title clauses into contracts of sale. Where property has not passed to the buyer under the contract of sale it is clear that the unpaid seller may simply withhold delivery of the goods in question, as stated in Sale of Goods Act 1979 s. 39(2).

7.3.2.   Invalidity/termination of the contract of sale

Questions may arise as to whether the contract of sale is void *ab initio*[440] or voidable.[441] In very general terms a void contract of sale has no effect in terms of passing property to the buyer, even where the buyer has taken delivery of the property, and the unpaid seller can therefore exercise his real rights against that property and call for its return. Where the contract is voidable, however, the right to rescind may be subject to certain

---

[438] See section 7.1.2.(b) on s. 239. See also, for a case in similar facts where the trust in question did not constitute a preference, *Re Kayford Ltd* [1975] 1 WLR 270.

[439] See section 12.

[440] For example, on the grounds of mistake.

[441] For example, because it was entered into as a result of a misrepresentation.

legal bars, including the fact that third party rights have intervened before rescission has taken place, or that the subject matter of the contract can no longer be restored.

7.3.3. The 'real' rights of the unpaid seller in the event of the buyer's insolvency

The Sale of Goods Act 1979 contains a raft of provisions which may assist an unpaid seller where property has passed to the buyer under the contract but delivery of that property has not yet occurred. The three major rights are a statutory lien,[442] a right of stoppage in transit[443] and a limited right of resale of the subject matter of the contract.[444] These will be briefly examined in turn, but first it is necessary to note that the 'unpaid seller' is quite broadly defined by the statute. Section 38 Sale of Goods Act 1979 provides:

'(1) The seller of goods is an unpaid seller within the meaning of this Act –

(a) when the whole of the price has not been paid or tendered;

(b) when a bill of exchange or other negotiable instrument has been received as conditional payment, and the condition on which it was received has not been fulfilled by reason of the dishonour of the instrument or otherwise.

(2) In this Part of this Act "seller" includes any person who is in the position of a seller, as, for instance, an agent of the seller to whom the bill of lading has been indorsed, or a consignor or agent who has himself paid (or is directly responsible for) the price.'

Thus, a seller includes certain agents of the seller, and there is no requirement for a total failure of consideration on the part of the buyer.[445]

(a)   The unpaid seller's lien

Section 41 Sale of Goods Act 1979 provides as follows:

'(1) Subject to this Act, the unpaid seller of goods who is in possession of them is entitled to retain possession of them until payment or tender of the price in the following cases: –

---

[442] *I.e.*, a right to retain possession of the subject matter of the contract: s. 41 Sale of Goods Act 1979.

[443] Section 44 Sale of Goods Act 1979.

[444] Section 48 Sale of Goods Act 1979.

[445] See, for further comment, Bridge, *The Sale of Goods* (1997), p 487.

(a) where the goods have been sold without any stipulation as to credit;
(b) where the goods have been sold on credit but the term of credit has ex-
      pired;
(c) where the buyer becomes insolvent.
(2) The seller may exercise his lien or right of retention notwithstanding that
he is in possession of the goods as agent or bailee or custodier for the buyer.'

Thus, notwithstanding that the buyer, by virtue of the contract of sale,
has become the owner of its subject matter, the unpaid seller need not
perform his delivery obligations under that contract, and has a complete
defence to any action for delivery by the buyer or the buyer's insolvency
office-holder. Even where the seller's continued possession of the goods is
in the capacity of the buyer's agent, the lien remains exercisable. The lien
is lost in three circumstances, these being where the seller delivers the
goods to a third party for the purposes of transmission to the buyer without reserving a right of disposal, where the buyer (or his agent) lawfully
acquires possession of the goods or where the seller waives his lien or
right of retention.[446] Bridge notes that the first two circumstances are
virtually co-terminous in that delivery to a third party for transmission
will almost certainly amount to the lawful acquisition of possession by the
buyer's agent.[447] There is no requirement that the seller 'prove' the fact of
the buyer's insolvency as such for the purposes of the section, as s. 61(4)
Sale of Goods Act 1979 deems the buyer to be insolvent when 'he has
either ceased to pay his debts in the ordinary course of business or he cannot pay his debts as they become due.' This latter test, sometimes referred
to as 'cash-flow insolvency', mirrors that found in s. 123(1)(e) Insolvency
Act 1986.

(b)   Right of stoppage in transit

Section 44 Sale of Goods Act 1979 provides:

> 'Subject to this Act, when the buyer of goods becomes insolvent the unpaid seller
> who has parted with the possession of the goods has the right of stopping them in
> transit, that is to say, he may resume possession of the goods as long as they are in
> course of transit, and may retain them until payment or tender of the price.'

Bridge notes that this particular right is most likely to be of use in the
context of international sales on credit terms, largely because of the logistical difficulties facing a seller attempting to issue a stop notice in rela-

---

[446] Sale of Goods Act 1979, s. 43(1).
[447] *Sale of Goods*, above n 445, pp 493-494.

tion to a carrier in the domestic context.[448] Moreover, he observes that in that context it will be the practice of sellers to explicitly reserve a right of disposal after shipment, to be surrendered only on some form of payment.[449] Therefore this right is probably little used in practice.

Bridge also questions the justification for what he describes as an 'extraordinary right', noting that it affords the seller priority over other unsecured creditors of the buyer without any real policy rationalisation.[450] Indeed, there is some force to this criticism, as, as noted above, a seller in these circumstance is able to protect himself by contractual stipulation reserving the right of disposal of the goods or, indeed, by recourse to retention of title. It is difficult to disagree with Bridge's conclusion that the continued existence of this statutory right is:

'... best explained by inertia and by the conviction that the buyer's creditors, secured and unsecured, should be denied access to goods that the buyer has never paid for and that have not come into his actual, visible possession.'[451]

The question of exactly *when* goods may be said to be in transit for the purposes of s. 44 Sale of Goods Act 1979 is addressed by s. 45:

'(1) Goods are deemed to be in course of transit from the time when they are delivered to a carrier or other bailee or custodier for the purpose of transmission to the buyer, until the buyer or his agent in that behalf takes delivery of them from the carrier or other bailee or custodier.
(2) If the buyer or his agent in that behalf obtains delivery of the goods before their arrival at the appointed destination, the transit is at an end.
(3) If, after the arrival of the goods at the appointed destination, the carrier or other bailee or custodier acknowledges to the buyer or his agent that he holds the goods on his behalf and continues in possession of them as bailee or custodier for the buyer or his agent, the transit is at an end, and it is immaterial that a further destination for the goods may have been indicated by the buyer.
(4) If the goods are rejected by the buyer, and the carrier or other bailee or custodier continues in possession of them, the transit is not deemed to be at an end, even if the seller has refused to receive them back.
(5) When goods are delivered to a ship chartered by the buyer it is a question depending on the circumstances of the particular case whether they are in the possession of the master as a carrier or as agent to the buyer.

---

[448] *Ibid*, pp 498-499.
[449] *Ibid*.
[450] *Ibid*, pp 499-500.
[451] *Ibid*.

(6) Where the carrier or other bailee or custodier wrongfully refuses to deliver the goods to the buyer or his agent in that behalf, the transit is deemed to be at an end.

(7) Where part delivery of the goods has been made to the buyer or his agent in that behalf, the remainder of the goods may be stopped in transit, unless such part delivery has been made under such circumstances as to show an agreement to give up possession of the whole of the goods.'

These provisions are largely self-explanatory.

(c)   Seller's right of resale

Section 48 Sale of Goods Act 1979 provides:

'(1) Subject to this section, a contract of sale is not rescinded by the mere exercise by an unpaid seller of his right of lien or retention or stoppage in transit.

(2) Where an unpaid seller who has exercised his right of lien or retention or stoppage in transit re-sells the goods, the buyer acquires a good title to them as against the original buyer.

(3) Where the goods are of a perishable nature, or where the unpaid seller gives notice to the buyer of his intention to re-sell, and the buyer does not within a reasonable time pay or tender the price, the unpaid seller may re-sell the goods and recover from the original buyer damages for any loss occasioned by his breach of contract.

(4) Where the seller expressly reserves the right of re-sale in case the buyer should make default, and on the buyer making default re-sells the goods, the original contract of sale is rescinded but without prejudice to any claim the seller may have for damages.'

The force of this section is that, whilst the exercise of an unpaid seller of rights under ss. 41 and 44 do not amount to a rescission of the contract, where they are actually exercised the seller may effect a re-sale of the goods in question and, in doing so, is able to pass the property rights in those goods to the 'second' buyer.

8.   Passing of property and risk in English Law

'The truth is that risk is a derivative, and essentially negative, concept – an elliptical way of saying that either or both of the primary obligations of one party shall be enforceable, and that those of the other party shall be deemed to have been discharged, even though the normally prerequisite conditions have not been satisfied. That is to say that the legal consequences attaching to the "risk" fall to be defined purely in terms of the parties' other duties and the corresponding rights and remedies: the sellers right to claim the price, and the buyer's right to resist payment or to demand its return; and the right to claim damages (e.g. for non delivery or non-acceptance) or to resist such a claim.'[452]

Prima facie English law treats the passing of property and risk as contemporaneous. This position is explicit in the Sale of Goods Act 1979, s. 20:

'(1) Unless otherwise agreed, the goods remain at the seller's risk until the property in them is transferred to the buyer, but when the property in them is transferred to the buyer the goods are at the buyer's risk whether delivery has been made or not.'

It should be noted that s. 20(1) is made expressly subject to contrary intention, so that it is open to seller and buyer to allocate risk howsoever they see fit, and to separate it from property altogether. There are, however, certain exceptions to the general rule in s. 20(1) in subsections (2) and (3) as follows:

'(2) Where delivery has been delayed through the fault of either buyer or seller the goods are at the risk of the party at fault as regards any loss which might not have occurred but for such fault.'
'(3) Nothing in this section affects the duties or liabilities of seller or buyer as bailee or custodier of the goods of the other party.'

Thus, where property has passed to the buyer under the contract of sale, but the goods are in the seller's possession due to a delay in delivery attributable to the seller, any loss or damage is the seller's responsibility. Equally, where property remains with the seller until the buyer takes delivery, and such delivery is delayed due to the fault of the buyer, the buyer bears the risk. Equally, where either seller or buyer can be characterised as a bailee of the goods, and loss or damage to them occurs as a result of their fault, they will be liable accordingly.

The linking of risk and property in English law has been subject to criticism on the ground that it may result in the position that risk is allocated to a party who, not having possession or control of the goods, cannot properly guard against it.[453] There is certainly some force in the argument that section 2-509 *United States' Uniform Commercial Code*, which separates risk and property and allocates risk to the party who has control of the goods, or is in a better position to insure against the risk in question, represents a more sensible and commercially realistic approach to

---

452 Sealy, '"Risk" In the Law of Sale', [1972] CLJ 225 at p 226.
453 See, e.g., Atiyah, *Sale of Goods* (2005), pp 357 *et seq.*

the matter. However, as noted above, it is open to the parties to reach this result by expressly providing for it.[454]

One English case, however, arguably subverts the approach of the Act in order to reflect the commercial realities of the situation. In *Stern v Vickers*[455] the defendant contracted to sell 120,000 gallons of white spirit out of a much larger quantity stored in a vast tank. The claimant was a sub-buyer from the original buyer of the spirit. The goods in question not being ascertained, property in them, and so risk, could not pass until ascertainment took place.[456] The defendant proffered, and the claimant accepted, a delivery warrant which would have allowed the claimant to take possession of the 120,000 gallons he had agreed to buy. The claimant delayed in taking delivery and the white spirit deteriorated badly. Under the scheme of the Sale of Goods Act 1979 it might appear that, property having yet to pass to the claimant, the risk of deterioration remained with the defendant. This was not, however, the conclusion of the Court of Appeal, Scrutton LJ observing:

> 'The vendor of a specified quantity out of a bulk in the possession of a third party discharges his obligation to the purchaser as soon as the third party undertakes to the purchaser to deliver him that quantity out of the bulk. In the present case, what happened was that at the date of the contract there was a bulk larger than the quantity sold, and it was of the contract quality according to sample. A delivery warrant was issued by the Thames Haven Company undertaking to deliver that quantity from the bulk which at that time corresponded with the sample. That warrant was accepted by the purchaser ... In those circumstances I come clearly to the conclusion that as between the plaintiffs and the defendants the risk was on the plaintiffs, the purchasers. The vendors had done all that they undertook to do. The purchasers had the right to go to the storage company and demand delivery, and if they had done so at the time they would have got all that the defendants had undertaken to sell them.'[457]

One explanation of this analysis is that the Court of Appeal was able to find an *implied* intention on the part of claimant and defendant that risk had passed to the claimant, but this seems ambitious to say the least.

---

[454] Although see the difficulties caused by such provision in *Leigh & Sillivan Shipping Ltd v Aliakmon Shipping Co Ltd (The Aliakmon)* [1986] AC 785.

[455] [1923] 1 KB 78.

[456] See the discussion on the passing of property in unascertained goods at sections 5.2 and 5.4 above.

[457] [1923] 1 KB 78, p 85.

Part III:
Original acquisition

9. Acquisition by commixture, processing etc

9.1. Fixtures (attachment of personalty to realty)

A general starting point for the law on the attachment of chattels to land is the maxim *quicquid plantatur solo, solo cedit* (whatever is attached to the soil becomes part of it).[458] It follows from this that any objects attached to a piece of land effectively undergo a change of legal state from personalty to realty, with property in the former chattel passing to the owner of the land. Within this concept three different stages might usefully be identified when a chattel is brought onto land:[459] first, the chattel might retain its independent identity as a chattel; secondly, it might be totally subordinated to the land so that it merges into it, losing its former identity completely; thirdly, it might become sufficiently annexed to the land that it is viewed as part of it, yet still retain, to some extent, its independent existence. It is this third class that represents the concept of a 'fixture'. The answer to the question of when a chattel is deemed to have undergone the transition into one of the latter two stages of this classification is to be found in the case law on the subject.

The test employed here has two limbs: the first concerns the mode of annexation, and the second the object and purpose of the annexation.[460] This test is one in which the circumstances of each particular case are crucial and its two limbs are relative so that strength in one limb can balance and compensate for weakness in the other, as demonstrated by a *dictum* of Blackburn J:

---

[458] *Minshall v Lloyd* (1837) 2 M & W 450 at p 459.

[459] See *Elitestone Ltd v Morris* [1997] 1 WLR 687 at p 691, *per* Lord Lloyd, where his Lordship adopted the classification found in Woodfall, *Landlord and Tenant*, vol 1, para 13.131.; see also Bennett, 'Attachment of Chattels to Land', in Palmer and McKendrick (eds), *Interests in Goods* (1998) at p 267. In theory, the test for determining whether a chattel passes into the second or third category is the same, the difference being presumably one of degree.

[460] See *Hellawell v Eastwood* (1851) 6 Ex 295 and *Holland v Hodgson* (1872) LR 7 CP 328.

'When the article in question is no further attached to the land, then by its own weight it is generally to be considered a mere chattel [...]. But even in such a case, if the intention is apparent to make the articles part of the land, they do become part of the land. Thus blocks of stone placed one on the top of another without any mortar or cement for the purpose of forming a dry stone wall would become part of the land, though the same stones, if deposited in a builder's yard and for convenience sake stacked on the top of each other in the form of a wall, would remain chattels. On the other hand, an article may be very firmly fixed to the land, and yet the circumstances may be such as to shew that it was never intended to be part of the land, and then it does not become part of the land.'[461]

Determining the first limb of the two-stage test in any given situation should normally be a matter of direct evidence of the method and extent of the attachment. The object of the annexation on the other hand is something to be inferred only from the surrounding circumstances. It is not concerned with the subjective intention of the fixer of the chattel,[462] nor is it concerned with the terms of any agreement between the fixer and the owner of the freehold.[463] Given that this is so, it might be asked how 'intention' is actually relevant, and indeed the use of the word has been labelled 'misleading' by the House of Lords.[464] A case that demonstrates not only the way in which the second limb is interpreted within a given set of facts, but also the arguably unsatisfactory consequences of that interpretation, is that of *Hobson v Gorringe*.[465]

Hobson involved a gas engine that was delivered under a hire purchase agreement on terms that it should not become the property of the hirer until all instalments had been paid. The hirer attached the engine, which was adorned with a plate identifying it as Hobson's property, to his freehold by means of bolts and screws. When the hirer defaulted on both the instalments and the mortgage payments the question of the status of the engine arose for determination. Hobson claimed that ownership of the engine still vested in him, while the mortgagee sought to recover on the basis that it had acceded to the freehold, and so fell within the mortgage. It was held by the Court of Appeal that the engine was sufficiently annexed to the land to become a fixture and that neither the plate nor the terms of the hire purchase prevented this. 'Circumstances to show Intention' in the second limb of the test meant the circumstances that were

---

[461] *Holland v Hodgson*, at pp 334-335.

[462] *Elitestone v Morris*, at p 693 *per* Lord Lloyd.

[463] *Melluish (Inspector of Taxes) v BMI (No 3) Ltd* [1996] AC 454 at p 473 *per* Lord Browne-Wilkinson.

[464] *Elitestone* at pp 693 and 698 *per* Lord Lloyd and Lord Clyde respectively, with whom the rest of the House agreed.

[465] [1897] 1 Ch 182.

'patent for all to see', and not the circumstances of a 'chance agreement that might or might not exist' between the owner of chattel and its hirer. The engine belonged to the mortgagee.

The above rules have been criticised as lacking coherence and certainty, with the interaction between the degree and purpose rules being particularly unsatisfactory.[466] The same writer suggested that a workable alternative might be to presume that all items attached to land will remain chattels unless it is unreasonable to remove them. However, it is submitted that such a test is only superficially attractive. When is it unreasonable to remove a chattel brought on the land? One answer is perhaps where the chattel is attached in such a way that its removal would damage the land. Another might be where there is evidenced an objective intention that the chattel remain in place. In this way one soon gets back to the old tests and case law; 'unreasonable' merely lifts the level of abstraction up a notch, embracing the old two-limb test with its ambiguity.

If the 'unreasonableness' test took into account an express agreement then it might, however, have a different effect, and meet a potential criticism revealed by the *Hobson* case, where the express agreement between the owner of the former chattel and the owner of the freehold was held to be of no consequence.[467] It might seem inconsistent to allow such intention as shown by a prior agreement to divert the operation of a rule of law in the field of *specificatio* and yet ignore a similar agreement in the related area of fixtures.[468] Both cases were fought in the context of insolvency, and so it is submitted that justifications based on that factor alone cannot explain the distinction. One explanation might be that fixtures involve land and that if it were possible to attach a chattel to the extent that it merges into the freehold and yet by express agreement still retain ownership of the former chattel it could cause problems for a potential purchaser of the land.

As an exception, three types of fixtures may be removed despite having acceded to the land: ornamental, trade and agricultural fixtures.[469] Some judges have treated this category not as an exception but as a collection of instances where a very liberal determination of the purpose of

---

[466] Haley, 'The Law of Fixtures: an Unprincipled Metamorphosis', [1998] Conv 137.

[467] A potential licence to re-enter and remove the engine was recognised but this was not something that could be enforced at law against a disponee from the licensor, nor could it be enforced in equity unless the disponee had notice of it. It was held in *Hobson* that in any event the entry of the mortgagee into possession determined that right.

[468] See *Clough Mill v Martin* below.

[469] For more detail see, for example, Harpum, *Megarry and Wade, The Law of Real Property* (2000), at pp 932 *et seq*.

annexation has led to the conclusion that the item in question remains a chattel.[470]

9.2.   Accessio (attachment of personalty to personalty)

It is said that the underdevelopment of English law in this area and in those related to it (*i.e. specificatio, commixitio, confusio*) is demonstrated by the fact that its vocabulary has been borrowed from Roman law; its substantive rules, however, have not.

Accessio involves the attachment of one chattel to another so that the identity of one (the 'subordinate') becomes lost to the other (the 'dominant'). Examples are the attachment of thread and buckles to a handbag,[471] or the welding of a replacement panel onto a car. The general rule here is that ownership of the new thing vests by way of operation of law in the owner of the dominant chattel.[472] Where the owner of the dominant thing has acted unlawfully in attaching the property of another then an action for conversion will still lie against him.

In order for the rule to operate two matters must be established. The first, in common with the law concerning fixtures, is whether the two (or more) chattels have become sufficiently attached so that it can be said that the identity of one has been subsumed into the other; the second, unlike the law of fixtures, where the answer is always clear, is which of the formerly separate chattels is the subordinate and which is the dominant.

The answer to the first of the questions is not clear in English law and the precise test for determining whether or not an accession has occurred is yet to be settled. It is submitted that by analogy with fixtures the test should focus on the mode and object of annexation. The only English case on the topic, albeit the accession point was not as fully argued as it could be, is *Hendy Lennox Ltd v Grahame Puttick Ltd*.[473] In that case engines were sold on retention of title terms, the agreement contemplating that the buyer would attach the engines to generating sets. The engines themselves remained substantively unchanged and could be identified by means of serial numbers marked onto them. Shortly after the goods were delivered the buyer went into receivership. By the time the claimant seller had taken steps to try to improve its position with regard to this situation, three of the engines remained in the buyer's possession. Of these, property in two had passed to sub-buyers leaving just one engine and the question of whether or not title to it was vested not in the seller

---

[470] See Gray and Gray, *Elements of Land Law* (2004).

[471] *Re Peachdart Ltd* [1984] Ch 131 at pp 141-142.

[472] Bridge, *Personal Property Law*, p 107.

[473] [1984] 1 WLR 485.

but in the insolvent buyer by virtue of its attachment to the generating set.

Having found that the bolts and other connectors that joined the engine to the set could be later undone, and indeed that it was normal practice for the engine to be removed and replaced, Staughton J distinguished the authorities of *Re Bond Worth*,[474] *Re Peachdart*,[475] and *Borden Ltd v Scottish Timber Products*[476] on the following basis:[477]

> 'Those reflections and the facts of this case persuade me that the proprietary rights of the sellers in the engines were not affected when the engines were wholly or partially incorporated into generator sets. They were not like the Acrilan which became the yarn and then carpet (the *Bond Worth* case), or the resin which became chipboard (*Borden's* case), or the leather which became handbags (the *Peachdart* case), or the grapes, olives, wheat and barley mentioned by *Crossley Vaines*. They just remained engines, albeit connected to other things.'

The result was that there had been no accession and the claimant sellers therefore had a valid proprietary claim to the remaining engine. With regard to the specific case, the point might be made that each of the three authorities Staughton J distinguished concern *specificatio* and not *accessio*. That the engines remained identifiable rather than forming some entirely new product, like chipboard, is only grounds for dismissing an argument of *specificatio*, and not grounds for ruling out the separate concept of *accessio*. By analogy with the law of fixtures, it is submitted that a chattel can remain separately identifiable and yet still accede to another. This minor criticism aside, the initial question, *i.e.* of the degree of attachment, is a valid one to ask in this field, given its obvious links to that of fixtures where such a consideration is part of the general test.

The second question, *i.e.* which is the dominant chattel, is generally not a difficult one. Where it is then factors such as relative size, value and purpose will be determinative. Aside from the general rule stated above, it appears that as a matter of English law, property in the offspring of an animal vests in the owner of the mother.[478]

---

[474] [1980] Ch 228.
[475] [1984] Ch 131.
[476] [1981] Ch 25.
[477] [1984] 1 WLR 485 at p 495.
[478] Blackstone. As an exception to this rule, Blackstone cites the *Case of Swans*, in which it was held that ownership of signets is to be divided equally between the owners of both the mother and father.

9.3.   Specificatio

Specificatio, also sometimes termed 'alteration', covers the situation where materials are processed so that they lose their former identity and are transformed into a new item. Examples from Blackstone's *Commentaries* include making wine from grapes or bread from wheat;[479] a more contemporary example is the working of leather into handbags (*Re Peachdart*).[480] The doctrine not only applies to the alteration of a single chattel, for example the slaughter of cattle,[481] but also to the mixture of two or more chattels, for example the combination of resin and wood chips to create chipboard.[482] Furthermore, the fact that *specificatio* can involve the combination of multiple chattels has led to some confusion between *specificatio* and *accessio*, an example of which is the *Hendy Lennox* case, dealt with in the previous section. It is clear, however, that the concepts are theoretically separate, albeit the question of whether and at what point a new item emerges from the combination of two of more chattels means that the boundary between them can be difficult to discern in practice.

Where the concept operates, title to the processed item is lost when it ceases to maintain an independent existence; title to the resultant product newly created vests, by operation of law, in the processor.[483] Faced with the problem of where title to newly manufactured products ought to vest, English law might have chosen either of the two solutions suggested in Roman jurisprudence, *i.e.* for ownership to vest in the provider of the materials, or alternatively in the manufacturer of the new item. That it appears to have chosen the latter is shown at least as early as the time of Blackstone, it has been said; however, correctly it is submitted, that this conclusion tends to be assumed rather than justified.[484] One answer might be that the processor invests time, knowledge and skill in the process leading to new goods and so, since title must vest in someone, it may as well be him. This option also avoids identification and quantification issues where multiple suppliers are involved, and such an explanation has been implicitly tendered in one case.[485] In the event however, it appears that this is a default rule that can be displaced by prior agreement.[486]

---

[479] *Commentaries on the Laws of England* at p 404.
[480] [1984] Ch 131.
[481] See *Chaigley Farms Ltd v Crawford Kaye & Grayshire Ltd* [1996] BCC 957, which decided that there was an 'inescapable difference between a live animal and a dead one', so that, upon slaughter a new product was created.
[482] *Borden (UK) Ltd v Scottish Timber Products Ltd* [1981] Ch 25.
[483] *Ibid* at p 44 *per* Templeman LJ; *Re Peachdart Ltd* [1984] Ch 131 at p 143.
[484] Bridge, *Personal Property Law* (2002), p 109.
[485] See *Clough Mill v Martin* [1985] 1 WLR 111 at p 121.
[486] *Ibid.*

There is uncertainty surrounding the situation where a manufacturer converts the goods of another, combining them with his own, to create something new. The way in which the law seems to have dealt with this situation provides for ownership to be shared proportionately between the innocent supplier and wrongful processor: *Glencore International v Metro Trading International Inc.*[487] The judge, having reviewed authorities on the topic, as well as a leading House of Lords authority on tracing,[488] settled on the conclusion that the new item is shared in common, in proportions that reflect the relative values of the contributions, with any doubts as to quantity or value, *etc.* being determined in favour of the 'innocent' party.[489] This approach avoids the 'all or nothing' results produced by an application of rules vesting outright ownership in either party. It also harmonises this area with that of mixtures, which seems desirable given that the doctrines of *specificatio* and *confusio/commixtio* shade into one another at their boundaries: It would seem illogical for the proprietary rights of the respective parties to depend upon the sometimes very difficult question of whether or not a new thing has emerged from a mixture of chattels. One obvious difficulty, however, is that this solution creates a stark division between lawful and unlawful *specificatio*.

Moreover, it was stated that such a solution would not be appropriate where the new product can not be divided between the parties. In this situation resort must be had to 'other principles in order to do substantial justice'.[490] What this entails has yet to be decided.

9.4.   Confusio and commixtio

In keeping with the Roman terminology, *confusio* is the term given to describe a mixture of fluids while *commixtio* refers to a mixture of dry goods. Again, however, it appears that English law does not follow precisely the distinctions found in Roman law.[491] The acquisition of ownership through intermingling can occur when both wet and dry goods are mixed, but only where separation of the mixed goods is either impossible or impracticable.[492]

---

[487] [2001] Lloyd's Rep 284.

[488] *Foskett v McKeown* [2001] 1 AC 102.

[489] *Glencore* at p 330.

[490] *Ibid.*

[491] *I.e.* fluid mixtures are owned in common while the constituent parts of dry mixtures are held by their respective owners.

[492] This reasoning appears in the *dictum* of Lord Moulton in *F S Sandeman & Sons v Tyzack & Branfoot Shipping Co* [1913] AC 680 at pp 694-695 as well as being the reasoning of Bovill CJ in *Spence v The Union Marine Insurance Co Ltd* (1868) LR 3 CP 427 at pp 438-439.

This will almost invariably be the case where fluids are combined and will sometimes occur when dry goods are combined. Where this does happen the mixture is held in common by those whose goods formed it and their respective shares will reflect their contributions to it.[493]

Some debate surrounds the situation where dry goods are mixed,[494] the question being whether the items continue in their original ownership or whether they are held in common. It is submitted however that the dividing line is not between wet and dry goods but rather, as in other areas, between items that retain their identities and those that do not. Where chattels are combined so that they remain distinct, identifiable and separable then there is no legally relevant 'mixture' and title to the items remains undisturbed in their original owners.[495] Where they do not then the legal rule comes into play and they are held in common. The doctrines in the areas discussed above (*i.e.* fixtures, *accessio*, *specificatio*) share the common feature that they are only called upon where for one reason or another a chattel loses its identity. Mixing of similar goods represents another way in which a chattel might cease to be identifiable, and when that happens resort must be had to the principles in this field.

Different considerations apply to the situation where one party wrongfully mixes his goods with those of another. Lord Moulton, in *F S Sandeman & Sons v Tyzack & Branfoot Shipping Co*,[496] said *obiter* that in this situation the 'innocent' party will ordinarily acquire ownership of the whole but that this rule might not prevail in extreme situations where its application would lead to injustice. His Lordship gave this example:

> 'For instance, if a small portion of the goods of "B." became mixed with the goods of "A." by a negligent act for which "A." alone was liable, I think it quite possible that the law would prefer to view it as a conversion by "A." of this small amount of "B.'s" goods rather than do the substantial injustice of treating "B." as the owner of the whole of the mixed mass.'[497]

---

[493] *Spence v The Union Marine Insurance Co Ltd; F S Sandeman & Sons v Tyzack & Branfoot Shipping Co.*

[494] See Bell, *The Modern Law of Personal Property In England and Ireland* (1989) at p 73; McCormack, 'Mixtures of Goods', 10 LS 293; Birks, 'Mixing and Tracing', [1992] CLP 69 at p 75; and Birks 'Mixtures', in Palmer and McKendrick (eds), *Interests in Goods* (1998), at p 238.

[495] See *Smith v Torr* (1862) 3 F & F 505 *per* Bramwell B; *Halsbury's Laws*, (4th ed reissue), vol 35, para 1239; and *Crossley Vaines* at p 434. This reasoning also seems implicit in the *dictum* of Lord Ellenbrough CJ in *Colwill v Reeves* (1811) 2 Camp 575 at pp 576-577, and in *Spence v The Union Marine Insurance Co Ltd* (1868) LR 3 CP 427 at pp 438-439 *per* Bovill CJ.

[496] [1913] AC 680.

[497] *Ibid* at p 695.

However, subsequent cases have sought to move away from this penal rule on the basis that such a primitive doctrine is no longer appropriate when modern and accurate methods of measuring respective contributions to a mixture are available. Thus, it was held in *Indian Oil Corporation v Greenstone Shipping SA* that:[498]

'where B wrongfully mixes the goods of A with goods of his own, which are substantially of the same nature and quality, and they cannot in practice be separated, the mixture is held in common and A is entitled to receive out of it a quantity equal to that of his goods which went into the mixture, any doubt as to that quantity being resolved in favour of A. He is also entitled to claim damages from B in respect of any loss he may have suffered, in respect of quality or otherwise, by reason of the admixture.'

Whether or not such a rule would pertain to a situation where the goods of A and B are not substantially of the same nature and quality was left to another case. It is submitted that in this situation a new product would emerge and the rules of *specificatio* would determine the outcome.

10. What are the rules of good faith acquisition and multiple selling?

10.1. The strength of legal interests

Where title conflicts arise English common law begins from the principle that the owner's interest is paramount and that *nemo dat non quod habet* ('no one can give that which he does not have'). A putative transferor cannot, generally, confer on another an interest greater than that vested in him. In the context of sale this rule is placed on a statutory footing by s. 21(1) of the Sale of Goods Act 1979:

'Subject to this Act, where goods are sold by a person who is not their owner, and who does not sell them under the authority or with the consent of the owner, the buyer acquires no better title to the goods than the seller had, unless the owner of the goods is by his conduct precluded from denying the seller's authority to sell.'

There are however some general exceptions to this rule that legal interests in chattels are good against the whole world. These exceptions stem from both the common law and statute.

---

[498] [1988] QB 345 at pp 370-371 *per* Staughton J.

10.1.1. Agency

It is clear from s. 21(1) that a sale of goods by an agent with actual or implied authority is effective to transfer title in spite of the fact that the
agent is not the owner. However, this is not a true exception: the acts of
the agent transfer his principal's title. The same is not true of apparent
authority.

10.1.2. Apparent authority

At common law, where an owner has by some act indicated to a third
party that another is acting with authority on his behalf, or has allowed
another to appear as the true owner while dealing with a third party then
he will be estopped from denying the title of the third party transferee.[499]
What is required here is some form of representation made by the owner to
the third party or the world at large that the 'agent' has his authority to
dispose of the chattel.[500] A common example is where the agent is placed
in a position that ordinarily carries with it a level of authority. The burden
is on the transferee to show that the owner made such a representation,
which in practice is a difficult requirement to meet.

The representation may take the form of words or conduct but must be
clear and unequivocal.[501] It is established that merely giving another possession does not amount to conduct that will give rise to an estoppel.[502]

10.1.3. Indicia of title

Where the non-owner transferor has been handed not only possession by
the owner but also something, like a log-book, that is suggestive of ownership of the chattel it has been argued that this adds an extra dimension
to the estoppel plea: *Central Newbury Car Auctions Ltd v Unity Finance
Ltd.*[503] Such an argument persuaded Lord Denning but not the majority of
the Court of Appeal, which held that the owner of the car was not estopped from denying the authority of the rogue purporting to transfer
ownership.

---

[499] See, *Eastern Distributors Ltd v Goldring* [1957] 2 QB 600, a rare example of the
estoppel argument succeeding.

[500] *Farquharson Brothers & Co v King & Co* [1902] AC 325 at p 333 *per* Earl of Halsbury LC.

[501] *Moorgate Mercantile v Twitchings* [1977] AC 890.

[502] *Farquharson Bros*, above; *Jerome v Bentley* [1952] 2 All ER 114.

[503] [1957] 1 QB 371.

It is clear that delivery of documents of title to the non-owner does not estop the true owner from asserting his title to the underlying goods because that has the same effect as delivery of the goods themselves, an act that does not amount to estoppel by conduct.[504] However, delivery of possession to the non-owner coupled with an acknowledgment that the non-owner has paid the price for the goods in full may be sufficient.[505]

10.1.4. Negligence

Similarly, it has been argued that where the owner has been careless and through his negligence he has allowed another to appear as though he was in fact the owner, the true owner should be estopped from asserting his title. Again however, this failed to convince a majority of the House of Lords in *Moorgate Mercantile Co Ltd v Twitchings*,[506] in which it was held that there was no duty of care owed by the true owner to the buyer and therefore no such estoppel could arise. As an aside, s. 11(1) of the TIGA 1977 makes it clear that in an action for conversion or intentional trespass contributory negligence of the owner is no defence.

10.1.5. Voidable title

In certain circumstances English law will treat a transaction as void (for example where it is the result of unilateral mistake as to identity), in others it will recognise the transaction but deem it to be voidable, *i.e.* capable of being avoided at the will of the transferor. This will occur where the transaction has been induced, for example, by a misrepresentation.[507] In the former situation the 'transferee' has no title at all to pass: It remains with the 'transferor',[508] by contrast, a transferee in the second situation does receive a title, albeit a somewhat fragile one. If he can pass the title on to a third party before the transferor avoids (rescinds) the transaction then that third party will acquire a good title, provided he acts in good faith and without notice of the defect of title.[509] The method and timing of rescission has therefore been the focus of litigation.

---

[504] See above.

[505] *Rimmer v Webster* [1902] 2 Ch 163 at p 173 *per* Farwell J.

[506] [1977] AC 890. A duty of care was recognised, but the argument of estoppel by negligence also ultimately failed, in *Mercantile Credit Co Ltd v Hamblin* [1965] 2 QB 242.

[507] Also by reason of fraud at common law or equity, non-disclosure, equitable mistake, duress, or undue influence: See *Benjamin's Sale of Goods* (2000) at 7-021.

[508] For example, *Cundy v Lindsay* (1878) 3 App Cas 459. *Ingram v Little* [1961] 1 QB 31.

[509] Sale of Goods Act 1979, s. 23.

For rescission to be effected the transferor must establish clearly and unequivocally that he terminates the contract and is no longer to be bound by it.[510] It is not necessary that the owner obtain a court order. The general rule is that this decision is to be communicated to the other party, but there are other ways of achieving rescission. One such way is where the transferor comes across the chattel and re-takes it without the knowledge of the transferee and before a resale to an innocent purchaser. Furthermore, in *Car & Universal Finance v Caldwell*[511] rescission was also achieved when a transferor, unable to find the fraudulent transferee by reason of his disappearance, contacted both the police and the Automobile Association and informed them of the fraud. As pragmatic as that decision is, however, it has been criticised and its effect limited.

Something is done in 'good faith' for the purposes of the SGA 1979 when it is done 'honestly, whether it is done negligently or not' (s. 61(3)), (for 'notice' requirements see below). The burden of showing the absence of good faith for the purposes of s. 23 of the SGA lies with the owner: *Whitehorn Brothers v Davison*.[512] However, this rule has been criticised, first because it does not fit with other aspects of *nemo dat* law which burdens the third party, and secondly because the third party is in a better position to provide information about his dealings with the rogue. It has also been asked why, public policy aside, a good faith requirement is necessary at all when the transferee and thus the third party gets a real, common law title, not an equitable one that requires clean hands.[513]

10.1.6. Mercantile agency

Certain statutes give life to exceptions that did not exist before enactment. The first is the Factors Act 1889, s. 2(1) of which provides that:

> 'Where a mercantile agent is, with the consent of the owner, in possession of goods or of the documents of title to goods, any sale pledge, or other disposition of the goods, made by him when acting in the ordinary course of business of a mercantile agent, shall, subject to the provisions of this Act, be as valid as if he were expressly authorised by the owner of the goods to make the same; provided that the person taking under the disposition acts in good faith, and has not at the same time of the disposition notice that the person making the disposition has not authority to make the same.'

---

[510] *Car & Universal Finance v Caldwell* [1965] 1 QB 525 at p 551 *per* Sellers LJ.

[511] *Ibid.*

[512] [1911] 1 KB 463.

[513] Bridge, *Personal Property Law* (2002), at p 124.

This exception, which is based on commercial convenience, has several facets. A 'mercantile agent' is defined as 'a mercantile agent having in the customary course of his business as such agent either to sell goods, or to consign goods for the purposes of sale, or to buy goods, or to raise money on the security of the goods'.[514] This definition embraces a number of commercial intermediaries whose possession of goods is suggestive of ownership.[515] A person can be a mercantile agent even if that is not his general occupation.[516]

The mercantile agent must be in possession of the goods in his capacity as such,[517] a judicial gloss on the statute designed to protect an owner who hands his goods over to an agent with a dual capacity, for example where a car repairer that also acts as a second-hand car dealer receives an owner's vehicle for the purposes of repair.

The statute requires that the agent be in possession with the consent of the owner,[518] but assists the third party recipient in several respects. First, the agent is deemed to be in possession of goods if he is in actual custody of them or if they are held by another for the agent and subject to his control.[519] Secondly, the consent of the owner is rebuttably presumed under s. 2(4), and the consent once granted is deemed to continue despite revocation by the owner, provided the third party has no notice of the withdrawal of consent at the time of the disposition (s. 2(2)).

The agent must be acting in the 'ordinary course of business of a mercantile agent', which is a concept that has been given a very wide meaning. The leading case is *Oppenheimer v Attenborough*,[520] in which the phrase was said to mean:[521]

> '"[A]cting in such a way as a mercantile agent acting in the ordinary course of business of a mercantile agent would act"; that is to say, within business hours, at a proper place of business, and in other respects in the ordinary way in which a mercantile agent would act, so that there is nothing to lead the pledgee to suppose that anything wrong is being done, or to give him notice that the disposition is one which the mercantile agent had no authority to make.'

---

[514] Factors Act 1889, s. 1(1).
[515] It does not include carriers and warehousemen since they do not perform any of the functions in s. 1(1).
[516] *Lowther v Harris* [1927] 1 KB 293.
[517] *Cole v North Western Bank* (1874-75) LR 10 CP 354.
[518] It has been held that the consent is valid even if obtained by agent using deceit: *Cole v North Western Bank*; *Cahn v Pockett's Bristol Channel Co* [1899] 1 QB 643.
[519] Factors Act 1889, s. 1(2).
[520] [1908] 1 KB 221.
[521] *Ibid* at pp 230-231 *per* Buckley LJ.

Good faith is not defined in the Act, but it is likely that it means the same thing as the absence of knowledge that the mercantile agent is exceeding the authority of the owner,[522] and that it coincides with dishonesty rather than mere carelessness.[523] Notice would appear to include actual and 'Nelsonian' notice, *i.e.* wilful blindness, but not constructive notice.[524] The burden of proof rests on the person dealing with the mercantile agent.[525]

10.1.7. Market overt

Prior January 3 1995 there was a market overt rule in English law. It provided protection to a purchaser, in good faith and without notice of the seller's defect in title, from a market overt (s. 22(1) SGA 1979) and applied to sales in shops in the city of London and, outside London to sale from any open, public and legally constituted market. The rule was abolished by the Sale of Goods (Amendment) Act 1994.

10.1.8. Seller in possession

A separate exception was deemed necessary when it was held that the mercantile agency exception did not apply to the case where a seller of goods remains in possession of them and resells them; section 8 of the Factors Act 1889 was the result,[526] the wording of which is almost identical to s. 24 of the Sale of Goods Act 1979.

Section 24 of the SGA states that:

'Where a person having sold goods continues or is in possession of the goods, or of the documents of title to the goods, the delivery or transfer by that person, or by a mercantile agent acting for him, of the goods or documents of title under any sale, pledge, or other disposition thereof, to any person receiving the same in good faith and without notice of the previous sale, has the same

---

[522] See Bridge, *Personal Property Law* (2002), at p 129.

[523] *Benjamin's Sale of Goods* at 7-044.

[524] *Forsythe International (UK) Ltd v Silver Shipping Co Ltd* [1994] 1 WLR 1334. See, *Benjamin's Sale of Goods* at 7-045.

[525] *Heap v Motorists' Advisory Agency Ltd* [1923] 1 KB 557.

[526] Strictly speaking s. 3 of the Factors Act 1877 was the result, but s. 8 of the 1889 is derived from that.

effect as if the person making the delivery or transfer were expressly authorised by the owner of the goods to make the same.'[527]

The reference to the 'owner' in the section is to the first buyer and the effect of the section is to bestow full title upon the second buyer at the expense of the first. Since the starting point of this section is a true relationship of sale it cannot apply where the seller himself could not pass title to the goods in the first place.

Two important points about the nature of the seller's possession arise from the Privy Council decision of *Pacific Motor Auctions Ltd v Motor Credits Ltd*.[528] In that case a car dealer sold its stock to a finance company at a discount, repaying it the price of individual vehicles as and when they were sold to customers. While title to the cars passed to the finance company, they never left the dealer's possession until the customers took the cars away. When the dealer ran into financial problems the finance company withdrew the authority that allowed the dealer to sell on its behalf, but on the same day the appellant, one of the dealer's creditors, without notice of the withdrawal of authority or the previous sale bought a number of cars, some of which were the property of the finance company. The cheque with which the cars were 'paid' for was indorsed on its reverse in favour of the appellant and was taken away with the cars.

The Privy Council advised that the appellant had gained good title to the cars, holding that the section required there to be continuous possession, which meant actual custody, and that it was irrelevant in what capacity the seller had possession. It is perhaps interesting to note that the Privy Council saw the purpose of the section as protecting the 'innocent purchaser who is deceived by the vendor's physical possession of goods or documents and who is inevitably unaware of legal rights which fetter the apparent power to dispose',[529] a purpose that mirrors the idea behind the mostly doomed estoppel arguments raised at common law. The situation of double-sale is different, but the third party cannot know of this if the section is to operate. If the focus is on the effect that the non-owner's possession has on the mind of the third party then it may be difficult to discern a difference, except, of course, that the section operates in much narrower confines.

---

[527] Section 8 reads almost identically, but for the addition of, 'or under any agreement for sale, pledge, or other disposition thereof' after 'under any sale, pledge, or other disposition thereof'. According to s. 21(2)(a) SGA 1979 nothing in the SGA 1979 affects the provisions of the Factors Acts 1889 (1979), so the two provisions can be used in the alternative.

[528] [1965] AC 867.

[529] *Ibid* at p 886.

The section contemplates sale, pledge or 'other disposition'. Where the second transaction involves a pledgee then all he will acquire against the first buyer is the special property of a pledgee. Light was shed on the term 'other disposition' in a complicated case again involving fraud: *Worcestor Works Finance v Cooden Engineering Co.*[530] In that case the respondent sold a car to a rogue for a cheque that was later dishonoured. Soon afterwards the same rogue then sold the car to the appellant on the basis that it would be let on hire-purchase terms to another (who happened to be in league with the rogue). However, this too was a fraud and the rogue remained in possession at all times, until, having discovered that the cheque had been dishonoured, the respondent repossessed the car. When the appellant knew of this it brought proceedings against the respondent. It was held by the Court of Appeal that the transactions fell within the section since the seller had been continually in possession and the re-taking by the respondent constituted a 'disposition' in that there was a transfer of the property by the seller:[531]

> 'It is said by Mr. Jacob that "disposition" in that context must mean something more than a mere transfer of possession. That is plainly right. "Disposition" must involve some transfer of an interest in property, in the technical sense of the word "property," as contrasted with mere possession.'

A constructive delivery will suffice as 'delivery or transfer'.[532] Moreover the presumption as to possession in s. 1(2) of the Factors Act that assists the third party under the mercantile agency exception also assists the second buyer here.[533]

Good faith carries the meaning given to it for the purposes of the SGA 1979 by s. 61(3) of that Act and 'notice' the same meaning as described under the 12.1.6 (above). Again, the burden rests on the party who seeks to rely on the section.

10.1.9. Buyer in possession

Another situation dealt with by statute is the case where a buyer, having bought or agreed to buy goods, takes delivery and then disposes of them before property has passed to him. Section 25(1) SGA 1979 (which re-enacts almost identically s. 9 of the Factors Act 1889) permits a sub-buyer to take good title:

---

[530] [1972] 1 QB 210.

[531] *Ibid* at p 220 *per* Megaw LJ.

[532] *Michael Gerson (Leasing) Ltd v Wilkinson* [2001] QB 514 (approved concession).

[533] *Forsythe International (UK) Ltd v Silver Shipping Co Ltd* [1994] 1 WLR 1334.

'Where a person having bought or agreed to buy good obtains, with the consent of the seller, possession of the goods or the documents of title to the goods, the delivery or transfer by that person, or by a mercantile agent acting for him, of the goods or documents of title, under any sale, pledge, or other disposition thereof, to any person receiving the same in good faith and without notice of any lien or other right of the original seller in respect of the goods, has the same effect as if the person making the delivery or transfer were a mercantile agent in possession of the goods or documents of title with the consent of the owner.'[534]

The reference to 'bought' seems at first odd and unnecessary but it may be that the seller retains an unpaid seller's lien on the goods and temporarily and for a limited purpose hands over the goods. The effect of s. 25 here would be to allow the sub-buyer to take free of that lien.

The question of delivery by the buyer has been the subject of litigation. First, in *Four Point Garage Ltd v Carter*[535] it was held that where a seller, at the first buyer's request, delivered a car directly to the second buyer that simultaneously gave rise to constructive possession of the first buyer and actual possession of the second, with the seller deemed to be the first buyer's agent; thus the section applied. Secondly, in *Forsythe International (UK) Ltd v Silver Shipping Co Ltd*[536] it was stated that there must be some voluntary act by the first buyer, so that a unilateral act of re-entry into possession by the second buyer did not satisfy s. 25. Furthermore, s. 1(2) of the Factors Act 1889 assists the second buyer with the presumption that the first buyer is in possession of the goods if he has actual custody of them or they are held by another subject to his control, *etc.* Similarly the question of consent is rebuttably presumed under s. 2(4) of the 1889 Act. Again, consent obtained by fraud is still good.[537]

Another contentious part of the section involves that which makes reference to the transaction taking effect 'as if' made by a mercantile agent. At first sight it does not appear to create any further hurdles in the application of the section. However, the opposite conclusion was reached by the Court of Appeal when considering s. 9 of the Factors Act 1889 in *Newtons of Wembley Ltd v Williams*.[538] In that case the words were taken to put the first buyer notionally in the position of a mercantile agent so that it was still necessary, in line with s. 2(1) of the Factors Act 1889, for

---

[534] Section 9 reads almost identically, but for the addition of, 'or under any agreement for sale, pledge, or other disposition thereof' after 'under any sale, pledge, or other disposition thereof'.

[535] [1985] 3 All ER 12.

[536] [1994] 1 WLR 1334.

[537] *Newtons of Wembley Ltd v Williams* [1965] 1 QB 560.

[538] *Ibid.*

the second buyer to show that the first was acting in the 'ordinary course of business of a mercantile agent'.[539] This interpretation of this part of the section is not one universally shared and its removal has been advocated.[540] The good faith and notice requirements are as found under 12.1.9 (above).

The effect of this section, and by analogy, section 24, is to vest in the protected buyer the title that was previously vested in the first buyer and the seller respectively. Thus, if A, who has stolen goods from X, sells goods to B and allows him to have possession, and B then sells to C, C will attain a title that will defeat A, but not X.[541] It has been argued, correctly, it is submitted, that this reasoning also applies to the other *nemo dat* exceptions.[542]

10.1.10. Hire-purchase

Hire-purchase agreements are structured so as to avoid the operation of the preceding exception. They involve a transfer of possession in return for the payment of hire instalments; upon payment of the all instalments the hirer is entitled to exercise an option to purchase the goods on hire at a nominal price. In this way the hirer, although in possession, has not agreed to buy the goods and so the section cannot operate.[543] This resulted in a clear distinction between a hire-purchase agreement and a conditional sale, which is in similar in substance. S. 25(2) and 9(2).

Furthermore, where the hire purchase or conditional sale of a motor vehicle is concerned Part III of the Hire Purchase Act 1964 provides a special *nemo dat* exception. Under this exception the first private (*i.e.* not a trade or finance purchaser, see ss. 27 and 29 of the 1964 Act) purchaser to buy in good faith and without notice from the rogue will gain good title.[544]

The way in which this narrow provision has been carved out illustrates the main difficulty with the current law of *nemo dat* and its exceptions.

---

[539] [1965] 1 QB 560 at pp 574 – 575 *per* Sellers LJ. This requirement therefore requires reference to *Oppenheimer v Attenborough* [1908] KB 221 (above).

[540] See, *Benjamin's Sale of Goods* (2000) at 7-079. The requirement was reluctantly followed in *Forstythe International (UK) Ltd.*

[541] *National Employers' Mutual General Insurance Association Ltd v Jones* [1990] 1 AC 24. See, Battersby, 'A Reconsideration of "Property" and "Title" in the Sale of Goods Act', [2001] JBL 1.

[542] Battersby, above n541, at p 8.

[543] *Helby v Matthews* [1895] AC 471.

[544] Hire Purchase Act 1964, s. 27(2). See further *Benjamin's Sale of Goods* at 7-08 *et seq.*

The area seems to be the result of piecemeal development, with aspects being designed to meet discrete situations. It is submitted that the scheme suffers from a lack of an overarching reconsideration of the how and when proprietary rights should be allowed to persist against a *bona fide* purchaser.

10.1.11. Money and the currency rule

Money is treated differently from other forms of property because of its place in the economy. Where a *bona fide* purchaser for value receives money he enjoys the benefits of the currency rule, which provides him with a fresh title and extinguishes the title of the previous owner.[545]

10.1.12. Miscellaneous

A number of other exceptions apply in specific circumstances.[546]

10.2.   The strength of equitable interests

Again the starting point here is the rule that *nemo dat non quod habet*, but, in contrast to the common law position, equity recognises a more general good faith purchase exception and as a result equitable interests in personal property are far more vulnerable than their common law counterparts. A *bona fide* purchaser of the legal interest in the property, for value without notice will take the legal estate free of any prior equitable interests.[547] The level of notice required is unclear. A purchaser with actual knowledge of the prior interest will lose the defence, however, it is unlikely that he will be deemed to possess constructive knowledge,[548] *i.e.* what the purchaser ought to have known had he made reasonable inquiries, given the judicial reluctance to allow the doctrine of constructive notice to disrupt the certainty of commerce.[549]

---

[545] *Miller v Race* (1758) 1 Burr 452; see, Fox, 'Bona Fide Purchase and the Currency of Money', [1996] CLJ 547.

[546] See further *Benjamin's Sale of Goods* at 7-107 *et seq.*

[547] *Pilcher v Rawlins* (1872) 7 Ch App 259. Thus, a donee (*i.e.* one who has not bought the legal interest) will take subject to equitable interests and mere equities; so too will the purchaser with notice of the prior interest.

[548] Cf. the position in respect of real property.

[549] See *Manchester Trust v Furness* [1895] 2 QB 39.

The *nemo dat* rule applies with full rigour to the purchaser of an equi-table interest, who will take subject to prior legal and equitable inter-ests;[550] however, the same is not true of mere equities, of which such a purchaser will take free.[551] Where equitable interests in an item of prop-erty compete for superiority the general rule is *'qui prior est tempore potior est iure'* ('that which is first in time is first in law').[552]

II.   Acquisitive prescription and other forms of original acquisition

II.1.   'Adverse' possession

English law has not developed a series of formal 'rules' relating to what would be recognised as 'adverse' possession of movables in the same way as such rules have developed in relation to real property.[553] Rather, as noted above in a number of sections of this report, the possession of any party, even one whose possession is wrongful, is treated as good against the whole world except a party who can demonstrate a superior right in the movable.

However, it could certainly be argued that, functionally, the rules as to limitation periods on action perform a role similar to that of rules which afford acquisitive prescription to be claimed.[554] In a situation where one party acquires possession of a movable, and that party's possession would be challengeable by the true 'owner' of the movable, the Limitation Act 1980 might well operate to extinguish the owner's title and, thereby, to indirectly afford the 'best' title to the party in possession. The starting point is section 2 of that Act, which imposes a limitation period of six years on all actions in tort. An action against a party in possession would normally be brought in the tort of conversion, so, *prima facie*, the owner of a movable has six years from the date of a conversion of it to bring an action.

Section 3(1) of the Limitation Act prevents an owner from extending the basic six year limitation period where a string of conversions has taken place by the starting time running as against *all potential defendants* at the same time. It provides:

---

[550] *Philips v Phillips* (1862) 4 De GF & J 208.

[551] *Ibid.*

[552] *Ibid.*

[553] For a treatment of the rules of adverse possession relating to land, see Gravells, *Land Law: Text & Materials* (2004), pp 86-108.

[554] See also section 1.4.2.(d) above.

'(1) Where any cause of action in respect of the conversion of a chattel has accrued to any person and, before he recovers possession of the chattel, a further conversion takes place, no action shall be brought in respect of the further conversion after the expiration of six years from the accrual of the cause of action in respect of the original conversion.'

Section 3(2) goes further, and effectively vests title to the movable in the person who, at the expiry of the limitation period, has the best claim (which will inevitably be based on possession or an immediate right to possession of the movable) to it.

'(2) Where any such cause of action has accrued to any person and the period prescribed for bringing that action has expired and he has not during that period recovered possession of the chattel, the title of that person to the chattel shall be extinguished.'

It should be noted at this stage that, if the six year limitation period has expired, the duration of possession of the party actually in possession at that point is irrelevant. To take an example, where the owner of the movable loses it, and it is found by one party who then sells it to another party 5 years and 11 months later, the month of possession enjoyed by the buyer will be adequate to protect him against any conversion action of the owner.

There is one exception to this general rule, found in section 4 of the Limitation Act. That section applies where the original conversion is a theft[555] of the movable from its owner. In such a case, the six year period does not begin to run from the date of the theft, but instead from the first conversion which is not related to the theft.[556] In essence, a party who acquires possession of the movable in good faith and for value does not acquire it through a conversion related to the theft.[557] It is therefore often stated that time begins to run for the purposes of limitation of actions from the date of the first 'innocent' conversion. As regards the original thief, or, indeed, any party acquiring the movable from him who is not in good faith, it would appear that there is no limitation period for the bringing of an action in conversion.[558]

---

[555] Defined as including the acquisition of the movable by blackmail or by fraud: s. 4(5)(b)(i)(ii) Limitation Act 1980.

[556] Limitation Act 1980, s. 3(1)

[557] *Ibid*, s. 3(2).

[558] *Ibid*, s. 4(1), (3).

11.2.   The rights of finders

11.2.1.   General

Any discussion of the rights of a finder of a movable presupposes that the movable in question has been lost by its owner or, indeed, abandoned by that owner.[559] It is important to distinguish between these two scenarios, as the legal consequences for the finder may differ. In very general terms, a finder of a movable acquires a good possessory title to it and may assert that title against all but the true owner of the property.[560] To the extent that the finder asserts rights inconsistent with those of the owner whilst in possession of the movable, he may well commit a conversion of it.[561] For example, the finder who sells the movable will clearly convert it, and any substantial alteration of the movable may also amount to a conversion. However, the provisions of the Limitation Act 1980, as discussed in the preceding section, will ultimately protect the finder who remains in possession for the applicable limitation period by extinguishing the owner's title after that time. This, arguably, has the indirect effect of conferring ownership rights on the finder whose possessory title will now be good as against the whole world. If English law admits that a movable may be abandoned,[562] it must follow that the finder of an abandoned chattel acquires a title that may be asserted against the world, including the abandoning owner, although no authority has determined this point.[563]

11.2.2.   The competition between finders and landowners

The rights of a finder may be subject to those of the owner of land upon which the movable is found. This competition is largely resolved by asking whether the landowner in question was in possession of the movable, in which case his possessory title is superior to that of the finder. As noted earlier in this report,[564] to assert possession requires the two elements of 'factual' possession and an intention to exclude all others from possession to be present. Thus, where a commercial traveller visiting a shop found a roll of banknotes on the floor, it was held that the shop owner, not being aware of their presence, could not demonstrate the

---

[559] As to abandonment, see below at section 13.

[560] See, *e.g.*, *Armory v Delamirie* (1722) 5 Stra 505.

[561] See above at section 1 for a discussion of the tort of conversion.

[562] As to which there may be some doubt: see below at section 13.

[563] But see Bridge, *Personal Property Law* (2002), p 23, citing Blackstone in support.

[564] See section 2.

necessary intention to exclude all others from the possession of them so as to be able to claim to be in possession himself.[565]

The leading case on the rights of finders, and on their obligations, is *Parker v British Airways Board*.[566] The claimant found a gold bracelet in the executive lounge of the defendant's airport, which he handed in to the airport authorities with an instruction to return it to him if the owner was not located. The defendant, having failed to find the owner of the bracelet, sold it and retained the proceeds. The Court of Appeal examined the question of whether the defendant was in possession of the bracelet at the time the claimant found it, and held that it was not. According to Donaldson LJ:

> 'An occupier of a building has rights superior to those of a finder over chattels upon or in, but not attached to, that building if, but only if, before the chattel is found, he has manifested an intention to exercise control over the building and the things which may be upon it or in it.'[567]

The requisite intention to control things that might be in or on the premises might, presumably, be demonstrated by placing notices requiring lost property to be handed in to the landowner or occupier. Further, where the finder in question is trespassing on the land in question there will, as a matter of public policy, be a finding in favour of the landowner.[568] It should further be noted that where the movable in question can be said to be attached or affixed to the land[569] then this will give the landowner or occupier a superior possessory title, as attached chattels become part of the land itself.[570]

11.2.3. The obligations of finders

It is clear from *Parker v British Airways Board* that the finder of a movable comes under an obligation to attempt to locate the owner of it and to inform him of its location:

> 'A person having a finder's rights has an obligation to take such measures as in all the circumstances are reasonable to acquaint the true owner of the finding and present whereabouts of the chattel and to care for it meanwhile.'[571]

---

[565] *Bridges v Hawksworth* (1851) 21 LJQB 75.
[566] [1982] QB 1004.
[567] *Ibid*, p 1018.
[568] *Ibid*, p 1010.
[569] See above, at section 9, as to fixtures.
[570] See *South Staffordshire Water Co v Sharman* [1896] 2 QB 44.
[571] [1982] QB 1004, 1017, *per* Donaldson LJ.

This might include placing advertisements in newspapers, but ultimately it will be a question of fact as to whether the content of this duty has been complied with in any given case.

11.2.4. Treasure

One further competition that might arise is between the finder of a movable and the Crown. At one time, the common law treated movables that had been 'hidden' by their owner and never recovered as vesting in the Crown. Therefore a finder of those movables would be vulnerable to a claim by the Crown, giving rise to an incentive to demonstrate that they had been abandoned rather than hidden.[572] This matter is now, however, governed by statute, in the form of the Treasure Act 1996. Section 4 of that Act provides that:

> '(1) When treasure is found, it vests, subject to prior interests and rights –
>   (a) in the franchisee, if there is one;
>   (b) otherwise, in the Crown ...
>   (4) This section applies –
>   (a) whatever the nature of the place where the treasure was found, and
>   (b) whatever the circumstances in which it was left (including being lost or being left with no intention of recovery)'.

Thus, the distinction between abandoned and hidden property is now irrelevant, as, if the property in question falls under the definition of 'treasure', it vests in the Crown in the absence of any franchisee. Treasure is defined in section 1 of the Act to include objects of at least 300 years old which are not coins but are at least 10% in weight of precious metal, precious metal being defined as gold or silver,[573] and coins of at least 300 years old and of 10% in weight of precious metal. The Secretary of State is given power, by section 2(2) of the Act, to designate as 'treasure' 'any class of object which he considers to be of outstanding historical, archaeological or cultural importance.'

---

[572] See *Attorney General v Trustees of the British Museum* [1903] 2 Ch 598.
[573] Treasure Act 1996, s. 3(3).

Part IV:
Additional issues

12. The rules on reservation of title

12.1. The doctrinal basis

In English law a security is regarded as being created:

> 'when a person ('the creditor') to whom an obligation is owed by another ('the debtor') by statute or contract, in addition to the promise of the debtor to discharge the obligation, obtains rights exercisable against some property in which the debtor has an interest in order to enforce the discharge of the debtor's obligation to the creditor.'[574]

A security right, in the English sense, is therefore a right of recourse *to the property of another* for the payment of a debt; the approach is one of form over function. For this reason, reservation or retention of title is termed a 'quasi-security': It functions as a security device, but, since the seller secures his position by retaining title to its own property, it is not classified as such.

The legal basis for these devices is to be found in the Sale of Goods Act 1979 and the English approach to the passing of personal property using contract.[575] By s. 17 of the SGA 1979 property passes from seller to buyer 'when it is intended to pass', and by s. 19 of the same Act, a seller may reserve the right of disposal of the goods, with property in them not passing until any conditions imposed by the seller are fulfilled. Thus, it is at first sight relatively straightforward for a supplier with sufficient bargaining power to protect its position in the event of a buyer's insolvency using this statutory basis. The rest of the rules relating to English retention of title are to be found in the case law.

---

[574] *Bristol Airport v Powdrill* [1990] 2 WLR 1362, *per* Browne-Wilkinson VC at p 1372.

[575] See, above at section 5.4.

12.2.   A taxonomy of retention of title clauses

12.2.1.   The 'simple' retention of title clause

As the name suggests, these are the most basic clauses in the taxonomy. Using them, the seller purports to reserve title to goods supplied that remain in the possession of the buyer in their original, identifiable state. The efficacy of this type of clause was established by the Court of Appeal in *Aluminium Industrie Vaasen BV v Romalpa Aluminium Ltd*,[576] and then confirmed by a different Court of Appeal in *Clough Mill Ltd v Martin*.[577] It rests on the legal basis outlined above and, so far as its mechanics are concerned, it is uncontroversial at law. The same is not true, however, of a clause that purports to retain equitable or beneficial ownership.

In *Re Bond Worth*[578] carpet fibre was supplied to Bond Worth on terms that 'equitable and beneficial ownership shall remain with [the supplier] until full payment has been received'. Further terms attempted to extend the reach of the equitable title to any proceeds of resale before payment to the seller, to any products made involving the goods supplied and to the proceeds of sale of such products. Such clauses will be considered in more detail below.

It was held by Slade J that the effect of the agreement was to create floating charges over all four types of asset,[579] and furthermore, since it was not possible to retain equitable title, full title to the goods had passed to the buyer, who then granted back to the seller the necessary equitable charges, which were void for non-registration.[580] *Romalpa* was distinguished on the basis that it involved the retention of legal title, which did not preclude the finding of a relationship of bailment between the parties (something that was, in any event, conceded by counsel for *Romalpa*).

Thus the limits of the device are already apparent. Reserving full (legal) title to goods that remain in their unaltered, identifiable state is possible using the 'simple' model, but this is of limited application when the subject matter of such clauses is destined for manufacture and/or resale. Spurred on by the success of *Romapla*, draftsmen of the supply contracts sought to extend the utility of reservation clauses further, meeting with mixed success.

---

[576] [1976] 1 WLR 676.

[577] [1985] 1 WLR 111.

[578] [1980] Ch 228.

[579] *I.e.* (i) the original goods, (ii) their proceeds of resale, (iii) their products, (iv) the proceeds of sale of (iii).

[580] Under what was then s. 95 of the Companies Act 1948.

12.2.2. 'All moneys clauses'

A straightforward method of maximising the utility of the 'simple' retention clause is to expand the scope of the stipulations that form the conditions precedent to property passing from an obligation to pay for the subject matter of the clause in question to the payment of *all* debts owed by the buyer to the seller. This is precisely what an 'all moneys clause' purports to do and the validity of such a device was upheld by the House of Lords in *Armour v Thyssen*.[581] There is a potential for argument to the effect that where the buyer has paid for all the goods under the contract and, because some other liability is outstanding, title to the goods has not passed, the supplier ought to be liable to refund the purchaser on the ground of total failure of consideration.[582]

12.2.3. 'Products clauses'

The aim of this type of clause is to 'retain' title to products made from the original goods supplied or to products incorporating those goods. The word 'retain' is put in inverted commas for the reason that the manufacturing process tends to destroy the original title, which cannot therefore logically be 'retained': A more apt term might be 'vesting of title'.[583] Thus a weakness inherent in this model of clause is that the original title is usually extinguished, leaving the seller vulnerable. An example of this can be seen in the case of *Borden (UK) Ltd v Scottish Timber Products Ltd*.[584] The claimant supplied resin to the defendant to be used in the manufacture of chipboard and the terms on which it was supplied included a reservation of title clause. The process of manufacture involved the irreversible mixing of the resin with certain other materials with the effect that the resultant chipboard was a wholly new product; when the identity of the resin was lost during this process so too was title to it. It was therefore held by the Court of Appeal that the claimant had no basis on which to claim any interest of whatever kind in the chipboard, which belonged entirely to the defendant.

---

[581] [1991] 2 AC 339.

[582] See, Goodhart and Jones, 'The Infiltration of Equitable Doctrine into English Commercial Law', (1980) 43 MLR 489; for a possible answer to this argument see Bradgate, 'Retention of Title in the House of Lords', [1991] MLR 726 and Mance, 'The Operation of an 'All Debts' Reservation of Title Clause', [1992] LMCLQ 35.

[583] For the same reason it is in this area that we see an interaction with and application of the rules regarding accessio, specificatio and commixtio.

[584] [1981] 1 Ch 25.

Although it was held that this was not the effect of the clause in *Borden*, a clause might provide for title to the newly produced goods to vest in the seller; however, this leaves room for an argument that the buyer/debtor has conferred on the seller an interest in the property. From this point it is relatively straightforward for the Court to reach the conclusion that the purpose behind the conferral was to provide the seller with security for the purchase price of the original materials and from there that the device is a registrable but unregistered, and so ineffective, charge. Such is the doctrinal difficulty inherent in products clauses that there are no reported cases in which such a clause has been upheld.

The leading authority in this area is *Clough Mill v Martin*,[585] in which a seller provided yarn to the insolvent on terms such that, *inter alia*, ownership of the yarn remained with the seller until payment for the yarn supplied had been made or title to it had been passed to a third party subbuyer under an exception to *nemo dat* (see above, 10.1.9.); and that if any of the yarn was incorporated into other goods before such payment the property in those goods should pass to the buyer until payment made or title passed to a *bona fide* sub-buyer. When the defendant was appointed receiver of the now insolvent buyer the seller attempted to re-possess a quantity of yarn still in the buyer's possession. The Court of Appeal held that the 'simple' part of the seller's retention of title clause entitled it to recover the yarn; in doing so it considered the effect of the, severable, 'products' part of the condition.

On this point, Goff LJ accepted that the operation of the doctrine of *specificatio* can be altered by agreement between the parties,[586] with the effect that title to the new products could vest directly in the seller without passing first through the buyer. This would then negate any argument that the buyer conferred a charge. However, the effect of the clause in the instant case was such that the seller would gain a windfall, in terms of both labour and materials added to create the new products. On that basis it was held that the only commercially-realistic construction of the second part of the clause was that it created a charge, albeit that this did 'violence to the language' of the provision.

It appears, therefore, that as a matter of theory, a products clause could, in certain circumstances, succeed. As stated, however, there is no reported case in which this has happened.

---

[585] [1985] 1 WLR 111.
[586] *Ibid* at p 120.

12.2.4. Proceeds clauses

The objective behind a proceeds clause (also termed 'tracing clause') is to obtain a proprietary interest in the proceeds that result from a sale of the goods supplied. Again, this form of clause has met with little success, having succeeded only in *Romalpa*,[587] a case widely considered to be wrongly decided. In that case it was conceded by the defendant that it held the goods as bailee for the supplier/bailor, from this it was held that there existed between the parties a fiduciary relationship, and therefore that the claimant was entitled to trace the proceeds of sale in equity according to the principle set out in *Re Hallett's Estate*.[588]

Romalpa was distinguished in the case of *Hendy Lennox v Grahame Puttick Ltd*,[589] which was discussed above in the context of accession. There the supplier of the engines argued that it could trace the proceeds of sale of the engines by virtue of the existence of a fiduciary relationship between it and the buyer as bailor and bailee. However, Staughton J held, *inter alia*, that the parties did not stand in such a position and accordingly the claimant's argument failed: The express terms of the agreement did not attempt to deal with mixed or manufactured objects; there was no obligation on the buyer that required to store the goods in such a way that they clearly manifested the property of the seller; there was no express mention in the contract of a fiduciary relationship, and in any event, the credit period allowed to the buyers negated a finding of any such relationship; and the proceeds of sale here related to not just the original goods supplied, *i.e.* the engines, but the generating sets to which they were attached.

Romalpa was again distinguished on very similar bases to those employed in *Hendy Lennox* in *Re Andrabell Ltd*.[590] In this case the relationship between the relevant parties was not fiduciary. First there was nothing in the contract obliging the purchaser to store the goods in a way that manifested the ownership of the seller; secondly, unlike in *Romalpa*, there is no express clause acknowledging that the parties stood in a fiduciary relationship; thirdly, there was no obligation on the buyer to keep the proceeds in a separate account; and an inference was to be drawn from the 45-day credit period that the buyer was free to use the proceeds as it wished until that term expired. Accordingly the claimant's argument failed.

In *E Pfeiffer Weinkellerei – Weineinkauf GmbH & Co v Arbuthnot Factors Ltd*[591] an express proceeds clause was held to be ineffective on the

---

587 [1976] 1 WLR 676.
588 (1880) 13 Ch D 696 *per* Sir George Jessel MR at p 708 *et seq.*
589 [1984] 1 WLR 485.
590 [1984] 3 All ER 407.
591 [1988] 1 WLR 150.

ground that where, as here, a buyer is permitted to sub-sell the goods supplied it does so on its own account, and not for the seller. Moreover, the agreement itself was inconsistent with a fiduciary relationship. Instead the agreement to transfer the claims to the proceeds of the sub-sale was in substance a charge void for non-registration. Again an express proceeds clause was employed without success in *Tatung (UK) Ltd v Galex Telesure Ltd*,[592] and *Modelboard Ltd v Outer Box Ltd*.[593]

13.   Abandonment of movables

13.1.   Introduction

Bridge describes the English law on abandonment as 'obscure and difficult to relate to modern conditions.' Indeed, there remains some doubt as to whether the notion of abandonment has or has not been accepted by the common law.[594] 'True' abandonment would seem to describe a situation where 'an owner or possessor unilaterally relinquishes possession ... intending to disclaim any interest he may have in them.'[595] This is to be distinguished from the position where a movable is lost and the search for it abandoned, as in this latter case the owner does not intend to disclaim his interest.

Two very early authorities appear to deny the possibility of abandoning ownership of movables in such a way as to constitute them *res nullius*.[596] Blackstone, however, asserts to the contrary:

'But a man who scatters his treasure into the sea, or upon the public surface of the earth, is construed to have absolutely abandoned his property, and returned it into the common stock, without any intention of reclaiming it: and therefore it belongs, as in a state of nature, to the first occupant or finder; unless the owner appear and assert his right, which then proves that the loss was by accident, and not with an intent to renounce his property.'[597]

---

[592] (1989) 5 BCC 325.

[593] [1992] BCC 945, in which the possibility of the supplier obtaining a windfall was held to point towards the clause being construed as a charge.

[594] For an excellent and lucid debate on this matter see Anthony Hudson, 'Abandonment', in: Palmer & McKendrick, *Interests in Goods* (1998), Chapter 23.

[595] *Ibid*, p 595.

[596] *Doctor and Student* (1551) 91 Seldon Society at pp 290-292; *Haynes's Case* (1614) 12 Co Rep 113.

[597] Commentaries on the Laws of England, Book 1, Chapter 8, p 285.

There is certainly House of Lords authority which appears to accept this proposition in *The Crystal*.[598] However, the law has tended to develop in a somewhat piecemeal and negative fashion, so that, for instance, a number of criminal cases allow that no offence is committed where property is taken in circumstances giving rise to a presumption of 'intended dereliction'.[599] Equally, discussion has taken place on the question of abandonment in the context of wrecks.[600] However, in the absence of any unequivocal statement on the matter, English law's position on the legal possibility of abandonment remains equivocal.

13.2. Requirements for and consequences of abandonment

Given the uncertainty as to whether abandonment is an accepted feature of English law, it is difficult to state what requirements are necessary to demonstrate the concept. However, Hudson's description of abandonment as covering the situation where possession is relinquished in circumstances where there is an accompanying intention to disclaim all interest seems to accurately describe the notion.

The consequences of abandonment will most likely turn on whether the movable in question is in any way hazardous or becomes so if abandoned. If this is the case, both the criminal law and the law of tort may well be relevant, as there are numerous statutory provisions which would apply to render the owner liable.

14.   Co-ownership of movables

14.1. Joint tenancy and tenancy in common

The common law on co-ownership of movables is reasonably well settled and relatively straightforward to state.[601] At law,[602] two forms of co-ownership are recognised, these being the joint tenancy and the tenancy in common. The major distinction between the two is that a joint ten-

---

[598] [1894] AC 508.

[599] See Hudson, above n 594, at pp 603-606.

[600] *Ibid*, pp 606-612.

[601] For a detailed exposition see Judith Hill and Elizabeth Bowes-Smith, 'Joint Ownership of Chattels', in: Palmer & McKendrick, *Interests in Goods* (1998), Chapter 10.

[602] Cf. the position in relation to real property, where the law recognises only a joint tenancy in land: s. 36 Law of Property Act 1925. Equity, however, both recognises a tenancy in common and operates a presumption in favour of the tenancy in common.

ancy treats the co-owners as, at one and the same time, entitled to the entirety of the interest in the movable, whereas the tenancy in common allocates to each co-owner a specific proportion as a share of the movable, according to their intention, which may be inferred from the proportion each contributed to the acquisition of the movable.

Joint tenancy will arise where the co-owners acquire the movable under such terms which do not suggest that they are to have divided shares in it. Certain circumstances may give rise to the presumption of co-ownership in shares however, most notably where the respective contributions to the acquisition of the movable are unequal. Moreover, where the co-owners are partners in a firm, there is an equitable presumption that any co-owned land will be held as tenants in common,[603] and there is no reason to suppose that the same presumption would not apply to movables. This presumption is, however, rebuttable by evidence of contrary intention.[604]

One further, important distinction between the joint tenancy and the tenancy in common is that only in relation to property held as tenants in common does any one co-owner have a 'share' in the property which may be bequeathed in a will. Property held on joint tenancy terms is subject to the doctrine of survivorship, which provides that any such property, on the death of one co-owner, automatically accrues to the surviving co-owner(s). The rather difficult logic of this position is that joint tenancy does not admit of the possibility that co-owners hold shares in the property, but, rather, that each is entitled to the whole. However, as will be seen, this does not in any way prevent a joint tenant from disposing of his interest, as such an act of alienation amounts to a severance of the joint tenancy.

14.1.1. Severance

Severance is a method by which a joint tenancy is effectively converted into a tenancy in common, at least as far as the severing co-owner and all other co-owners are concerned. At common law, a joint tenancy of movables could be severed by any of the methods described in the *Williams v Hensman*[605] catalogue. These methods are by way of mutual agreement, by a course of dealing with the property demonstrating that the parties have agreed to treat their interests in it as severed, and by the unilateral act of one co-owner 'operating upon his own share'. This last method will in-

---

[603] See *Malayan Credit Ltd v Jack Chia-MPH Ltd* [1986] 1 AC 549.

[604] See *Bathurst v Scarborow* [2004] EWCA Civ 411.

[605] (1861) 1 Johns & Hem 546.

clude any acts of a joint owner which purport to transfer his 'share',[606] such as an outright transfer of that share. Equally, it is settled that the bankruptcy of a joint owner is a severing event, as the joint owner's interest in any property is, by virtue of the bankruptcy, vested in the trustee in bankruptcy.

14.2. Division of the legal and equitable title to movables

One further method by which property could be said to be co-owned is where that property is subject to a trust, so that the legal title vests in the trustee and the beneficial title in the beneficiary. The institution of the trust, as noted elsewhere in this Report,[607] is the paradigm equitable device for redressing the perceived injustice caused by the common law's exclusive regard to legal 'paper' titles in determining who may claim rights in property. Trusts may arise in a variety of circumstances, and, indeed, equitable proprietary rights may arise in circumstances which do not, *stricto sensu*, require the recognition of a trust. This is not the place for a detailed exposition of this very complex area of law,[608] but it is necessary to note that it may give rise to separate property rights to movables vested in the 'trustee' and the 'beneficiary' respectively.

14.3. Transfer of co-owned movables

14.3.1. Joint tenancy and tenancy in common

There is no difficulty associated with the transfer of an interest in movables held as either a joint tenant or a tenant in common. In both cases the co-owner is able to dispose of his 'share' by any of the methods discussed in earlier sections of this report.[609]

---

[606] Which, logically and in accordance of the basis of a joint tenancy, he does not actually have! The common law is intensely pragmatic in that it treats the transfer as a severing act which effectively 'creates' the share.

[607] See, particularly, section 1.1.

[608] For detailed treatment see Maitland, *Equity: A Course of Lectures* (1969); Meagher, Heydon and Leeming, *Meagher, Gummow and Lehane's Equity: Doctrines and Remedies* (2002); McGhee, *Snell's Equity* (2005).

[609] For example, by sale, by gift, by way of security or by any other method, such as barter or exchange.

14.3.2. Transfer where legal and equitable title are divided

This is a complex area of law and the treatment here is basic in the extreme. Further reference should be made to the works in n 611 above for a full exposition. A trustee of property may, by the terms of the trust, be entitled to dispose of the legal title to that property, although he will hold proceeds or any substitute property on trust for the beneficiary or beneficiaries as the case may be. The *unauthorised* transfer of property will still be effective to vest title in the transferee: The trustee, however, breaches his fiduciary duty and will be liable to account to the beneficiary for any loss caused by the unauthorised disposal. Equally, the beneficiary will be entitled to 'trace' into the proceeds or substitute property, including any enhanced value represented by those proceeds or property.[610]

One further point should be noted here. Where a transferee appreciates that the transfer of property held on trust is unauthorised or in some other way in breach of fiduciary duty, the transferee may be held liable for *knowing receipt of trust property*, which may lead to the imposition of a constructive trust in favour of the beneficiary on the transferee. The most recent authority of the matter appears to suggest that it is not necessary in all cases to demonstrate that the transferee acted dishonestly in relation to the transfer.[611]

A beneficial 'owner' of property held on trust may dispose of it, but the disposition must be in writing by virtue of s. 53(1)(c) Law of Property Act 1925.[612]

15. The floating charge

15.1. Recognition and nature of the floating charge in English Law

The floating charge is a well established and recognised feature of English law.[613] It is an equitable proprietary right which confers upon its holder the right to have recourse to the property subject to it in the event of the

---

[610] For a commentary on the process of tracing, see Lionel Smith, *The Law of Tracing* (1997).

[611] See *Bank of Credit and Commerce International (Overseas) Ltd v Akindele* [2001] Ch 437.

[612] Subject to the exception found in s. 53(2) of the Law of Property Act 1925.

[613] What follows is a basic description of the history of the floating charge and its characteristics. An excellent series of discussions of all aspects of company charges can be found in Joshua Getzler and Jennifer Payne, *Company Charges: Spectrum and Beyond* (2006).

default of the debtor company.[614] The collateral covered by the floating charge remains in the possession of the debtor and, most notably, the debtor is entitled to dispose of the property in the ordinary course of its business. This right persists until *crystallisation*[615] of the charge occurs.

Perhaps remarkably, it appears that the floating charge originated in the Court of Chancery. With the emergence of the limited liability company in the mid-19th century, lenders to corporations were able to take advantage of the mortgage transaction, which itself had existed for many centuries prior to this development, to lend on secured terms to corporations. The mortgage transaction was adapted and evolved, in the context of corporate lending, into the *fixed charge*, a security interest which did not involve, as did the mortgage, an outright transfer of the borrower's title to the collateral subject to a right in the borrower to call for retransfer on the discharge of all indebtedness. Instead, the fixed charge simply conferred a right of recourse to the collateral:

'An equitable charge is a species of charge, which is a proprietary interest granted by way of security ... A proprietary interest provided by way of security entitles the holder to resort to the property only for the purpose of satisfying some liability due to him ... and, whatever the form of the transaction, the owner of the property retains an equity of redemption to have the property restored to him when the liability has been discharged ... A charge is a security interest created without any transfer of title or possession to the beneficiary.'[616]

However, the *fixed charge* (whether of land or of movables) was an inappropriate form of security where the collateral would be expected to be turned over regularly. Whilst it could be drafted to extend not only to property already owned by the chargor company but also that to be acquired in future,[617] it was considered that a fixed charge purporting to extend to *all* property of the company would necessarily paralyse the business of that company. One of the defining features of the fixed charge is that the debtor cannot dispose of or otherwise deal with the collateral subject to the charge without the creditor's permission: Whilst this might be perfectly workable in relation to property such as land and fixed machinery or plant, a good many corporate assets would be regularly disposed of as part of the company's business operations. To require the chargee's consent to each disposal would be logistically impossible.

---

[614] Only corporations, and not individuals, may grant floating charges.

[615] See below.

[616] *Re BCCI (No 8)* [1997] 4 All ER 568, *per* Lord Hoffmann, 576-577.

[617] See *Holroyd v Marshall* (1862) 10 HL Cas 191; *Tailby v Official Receiver* (1883) 13 App Cas 523.

This conundrum was addressed in the case of *Re Panama, New Zealand and Australian Royal Mail Co.*[618] The case involved the construction of a charge stated to extend to the 'entire undertaking' of the chargor. It was characterised by the court as a floating charge in order to avoid the conclusion that otherwise the business of the chargor would be paralysed, which, inevitably, could not have been the intention of the parties. Some thirty years later, Romer LJ described the floating charge in the following terms:

'... I certainly think that if a charge has the three characteristics I am about to mention it is a floating charge. (1) If it is a charge on a class of assets of a company present and future; (2) if that class is one which, in the ordinary course of the business of the company, would be changing from time to time; and (3) if you find that by the charge it is contemplated that, until some future step is taken by or on behalf of those interested in the charge, the company may carry on its business in the ordinary way as far as concerns that particular class of assets I am dealing with.'[619]

The floating charge, therefore, allows the chargor not only to remain in possession of the collateral, and to use it in the ordinary course of its business, but also to dispose of that collateral free of the interest of the chargee. This state of affairs continues unless and until the charge *crystallises*, which the courts considered would occur on the liquidation of the chargor,[620] the cessation of its business,[621] or the intervention of the chargee in such a way as to withdraw the right of free disposal.[622] Thus, the floating charge, on crystallisation, affords its holder priority over other creditors of the chargor by terminating the chargor's permission to deal with the collateral free of the chargee's interest:

'A floating security is not a future security; it is a present security, which presently affects all the assets of the company expressed to be included in it. On the other hand, it is not a specific security; the holder cannot affirm that the assets are specifically mortgaged to him. The assets are mortgaged in such a way that the mortgagor can deal with them without the concurrence of the mortgagee. A floating security is not a specific mortgage of the assets, plus a licence to the mortgagor to dispose of them in the course of his business, but is a floating mortgage applying to every item comprised in the security, but not specifically affecting any item *until some event occurs or some act on the part of*

---

[618] (1870) 5 Ch App 318.

[619] *Re Yorkshire Woolcombers Association* [1903] 2 Ch 284.

[620] *Wallace v Universal Automatic Machines Co* [1894] 2 Ch 547.

[621] *Government Stocks Investment v Manila Railway Co* [1897] AC 81.

[622] *Evans v Rival Granite Quarries Ltd* [1910] 2 KB 979.

the mortgagee is done which causes it to crystallise into a fixed security ... This crystallisation may be brought about in various ways. A receiver may be appointed, or the company may go into liquidation and a liquidator be appointed, or any event may happen which is defined as bringing to an end the licence to the company to carry on business.'[623]

15.2. The significance of the fixed/floating charge dichotomy

15.2.1. The vulnerability of the floating charge

The priority enjoyed by the chargee under both fixed and floating charges over unsecured creditors may only be asserted if the charge is registered under s. 395 Companies Act 1985. To the extent that the charge is not registered within 21 days of its creation it will be 'void against the liquidator or administrator and any creditor of the company'. However, the floating charge is, in liquidation, administration and administrative receivership, also vulnerable to other claims which are elevated by statute over those of the floating charge holder. By virtue of s. 175(2) Insolvency Act 1986:

> '(2) Preferential debts –
> (b) so far as the assets of the company available for payment of general creditors are insufficient to meet them, have priority over the claims of holders of debentures secured by, or holders of, any floating charge created by the company, and shall be paid accordingly out of any property comprised in or subject to that charge.'

Preferential debts thus take priority as regards the proceeds of property secured by floating charge. Preferential debts, up until very recently, included taxes *collected* by the company. This category was, however, abolished by s. 251 Enterprise Act 2002. However, certain claims of the company's employees remain preferential, and so will be paid out of the proceeds of property subject to a floating charge in priority to the claims of the charge holder.

Moreover, section 252 of the Enterprise Act 2002 inserted section 176A into the Insolvency Act 1986, which effectively introduces a 'ring-fenced' fund for any unsecured creditors of the insolvent company. This fund also takes priority over the claims of the floating charge holder. The overall effect of s. 176A is that the presiding insolvency official must set aside out of the proceeds of property subject to a floating charge an amount (the 'prescribed part') to be distributed to the company's unse-

---

[623] *Ibid, per* Buckley LJ, 999-1000, italics added.

cured creditors. The level of the prescribed part is 50% of the first £10,000 and 20% of any amount over that as regards the company's net property, with a ceiling of £600,000 (SI 2003/2097). This will not apply where the company's property is worth less than £10,000 (the 'prescribed minimum', as provided for in SI 2003/2097) or where the costs of making such a distribution would be disproportionate to the benefits (s. 176A(5)). More importantly, however, is that s. 176A does not apply to any floating charge in existence before the provision came into force (s. 176A(2) – the relevant date is 15 September 2003). This means that floating charge holders whose charges were executed prior to that date will reap the benefit of the abolition of the Crown preference without having to shoulder the burden of the payment of the prescribed part. However, the critical point to note is that neither preferential debts nor the prescribed part can be extracted from the proceeds of a *fixed charge*. Therefore, the distinction between the two types of charge remains significant.

Finally, where the company enters administration the expenses of the administration are also payable in priority to the claims of the floating charge holder. The decision of the House of Lords in *Buchler v Talbot*[624] determined that this was not the case in a liquidation of the company *unless* the expenses in question were incurred in the realisation of property subject to the floating charge.[625] However, s. 1282 of the Companies Act 2006, which is intended to reverse the *Buchler v Talbot* decision, will insert into the Insolvency Act 1986 a new s. 176ZA, the effect being that assets subject to a floating charge will be available to fund liquidation expenses. As presently advised, the earliest that this provision will enter into force is October 2007.

15.2.2. Characterisation of the charge: the significance of control

The test for distinguishing between fixed and floating charges has been the subject of much judicial and academic debate over the years, and particularly in the context of the legal possibility of taking a fixed charge over receivables (or book debts). The nature of the test, if not its application in all circumstances, has been resolved by the decision of the House of Lords in *Re Spectrum Plus Ltd.*[626] According to Lord Scott:

> 'In my opinion, the essential characteristic of a floating charge, the characteristic that distinguishes it from a fixed charge, is that the asset subject to the

---

[624] [2004] 2 AC 298.

[625] Reversing the decision of the Court of Appeal to the opposite effect in *Re Barleycorn Enterprises Ltd* [1970] Ch 465.

[626] [2005] UKHL 41.

charge is not finally appropriated as a security for the payment of the debt until the occurrence of some future event. In the meantime the chargor is left free to use the charged asset and to remove it from the security.'[627]

This reflects the view of Millett LJ in *Re Cosslett Contractors Ltd*:[628]

'The essence of a fixed charge is that the charge is on a particular asset or class of assets which the chargor cannot deal with free from the charge without the consent of the chargee. The question is not whether the chargor has complete freedom to carry on his business as he chooses, but whether the chargee is in control of the charged assets.'

The *Spectrum* case involved a charge, stated in the loan agreement conferring it to be a 'specific' (*i.e.* fixed) over debts owed to the company. The company was allowed to collect the debts, but was required to pay the proceeds into an account with the chargee bank. Whilst the account was described as 'blocked', and was at all materials times overdrawn, the company was entitled to continue to draw on it. This, according to Lord Scott, led to the inevitable conclusion that the charge in question was not fixed but floating:

'The critical question, in my opinion, is whether the chargor can draw on the account. If the chargor's bank account were in debit and the chargor had no right to draw on it, the account would have become, and would remain until the drawing rights were restored, a blocked account ... But so long as the chargor can draw on the account, and whether the account is in credit or debit, the money paid in is not being appropriated to the repayment of the debt owing to the debenture holder but is being made available for drawings on the account by the chargor.'[629]

Whilst the *Spectrum Plus* decision concerned a purported fixed charge over book debts, the test of control is clearly applicable to charges over tangible movables.

---

[627] *Ibid*, para 111.
[628] [1998] Ch 495.
[629] [2005] UKHL 41, para 117.

16.   Consequences of restitution of movables to the owner

16.1.   General

As noted above, at 1.4.1, the common law, as distinct from equity, lacks
an action akin to the Roman law concept of *vindicatio*. An owner of a
chattel has no right to specific restitution of it, and instead must usually
be content with an award of damages representing the value of the thing
lost. However, if the defendant retains the owner's goods the court has a
discretion under s. 3(2)(a) TIGA 1977 to order specific relief (see
1.4.2.(b)). It should be noted, however, that this is an extraordinary remedy. Normally damages will be an adequate form of compensation, and
the 'forced judicial sale' is completed.

The position in equity is different. It is possible for an owner to establish equitable title to a thing and, on that basis, seek a declaration from
the court that a party in possession holds the chattel on trust for him.[630]
Once this is done the claimant can ask the court to order the transfer of
it to him in line with the principle in *Saunders v Vautier*.[631] The availability of this remedy is, of course, dependent on the claimant being able to
establish equitable title to the thing in question.

16.1.1. Two-party situations

(a)   Voidable contracts

The consequences of the avoidance of a voidable contract that purported
to transfer ownership of a chattel has been explored above at 10.1.5.
Where it is said that the transferor has successfully effected rescission,
and has thereby revested title to the chattel in himself, the question of
how his rights might be enforced arises. The answer at common law is
that the claimant can bring an action in conversion against the party in
possession of the chattel, and, as set out in 15.1, the court has a discretion to order specific restitution.

Where the claimant's rights lie in equity then the position is as outlined in the second part of 15.1.

---

[630] See, for example, *Macmillan v Bishopsgate Investment Trust* [1996] 1 All ER 585.
[631] (1841) 4 Beav 115, affirmed Cr & Ph 240.

(b)   When a right to use has ended

In this case the status of the party in possession of the chattel will alter from that of a bailee for a term to that of a bailee at will. General principles of the law of conversion apply, so that if, following requests for the return of the chattel, the bailee at will fails to return the thing then an action for conversion lies.

It is unlikely, although not inconceivable, that the equitable route would be open to a claimant here.

(c)   Theft

It is somewhat surprising that this situation is as analytically unclear as it is. The most obvious analysis is that the act of theft is the clearest example of conversion there is. The consequences of such an action are as set out above.

The water here is muddied, however, by an *obiter dictum* of Lord Browne-Wilkinson in *Westdeutsche Landesbank Zentrale v Islington London Borough Council*[632] to the effect that a thief holds stolen good on constructive trust for the true owner. If this is correct, which must be doubted, then the claimant would instead pursue the matter in equity.

(d)   Finders

The situation with respect to finders is merely a variation on a theme. If the finder commits an act that amounts to a conversion then the owner has an obvious right of action, with the attendant remedial consequences set out above.

16.1.2. Three-party situations

The analytical structure of actions in this area means that there is very little difference between two and three-party scenarios.

(a)   Restitution of a movable acquired from non-owner

Again, an action in conversion may lie against the party in possession. As discussed above at 1.4.1, liability in conversion is strict; good faith is

---

[632] [1996] AC 669 at p 716.

therefore irrelevant in this regard. However, the successful application of any of the *nemo dat* exceptions addressed above (see section 10) will affect a conversion action, and for that reason both good faith and the payment of a price for the chattel by the defendant possessor may be important.

A claimant may also rely, where appropriate, on his equitable title against a third party who acquired the movable in question from a non-owner, although such a claim would, of course, fail against a defendant who buys the chattel in good faith without notice of the claimant's title.[633] For this reason, the fact that the third party possessor has paid a price to the non-owner in good faith is highly relevant.

(b)   'Garage' cases

Where a chattel is deposited with a repairer, who then carries out repairs or improvements to the chattel, there exits a lien over the property to secure the expenses of repair.[634] The effectiveness of the lien is not affected by the fact that the chattel was delivered into the possession of the repairer by someone other than its owner. In such a case the lien is good against the true owner,[635] who must discharge it before he can regain possession.

16.2.   Loss and deterioration of the movable

Where damages are awarded to the claimant these reflect the value of the chattel at the date of conversion. It follows that in this case subsequent deterioration of the movable will not matter. Where, however, the chattels in issue warrant the grant of specific relief then subsequent loss might be compensated by means of damages for consequential loss (s. 3(2)(a) TIGA 1977).

The same loss might be remedied in equity by means of equitable compensation akin to damages for any consequential loss suffered.

The only defences available to a defendant in these situations are ones that might be raised against the underlying actions; however, a defendant might also attempt to reduce his exposure to liability by raising issues of causation and remoteness.

---

[633] See section 10.2, above.

[634] See Bridge, M, *Personal Property Law* (2002), pp 171-175.

[635] *Tappenden v Artus* [1964] 2 QB 185.

16.3. Improvements

If an improvement to a chattel has become part of it according to the rules set out in section 9 of this Report, then that improvement belongs to the owner of the chattel. Clearly, if this is not the case then the improver is entitled to retain the improvement.

TIGA 1977 contains provisions designed to prevent the unjust enrichment of the claimant at the expense of the mistaken improver: s. 6(1). The improver must show that he acted in the mistaken but honest belief that he had good title to the chattel in question. If he can do so then there will be a reduction in the quantum of damages to reflect the value of any improvements. A similar provision is made to protect a good faith transferee from the improver. Reference should be made to section 1.4.2.3 of this Report for details.

Where the 1977 Act does not apply, for example where an owner exercises a right of recaption, an improver must rely upon common law principles of restitution.[636]

It might be argued that an 'equitable allowance'[637] can have the same effect where a claimant relies upon his equitable title to the chattel. However, there will be fewer situations in which such a question will arise because of the availability of the *bona fide* purchaser defence: If the improver buys in good faith then he defeats the claimant's title. If he improves with notice then he ought not to be entitled to any allowance. Obviously, this leaves the situation where the improver is a donee who took in good faith.

16.4. Owner's right to 'benefits'

Albeit there is much debate surrounding the subject of restitution for wrongs, there have been instances in which a claim for wrongful interference with goods has been met with what can be described as a restitutionary remedy.[638] Moreover, as noted above,[639] there has been a recent indication at the highest judicial level that a claim in conversion can lead to the recovery of benefits enjoyed by the defendant at the expense

---

[636] See *Greenwood v Bennett* [1973] QB 195, in which such a claim was discussed; see also McKendrick, 'Restitution and the Misuse of Chattels – The Need for a Principled Approach', in: *Interests in Goods* (1998).

[637] See *Halsbury's Laws*, (4th ed reissue), vol 48, para 830.

[638] See, for example, *Strand Electric and Engineering Co v Brisford Entertainments* [1952] 2 QB 246; *United Australia Ltd v Barclays Bank Ltd* [1941] AC 1.

[639] At para 1.4.2.(b).

of the claimant. In *Kuwait Airways Corpn v Iraqi Airways Co*[640] Lord Nicholls contemplated the possibility that the owner of several aircraft wrongfully seized by the defendant might, in appropriate circumstances, be awarded damages based not only on the value of the aircraft at the time of the conversion but also on any benefit the defendant had gained through use of the aircraft.[641] Such a claim would appear to be based on general principles of restitution in English law, and particularly on the fact of the defendant's unjust enrichment.[642] In the absence of further authority on this point, it remains to be seen whether the principle will be further developed.

16.5. Expenses of restitution

It is submitted that, if restitution is ordered, the expenses of effecting transfer would generally be borne by the defendant, although it would be a matter for argument in each individual case.

---

[640] [2002] 2 AC 883 at p 1094.

[641] In the case itself no claim for such so-called 'user damages' was pleaded.

[642] See p 1093.

National Report on the Transfer of Movables in Ireland

Caterina Gardiner

Table of Contents

2. Possession

3. Rights to hold and use movables

4. Field of application and definitions

Part I:
Basic information on property law

1. Introduction

1.1. General basics

The Irish legal system belongs to the family of legal systems known as common law systems. It derived its legal system including its system of property law from England. Irish property law is therefore a mixture of different elements: English common law which was introduced to Ireland in the twelfth century and developed by judges over the ensuing centuries, English statute law, which includes statutes passed at Westminster for both England and Ireland prior to 1922, Irish statute law after 1922, Irish common law, in the sense of principles developed by Irish judges exclusively for Ireland, and the Irish Constitution of 1937.[1]

1.1.1. Characteristics of rights in rem in contrast to obligations

Rights are classified as either real (*in rem*) or personal. Possession and ownership of a chattel are real rights rather than personal ones. The main significance of this is that they survive the bankruptcy of the person against whom they are asserted (or liquidation in the case of a company), so that the asset can be held against or reclaimed from his trustee in bankruptcy (or the liquidator of the company).

Goode explains that the distinction between real and personal rights may also be expressed as the distinction between property and obligation, *i.e.*, between what I *own* and what I am *owed*.[2] The common law has always maintained this distinction strictly. A contract to transfer an asset is not the same as an actual transfer. Until the actual transfer is made, the transferee has no proprietary interest in the asset, merely a contractual right to have it transferred. So, if the transferor becomes bankrupt before executing the transfer, the transferee's status is just that of an unsecured

---

1   For an account of the development of the Irish legal system, see Byrne & McCutcheon, *The Irish Legal System* (2001), Chapter 2.
2   Goode, R M, *Commercial Law* (1995), p 31. See also Goode, R M, 'Ownership and Obligation in Commercial Transactions', (1987) 103 LQR 433.

creditor. The impact of this distinction is lessened by the intervention of equity and the development of equitable real rights. Thus, in equity, the agreement to transfer is treated as if it was an actual transfer and the proprietary interest that is created is as effective as a transfer at law except that it will be defeated by a *bona fide* purchaser for value without notice of the interest. Equitable proprietary rights play an important part in the creation of security in the provision of finance in commercial transactions – equitable mortgages, charges *etc.*

1.1.2. Numerus clausus

There is no express recognition of the *numerus clausus* principle in Irish law. However, it is clear that common law courts treat property rights very much like civil law courts do. They acknowledge that there is a category of previously recognised forms of property which is a closed category and cannot be extended except by the legislature. There are cases which lend support to the view that there exists a numerus clausus principle in our property law. In *Hill v Tupper*,[3] Pollock CB stated:

> 'It is an old and well-established principle of our law that new estates cannot be created ... New rights or incidents of property cannot be created, nor can a new species of burden be imposed upon land at the pleasure of the owners ... The owner of an estate must be content to take it with the rights and incidents known to and allowed by law.'[4]

In *Keppel v Bailey*,[5] Lord Brougham LC stated:

> '... it must not be supposed that incidents of a novel kind can be devised and attached to property at the fancy or caprice of any owner. It is clearly inconvenient both to the science of the law and to the public weal that such a latitude be given ...'[6]

In *Tulk v Moxhay*,[7] however, Lord Cottenham LC did extend the list of property rights by holding that the burden of certain covenants would 'run' with the land so as to bind successors in title of the original convenantor, except a *bona fide* purchaser of the land without notice of the covenant. However, since this case was decided, case law has restricted

[3]   (1863) 2 H & C 121.
[4]   *Ibid*, p 127.
[5]   (1834) 2 My & K 517.
[6]   *Ibid*, p 535.
[7]   (1848) 2 Ph 774.

the operation of the principle and certain prerequisites to the binding effects of such covenants were laid down.[8]

Some commentators have described this closed category of rights as a 'norm of judicial self-governance'.[9] There are differences of opinion as to the reason for the existence of the concept. For example, Merrill and Smith argue that the *numerus clausus* is the expression of 'optimal standardisation' of property rights and of balancing the economic benefits of a new property right against the cost for third parties to become informed about the new right.[10] Other commentators suggest that the *numerus clausus* doctrine insofar as it applies in the common law is not about standardisation but is about regulation of the types and degree of notice required to establish different types of property rights. The purpose of the regulation is to enable third parties to verify ownership of rights.[11] Van Erp argues that the number of property rights in the common law and in equity is still so open that it could not be said that a *numerus clausus* principle exists, rather that there is a standardisation, *i.e.*, that for practical reasons, a limited category of property rights exists but that it does not mean that it is completely closed. Courts may still decide that certain rights, created by two parties and not to be found in the existing categories bind certain third parties. So, the contents of the various categories is not as fixed as it is in the civil law.[12] This proposition is supported by the statement of Wilberforce LJ in *National Provincial Bank Ltd v Ainsworth*:[13]

'Before a right or interest can be admitted into the category of property, or a right affecting property, it must be definable, identifiable by third parties, capable in its nature of assumption by third parties and have some degree of permanence or stability.'[14]

---

[8] See further Wylie, *Irish Land Law* (1997), Chapter 19.

[9] Merrill and Smith, 'Optimal Standardisation in the Law of Property: The Numerus Clausus Principle', 110 Yale Law Journal (2000).

[10] *Ibid.*

[11] Hansmann and Kraakman, 'Property, Contract and Verification: The Numerus Clausus Problem and the Divisibility of Rights', Harvard Law School Public Law Research Paper 037, at http://www.ssrn.com/lsn/index.html.

[12] Sjef van Erp, 'A Numerus Quasi-Clausus of Property Rights As a Consitutive Element of a Future European Property Law?', EJCL, Vol 7 (2003).

[13] [1965] AC 1175.

[14] *Ibid*, p 1247.

1.1.3. Historical background

The English common law developed in a feudal system of land tenure under the reign of William I. Under this system, all land in the kingdom ultimately belonged to the King. All other ownership of the land could be derived from the Crown only. The major tenants in chief held land directly from the Crown in return for feudal dues and service. By a process called subinfeudation, lesser tenants held portions of the same land from the tenants in chief. There was no such thing as absolute ownership. The concept of tenure was introduced to Ireland in the twelfth century by Henry II and his Norman followers. Although not existing in the same form, the basic principles of the feudal system are still of considerable importance in the land laws of England and Ireland and the system of tenure through a hierarchical system of landholding survives today.[15] According to the common law system, the subject of ownership is not land directly but estates and interests in land. All these estates existed at common law as legal estates, *i.e.*, the legal title to the land could be split up amongst the different estate owners. But by the side of the common law grew up the system of *equity* administered mainly by the Court of Chancery. The principal feature of equity was the concept of the *trust*, *i.e.*, the vesting of the legal estate in a trustee who would hold it for the enjoyment of a beneficiary (*cestui que trust*). The common law recognised only the trustee, because it looked only to the legal owner, but the Court of Chancery protected the interest of the beneficiary by obliging the trustee to adhere to the terms of the trust. The interest of the beneficiary was an equitable one. This hierarchical structure of tenure and estates never applied to property other than land. Chattels are not the subject of tenurial rights; they can be fully owned and estates in chattels are not possible at law, although limited interests may now exist in personal property by way of trust in essentially the same way as is the case for real property.

The common law makes a distinction between real property and personal property. Property in Irish law is therefore either real or personal. For the most part, real property comprises all forms of land including things built on land. Most other kinds of property are personal property. The reason for the distinction between the two forms of property lies in the history of the development of the common law in the English courts and the procedure in relation to forms of action. The common law allowed actions for the recovery of property and these were called real actions. All other actions were personal, seeking a remedy against the defendant himself as opposed to over the property in his hands. In these cases, the plaintiff could not insist on specific restitution if were successful in his action, it was only a personal action against the defendant him-

---

[15] See Wylie, *Irish Land Law*, Chapter 1.

self for which he could recover damages. A real action could only be brought in respect of freehold land, and therefore, it alone was classified as real property. Property in relation to which a personal action could be brought was classified as personal property. That meant that leaseholds were classified as personal property although in time, they came to be called chattels real. Eventually, leaseholders did acquire an action by which they could recover land – the personal action of ejectment based on a writ of trespass. The leaseholder's interest is still, however considered to be a personalty rather than realty.

Historically, there were different rules as far as disposition on death were concerned for real and personal property. Land devolved to the heir at law automatically and he became entitled to such property in the event of total or partial intestacy. Personal property devolved on the testator's personal representatives and property not disposed of by will fell to the State. These differences do not apply any more and the rules for realty and personalty are the same under the Succession Act 1965.

1.1.4. Sources of Irish property law

As outlined above, the rules on Irish property law are derived from various different sources. Irish property law is partly based on English common law, English statute law, which includes statutes passed at Westminster for both England and Ireland prior to 1922, Irish statute law after 1922, Irish common law, and the Irish Constitution of 1937. The legislation concerning movable property is subject-specific and there is no one body of legislation dealing with movable property in general. The more important statutes are: The Sale of Goods Act 1893, The Sale of Goods and Supply of Services Act 1980, The Bankruptcy Act 1988, The Bills of Exchange Act 1882, The Bills of Sale (Ireland) Act 1879 and Bills of Sale (Amendment) Act 1883, The Consumer Credit Act 1995, and The Succession Act 1965.

1.2. Notion of ownership and property ights

1.2.1. Ownership and possession

Proprietary interests in chattels (*i.e.* tangible personal property) are defined in terms of possession and ownership. Both possession and ownership are difficult concepts and not easily defined. Ownership is inevitably linked to possession. Under the common law, great significance is attached to possession. In certain circumstances, possession is conclusive evidence of ownership. The common law principle is to be found in *Jeffries v Great*

Western Railway Co.[16] A person in possession with the intention of assuming ownership is treated as owner, and given all the rights and remedies available for the protection of the owner, against the whole world apart from the true owner himself who has a better title. In Ireland, this rule was accepted as good law in *Haggan v Pasley*.[17] There, the owner of a piano mortgaged it, retaining possession and subsequently sold it to the plaintiff without informing him of the existence of the mortgage. The plaintiff took possession. The original owner's landlord seized possession of the piano from the plaintiff in an attempt to recover arrears of rent from the original owner. The plaintiff sued the landlord in trespass and conversion. The landlord pleaded that the piano belonged to the mortgagee, not to the plaintiff. However, following the decision in *Jeffries*, the court held that it was not possible for the defendant to raise the defence of *jus tertii*, and argue that a third party was the true owner of the goods.

1.2.2.   The notion of ownership

The question of what is ownership is a difficult one and has been much debated by jurisprudential scholars.[18] According to Bell, ownership is the greatest right or bundle of rights that can exist in relation to property.[19] The rights of an owner are not absolute and must be exercised subject to restrictions such as the need to comply with criminal law and the private rights of others. Ownership is also restricted by the existence of other lesser property rights such as possession under a pledge or bailment. For this reason, most commentators define ownership in terms of what is left after lesser rights have been granted. Thus, ownership could be said to be the residue of legal rights in an asset remaining in a person, or in persons concurrently, after specific rights over the asset have been granted to others.[20] A person in whom such residue of rights is vested is said to have an absolute interest in the asset. One who enjoys merely specific rights *e.g.* possession under a bailment has only a limited interest.

---

[16]   (1856) 5 El & Bl 802.

[17]   (1878) 2 LR Ir 573.

[18]   See Guest, A G (ed), *Oxford Essays in Jurisprudence* (1961). See also discussion of ownership in Bell, A P, *Modern Law of Personal Property in England and Ireland* (1989), Chapter 4.

[19]   Bell, *op cit*, p 66.

[20]   See further Goode, *Commercial Law* (1995), at p 35; Bridge, *Personal Property Law* (1996), p 15; Bell, *op cit*, p 66.

(a)   Ownership is indivisible

In the case of land, ownership can be divided according to the doctrine of estates and a lesser legal title can be carved out of a larger one and the two interests can exist concurrently as legal interests.[21] This is not the case with chattels. Legal title to an interest in a chattel can only be held or transferred entire. It is of course possible to transfer possession of a chattel to someone else but the transfer of possession by the owner does not grant ownership rights.

Chattels may be the subject of co-ownership in the form of either joint tenancy or tenancy in common. In the case of a joint tenancy, the interests of the joint tenants are acquired at the same time as a single interest, as where the goods are bought 'in equal shares' or are to be held 'equally'. The rights of a joint tenant descend on death to the other joint tenant(s). Where their interests are acquired at different times, they are tenants in common. In this case, each tenant owns only his share of the whole which goes to his next of kin on death.

The principle that ownership is indivisible is subject to the important exception applying to equitable ownership.

(b)   Equitable ownership

There is an important exception to the rule that ownership is indivisible. All interests in property recognised at common law may be the subject of divided ownership whereby one person has the bare legal ownership and the other the beneficial ownership. Thus, the beneficial owner has the enjoyment and use of the thing. The most common example is where property is held on trust. The usual way in which a trust comes into being is where the owner of property transfers property on trust in favour of a beneficiary or beneficiaries. The owner may himself be the trustee or he may transfer the property to someone else on the express condition that he shall act as trustee. The legal title vests in the trustee while the beneficial interest is held by the beneficiary. Trusts may also arise by operation of law.[22]

Equity treats the beneficiary as owner of the property and protects his interest in it accordingly, providing equitable remedies parallel to those available to a legal owner. The only interests in personal property recognised at common law are rights of ownership and possession. Any other interests only exist as rights in equity. Such equitable rights are overridden by the

---

21 Goode gives the example of a leasehold interest or mortgage by demise being carved out of a fee simple, *op cit*, at p 37 *et seq*.

22 See Bell, *Modern Law of Personal Property in England and Ireland*, Chapter 7.

rights of the *bona fide* purchaser of the legal estate who does not have notice of the equitable interest.

1.3.   Other property rights

The law recognises many other kinds of right aside from ownership. The traditional classification of property rights makes a distinction between legal and equitable interests. In relation to personal property, the legal interests recognised by the common law are ownership and the bailee's special property (including liens and rights arising under pledges.) All other rights exist in equity only: The rights of a beneficiary under a trust, charges, non-possessory liens and the mortgagor's right of redemption. There is another category of remedial rights called mere equities. They are regarded as property rights but are more like rights to interests rather than interests themselves. It is also possible to adopt a functional classification of property rights. By using a functional approach, Bell identifies property rights as security, beneficial, managerial or remedial rights.[23]

1.3.1.   Security rights

These exist to ensure performance of an obligation, usually to pay money. Security rights can be divided into possessory and non-possessory securities. Possessory securities include pledges and liens. Non-possessory securities are charges, equitable liens and mortgages. A charge is the right to have the property sold in the case of default, but until that happens, the property remains in the hands of the debtor. Charges can be fixed or floating. An equitable lien is a non-possessory security conferred by operation of law. It differs from a charge in that it is not based on consent between the parties. It could be said that security rights are secondary rights. The primary right is the personal right of the creditor against the debtor to be paid. The property right exists just to ensure that the primary right is satisfied.

1.3.2.   Beneficial rights

Beneficial rights on the other hand are primary rights. These are rights in themselves as opposed to rights to secure a right to a benefit. Ownership is the main example of a beneficial right, as outlined above, the most basic right to enjoy and have the benefit of the property. Other rights

---

[23]   *Ibid*, Chapter 1, p 4.

may also be beneficial rights, for example, the rights of the hirer of a car, the rights of a beneficiary under a trust.

1.3.3. Managerial rights

Bell also identifies the existence of managerial rights. One example is the position of the trustee under a trust. The trustee has a managerial right, *i.e.*, a right excercised for the benefit of another. Where a person is entrusted with the possession of goods he has limited property rights over them, for example the bailee's special property in goods. If the purpose of the bailment is for the bailee to perform some service for the owner, *e.g.*, to look after the goods, the bailee merely has managerial rights.

1.3.4. Remedial rights

Certain remedial rights could also be seen as property rights. For example, the right to rescind a contract of sale is a property right.

1.4. Protection of property interests – personal actions

The common law has no equivalent of the Roman Law *vindicatio* and there is no special claim available to an 'owner' in terms of protection of property rights. The system of protection of property interests does not attempt to identify an individual as an 'owner'. In the context of protection of property rights, possession is more important than ownership. Property interests are protected through the law of torts. A plaintiff can bring an action in conversion, tort, trespass or detinue. To succeed in these claims, the plaintiff does not need to establish ownership of the property, merely that they were in possession of the property. The main remedy at common law for the protection of personal property interests is not the return of the property to the claimant but instead, damages.

1.4.1. Trespass to chattels

Trespass to chattels consists of any legally unjustifiable act of direct physical interference with chattels in the possession of another.[24] A direct

---

[24] See Tyler & Palmer, *Crossley Vaines on Personal Property* (1973), p 22 and citations therein. On trespass to chattels generally, see McMahon & Binchy, *The Law of Torts* (2000), Chapter 28.

link between the behaviour of the defendant and the chattel is required. In *McDonagh v West of Ireland Fisheries Ltd*,[25] the defendant was held not liable in trespass where a boat which the defendant had temporarily removed from the moorings in a harbour was later damaged in uncertain circumstances. The Court held that the injury to the boat was not direct and therefore did not constitute trespass. It is generally agreed that trespass is actionable *per se* and without proof of special damage.[26] In order to be actionable, trespass must be either wilful (*i.e.* intentional) or negligent. Trespass will not lie against a defendant entirely free from fault.[27] The right to sue in trespass exists only in favour of a plaintiff who has possession or the immediate right to possession enjoyed by a bailor where the bailment is at will.[28] In *ESB v Hastings & Co Ltd*,[29] the defendant when resurfacing a road, opened a trench and allowed a mechanical shovel to damage a cable. The defendant was made aware by the plaintiffs of the presence of the cable in the general vicinity of its operation. The High Court awarded damages for trespass to goods.

1.4.2. Conversion

The tort of conversion has its origins in the old writ of trover which was a branch of the writ of trespass on the case.[30] Trover originally contained four averments by the plaintiff. Firstly that the plaintiff possessed the chattel, secondly that the plaintiff casually lost it, thirdly that the defendant found it; and fourthly that the defendant converted it to his own use. Eventually the second and third requirements were dropped and the right to sue was extended beyond those who were in actual possession at the time of the conversion. It developed to include those with a right to immediate possession, including bailors at will and unlawfully dispossessed owners following chattels down a chain of transactions involving their transfer.

It is difficult to define conversion but the statement of Atkin LJ in *Lancashire and Yorkshire Railway Co v MacNicoll* is helpful: '... dealing with

---

[25] Unreported High Court, Blayney J, 19th December 1986 (1983-3887P).

[26] See McMahon & Binchy, *op cit*, p 771.

[27] *ESB v Hastings & Co Ltd* [1965] Ir Jur Rep 51; *National Coal Board v Evans* [1951] 2 KB 861.

[28] *Keenan Bros Ltd v CIE* (year) 97 ILTR 54 (High Ct Budd J) *Wilson v Lombank* [1963] 1 WLR 1294. However, in *Penfolds Wines Pty Ltd v Elliot*, the Australian High Court concluded that actual possession, not a right to immediate possession was needed for a trespass action.

[29] [1965] Ir Jur Rep 51.

[30] On conversion generally see McMahon & Binchy, *op cit*, chapter 30.

goods in a manner inconsistent with the right of the true owner amounts to a conversion, provided that it is also established that there is also an intention on the part of the defendant in so doing to deny the owner's right or to assert a right which is inconsistent with the owner's right.'[31]

There are two essential ingredients. There must be a dealing with the goods and there must be an intention to deny the right of ownership. The key to this tort is that it protects ownership and not possession. Conversion may be committed by the wrongful taking of possession of the goods, abusing possession already acquired, or otherwise denying the title of the other person to them, whether or not possession has been acquired.

(a) Taking possession

Taking possession of another's property may constitute conversion; however this is not always the case. It is only where the defendant deals with the goods in a manner inconsistent with the right of the true owner, conversion will be committed.[32] Dealing with goods in a manner inconsistent with the right of the true owner need not involve any intention on the part of the defendant permanently to deprive the owner of the goods. In general, the voluntary reception of another's goods without his authority constitutes conversion. An involuntary reception does not, however constitute conversion.[33]

(b) Abusing possession

Where possession has been lawfully acquired, subsequent abuse of it may constitute conversion. Pawning another's goods or sale and delivery of them are examples of such abuse. The delivery of goods to some other third party may not constitute conversion in certain cases. The tort is actionable *per se* but not every interference with chattels will ground an action in conversion. The interference must be so serious as to amount to

---

[31] (1918) 88 LJKB 601.

[32] See, for example, *Fouldes v Willoughby* (1841) 89 M&W 540, 151 ER 1153 where, after a dispute about fares with a passenger, a ferry boat operator turned two horses that he was transporting loose on the landing-place. He was held not to have been guilty of conversion of the animals. Lord Abinger CB held that the simple removal of a chattel, independent of any claim over it, does not amount to conversion of a chattel. The removal of the horses was not connected with the denial of the right of the plaintiff to the possession and enjoyment of them.

[33] See *Elvin & Powelle Ltd v Plummer Roddis* (1933) 50 TLR 158; *Hiort v Bott* (1874) LR 9 Ex 86; *London & NW Ry Co v Hughes* (year) 26 LR Ir 165.

a denial of the claimant's title. In *Morgan v Maurer & Son*,[34] a watch-maker sent a watch left for repairs to Dublin without the consent of the owner. When the watch was lost in the post, the owner sued for conversion. It was held that the defendant was not guilty of conversion, although he was liable for breach of the terms of the contract of bailment.

The refusal to return goods to their owner in response to a demand to do so is normally conclusive evidence of conversion, unless the refusal is reasonable. In *British Wagon Co Ltd v Shortt*,[35] the plaintiff leased a bull-dozer to the hirer who later sold it to the defendant. The High Court held that the defendant's refusal to return the machine amounted to a conversion.

(c)   Denying title

Where the defendant has never been in possession (actual or constructive) of the goods of another, he may nonetheless be guilty of conversion if he deals with them in such a way as to amount to an absolute denial of that other's title to them. An honest but mistaken belief of the defendant that he has the right to deal with the goods generally does not excuse him.[36]

(d)   Entitlement to sue in conversion

A plaintiff may maintain an action if, at the time of the defendant's act, he has either (a) ownership and possession of the goods; or (b) possession of them; or (c) merely an immediate right to possess them, unless the defendant can prove that the title to the goods is in some other party. As between co-owners, there is unity of possession so one co-owner cannot be guilty of conversion as against the other merely by using the goods in a particular way, unless he actually destroys them, sells them in market overt or completely excludes the other from possession of them. Protection against the unreasonable or vindictive disposal of household chattels by a spouse is afforded by the Family Home Protection Act 1976, s. 9. Where the plaintiff establishes ownership and possession or possession of the goods at the time of their conversion, the plea of *jus tertii* is not available. This means that it is no defence for the wrongdoer to plead that someone else (the *tertius*) has, in relative terms, a better possessory right than the plaintiff. If, however, the plaintiff is relying on a right to immediate possession, *jus tertii* may be pleaded. There is an exception relating to bailment. A bailee is estopped,

---

[34]   [1964] Ir Jur Rep 31.

[35]   [1961] IR 164.

[36]   *Hollins v Fowler* (1875) LR 7 HL 757.

when sued by the bailor from pleading the superior entitlement of a third party, though the bailee has a good defence if actually evicted by title paramount by the true owner. Where the bailee is subjected to competing claims by the bailor and a third party, he may have the issue resolved by interpleader proceedings, *i.e.* to pay the chattel into court to permit the bailor and the other plaintiff to fight it out between them.[37]

(e)　Remedies

The remedy for conversion lies in the forced judicial sale of the chattel to the defendant.[38] The value of the chattel at the date of the conversion award therefore defines the damages award. This is the price the defendant has to pay to buy out the plaintiff's interest. Consequential damages may also be awarded to the plaintiff. These might include the loss of the post-conversion appreciation in value of the chattel, so that in substance, the plaintiff would recover damages representing the value of the chattel at the judgment date. If the plaintiff consents to the return of the chattel before judgment, then nominal damages would be an appropriate measure. Nominal damages would also be the correct measure where the chattel would, even without the defendant's conversion been lost.[39]

1.4.3.　Detinue

(a)　General

The essential element of the tort of detinue is the wrongful refusal by the defendant to deliver up to the plaintiff a chattel after demand has been made by the plaintiff to do so.[40] It therefore consists of the withholding of goods from one who is immediately entitled to their possession. It differs from trespass in that the element of detention is essential. It differs from conversion in the following respects: Conversion consists of denial of title whereas a party who loses the goods may be liable in detinue; conversion consists of a single act of denial of ownership, whereas detinue is a continuing denial; and in detinue, the return of specific goods is central, whereas in conversion, damages to compensate the owner for the loss are sufficient.

---

[37] The law on *jus tertii* in the UK has been amended by the Torts (Interference with Goods) Act 1977. S. 8 provides that any rule of law preventing the defendant from pleading the *jus tertii* is abolished.

[38] See generally, Bridge, *Personal Property Law* (1996), p 72 *et seq.*

[39] See *Kuwait Airways Corpn v Iraqi Airways Co* [2002] UKHL 19.

[40] See generally, McMahon & Binchy, *op cit*, chapter 29.

A detention is not wrongful unless the defendant's possession is adverse to or in defiance of the plaintiff's right. A bailee who merely holds onto a chattel after termination of the contract of bailment may be liable for breach of contract but not in detinue. Normally, adverse possession will be proved by evidence that a demand for the return of the goods was made by the owner which is followed by a refusal by the detainer to deliver them up.[41] For a demand for the return of a chattel to be effective, it must as a general rule be brought to the knowledge of the person of whom it is made.[42] There is no liability if the refusal to return the goods is reasonable, as for example, where the defendant wishes to investigate the legality of the plaintiff's claim.[43] The necessity of a demand and refusal may be dispensed with where it is clear that the demand would have been futile.[44]

(b)   Remedies

One of the advantages of an action for detinue over that of conversion lies in the breadth of the remedies available to the plaintiff. Three possible forms of remedy exist:

(i)   Order for the value of the chattel as assessed (at the date of the judgment)

This is the appropriate remedy where the chattel is an ordinary article of commerce, or where the plaintiff does not want the goods back or where it is not possible for them to be returned.

(ii)   Order for the return of the chattel or its value as assessed and damages

This is a discretionary power of the court and it has been held that it will not be exercised 'when the chattel is an ordinary article of commerce and is of no special value or interest and is not alleged to be of any special value to the plaintiff and where damages would fully compensate'.[45]

---

[41] See *Cullen, Allen & Co v Barclay* (1881) LR Ir 224, and *King v Walsh* [1932] IR 178.

[42] *King v Walsh* [1932] IR 178.

[43] See *Poole v Burns* (1944) Ir Jur Rep 20.

[44] *Baud Corporation NV v Brook* 40 DLR (1974) (3d) 418.

[45] *Whitely Ltd v Hilt* [1918] 2 KB 808; see also *Waterford Corporation v O'Toole* Unreported, High Court, Finlay J 9 November 1979 (1969-271 Sp) for an example of the exercise of the judicial discretion.

(iii)   Order for the return of the chattel and damages for its detention

This remedy is similar to the previous but lacks the element of assessment of the value of the chattel. The only pecuniary redress that may be given is damages for detention.

1.4.4.   Reversionary interests

If an owner has no right to the immediate possession of his chattel, he may not bring an action based on conversion, detinue or trespass. However, such a person may bring an action for any damage done to his reversionary interest in the goods. So, for example, in *Mears v London and South Western Rail Co*,[46] the bailor of a barge was allowed to sue the railway company, who by their negligence had allowed a boiler to drop through the bottom of the barge. The court found that the bailor who had merely a suspended right to possession at the time of the wrongful act nevertheless could sue if it causes permanent injury.

1.4.5.   Self-help

Self-help is the extra-judicial recovery of chattels and is technically known as recaption. This right of recaption is limited in the sense that reasonable means must be used to recover the chattels. For example, the owner may first have to notify the wrongful possessor of the chattel of an intention to recover it if the use of force is to be regarded as reasonable means.[47] It appears that reasonable force may be used even if the wrongful possessor has not committed a trespass against the owner seeking recaption.[48] Entry onto the land of another to effect recaption is permitted where the occupier of the land is guilty of a trespassory taking as against the owner and it may be permissible in other cases too.[49] The nature of the right of recaption is somewhat unclear and there have been few cases. Bridge offers the practical advice that if recaption is to be exercised, then it should be done quickly and effectively without causing a breach of the peace or incidental damage to the property of the occupier.[50]

---

[46]   (1862) 11 CBNS 850.

[47]   See Bridge, *Personal Property Law*, p 77.

[48]   *Blades v Higgs* (1861) 10 CB (NS) 713.

[49]   *Patrick v Colerick* (1838) 3 M & W 483; *Anthony v Haney* (1832) 8 Bing 186.

[50]   See Bridge, *op cit*, p. 78.

2.   Possession

2.1.   The notion of possession

At common law, there is no precise definition of possession. The meaning
of possession varies according to the context in which it arises. It is necessary at the outset to make the distinction between possession in fact and
possession in law. As understood in everyday language, possession usually
denotes exercise of physical control over a chattel. For the purposes of the
law, possession can be said to consist of both physical control over the
chattel and an intention to exclude others from the exercise of control.[51]
It is possible to recognise different degrees of possession: Actual possession, constructive possession and custody.

2.1.1.   Actual possession

This requires both intention to control and control in fact, or physical
control. The question of whether a person has sufficient physical control
of the chattel is determined according to the facts of each individual case.
The degree of control required is relative to the nature of the property
involved and can be established when such control has been acquired as
the nature of the case allows. In *The Tubantia*[52] where a salvage company
was found to have acquired possession of a wreck, having had contact with
the vessel for only short periods of time because of the weather and the
roughness of the seas. It was held that they had exercised 'the use and
occupation of which the subject matter was capable.' A contrasting case is
that of *Young v Hichens*.[53] There, the plaintiff while fishing for pilchards
had nearly caught a shoal with a seine net when the defendant by rowing
his boat into the opening of the net, disturbed the fish and prevented the
plaintiff from catching them. The plaintiff sued in trespass but it was held
that he was not entitled to recover. The plaintiff argued that he had a
'strong probability of complete capture' and that this was enough to give a
right of possession against a party preventing the capture. However, the
court held that he did not have possession. It was not enough that it was
'almost certain' that he would have had the fish without the defendant's
actions.

---

[51] Goode describes possession of an asset as '*control, directly or through another, either of
      the asset itself or of some larger object in which it is contained or of land or buildings on or
      beneath which it is situated, with the intention of asserting such control against others,
      whether temporarily or permanently.*' Goode, R M, *Commercial Law*, p 47.
[52] [1924] All ER 615.
[53] (1844) 6 QB 606.

The degree of control needed to acquire possession is not necessary for possession to be maintained. Bell gives the example of a person going into a shop and leaving their bicycle outside. That person does not lose possession of the bicycle and, if someone interferes with it, they can be sued for trespass, the tort that protects possession. If this was not the case, peace and social order would be threatened and the rights of possessors would always be at risk. The full test of control is only applied to those who claim to have acquired possession. Once possession has been acquired, a mere intention to control (or the absence of intention to relinquish control) will be sufficient for possession to continue. Possession only comes to an end if both intention and control are relinquished, if someone else acquires the degree of control necessary for possession, or if the property is animate and asserts its own independence.[54]

2.1.2. Possession is indivisible

There is a rule that possession is indivisible, but it is important to bear in mind the distinction between possession and the right to possess. The latter is not exclusive and for example, a person in possession of a chattel at the will of the owner has a right of possession as against all but the owner, whereas the owner has a right of possession against everyone. In addition, it has been accepted that a bailor and a bailee can be recognised as being in possession of the chattel bailed, although the possession of the bailor may more accurately be described as constructive possession.[55]

2.1.3. Constructive possession

Falling short of actual possession, a person may have constructive possession of property if he has the right to take actual possession. Where things are in the hands of a bailee at will, the bailor has a constructive possession of the property. The bailee acknowledges the superior right of the bailor and reserves no right to retain possession of the property if it is recalled. In those circumstances the law treats the bailee as exercising his control over the property as agent for the bailor so that the control is deemed to be that of the bailor. This constructive possession is sufficient

---

[54] See Bell, *Modern Law of Personal Property in England and Ireland*, p 36.

[55] See *Ancona v Rogers* (1876) 1 Ex D 285. For the purpose of a suit in trespass, Mellish LJ held that a bailor who delivered goods to a bailee to keep them on account of the bailor, may still treat the goods as being in his own possession.

to sue third parties in trespass and the bailor will have possession for the purposes of the rules on possessory title.[56]

Where things are held by a beneficiary, it has been held that the trustee may sue in trespass. The trustee is recognised as having constructive possession in the same way as in the case of bailments at will.[57]

The State has the constitutional right to take wrecks and treasure trove. The right is an immediate right to possession and it can be conferred on a franchise holder by the State. The franchise holder can then sue in trespass. It is recognised as a form of constructive possession.[58]

Where things are in adverse actual possession, (*i.e.* where they are held by an unauthorised person), the owner of the goods has an immediate right to possession where they are held by an unauthorised person. This right can be enforced by suing in conversion and in detinue.[59]

A person may also have a qualified constructive possession where his right to possession is not immediate. For example, in the case of security rights, a pledgee can deal with the property so as to confer a lien over it and can create a sub-pledge.[60]

Qualified constructive possession also arises in the case of the unpaid seller's right to stop goods in transit. This right is lost when the goods come into the possession of the buyer, and the buyer is said to be in possession if the carrier acknowledges that he holds the goods as bailee for him.[61]

2.1.4. Custody

An employee does not possess the employer's chattels but only has custody of them. Possession is attributed to the employer. Therefore, if an employee finds lost property while at work, it is his employer who is entitled to keep it as against everyone except its true owner and the employee must surrender it to him.[62] If an employee allows the property he has found to be stolen, it will be the employer who is liable as bailee to its owner.[63] This rule on custody was formulated at a time when the offence of larceny required removal of the chattel from the possession of the owner. Thus, if it

---

[56] See *Wilson v Lombank* [1963] 1 All ER 740, *USA v Dolfus Mieg et Compagnie SA* [1952] AC 582. See also Bell, *op cit*, at p 54.

[57] *White v Morris* (1852) 11 CB 1015.

[58] *Bailiffs of Dunwich v Sterry* (1831) 1 B & Ad 831. See also para 11.2.2. below.

[59] See para 1.4. above.

[60] See Bell, *op cit*, at p 57.

[61] Sections 41-43 Sale of Goods Act 1893. See para 7.4.2. below.

[62] *McDowell v Ulster Bank Ltd* (1899) 33 ILT Jo 223; *Crinion v Minister for Justice* [1959] Ir Jur 15.

[63] *Mullins v Laird* (1915) 50 ILTR 7.

was the case that the employee was in possession of the employer's chattel before forming an intention to steal it, he could not be convicted of larceny. The rule on custody meant that the law on larceny could work to protect the employer's property.[64] Similarly, a hotel guest does not have possession of the chattels in the hotel room, merely custody, nor does a dinner guest have possession over his hosts cutlery or glassware.

2.2. Bailment

Bailment is a possessory relationship by which a bailor transfers possession of a chattel to a bailee. The bailment confers on the bailee a limited interest in the goods he holds, usually referred to as special property, and it also creates a relationship between him and the person from whom he derives possession (the bailor). Bailment covers a wide range of common situations in commercial life. It includes contracts of warehousing, carriage, dry cleaning, hire purchase, hire and pledge as well as gratuitous arrangements such as borrowing, safekeeping and holding lost property. The bailment may be at will, in which case the bailor has the right to call for the return of the goods at any time, or it may be for a fixed determinable period, in which case, the bailee has the right to resist a demand for the early return of the chattel. If the bailment is executed according to a contract, the contract will govern the relationship along with the rules of property that apply. If no contract exists, the rights and duties of the bailor and bailee *inter se* may be defined according to the law of torts.

For a bailment to exist, it is essential that one person (the bailee) is in possession of goods to which another (the bailor) has better title. If possession of a chattel is not transferred, there can be no bailment.[65] Bell supplies the following definition of bailment: 'a bailment arises when one person (the bailee) is willingly and with authority in possession of goods to which another (the bailor) retains better title; and the necessary authority to possess may be supplied either by the bailor's consent, actual or implied, or by operation of law.'[66] Where the bailor consents, the bailee may sub-bail the chattel to another party. The original bailee continues to act as such and the third party will become his bailee. The relationship between bailor and sub-bailee is complex and many of the issues which arise in relation to this relationship have not yet been resolved.[67]

---

[64] See Bell, *Modern Law of Personal Property in England and Ireland*, pp 20-21.

[65] *Ashby v Tolhurst* [1937] 2 KB 242.

[66] See Bell, *Modern Law of Personal Property in England and Ireland*, p 87.

[67] See *The Pioneer Container* [1994] 2 AC 324; *Morris v CW Martin & Sons Ltd* [1966] 1 QB 716. See also Bell, 'Sub-Bailment on Terms', in Palmer, N and McKendrick, E (eds) *Interests in Goods* (1998).

2.2.1.   The property rights of the parties under a bailment

(a)   The bailor

Where the bailor is the owner of the goods before the bailment, he will continue to be owner of the goods despite the transfer of possession. However, if the bailment is not at will, the bailor's rights as owner will be restricted. He may not be able to sue third parties for interference with it during the currency of the bailment. He will not have sufficient constructive possession to sue for trespass and he will not have the right to immediate possession required to sue in conversion.[68] However, if the interference persists after the term of the bailment has expired, the bailor can bring a special action for any damage done to his reversionary interest in the goods.[69] As far as negligence is concerned, it is not confined to situations where there is an immediate right to possession, but without loss, there is no cause of action and if the bailment is for a term, any temporary injury will affect the bailee rather than the bailor.

(b)   The bailee

The bailee has a special property in the goods he holds but the nature of his interest varies according to the type of bailment involved. All bailees have defensive rights against third parties who interfere with the goods, but not all have rights that run with the goods and only some rights are assignable. The bailee can sue third parties who interfere with the goods in torts which require a property interest such as conversion and negligence. This is based on his possessory title to the goods. A bailee, like any other possessor is entitled to assert the rights of an owner against wrongdoers by virtue of the rules of possessory title. It is also accepted, however that the bailee has a real, proprietary interest in the goods.[70] This will be relevant only in cases where the possessory title cannot be relied upon such as where the bailee has entrusted the goods to a sub-bailee, giving him exclusive right to possession, or where the goods have been taken by someone who is not a wrongdoer, *e.g.* the police. In these circumstances, the bailee cannot rely on his possessory interest and would have to rely on his true interest so that he can only recover for his own personal loss. The extent of the bailee's loss will depend on the nature of the bailment. A pledgee or lienee will recover the amount for which the goods were secured. A hirer will recover the value of the use of the goods, and any

---

[68]   *Gordon v Harper* (1796) 7 Tr 9.

[69]   *Mears v London & South Western Railway Co* (1862) 22 CB (NS) 850.

[70]   See Bell, *Modern Law of Personal Property in England and Ireland*, p 98.

bailee will recover the amount for which he is liable to his bailor. The bailee may also have rights as against the bailor directly affecting the property. He may have a right to possession, a power of sale in the event of failure to repay (in the case of pledges and liens) or to collect (in the case of other bailments). The other rights of the bailee which do not affect the property bind only the bailor. Such rights include his right to remuneration or expenses in respect of the holding of the property.

2.3. Acquisition of possession

Transfer of possession by manual means takes place by delivery. Delivery can be either actual, constructive or symbolic.

2.3.1. Actual delivery

This confers actual possession on the deliveree. It can take place either by the deliveror or his agent handing the property over to the deliveree or the deliveree may simply take it with the deliveror's permission from the place where it is.

2.3.2. Constructive delivery

Constructive delivery occurs in various ways:

It may occur where the deliveror in actual possession agrees with the deliveree to hold the property as his bailee, thereby conferring constructive possession on him. For example, in *Elmore v Stone*,[71] the owner of a livery stable sold two horses. The buyer had no stable of his own and therefore asked the seller to keep them at livery for him. It was held that although there was no actual delivery of the horses, there had been a constructive delivery.

Constructive delivery also occurs if a third party such as a warehouseman is in actual possession as bailee for the deliveror, if, with the deliveror's consent, he attorns to the deliveree. This means that he must acknowledge that he holds no longer as bailee for the deliveror, but as bailee for the deliveree. This results in the deliveree having constructive possession. If the deliveree is already in actual possession as bailee for the deliveror, there will be a constructive delivery if the deliveror agrees to his holding the property henceforth in his own right.[72] There will also be

---

[71] (1809) 1 Taunt 458.
[72] *Pascoe v Turner* [1979] 2 All ER 945.

constructive delivery where the deliveree initially has merely possession in fact, and then the deliveror agrees to his having possession in law. So, for example, in *Winter v Winter*,[73] the owner of a barge told his son, who was working on the barge as an employee, that it was his. This was held to be sufficient delivery to constitute a good gift.

2.3.3.   Symbolic delivery

Symbolic delivery may occur in two ways: The delivery of a symbol or the performance of an act or gesture symbolising delivery.

(a)   Documents of title

In general, where property is held by a third party, for example, a warehouseman, the possession of a document of title to it will not carry with it constructive possession of the document itself. For there to be constructive possession, there would need to be attornment. In the absence of attornment, goods in a warehouse are not delivered by the transfer of a delivery order. However, certain documents are either by virtue of a mercantile custom or by statute, in the eyes of the law symbols representing the property to which they refer, so that possession of the document is equivalent to constructive possession of the property itself. The first of these documents to be recognised is the bill of lading. Bills of lading have long been accepted as negotiable documents of title in that the carrier's delivery obligation is transferred to the holder of the bill when it is negotiated.[74] A bill of lading is a document issued by a carrier attesting to the fact that the cargo has actually been shipped on board and not merely received for shipment.[75] The recognition of the bill of lading as a symbol representing the property to which it refers is founded on mercantile custom. Other documents may be given similar effect provided that a clear custom could be established.

The Factors Act 1889 extends the category of documents of title which may be deemed to be symbols of the goods. Under this Act, for the purposes of mercantile agency, the expression 'documents of title' includes a wide array of documents whose possession is suggestive of authority or ownership. S. 1(4) of the Factors Act 1889 defines the expression as including: *Any bill of lading, dock warrant, warehouse keeper's certificate, and warrant or order for the delivery of the goods, and … any other document used*

---

73   (1861) 4 LT 639.

74   *Lickbarrow v Mason* (1787) 2 Tr 63.

75   *Diamond Alkali Export Corpn v Fl Bourgeois* [1923] 3 KB 443.

in the ordinary course of business as proof of the possession or control of the goods, or authorising or purporting to authorise, either by endorsement or by delivery, the possessor of the document to transfer or receive goods thereby represented.

S. 3 provides that a pledge of the documents of title to goods shall be deemed to be a pledge of the goods. This provision however, only applies to pledges made by a mercantile agent.[76] S. 3 however, can be relied on indirectly when the disposition is made by the buyer of the goods. Under s. 9, it is provided that: 'where a person, having bought or agreed to buy goods, obtains with the consent of the seller possession of ... the documents of title to goods, the transfer by that person ..., of ... the documents of title, under any... pledge...thereof, to any person receiving the same in good faith and without notice of any lien or other right of the original seller in respect of the goods, shall have the same effect as if the person making the transfer were a mercantile agent ...'[77]

(b)   Keys

The delivery of a key may give the deliveree symbolic possession of the property to which it gives access.[78] However, this may be properly viewed as actual possession for the key gives real, and not deemed control.[79] There is a view that in the case of bulky goods, where they are incapable of manual delivery, the delivery of a key as a symbol will suffice.[80] Bell is critical of this approach, however, arguing that it is not necessary to invoke the symbolism of a key. The reasoning for doing so is the assumption that there is a minimum standard of control required for actual possession which is not satisfied here because of the nature of the goods. Bell argues that such assumption is not well founded, the true test for actual possession being whether there is the 'use and occupation of which the subject matter is capable' as set out in *The Tubantia*.[81]

---

[76] A mercantile agent is 'a mercantile agent having in the customary course of his business as such agent authority either to sell goods, or to consign goods for the purpose of sale, or to buy goods, or to raise money on the security of goods.' S. 1(1) Factors Act 1889.

[77] For further discussion of the Factors Act 1889, see Bell, *Modern Law of Personal Property in England and Ireland*, p 60.

[78] *Jones v Selby* (1710) Prec Ch 300.

[79] *Ward v Turner* (1752) 1 Dick 170.

[80] *Re Wasserberg* [1915] 1 Ch 195; *Ward v Turner, ibid.*

[81] [1924] All ER 615. See Bell, *op cit*, p 58.

2.4.   Protection of possession

Possession is protected under the law of torts, and specifically the law relating to trespass to goods, conversion and detinue. These have been considered above.[82]

3.   Rights to hold and use movables

3.1.   General

Not all rights relating to the holding and use of movables are property rights. What characterises a property right as such is that it is a right against the world, *i.e.*, against persons in general; and it that it is assignable. How can such a right be identified? As discussed above, some commentators argue that there is a *numerus clausus* or closed list of such rights.[83] A different view is that the list of rights is not closed, but if a right satisfies certain criteria, it could be recognised as a property right. This view was expressed by Wilberforce LJ in *National Provincial Bank Ltd v Ainsworth*,[84] who stated that before a right can be admitted within the category of 'property' it must be:

> 'definable, identifiable by third parties, capable in nature of assumption by third parties, and have some degree of permanence or stability.'[85]

As Swadling points out, Wilberforce LJ's test has never been used to admit a right to the list and there are many rights which may satisfy this test but have not been recognised as property rights.[86]

3.2.   Are contracts of lease, hire and hire purchase proprietary in nature?

The question of whether a lease (or hire) of goods or a hire purchase of goods give rise to personal or proprietary rights is a controversial one. Contracts of lease or hire of goods involve the use of goods without purchase under which the owner allows the lessee to use the goods in return

---

[82] See above, paragraph 1.4.

[83] Paragraph 1.1.2.

[84] [1965] AC 1175.

[85] *Ibid*, p 1247-1248.

[86] Swadling, 'Property: General Principles', Chapter 4 in Birks (ed), *English Private Law* (Oxford 2000).

for rental payments. Such agreements vary from short-term hire of goods to long term financial or operating leases. In such contracts, there is no provision for legal title to the goods to pass to the lessee. These agreements are bailments of goods for reward.[87] A hire purchase agreement is a contract in which the owner gives possession and the use of goods to the hirer in return for the payment of rental instalments and in which the hirer is given the option to buy the goods by paying the final instalment or by paying a nominal sum in addition to the instalments. It is a bailment of goods with an option to purchase.

There has been much debate about whether such agreements give rise to merely personal rights or whether the interests are proprietary in nature. If the hirer hires property from the owner, and before the period of hire is over, the owner sells the same property to a third party, can the hirer assert proprietary rights against the third party based on his possessory interest in the goods; or is his interest merely personal in nature? If the interest is merely personal in nature, then the hirer's rights lie in contract against the owner only. He will have no proprietary claim against the third party, nor can he have any contractual claim against the third party, there being no privity of contract between them. There is no doubt that it would be possible for the hirer to claim against the third party in respect of the tort of conversion. As outlined above, the tort of conversion protects possession rather than ownership.[88] The right of possession can be asserted against all those who cannot prove a better right. A party in possession, such as the hirer, if wrongfully dispossessed, may bring an action in conversion. The hirer can sue in conversion because he has possession. However, this does not answer the question of the proprietary status of the lease. It has been argued that in the above scenario, the application of the rules of *nemo dat quod non habet* must result in the lease of goods having proprietary effect.[89] If the general rule of *nemo dat quod non habet* is applied, this means that the owner cannot give a better title than he has to give. This would mean that the owner cannot give the third party a title to an interest in the property which conflicts with the possessory interest already given to the hirer. Unless the third party can bring himself within one of the exceptions to *nemo dat*, the hirer's interest should get priority over the third party's. According to Swadling, however, the problem with this approach is that it takes no account of the *numerus clausus* principle. There is no room to invoke a *nemo dat* exception where the right in question is not a proprietary one.[90]

---

[87] See paragraph 2.2.

[88] See paragraph 1.4.

[89] See paragraph 10.

[90] Swadling, 'The Proprietary Effect of a Hire of Goods', in Palmer & McKendrick, *Interests in Goods*, Chapter 20, see also Swadling, 'Property: General Principles', Chapter 4 in Birks, P (ed), *English Private Law* (2000).

There is an equitable maxim 'Equity looks upon that as done which ought to be done'. It has been recognised that this can create a property right out of a contract to convey a property right.[91] The precondition is that performance of the contract would eventually entail the creation of a legal property right. This maxim was applied in *Bristol Airport plc v Powdrill*.[92] There, an airline company was the lessee of a number of aircraft. It owed Bristol Airport certain airport charges. The airport sought to exercise a statutory lien over the aircraft in respect of these charges. The company was insolvent but had been placed under an administration order under s. 8 UK Insolvency Act 1986. This meant that no steps could be taken to enforce any security over the company's property without the consent of the administrator or the leave of the court. The airport argued that they did not need the consent of the court before detaining the aircraft on the ground that the aircraft, being held under leases, were not the property of the company. The Court of Appeal held that the aircraft were indeed the property of the company and that the consent of the court was required. Browne Wilkinson V-C stated:

> 'Although a chattel lease is a contract, it does not follow that no property interest is created in the chattel. The basic equitable principle is that if, under a contract, A has certain rights over property as against the legal owner, which rights are specifically enforceable in equity, A has an equitable interest in such property. I have no doubt that a court would order specific performance of a contract to lease an aircraft, since each aircraft has unique features peculiar to itself. Accordingly in my judgment, the lessee has at least an equitable right of some kind in that aircraft which falls within the statutory definition as being some 'description of interest ... arising out of or 'incidental to' that aircraft.'[93]

So, the judgment seems to support the argument that rights under a lease of goods are proprietary in nature. However, it should be noted that the decision was made in the context of whether the possessory rights of the insolvent company over the aircraft could be construed as property rights for the purposes of the Insolvency Act 1986. Swadling argues that the conclusion that a chattel lease is a property right may well be right in this specialised context, particularly in view of the very wide definition of property contained in that Act and the aims of the legislation. However, he criticises the reasoning. Equity treats a contract for the sale of land as effective to pass title to the land so long as the contract is specifically enforceable in accordance with the maxim that equity looks upon that as done which ought to be done. Thus, equity anticipates the final result in

---

[91] See *Walsh v Lonsdale* (1882) 21 Ch D 9.
[92] [1990] 1 Ch 744.
[93] *Ibid*, p 759.

law which is that property rights will pass to the purchaser under the contract. However, Swadling argues that the same reasoning does not apply to a lease of chattels. He points out that if a contract to lease chattels when executed does not create a proprietary right in the lessee, how can equity hold that it does when merely executory? Since actual performance cannot create property rights, anticipated performance cannot do so either. If it did, equity would be destroying the dividing line between personal and proprietary rights.[94] According to Swadling, the reasoning in the *Bristol Airport Case* was flawed, the court equating the availability of the equitable relief of specific performance with the existence of an equitable proprietary interest.[95] Swadling also compares possessory covenants over land and chattels and draws the conclusion that the mere fact that a covenantee has a right to possession of the subject matter of the contract does not mean that he has a proprietary right. This he demonstrated by examining land law cases showing that while an occupational licensee of land can sue third parties in trespass he does not have a proprietary right in the land. The same reasoning applies to chattels.[96]

The question of the proprietary effect of a hire of goods remains unclear as it has never been directly addressed in English and Irish law. However, Swadling's arguments are cogent and his conclusion is persuasive: That our law of property works on a *numerus clausus* principle and that the rights of a hirer of goods have not been admitted to the list of recognised property rights. Whether such rights should be admitted to the list of recognised property rights is another question as is the question of whether the courts have the power to do so.[97]

4. Field of application and definitions

4.1. Choses in possession/tangible property

These are corporeal things, moveable tangible items. The term 'chose in possession' indicated that the thing could be possessed and that ownership of them could be asserted by taking possession, as opposed to having to go to court. The term 'chattel' is also used to denote 'chose in possession'. In the more modern statutes such as the Sale of Goods Acts, the word 'goods' is normally used to denote tangible personal property. Under s. 62 Sale of Goods Act 1893, 'goods' are defined as:

---

94 Swadling, 'The Proprietary Effect of a Hire of Goods', in Palmer & McKendrick, *Interests in Goods*, p 506.
95 *Ibid*, p 507.
96 *Ibid*, pp 509-524.
97 See above paragraph 1.1.2.

'all chattels personal other than things in action and money, and in particular, "goods" includes emblements, industrial growing crops, and things attached to or forming part of the land which are agreed to be severed before sale or under the contract of sale'.

Apart, therefore from things in action and money, the definition of goods embraces all personal chattels. The definition is thus very wide, including, for example large and unusual items such as ships and aircraft.[98]

(a)   Money

A contract for the sale of money is not a contract for the sale of goods. However, where the money is no longer legal tender, and has a curiosity value or an inherent value, it can be considered as 'goods' under the Act.[99]

(b)   Electricity and gas

The situation with regard to sales of electricity and gas is not altogether certain. These forms of energy are less easily categorised as tangible personal chattels. However, in *Bentley Bros v Metcalfe & Co*,[100] it was held that the supply of power (whether in the form of gas, electricity or any other motive power) was a sale and therefore the implied term as to fitness for buyer's purpose applied to the contract. The court did not, however, address the precise definition of the subject matter of the contract. The question whether the supply of electricity was a sale of goods was left open in *County of Durham Electrical Power Distribution Co v IRC*.[101] The sale of gas would appear to be covered by the Acts.[102] For the purposes of VAT law, the supply of gas and electricity is treated as a supply of goods rather than services.[103]

---

[98] *Behnke v Bede Shipping Co Ltd* [1927] 1 KB 649; *United Dominions Trust (Commercial) Ltd v Eagle Aircraft Services Ltd* [1968] 1 All ER 104.

[99] *Moss v Hancock* [1899] 2 QB 111.

[100] [1906] 2 KB 548.

[101] [1909] 2 KB 604.

[102] *Marleau v People's Gas Supply Co Ltd* [1940] 4 DLR 433; *Erie County Natural Gas and Fuel Co Ltd v Carroll* [1911] AC 105.

[103] Finance Act 2004, s. 56.

(c)   Crops and fixtures

Crops and structures on the land amounting to fixtures, may come within the definition of goods provided they are severed before the sale or under the contract of sale. The definition of goods makes specific reference to 'emblements' and 'industrial growing crops'. Emblements are annual crops grown by agricultural labour, as opposed to naturally occurring crops. Industrial growing crops are also cultivated, but are not expected to mature in one year. Emblements and industrial growing crops can be classified as *'fructus industriales'*. They are to be contrasted with *'fructus naturales'* which is the natural produce of the land such as trees, grass, timber or fruit from trees. *Fructus naturales* are included in the definition within the expression 'things attached to and forming part of the land'. Minerals, gravel and the soil itself would also be included in this expression, forming part of the land and are capable of being the subject of a sale of goods. Provided such things are severed before the sale or under the contract of sale, they can be goods under the Acts.

Some difficulty has arisen, however, with regard to whether particular transactions constitute a disposition of land or a sale of goods. In cases where the 'seller' is to sever or extract the materials in question and supply them at a price, there is no difficulty and the transaction will be a sale of goods. In cases where the 'buyer' is to be given a right to extract or sever the materials from the land, does this amount to a sale of goods? In *Morgan v Russell*,[104] the defendant, a tenant of land, entered into a contract to allow the plaintiff to enter onto the land to remove heaps of slag and cinders resting on the land. The heaps were about fifty years old and the slag composing them had become part of the land. The defendant's landlord prevented the plaintiff from entering the land, and the plaintiff sued for damages for breach of contract. It was held that the contract was one for the disposal of an interest in the land, not a sale of goods. It is thought that the case does not establish a general rule that the sale of minerals to be extracted can never be a sale of goods,[105] however, there would appear to be a general reluctance to treat such contracts where the buyer is to extract minerals under a contract as contracts for the sale of goods.[106] Goode suggests that in a situation where the 'buyer' is to extract

---

[104] [1909] 1 KB 357.

[105] See comments of Walton J: 'I wish to guard myself against any expression of opinion that a contract for the sale of minerals ungotten at the date of the contract may not be a sale of goods within the meaning of s. 62 of the Sale of Goods Act 1893. We have to decide, not whether any such contract may be, but whether this particular contract is, a contract for the sale of goods.', *ibid*, p 366.

[106] In the Australian case of *Mills v Stockman* (1967) 41 AJLR 16, a quantity of slate which had been left on land was held to be part of the land and not goods. It had

the material, it will be a sale if he is under an obligation to extract and pay for the materials extracted and is not intended to acquire any interest in the materials prior to extraction. If the buyer is not under an obligation to sever the materials, but is given an interest in the materials *in situ*, then the transaction will be a profit a prendre and not a sale of goods.[107]

4.2.   Choses in action/intangible property

Choses in action are defined in terms of what is not a chose in possession. Thus choses in action could be said to be all rights and incorporeal things not being chattels real or choses in possession, which make up personalty. There is a diverse range of such intangible property. Examples would include debts, goodwill, intellectual property, company shares, bills of exchange. It is not possible to take physical possession of such property. The only way to assert title to it is through legal action. A chose in action could be said to be *'a general term for intangible property of all kinds, any right that can be protected by legal action rather than by taking possession.'*[108]

4.2.1.   Legal/equitable choses in action

A further distinction is made between legal and equitable choses in action. Equitable choses in action are those that were recognised only by equity such as the beneficial interest under a trust. The original legal chose in action was the debt. Originally this was not considered property at all because it could not be assigned. However, as assignment of debts became possible, it was recognised as proprietary in nature. Other kinds of intangible property rights subsequently were developed at common law such as shares and eventually, chose in action came to be a general term for intangible property of all kinds. Equity took a more realistic approach to the assignment of choses in action. Equitable choses in action such as interests under a trust were freely assignable, allowing the assignee to sue in his own name without involving the assignor. Legal choses in action, however posed difficulties because the courts of equity could not interfere with the legal title as this was a matter for the common law courts. They did, however compel the assignor to allow the assignee to sue at law in his name. Ultimately Parliament intervened to allow for simpler proce-

---

been left for many years and treated as waste material. It was held that the intention was that the slate would remain indefinitely on the land and by implication it was part of the land.

[107] Goode, R, *Commercial Law* p 202.

[108] *Torkington v Magee* [1902] 2 KB 427, *per* Channell J at 430.

dures and in practice most assignments are now made by statute. There are specific statutes which apply to specific types of chose. For example, in the case of shares, legal assignments are dealt with partly by The Stock Transfer Act 1963 and by the articles of association of the company. The Companies Act 1963 stipulates that there must be 'a proper instrument of transfer', and this is a requirement that cannot be altered by the company's articles.[109] In the case of insurance policies, special methods of transfer can be used in the case of marine insurance and life insurance.[110] Where there is no specific statute dealing with assignment of choses in action, there is a general method of assignment provided for in the Supreme Court of Judicature (Ireland) Act 1877.

4.2.2. Negotiable instruments

Negotiable instruments are documents embodying legal choses in action. The meaning of 'negotiable' is that the rights embodied in the document can be transferred at common law simply by delivery, sometimes with an endorsement. The rules governing their transfer are therefore different to the assignment of other choses in action. The primary forms of negotiable instrument are the bill of exchange and the promissory note. The law relating to these instruments is contained in the Bills of Exchange Act 1882.

---

[109] S. 81 Companies Act 1963.
[110] S. 50 Marine Insurance Act 1906 and Policies of Assurance Act 1867.

5. Which system of transfer is used?

5.1. Basic characteristics/overview

5.1.1. The unitary system of transfer

Generally speaking, a transfer of movables will operate to transfer all rights associated with ownership from transferor to transferee at one single moment. However, the parties are generally free to make whatever arrangements they see fit. So, for example, the terms of their agreement may provide that possession is to remain with the transferor.

5.1.2. Are the same rules applicable to all kinds of obligations?

Proprietary interests can be transferred from one party to another by gift, barter or sale. There are common law rules which govern each mechanism and determine whether the parties' acts have been sufficient to effect a transfer of the property interest at law.

5.1.3. Basic transfer requirements

Is the system of transfer consensual or does it require some form of *traditio*?
Historically, for every transfer of movables, English law, and hence Irish law, required delivery of the goods, *i.e.*, transfer of possession. The same applied to transfer of land. There was a unitary transfer system that could be classified as a tradition system, *i.e.*, it required a form of '*traditio*'. However, two exceptions to the delivery rule developed. It was accepted that a gift could be made by deed rather than delivery,[111] and it was

---

[111] *Standing v Bowring* (1885) 31 ChD 282. In the absence of a deed, delivery is essential. This rule was laid down in *Irons v Smallpiece* (1819) 2 B & Ald 551.

gradually accepted that in the case of sale, ownership of the goods could pass to the buyer when the contract is made even if the goods have not yet been delivered to the buyer. This is now reflected in the Sale of Goods Act 1893 and the Irish Sale of Goods and Supply of Services Act 1980. As such, therefore, in the case of transfers of gifts by deed and for certain contracts of sale,[112] there is a *consensual* transfer system. In relation to all other transfers, the tradition system applies.

5.1.4. Is the concept abstract or causal?

This is not a question which has been the subject of discussion in the common law literature or case law. In a causal transfer system, a valid contract is required as cause so that the transfer of ownership necessarily depends on the validity of the contract. Van Vliet[113] suggests that by examining the effect of the invalidity of the underlying contract on the validity of the transfer it is possible to establish whether the system of transfer could be described as a causal or abstract system. In particular, it is necessary to examine the effects in Irish law of various defects which render contracts void, voidable and unenforceable.

(a) Void contract

A contract may be void for lack of consideration, or because of mistake or it can be declared void by statute, for example where it is a wagering contract. A contract which is void produces no legal relationship between the parties and has no legal consequences. Ownership cannot pass under a void contract.[114] This would suggest that the transfer system of the Irish Sale of Goods legislation is causal and not abstract.

(b) Voidable contract

A voidable contract is one which a party is entitled to rescind, or to have set aside by the court by reason of a factor such as fraud, misrepresentation, duress, or undue influence. The contract is valid until it is rescinded. Rescission cancels the contract from the beginning, so that each party is obliged to

---

[112] *I.e.*, for the sale of specific goods. Different rules apply to the sale of unascertained goods, see para 5.5.2. below.

[113] Van Vliet, *Transfer of Movables in German, French, English and Dutch Law* (2000), Chapter 4, p 111.

[114] *Cundy v Lindsay* (1878) 3 App Cas 459; *Ingram v Little* [1960] 3 All ER 332.

return the benefits he has received and in so far as possible, the parties are restored to the position they were in had no contract been entered into. S. 23 of the Sale of Goods Act is illustrative of the effect of a voidable contract on the validity of transfer. The section protects the buyer against the seller having a voidable title. The seller has a voidable title when he acquires ownership under a voidable legal act, for example, a contract which was voidable as a result of misrepresentation, duress or undue influence. S. 23 provides that:

> 'when the seller of goods has a voidable title thereto, but his title has not been avoided at the time of the sale, the buyer acquires a good title to the goods, provided he buys them in good faith and without notice of the seller's defect in title.'

So, where A is the owner of goods and B fraudulently induces A to sell the goods to him, the contract of sale is voidable at the option of A. If, before A avoids the contract, B resells the goods to C, avoidance of the first contract will revest C's ownership in A. DelS. 23 protects the second buyer C against the *nemo dat* rule by providing that B is nonetheless able to pass ownership to him provided C is acting in good faith without notice.[115] DelS. 23 therefore reinforces the proposition that the transfer system in the Sale of Goods Act is causal. If the system was abstract, avoidance of the contract could not return ownership to the seller and s. 23 would be superfluous.[116]

(c)   Unenforceable contract

An unenforceable contract is one which is valid and therefore effective to produce a legal relationship between the parties, but for some reason cannot be legally enforced by one party (and sometimes the other as well). An illegal contract is generally unenforceable as opposed to void. To the extent that the obligations of a party under the contract have been performed, the question of enforcement of those obligations does not arise and the illegality has no impact. However, where money has been paid or property transferred under the illegal contract, title passes to the transferee, despite the illegality.[117] So, ownership can pass on the basis of an illegal contract. This might suggest that a transfer under an illegal contract is an abstract transfer, however it must be remembered that illegal contracts are unenforceable rather than void. The contract is valid but cannot be enforced by the parties.[118]

---

[115] See further below, paragraph 10.

[116] See further, Van Vliet, *op cit*, p 110.

[117] *Singh v Ali* [1960] AC 167; *Belvoir Finance Co Ltd v Stapleton* [1971] 1 QB 210.

[118] See further Van Vliet, *op cit*, p 111 *et seq*.

5.1.5. Does the system recognise a real agreement?

Within the statutory regime for the sale of goods, there is recognition of the real agreement in the context of the rules for the passing of property in unascertained/generic goods. This is considered below.[119]

5.1.6. Is there a requirement of payment?

There is no requirement of payment in Irish law, although the parties may specify payment as a condition of the passing of transferor's ownership rights to the transferee under a retention of title clause.[120]

5.2. General issues

5.2.1. Specific, quasi-specific and unascertained/generic goods

Irish law distinguishes between specific, quasi-specific and unascertained goods or generic goods. There is a principle that rights *in rem* can exist in relation to specific assets only. So, where the contract is for the sale of unascertained or quasi-specific goods, no property interest of any kind vests in the buyer until the goods have become ascertained. The statutory rules make it clear that precise identification of the goods is crucial if the purchaser is to be able to assert legal title to them.

Specific goods are those which are 'identified and agreed on at the time a contract of sale is made.'[121] Unascertained or generic goods are not identified at the time of the contract but depend on some subsequent agreed act of appropriation by the seller or by the buyer. Quasi-specific goods are, strictly speaking, unascertained goods but from a source identified when the contract is made. For example, a contract to sell 500 tons of wheat, out of an identified bulk cargo of 10,000 tons. So, the goods are partially identified.

The statutory rules on the transfer of ownership of specific and unascertained goods are based on rules developed at common law prior to the 1893 Act and are to be found in sections 16 to 26 of the Sale of Goods Acts 1893

---

[119] Paragraph 5.6.

[120] S. 19 Sale of Goods and Supply of Services Act 1893 provides that the seller may impose a condition on the passing of property in goods. The seller will frequently include a retention of title clause in the sales contract. See further below, paragraph 12.

[121] S. 61(1) Sale of Goods Act 1893.

to 1980. The rules are considered in detail below.[122] The basic rule is to be found in s. 17, which provides that property passes when the parties intend it to pass. Where the parties' intention as to the passing of property is not clear, s. 18 provides a set of rules of presumed intent. These rules can be negatived or varied by the contrary intention of the parties. However, s. 17 and s. 18 are subject to s. 16 which is mandatory in application. S. 16 is limited to the sale of unascertained goods and provides that property cannot pass until the goods are first ascertained. Goods become ascertained when they are 'unconditionally appropriated to the contract.' The process of un-conditional appropriation is dealt with below.[123] S. 16 has significant conse-quences for the pre-paying buyer of unascertained goods where the seller becomes insolvent. The buyer, as an unsecured creditor of the seller seeking a refund of the price and damages for non-delivery will rank alongside the other unsecured creditors in the insolvency. In addition, where goods are destroyed or damaged, the general rule is that risk passes with property so that a seller of unascertained goods will bear the risk of damage or destruc-tion of the goods. The consequences of s. 16 are considered further below.[124]

5.2.2. Party autonomy

Party autonomy plays an important role in Irish law on transfer of movables. It is particularly important in the context of the sale of goods. As outlined below, s. 17 of the Sale of Goods Act 1893 provides that it is the intent of the parties as evidenced from the terms of their contract which is relevant and determines when property in the goods passes to the buyer. The general rule therefore is that title to goods passes when the parties intend it to pass. An exception to this general rule exists in relation to unascertained goods. S. 16 of the 1893 Act provides that where there is a contract for the sale of unascertained goods, no property in the goods is transferred to the buyer unless and until the goods are ascertained. This rule cannot be excluded or varied by the parties. In relation to other types of transfer, party autonomy is more restricted. For example, gifts of property must be perfected by delivery or a delivery equivalent to be enforceable.

In a transfer of movables by sale, because ownership rights can be transferred without possession, there will inevitably be an effect on third parties, where the same property can be the subject of several purported transfers. There are rules on good faith acquisition to deal with resulting title conflicts.[125]

---

[122] See paragraphs 5.5.1. and 5.5.2.
[123] See paragraph 5.5.3.(b).
[124] See paragraph 5.5.2.
[125] See paragraph 10.

5.3. Requirement of a valid obligation to transfer ownership

5.3.1. Types of obligations

(a) Contract

There are many different ways in which a transfer of legal ownership can be made for value. The most common method is sale, but there are others, for example, hire purchase and barter. Contracts for the sale of goods are governed by the Sale of Goods Act 1893 as amended by Part II of the Sale of Goods and Supply of Services Act 1980. Together this legislation is referred to as the Sale of Goods Acts 1893 and 1980. These Acts set out the rights and duties of the parties. However, they are not codes and do not contain all the rules applicable to sales contracts. S. 61(2) of the 1893 Act provides that:

'the rules of the common law, including the law of the merchant ... shall apply to contracts for the sale of goods, except insofar as they are modified by the Act.'

The Acts are described as optional rather than peremptory law, laying down rules which apply in the absence of a contrary agreement by the parties.

The definition of a contract of sale is:

'A contract of sale of goods is a contract whereby the seller transfers or agrees to transfer the property in the goods to the buyer for a money consideration, called the price.'[126]

A contract for hire purchase does not fall to be considered under the Sale of Goods Act, as the agreement is not one of sale under this definition but a contract to hire the goods with an option to buy them. Hire purchase contracts are governed by the Consumer Credit Act 1995.

A contract for work and materials will usually involve the transfer of ownership of material goods but it is a contract for services and is not governed by the Sale of Goods Act. The distinction between the two types of contract is based on whether the main object of the agreement is to sell goods or to provide labour or other services. The question that must be answered in every case is whether the contract is primarily for the supply of goods, in which case it is a contract of sale, or whether the work or services are just as important, if not more so. Thus, an agreement whereby a carpet was to be supplied and laid has been held to be a contract of

---

[126] S. 1(1) 1893 Act.

sale,[127] while the supply and installation of roofing tiles has been held to be a contract for work and materials.[128] The nature of the transaction will depend on the particular facts of the case and the intention of the parties. Accordingly, case law, though useful as guidance, needs to be treated with care. Where a contract is held to be one for work and materials, it is governed by the Sale of Goods and Supply of Services Act 1980.

A bailment is a transaction whereby one party (the bailor) delivers goods to another party on terms which normally require the bailee to hold the goods and eventually to redeliver the goods to the bailor, or in accordance with his directions. The notable feature of a bailment is that there is no transfer of property or ownership in the goods, merely possession and further, this transfer of possession is temporary. Everyday examples of bailment include leaving a coat in a cloakroom for later collection, transporting goods with a carrier, contracts of hire. Bailments can be contractual, for example, when you pay to leave your coat at a cloakroom, or gratuitous. The basis of liability under a bailment is negligence. The bailee must exercise due care in the handling of goods in his possession. A contract of hire or lease is a type of bailment. Where the letting is financed by credit with a consumer hirer, the arrangement is regulated under Part VII of the Consumer Credit Act 1995.

In a contract of sale, the consideration for the transfer of property in the goods must be money consideration. This is the main distinguishing feature between a contract of barter or exchange and a contract of sale. The traditional barter arrangement occurs where goods are exchanged in return for other goods. The distinction between sale and barter becomes less clear where goods are transferred in return for goods plus money. A common example is where a second hand car is traded in, in return for a new car plus money. In *Flynn v Mackin & Mahon*,[129] a car was traded for another car plus £250. It was held that this was a barter because no value was, nor could be, placed on the goods. It would seem that if a value, even a notional value can be placed on the goods, the transaction will be a sale.

(b)   Gift

With a gift of goods, there is no consideration provided for the transfer of property in the goods, even though there may be a valid transfer of property where the gift is executed, *i.e.*, where the goods are delivered to the donee. Where the gift is executory (yet to be performed), the promise of a gift is not binding unless it is made by deed.

---

[127] *Phillip Head & Sons Ltd v Showfronts Ltd* [1970] 1 Lloyds Rep 140.

[128] *Norta Wallpapers (Ireland) Ltd v John Sisk & Sons (Dublin) Ltd* [1978] IR 114.

[129] [1974] IR 101. Cf *Aldridge v Johnson* (1857) 7 E & B 885.

(c)   Unjust enrichment

It is not settled whether or not proprietary rights including ownership can be created as a result of unjust enrichment. There is authority that money paid on the basis of mistake is held on trust by the payee for the payor. In *Chase Manhattan Bank v Israel-British Bank*,[130] a New York bank had, by mistake paid the same sum twice to the credit of the defendant, a London bank. Shortly thereafter, the defendant bank went into insolvent liquidation. The question was whether the New York bank had a claim *in rem* against the assets of the London bank to recover the second payment. It was held that where money was paid under a mistake, the receipt of such money without more constituted the recipient a trustee, the payer retaining an equitable property in it, the recipient subject to a fiduciary duty to respect his proprietary right. The reasoning in the case was later criticised by Lord Browne-Wilkinson in *Westdeutsche Landesbank Zentrale v Islington London Borough Council*.[131]

(d)   Breach of obligation

The question of whether breaches of obligation can give rise to property rights is a controversial one. In *Attorney General of Hong Kong v Reid*,[132] the Privy Council held that that a gift accepted by a person in a fiduciary position as an incentive for his breach of duty constituted a bribe and, although in law it belonged to the fiduciary, in equity he not only became a debtor for the amount of the bribe to the person to whom the duty was owed but he also held the bribe and any property acquired therewith on constructive trust for that person; that if the value of the property representing the bribe depreciated the fiduciary had to pay to the injured person the difference between that value and the initial amount of the bribe, and if the property increased in value the fiduciary was not entitled to retain the excess since equity would not allow him to make any profit from his breach of duty. Many commentators do not agree with the existence of a proprietary remedy for breach of a fiduciary obligation.[133]

---

[130] [1981] 1 Ch 105.

[131] [1996] AC 669 at 715.

[132] [1994] 1 AC 324.

[133] See Goode, 'Proprietary Restitutionary Claims' in WR Cornish, R Nolan, J O'Sullivan and G Virgo (eds), *Restititution: Past, Present and Future* (1998), Chapter 5.

5.3.2.   Validity of the obligation

(a)   Lack of capacity

According to s. 2 of the 1893 Act, capacity to buy and sell is regulated by the general law concerning capacity to contract, and to transfer and acquire property. S. 2 also provides that where necessaries are sold and delivered to an infant, or minor, or to a person who by reason of mental incapacity or drunkenness is incompetent to contract, he must pay a reasonable price for them. 'Necessaries' in this section mean 'goods suitable to the condition in life of such infant or minor or other person, and to his actual requirements at the time of the sale and delivery.' A minor is a person under the age of 18. Minors may enter valid contracts for necessary goods. The contract will not be enforceable if the minor has enough of the goods already. A minor is only required to pay a reasonable price for necessaries and this may be less than the contract price. Trade goods bought for resale are not necessaries. Certain long-term contracts may be avoided by the minor while still a minor or within a reasonable time of reaching the age of majority. These include contracts involving an interest in land, or the acquisition of securities on the stock exchange, or a partnership agreement. Although he may repudiate such contracts, he may not be able to recover money paid if he has received consideration such as enjoyment of a lease or the shares contracted for.[134] Under the Infants Relief Act 1874, loans, contracts for goods other than necessaries and book debts are 'absolutely void.' In practice, however, they are regarded by the courts as being merely unenforceable against the minor or voidable although he will not be allowed to recover back what he has already given where he has received consideration for it.

If a person when he contracts, is so mentally disordered as to be unable to understand the nature of a contract, or if he is in such a state of drunkenness as not to know what he is doing, the contract is voidable if it can be shown that his condition was known to the other party.

Where a company enters into a contract which is *ultra vires, i.e.,* outside of the stated objects in its memorandum of association, the result is that the contract is void, not merely as between the company and its members but also as between the company and the other party to the contract. Furthermore, persons dealing with the company are presumed to know the contents of the memorandum under the doctrine of constructive notice. The harshness of this rule is tempered significantly by the legislature in favour of outsiders dealing with the company. S. 8(1) Companies Act 1963 provides that:

---

[134] *Blake v Concannon* (1870) Ir Ex.

'Any act or thing done by a company which if the company had been empowered to do the same would have been lawfully and effectively done, shall, notwithstanding that the company had no power to do such act or thing, be effective in favour of any person relying on such act or thing who is not shown to
have been actually aware, at the time when he so relied thereon, that such act
or thing was not within the powers of the company, but any director or officer
of the company who was responsible for the doing by the company of such act
or thing shall be liable to the company of such act or thing shall be liable to
the company for any loss or damage suffered by the company in consequence
thereof.'

Thus, an outsider who enters into a transaction unaware of the contents
of the memorandum and articles is now able to enforce the transaction
against the company even though it is *ultra vires*. In addition, Article 6 of
the European Communities (Companies) Regulations 1973 provides that:

1. In favour of a person dealing with a company in good faith, any transaction entered into by an organ of the company, being its board of directors or any person registered under these regulations as a person
   authorised to bind the company, shall be deemed to be within the capacity of the company and any limitation of the powers of that board
   or person whether imposed by the memorandum or articles of association or otherwise may not be relied upon as against any person so
   dealing with the company.
2. Any such person shall be presumed to have acted in good faith unless
   the contrary is proved.

The scope of this regulation and its relationship to s. 8 of the 1963 Act is
not clear. It is more limited than s. 8 in that it is confined to contracts
entered into by the board of directors and registered agents and does not
apply to unlimited companies. Such contracts are enforceable under the
terms of article 6 even though *ultra vires*, provided outsiders entered into
them 'in good faith.' Where the person is not aware of the lack of capacity of the company, it seems clear that he should be treated as having
acted in good faith.[135]

---

[135] The Company Law Review Group has recommended that private companies limited by shares should be granted the legal capacity of a natural person with the
consequent effect that the doctrine of *ultra vires* should be disapplied from such
companies. (Company Law Review Group, First Report, Recommendation 10.9.2
at p 226) For further detail on the *ultra vires* doctrine, see Keane, *Company Law*
(2000), Chapter 12.

(b)   Void contract

A contract may be void for lack of consideration, or because of mistake or
it can be declared void by statute, for example where it is a wagering
contract. A contract which is void produces no legal relationship between the parties and has no legal consequences. Ownership cannot pass
under a void contract.[136]

(c)   Voidable contract

A voidable contract is one which a party is entitled to rescind, or to have
set aside by the court by reason of a factor such as fraud, misrepresentation, duress, or undue influence. The contract is valid until it is rescinded. Rescission cancels the contract from the beginning, so that each
party is obliged to return the benefits he has received and in so far as
possible, the parties are restored to the position they were in had no contract been entered into. S. 23 of the Sale of Goods Act is illustrative of
the effect of a voidable contract on the validity of transfer.[137] The section
protects the buyer against the seller having a voidable title.

(d)   Termination of the contract

The termination or discharge of the contract has no retroactive effect. It
works *ex nunc*. If ownership of a thing has passed to the buyer before the
termination of the contract, the legal basis for this transfer remains intact.
Ownership of the thing cannot automatically revert back to the seller.
This must be distinguished from the situation where a buyer exercises his
right of rejection. A buyer can reject goods in four circumstances. First,
where there is an express right to reject under the contract. Second, the
legislation provides a specific right where, for example, the seller delivers
the wrong quantity.[138] Third, the legislation provides a general right to
reject where the seller has breached a condition, for example, where he
has delivered defective goods.[139] Fourth, the common law also allows rejection for serious breach of contract.[140] If ownership has not yet passed to
the buyer, the exercise of the right of rejection prevents ownership from

---

[136] *Cundy v Lindsay* (1878) 3 App Cas 459; *Ingram v Little* [1960] 3 All ER 332.
[137] See below, paragraph 10.2.5.
[138] S. 30 Sale of Goods Act 1893.
[139] S. 11(2) Sale of Goods Act 1893.
[140] *The Hansa Nord* [1976] QB 44; *Irish Telephone Rentals v ICS Building Society* [1991]
   ILRM 880.

passing to the buyer. If the buyer has already acquired ownership, the exercise of the right of rejection revests ownership in the seller. The risk of loss or damage to the goods also revests in the seller. Where the buyer remains in possession following rejection, he would be liable as an involuntary bailee. This revesting of ownership in the seller has been explained as follows: Property in goods passes to the buyer subject to the condition that they revest if upon examination he finds them to be not in accordance with the contract. That means that he gets only conditional property in the goods, the condition being a condition subsequent.[141]

S. 11(3) of the Sale of Goods Act 1893 recognises that a breach of condition may entitle the buyer to treat the contract as repudiated or terminated. The buyer is not obliged to treat the contract as terminated. He may reject the goods without terminating the contract. In many cases, it is in the interests of buyers, especially commercial buyers to maintain the contract and accept a re-tender of the goods. The contract may expressly give the seller the right to repair or replace defective goods. In the absence of such an express provision, it is not clear whether there is a legal right for either party to insist on cure. Some commentators argue that since the effect of rejection is to put the parties in the same position as if the seller had not delivered, the seller is entitled to make a replacement delivery provided that the time for performance has not expired and that the seller has not otherwise repudiated the contract. Under a contract for unascertained goods, the seller could cure by delivering replacement goods matching the contract description. Under a contract for specific goods, the seller could only cure by repairing the goods.[142]

5.4. Delivery and delivery equivalents

5.4.1. Gifts

Where a deed of gift is signed, sealed and delivered, the transfer is immediately effective, subject to disclaimer by the donee. In practice, this type of transfer is only used when vesting property in trustees on the creation of a settlement. In the absence of a deed, delivery is essential for a valid transfer by way of gift. This rule was established in *Irons v Smallpiece*.[143] There, a father had purported to give two horses to his son but retained possession of them. When the father died, it was held that the animals formed part of his estate, the gift having been ineffective to transfer ownership.

---

[141] Per Devlin J in *Kwei Tek Chao v British Traders and Shippers Ltd* [1954] 1 All ER 779.

[142] See Goode, *Commercial Law*, p 363.

[143] (1819) 2 B & Ald 551.

Actual delivery of the goods is an acceptable form of delivery, whether this involves the donor handing over the property or the donee taking possession of it with the donor's permission. Where the donee is already in possession as bailee or has custody of the property, a constructive delivery changing the character of his holding will be effective.[144] Any constructive delivery conferring on the donee an immediate right to possession will also be effective. This can include some forms of symbolic delivery. For example, in *Lock v Heath*,[145] a husband purported to make a gift to his wife of all his furniture by handing one chair to her. This was held to be a good gift.

5.4.2. Sale

Delivery is not necessary in order to transfer property in goods from seller to buyer. In the case of sale, ownership of specific goods can pass to the buyer when the contract is made even if the goods have not yet been delivered to the buyer. The detailed rules are considered below.[146]

5.5.   Consensual system

5.5.1. Passing of property in specific goods

As outlined above, s. 1(1) of the 1893 Act defines a contract for the sale of goods as:

> 'a contract whereby the seller transfers or agrees to transfer the property in goods to the buyer for a money consideration, called the price.'

A contract of sale can be in one of two forms: A sale, or an agreement to sell. S. 1(3) provides:

> 'where under a contract of sale, the property in the goods is transferred from the seller to the buyer the contract is called a sale; but where the transfer of the property in the goods is to take place at a future time or subject to some condition thereafter to be fulfilled the contract is called an agreement to sell.'

---

[144] See *Pascoe v Turner* [1979] 2 All ER 945 where the plaintiff had been living with the defendant and having abandoned her for another woman, told her that the contents of the house were hers. The Court of Appeal held that this was a valid gift.

[145] (1892) 8 TLR 295.

[146] See paragraph 5.5.1.

In Irish law, property and possession are separated so that the buyer may own goods which he does not physically control or possess. Irish law allows the contract of sale to act as such in creating rights *in personam* between seller and buyer and as a simultaneous conveyance of the property in the goods to the buyer, thus creating rights *in rem*. As outlined above, where the contract passes the property immediately, it is referred to as a 'sale'. Where property passes at some time after the contract, it is known as an 'agreement to sell.' Concepts such as delivery of the goods and payment for them are not essential features in the distinction between an agreement to sell and a sale which passes property in the goods to the buyer.

'Property' is defined in s. 62 of the 1893 Act as meaning the 'general property' in the goods, and not merely a 'special property'. In this sense, property means the absolute legal interest in the goods, or ownership.[147] The legislation does not apply to any transaction in the form of a sale that is intended to operate by way of mortgage, pledge, charge or other security.[148]

'Goods' are defined in s. 62 of the 1893 Act as including

> 'all personal chattels other than things in action and money, and in Scotland all corporeal moveables except money; and in particular "goods" includes emblements, industrial growing crops, and things attached to or forming part of the land which are agreed to be severed before sale or under the contract of sale and includes an undivided share in goods.'

Choses in action such as debts, bills of exchange, bills of lading, shares and other securities, trade marks, patents, and insurance policies are outside the definition of goods for the purposes of the Sale of Goods Acts. Likewise, intangibles such as information are not classifiable as 'goods'.

Sections 16 to 26 of the Sale of Goods Act 1893 contain the provisions on transfer of ownership. In Irish law, it is the intent of the parties as evidenced from the terms of their contract which is relevant and determines when property in the goods passes to the buyer. The general rule therefore is that title to goods passes when the parties intend it to pass. This rule appears in s. 17 of the 1893 Act which states that the moment when property (*i.e.* ownership) in the goods passes to the buyer depends on the intention of the parties to the contract. If no intention appears, then the rules in s. 18 will apply. Because these are rules of presumed intent, they can be excluded or negatived expressly or impliedly, by the contrary intention of the parties.

The principal rule in s. 18 is Rule 1 states:

---

[147] See further Goode, 'Ownership and Obligations in Commercial Transactions', (1987) 103 LQR 433.

[148] S. 61(4) 1893 Act.

'Where there is an unconditional contract for the sale of specific goods in a deliverable state the property in the goods passes to the buyer when the contract is made, and it is immaterial whether the time of payment or the time of delivery, or both, be postponed.'

The effect of this rule is that ownership passes to the buyer the moment the contract is created. It is not needed to transfer possession of the goods to the buyer. No *traditio* is needed and ownership passes simply as a result of consensus between the parties, *i.e.*, it is a consensual as opposed to tradition system of transfer.[149] A contract for the sale of specific goods therefore can have a dual function as a contract and a simultaneous conveyance of the property in the goods to the buyer. It is quite possible therefore, for property in specific goods to pass to the buyer on contract under s. 18, Rule 1 even though the buyer has neither paid for the goods nor obtained physical possession of them. However, the consensual system is confined to *existing specific goods*. Other rules apply to *unascertained* goods. An agreement to sell unascertained goods could not act as an instantaneous conveyance of the property in the goods to the buyer for the reason that the goods must be physically ascertained before the buyer can own them.

'Deliverable state' is defined in s. 62(4) as:

'such a state that the buyer would under the contract be bound to take delivery of them'.

Deliverable state has been given a restricted meaning. It is clear that goods can be in a deliverable state and be defective. Defects in goods do not prevent property passing. Goods will not be in a deliverable state if the seller has agreed to do something to the goods before delivery under the contract.[150]

S. 18 Rule 2 provides:

'Where there is a contract for the sale of specific goods and the seller is bound to do something to the goods for the purposes of putting them into a deliverable state, the property does not pass until the thing is done and the buyer has notice that it has been done'.

The phrase 'deliverable state' has the same meaning as Rule 1.

S. 18 Rule 3 states that where the contract is for

'the sale of specific goods in a deliverable state but the seller is bound to weigh, measure, test or do some other act or thing with reference to the goods

---

[149] Assuming that the transferor has the right to sell the goods.

[150] *Underwood Ltd v Burgh Castle Brick and Cement Syndicate* [1922] 1 KB 343.

for the purpose of ascertaining the price, the property does not pass until the act or thing is done and the buyer has notice that it has been done.'

S. 18 Rule 4 applies where goods are delivered to the buyer 'on approval or on sale or return or other similar terms'. In those cases property passes to the buyer:

(a) When he signifies his approval or acceptance to the seller or does any other act adopting the transaction; or
(b) If he does not signify his approval or acceptance to the seller but retains the goods without giving notice of rejection then, if a time has been fixed for the return of the goods, on the expiration of that time, and if no time has been fixed, on the expiration of a reasonable time.

5.5.2. Passing of property in unascertained/generic goods

(a) General

The overriding rule in relation to contracts for the sale of unascertained goods is contained in s. 16 and provides that in such a contract, no property in the goods is transferred to the buyer unless and until the goods are ascertained. Subject to this, the passing of property in unascertained goods is governed by s. 18, Rule 5 which provides:

> 'Where there is a contract for the sale of unascertained or future goods by description, and goods of that description in a deliverable state are unconditionally appropriated to the contract, either by the seller with the assent of the buyer, or by the buyer with the assent of the seller, the property in the goods then passes to the buyer.'

Like the other rules on the passing of property, this is a rule of presumed intention and can be excluded or varied by the parties. The rules in s. 16 and s. 18, Rule 5 apply to sales of wholly unascertained goods and to contracts to sell 'quasi-specific' goods.

S. 16 provides that property in unascertained goods cannot pass until the goods are identified or 'ascertained'.

There is no definition of 'ascertained' in the Sale of Goods Act, but it is accepted that it means 'identified in accordance with the agreement after the time a contract of sale is made.'[151]

S. 16 can cause problems where part of a bulk is being sold. In *Re Wait*,[152] the owner of a cargo sold 500 tons out of a total bulk of 1000 tons

---

[151] *Re Wait* [1927] 1 Ch 606.

on a particular ship to a buyer who paid for that part of the cargo in advance. The owner became bankrupt before the ship reached its destination. It was held that the buyer was unable to claim any part of the cargo. He had agreed to buy unascertained goods (although they were quasi-specific) which had not been separated from the bulk and hence were not identified with the buyer's contract. Under s. 16, ownership cannot pass to the buyer until the goods have been appropriated as the assets to be transferred to that particular buyer. In order for the part of a bulk being sold to be ascertained, it must be physically separated from the bulk.

Another example of the effects of s. 16 can be illustrated by examining the New Zealand case of *Re Goldcorp Exchange Ltd.*[153] The company had invited members of the public to invest in gold and other precious metals. Purchasers paid the price and received a certificate of ownership detailing the amount bought and giving them the right to call for delivery of the gold on giving seven days notice. The company also made assurances about the physical presence of the gold sold which was not stored separately for each contract but as part of a larger bulk. The company promised that it would have enough gold in stock to satisfy demand and to ensure this, the stock would be audited monthly by a firm of accountants. However, the company became insolvent and a bank holding a debenture secured by a floating charge appointed receivers. The purchasers claimed that under the contracts of sale, ownership had passed to them. However, the court held that the customers were purchasers of unascertained goods which were never ascertained and so they had no property rights in the gold. Lord Mustill explained the reason why ownership in unascertained goods cannot pass. He stated '... common sense dictates that the buyer cannot acquire title until it is known to what goods the title relates.' This reflects the principle that rights *in rem* can only exist in relation to specific assets. The object of the right of ownership or any right *in rem* must be a specific object.

(b)   Reform of s. 16

These cases illustrate the difficulties for the pre-paying buyer of unascertained goods. Such a buyer will have no proprietary claim to the goods bought under the contract and the price that he has paid for the goods and the remaining assets of the insolvent seller will be used to pay the creditors of the seller. The buyer, as an unsecured creditor of the seller seeking a refund of the price paid, will rank at the bottom of the list of creditors to be paid.

---

[152] *Ibid.*
[153] [1994] 2 All ER 806.

S. 16 can lead to some arbitrary results. For example, we have seen how s. 16 applies to quasi-specific goods, *i.e.*, where goods are sold as part of an identified bulk. In the case of a pre-paying buyer of such goods, where the seller becomes insolvent, the application of s. 16 means that the buyer is left as an unsecured creditor with little opportunity to recoup the price paid. However, s. 16 may not apply where the proportion of the bulk is represented as a fraction as where, for example, the seller sells a 50% share in the bulk. In that case, property in the share passes to the buyer when the contract of sale is made. No appropriation is necessary because the share relates to the whole of the bulk and consequently to every item in the bulk. So, the buyer of a share acquires a proprietary interest whereas the buyer of a certain amount merely has a personal right to delivery of the goods. Where one buyer purchases the whole bulk under several contracts, the goods will be ascertained but where two or more buyers purchase the whole bulk there is no ascertainment.

As a result of these difficulties, in the UK, the law has been amended following a Law Commission Report.[154] The amendments are contained in sections 20A and 20B of the Sale of Goods (Amendment) Act 1995. The amendments relate to sales of quasi-specific goods which have been paid for. Under the new sections, a pre-paying buyer of a specified quantity from an identified bulk is recognised under certain conditions, as having a proprietary interest in the goods in the form of an undivided share in the bulk and he becomes a co-owner with the other owners.[155]

There have been calls for similar reform in Ireland.[156] With the modern trend to bulk storage and carriage of goods, contracts for sale of goods from bulk are more common especially in the commodity trades. The application of s. 16 as illustrated in cases like *Re Wait* is not in accordance with commercial expectations of such transactions. Thus, it is generally accepted that the law in Ireland should be reformed to protect the pre-paying buyer of unascertained goods from a designated bulk source.

Critics of the UK amendment argue that the scope of the sections is too limited. Although they offer some protection to a buyer who contracts to buy goods from bulk, they have no application where the contract is for wholly unascertained goods and no agreement is made to satisfy the con-

---

[154] 'Sale of Goods Forming Part of a Bulk' (Law Com No 215; Scot Law Com No 145, HC 807, 1993).

[155] See further Bradgate & White, 'Sale of Goods Forming Part of a Bulk: Proposals for Reform', [1994] Lloyd's Maritime and Commercial Law Quarterly 315; Ulph, 'The Sale of Goods (Amendment) Act 1995: co-ownership and the rogue seller', [1996] Lloyd's Maritime and Commercial Law Quarterly 93; Burns, 'Better Late than Never: the Reform of the Law on the Sale of Goods Forming Part of a Bulk', (1996) 59 MLR, 260-271.

[156] White, *Commercial Law* (2002), p 380.

tract from any particular source. Thus, for example, the buyers in *Re Gold-corp Exchange* would not have benefited from the new provisions. It is argued that the law should protect consumers given the growth in online trading and the development of e-commerce generally. There is a need to protect such consumers who pre-pay for unascertained goods prior to delivery.[157]

5.5.3. Appropriation of unascertained goods

(a)   General

As outlined above, in order for ownership of unascertained goods to pass to the buyer, it is required that the goods be ascertained. This means that the goods must be irrevocably appropriated to the contract. This process of appropriation converts the unascertained goods into specific goods. This therefore operates as a major exception to the *solu consensu* principle.

Subject to the requirement that the goods must have been ascertained, property will pass when the parties intend it to pass. In the absence of an express or implied intention, s. 18, Rule 5 applies:

> 'Where there is a contract for the sale of unascertained or future goods by description and goods of that description and in a deliverable state are unconditionally appropriated to the contract, either by the seller with the assent of the buyer or by the buyer with the assent of the seller, the property in the goods then passes to the buyer, and the assent may be express or implied, and may be given either before or after the appropriation is made.'

(b)   'Unconditional appropriation'

The key to Rule 5 is 'unconditional appropriation'. Some act must be done by the seller or the buyer whereby the goods are irrevocably earmarked to the contract. Generally this requires the seller to do some act which puts the goods out of his control so that he cannot use them in the performance of another contract. The earmarking must be unequivocal and unconditional. An act of constructive delivery which puts the goods out of the control of the seller, for example, delivery to a carrier without reserving a right of disposal, almost always constitutes an unconditional appropriation.

Where an unidentified part of a bulk is sold, there is no appropriation until there is a severance of the part sold from the rest and therefore no

---

[157] See further Bradgate, R, *Commercial Law* (2000), p 390-391.

passing of property.[158] The only thing necessary for appropriation is the separation of the part sold from the rest with the assent of the parties.[159]

The meaning of the term 'unconditional appropriation' has been considered on many occasions by the courts.

In *Carlos Federspiel & Co v Charles Twigg & Co Ltd*,[160] the sellers manufactured bicycles to the buyer's order. The buyer paid for the goods in advance. The bicycles were made and packed in containers with the buyer's name and address on them. But before the goods could be shipped, the sellers became insolvent. The issue before the court was who owned the goods. Had they been unconditionally appropriated to the contract? It was held that the property had not passed to the buyers. Pearson J held that a mere setting apart or selection of the goods by the seller which he expects to use in the performance of the contract is not enough. Such conduct was merely an aspect of the internal administration of the seller's business. If that is all he can change his mind and use some other goods in the performance of the contract.

To constitute an appropriation of goods, the parties must have had or be reasonably supposed to have had an intention to attach the contract irrevocably to those goods so that those goods and no others are the subject of the sale and become the property of the buyer.

Usually the appropriating act is the last act to be performed by the seller. For example, if delivery is to be taken at the seller's premises and the seller has put the goods aside, identifies them, informs the buyer that they are ready and buyer agrees to come and take them, that is appropriation and assent to appropriation. But if there is a further act to be done by the seller then there is *prima facie* evidence that property does not pass until the final act is done. Probably in the *Carlos Federspiel* case, the decisive factor was that the sellers were responsible for arranging shipment of the goods and the last act that the seller had to perform was therefore to place the goods on board ship. Hence, the receiver was entitled to remove the bicycles from the crates and sell them to another customer, leaving the buyer an unsecured creditor.

The *Carlos Federspiel* case can be contrasted with *Hendy Lennox Ltd v Graham Puttick Engines Ltd*.[161] There, the agreement was to sell generators. The generators were set aside at seller's premises and marked with the buyer's name. It was held that the generators were appropriated to the contract when S sent B an invoice and delivery note with the serial numbers of the generators. At that stage, the seller had done everything that was needed under the contract. The serial numbers would allow the par-

---

[158] *Laurie & Morewood v John Dudin & Son* [1926] 1 KB 223.

[159] *Aldridge v Johnson* (1857) 7 E & B 885.

[160] [1957] 1 Lloyds Rep 240.

[161] [1984] 1 WLR 485.

ticular generators sold to be identified and nothing remained to be done except for the buyer to pay the invoices and take delivery.

It is important to remember that before goods can be unconditionally appropriated to the contract, they must first be ascertained under s. 16. It is clear that where an unidentified part of a bulk of goods is sold, there can be no appropriation until there is a severance from the rest, as outlined above. So, for example, where goods are delivered to a carrier still mixed with other goods, no property can pass because the goods are still unascertained.[162]

The appropriation must be unconditional. Appropriation is not unconditional if the seller only means to let the buyer have the goods on payment. Any express or implied term of the contract showing that the seller intends to reserve some rights over the goods themselves until he has been fully paid makes the appropriation conditional and no property in the goods passes until this happens.[163]

Rule 5 requires that assent must be given before or after the appropriation is made. The assent may be express or implied. It can be inferred from the circumstances of the case and the nature of the transaction. So, for example, where goods are delivered to a carrier for shipment to the buyer, the goods are taken to be unconditionally appropriated to the contract even where there is no express assent. The buyer's assent is to be inferred from the nature of the transaction itself.

5.6.   The real agreement

Within the Sale of Goods Acts, there is recognition of the concept of the real agreement. Where there is a contract for the sale of unascertained or future goods, for example, s. 18 Rule 5 (1) provides that in order for ownership of unascertained goods to pass to the buyer it is necessary that the goods be unconditionally appropriated to the contract by one party with the consent of the other. In the absence of agreement as to when ownership will pass therefore, apart from the contract itself, a real agreement is required in which the parties agree about the passing of ownership. The 'unconditional appropriation' could be regarded as a real agreement.

5.7.   Right to dispose

In Irish law, ownership can be transferred by someone other than the owner. For example, the law of agency provides that an agent with authority (either express or implied) may enter into valid contracts for the

---

[162] See *Healy v Howlett & Sons* [1917] 1 KB 337.
[163] See *Re Shipton Anderson & Co Ltd and Harrison Bros & Co Ltd* [1915] 3 KB 676.

sale of property on behalf of his principal. Authority of agents may be actual or apparent. Apparent authority is founded on a representation made by the principal or someone acting on behalf of the principal that the agent has the authority to enter into the contract in question. It is possible for a principal to ratify an unauthorised act, provided the requirements for a valid ratification are met. The rules on agency are considered in more detail below.[164]

6. Transfer or acquisition by means of indirect representation

In Irish law, agency is the relationship arising where one person, the principal, appoints another, the agent to bring about, modify or terminate legal relations between the principal and one or more third parties.[165] This includes cases of direct and indirect representation. Irish law draws a distinction between situations where the agency is disclosed and where it is undisclosed. Where the agent contracts as principal so that the agency is undisclosed, the true principal has a right to intervene to enforce the contract and can be sued on it by the other contracting party. In this respect, the common law concept of agency is broader than that of the civil law which generally confines agency to direct representation and treats indirect representation as incapable of conferring rights or imposing liabilities on the principal.

6.1. Where agency is disclosed

Where an agent, with the principal's actual authority, concludes a contract on the principal's behalf with a third party and the agency is disclosed, a direct contractual relationship is created between the principal and the third party, and each party can sue the other on the contract. The agent is not liable on this contract to either the third party or the principal.

If an agent concludes a contract outside his actual authority, but within his apparent authority, the principal will be bound by the contract but cannot enforce it: As apparent authority is based on a form of estoppel it does not give rise to an independent cause of action. Since apparent authority depends on a representation from the principal that the agent has authority, apparent authority can only arise where the purported agency is disclosed.

---

[164] Paragraph 6.
[165] On Agency generally, see White, *Commercial Law*, Chapters 4-7; *Bowstead and Reynolds on Agency* (2001).

If an agent acts without the principal's actual authority, the principal can ratify his actions provided the agent purported to act on his behalf; only a disclosed principal can ratify an unauthorised contract. A direct contractual relationship is created between the principal and the third party and each party can sue the other on the contract. The agent is not liable on this contract to either the third party or to the principal.

6.2.   Where agency is undisclosed

Where an agent contracts with a third party without disclosing that he is acting as an agent, the contract is initially between the agent and the third party. Therefore, the third party can enforce the contract against the agent, and providing the principal does not intervene, the agent can enforce it against the third party. If the third party discovers the identity of the principal, the third party has a choice. The agent remains liable on the contract and the third party may choose to enforce it against either the principal or the agent but not both. In addition, the principal is allowed to intervene and enforce the contract on his own behalf as long as the agent acted with actual authority. This right to intervene is limited in several respects in order to protect the position of third parties. So, an undisclosed principal can only intervene if he was in existence and had capacity to make the contract at the time that it was made. An undisclosed principal can only intervene if the agent had actual authority to conclude the contract. An undisclosed principal cannot intervene if such intervention is prohibited by the contract either expressly or impliedly.[166] An undisclosed principal cannot intervene if it can be shown that the third party contracted with the agent for personal reasons, for example, where it is clear that the third party intended only to contract with the agent due to some personal skill or due to the solvency of the agent.[167]

Where an agent acquires property on behalf of a principal, the question as to whether the principal obtains rights directly in that property or whether the agent acquires those rights for some time and then has to

---

[166] *Humble v Hunter* (1848) 12 QB 310: Where the contract relates to property and describes the agent as having a proprietary interest in the property, the agent may be taken impliedly to have undertaken that no one else has an interest in the contract so that the undisclosed principal will be excluded. See also *Sui Yin Kwan v Eastern Insurance* [1994] 2 AC 199. Here, an undisclosed principal was allowed to intervene to enforce an insurance contract. The insurance contract described the agent as 'the insured'. The Privy Council held that the language of the policy was not such as to exclude intervention. This judgment suggests that in commercial contracts, a court will be slow to exclude an undisclosed principal.

[167] See *Said v Butt* [1920] 3 KB 49; *Dyster v Randall & Sons* [1926] Ch 932.

transfer them to the principal is not clear. It is difficult to say when property passes to the principal where the agent has acquired the goods on the principal's behalf. It is clear that the agent stands in a fiduciary relationship to the principal. On this basis, it has been argued that a person can acquire proprietary rights in equity by operation of law so that where an agent acquires property for an undisclosed principal, he has an equitable duty (arising from the fiduciary duty to act in the best interests of the principal), to deliver that property to the principal or to hold it on behalf of the principal. It could be argued that from the time when the agent acquires the legal property in the goods, then he holds the goods on trust for the principal. The principal would thus have an immediate equitable proprietary right in the movable. In *AG for Hong Kong v Reid*,[168] it was held that an agent who accepted a bribe in breach of his fiduciary duty holds that bribe in trust for the person to whom the duty is owed. However, in *Lister v Stubbs*,[169] it was held that a principal was held to have no proprietary interest in a bribe taken by his employee. There was a duty to account for the bribe but the remedy was characterised *in personam* only. The decision in *AG for Hong Kong v Reid* is controversial for the award of a proprietary remedy has the effect of excluding from the agent's estate an asset which would otherwise be available for its general creditors.[170]

It could also be said that any proprietary interest must relate to an identified asset. For a proprietary interest to arise by operation of law, there must be an obligation imposed on the defendant to transfer an identified asset to the plaintiff. In the context of a breach of the plaintiff's obligations, this will only ever be the case if the remedy for the breach obliges the defendant to transfer a specific asset to the claimant. An award of expectation damages for breach of contractual obligations is not of this form. An award of specific performance would be such a remedy. However, contracts for the sale of goods are rarely specifically enforceable and this would suggest that in the context of a breach of a sales contract, no equitable proprietary interest would arise.[171]

---

[168] [1994] 1 AC 324.

[169] (1890) 45 ChD 1.

[170] Goode argues that the principal's claim should not be recognised as proprietary. See R Goode, 'Proprietary Restitution Claims', in WR Cornish, R Nolan, J O'Sullivan and G Virgo (eds), *Restitution: Past, Present and Future*, (1998), Chapter 5.

[171] See further Worthington, *Personal Property Law, Text and Materials*, Chapter 5.

7.   Consequences of insolvency of transferor or transferee

7.1.   Overview of Irish insolvency procedures

Insolvency law in Ireland can be categorised according to whether the insolvency is that of an individual or of a company. The insolvency of an individual is termed 'bankruptcy'. The term insolvency is mainly used in connection with companies.

7.1.1.   Bankruptcy

Bankruptcy is dealt with by the Bankruptcy Act 1988.[172] A debtor may bring a petition for his/her own adjudication as a bankrupt where s(he) is unable to meet obligations to creditors and where his/her available estate is sufficient to produce at least € 1900.00. A creditor may bring a petition for bankruptcy against a debtor where the debtor has committed an 'act of bankruptcy' within three months beforehand. An act of bankruptcy is an act or default on the debtor's part which makes the debtor liable to be adjudged bankrupt by the court. The various acts of bankruptcy are listed in Section 7 of the Bankruptcy Act 1988, but the most common acts of bankruptcy relied upon by a creditor are (a) failure by the debtor to comply with a bankruptcy summons requesting payment, within fourteen days from service of the summons on the debtor, of a specific sum due; and (b) the seizure of the debtor's goods, or the making of a return of no goods in respect of the debtor, by the sheriff or county registrar.

Once a bankruptcy order has been made, the creditors may appoint an Official Assignee in bankruptcy whose functions are to get in, realise and distribute the bankrupt's estate in accordance with the general scheme on insolvency.

7.1.2.   Company insolvency

There are a number of different procedures in relation to corporate insolvency. These are liquidation, receivership and examinership. Each is provided for in the Companies Act 1963. [173]

The predominant procedure is liquidation. There are three types of liquidation procedure: Members' voluntary winding up, creditors' voluntary

---

[172] On bankruptcy generally, see Forde, *Bankruptcy Law in Ireland* (1990).

[173] On company insolvercny generally, see Courtney, *The Law of Private Companies* (2002); Keane, *Company Law* 3rd ed. (2000); Lynch, Marshall & O'Farrell, *Corporate Insolvency and Rescue: Law and Practice* (1996).

winding up and winding up by order of the court (Official Liquidation). In a member's voluntary winding up the company is solvent, but for whatever reason, the members resolve to wind up the company. A creditor's voluntary winding up occurs where the company resolves at general meeting that it cannot, by reason of its liabilities, continue in business. A winding up by the court occurs where the High Court orders that a company be wound up. The court directly supervises the liquidator. The procedure can however be initiated by a creditor. The court will order that a company be wound up on the grounds set out in s. 213 Companies Act 1963;

(a) where the company resolves to be wound up by special resolution;
(b) where the company does not commence business within one year of incorporation or suspends its business for one year;
(c) where the membership falls below the statutory minimum;
(d) where the company is unable to pay its debts;
(e) where there is 'oppression' that would justify making an order under s. 205 CA63;
(f) where it is 'just and equitable' to order a winding up.

The petition may be presented by the company, a creditor, a contributory, the Minister for Enterprise and Employment or an oppressed person. For all types of liquidation, a liquidator is appointed to the company who will take possession of the company's assets and protect them, make out lists of the creditors and contributories, have disputed claims adjudicated on by the court, realise the assets and apply the proceeds in payment of the company's debts and liabilities in the proper order of priority.

7.1.3. Receivership

A receiver may be appointed by a secured creditor under a debenture. The main function of the receiver is to receive or get in all the assets of the company on behalf of the debenture holder and dispose of them in due course in order to pay off the debt due to the debenture holder. In addition, he is also frequently appointed manager of the company's affairs with power to carry on its business for as long as is necessary. The receiver may be appointed either on application to court or by the debenture holder himself, without any application to the court, in circumstances in which the debenture provides for such appointment. The grounds for appointment will depend on the terms of the debenture itself, and will vary from debenture to debenture. Before a receiver can be appointed on foot of a debenture, there must usually have occurred an act or event of default by the borrower company. These events of default will usually be set out in the debenture. They may include the following;

- whenever the principal sum falling due becomes payable;
- whenever the company fails to pay any instalment or interest;
- whenever the company ceases, or threatens to cease carrying on its business;
- whenever a resolution is passed to wind-up the company;
- whenever the company acts in such a way as to endanger or jeopardise the security created by the debenture; or
- whenever the company is unable to pay its debts.

The receiver's principal function is to realise the debenture holder's security. Under the terms of the debenture, the receiver is usually designated as the company's agent and will obviously owe duties to the company. However, he will also have obligations to the debenture holder to get in the charged assets and realise them and to pay off what is owed to the debenture holder. His primary duty is owed to the debenture holder.

7.1.4. Examinership

This procedure was introduced by the Companies (Amendment) Act 1990. The regime was amended by the Companies (Amendment) Act 1999. A company that is *inter alia*, unable to pay its debts may be placed under the protection of the court for a period of time not exceeding 70 days. The object of such protection is to protect the company from actions by creditors and to allow the appointment of a court official called an 'Examiner' to investigate the affairs of the company and make proposals for its survival through a compromise or scheme of arrangement so as to keep the company (or part of it) alive as a going concern. It is for the court to decide whether any such scheme should be implemented. The examiner's role is an investigating and reporting one. The petition to appoint an examiner may be presented by the company, its directors, a creditor or contingent or prospective creditor, including an employee or a member holding not less than one quarter of the voting shares. The petition must be accompanied by a report of an independent accountant which must contain a statement of affairs of the company and a statement as to whether the company would have a reasonable prospect of survival as a going concern.

7.2.   Avoidance of transactions

7.2.1.   Disclaimer of onerous obligations

Under s. 290 of the Companies Act 1963, the liquidator, with the consent of the court, may disclaim the company's obligations to certain creditors on the grounds that performance of such obligations would be unduly burdensome to the company. Persons whose contracts were disclaimed now have the right to prove in the winding up for a dividend. Almost any contract may be disclaimed including 'unprofitable contracts'. S. 290(1) defines the property and interests which are capable of being disclaimed as that which consists of:

> 'Land of any tenure burdened with onerous covenants, of shares or stock in companies, of unprofitable contracts or any other property which is unsaleable or not readily saleable by reason of its binding the possessor thereof to the performance of any onerous act or to the repayment of any sum of money.'

In *Re Ranks Ireland Ltd*[174] Murphy J restated the principle that all those who had contracted with the company, and whose rights were effected by a disclaimer, could prove in a winding up. It appears that a contract will not be unprofitable merely because the company could have made a better bargain.[175] The Bankruptcy Act 1988 gives a similar power to the Official Assignee in bankruptcy proceedings.[176]

There is no statutory mechanism by which a Receiver may disclaim onerous contracts in a receivership. However, the Receiver is entitled to prevent the company from performing its contractual obligations. The Receiver will not as a general rule, in the absence of bad faith, be liable for a breach of contract by the company, nor be guilty of inducing breach of contract. This is illustrated by *Lathia v Dronsfield Bros Ltd*.[177] According to Sir Neil Lawson:

> 'The receivers can adopt or decline to adopt a contract which the company has entered into and which is unexecuted. It follows from this, and the agency clause, that the agent is personally immune from claims for damages for breach of contract or procurement of breach of contract. The agent has immunity from a claim for inducing breach of contract unless he has not acted bona fide or acted outside the scope of his authority, i.e. has not acted as agent.'[178]

---

174 [1988] ILRM 751.
175 *Squires v AIG Europe (UK) Ltd* [2006] EWCA Civ 7.
176 S. 56 Bankruptcy Act 1988.
177 [1987] BCLC 321.
178 *Ibid*, p 324.

It seems that where a receiver prevents a company from honouring its contracts, he will not be liable in tort for interference with contractual relations if he acted as agent of the company, unless he acted *mala fides* or beyond the scope of his authority.[179]

An Examiner is given statutory power to repudiate contracts. Under s. 7 Companies (Amendment) Act 1990, where an Examiner becomes aware of any actual or proposed act, omission, course of conduct, decision or contract, by or on behalf of the company to which he has been appointed, in relation to the income, assets or liabilities of that company which, in his opinion, is or is likely to be to the detriment of that company, he has full power to take whatever steps are necessary to halt, prevent or rectify the effects of such act, omission, course of conduct, decision or contract. This power is stated to be subject to the rights of parties acquiring an interest in good faith and for value in such income, assets or liabilities. This section was amended by the Companies (Amendment) (No.2) Act 1999, s. 18 which inserted a new section 7 (5A) in to the Companies Amendment Act 1990. This new section provides that examiners may not repudiate contracts entered into by the company prior to its being placed under the protection of the court.

One of the most important principles of Irish insolvency law is that creditors share *pari passu* on the winding up of a company. It is essential that the company should not be allowed to defeat this principle by unfairly preferring one creditor over another before the winding up takes place. In such a case one creditor is enriched at the expense of the general body of creditors. Irish company law legislation provides that the liquidator may investigate such transactions and in some instances, avoid them.

7.2.2.   Fraudulent dispositions of property

Under s. 139 Companies Act 1990, if any assets of the company have been disposed of wrongfully, the company or liquidator may recover them. There would be a remedy in tort or restitution in any event, but s. 139 makes it easier to recover such property. Thus, if company property has been disposed of in any way that defrauded the company, its creditors or members, an application may be made to the court by the creditor or liquidator. If the court is satisfied that the property has been disposed of in this way, it will order its replacement or recovery on such terms and conditions as the court sees fit. S. 139(3) provides that in exercising its discretion, the court must have regard to the rights of persons who have *bona fide* and for value acquired an interest in the property that is the subject matter of the application. Receiv-

---

[179] *Welsh Development Agency v Export Finance Co Ltd* [1992] BCC 270; *Said v Butt* [1920] 2 KB 497.

ers and Examiners may also apply for recovery of property under s. 139.[180] The applicant under s. 139 is not required to prove an intention to defraud, merely that the effect of the disposition was to perpetrate a fraud on the company, its creditors or members. In this context, it seems that fraud means the diversion of property from the entity or person who is lawfully entitled to it. An example would be a gratuitous transfer of company property in favour of its controllers.

It is clear that, under this section, where the effect of a transfer of a movable is to defraud the company, the court may order the revesting of that property in the company.

7.2.3. Bankruptcy – transactions at an undervalue

Under s. 58 of the Bankruptcy Act 1988, in relation to an individual's insolvency, if within three months before he is adjudicated bankrupt a debtor commits an act of bankruptcy and thereafter either sells any of his property at a price which, in the opinion of the Court, is substantially below its market value or enters into or is a party to any other transaction which, in the opinion of the Court, has the effect of substantially reducing the sum available for distribution to the creditors, such transaction shall be void as against the Official Assignee, unless the transaction was *bona fide* entered into and the other party had not at the time of the transaction notice of any prior act of bankruptcy committed by the bankrupt. This is stated not to affect the rights of any person making title in good faith and for valuable consideration through or under a person (other than the bankrupt) who is party to a transaction mentioned therein.[181] Again, this section would have an impact where the sale of a movable was made at an undervalue.

7.2.4. Fraudulent preference

(a)   General

This is the paying or giving of security to one creditor in preference to the others. It is a principle of bankruptcy law made applicable to companies by s. 286 Companies Act 1963.[182]

S. 286(1) Companies Act 1963 provides that:

---

[180] S. 178 and s. 180(2) of Companies Act 1990.

[181] S. 58(2) Bankruptcy Act 1988.

[182] S. 57 Bankruptcy Act 1988 deals with fraudulent preference in the insolvency of an individual.

'Any conveyance, mortgage, delivery of goods, payment, execution or other act relating to property made or done by or against a company which is unable to pay its debts as they become due, in favour of any creditor, with a view to giving such creditor a preference over the other creditors, shall, if the winding up of the company commences within six months, be deemed a fraudulent preference and be invalid.'

In order for this section to apply, the company must have been insolvent at the time the transfer was made, meaning that it was unable to pay its debts as they fell due. It doesn't matter that the directors believed that the company was solvent or that its financial position would shortly improve and it would not have to be wound up. Although most preferences falling within this section are cash payments, transfers of any kind of property can be caught. So, for example, where the company receives goods but hasn't yet paid for them, and then returns the goods to the seller, the return could amount to a preference.

The liquidator (unless dealing with 'connected persons') must prove that the predominant intention of the company when transferring the property to the creditor was to deliberately place that creditor at an advantage over the other creditors.

It is not sufficient that the effect or consequence of the transfer was to place that creditor at an advantage. The motive must have been to prefer. The mere fact of preference does not demonstrate the intent. There are certain stock situations where the courts readily infer an intent to prefer – most notably where a company's directors have given personal guarantees for the company's debts and shortly before the winding up, they arranged to have those debts paid off and the security cancelled. Where there is no direct evidence of intention to prefer, the court may draw an inference of an intention to prefer from the circumstances.[183]

It is now well accepted that where a creditor exerts such pressure on the company so as to overbear the free will of the company, there will be no fraudulent preference.[184]

Under the Companies Act 1990, s. 286 was amended to provide for payments to connected persons. Now, under s. 286(3) Companies Act 1963,[185] a preferential transaction made in favour of a connected person will be invalid if made within two years of the winding up of the company. A transaction will be deemed improper unless the contrary can be shown, therefore the connected person must demonstrate a genuine commercial justification for the company's preferring him over other creditors. 'Con-

---

[183] *Re Station Motors Ltd* [1985] IR 756.

[184] *Re John Daly & Co Ltd* (1886) 19 LR Ir 83; *Corran Construction Ltd v Bank of Ireland Finance Ltd* [1976] ILRM 175.

[185] Inserted by s. 138(3) Companies Act 1990.

nected person' includes a director or shadow director, a director's spouse, parent, sibling or child, a related company, any trustee of or surety or guarantor for the debt due to any person referred to above.[186] In this way the legislature has broadened the scope of the provision by targeting persons who are perceived to be in a special position of trust to the company.

(b) The effect of a fraudulent preference

Where a fraudulent preference is deemed or found to have been made, then the transaction is invalid. S. 286(4) provides that the rights of any person taking title in good faith and for valuable consideration through or under a creditor of the company shall not be affected.

7.3. Effect of insolvency of the transferor

There is relatively little protection provided under Irish law for the transferee against the insolvency of the transferor. If the seller becomes bankrupt or goes into liquidation without having delivered goods, the buyer's ability to enforce against the liquidator or official assignee will depend on whether the property has passed to the buyer. If the property in the goods was still in the seller at the date of the commencement of the winding up, the buyer is restricted to a right to prove in competition with all the other creditors. The rules for the passing of property have been described above and the particular difficulties for the pre-paying buyer of unascertained goods have been noted.[187]

It has been argued that pre-paying buyers of unascertained goods may have an equitable interest in the subject matter of the contract. In *Re Wait*,[188] however, such a claim was unsuccessful. The court found that the mere fact of a sale or an agreement to sell part of a specified bulk did not give the buyer an equitable interest in the goods. The Court of Appeal held that the Sale of Goods legislation represented a definitive and comprehensive statement of the proprietary rights conferred by a sale of goods contract. This decision was approved more recently in *Re Goldcorp*.[189] It is open to the parties to a contract to expressly agree to the creation of equitable rights and include such a term in the sales contract. It should be noted that both *Re Wait* and *Re Goldcorp* were cases which concerned contracts for the sale of unascertained goods. It is possible that in relation

---

[186] S. 286(5) Companies Act 1963.
[187] See above paragraph 4.5.2.
[188] [1927] 1 Ch 606.
[189] [1995] 1 AC 74.

to sales of specific goods, for example, the contract of sale could give rise to an equitable interest before the passing of property. However, the creation of an equitable interest usually depends on the contract being specifically enforceable. It is rare that a sales contract will be held to be specifically enforceable so that such an equitable interest would only arise in exceptional circumstances.

7.4.   Effect of insolvency of the transferee

7.4.1.   General

The insolvency of the transferee will have an impact on the transferor where the property in the goods has been transferred but not yet paid for. The rules for the passing of property in goods have been outlined above, the basic rule in s. 17 being that the property passes when the parties intend it to pass. S. 19(1) provides that the seller may reserve the right of disposal of the goods until certain conditions are fulfilled. Under this provision, it is common for sellers to include an express term in the contract retaining title in the goods until they are paid for. Retention of title clauses are considered below.[190]

7.4.2.   Real remedies of the seller

Sections 38-48 of the 1893 Act give the unpaid seller real remedies which provide some protection against the buyer's inability to pay due to insolvency.

S. 39 gives an unpaid seller three rights:

(a) A lien on the goods or the right to retain them for the price while he is still in possession of them;
(b) A right of stopping the goods in transit after he has parted with possession of them;
(c) A right of resale in certain circumstances.

These rights are available to the 'unpaid seller.' A seller is unpaid where the whole of the price has not been paid or tendered; when a bill of exchange or other negotiable instrument has been received as conditional payment, and the condition on which it was received has not been fulfilled by reason of the dishonour of the instrument or otherwise. Seller includes a person who is acting as an agent of the seller. This definition is

---

[190] Paragraph 12.

wide – so, for example, where goods are sold on credit, a seller remains unpaid until the whole of the price has been paid or tendered. Where the seller has received a conditional payment such as a cheque, the seller is unpaid until the condition is fulfilled.

(a)   Unpaid seller's lien

The seller's lien is a right to retain the goods until the whole of the purchase price has been paid or tendered.[191] A lien is simply a right to retain possession of the goods. An unpaid seller is given a lien in three situations:

(a) Where goods are sold without the parties making any agreement about credit;
(b) Where goods are sold on credit but the agreed terms of the credit expired;
(c) Where the buyer becomes insolvent.

The combined effect of (a) and (b) is that if the goods were sold on credit, the seller cannot exercise a lien until the credit period has expired.

Insolvency is defined as a situation where the person either ceased to pay his debts in the ordinary course of business or he cannot pay his debts as they become due.[192]

A lien may be lost in several ways:

It will be lost where possession is lost and a seller does not regain his lien merely because he obtains possession of the goods again. Hence, the lien is lost, for example, where the seller delivers the goods to the buyer, his agent or an independent carrier for transmission to the buyer.[193] The seller loses the lien where he has waived it. Where the full price is paid, the seller ceases to be an unpaid seller and therefore loses the lien.

(b)   Stoppage in transit

If the buyer becomes insolvent, s. 44 gives the unpaid seller a right of stoppage in transit. He has the right to 'resume possession of the goods as long as they are in the course of transit' and to retain them until payment is made or tendered.

The right is exercised by the seller taking possession of the goods or giving notice to the carrier. It is lost when the transit ends and the goods

---

[191] S. 41 1893 Act.
[192] S. 62(3) 1893 Act.
[193] S. 43 1893 Act.

are delivered to the buyer or his agent. Once the carrier is notified that this right is being exercised, he must redeliver the goods in accordance with the seller's directions but the cost of such redelivery will be borne by the seller. Goods are in transit when they have passed out of the possession of the seller into the possession of an independent carrier, but have not yet reached the destination of the buyer.[194] The transit is deemed to have ended where the buyer or his agent obtains delivery of the goods before their arrival at the appointed destination, or where the carrier wrongfully refused to deliver the goods to the buyer or his agent.[195]

(c)   Right of re-sale

Under s. 48(2) a seller who has exercised his right of lien or stoppage in transit may, in certain circumstances re-sell the goods.
    This right of resale is available where:

(a) The goods are perishable; or
(b) The seller gives the buyer notice that he intends to resell the goods and the buyer fails within a reasonable time to tender the price; or
(c) Resale is authorised by the contract.[196]

The consequences of a resale are that:

(a) The original contract of sale is terminated and the seller may claim damages from the buyer for any losses he suffers as a result of the buyer's breach of contract: For instance, the difference between the original contract price and the amount realised on the resale; and
(b) The resale passes a good title to the goods to the second buyer to whom the goods are resold even if property in the goods had already passed to the first buyer.[197]

If the seller exercises his right to resell, he does so for his own benefit and he is entitled to any profit made on re-sale. He also may claim damages for losses suffered as a result of the buyer's failure to pay.

---

[194] S. 45(1).
[195] S. 45(6).
[196] S. 48(4).
[197] S. 48(2).

8. Passing of property and risk

8.1. General rule

The basic common law rule that applies in Irish law is that the owner of property bears the risk of its damage, deterioration or destruction. This is summed up in the maxim *res perit domino*: The risk is with the owner unless the parties have agreed otherwise. This is reflected in s. 20 of the 1893 Act which provides that in the absence of agreement to the contrary, the goods are at the seller's risk until the property is transferred, whereupon the risk will transfer to the buyer, regardless of whether the goods were or were not delivered. Thus, it is the rules on the passing of property considered above, which will determine who must bear the loss of accidental damage or destruction. In the absence of express agreement, generally, the risk in specific goods in a deliverable state passes once the contract is made, and the risk in unascertained goods passes when they are unconditionally appropriated to the contract in accordance with s. 18, Rule 5.

In *Clarke v Michael Reilly & Sons*,[198] the plaintiff agreed to buy a new car in exchange for his old car and cash. He was permitted to retain his old car until the one he had bought could be delivered. Before he took delivery of the new car, he crashed and damaged the old car. It was held that the property in the old car had passed to the buyers once the contract was made, and therefore the risk passed to the buyers at that time.

In *Healey v Howlett & Sons*,[199] the issue was who should bear the loss caused by the deterioration of a consignment of fish being sent from Kerry to London. It was held that the risk was still with the seller when the defective consignment was discovered. Property and risk would not pass until the goods were ascertained and unconditionally appropriated to the contract.

8.2. Exceptions to the general rule

The rule in s. 20 may be excluded by express or implied agreement. It is also subject to some exceptions and modifications. The parties may, by express agreement, allocate the risk according to how they see fit. Even where the contract contains no express term as to the allocation of risk, it may be possible to find an implied agreement based on the circumstances of the case. For example, in *Stern v Vickers Ltd*,[200] the purchaser agreed to buy a part of a larger bulk (120,000 gallons of spirit from a total quantity

---

[198] 94 ILTR 96.
[199] [1917] 1 KB 337.
[200] [1923] 1 KB 78.

of 200,000 gallons in a storage tank) and obtained a delivery order in respect of the goods. It was held that the risk passed to him at that point even though the property had not yet passed. The case may be explained in that, by exchanging the delivery order, which would help the buyer transfer the goods to third parties, the parties intended that the risk should pass at that time.

Where delivery of the goods was delayed due to the fault of the buyer or of the seller, s. 20(2) stipulates that the party at fault bears the risk of loss which resulted directly from that delay. It must be shown that the loss in question would not have occurred but for the delayed delivery. In that event, the party who caused the delay incurs the loss.[201]

Under s. 20(3), where either seller or buyer is a bailee of the goods for the other party, and loss or damage to the goods occurs as a result of their fault, they will be liable accordingly.

---

[201] *Demby Hamilton & Co Ltd v Barden* [1949] 1 All ER 435.

Part III:
Original acquisition

9. Acquisition by accession, commixture, specification

There is little common law authority on the rules applying to alterations and mixtures. Where such issues arise, judges have often therefore had regard to the traditional Roman law doctrines. The Roman law divides the problem into three scenarios. *Accessio*: Where property might become attached to the property of another owner. *Confusio* and *Commixtio*: Where the original owner's property might become confused or mingled with property belonging to other owners and *Specificatio*: Where the original owner's property might lose its physical identity because it is used in some manufacturing process. The Roman law solutions do not necessarily accord with those of the common law however, the different categories remain relevant to the treatment of the topic.

9.1. Accessio

The traditional Roman rule is that the right of accession gives the property in the whole to the owner of the principal chattel, which is probably that which is the greater in value.[202] The degree of annexation sufficient to constitute an accession must be decided and in addition, it must also be established which of the chattels is the principal one.

In *Hendy Lennox Ltd v Grahame Puttick Ltd*[203] the seller supplied diesel engines to the buyer which were to be incorporated in 'diesel generating sets' but which could be detached in 'several hours' by removing bolts and connections, both the engines and generating sets remaining intact. The engines could be identified by the serial numbers marked on them. Staughton J held that the proprietary rights of the seller to the engines were unaffected by this incorporation as 'they just remained engines albeit connected to other things.' There had been no accession and the sellers therefore had a proprietary claim to the engines. So the test used here was that of severability or 'injurious removal', *i.e.*, could there be a

---

[202] *Crossley Vaines on Personal Property*, *op cit*, Chapter 19, p 432.
[203] [1984] Ch 131.

separation of the original chattels without destroying or seriously injuring the whole? Other tests have been suggested which are derived from commonwealth and U.S. decisions: The test of 'separate existence', *i.e.*, whether the incorporated chattel ceased to exist as a separate chattel; whether the removal of the incorporated chattel would destroy the utility of the principal chattel, and finally, the test of the degree and purpose of annexation.[204]

There is also the possibility that the common law may resolve the problem by providing that where the parties' respective contributions can be assessed, they should become co-owners of the merged whole. However, there is little support for this approach in the case-law.[205]

It should be noted that contractual terms may provide that the owner shall acquire any additions made to the goods or that the end product is to belong exclusively to one party.

9.2.   Commixture or confusion

In this situation, goods belonging to different owners are mixed so that they can no longer be identified and separated, even though their physical identity remains intact. Traditionally, Roman law distinguished between *confusio* (wet mixtures) and *commixtio* (dry mixtures). Roman law considered that the elements of wet mixtures lost their physical identity but that the elements of dry mixtures did not. Thus, different considerations applied to each type of mixture. Common law does not make this distinction. The acquisition of ownership through intermixture can occur when both types of goods are mixed, but only where separation of the mixed goods is impossible or impracticable.

Where the mixing of the goods is not the fault of any of the parties, provided the goods are of substantially the same nature and quality, the mixture will belong to them both as tenants in common, their shares being in the same proportion as their contributions.[206]

Where the mixing was the wrongful act of one of the parties, the rule is apparently the same. In *Indian Oil Corporation Ltd v Greenstone Shipping Company SA*,[207] the owners of an oil tanker wrongfully mixed cargo they were carrying with some of their own oil. Staughton J held that the mixture was held in common by them and the persons entitled to the cargo. He held

---

[204] *Ibid.*

[205] See further Bell, *Modern Law of Personal Property in England and Ireland*, Chapter 4, p 73, and Worthington, *Proprietary Interests in Commercial Transactions* (1996), pp 135-143.

[206] *Spence v The Union Marine Insurance Co Ltd* (1868) LR 3 CP 427.

[207] [1987] 3 All ER 893.

that where one of the parties wrongfully mixes the goods with the goods of the other which are substantially of the same nature and quality, and they cannot in practice be separated, the mixture is held in common and the innocent party is entitled to receive out of it a quantity equal to that of his goods which went into the mixture. If there is a doubt as to the quantity, this is resolved in favour of the innocent party. The innocent party is also entitled to claim damages from the other for any loss he may have suffered, in respect of quality or otherwise, by reason of the mixing of the goods.

If the elements mixed are of different qualities, and the difference is a substantial one, the mixture will be a new entity and the rules as to *specificatio* will apply.

9.3. Specificatio

This applies to a situation where the property ceases to be identifiable because it is processed to create a new product. In this case, the question to be answered is whether the materials used have truly lost their identity. If they have, then they, and any property rights in them will have ceased to exist and the ownership of the new product will vest in the creator, unless he is a wrongdoer. In *Borden (UK) Ltd v Scottish Timber Products Ltd*,[208] the plaintiff supplied resin to manufacturers subject to a retention of title clause. It was used with other materials in the making of chipboard. The Court of Appeal held that this processing destroyed the identity of the resin and the processed chipboard belonged solely to the manufacturers.

This right of the manufacturer to the processed goods may be varied by agreement. This is particularly relevant in the context of retention of title clauses. Where a manufacturer buys materials subject to such a clause, the supplier may stipulate that he shall be the owner of any products made with them until they are paid for. The validity of such terms in retention of title clauses is subject to some debate.[209]

If the manufacturer is using materials he is not entitled to use, combining them with his own to create a new product, the question as to ownership is not clear. It has been argued that the product is owned by those whose materials have been used and that the creator has no interest in it.[210] This is an application of the principle that a person cannot acquire property rights by a wrongful act.[211] An alternative view is that the creator owns the product but is liable in conversion for the materials used. However, in a recent case, a different approach was taken. In *Glen-*

---

[208] [1981] Ch 25.

[209] This point is considered in more detail below at para 12.

[210] See Goode, *Proprietary Rights and Insolvency in Sales Transactions* (1989), p 80.

[211] *Blades v Higgs* (1865) 11 HLC 621.

core International v Metro Trading International Inc,[212] it was held that the new product is shared in common, in accordance with the respective contributions of the parties and with any doubt as to the value of the contributions being resolved in favour of the innocent party.

10.   The rules of good faith acquisition

10.1.   The nemo dat principle

'In the development of our law, two principles have striven for mastery. The first is for the protection of property: no one can give better title than he himself possesses. The second is for the protection of commercial transactions: the person who takes in good faith and for value without notice should get a better title. The first principle has held sway for a long time, but it has been modified by the common law itself and by statute so as to meet the needs of our time.'[213] per Denning LJ in *Bishopsgate Motor Finance Corpn Ltd v Transport Brakes Ltd.*

This extract summarises the common law position with regard to title conflicts. It is a basic rule of property law that no one can transfer a better title than he himself has: *Nemo dat quod non habet*. This rule applies to sales of goods and other forms of property, gifts, bailments and other contracts such as hire and hire-purchase. However, over time, a number of exceptions have been established both by common law and by statute to protect the *bona fide* purchaser for value. The statutory exceptions are to be found in the Sale of Goods Act 1893, the Factors Act 1889 and the Consumer Credit Act 1995.

The fundamental rule in relation to sales is re-stated in s. 21 Sale of Goods Act 1893:

'Subject to the provisions of this Act, where goods are sold by a person who is not the owner thereof ... the buyer acquires no better title to the goods than the seller had ...'

In situations of title conflict, the buyer (B) may discover that having acquired goods, they are claimed by another person, (O) who claims that he is the true owner of the goods, or has a prior right to possession of them and was dispossessed of them by the wrongful act of the seller (S) or of a third party. B may be entirely innocent but the owner will generally seek to recover the goods from him by suing in the tort of conversion. The court must decide on these conflict disputes applying the *nemo dat* principle and the exceptions thereto. If B succeeds in a defence based on the exceptions to the

---

[212] [2001] 1 Lloyds Rep 284.
[213] [1949] 1 KB 322.

nemo dat principle, he will acquire a title to the goods superior to that of O. Where the goods are sold in a chain, B must examine each of the transactions in the chain to see if any fall within the exceptions to *nemo dat*. If any of the transactions fall within any of the exceptions, all subsequent parties in the chain will have a good defence to O's claim.

10.2. Exceptions to the nemo dat rule

10.2.1. The Factors Act 1889

From the eighteenth century onwards, it became common for trade to be carried on through 'factors' – agents who sold goods for their principals. Factors generally contracted in their own names without disclosing the principal's identity and often also traded on their own behalf. It was established that these factors had general authority to sell and that if a factor sold disregarding an instruction from his principal, the sale would be nonetheless effective. However, it became common for factors to dispose of goods by pledging them pending an eventual sale. The courts refused to recognise the authority of the factor to bind his principal to make such a pledge effective against the principal without his express consent. In 1823, the first of five Factors Acts was passed to extend the common law protection of persons dealing with factors.

The Factors Act of 1889 remains in force. It does not limit itself to dealing with factors as such but lays down the power of disposition of the 'mercantile agent'. S. 2(1) provides:

'Where a mercantile agent is, with the consent of the owner, in possession of goods or of the documents of title to the goods, any sale, pledge or other disposition of the goods made by him when acting in the ordinary course of business as a mercantile agent, shall, subject to the provisions of this Act, be as valid as if he were expressly authorised by the owner of the goods to make the same; provided that the person taking under the disposition acts in good faith, and has not, at the time of the disposition, notice that the person making the disposition has not authority to take same.'

Thus, where the facts of a case come within this provision, the effect of a disposition by a mercantile agent is as if the agent was expressly authorised to dispose of the goods. Hence, the owner of the goods is bound by the disposition even where the agent lacks any form of authority. The original owner's title is extinguished and the *bona fide* purchaser or disponee acquires good title and is protected against any claims by the original owner.

There are a number of matters to be considered in relation to this provision:

(a)   The meaning of mercantile agent

S. 1(1) Defines a mercantile agent as:

> 'a mercantile agent having in the customary course of his business as such
> agent authority either to sell goods or to consign goods for the purpose of sale,
> or to buy goods, or to raise money on the security of goods.'

The mercantile agent must be an agent. He may act for a disclosed or an
undisclosed principal. He must act as an agent for the purposes of making
dispositions. This does not necessarily mean that he must be an agent for
sale. The definition includes agents whose business is the pledging, mort-
gaging or charging of goods. The mercantile agent must have a business
or at least be acting in a business capacity with the owner of goods.[214]

(b)   The mercantile agent must be in possession

S. 1(2) of the Factors Act provides that a person shall be deemed to be in
possession of the goods if the goods (or documents of title) are in his
actual custody or are held by any other person subject to his control or on
his behalf.

It has been held that the mercantile agent must be in possession of the
goods at the time the disposition is made.[215] In addition, the mercantile
agent must be in possession of the goods in his capacity as such.[216]

Documents of title include not just those documents recognised at
common law as documents of title but are defined to include many other
documents including:

> 'any bill of lading, dock, warrant, warehouse-keeper's certificate, and warrant
> or order for the delivery of goods, and any other document used in the ordi-
> nary course of business as proof of possession or control of goods, or authoris-
> ing or purporting to authorise, either by endorsement or by delivery, the pos-
> sessor of the document to transfer or receive goods thereby represented.'[217]

---

[214] *Budberg v Jerwood* (1934) 51 TLR 99.
[215] *Beverley Acceptances Ltd v Oakley* [1982] RTR 417.
[216] *Heap v Motorists Advisory Agency Ltd* [1923] 1 KB 147.
[217] S. 1(4) 1889 Act.

(c)   In possession with the consent of the owner

S. 2(1) requires that the mercantile agent must have possession with the consent of the owner. The owner's consent is presumed to exist unless disproved.[218] Withdrawal of consent is ineffective unless the third party has notice of the fact.[219] Provided that the owner has given consent to the mercantile agent's possession, it is irrelevant that the mercantile agent obtained this consent by deception.[220] It has been held, however that this exception to the *nemo dat* principle does not apply where the goods or documents of title to them were stolen from the owner.[221]

(d)   Ordinary course of business

The disposition must have been made in the ordinary course of business of a mercantile agent. This has been interpreted widely to mean that the agent '...should act within business hours, at a proper place of business and in other respects in the ordinary way in which a mercantile agent would act, so that there is nothing to lead the pledge to suppose that anything wrong is being done, or to give him notice that the disposition is one which the mercantile agent has no authority to make.'[222]

(e)   Good faith and without notice

To avail of this exception to the *nemo dat* principle, the person who deals with the mercantile agent must do so in good faith and without notice of the agent's lack of authority. Good faith is not defined in the Act, however, it seems that the requirement is related to the 'ordinary course of business' requirement. Thus, if there is a departure from the ordinary course of business, this may suggest dishonesty and put the third party on notice that the circumstances are suspicious. The burden of proof is on the person dealing with the mercantile agent to show good faith and lack of notice.[223] The equitable doctrine of constructive notice is not sufficient to constitute notice in this context.[224]

---

[218] *Ibid*, s. 2(4).

[219] *Ibid*, s. 2(2).

[220] See *Pearson v Rose Young Ltd* [1951] 1 KB 275.

[221] See *National Employers Mutual General Insurance Association Ltd v Jones* [1990] 1 AC 24.

[222] *Oppenheimer v Attenborough & Son* [1908] 1 KB 560.

[223] S. 2(1); see *Heap v Motorists Advisory Agency Ltd* [1923] 1 KB 557.

[224] *Forsythe International (UK) Ltd v Silver Shipping Co. Ltd* [1994] 1 WLR 1334.

10.2.2. Agency

Under the Sale of Goods Act 1893, an owner will be bound by any disposition of goods made by an agent acting within his authority. S. 21(1) provides that:

> 'subject to this Act, where goods are sold by a person who is not their owner, and who does not sell them under the authority of or with the consent of the owner, the buyer acquires no better title to the goods than the seller had, unless the owner of the goods is by his conduct precluded from denying the seller's authority to sell.'

In addition to this provision, s. 61 of the Act preserves the common law rules of agency. Thus an owner is bound by any disposition of his goods by an agent acting with his authority or consent. Where an agent has any of the recognised forms of authority, whether actual, apparent, usual or by ratification, the owner will be bound by a disposition of his goods. Where an agent exceeds his authority or consent, the disposition will not bind the principal and the principal will be able to recover the goods from a purchaser. However, in many cases, the agent will be a mercantile agent within the meaning of the Factors Act 1889 and may have the power under that Act to dispose of the principal's goods.

10.2.3. Estoppel

S. 21 provides that the *nemo dat* rule applies 'unless the owner of the goods is by his conduct precluded from denying the seller's authority to sell.' This reproduces the common law principle of estoppel. A person who buys from someone other than the owner may acquire a title to the goods where the owner is precluded or estopped from denying the seller's right to sell the goods. This exception may apply in a case where the owner represents that the seller is the owner's agent as in cases of apparent authority. However, it also includes a situation where the owner's conduct makes it appear that the seller is the true owner of the goods. This may be described as 'apparent ownership'. An estoppel is generally created by a representation made by the person estopped which is relied upon by the person to whom it is made. It is clear that the owner's representation may be by words or conduct. The representation must be one of fact and must be unambiguous, and must be relied upon. The exception has in general, been narrowly interpreted. In *Central Newbury Car Auctions Ltd v Unity Finance Ltd*,[225] the plaintiffs, dealers in motor cars, had

---

[225] [1957] 1 QB 371.

been tricked by a rogue into allowing him to take possession of a car and its registration book, believing that he was intending to purchase the car on hire purchase terms. The rogue sold the car to the first defendants, who in turn, sold it to the second defendants. The plaintiff traced the car and sued the defendants in conversion. The Court of Appeal held that there was no estoppel. Simply handing over the car to use it as a potential hirer was no representation to the world of any general authority. The handing over of the registration book was not relevant as it was not a document of title.

Estoppel may be based on the owner's negligence. Where the owner has been careless and through his negligence he has allowed another to appear as if he was in fact the owner, it may be that the true owner will be estopped from asserting his title. However, it seems that the owner's negligence in dealing with his property will not estop him from recovering it from an innocent buyer unless he owes a duty of care to the buyer. In addition, the purchaser would have to prove that the duty of care was breached and that the breach of duty was the proximate and effective cause of the purchaser entering the transaction by which he obtained the goods. In *Moorgate Mercantile Co v Twitchings*,[226] the plaintiff was a hire purchase company which had let a vehicle on hire purchase. The plaintiff had failed to inform the Hire Purchase Information (HPI), an organisation of which the plaintiff was a member, which kept a register of vehicles subject to hire purchase agreements. The hirer sold the vehicle to a motor dealer, also a member of HPI, who had checked the register and found no entry with respect to it. The dealer then sold the vehicle to a private purchaser. The plaintiff company sued the dealer in conversion and succeeded. The House of Lords held that the company was under no duty to register the hire purchase agreement with HPI. Although registration was general practice, the HPI rules did not actually require registration to be made. The failure to register did not amount to estoppel by negligence and the purchaser did not get good title. Under English law, it appears that the courts will be reluctant to allow an estoppel based on the owner's negligence. It has been suggested that the Irish courts may be more willing to allow such a claim, being in principle more amenable to recognising a duty of care to avoid economic loss and to compensate for pure economic loss.[227]

---

[226] [1977] AC 890.
[227] See White, *Commercial Law* (2002), Chapter 19. See also McMahon & Binchy, *Law of Torts*, Chapter 10.

10.2.4. Market overt

S. 22 of the 1893 Act provides:

> 'Where goods are sold in market overt, according to the usage of the market,
> the buyer acquires a good title to the goods, provided he buys them in good
> faith and without notice of any defect or want of title on the part of the seller.'

This exception has been part of the common law since the fifteenth century. In the Middle Ages, the buying and selling of goods took place in
only limited situations. The important places of commerce were the public fairs and markets and the major ports, such as London and Bristol.
Sales in these places came to be protected by the Market Overt rule
which conferred on the buyer a good title even if the goods were stolen
property. The rationale for the rule was that where goods were stolen, the
onus was placed on the owner to go to the markets to seek his goods. If an
owner failed in this endeavour, and the goods were sold at market, the
buyer took a good title. This encouraged trading at markets and thus
promoted commercial dealings. In addition, the rule distinguished between those who bought honestly and those who did not. A purchase in a
public market was open for all to see whereas private transactions were
viewed as being open to suspicion.

For the rule to apply, the sale must take place in an open, public and
legally constituted market established by Royal Charter, statute or custom. A private market or a car-boot sale, for example, would not qualify
as a market overt. The sale must take place between sunrise and sunset.
The buyer must act in good faith and without notice of any defect in the
seller's title to the goods.

This rule is an anachronism and the rationale for its existence no
longer applies. It was abolished in England by the Sale of Goods (Amendment) Act 1994.[228] It has been acknowledged by many that this section is
in need of urgent review in Ireland.[229] Commentators argue that it should
either be abolished or extended to encompass sales from all retail out-
lets.[230]

---

[228] See Twelfth Report of the Law Reform Committee, 'Transfer of Title to Chattels'
(1966); Prof Diamond's *Review of Security Interests in Property* (1989).

[229] See White, *op cit*, Chapter 19, p 414; Bell, *Modern Law of Personal Property in
England and Ireland*, Chapter 21, p 479.

[230] See White, *op cit*, Chapter 19, p 415.

10.2.5. Voidable title

S. 23 of the 1893 Act provides:

> 'when the seller of goods has a voidable title thereto, but his title has not been avoided at the time of the sale, the buyer acquires a good title to the goods, provided he buys them in good faith and without notice of the seller's defect in title.'

The section only applies where the seller's title is voidable. This can apply where the transaction was induced by misrepresentation or duress or undue influence; or where the seller's title is defective because one of his predecessors in title acquired the goods under a voidable contract. So, for example, where A sells goods to O, but is induced to do so, for example because of misrepresentation, A has a right to rescind. If O then sells the goods on to B and O's title has not been avoided at the time of the sale to B, B may nevertheless acquire a good title to the goods provided he buys them in good faith and without notice of O's defect in title.

Anderson v Ryan[231] provides a good example of the operation of the section. In this case, Davis owned a mini car. He answered an advertisement offering a Sprite car for sale. The parties agreed to swap vehicles without monetary consideration. The Sprite was a stolen car. Davis was dispossessed of the Sprite but the police eventually returned the Mini car to him. In the meantime, the Mini had been the subject of two subsequent deals. The defendant, Ryan bought the car from a person representing himself as Davis. This person was probably the person who had misrepresented himself as the owner of the Sprite. The defendant then sold the mini to the plaintiff, Anderson, who was dispossessed of it by the police. Anderson sued Ryan claiming that under s. 12(1) and s. 21(1) of the Sale of Goods Act 1893, Ryan lacked title to the goods at the time of transfer of the property to him, Anderson. The High Court found that the issue to be decided was whether Ryan had good title to the car when he sold it to Anderson. Davis, the original owner had parted with the car relying on a fraudulent misrepresentation. This rendered the contract voidable. The contract between Davis and rogue had not been avoided before the sale between Anderson and Ryan had been concluded. As a result, Ryan had a valid but voidable title to the car under s. 23(1) of the Sale of Goods Act 1893. This voidable title was transferred to Anderson. The court found that the seizure of the Mini by the police was a wrongful act and redress should be sought from that direction.

An important issue is when exactly is a contract rescinded. It has been held that the transferor (A) must establish clearly and unequivocally that

---

[231] [1967] IR 34.

he terminates the contract and is no longer bound by it. There is no need to obtain a formal court order. The general rule is that the transferor must communicate his decision to the transferee, however, in *Car and Universal Finance Ltd v Caldwell*,[232] the English Court of Appeal held that if the transferee dishonestly absconds or hides so that he cannot be traced by the transferor, it is enough for the transferor to take all steps possible to regain the goods. In that case, when unable to trace the fraudulent transferee, the transferor contacted the police and the automobile association and informed them of the fraud. This was sufficient to achieve rescission. This decision has been criticised on the basis that it makes the innocent third party suffer because of the transferee's dishonesty in making himself untraceable. The effect of the decision is limited in any event because of the decision in *Newtons of Wembley v Williams*,[233] where it was held that if the transferor exercises his right to rescind, but the transferor retains possession of the goods, he is still a buyer in possession who can confer a good title under s. 25(2) Sale of Goods Acts.

The buyer must act in good faith and without notice of the seller's defect in title. However, the burden of proof under s. 23 is different from the other exceptions to the *nemo dat* rule. It is for the original owner to prove that the purchaser did not act in good faith.[234] This rule has been criticised on the basis that requiring an owner to prove a third party's bad faith is more difficult than requiring a third party to prove his good faith.[235]

S. 23 does not apply where the seller has no title at all, such as where the goods are stolen, nor does it apply to void, as opposed to voidable contracts.

10.2.6. Seller in possession

S. 25 of the 1893 Act is designed to protect persons who deal with sellers or buyers in possession of goods but who no longer, or do not yet, own them. It provides that:

'Where a person having sold goods continues or is in possession of the goods, or of the documents of title to the goods, the delivery or transfer by that person, or by a mercantile agent acting for him, of the goods or documents of title under any sale, pledge or other disposition thereof, to any person receiving the

---

[232] [1965] 1 QB 525.

[233] [1965] 1 QB 560.

[234] See *Whitehorn Brothers v Davison* [1911] 1 KB 463.

[235] The UK Law Reform Committee recommended reversal of this burden of proof, see Twelfth Report of the Law Reform Committee, 'Transfer of Title to Chattels' (1966), paragraph 25.

same in good faith and without notice of the previous sale, shall have the same effect as if the person making the delivery or transfer were expressly authorised by the owner of the goods to make the same.'

This provision was found necessary as the mercantile agent's exception was held not to apply to the case where a seller of goods remains in possession of them and resells them. As a result, s. 8 Factors Act 1889 was enacted and remains in force. The wording of s. 25 of the Sale of Goods Act is almost identical and the two provisions can be used in the alternative.

The provision covers a situation where a person (S) who has contracted to sell goods, retains possession of them even after the contract of sale and thus appears to own the goods, even if property in them has already passed to the first buyer (B1). A second buyer (B2) may deal with the seller as if he were still the owner of the goods and agree to buy the same goods. S. 25 may protect B2 and bestow full title on him.

S must be in possession at the time of the sale and there must be continuity of possession prior to the sale. The provision applies regardless of the capacity in which S remains in possession of the goods. In *Pacific Motor Auctions Property Ltd v Motor Credits (Hire Finance) Ltd*,[236] a motor dealer, S, transferred cars to B1, a finance company, under a financing arrangement, but retained possession as B1's agent. It was held that seller in possession exception applied. It was irrelevant in what capacity the seller had possession. In *Worcester Works Finance Ltd v Cooden Engineering Ltd*,[237] the court confirmed that continuity of physical possession is sufficient. The capacity in which the seller is in possession is not relevant. This case was approved in Ireland in *Hanley v ICC Finance*.[238] In this case, the defendant purchased a car from the seller, a car dealer, and then leased the car back to a company wholly owned by the seller. At the end of the leasing period, the seller was to re-purchase the car. The defendant retained the car's registration book but it was returned to the lessee for the purpose of allowing it to tax the car. While in the lessee's possession, the plaintiff purchased the car. The lessee then went into liquidation. The court found that the car was at all relevant times in the possession of the seller. Accordingly, the motor dealers gave good title to the car to the plaintiff under s. 25.

S. 25 requires that the goods be delivered or transferred to B2 if he is to get priority. It has been held that a constructive delivery will suffice as delivery or transfer.[239]

---

[236] [1965] AC 867.

[237] [1972] 1 QB 210.

[238] [1996] ILRM 463.

[239] *Michael Gerson (Leasing) Ltd v Wilkinson* [2001] QB 514.

S. 25 refers to a sale, pledge or 'other disposition'. 'Other disposition' has been given a wide meaning but the disposition to B2 must involve the creation of a proprietary interest, rather than a mere possessory interest.[240] Where B2 takes the goods under 'any other disposition', the nature of B2's interest will depend on the nature of the disposition. For example, where B2 takes the goods under a pledge, B1 will own the goods subject to a pledge.

The section applies where B2 acquires the goods in good faith and without notice of S's defect in title. The burden of proof is on B2 to prove that he acted in good faith and without notice.

10.2.7. Buyer in possession

S. 25(2) states:

> 'where a person having bought or agreed to buy goods obtains, with the consent of the seller, possession of the goods or the documents of title to the goods, the delivery or transfer by that person, or by a mercantile agent acting for him, of the goods or documents of title, under any sale pledge or other disposition thereof, to any person receiving the same in good faith and without notice of any lien, or other right of the original seller in respect of the goods, shall have the same effect as if the person making the delivery or transfer were a mercantile agent in possession of the goods or documents of title with the consent of the owner.'

This is designed to deal with the situation where a buyer having bought or agreed to buy goods, takes delivery and then disposes of them before the property in the goods has passed to him.

The buyer must have bought or agreed to buy the goods. S. 25(2) only applies where possession of the goods was acquired under a sale or agreement for a sale. It does not apply therefore to hire purchase agreements or agency agreements, or contracts for work and materials.

The buyer must be in possession of the goods or the documents of title to the goods with the consent of the seller. So, a thief cannot pass good title under s. 25(2). At the time of the disposition to the second buyer, the first buyer must be in actual or constructive possession of the goods or documents of title to them. Provided that the first buyer acquired possession of the goods with the seller's consent, it is irrelevant that the seller withdraws his consent prior to the first buyer's disposition of them. It is also irrelevant that the first buyer obtained his consent by deceiving

---

[240] *Worcester Works Finance Ltd v Cooden Engineering Ltd* [1972] 1 QB 210.

him.[241] However, it has been held that this exception to the *nemo dat* principle does not apply where the goods or documents of title were stolen from the owner.[242]

As with s. 25(1) there must be delivery of the goods or transfer of documents of title. In *Four Point Garage Ltd v Carter*,[243] it was held that where the seller, at the request of the first buyer, himself delivers the goods directly to the second buyer, this is enough to bring the second buyer within the protection of s. 25(2). The first buyer is in constructive possession at the time of his instruction to the seller and there is a constructive delivery from the first buyer to the second buyer that is sufficient for the application of the section.

As with the other exceptions, the second buyer must act in good faith and without notice of any rights of the seller. The burden of proof is on the second buyer to prove that he acted in good faith and without notice.

S. 25(2) makes reference to the disposition by the first buyer to the second buyer having the same effect as if the first buyer 'were a mercantile agent in possession of goods with the consent of the owner.' The English courts have interpreted this to mean that the first buyer must act in the way in which a mercantile agent acting in the ordinary course of business would act in disposing of the goods.[244] So, for example, where goods are sold in unusual circumstances, a court might find that s. 25(2) would not apply. This interpretation has been criticised as reading into the statute a meaning which is not there.[245] The question has not come before an Irish court and it is not clear whether the same interpretation would be adopted if it did.

It has also been held that since a disposition by a mercantile agent is only binding on the owner of the goods if the agent is in possession of them with the consent of the owner, s. 25(2) only applies where the first buyer is in possession with the consent of the owner. Therefore, if the seller steals goods from the owner and sells them to the first buyer, a re-sale by the first buyer to the second buyer and any subsequent re-sales are not within s. 25(2) as the first buyer, although in possession with the consent of the seller, is not in possession with the consent of the owner.[246]

---

241 *Pearson v Rose Young Ltd* [1951] 1 KB 275.

242 *National Employers Mutual General Insurance Association Ltd v Jones* [1990] 1 AC 24.

243 [1985] 3 All ER 12.

244 *Newtons of Wembley Ltd v Williams* [1965] 1 QB 560.

245 See White, *Commercial Law*, Chapter 19, p 428. See also *Benjamin's Sale of Goods* (2006), at 7-079.

246 *National Employers Mutual General Insurance Association Ltd v Jones* [1990] 1 AC 24.

10.2.8. Hire purchase

A hirer under a hire-purchase agreement is not a 'buyer in possession'. In general such a person cannot pass a better title than he himself has, however a statutory exception is made in certain circumstances.

S. 70 Consumer Credit Act 1995 provides:

> Where goods of any class or description are let under a hire-purchase agreement to a dealer who deals in goods of that class or description and the dealer sells the goods when ostensibly acting in the ordinary course of his business, the sale shall be valid as if the dealer were expressly authorised by the owner to make the sale: Provided that the buyer acts in good faith and has not at the time of the sale notice that the dealer has no authority to make the sale.

The equivalent English provision is much narrower, applying only in the case of motor vehicles disposed to private purchasers. However, it is not restricted to hirers who are dealers nor is it confined to sales.[247]

10.2.9. Sales under special powers of sale or orders of the court

S. 21(2)(b) of the Act provides that nothing in the Act shall affect the validity of any contract of sale under any special common law or statutory power of sale or under the order of a court of competent jurisdiction. Examples of common law powers are a pledgee's right to sell goods pledged to him and an agent of necessity's power of sale. Statutory powers are numerous and include powers unpaid sellers of goods, powers of sheriffs and bailiffs who sell goods of debtors seized under warrants of execution, and powers of landlords who have distrained upon their tenant's goods.[248]

10.2.10. Money and the currency rule

According to the currency rule, once money passes into circulation, the very act of circulation destroys the title of the original owner and creates a new title in the person acquiring the money *bona fide* and for value and without notice of a defect in the title of the transferor.[249] The same rule applies to negotiable instruments.

---

[247] S. 27 and s. 29 Hire Purchase Act 1964.

[248] See further White, *Commercial Law*, Chapter 19, p 429.

[249] *Miller v Race* (1758) 1 Burr 452.

10.3.   Title conflicts and reform

Development of the law on title conflicts has been piecemeal and has resulted in a body of law which is not coherent. The exceptions to the *nemo dat* principle are difficult to apply. There is considerable overlap between them and the rules are technical and outdated. Suggestions for reform have been made by the Law Reform Committee in England in 1966[250] and in 1989 by Professor Diamond in his *Review of Security Interests in Property*.[251] To date, the only reform proposal that has been implemented is the abolition of the Market Overt rule in England. There have also been calls for reform of this rule in Ireland.[252]

11.   Acquisitive prescription

11.1.   Statutory limitation provisions

There are no formal rules in Irish law as to acquisitive prescription of movables. However, in this context, a discussion of the statutory limitation provisions is relevant as a person's ability to bring an action to assert his rights to a movable may be lost by virtue of the statutory limitation provisions. This barring of a right of action may result in the extinction of the owner's interest in the property and operate to afford the best title to the party in possession. The relevant statute is the Statute of Limitations Act 1957.

Legal interests in property are protected through the law of tort. S. 11(2) of the 1957 Act places a limitation period of six years on tort claims. An action against a party in possession would normally be brought in the tort of conversion. So, under the Act, the owner of a movable has six years in order to bring an action. Once the limitation period has elapsed after the original conversion, and provided that the owner has not during that time recovered possession of the goods, no action can be brought in respect of any subsequent conversion and the owner's title is extinguished.[253] In England, there are special provisions where the interference with the goods is not merely tortious, but criminal. Where the goods are stolen, there are no time limits for bringing an action, and so, without more, there is no extinction of the owner's title.[254] There are no comparable provisions in Ireland dealing spe-

---

250 Twelfth Report of the Law Reform Committee, 'Transfer of Title to Chattels' (1966).

251 (London, H.M.S.O., 1989).

252 White, *op cit*, Chapter 19, p 430.

253 S. 12(1) and s. 12(2) 1957 Act.

254 S. 4(4) Limitation Act 1980.

cifically with theft. The situation falls to be considered under other provisions extending the limitation period where there is fraud or deliberate concealment of facts relevant to the bringing of an action.[255] Under these provisions, time begins to run from the time the plaintiff could reasonably have discovered the fraud or concealment. The time limit is extended not just against the thief, but also against subsequent converters, excluding innocent purchasers for value.[256]

11.2. Other forms of original acquisition

11.2.1. Occupation of goods

A basic method of acquiring ownership is taking possession of something that has no owner, or occupancy. Under the common law, all chattels are capable of acquisition, and most 'ownerless' things are the subject of landowner's rights. Therefore, in Irish and English law, historically occupancy is not of great importance and mostly relates to the way that fish and wild animals become owned. In the case of animals, a distinction is drawn between those which are found tame in which full property can exist and those found wild. In wild animals, ownership may be acquired by industry – *i.e.* – by taming or reclaiming them.[257] In certain situations, a person may acquire ownership when a third party takes possession. If a trespasser on land catches or kills wild animals he finds there, the animals become the property of the person having the exclusive right to take them, which normally means the occupier of the land.[258] In the case of naturally occurring inanimate things such as plants, these rules do not apply. If they are brought by the forces of nature onto a person's land, they will automatically belong to him whether or not he or anyone else has taken possession of them.[259]

---

[255] S. 71 1957 Act.

[256] S. 71(2) 1957 Act.

[257] In *Kearry v Pattinson* [1939] 1 All ER 65, it was held that bees which swarm remain the property of their owner so long as they are in his sight and he has power to pursue them. But when they have flown on to another's land, they are wild, the power of pursuit being ended. Thereafter, they may become the property of anyone who hives them.

[258] *Blade v Higgs* (1865) 11 HLC 621.

[259] *Brew v Haren* (1877) IR 11 CL 198.

11.2.2. Finding

It is a general rule that the finder of chattels acquires possessory title to them as against all but the true owner. There are exceptions to this rule:

(a)   Treasure trove

In the UK, treasure trove consists of money, coin, gold, silver, plate or bullion hidden in the earth or other private place the owner thereof being unknown. It belongs to the Crown by virtue of a common law prerogative.[260] It is an offence in the UK at common law to fail to disclose treasure trove. In Ireland, it has been held that such Crown prerogatives did not survive the enactment of the 1937 Constitution and did not exist in Ireland. However, in *Webb and Webb v Ireland and the Attorney General*[261] it was held that in certain instances, the Constitution substituted new versions of the old prerogatives. A right to treasure trove comparable to the royal prerogative was found in the provisions of Article 10.1 and Article 5 of the Constitution. Finlay CJ said:

'It would, I think, now be universally accepted, certainly by the people of Ireland, and by the people of most modern states, that one of the most important national assets belonging to the people is their heritage and knowledge of its true origins and the buildings and objects which constitute keys to their ancient history. If this be so, then it would appear to me to follow that it is a necessary ingredient of sovereignty in a modern state, and certainly in this State, having regard to the terms of the Constitution, with an emphasis on its historical origins and a constant concern for the common good is and should be an ownership by the State of objects which constitute antiquities of importance which are discovered and which have no known owner. It would appear to me to be inconsistent with the framework of society sought to be created and sought to be protected by the Constitution that such objects should become the exclusive property of those who by chance may find them.'[262]

This constitutional right may be wider than the crown prerogative. It appears to cover the finding of other objects in addition to gold and silver. Finlay CJ referred to the State's ownership of *'antiquities of importance'* and Walsh J referred to *'all objects forming part of the national heritage.'*[263]

---

[260] See Tyler & Palmer, *Crossley Vaines on Personal Property* (1973), p 419 *et seq.*
[261] [1988] ILRM 565.
[262] *Ibid*, p 593-594.
[263] *Ibid*, p 604.

(b)   Chattels found by an employee in the course of his employment

As outlined above, if an employee finds chattels in the course of his employment, these belong to his employer. In *London Corporation v Appleyard*,[264] the general principle was established that an employee who receives property or money whether corruptly or honestly by reason of his employment is accountable therefore to his employer. The finder does not acquire a title as against a person, other than the true owner, who has a prior possessory right by virtue of *de facto* control and a presumed intention to exclude. The finder therefore, does not obtain possessory title as against the owner of a chattel in which the goods are found. For example, in *Cartwright v Green*,[265] a bureau was given to a carpenter to repair, which unknown to the owner had a very large sum of money hidden in it by its original owner. The carpenter found the money and divided it among himself, his wife and a third person. The question arose as to whether this was larceny. It was held that as he was only entrusted with the bureau for the purpose of repairing it, he committed a trespassory taking when he removed the money. In addition, where an article is sold, unless it is clearly sold with all its contents, the purchaser who finds valuables in it cannot claim against the seller.[266]

(c)   Chattels found on land

The basic rule is that occupation of land does not automatically entail possession of things found on it. The occupier must take active steps to exercise control over them before he possesses them. This rule was established in *Parker v British Airways Board*.[267] The plaintiff found a gold bracelet in an executive lounge at an airport. He handed the bracelet to an official of British Airways, who leased and occupied the lounge, and asked for it to be returned to him if the owner was not found. The bracelet was not claimed and the bracelet was sold, the airline keeping the proceeds. The court found in favour of the passenger. According to the Court of Appeal, the issue depended on whether the airline had already acquired a possessory title to the bracelet before the passenger found it. If not, the law would protect the finder's claim against subsequent claimants. The question of whether the airline already had possession of the property before it was found depended on whether it had shown a suffi-

---

[264] [1963] 2 All ER 834.

[265] (1803) 8 Ves Jun 405.

[266] See *Merry v Green* (1841) 7 M & W 623, discussed further in Tyler & Palmer, *op cit* at p 421.

[267] [1982] 1 All ER 834.

ciently strong intention to control both the premises on which the bracelet was found and the 'things which may be on or in it.' No such intention was shown. The only step that the airline had taken with respect to
lost property was to instruct their employees what to do with things that
had already been found. The court found that in order to have possession,
the airline would have had to take an active step to make searches for lost
property. The passenger therefore established a prior and superior possessory claim.

The situation may be different where property not in the possession of
the occupier according to these rules is found by a trespasser on the land.
Here, it seems that public policy requires a different result. It was suggested by Donaldson LJ in *Parker* that the law will rule in favour of the
occupier in this situation and the finder will not be allowed to profit from
his wrongdoing.[268] There is clear Irish authority for this proposition in the
case of *Webb and Webb v Ireland and the Attorney General* where the Irish
Supreme Court approved of this suggestion and held that the occupier
had a better claim than trespassing finders.[269]

(d)   Things attached to or under the land

The rule here is that a finder cannot acquire a possessory title against the
owner or occupier of land when the chattels are under the land or attached thereto. The leading case is *South Staffs Water Co v Sharman*[270]
where the defendant was employed to clean out a pool situated on land
belonging to the plaintiff. In the mud at the bottom of the pool, the defendant found two gold rings. It was held that the defendant had not title
as against the plaintiff. The decision was based on a passage from Pollock
and Wright's *Essay on Possession in the Common Law,*: '*The possession of
land carries with it in general, by our law, possession of everything which is
attached to or under that land, and, in the absence of a better title elsewhere,
the right to possess it also. And it makes no difference that the possessor is not
aware of its existence.*'[271]

The Irish case of *Webb*[272] is also relevant here. The plaintiffs had lawfully entered someone else's land and used metal detectors to search for
buried objects. They discovered extremely valuable historical artefacts,
known collectively as the 'Derrynaflan Hoard' and valued at £5,500,000.
It was held that the excavations were unauthorised and this made the

---

[268] *Ibid*, p 837.
[269] [1988] ILRM 565.
[270] [1896] 2 QB 44.
[271] *Ibid*, cited by Lord Russell of Killowen at p 41.
[272] [1988] ILRM 565.

plaintiffs trespassers. The Supreme Court found on this basis that the landowners had a better claim to the hoard. In the course of the judgment, the Supreme Court referred to the decision in *Parker* and to the distinction between things on land and things attached to or under land. The Court found that when examining cases where objects are attached to or under the land, the extent to which absence of control may deprive the owner against the finder is limited to cases such as *Hanna v Peel*.[273] That case related to a situation where the owner of a house had never entered into possession of it though the title had developed upon him. The Supreme Court approved of the propositions set out by Donaldson LJ in *Parker*. In particular, two of the propositions stated in *Parker* were relevant: First, that an occupier of land has rights superior to those of a finder over chattels in or attached to that land; and second, that the finder of a chattel acquires very limited rights over it if he takes it into his care and control ... in the course of trespassing.[274]

---

[273] [1945] KB 509.
[274] Per Finlay CJ, p 588-590.

Part IV:
Additional issues

12. Reservation of title

The use of reservation of title (or retention of title) clauses is common in sales contracts in order to provide additional protection against a buyer's inability to pay.[275] This is particularly important in the context of the buyer's insolvency where the seller's personal remedies may be worthless. Under s. 17 of the Sale of Goods Act 1893, the passing of property from seller to buyer depends on the intention of the parties. S. 19 allows the seller to impose a condition on the passing of property. By including a retention of title clause, the seller imposes such a condition.

12.1. The purpose of a retention of title clause

The purpose of a retention of title clause has been explained as follows:

> 'The broad purpose of an agreement that a seller retains title to goods pending payment of the purchase price and other moneys owing to him is to protect the seller from the insolvency of the buyer in circumstances where the price and other moneys remain unpaid. The seller's aim in insisting on a retention of title clause is to prevent the goods and the proceeds of sale of the goods from becoming part of the assets of an insolvent buyer, available to satisfy the claims of the general body of creditors.' *Per* Mummery J in *Compaq Computer v Abercorn Group*.[276]

12.2. Types of retention of title clause

The traditional method of reserving property in goods was by way of conditional sale agreement, retaining title to the goods until they were paid for.

---

[275] See generally, McCormack, *Retention of Title Clauses* (1995); Benjamin's Sale of Goods, chapter 5; White, *Commercial Law*, chapter 15.

[276] See *Compaq Computer v Abercorn Group* [1993] BCLC 602 at p. 611 *per* Mummery J.

Under this method of sale, it is assumed as is the case with hire purchase that the debtor will retain the goods unaltered. However, in the *Romalpa Case (Aluminium Industrie Vaassen BV v Romalpa Aluminium Ltd)*,[277] it was held that a conditional sale agreement could be effective to reserve property in the goods even where the goods were supplied on the understanding that they would be *consumed* or *resold*. Therefore it was recognised that by supplying goods on conditional sale terms, subject to a reservation of property, suppliers could protect themselves against their customers becoming insolvent.

The full impact of reservation of title was not felt until this case was decided. The Court of Appeal held that through a reservation of title clause, the seller was allowed to trace goods to proceeds of sale under equitable tracing principles. These clauses became known as retention of title or '*Romalpa*' clauses.

There is now a wide variety of types of Retention of Title clauses in common use:

1. simple retention of title clauses
2. 'all sums due' retention of title clauses
3. manufactured goods clauses
4. proceeds of sale clauses

12.2.1. Simple retention of title clauses

A simple retention of title clause seeks to retain title to the goods supplied under the contract until their price is paid. The clause reserves title in the *original identifiable goods* until payment is made by the buyer for the goods.

Retention of title is such a condition. It was conceded in *Romalpa* that a simple retention of title clause which retained title to the goods supplied would be effective. This was confirmed in *Clough Mill Ltd v Geoffrey Martin*.[278] In that case, the seller supplied yarn to the buyer on terms that risk should pass to the buyer on delivery but that '*ownership of the material shall remain with the seller which reserves the right to dispose of the material until payment in full for all the material has been received by it.*' This validity of this clause was upheld. The decision clearly establishes that a simple retention of title clause, reserving title to the goods *in their original form* until they are paid for, will be effective.

---

[277] [1976] 1 WLR 676.
[278] [1984] 2 All ER 982.

However, a clause that purports to retain equitable or beneficial ownership in the goods will not be effective. In *Re Bond Worth*,[279] the seller sought to retain 'equitable and beneficial ownership' until full payment by the buyer or until resale in which case the seller's beneficial entitlement would attach to the proceeds of sale. There, it was held that the property had passed to the buyer and an equitable charge had been created in favour of the seller which was void for non-registration.[280]

A simple clause like that used in *Clough Mill* only protects the seller as long as he can *identify* the goods as his property under the retention of title clause. If the goods have been so altered as to become a different item, they will be irrecoverable. The difficult question is to know when goods have become so altered. In *Re Peachdart Ltd*,[281] the seller had supplied leather to make handbags. Although there was evidence that the leather remained identifiable throughout the manufacturing process, so that the seller could prove that a particular bag was made from leather from a particular contract, it was held that the parties must have intended that the leather would cease to be the seller's property as soon as it entered the manufacturing process.

It has been held that the seller's goods do not lose their identity where they are attached to other property but can be detached without damage either to the goods or to the property.[282] However, the seller's ownership will be terminated if his goods are used in a manufacturing process and become irreversibly mixed with other goods. So, for example, in *Borden (UK) Ltd v Scottish Timber Products Ltd*[283] the seller supplied resin which was used in the manufacture of chipboard. The seller claimed that its retention of title clause to the resin allowed it to trace the resin into the finished product and claim a share of the chipboard. However, the court of appeal rejected this claim holding that the seller lost its title to resin when it was mixed with wood chips to make chipboard.

12.2.2. Claims to manufactured products

(a)   General

In order to overcome the problem of the original goods supplied losing their identity in a manufacturing process, retention of title clauses have been drafted to claim title to the products manufactured using the origi-

---

[279] [1980] Ch 228.
[280] Under s. 95 Companies Act 1948.
[281] [1984] Ch 131.
[282] *Hendy Lennox (Industrial Engines) Ltd v Grahame Puttick Ltd* [1984] 1 WLR 485.
[283] [1981] Ch 25.

nal goods supplied. However, such a claim is likely to be regarded as creating a charge. The clause in Clough Mill contained such a provision and the Court of Appeal *obiter*, considered its effect. Goff LJ held that it is open to the parties to make any agreement they wish about the ownership of the new product, so they could theoretically agree that the seller is to be the owner as soon as they are manufactured. In practice, it is assumed that the intention of the parties is that the new products should initially belong to the buyer. The court emphasised that the new product will normally be worth more than the value of the seller's materials included in it. The buyer will have contributed labour. To recognise the seller as owner of the new product would therefore be to give him a windfall profit. The expectation of the parties would normally be that the seller's interest in the product should be limited to the payment of the sum due to him for his goods and defeasible on such payment and so a clause which provides that new products are to belong to the seller will normally be construed as creating a charge to secure the payment. So, in several cases, such a clause has been held to create a charge over the new goods which was void for non-registration.[284]

In rare circumstances, a 'new products' clause might vest ownership of the goods in the seller. In *Clough Mill*, the court stated that if the contract terms are unequivocal, if the seller's goods remain in a separate and identifiable state, if the buyer supplies no material of his own, or at least only inexpensive items, and only the seller's materials are incorporated in the goods and none from other suppliers, the clause may be effective.

(b)   Joint ownership of the new product

In order to avoid problems involved with ownership of manufactured goods, the draftsmen came up with another type of provision that the seller and buyer were to hold the new product jointly in proportion to the value of the seller's goods and the value of the buyer's goods.

This type of clause was used in an Irish case: *Kruppstahl AG v Quitmann Products Ltd.*[285] However, the court held that this was a registrable charge. If the seller seeks to claim only a proportionate share in the new product, he expressly recognises that he has only a limited interest in the product to secure payment of the outstanding debt and so is likely to be regarded as having only a charge over the product.

---

[284] *Specialist Plant Services Ltd v Braithwaite Ltd* [1987] BCLC 1; *Modelboard Ltd v Outerbox Ltd* [1993] BCLC 623.

[285] [1982] ILRM 551.

12.2.3. Retention of title to secure 'all sums due'

In order to avoid problems of identification, the seller may include a term in the contract that the goods supplied remain his property until all sums due (not just those due under the particular sales contract) have been paid for. The idea of these clauses is that they help to resolve the seller's practical difficulties in identifying and separating the goods which have not been paid for because, under such a provision, he can retake all the goods in the buyer's possession. The validity of such clauses was upheld in *Armour v Thyssen*.[286] The case has been criticised as leaving some questions unanswered. For example, if the seller retakes goods which the buyer has paid for in full in order to settle an outstanding debt under a separate contract, the seller would immediately have to refund the price of those goods to the buyer on the grounds of failure of consideration. This would defeat the object of the clause. This point was not addressed. The case was argued and technically decided on a point of Scots law. The effectiveness of these clauses cannot be regarded as being effectively settled in Irish law.

12.2.4. Resale of goods and claims to proceeds

If the buyer resells the goods before paying for them, the seller's rights over the goods will normally be extinguished because the sub-buyer will take a good title to the goods normally by virtue of s. 25(2) of the 1893 Act. In order to overcome this problem, the seller may try to claim an interest in the proceeds of the resale. In *Romalpa*, the Court of Appeal held that the buyer had an implied right to resell the foil, subject to an implied duty to account for the proceeds in equity. In certain circumstances, the seller was entitled to *trace* his goods into the proceeds of their resale.

In order to succeed against a receiver or liquidator, the seller must establish a proprietary claim to the proceeds of sale. He must therefore establish that the goods were sold by the buyer on his behalf and the proceeds of sale received by the buyer in a fiduciary capacity. If so, he may be able to trace his property in the goods into the proceeds of sale according to equitable principles set out in *Re Hallett's Estate*.[287]

The first obstacle for the seller to overcome is to establish that the buyer effected the sale and received the proceeds in a fiduciary capacity. The wording and construction of the particular clause will be important. In *Romalpa*, a Dutch company supplied aluminium foil to an English company on terms which provided that the foil remained the seller's property until the buyer had paid all debts due to the seller. The clause provided that:

---

[286] [1990] 3 All ER 481.
[287] (1880) 13 ChD 696.

1. The foil should be stored in such a way as to identify it as the seller's property;
2. Products made from the seller's foil were to belong to the seller and be stored so as to make them identifiable as such;
3. Until resale, the buyer was to hold manufactured products in the capacity of 'fiduciary owner' for the seller; and
4. On demand the buyer should 'hand over' to the seller claims against its customers who bought manufactured products.

The buyer became insolvent and a receiver was appointed. However, prior to insolvency, the buyer had sold a quantity of foil and the price of that foil was paid by the buyer to the receiver. The seller claimed the proceeds of sale from the receiver. The contract contained no stipulation for this situation. The receiver conceded that the buyer held the foil as bailee for the seller pending payment. The court of appeal therefore concluded that when re-selling the foil, the buyer acted as the seller's agent and that as a result of the bailment and agency relationships between them, there was a fiduciary relationship between the parties. That relationship allowed the seller to trace its property into the proceeds of sale in accordance with the principle of tracing in *Re Hallet's Estate*.

However, despite this decision, subsequent decisions have refused to follow this line. The courts are very reluctant to recognise a fiduciary relationship between a buyer and seller when in truth the relationship is really one of debtor and creditor. Generally it seems that a fiduciary relationship will be held to be inconsistent with the express terms of the contract and the essential nature of the transaction as a sale of goods on credit terms. In *Re Andrabell Ltd*[288] the fact that the buyer was allowed credit and so could use the proceeds of sale in his own business negated the existence of a fiduciary relationship. In addition, the buyer did not have to store the seller's goods or the proceeds of sale separately. Even where the clause is carefully drafted, the courts will be reluctant to recognise the clause In *Compaq Computers Ltd v Abercorn Group Ltd*,[289] the retention of title clause stipulated (i) that the seller's goods should be stored separately so that they were identifiable, (ii), the buyer held the goods as 'bailee' and 'agent'; (iii) the buyer had to account to the seller as bailee or agent for the full proceeds of resale; and (iv) the buyer had to keep separate account of such proceeds. Despite these provisions, the court held that a charge was created over the proceeds of resale because the seller's interest in the proceeds was limited to the amounts owing by the buyer and was determinable on the buyer's payment of the outstanding debt. The Irish courts

---

[288] [1984] 3 All ER 407.
[289] [1991] BCC 484.

have similarly been reluctant to uphold the validity of such clauses.[290] It seems unlikely that an Irish court will in future uphold a seller's claim to an interest in the proceeds of the buyer's resale.

12.3. Reform of the law on retention of title

The law on retention of title has developed on a case by case basis – this makes it very difficult to predict with complete certainty whether a particular clause is or is not effective. The courts have shown themselves relatively willing to make use of established concepts such as agency, bailment and fiduciary relationships to make effective such clauses. However, although some commentators argue that the principle of freedom of contract should allow the parties to reach any agreement they like about the passing of property, there are some policy considerations with regard to the impact of these clauses on third parties.

By inserting a retention of title clause, a seller can improve his position in the insolvency of the buyer – he can effectively jump the queue prescribed by statute and deplete the pool of assets available to other creditors. This form of protection is not available to all creditors. For example suppliers of services cannot use it. In addition, a retention of title clause gives security without publicity. Where a bank has a floating charge, it must be registered and its existence can be discovered by any potential creditors by searching in the appropriate register. The absence of any provisions requiring disclosure of retention of title clauses is thought not to be satisfactory. However, exactly the same type of objections can be directed at hire purchase, leasing and other arrangements. The problem appears to be that these arrangements are intended to provide goods on credit with security against non-payment, but the law adopts a formalistic approach and treats different security arrangements in different ways.

In England, the use of reservation of title clauses was reviewed in the Crowther Committee Report in 1971 and the Diamond Report in 1989.[291] It was recommended that a more substantive approach should be adopted and that all security arrangements should be subject to a registration requirement. Diamond recommended a new 'notice filing' registration

---

[290] In *Carroll Group Distributors v G & JF Burke* [1990] ILRM 285, it was held that the clause possessed all the characteristics of a charge which was void for non-registration under the Companies Act 1963. The basis for this decision appears to be that the clause provided that when the buyer resold the goods, it did so on his own account and not as agent for the seller, therefore no fiduciary duty was imposed by the clause.

[291] Report of the Crowther Committee on Consumer Credit (1971); Diamond, *Review of Security Interests in Property* (1989).

system applicable to all security devices including retention of title, hire purchase, conditional sale and chattel leases for a period of three years or more. He drew a distinction between simple and proceeds clauses which would be subject to this notice filing system and on the other hand all sums due and manufactured products clauses which would be regarded as creating a charge and need to be registered for each individual transaction. To date, nothing has been done to implement these proposals.

In Ireland, the issue of reservation of title was reviewed by the Law Reform Commission in 1989.[292] It proposed that retention of title clauses should not be enforceable unless evidenced in writing and signed by the buyer; and that such clauses would not be deemed to create any form of charge over the goods unless expressly stipulated at the time the contract was concluded between the parties. It further proposed a system of registration of retention of title clauses and did not rule out a more comprehensive system of registration for other types of security interests in goods. The proposed reforms have not been implemented.[293]

13.   Abandonment

The proposition that possession, and therefore ownership can be abandoned is controversial and the law in this area is unclear. Some commentators have accepted the idea of abandonment; others do not accept its possibility.[294]

---

[292] Law Reform Commission, 'Report on Debt Collection (2) Retention of Title', (1989).

[293] For further detail on retention of title clauses, see Jones, 'Retention of Title Clauses: Ten Years from Romalpa', (1986) 7 Co Law 233; Goode, 'The Modernization of Personal Security Law', (1984) 100 LQR 234; Gregory, 'Romalpa Clauses as Unregistered Charges – A Fundamental Shift?', (1990) 106 LQR 551; Ogowewo, 'When is a Cow not a Cow? Loss of Title and Retention of Title Clauses', [1996] ICCLR (No. 12) Analysis Section; Webb, 'Title and Transformation: Who Owns Manufactured Goods?', [2000] Journal of Business Law 513; Farrar & Chai, 'Romalpa Revisited Again', [1985] Journal of Business Law 160; De Lacy, 'The Anglocisation of Irish Retention of Title', [1990] Irish Law Times 279; Bradgate, 'Retention of Title in the House of Lords: Unanswered Questions', (1991) 54 Modern Law Review 726, Donnelly, 'Reforming Personal Property Securities Law; Is there a Case for a Single Securities Register?', (2000) 7 (1) DULJ 50.

[294] See Bell, *Modern Law of Personal Property in England and Ireland*, p 52; Tyler & Palmer, *Crossley Vaines on Personal Property*, p 419 *et seq*, and Bridge, *Personal Property Law*, p 22.

There is an extremely old authority for a rule that abandonment in fact is not abandonment in law. In *Haynes Case*,[295] a criminal dug up the bodies of four people in a graveyard and stole the shrouds from the bodies. It was held that each shroud remained the property of the person to whom it belonged when the body was wrapped in it. The court held that a person could not relinquish his property in goods 'unless the thing be vested in another.' Bell points out that this does not represent the modern criminal law in which it is accepted that one does not possess what one has abandoned and that you cannot be charged with stealing abandoned property. He is critical of the fact that the *Haynes* case is still regarded by commentators as an authority for civil cases.[296]

There are civil cases which recognise abandonment. Many of these involve shipwrecks. In *The Crystal*,[297] a claim was made by harbour commissioners against the owner of a sunken ship for their expenses in connection with blowing up the wreck. The court held that at the time the work was done the defendants no longer owned the wreck having given notice of abandonment prior to the incurring of expenses. It is not clear whether this is a general authority for the recognition of abandonment or whether shipwrecks may be in a special category. There are other cases, however which do not involve shipwrecks. For example in *Elwes v Briggs*,[298] the owner of the land beneath which a prehistoric boat was found was held to be the true owner. The rights of the original owner were said to have been abandoned. In the *Webb* case, the Irish Supreme Court also recognised albeit *obiter* the possibility of chattels being abandoned.[299] While Tyler and Palmer accept the authority of the *Haynes* Case and state that 'once owned, a thing remains owned',[300] the majority of commentators are of the view that ownership of a chattel can be abandoned effectively by the true owner. If this is the case and ownership can be abandoned, then the finder first to take possession succeeds to the position of true owner.[301] The requirements of abandonment are not clear but would seem to involve relinquishment of possession in circumstances where there is an accompanying intention to disclaim all interest in the goods.[302]

---

[295] (1614) 12 Co Rep 113.

[296] Bell, *op cit*, p 52.

[297] [1894] AC 508 HL.

[298] (1886) 33 Ch D 562.

[299] [1988] ILRM 565, *per* Walsh J, p 600.

[300] See Tyler & Palmer, *op cit*, p 427.

[301] See Bridge, *op cit*, p 23.

[302] See Hudson, 'Is Divesting Abandonment Possible at Common Law?', (1984) 100 LQR 110.

14.   Co-ownership

14.1.   Legal co-ownerhsip

Two forms of co-ownership are recognised at law: A tenancy in common and a joint tenancy. The essential difference between these forms of co-ownership is that where A and B hold as tenants in common and A dies, A's share forms part of his estate and passes under his will or intestacy. If they hold as joint tenants, B becomes sole owner of the property. Both types of tenancy exist in relation to movables but it appears that in the case of choses in action, there can only be joint tenancy.

A joint tenancy arises where the co-owners acquire the movable under such terms which do not suggest that they are to have divided shares in it. To establish a tenancy in common, the transferor must use words of severance, *i.e.* words that indicate an intention that they should have independent shares. Such words could be, for example, 'in equal shares', 'to be distributed amongst them in joint and equal proportions', 'to be divided between'. A joint tenancy can become a tenancy in common by severance. So, there will be a severance where one joint tenant disposes of his share, where the tenants agree to hold in common; and where the conduct of the tenants is such as to show that they treat the property as if it were held in common.[303]

14.2.   Equitable co-ownership

Equitable ownership may also be divided between several persons. Both joint tenancies and tenancies in common are possible. So, where property is settled on A in trust for B and C, both types of co-ownership of the beneficial interest can arise. Equity is hostile to joint tenancies, however, on the grounds that the death of one tenant gives the survivor a windfall. Equity leans in favour of tenancies in common. At common law the presumption is in favour of joint tenancies, so that when property is vested in two or more persons, a tenancy in common will only arise if the intention to create one is made clear. In equity, this presumption only operates if the shares of the co-owners are equal. If they are unequal, a tenancy in common is presumed.[304] Even where property is held by joint tenants at common law, equity will regard them as trustees for themselves as tenants in common. So, for example, if A and B buy property, with A paying €1000 and B paying €2000, although they may hold the legal interest as

---

[303] *Connolly v Connolly* (1866) 17 Ir Ch R 208; *Re Armstrong* [1920] 1 IR 208; see further Bell, p 75.

[304] *O'Connell v Harrison* [1927] IR 330.

joint tenants, they are viewed as having the beneficial ownership vested in them as tenants in common.[305]

14.3.   The rules on transfer

The rules on transfer with regard to co-ownership are straightforward. In the case of both joint tenancies and tenancies in common, the co-owner transfers his share of the goods under the same rules for the transfer of movables as apply to single owners.

15.   Floating charge

The law recognises two kinds of charge, fixed and floating. The distinction between the two is extremely significant in the context of security given for loans to companies.[306] Under a fixed charge, a particular asset is appropriated to the satisfaction of a debt. The charge is attached to that asset and the asset cannot be used in the ordinary course of business. The asset is a specific identifiable item of property like specific plant machinery, motor vehicles, shares, insurance policies, intellectual property. Under the floating charge, there is a charge, not over a particular asset, but over a constantly changing fund of assets. The charge hovers above the fund of assets until an event occurs which causes it to crystallize. When it crystallizes it fastens over all the assets contained in the fund at that moment and attached to them. It then becomes a quasi fixed charge. For example, a floating charge can be given over a company's motor vehicles, stock in trade and raw materials, and although these items are subject to the charge, the company is permitted to use them and even dispose of them in the ordinary course of its business and replace them with new vehicles, stock machinery, etc. The floating charge is a nineteenth century creation. Its validity was recognised in Re Panama, New Zealand & Australian Royal Mail Co.[307]

There is no statutory definition of the term floating charge, but it has long been recognised that they contain three essential characteristics. These were set out by Romer J in Re Yorkshire Woolcombers Assoc Ltd:[308]

'If a charge has three characteristics I am about to mention it is a floating charge:

---

[305] Lake v Gibson (1729) 1 Eq Ca Abr 290; see further Bell, p 167.

[306] For a detailed consideration of the law on fixed and floating charges as it applies in Ireland, see Courtney, The Law of Private Companies (2002) and Keane, R, Company Law (2000).

[307] (1870) 5 Ch 318.

[308] [1903] 2 Ch 284.

1. If it is a charge on a class of assets in a company present and future;
2. If that class is one which in the ordinary course of the business of the company would be changing from time to time; and
3. If you find that by the charge it is contemplated that until some future step is taken by or on behalf of those interested in the charge, the company may carry on its business in the ordinary way so far as concerns the particular assets I am dealing with.'

15.1.   Significance of fixed v. floating charges

Companies typically grant fixed and floating charges over a wide variety of assets. Whether the charge is fixed or floating will be of considerable significance particularly in determining the priority accorded to the security on insolvency. So, for example, in insolvency, fixed charges rank ahead of floating charges. Under sections 98 and 285 Companies Act 1963, if a charge crystallizes on the appointment of a receiver or liquidator, preferential debts have priority over the floating charge. In addition, in certain circumstances, a floating charge will be invalid if the company goes into liquidation within a specified period. (Within 12 months of liquidation, unless company solvent at the time; within 24 months of liquidation to a connected person, unless company solvent at that time.)[309]

Given that a fixed charge offers greater security than a floating charge, much of the litigation to date has involved disputes between creditors as to their respective places in the queue to claim the company's assets on insolvency.

15.2.   Crystallization of floating charges

15.2.1. General

A floating charge may never crystallize. For example, where the debt secured by the floating charge is repaid. However, it doesn't float on indefinitely. A time may come when it is said to crystallise. If this happens, it is as if a net drops over whatever assets the company has within the assets or class of assets which are the subject of the floating charge. The effect is that the charge becomes a fixed charge attaching to whatever assets happen to be within its grasp at the time. Crystallisation can occur in a number of ways. As a matter of law, a floating charge will crystallise on the appointment of a receiver, or when the company goes into liquidation (on a resolution being passed or a compulsory winding up ordered),

---

[309] See Rules on fraudulent preference as outlined above at paragraph 7.2.4.

or there is otherwise a cessation of business on the part of the company. The effect of those circumstances is to bring to an end the company's freedom to carry on business in the ordinary way. Equally the bank may prescribe situations where the charge will crystallise which may or not require intervention of the chargee.

On crystallization the charge attaches to all assets which are the property of the company at the time and are of the type identified in the debenture. Once crystallized, a floating charge ranks as a fixed charge. The exception to this is if the charge crystallized on the appointment of a receiver, or the commencement of a winding-up. In such cases, sections 98 and 285 Companies Act 1963 give priority to preferential creditors. If crystallization occurs for any other reason, the holders of a crystallized floating charge rank with fixed charge holders. On crystallization the company is no longer entitled to manage the charged assets. The charge is now fixed.

15.2.2. De-crystallization

Until recently, it was generally thought that once a floating charge had crystalllised, it could not de-crystallise. However, in *Re Holidair*,[310] the Supreme Court held that the appointment of an examiner automatically de-crystallizes a floating charge. The discharge of the examiner automatically re-crystallizes it. A floating charge had been created over the company's book debts. Blayney J acknowledged that it had crystallised upon the appointment of a receiver. However, he went on to hold that the appointment of the examiner the crystallised floating charge de-crystallised.

15.3. Charges over book debts

A particularly contentious issue in recent years has been the nature of charges over book debts (or sometimes called receivables).[311] These are sums due to the company and arising from goods or services supplied by the company in the course of its business. These book debts are a valuable asset (assuming they are bad debts) for they represent an income stream for the company and therefore creditors are anxious to obtain security

---

[310] [1994] 1 IR 434.

[311] See generally, Breslin, 'Brumark Investments Ltd: Charges Over Book Debts, Divisibility of Assets, and the Role of Conduct in Interpretation of Contracts', (2001) 8 (9) CLP 207; Breslin & Smith, 'The House of Lords Decision in Spectrum Plus – the Implications for Irish Banking Law', (2005) 12 (9) CLP 228; Ali, 'Developments in Fixed and Floating Charges: Legal Principles, Policy Issues and Implications for Structured Financing', (2006) 13 (2) CLP 46.

over them. Equally, of course book debts are the type of assets where the company is anxious to preserve its freedom to control the assets to the greatest extent possible – they represent part of the company's cash flow.

Until 1978 it was believed that a fixed charge could not be taken over circulating assets such as book debts. It was felt that only a floating charge could be taken over such assets. However, the changing nature of the subject matter of the charge is not the only prerequisite of a floating charge. It is also important that the creditor undertake to leave management of the fund in the hands of the debtor prior to crystallization. The validity of fixed charges over book debts was recognised in *Siebe Gorman v Barclays Bank*[312] where it was held that provided that there are express restrictions on the company's freedom to deal with the assets it could be a fixed charge. The restrictions imposed in Siebe were a requirement that the charger pay all monies received in such book debts into a special bank account and there was a prohibition on charging or assigning those sums without prior consent of chargee. There was no restriction by the company on the proceeds once collected but the company could not access those funds without consent of bank. The restrictions were such that the charge was a fixed charge.

In Ireland, the courts also recognised the possibility of creating a fixed charge over book debts. In *Re Keenan Bros Ltd*,[313] the debenture provided that 'the company shall pay into a designated account with the bank all moneys it receives in respect of book debts and other debts charged and shall not withdraw or direct any payment from the account without consent of bank. This segregation meant that the book debts were unusable by the charger save with the prior written consent of the bank so that a fixed charge had been created. The charged assets were so withdrawn from their ordinary trade use by putting them in the control of the debenture holder that the charge constituted a fixed charge.

In *Re Wogan's (Drogheda) Ltd*,[314] the clause prohibited any withdrawal of monies from the account specified by the lender into which the monies collected were to be paid without the consent of the lender. This was sufficient to categorise the charge as a fixed charge even where such account had never been operated.

The latest decision of the House of Lords in *National Westminster Bank Ltd v Spectrum Plus Ltd*,[315] clarifies the application of the test for distinguishing between fixed and floating charges. The company obtained an overdraft facility from the bank. The overdraft was secured by a debenture. The debenture purported to create a fixed charge and provided for a

---

[312] [1979] 2 LLR 142.
[313] [1985] IR 401.
[314] [1993] 1 IR 157.
[315] [2005] UKHL 41.

number of restrictions on the company's ability to deal with its book debts: The company was prohibited from disposing of the book debts before they were collected and once collected the proceeds had to be paid into an account with the bank. However, there was no restriction on the company's ability to use the book debts and their proceeds in the ordinary course of business. The central issue was whether it was necessary for the bank account to be blocked for a legally effective fixed charge.

The House of Lords held that the charge created a floating charge – not a fixed charge. In spite of the requirement to pay the proceeds of the book debts into an account with the bank, the security amounted to a floating charge. The House of Lords held that it is possible to take a fixed charge over present and future book debts provided the nature of the borrower and the lender's rights in respect of the charged asset are consistent with a fixed charge. It was held that it is an essential characteristic of a fixed charge over book debts that the borrower is restricted in its use of the book debts and their proceeds in the ordinary course of its business. Restrictions on a borrower's ability to deal with its uncollected book debts are not decisive. It is the restrictions on the company's use of the proceeds that are important. In particular, the House of Lords held that it was essential that the borrower be required to pay the proceeds into a blocked account from which it cannot withdraw monies without the lender's consent. The decision of Slade J in *Siebe Gorman* was emphatically overruled.

In summary, Irish and UK law are united in the sense that a charge which does not provide for a restriction on the borrower enjoying access to the proceeds of the book debts will be classified as a floating charge even though it is termed a legal charge in the contractual documentation. An area of uncertainty exists because where Irish and UK law apparently differ now is in the manner in which the actual behaviour of the parties is viewed. In the United Kingdom, conduct which permits the chargor to enjoy the proceeds of the debts is a badge of a floating charge. In Ireland, following the *Wogans* case, a consideration of the conduct of the parties is not an appropriate means of contractual interpretation. So, in Ireland, where a debenture specifies that a separate bank account must be maintained, it will not be fatal to the creation of a fixed charge where the separate bank account is not actually maintained.[316]

Thus, it seems that the essential characteristic of a floating charge and that which distinguishes it from a fixed charge will be that the chargor is left free to use the charged asset and to remove it from the security. This test of control will be relevant both to the classification of charges over book debts and to charges over other types of movable property.

---

[316] For further discussion, see: Breslin and Smith, 'The House of Lords decision in Spectrum Plus – the Implications for Irish Banking Law', (2005) 12 (9) CLP 228.

16.   Consequences of restitution of the movable
to the owner

The consequences arising when a movable has to be restored to the owner in cases involving damage to goods or interests in goods are complex and at common law, there is a wide variety of claims that can be made in the case of misuse of chattels. These claims involve tort, breach of contract and restitution. These different claims often overlap and this area of the law is often unclear and lacks consistency. Some moderate reforms have been enacted in England by the Torts (Interference with Goods) Act 1977. There has not yet been any legislative reform in Ireland. It is proposed first to make a brief overview of the remedies available in each of these areas.

16.1.   Tort

The general law in relation to trespass, conversion and detinue has been examined above.[317] As far as remedies are concerned, the general rule for damages in tort is that the plaintiff should be placed in the same position as if the loss had not occurred insofar as this is possible.

16.1.1. Conversion

The tort of conversion can be committed in a wide variety of ways. It is generally said to consist of any act relating to the goods of another that constitutes an unjustifiable denial of his or her title to them. It may be committed by the wrongful taking possession of the goods, abusing possession already acquired or otherwise denying title of the other person to them, whether or not possession has been acquired.[318] Abusing possession may consist of pawning another's goods, sale and delivery of them, or the wilful destruction of the goods. If the goods have been destroyed, but have retained their identity, the defendant will not be liable for conversion though he or she will be liable in trespass.[319] Whatever the method of commission of the tort, in claims for conversion, the ordinary measure of damages is the full value of the chattel, and so consists of a forced judicial sale of the goods. In this context, full value means market value. Whereas for detinue, the value is assessed at the time of the trial; for conversion, the value is assessed at the time the goods were wrongfully

---

[317] See paragraph 1.4.

[318] See McMahon & Binchy, *The Law of Torts*, Chapter 30.

[319] *Simmons v Lilystone* (1853) 8 Ex 431.

converted.[320] A reference will be made to the market where one exists to calculate the value of the chattel, but if, through the wrongdoing of the defendant, the value cannot be determined, any doubt will be resolved in the plaintiff's favour.[321] For example, where the chattel has disappeared, it will be ascribed the highest value that it could possess, provided the other evidence in the case is consistent with this approach.[322] Consequential damages can be awarded as long as principles of mitigation have been followed and unless they are too remote.[323] Such damages may include the loss of post-conversion appreciation in value of the converted chattel, so that in fact the plaintiff will recover damages representing the value of the chattel at the date of judgment. Where the defendant has carried out improvements to the goods, if he was acting in the mistaken but honest belief that he had good title to the goods, then in assessing damages, an allowance will be made for the amount of expenditure on the improvement. This assessment will be made at the time of the conversion and not at the time of the judgment.[324] If the owner recapts the goods, it seems that the defendant may sue the owner for the amount of the expenditure, although there is some conflict of judicial opinion on this.[325] It also appears that where an order for specific delivery is made, the plaintiff owner may be required to pay for any improvement.[326]

16.1.2. Detinue

Detinue consists of the wrongful refusal by the defendant to deliver up to the plaintiff a chattel after demand has been made by the plaintiff to do so. A detention is not wrongful unless the defendant's possession is adverse to or in defiance of the plaintiff's right. Thus, for example, a bailee who merely holds on to a chattel after the termination of the contract of bailment may be liable for breach of contract but not in detinue. One of the advantages of an action for detinue over that of conversion lies in the available remedies. Three possible forms of remedy exist:

---

[320] Johnson and Johnson (Ireland) Ltd v CP Security Ltd [1985] IR 362.

[321] Armory v Delamirie (1722) 1 Stra 505.

[322] Colbeck v Diamanta Ltd [2002] EWHC 616.

[323] See Kuwait Airways Corpn v Iraqi Airways Co [2002] UKHL 19.

[324] Greenwood v Bennett [1973] QB 195.

[325] Greenwood v Bennett – the judges were divided on whether this was possible.

[326] Ibid.

(a)   For the value of the chattel to be assessed and damages for its detention

This is appropriate where the chattel is an ordinary article of commerce, or where the plaintiff does not want the goods back or where it is not possible for them to be returned.

(b)   Order for the return of the chattel or its value as assessed and damages

This is a discretionary power of the court and the court will not exercise this discretion where the article is an ordinary article of commerce and of no special value or interest, and not alleged to be of any special value to the plaintiff and where damages would be an adequate remedy.[327]

Where a court orders return of a chattel in circumstances where the defendant has added to its value by his or her own work, creativity or expenditure, the court will make an allowance to the defendant for this increase in value. The leading Irish case is *Webb v Ireland*.[328] Here, the finders of a hoard of ecclesiastical artefacts sued to recover them from the National Museum of Ireland. Blayney J in the High Court held that the Irish State had no property in the objects and ordered that they be returned to the finders or that they should recover its value (£5,536,000). He held that the State was entitled to an allowance (£25,800) for the preservation and restoration it had carried out on the hoard while in its possession. Blayney J followed *Greenwood v Bennett*[329] and held that an award of an allowance depended on the improver's ignorance of the owner's title and his belief in his own. However, he also held that the improver can lose his right to an allowance where he makes the improvements after getting notice of a rival claim, even though his belief in his own title persists. The result was that the National Museum could not recover those preservation costs which were incurred after they had received a solicitor's letter from the finders making claim to the hoard. According to Blayney J, the letter consisted of notice of a possible defect in the State's title and therefore distinguished the State's position from that of the innocent purchaser in *Greenwood v Bennett*.[330] The case was appealed to the Supreme Court where it was held that the hoard be-

---

[327] *Whitely Ltd v Hilt* [1918] 2 KB 808; *Waterford Corporation v O'Toole*, High Court, 9 November 1979, Finlay J.

[328] [1988] IR 353.

[329] [1973] QB 195.

[330] [1988] IR 353, p 370.

longed to the State. There was no further consideration of the issue of the finder's obligation to compensate for improvement.

(c) Order for return of the chattel and damages for its detention

This is similar to the second remedy but does not involve an assessment of the value of the chattel.

16.1.3. Trespass

As discussed above,[331] trespass to goods requires proof that the plaintiff's possession of his goods was wrongfully and directly interfered with by the defendant.[332] The interference can consist of taking the goods out of the possession of another, wrongful seizure of goods or doing damage to goods with one's person or property. It is one of the requirements of the law of trespass to goods that the interference must be direct.[333] A trespass may coincide with a conversion, however trespass can be committed without any denial of or interference with title. Trespass lies only in favour of a plaintiff who has possession or the immediate right to possession enjoyed by a bailor where the bailment is at will. Damages are the primary remedy, however remedies may also include injunctions, orders for re-delivery of goods, and recaption. Where the plaintiff is the owner and has been wholly deprived of the goods, he can recover the full market value and any consequential loss. If he only owns a part interest, he can recover the value of that interest. For partial loss or damage to the goods, the diminution in the value of the property will be recoverable. It is also possible to recover damages for loss of use of the goods.[334] There is some authority to the effect that if an order for re-delivery of the goods is made, this will reduce the damages available in conversion, but not in trespass.[335]

16.2. Restitution

There is a body of law in the common law known as the Law of Restitution. It is concerned with the award of remedies which do not operate to compensate the plaintiff but rather serve to deprive the defendant of a

---

[331] See above, paragraph 1.4.1.
[332] Cf. *Farrell v Minister for Agriculture and Food High Court*, 11 October 1995.
[333] See above, paragraph 1.4.1.
[334] *The Mediana* [1900] AC 113.
[335] *Rundle v Little* (1844) 6 QB 174.

gain. For many years, restitution was seen as being a part of the law of contract. UK and Irish law now recognise the existence of an independent law of restitution based on the concept of unjust enrichment.[336] The first Irish case to definitively recognise an independent cause of action in unjust enrichment was *Dublin Corporation v Building and Allied Trade Union*.[337] According to Keane J:

> 'It is clear that, under our law, a person can in certain circumstances be obliged to effect restitution of money or other property to another where it would be unjust for him to retain the property ... This principle no longer rests on the fiction of an implied promise to return the property, which in the days when the forms of action still ruled English law, led to its tortuous rationalisation as "quasi-contractual" in nature.'

Keane J outlined four essential pre-conditions on the obligation to make restitution. There must be: (i) an enrichment to the defendant (ii) at the expense of the plaintiff (iii) in circumstances in which the law will require restitution (*i.e.* whether the enrichment was 'unjust') (iv) where there is no reason why restitution will be withheld).

16.2.1. Restitution for unjust enrichment

The 'unjust' element of the enquiry is satisfied by establishing a recognised cause of action such as mistake, duress or total failure of consideration.

(a)   Mistake of fact

Payments made on the basis of a mistaken belief are generally recoverable if the mistake is fundamental and relates to the terms of the contract. This general rule was established in *Kelly v Solari*[338] and endorsed in Ireland in *National Bank Ltd v O'Connor & Bowmaker Ireland Ltd*.[339] Thus, in *O'Connor*, for example, a bank which paid the defendant on foot of fraudulent drafts in the mistaken belief that they were valid could recover the money. Traditionally, it was the case that this cause of action only lay where the mistake was one of fact. The common law made a distinction between mis-

---

[336] In the UK, the House of Lords recognised the existence of an independent law of restitution based on unjust enrichment in the case of *Lipkin Gorman (a firm) v Karpnale Ltd* [1991] 2 AC 548.

[337] [1996] 2 ILRM 547.

[338] (1841) 9 M & W 54.

[339] (1966) 103 ILTR 73.

takes of fact and mistakes of law. If the mistake could be characterised as one of law, then it may not be possible to order restitution. For example, a mistake as to the interpretation of a statute or statutory instrument is a mistake of law.[340] The general rule was that a payment made in such circumstances could not be recovered. This rule was often criticised as creating an irrational and arbitrary distinction. It was described as 'a rule built on inadequate foundations, lacking in clarity (the distinction between mistake of fact and mistake of law can best be described as a fluttering, shadowy will-o'-the-wisp), and whose harshness had led to a luxuriant growth of exceptions.'[341] This rule has now been abolished in the UK. In *Kleinwort Benson Ltd v Lincoln CC*[342] the House of Lords removed the bar to recovery for mistake of law. Many other common law countries have also abolished the bar.[343] The position in Ireland remains somewhat unclear. Irish cases had followed the English position and held that there may be some circumstances in cases of mistake of law in which an order for restitution may be made. For example, there was some English authority to the effect that restitution could be ordered following a mistake of law where there had been a breach of trust by the defendant.[344] In these cases, it was held that where the parties are not equally situated and when the payee has either a duty to the plaintiff or is in a better position to know the law, or is primarily responsible for the mistaken interpretation of the law, then the payee may be obliged to make restitution. This approach was adopted by the Irish Courts in *Dolan v Neligan*.[345] In this case, overpayments to the Revenue Commissioners based on a mistaken interpretation of the relevant statutes were held to be recoverable.

However, it is now acknowledged that the distinction between mistake of fact and mistake of law has '*collapsed under the weight of its exceptions*'.[346] In Ireland, it seems to be the case that an enrichment conferred under mistake of fact *or* law is probably recoverable. This was accepted by Keane J in *Dublin Corporation v Building and Allied Trades Union*.[347] Some uncertainty has

---

[340] See *O'Loghlen v O'Callaghan* (1874) IR 8 CL 116; *Holt v Markham* [1923] 1 KB 504; *Casey v The Irish Sailors and Soldiers Land Trust* [1937] IR 208.

[341] *Air Canada v British Columbia* (1989) 59 DLR (4th) 161, 191, *per* Forest J.

[342] [1999] 2 AC 349.

[343] The rule was abolished by the Supreme Court of Canada in *Air Canada v British Columbia* (1989) 59 DLR (4d) 161, by the Australian High Court in *David Securities Pty Ltd v Commonwealth Bank of Australia* (1992) 175 CLR 353, by the South African Supreme Court in *Willis Faber Enthoven Pty Ltd v Receiver of Revenue* 1992 (4) SA 202 (A) and in Scotland in *Morgan Guaranty Trust Co of New York v Lothian Regional Council* 1995 SLT 299.

[344] *Kiriri Cotton Co v Dewani* [1969] AC 192; *Rogers v Ingham* (1876) 3 ChD 351.

[345] [1967] IR 247; See also *Rogers v Louth County Council* [1981] ILRM 144.

[346] O'Dell, *Annual Review of Irish Law* (1997), p 619.

[347] [1996] 2 IR 468.

been added to the situation, however by the decision of the Supreme Court in *Duff v Minister for Agriculture (No 2)*.[348] Here, the Minister for Agriculture implemented a European Regulation erroneously and thereby excluded the plaintiff farmers from milk quotas. The Supreme Court held that the plaintiffs were entitled to damages and remitted the matter to the High Court for the assessment of those damages. However, the basis of the liability is unclear. The erroneous implementation was described by the Supreme Court as a mistake of law and it was concluded that 'just as money paid under a mistake of law can be recovered if the responsibility for the mistake lies more on the one party than the other and the one with the responsibility is in a more powerful position, so I believe should the plaintiffs be entitled to a remedy at the hands of the Minister for the wrongs they have suffered.'[349] According to Barrington J 'if the plaintiffs have suffered loss and damage as a result of the Minister's mistake of law, it appears to me just and proper in the circumstances of this case, that the Minister should pay them compensation.'[350] The reasoning has been criticised. O'Dell is of the opinion that it is *'odd to say the least, first, to see life being breathed into a doctrine which has been abolished in many jurisdictions and is on its last legs in many others, and then to see the rejuvenated doctrine transmuted from a bar into a cause of action.'*[351] Later cases call into question the 'mistake of law' reasoning, and suggest that the correct basis of liability in *Duff* should have been that the farmers had a legitimate expectation as a matter of national law which the Minister's error had frustrated.[352]

(b)   Total failure of consideration

Where a plaintiff has not received any part of that contracted for, this is said to be a total failure of consideration. So, if a plaintiff has paid money in pursuance of his obligations under a contract and the consideration for which he entered the contract totally fails, he may bring an action for the return of the money so paid.[353] If the plaintiff received any part of the promised consideration, a claim for restitution of money paid will fail.[354] For

---

[348] [1997] 2 IR 22, *per* O'Flaherty J.

[349] *Ibid*, at 75.

[350] *Ibid*, at 90.

[351] O'Dell, *Annual Review of Irish Law* (1997), p 623.

[352] See *Glencar Exploration v Mayo CC* Supreme Court July 19 2001, and analysis by O'Dell in *Annual Review of Irish Law* (2001), p 505.

[353] See *Hayes v Stirling* (1863) Ir CLR 277; *Griffin v Caddell* (1875) IR 9 CL 488.

[354] See *Lecky v Walter* [1914] IR 378; *Stapleton v Prudential Assurance* (1928) 62 ILTR 56.

example, in *Stapleton v Prudential Assurance*,[355] the plaintiff could not recover insurance premiums paid under a voidable contract because she was covered by the policy throughout the duration of the time when the contract was valid. Therefore there was no failure of consideration. It is important to note however, that just because the plaintiff received some benefit from the transaction that a court will find that there has not been a total failure of consideration. The leading English case is *Rowland v Divall*.[356] There, the defendant, S. bought a car in good faith from a thief, T., and resold it to the plaintiff B1, a car-dealer for £334. The car dealer plaintiff repainted the car and two months later, sold it a third party, B2 for £400. Two months after that, the police took possession of the car on behalf of the true owner. B1 returned the price of the car to B2 and then brought an action to recover the £334 from the defendant. The Court of Appeal held that his action should succeed. The decision was reached on the basis that notwithstanding that B1 had obtained a benefit of four months use of the car and that the car could not be restored to the defendant, that the consideration for the payment had totally failed. According to Atkin LJ:

> 'the buyer has not received any part of that which he contracted to receive – namely, the property and right to possession – and, that being so, there has been a total failure of consideration.'[357]

The case has been criticised on the basis that the result seemed to unjustly enrich B1 who had use of the goods and yet was entitled to a full refund of the price. It has been suggested that the rule in *Rowland v Divall* should be reconsidered and that any claim by the buyer should be limited to the recovery of the actual loss which he has sustained by reason of the defect of title.[358] In addition there is some doubt as to whether the rule could apply in a case where the buyer cannot return the goods not because they were stolen, but because they have been consumed or resold by him. *Rowland v Divall* was followed in Ireland in *United Dominions Trust (Ireland) v Shannon Caravans Ltd*[359] and *Chartered Trust Ireland Ltd v Healy & Commins*.[360]

---

[355] (1928) 62 ILTR 56.
[356] [1923] 2 KB 500.
[357] *Ibid*, p 507.
[358] *Benjamin's Sale of Goods*, Chapter 4, p 181.
[359] [1976] IR 225.
[360] Unreported, High Court December 10 1985.

(c)   Ignorance

Ignorance has never been expressly recognised by the Irish courts as a ground of restitution in its own right, however, many commentators argue that it is another possible ground of restitution. If a plaintiff has paid money to a defendant in the mistaken belief that he is liable to pay the defendant, then he will be able to obtain restitution of the money. This is because the mistake is taken to have vitiated the plaintiff's intention that the defendant should receive the money. Thus, it is argued that if mistake is sufficient to vitiate the claimant's intention, it should also be possible to justify restitution where the defendant received the money in circumstances where the plaintiff was ignorant of the transfer.[361] Where money is stolen from a plaintiff, the plaintiff is unaware of the thief's enrichment at his expense, but can have restitution from the thief. There is some support for this theory in Irish law. In *Kelly v Cahill*, by his will dated 1969, the testator left his property jointly to his wife and brother for life, with remainder in trust for his nephew. In 1994, he changed his mind and instructed his solicitor that he wished to leave all of his property to his wife instead of to his nephew. The solicitor advised him that the most tax efficient way to do this was to leave the will unaltered but to put the property into the joint names of himself and his wife. A deed of transfer was drawn up and executed by the parties. However, due to the solicitor's mistake, without the knowledge of the testator and his wife, the deed excluded much of the testator's property. When the testator died, these excluded lands passed under the will to the nephew. Barr J held that the nephew would be unjustly enriched by the receipt of the property and therefore that he held it on remedial constructive trust for the testator's widow. O'Dell argues that since Barr J held that the plaintiff and her husband could not reasonably have known of the solicitor's error, which had the effect of enriching the nephew, this must constitute a strong endorsement of ignorance as an unjust factor as a matter of Irish law.[362]

(d)   Compulsion

The principle of compulsion underlies a number of specific grounds of restitution such as duress and undue influence. It arises where a pressure has been placed on the plaintiff to transfer a benefit to the defendant. The effect of such pressure is to vitiate the plaintiff's intention that the defendant should receive the enrichment.[363]

---

[361] See Virgo, *The Principles of the Law of Restitution* (2006), Chapter 7, p 131.

[362] O'Dell, *Annual Review of Irish Law* (1998), p 508.

[363] See *Hogan v Steele and the ESB* Supreme Court November 1 2000.

(e)   Incapacity

Where the plaintiff lacks capacity to enter a transaction this will constitute a ground of restitution to enable him to recover any benefits transferred to the defendant pursuant to the transaction. The effect of the incapacity is to vitiate the plaintiff's intention that the defendant should receive a benefit. Moreover, there are strong policy reasons to protect incapacitated people from the consequences of their actions. Incapacity includes mental disorder, intoxication, and minority.

16.2.2. Restitution for wrongs

This category relates to restitutionary claims which are founded on the commission of a wrong by the defendant. Certain types of wrongdoing may trigger the award of restitutionary remedies. The concept is based on the principle that no one should be allowed to profit from wrongdoing and damages in the restitution measure for a wrong have the effect of requiring the defendant to disgorge that profit regardless of the type of wrong committed. The Law Reform Commission Report on Aggravated, Exemplary and Restitutionary Damages[364] concluded that restitutionary damages were available in Irish law for all torts and breach of contract, in cases where the defendant has derived a profit from the commission of the tortious or contractual wrong against the plaintiff. The Commission did not recommend the enactment of legislation on this matter but considered that the development of the law should be left to the common law.[365] Earlier Irish cases had already recognised the availability of such damages in Irish law. For example, in *Hickey v Roches Stores (No 1)*,[366] Finlay J held that there were exceptions to the traditional measures of damages in contract and tort as to the general rule with regard to the assessment of damages. He stated that:

> 'Where a wrongdoer has calculated and intended by his wrongdoing to achieve a gain or a profit which he could not otherwise achieve and has in that way acted mala fide, then irrespective of whether the form of his wrongdoing constitutes a tort or breach of contract the Court should in assessing damages look not only to the loss suffered by the injured party but also to the profit or gain unjustly or wrongly obtained by the wrongdoer. If the assessment of damages confined to the loss of the injured party should still leave the wrongdoer profiting from his calculated breach of the law, damages should be assessed so as to deprive him of that profit.'

---

[364] LRC 60-2000; LRC, Dublin, 2000.
[365] *Ibid*, para 6.48; p 103.
[366] High Court, July 14 1976.

In *Maher v Collins*,[367] the Supreme Court held that the primary measure of damages in tort is the compensation measure but found that there may be exceptional circumstances where the defendant's conduct is designed by him to make a profit for himself which may exceed any compensation he may be liable for. In those circumstances, the Court seems to envisage the reversal of such unjust enrichment from the defendant.[368]

16.2.3. The characteristics of restitutionary remedies

Restitutionary remedies are assessed by reference to the defendant's gain and the effect of a restitutionary remedy in many cases is to restore to the plaintiff what he has lost. In some cases, the defendant may be required to disgorge benefits to the plaintiff rather than to restore to the plaintiff what he has lost. This occurs where the defendant has committed a wrong against the plaintiff. This reflects the fundamental principle of restitution that no defendant should profit from his wrongdoing.

Restitutionary remedies can be divided into two broad categories; personal restitutionary remedies and proprietary restitutionary remedies.

(a)   Personal restitutionary remedies

These remedies restore to the plaintiff the value of a benefit which the defendant has received. These remedies operate *in personam*. The defendant is liable to pay the value of the benefit to the plaintiff rather than transfer the benefit itself. The plaintiff has a right as against a person rather than a thing. This means that the award of such a remedy creates a relationship of creditor and debtor between the parties. This type of remedy does not depend on the defendant retaining the benefit which he received from the plaintiff.

(b)   Proprietary restitutionary remedies

These remedies operate to enable the plaintiff to assert his property rights in an asset which is held by the defendant. These remedies operate *in rem*. These remedies can be divided into those which enable the plaintiff to recover property which is held by the defendant and those that recognise that the plaintiff has a security interest in the property which is held by the defendant. The advantage of a proprietary restitutionary remedy is

---

[367] [1975] IR 232.
[368] See O'Dell, *Annual Review of Irish Law* (1998), p 559.

that in the event of the defendant's insolvency, the plaintiff's claim to the asset ranks above other creditors of the defendant. The plaintiff is therefore more likely to recover the value of the asset if the defendant becomes insolvent. This category of remedy depends on the defendant retaining the property in which the plaintiff has an interest. If the defendant has dissipated the property which he had received before the plaintiff brought his action, the plaintiff will have to rely on personal remedies. However, proprietary restitutionary remedies may still be awarded where the property has been dissipated so long as the defendant retains the product of the property or a substitute for it in accordance with the rules for tracing.[369]

16.2.4. Types of restitutionary remedies

(a) Money had and received

This is a common law restitutionary remedy which applies where the plaintiff wishes to recover money which had been paid to the defendant. It is a personal remedy which exists only at common law. It allows the plaintiff to recover the value of the money received by the defendant.

(b) Account of profits

Where the defendant has committed a wrong against the plaintiff such as a breach of fiduciary duty, the defendant may be ordered to make an account of profits which the defendant made as a result of the wrongdoing to the plaintiff. This is a personal remedy however, the profit may be held on constructive trust so that the plaintiff has an equitable proprietary interest in the profit.

(c) Restitutionary damages

The term restitutionary damages refers to the situation where the defendant has benefited from wrongdoing by saving expenditure. This head of damages deprives the defendant of this benefit by means of a restitutionary remedy. It can be contrasted with the situation where the defendant has profited from his wrongdoing in which case an order for account of profits is made.

---

[369] See below para 16.3.1.(d).

(d)   Recognition of beneficial interest

Unjust enrichment of the defendant at the expense of the plaintiff simply
gives rise to a personal obligation on the part of the defendant to make
restitution to the plaintiff of the value of the enrichment received. It is
therefore a legal personal claim, giving rise to no proprietary obligation to
hold the goods property received for the plaintiff. However, where the
defendant retains property in which the plaintiff has an equitable proprietary interest, a court may order that a defendant hold this property on
trust for the plaintiff. The plaintiff can call for the return of the property
whenever he wishes. This is a proprietary restitutionary remedy. In order
to avail of this the plaintiff must first establish an equitable proprietary
interest in the property which was received by the defendant. The trust is
often used in order to justify this type of proprietary restitution.[370] For
example, the court may order that property is to be held on constructive
trust for the plaintiff's case.

(e)   Rescission

Where a transaction is voidable for fraudulent or innocent misrepresentation, duress or undue influence, the plaintiff can seek to have the contract rescinded. Rescission operates to avoid or nullify the contract *ab
initio* which means that the parties should be returned to the position
they were in before it was entered into. In the case of an executed or
partly executed contract, then, rescission involves the restoration of
benefits transferred under the transaction and the recovery by the plaintiff of property with which he has parted under the transaction and the
return of any benefit which he received to the defendant. Rescission can
occur both at common law and in equity. Where the transaction is voidable for fraudulent misrepresentation, duress or non-disclosure, the plaintiff can have the transaction set aside in law. Where the transaction is
voidable for non-fraudulent misrepresentation, or undue influence, it can
be set aside in equity. Rescission at law theoretically can occur without
the plaintiff obtaining a court order, although in practice this will frequently be necessary, where, for example, the other party disputes the
entitlement to rescind. It is essentially a self-help procedure. In general to
be effective, recission requires notice to the defendant.[371] Rescission in
equity only occurs by order of the court.

---

[370] See further Virgo, *The Principles of Restitution*, Chapters 20 and 21.

[371] However, in exceptional circumstances, the plaintiff may be able to rescind without communicating directly to the other party. See *Car and Universal Finance Co
Ltd v Caldwell* [1965] 1 QB 525.

The restitutionary implications of recission can be either proprietary or personal. If the transaction is rescinded at law, legal title to the property will be re-vested in the plaintiff. Where the transaction is rescinded in equity, the property which the plaintiff transferred will be held on trust for the plaintiff who will have a proprietary interest in it. Where the circumstances are such that the defendant has not retained the property or its traceable substitute, a proprietary claim will not be available. The plaintiff will instead be able to make a personal restitutionary claim to recover the value of the benefits transferred. This is an illustration of the unjust enrichment principle operating to ensure that the consequence of rescission is that the defendant will not be able to obtain a benefit where the plaintiff had not intended the defendant to receive the benefit in those circumstances.[372]

The plaintiff may lose the right to rescind the contract in certain circumstances:

(i)   Restitutio in integrum is impossible

The traditional view of rescission is that an essential requirement of the remedy where the contract has been partly or wholly performed is the restoration of the parties to their original positions. It is said that 'restitutio in integrum' is essential. The general rule is that rescission cannot be enforced if the plaintiff and defendant cannot restore the benefits received under the voidable transaction.[373] Thus, for example when goods delivered under a voidable contract have been radically changed or consumed by the plaintiff buyer, the plaintiff will be barred from rescinding the contract because counter-restitution cannot be made.[374] Where, for example, the buyer of a car has substantially modified it after purchase, or where it has been seriously damaged in an accident, restitution *in integrum* will not be possible. Traditionally equity was more flexible in its approach to the requirement of restitution in integrum. Equity had the

---

[372] See Virgo, *op cit*, p 31.

[373] '... though the defendant has been fraudulent, he must not be robbed, nor must the plaintiff be unjustly enriched, as he would be if he both got back what he had parted with and kept what he had received in return. The purpose of the relief is not punishment, but compensation.' Per Lord Wright in *Spence v Crawford* [1939] 3 All ER 271 at 288-289.

[374] *Clarke v Dickson* (1858) EB & E 148; see also *Smith New Court Securities Ltd v Scrimgeour Vickers (Asset Management) Ltd* [1994] 2 BCLC 212. The plaintiff bought shares acting on the defendant's fraudulent misrepresentation. The plaintiff was unable to rescind the contract and recover the purchase price of the shares because the shares had been sold to a third party.

flexibility to recognise the value of benefits received so that even if it is no longer possible to restore property itself, the reasonable value of that property can be paid. If property transferred by the defendant has deteriorated in the hands of the plaintiff so that it cannot be restored in its original state, provided that its substantial identity remains, its restoration will be ordered on terms that the plaintiff pay compensation for its deterioration. In *Erlanger v New Sombrero Phosphate Co.*,[375] the plaintiff wished to rescind a contract for the purchase of a mine on the grounds of non-disclosure of a material fact by the defendant. The plaintiff had worked the mine and obtained a benefit from it. The court held that the plaintiff could rescind the contract, returning the mine to the defendant and making an account of profits for the benefit received from working the mine. According to Lord Blackburn, the court, in the exercise of its equitable jurisdiction 'can take account of profits and make allowance for deterioration. And I think the practice has always been for a court of equity to give this relief whenever, by the exercise of its power, it can do what is practically just, though it cannot restore the parties precisely to the state they were in before the contract.'[376] It follows that in equity, rescission will hardly ever be prevented by the operation of the restitution *in integrum* requirement. Restitution can be made in respect of practically all benefits received if they can be valued. Virgo argues that a similar approach to restitution should be recognised for rescission at common law and the bar of not being able to make restitution should only be relevant where the value of the benefit cannot be restored. This would only occur where the benefit obtained could not be valued.[377]

(ii) Third party rights

Rescission will not be available if a third party acquires an interest in the property which was transferred under a voidable transaction and can show he is a *bona fide* purchaser for valuable consideration. The leading Irish case is *Anderson v Ryan*.[378] Here, Davis owned a mini car. He answered an advertisement offering a Sprite car for sale. The parties agreed to swap vehicles without monetary consideration. The Sprite was a stolen car. Davis was dispossessed of the Sprite but the police eventually returned the Mini car to him. In the meantime, the Mini had been the subject of two subsequent deals. The defendant, Ryan bought the car from a person representing him-

---

[375] (1878) 3 App Cas 1218.

[376] *Ibid*, 1278-1279.

[377] See Virgo, *The Principles of the Law of Restitution*, Chapter 1, p 33. See also Halson, 'Rescission for Misrepresentation', [1997] RLR 89.

[378] [1967] IR 34.

self as Davis. This person was probably the person who had misrepresented himself as the owner of the Sprite. The defendant then sold the mini to the plaintiff, Anderson, who was dispossessed of it by the police. Anderson sued Ryan claiming that under s. 12(1) and s. 21(1) of the Sale of Goods Act 1893, Ryan lacked title to the goods at the time of transfer of the property to him, Anderson. The High Court found that the issue to be decided was whether Ryan had good title to the car when he sold it to Anderson. Davis, the original owner had parted with the car relying on a fraudulent misrepresentation. This rendered the contract voidable. The contract between Davis and rogue had not been avoided before the sale between Anderson and Ryan had been concluded. As a result, Ryan had a valid but voidable title to the car under s. 23(1) of the Sale of Goods Act 1893. This voidable title was transferred to Anderson. The court found that the seizure of the Mini by the police was a wrongful act and redress should be sought from that direction. If property is transferred under a voidable transaction to a person who subsequently cannot be traced, the owner may be able to rescind the contract by taking steps to recover his property such as notifying the police. This will prevent further transactions involving the property from passing good title to the transferee, even if he is an innocent third party.[379]

(iii)   Affirmation

The plaintiff cannot rescind the transaction where he is held to have affirmed the contract. Affirmation can occur if the plaintiff has full knowledge of the facts and the existence of the circumstances allowing rescission. For example, this will be the case, if he knows that there has been a misrepresentation. In addition, the plaintiff must show that he has decided not to rescind the contract. It is not necessary for any affirmation to be communicated to the defendant.[380] In *Sharpley v Louth and East Coast Railway Co,*[381] the plaintiff was induced to purchase shares in the defendant company by a misrepresentation. The plaintiff sought to rescind the contract but was unable to do so because he knew that there had been a misrepresentation, yet continued to act as a shareholder. This was considered by the court to be conduct amounting to affirmation. Loss of the right to rescission due to affirmation of the contract does not prevent the plaintiff from obtaining a remedy in damages.[382]

---

[379] *Car and Universal Finance Co Ltd v Caldwell* [1965] 1 QB 525.

[380] *Ibid.*

[381] (1876) 2 Ch D 663.

[382] See *Production Technology Consultants v Bartlett* [1988] 1 EGLR 182.

(iv)   Delay in seeking relief

The plaintiff may be barred from rescinding a contract if the court considers that a reasonable period of time has elapsed before the attempt to rescind it. Rescission is generally sought in equity and the equitable doctrine that litigants should seek equitable relief promptly may operate. In *Leaf v International Galleries*[383] an innocent misrepresentation was made by the vendor that a painting was by John Constable. Five years later, the purchaser, on learning that the statement was false claimed rescission on the grounds of innocent misrepresentation. The Court of Appeal dismissed the claim. The right to rescind was lost where it was not sought within a reasonable time of the sale. In sale of goods cases, the courts will also consider whether a right to rescind can be lost through acceptance of the goods.[384]

16.2.5. Defences

There are a number of defences to a restitutionary claim. These include estoppel and change of position as well as the defence of *bona fide* purchase for value.[385] The defence of change of position involves a denial that the defendant has been enriched on the basis that the enrichment is no longer in his hands. This defence has been recognised in English law in *Lipkin Gorman v Karpnale*.[386] In the New Zealand case of *National Bank of New Zealand v Waitaki International Processing*,[387] the plaintiffs mistakenly paid a sum of money to the defendants. Pending resolution of the issue of whether the money was in fact due, the defendants deposited the money with a finance company. The finance company went into liquidation and the money was lost. It was held that the defendant did not derive a benefit from the money because it had been lost by the failure of the ultimate recipient. It was not spent or used by the defendant. The defendant was therefore allowed to rely on the defence of change of position. The defence of change of position has been recognised in Ireland in *Murphy v AG*[388] and *McDonnell v Ireland*.[389]

---

[383] [1950] 2 KB 86.

[384] S. 34 and s. 35 Sale of Goods Act.

[385] See further Virgo, *The Principles of The Law of Restitution*, Chapters 23 to 28.

[386] [1991] 2 AC 548.

[387] [1997] 1 NZLR 724.

[388] [1982] IR 241.

[389] Unreported, Supreme Court July 23 1997.

16.3. Acquisition of movable from non-owner

The rules on transfer of title by non-owners have been examined above. The general rule is that no-one can transfer a better title to goods than he himself possesses, (*nemo dat quod non habet*). Exceptions to this rule have been progressively introduced both by common law and by statute.

16.3.1. Remedies of the owner and consequences for possessor

(a)   Conversion

An owner who has an immediate right to possession of the goods is entitled to recover possession of them from a person who is wrongfully in possession of the goods. He may bring an action in the tort of conversion against any person who deprives him of possession or who, without his authority deals with the goods intending to assert a right to them inconsistent with his right. Provided that the defendant has this intention, liability in the tort of conversion is strict. So, a defendant may be liable even though he was unaware of the plaintiff's right to the goods or honestly believed that he himself was the true owner. The owner may retake the goods without action if he can do so lawfully. (Right of Recaption – see above) However, if the defendant resists the owner's claim, the owner will need to bring an action in conversion. In his defence, the defendant can rely on any of the exceptions to the *nemo dat* rule. Where he cannot rely on any of the *nemo dat* exceptions, the defendant will be forced to surrender the goods, or pay their value to the owner. Even where the owner has been deprived of his title by the operation of one of the *nemo dat* exceptions, the owner will nevertheless be able to institute proceedings in tort for conversion against any person who converted the goods before his title was extinguished.

(b)   Improvements

Where an action is taken in conversion against a person who has improved the goods, for example, by servicing or repairing the goods, if it is shown that the improver acted in the mistaken but honest belief that he had good title to them, then damages in a conversion action against the defendant improver will be reduced to give the latter credit for the improved value.[390] If the goods are improved by an intermediary after leaving the possession of the claimant but before the goods come into the possession of the defendant, it seems that the defendant, having paid a price

---

[390] See *Reid v Fairbanks* (1853) 13 CB 692; *Munro v Wilmott* [1949] 1 KB 295.

which reflects those improvements is entitled to a reduction in damages on the same principle. In addition, if the court makes an order for delivery up of the goods, it may assess the allowance to be made in respect of the improvement and require as a condition of delivery of the goods that allowance is to be made by the plaintiff.[391] A person who has improved the goods may also have a direct restitutionary claim against the owner if the necessary elements of a such a claim can be established.[392]

(c) Restitution

Alternatively, the owner may elect to pursue a restitutionary claim to recover any sum received as a result of the sale or use of the goods by the wrongdoer in an action in restitution for monies had and received.[393]

(d) Tracing

In addition, the proprietary right of the owner is recognised both at common law and in equity by allowing the owner to 'trace' his property into the proceeds of its sale so long as these have not been dissipated.[394] He may also trace into other identifiable assets which have been purchased with those proceeds.[395] This will be important where the defendant is insolvent and the owner is trying to establish a claim in priority to the defendant's general creditors. At common law, tracing is only available where the proceeds of sale have not been mixed with other monies, *e.g.* in a bank account, or (if a claim is made to other assets) where these have been purchased exclusively with the unmixed proceeds.[396] However, in equity, tracing is available into a mixed fund or into assets purchased with the mixed fund and will follow the moneys into the hands of anyone other than a *bona fide* purchaser for value without notice. Equity gives the owner a charge over the fund or assets in

---

[391] See *Greenwood v Bennett* [1973] 1 QB 195; see also Irish case of *Webb v Ireland* [1988] IR 353, discussed above paragraph 16.1.2.(b)

[392] See above paragraph 16.3.1.(c). See also discussion by McKendrick, 'Restitution and the Misuse of Chattels – The Need for a Principled Approach', in Palmer & McKendrick, *Interests in Goods*, Chapter 35 and discussion by Palmer and Hudson, 'Improving Stolen Chattels', Chapter 36.

[393] See above paragraph 16.2.4.(a).

[394] *Re Diplock* [1948] Ch 465. On tracing generally, see Virgo, *op cit*, p 619 *et seq*; Smith, *The Law of Tracing* (1997); Worthington, *Personal Property Law*, p 476 *et seq*.

[395] *Foskett v McKeown* [2001] 1 AC 182.

[396] *Taylor v Plumer* (1815) 3 M & S 562; *Banque Belge pour L'Etranger v Hambrouck* [1921] 1 KB 321; *Lipkin Gorman v Karpnale Ltd* [1991] 2 AC 548.

question.[397] In order to trace in equity, the owner must establish that the defendant or a third party is in a fiduciary relationship to him and that he has an equitable proprietary interest in the property claimed.[398]

As outlined above,[399] where goods of the owner are wrongfully mixed by the defendant with goods of his own, and the goods are substantially of the same nature and quality, and they cannot in practice be separated, the mixture is held in common and the innocent party is entitled to receive out of it a quantity equal to that of his goods which went into the mixture. If there is a doubt as to the quantity, this is resolved in favour of the innocent party. The innocent party is also entitled to claim damages from the other for any loss he may have suffered, in respect of quality or otherwise, by reason of the mixing of the goods.[400]

16.4. Contract

16.4.1. Acquisition of movable under voidable contracts

A contract will be voidable where it is induced by a misrepresentation or entered into under duress, undue influence, or fraud. In the case of misrepresentation, the plaintiff may be entitled to statutory damages under the s. 45(1) Sale of Goods Act 1980. Prior to 1980, damages were only available for misrepresentation where the false statement was made fraudulently or negligently. The misrepresentee may also be entitled to an indemnity, and is entitled to rescind the contract in accordance with the principles set out above.[401] The Sale of Goods and Supply of Services Act 1980, s. 45(2) permits a court to declare a contract subsisting and award damages in lieu of rescission if the court 'is of the opinion that it would be equitable to do so.' If rescission has been lost through lapse of time, affirmation or waiver it is not possible to award damages under s. 45(2). Restitutionary remedies may be available as set out above in the case of unjust enrichment or for restitutionary wrongs.[402]

The Sale of Goods legislation makes provision for the case of sale of goods under a voidable title. S. 23 provides that 'when the seller of goods has a voidable title thereto, but his title has not been avoided at the time of the sale, the buyer acquires a good title to the goods, provided he buys them

---

[397] Re Hallet's Estate (1880) 13 ChD 696; Re Oatway [1903] 2 Ch 356.

[398] Re Diplock, above; Westdeutsche Landesbank Girozentrale v Islington London BC [1996] AC 669.

[399] See paragraph 9.

[400] See Indian Oil Corp Ltd v Greenstone Shipping SA (Panama) [1988] QB 345.

[401] See paragraph 9.

[402] See paragraph 16.2.4.

in good faith and without notice of the seller's defect in title.' This operates as an exception to the *'nemo dat'* rule and is examined in detail above at paragraph 9. The section applies where the seller's title is voidable, *i.e.* where the seller acquired the goods under a transaction affected by misrepresentation, duress, undue influence; or where the seller's title is defective because one of his predecessors in title acquired the goods under a voidable contract. S. 23 does not apply where the seller has no title at all, such as where the goods were stolen. It also does not apply where the contract under which the seller acquired the goods purported to transfer nothing more than possession of the goods. So, if the agreement between true owner and seller is only an agreement to sell, or if the transaction is one of hire purchase or conditional sale, or if the seller is in possession of the goods on sale or return or approval terms, and at the time of the sale to the innocent buyer the property has not yet passed to the seller, s. 23 will not apply.

If the transaction under which the seller acquired the goods was void as opposed to voidable, s. 23 does not apply since a void contract has no effect at all. The title of the seller may be voidable at the option of the true owner on the grounds of fraud, misprepresentation, duress, undue influence, non-disclosure. In these cases, the true owner is entitled to rescind the contract between himself and the seller. If, however, the contract is completely void, no property in the goods will pass to the seller and the buyer will not acquire good title under s. 23 even if he purchases the goods in good faith and without notice of the seller's defect in title. A contract may be void for example on the grounds of mistake, illegality or incapacity.

S. 23 provides that purchaser in good faith will succeed in a title conflict with the owner where the seller has a voidable title and the title has not been avoided at the time of the sale. The true owner can defeat this claim by avoiding the seller's title before the seller re-sells the goods to the buyer. The owner may do this by rescinding the contract between himself and the seller. This may be done by simply notifying the seller of his intention to avoid the contract or by retaking possession of the goods. Where the seller cannot be traced, the owner may be able to rescind by taking some step to recover the property such as notifying the police.[403] In order to avoid the seller's title, the true owner must be in a position to rescind the contract and none of the bars to rescission must apply.[404]

At common law, a similar rule to s. 23 applies to a person with voidable title who pledges goods with an innocent pledge or who creates an equitable right by an incomplete pledge.[405] However, an assignee in bankruptcy is not an innocent buyer, because he takes 'subject to equities'. Therefore, if the

---

[403] See *Car and Universal Finance Co Ltd v Caldwell* [1965] 1 QB 525.

[404] See above paragraph 16.2.4.(e).

[405] *Parker v Patrick* (1793) 5 TR 715; *Attenborough v London & St Katherine's Docks* (1878) 3 CPD 450.

true owner of goods is fraudulently induced to sell them to another, who subsequently becomes bankrupt, he can rescind the contract of sale and recover the goods.[406]

16.4.2. Acquisition of movable under void contracts

(a) Money paid or property transferred under an illegal contract

A contract may be unenforceable on the grounds of illegality. A contract is illegal if it involves the commission of a legal wrong or if it is contrary to public policy. Such contracts are commonly said to be 'void', although they may be enforceable in certain circumstances for example by an innocent party to the contract. The illegality may relate to the terms of the contract, the manner of its performance or the purpose for which the contract was made. An illegal contract cannot be enforced by a party who was aware of the illegality. If both parties are aware of it, it cannot be enforced by either of them.[407] A party who is unaware of the illegality may have a remedy in terms of an action for the price, or an action for damages for breach of contract.[408]

It has been established that property in goods may pass under an illegal contract of sale. Where physical possession of the goods has been transferred to the purchaser, they cannot be recovered back by the seller. The buyer may assert his proprietary rights against both the seller and against a stranger.[409] This principle applies even where the transferee has not taken possession of the property as long as the title was intended under the contract to pass to him and had so passed. This was established in *Belvoir Finance v Stapleton*,[410] and followed in Ireland by Costello J in *Hortensius Ltd & Durack v Bishops and Others*.[411]

Where a contract has been tainted by illegality, neither party may sue to recover money paid or property transferred pursuant to it. The law was stated thus by Lindley LJ in *Scott v Brown Doering*:[412]

> '*Ex turpi causa non oritur actio* ... No court ought to enforce an illegal contract or allow itself to be made the instrument of enforcing obligations alleged to arise out of a contract or transaction which is illegal if the illegality is duly

---

[406] *Re Eastgate* [1905] 1 KB 465; see also *Benjamin's Sale of Goods*, Chapter 7.
[407] *Scott v Brown Doering* [1892] 2 QB 724.
[408] *Sumner v Sumner* (1935) 69 ILTR 101.
[409] *Singh v Ali* [1960] AC 167.
[410] [1971] 1 QB 210.
[411] [1989] ILRM 294.
[412] [1892] 2 QB 724.

brought to the notice of the court and if the person invoking the aid of the court is himself implicated in the illegality.'[413]

This rule applies where the parties are '*in pari delicto*' which means that both parties are equally at fault. There are certain exceptions to this rule. For example it appears that the owner of property may bring an action based on his proprietary rights provided that he is not obliged to rely on the illegal transaction in support of his claim but sues independently of it. In *Bowmaker v Barnet's Instruments*,[414] S sold three machine tools under a contract to the plaintiffs who then let them to the defendants on hire purchase. The initial sale to the plaintiffs was illegal. The defendants wrongly sold machine tools one and three to third parties and failed to pay hire charges due under the contract in respect of machine tool two. The plaintiffs sued for conversion. The defendants resisted the action on the ground that the initial illegal contract also attached to the hiring contracts. The Court of Appeal noted that neither party was aware of the illegality with regard to the contract of sale. It upheld the action in conversion. The wrongful sale of tools one and three had the effect of terminating the defendant's right to possession and, because it was conceded that ownership had passed to plaintiff from S. Notwithstanding the initial illegality, the plaintiffs could rely on their rights of ownership and were not constrained to plead the illegal contract.

The general rule does not apply where the parties are not *in pari delicto*. A party will be allowed to sue to recover his property where, for instance, he is not aware of the facts which render the contract illegal or where he is not aware of the intention of the defendant to perform the contract in an illegal manner. A plaintiff will not be *in pari delicto* if he entered the bargain because of fraud, duress or undue influence on the part of the defendant.[415] In addition the courts will generally permit relief if the plaintiff can show that he was a member of the class which the statute was designed to protect.[416] Where this is the case, normal restitution proceedings may be instituted to recover property transferred or money paid even after the contract has been executed.[417]

---

[413] *Ibid*, at 726.
[414] [1945] KB 65.
[415] *Sumner v Sumner* (1935) 69 ILTR 101.
[416] *Browning v Morris* (1778) 2 Comp 790.
[417] See above paragraph 16.2.

(b) Mistake

A mistake operative at common law leads to the contract being declared void *ab initio*.[418] At law, a mistake which is common to both parties and which relates to a fundamental matter of fact such as the continued existence of the goods will prevent a contract coming into being. The price paid will be returnable. It is open to a party who alleges a mistake to make application to a court of equity to have the contract set rescinded. The court will refuse specific performance of such a contract. Rectification of the contract may also be available. Restitutionary remedies may also apply to a contract which is void for mistake.[419]

16.5. Restitution of movable in case of theft

16.5.1. Remedies of buyer of stolen goods

The buyer of a stolen object who improves it or spends money on its preservation may have some remedies. Assuming that the buyer gets no title to the stolen goods, and the owner has an action against him for conversion, trespass or detinue, then the court has two options. It can make an order for damages or it can make an order for specific redelivery of the goods and any consequential damages. The court will only order specific redelivery of the goods where the goods are unique in some way and not ordinary articles of commerce replaceable in the market. In other words, where damages are an adequate remedy, the court will not order specific redelivery of the goods. In this case, the court may order that the buyer receives a credit for the improvements as set out above. Where the improved goods are in some way unique, and the court makes an order for specific redelivery, the case of *Greenwood v Bennett*[420] suggests that the court will order the reimbursement of the improver to the extent of the costs incurred on the improvement. The *Webb*[421] case is also authority for the proposition that where the court orders return of goods, the possessor is entitled to a fair and just allowance for the restoration which has been carried out on the goods while in their possession. However, Palmer and Hudson suggest that if the result of ordering such an allowance was that the owner would be compelled to sell the goods in order to pay for the unrequested improve-

---

[418] *Cundy v Lindsay* (1878) 3 App Cas 459.
[419] See above paragraph 16.2.
[420] [1973] 1 QB 195.
[421] [1988] IR 353.

ment, the allowance being equitable, the court may exercise its discretion not to make such an order and to deny the restitutionary claim.[422]

16.5.2. Remedies of owner of stolen goods

Where a person buys goods which turn out to be stolen, it is a fundamental principle of the law of restitution that no criminal can retain a benefit which accrues to him or her as a result of the commission of a crime.[423] In order to recover the benefit which the defendant obtains, however, the victim of the crime must base his restitutionary claim on one of the principles which underlie the law of restitution.

This means that the defendant must found his claim on for example, unjust enrichment, vindication of property rights, or tort as outlined above. So, for example, if the commission of the crime also consists of the commission of a tort, the claimant may sue the defendant in tort (for example conversion) for a restitutionary remedy.[424]

It may be possible for the victim to bring a restitutionary claim on the basis that the defendant was unjustly enriched at his expense. The commission of the crime may enable the victim to establish one of the recognised grounds of restitution.

(a)   Claims founded on vindication of property rights

The victim may be able to establish a restitutionary claim against the criminal on the basis that the victim seeks to vindicate his or her continuing proprietary rights. This will often be the case where the defendant steals the claimant's property or handles stolen property. In *Lipkin Gorman v Karpnale Ltd*,[425] money was stolen from the claimant, a firm of solicitors, by one of its partners. The partner gambled with the money at the defendant's casino. The claimant firm of solicitors recovered much of the money stolen on the basis that the defendant had received money which belonged to the claimant. It was irrelevant that the defendant was not the criminal. It was sufficient that the defendant had received the proceeds of crime from the criminal.

---

[422] Palmer and Hudson, 'Improving Stolen Chattels', in Palmer & McKendrick, *Interests in Goods*, Chapter 36.

[423] *St John Shipping Corp v Joseph Rank Ltd* [1957] 1 QB 267.

[424] See above paragraph 15.3.1.

[425] [1991] 2 AC 548.

(b) Claims founded on wrongdoing

The victim of the crime may found his restitutionary claim on the commission of a wrong. This could occur where the crime also constitutes the commission of a tort which gives rise to a claim for restitution. The plaintiff may sue the defendant in tort for a restitutionary remedy. For example, where the defendant obtains property by deception, this would constitute the tort of deceit and the claimant can obtain a restitutionary remedy.

The question as to whether the plaintiff may found a claim for restitution on the crime itself is more controversial. Where the victim of the crime is unable to sue the criminal for the commission of a tort, is a restitutionary claim based on the crime itself possible? There are few cases which deal with this question, mainly because in many cases the victim will have a compensatory claim from the defendant. Where the victim's loss is equivalent to the defendant's gain and it is clear that the victim can obtain compensation for the loss suffered as a result of the crime under relevant common law and statutory provisions, it is clear that there is no need for the victim to bring a restitutionary claim. Sometimes the defendant's gain may exceed the victim's loss, however, the courts have been reluctant to recognise a restitutionary claim in such circumstances. The reason for this lies in the policy argument that preventing the criminal from profiting from the crime should be a matter for Parliament, by way of statutory provisions on fines and confiscation. So, for example in *Halifax Building Society v Thomas* [1996] Ch 217, Gibson LJ stated:

> 'In considering whether to extend the law of constructive trusts in order to prevent a fraudster benefiting from his wrong, it is also appropriate to bear in mind that Parliament has acted in recent years on the footing that without statutory intervention, the criminal might keep the benefit of his crime. Moreover, Parliament has given the courts the power in specific circumstances to confiscate the benefit rather than reward the person against whom the crime has been committed.'

Virgo contends that there is no obvious objection to the common law and equity recognising that the victim of a crime ought to have a right to obtain the proceeds of the crime from the criminal, albeit that this right should be subsidiary to the power of the State to obtain such proceeds. Where the State has not deprived the criminal of the profits of the crime, he argues that it is appropriate that the victim should be allowed to instigate an action to do so as 'the instrument of social purpose.'[426]

The restitutionary relief available in such cases would take the form of an account of the profits obtained as a result of the crime. It is also possible that

---

[426] Virgo, Graham, *The Principles of the Law of Restitution*, p 542.

the court would find that the defendant holds the proceeds of crime on constructive trust for the claimant on the basis of the principles laid down in *Westdeutsche Landesbank Girozentrale v Islington London Borough Council*.[427]

---

[427] [1996] AC 669.

National Report on the Transfer of Movables in Scotland

David L Carey Miller
Malcolm M Combe
Andrew J M Steven
Scott Wortley

Preface

This report aims to state the Scottish rules governing transfer of movables. Scotland is an unusual jurisdiction in Europe, because it is uncodified and is also a mixed legal system. The lack of code means that the rules come from statute and common law. For the avoidance of doubt, the expression 'common law' in this report means non-statute law, in particular case law and the works of the institutional writers such as Stair, Erskine and Bell from the seventeenth, eighteenth and nineteenth centuries.

The published version of the report does not contain the full text of statutory provisions. But all Scottish and UK statutes are now available online at http://www.statutelaw.gov.uk. We would also note that the accepted spelling of 'movable' in Scotland is 'moveable' and we follow this in the Report.

Our thanks go to Candice Donnelly and Louise Crawford for research assistance and for providing initial drafts of chapters 2 and 19.

We have attempted to state the law as of 1 July 2007, but it has been possible to take account of some later developments.

Aberdeen/Edinburgh, August 2007

David L Carey Miller
Malcolm M Combe
Andrew J M Steven
Scott Wortley

Table of Contents

2. Possession

3. Rights to hold, use or acquire moveables

17. Co-ownership

18. Further rules applying to unspecified goods

19. Consequences of restitution of moveable to the owner

Part I:
Basic information on property law

1. The notion of ownership and other property rights

1.1. General basics

1.1.1. Characteristics of rights in rem in contrast to obligations

Scotland, while part of the United Kingdom of Great Britain and Northern Ireland, has her own separate legal system. Although the Parliaments of England and Scotland were united three hundred years ago, the Treaty of Union of 1707 expressly preserved the independence of Scottish law.[1] Since 1999, this position has been strengthened by the establishment of the devolved Scottish Parliament. It has legislative power over private law.[2] The country is also distinctive in Europe as it is a mixed legal system. Roman (civil) law and English (common) law have both influenced the development of Scottish law significantly. There are a relatively small number of mixed legal systems worldwide, notably Israel, Louisiana, Quebec, South Africa and Sri Lanka.[3] Naturally, the mix in such systems tends to be an uneven one and Scotland is a good example of this.[4] For the most part, her property law is resolutely civilian and shares far more in common with the legal systems of continental Europe than with England.[5]

---

[1] Treaty of Union, articles XVIII and XIX. On the historical development of Scottish law both before and after 1707, see Cairns, J W, 'Historical Introduction' in Reid & Zimmermann, *History*, vol 1, pp 14-184.

[2] See below, para 1.1.4(a).

[3] See Palmer, V V (ed), *Mixed Jurisdictions Worldwide: The Third Legal Family* (2001); Smits, J (ed), *The Contribution of Mixed Legal Systems to European Private Law* (2001) and K G C Reid, 'The Idea of Mixed Legal Systems', (2003) 78 Tulane Law Review 5.

[4] See, for example, Whitty, N R, 'The Civilian Tradition and Debates on Scots Law', 1996 Tydskryf vir die Suid-Afrikaanse Reg 227 and 442; MacQueen, H L, 'Mixture or Muddle? – Teaching and Research in Scottish Legal History', (1997) 5 Zeitschrift für Europäisches Privatrecht 369; and du Plessis, J, 'The promises and pitfalls of mixed legal systems: the South African and Scottish experiences', (1998) 3 Stellenbosch Law Review 338.

[5] See further Reid, K, 'Property Law: Sources and Doctrine' in Reid & Zimmermann, *History*, pp 185-219. The picture of course is more complex. The key area of English influence has been the Sale of Goods Act. See below, chapter 5.

In line with civilian property law systems, a distinction is recognised between (a) real rights and (b) personal rights.[6] In the important recent case of *Burnett's Trustee v Grainger*[7] Lord Rodger of Earlsferry refers to the 'unbridgeable division' between the two.[8] In essence, real rights are rights in things. Such rights are 'good against the world'. The principal real right is of course ownership. In contrast, personal rights are only good against a particular person or limited class of persons. They are the basis of the law of obligations.[9] Examples are:

(a) a right under a contract, for example the buyer's right to delivery of the goods under a contract of sale;
(b) a right under delict, for example the right to compensation for injury suffered in a car accident caused by another;
(c) a right under unjustified enrichment, for example the right to be repaid money handed over in error; and
(d) the right of a beneficiary under a trust.[10]

As personal rights are only enforceable against the particular person (or limited class of persons) who are bound by the obligation, they are ineffective if that person becomes insolvent. Similarly a personal obligation relating to a piece of property cannot be enforced against a successor owner. In contrast, a real right can. An example illustrates this. Alan lends Belle £100. In security of the debt, Belle hands over her gold watch. This gives Alan the real right of pledge. If Belle becomes insolvent, Alan can recover his money by selling the watch. If he did not have this real right, he would be left to rank in Belle's insolvency as an unsecured creditor and could recover very little or even nothing. The real right is good in insolvency. It also remains good if Belle transfers ownership of the watch to Carol. Alan still has his real right as long as he holds possession. He can still take action against the watch and recover the debt. In contrast he has no contractual right against Carol. Carol is not personally liable under the contract of loan but her property has real liability, because the pledge was not discharged prior to the transfer to her.

---

[6] Stair, I.1.22; Bankton, II.1.1; Erskine, III.1.2; Hume, *Lectures*, I, 10; Bell, *Principles*, § 3; Reid, *Property*, para 3; Carey Miller with Irvine, *Corporeal Moveables*, para 10.01; Reid, K G C, 'Obligations and property: exploring the border', 1997 Acta Juridica 225; MacCormick, N, *Institutions of Law: An Essay in Legal Theory* (2007), pp 135-139.

[7] 2004 SC (HL) 19 at para 87.

[8] Borrowing from Nicholas, B, *An Introduction to Roman Law* (1962), p 100.

[9] See, for example, Hogg, M, *Obligations* (2nd ed, 2006).

[10] The personal right of a beneficiary is an unusual personal right in that it appears to take priority over unsecured creditors of the trustee (in his or her personal capacity) in insolvency. This is because it is a right against the trust patrimony.

1.1.2. The *numerus clausus* principle

Scottish law, unlike the laws of most other European countries, is uncodified.[11] There is no statutory list of real rights, nor indeed has one been set out by the courts. The better view, however, is that there is a *numerus clausus*.[12] The real rights recognised are as follows:[13] (a) ownership; (b) real security;[14] (c) proper liferent;[15] (d) servitude;[16] (e) negative real burden;[17] (f) lease of land, but not hire of moveables;[18] (g) possession;[19] (h) certain rights held by the public, for example public rights of way; (i) intellectual property rights;[20] and (j) various statutory rights, for example the right to install pipes into other apartments in a block.[21] A number of these rights, in particular lease, servitude and negative real burden are limited to immoveable property. The effect of the *numerus clausus* is that it is incompetent for parties to invent new real rights. But it is always open to the legislature to create new real rights. It is debatable whether a new real right could be recognised at common law. The courts have done this in the past, but not recently.[22]

---

[11] See for example, Steven, A J M, 'Transfer of Title in Scottish Law' in Rainer, J M and Filip-Fröschl, J (eds), *Transfer in Title Concerning Movables Part 1 – Eigentumsübertragung an beweglichen Sachen in Europa* (2006), p 155 at 156.

[12] Reid, K and Van der Merwe, C G, 'Property Law: Some Themes and Some Variations' in Zimmermann, Visser & Reid, *Mixed Legal Systems*, p 637 at 654.

[13] This list is drawn from Reid, *Property*, para 5 and Reid and Van der Merwe, 'Property Law: Some Themes and Some Variations' at pp 651-654.

[14] In contrast there is personal security where a third party guarantees the debt. This is known as caution.

[15] This is the equivalent of *usufructus* in Roman law.

[16] The right of one landowner to make limited use of the land of a neighbour. The leading text is Cusine, D J and Paisley, R R M, *Servitudes and Rights of Way* (1998).

[17] This is a restriction on the use of land, normally enforceable by a neighbouring landowner. See the Title Conditions (Scotland) Act 2003, s. 9.

[18] See below, para 3.1.3(a). The real nature of a lease of land was conferred by a very early statute, the Leases Act 1449.

[19] See below, chapter 2. Strictly speaking, only the right to possession based on another real right, such as ownership or liferent, is real. See Reid, *Property*, para 127.

[20] The issue of whether intellectual property rights are real is a controversial one. Although such rights satisfy the test of being good against the world there is no actual thing that the right is in. See below, para 4.1.3.

[21] Civic Government (Scotland) Act 1982, s. 88.

[22] As Reid and Van der Merwe, 'Property Law: Some Themes and Some Variations' at p 654 have commented, the last time this happened was 1840, when the real burden was recognised.

1.1.3. General principles of property law

A number of general principles may be identified.[23]

(a)   A unitary law

In principle both moveable and immoveable (heritable)[24] property are governed by the same fundamental legal principles. As the leading modern text states: '[T]he law of property is unitary in nature. There is only one set of rules ... subject to local variations in particular cases.'[25] For example, registration is a fundamental aspect of the transfer of land,[26] but this is merely an instance of a more general principle, namely that real rights normally require publicity for their creation, transfer and extinction.

(b)   Intention

It is an axiomatic feature of property law that real rights cannot usually be dealt with unless the relevant party or parties have the required intention. In the context of derivative acquisition, intention is an obvious requirement. For example, Colin cannot voluntarily transfer property to Deborah unless Colin intends to give ownership and Deborah intends to receive ownership. Only in a small number of cases, such as transfer on death or insolvency, or where public bodies have powers to acquire property compulsorily, is intention not required.[27] In some instances of original acquisition (for example, occupation) intention is required.[28] In others, matters are more complex.[29]

---

[23] See further Steven, 'Transfer of Title in Scottish Law' at 158-161 and Farran, S and Cabrelli, D, 'Exploring the Interfaces between Contract Law and Property Law: A UK Comparative Approach', (2006) 13 Maastricht Journal of European and Comparative Law 403.

[24] The formal name for immoveable property in Scotland is 'heritable property'. See Steven, 'Transfer of Title in Scottish Law' at p 157.

[25] Reid, *Property*, para 1.

[26] Abolition of Feudal Tenure etc (Scotland) Act 2000, s. 4.

[27] See Reid, *Property*, paras 663ff.

[28] See below, para 14.2.

[29] See below, chapter 11.

(c)   Publicity

Real rights normally require to be publicised. For example, for a corporeal moveable to be pledged it must be delivered to the creditor. The publicity principle protects third parties, letting them know who has the right of ownership or limited real right. It is not applied universally in Scotland, because where corporeal moveables are sold the intention of the parties alone is sufficient to allow transfer.[30] However, as shall be seen, the rules here have an English common law rather than civilian background, which explains the lack of adherence to the norm.

(d)   Certainty

As the rules of property affect everyone dealing with the property, they need to be certain. For example, it needs to be clear whether certain moveable property has acceded to land, in order that a potential acquirer knows what he or she is getting if they contract to purchase the land.[31] As a leading writer has commented: 'A fixture should be a fixture if it is patent for all the world to see.'[32]

(e)   Specificity

In order to be dealt with, property must be identified. Where corporeal moveables are being sold, they must normally be ascertained before transfer can take place. Therefore, if a buyer agrees to buy twelve bottles of whisky and the seller becomes insolvent before separating these from the rest of his stock, title cannot have passed.[33] The specificity principle is associated with the aforementioned principle of certainty which pervades civilian property law systems.

---

[30] See below, para 5.1.2.

[31] See below, para 11.1.5.

[32] Van der Merwe, C G, 'Accession by Building' in Reid & Zimmermann, *History*, vol 1, p 245 at 268.

[33] Sale of Goods Act 1979, s. 16. See *Hayman & Son v McLintock* 1907 SC 936. There is now a limited exception to this rule for bulk goods where the buyer has prepaid. See 1979 Act, s. 20A and 20B. See below, para 5.2.2(d).

(f)   Contract versus conveyance

In accordance with Roman law, a fundamental distinction is made between the contract made by a prospective transferor and transferee, the *causa*, and the conveyance: *traditionibus non nudis pactis dominia rerum transferuntur*. The contract alone is insufficient to pass ownership.[34] A separate conveyance is required. The result is that if the parties have contracted to transfer, there needs to be both *consensus in idem* as regards the contract and as the conveyance.[35] The contract/conveyance distinction has been somewhat eroded by the Sale of Goods Act but is still fundamentally present.[36]

(g)   Instantaneity

Real rights are created at one point in time. For example, if the relevant requirements are met, then the seller will be entirely divested of ownership and the buyer invested with ownership simultaneously.[37] At no point do both share title. A suitable analogy is a light being switched off, rather than slowly faded out. The English law notion of a division between legal and equitable ownership is not recognised north of the border. The only way ownership can be held by more than the one person at the one time is where there is co-ownership.[38]

(h)   Abstract system of transfer

It is accepted that an abstract system applies to transfers of land. In other words, the conveyance is viewed separately from the contract. The leading institutional writer, Stair, wrote that 'we do not follow that subtility of annulling deeds because they are *sine causa*'.[39] Authority for the position as regards moveable property is more sparse,[40] but as property law is considered to be a unitary subject, it is submitted that the same rule ap-

---

[34] See, for example, *Gibson v Hunter Home Designs Ltd* 1976 SC 23.

[35] See below, para 5.3.1. In some cases, typically donation, there will be no contract.

[36] See below, para 5.1.2.

[37] Reid, *Property*, para 603, followed by Lord President Hope in *Sharp v Thomson* 1995 SC 455 at 469. The decision of the Inner House of the Court of Session in *Sharp* was reversed on appeal, but not on this point. See 1997 SC (HL) 66.

[38] See below, chapter 17.

[39] Stair, II.3.14.

[40] Reid, *Property*, paras 608-612.

plies at common law. Under the Sale of Goods Act, the position is rather different.[41]

(i)   The *nemo plus* rule

For a transferor to be able to confer a good title on a transferee he or she must have such a title in the first place. A non owner can normally not validly transfer: *nemo plus juris ad alienum transferre potest, quam ipse haberet.*[42] Compared with other European countries, good faith rarely rescues a purchaser who buys from a party who does not have title.[43] The position in Scotland is well summed up in a statement by Lord Braxfield in the 1781 case of *Mitchells v Ferguson:* 'As to *bona fides,* although *mala fides* may cut down a right, *bona fides* cannot establish a right'.[44] It can be said in fact that the strong application of the *nemo plus* rule makes Scottish law more civilian than modern codified civilian systems.[45]

1.1.4. *Sedis materiae*

As already mentioned, Scotland is an uncodified jurisdiction. The rules on property law as regards corporeal moveables are a mixture of (a) statute and (b) common law.[46]

---

41 For a more detailed discussion, see below, para 5.1.6.

42 D 50.17.54 (Ulpian). The alternative formulation is *nemo dat quod non habet.* See Reid, *Property,* paras 669-670.

43 Notable exceptions are the Sale of Goods Act 1979, ss. 24 and 25. Compare the greater protection given, for example, in France by the Code Civil, art. 2279, in Germany by the BGB arts. 932 and 935 and in the Netherlands by the BW art. 3.86. See below, chapter 12.

44 (1781) 3 Ross's Leading Cases 120 at 127. For discussion, see Carey Miller, D L, 'Good Faith in Scots Property Law' in Forte, A D M (ed), *Good Faith in Contract and Property Law* (1999), pp 103-127.

45 This point has recently been made with regard to the protection of owners by the Sale of Goods Act 1979, which, as discussed below, applies in England too. See Carey Miller, D L, 'Plausible Rogues: Contract and Property', (2005) 9 Edinburgh Law Review 150 at 155-156.

46 By 'common law' is meant unenacted law, not English common law.

(a)   Statutes

Until 1707 Scotland had her own Parliament, which legislated on property law matters.[47] Thereafter there was the one Parliament for the
United Kingdom, namely Westminster. The Scotland Act 1998 established a devolved Parliament in Edinburgh which has legislative competence as regards property law.[48] The number of statutes directly relating to
corporeal moveable property is relatively small, as a look at the index in
the leading modern text confirms.[49] The most important is undoubtedly
the Sale of Goods Act 1979, the title of which is self-explanatory. Other
statutes which are worth noting include the Consumer Credit Act 1974
which regulates pawnbroking, the Civic Government (Scotland) Act
1982 which provides rules for the disposal of lost property and the Age of
Legal Capacity (Scotland) Act 1991, which again has a self-explanatory
name. Lastly, Scottish property law is subject to the European Convention on Human Rights as a result of the Human Rights Act 1998.[50]

(b)   Common law

The common law is developed by the courts. Most cases[51] of course involve decisions of fact only and do not create new law. But many cases,
particularly those before the superior courts, require a decision of law.
That decision is then itself law. Under the doctrine of *stare decisis* a decision binds future courts of equal or inferior status.

The court has to consider all the previous relevant case law. The doctrine of precedent means that a judge is obliged to follow the previous
decisions of courts above him or her within the system of hierarchy, provided that the facts and legal issues are the same. Judges may decline to
do so if they can distinguish the previous case on its facts. If a judge has
disregarded precedent in reaching a decision, that decision may be overturned on appeal as *per incuriam*.

Case reports from the Court of Session and selected cases in the Sheriff
(local) Court are available at http://www.scotcourts.gov.uk. House of Lords

---

[47] See for example the Royal Mines Act 1424 and the Leases Act 1449, which are
still in force.

[48] Scotland Act 1998, s. 129.

[49] Carey Miller with Irvine, *Corporeal Moveables*, xxix-xxxii.

[50] Carey Miller with Irvine, *Corporeal Moveables*, paras 1.23-1.25; Steven, A J M,
'Property Law and Human Rights', 2005 Juridical Review 293.

[51] In a case, the party who raises the action is known as the 'pursuer'. The party
against whom the action is raised is known as the 'defender'.

decisions are found at http://www.parliament.the-stationery-office.co.uk/pa/ld199697/ldjudgmt/ldjudgmt.htm.

Works of the institutional writers, (for example, Stair, Bankton, Erskine, and Bell) are frequently cited in the modern courts in cases on property law. Contemporary academic writing until about 20 years ago enjoyed very little recognition in the courts. This pattern is, however, changing.[52]

1.2. Notion of ownership

1.2.1. Definition and restrictions

The standard Scottish definition of ownership is that of the institutional writer, Erskine: 'the right of using and disposing of a subject as our own, except in so far as we are restrained by law or paction'.[53] This is based on the classic *ius commune* definition of Bartolus and others.[54] It makes it clear that ownership may be either limited by law or paction (agreement). An example of a restraint by law is the Guard Dogs Act 1975 which lays down rules on how such animals may be used.[55] An example of a restraint by agreement would be a contract to hire a car to another person for a month. During that period the owner would not be able to use the car. A similar definition in relation to moveable property is given by a later institutional writer, Bell:

> 'Ownership in moveables is a right of exclusive and absolute use and enjoyment, with uncontrollable powers of disposal, provided no use be made of the subject and no alienation attempted, which for purposes of public policy, convenience, or justice, are, by the general disposition of the common law or by special enactments of the Legislature, forbidden; or from which, by obligation or contract, the owner has bound himself to abstain'.[56]

---

[52] See for example *Boskabelle Ltd v Laird* [2006] CSOH 173, 2006 SLT 1079 commented on by Carey Miller, D L, 'Right to Annual Crops', (2007) 11 Edinburgh Law Review 274. See more generally Reid, K G C, 'Rise of the third branch of the profession' in MacQueen, H L (ed), *Scots Law into the Twenty First Century: Essays in Honour of W A Wilson* (1996), p 39.

[53] Erskine, II.1.1. See also Reid, *Property*, para 5.

[54] Schrage, E J H, 'Property from Bartolus to the New Dutch Civil Code' in van Maanen, G E and van der Walt, A J (eds), *Property Law on the Threshhold of the 21ˢᵗ Century* (1996), pp 43-46 and Reid, 'Property Law: Sources and Doctrine' in Reid & Zimmermann, *History*, vol 1, p 185 at 198.

[55] Reid, *Property*, para 184.

[56] Bell, *Principles*, § 1284.

Once more the idea of ownership being restricted by the law or agreement can be seen.

1.2.2. Interests

Professor Gordon has commented that 'It is not profitable to attempt to enumerate the rights of an owner – it is simpler to say that he has any right to deal with property of which he is not deprived by law or by his own contract'.[57] The point is a good one. Nevertheless, the main rights of an owner can be mentioned:[58]

(a) the right to transfer the property during life or on death;
(b) the right to grant subordinate real rights or contractual rights in relation to the property;
(c) the right to recover the property from a third party, even if that party is insolvent;
(d) the right to use the property;
(e) the right to the fruits of the property; and
(f) the right to destroy the property.

Ownership also brings with it certain responsibilities. One cannot use one's property as a weapon to harm someone else. An owner of animals cannot subject them to cruelty. Motor vehicles must be driven responsibly. Other examples can be given.

1.3.   Other property rights

Three real rights in respect of corporeal moveable property should be mentioned. The first is security. A number of different security rights are recognised, notably pledge, lien and the hypothec of the landlord (lessor).[59] The second is proper liferent, under which the liferenter is given the right to use the property for the duration of his or her life. Proper liferents of corporeal moveables are relatively rare. The third right is possession. On one view, this right is strictly only real where it is held on the basis of another real right, such as ownership.[60] The law of possession,

---

[57] Reid, *Property*, para 533.
[58] For a recent theoretical account, see MacCormick, *Institutions of Law: An Essay in Legal Theory*, pp 141-146.
[59] Carey Miller with Irvine, *Corporeal Moveables*, chapter 11.
[60] Reid, *Property*, para 127.

however, is underdeveloped[61] and it is arguable that a party with an honest belief in his or her right who is dispossessed may recover the property from any party other than one establishing ownership.

1.4. Protection of property rights

The owner of property is entitled to vindicate that ownership against a third party who is holding the property. For there to be a successful claim, the pursuer must establish his or her ownership as well as the possession of the defender.[62] The name of the remedy here is restitution.[63]

A claim is available in delict against someone who has caused the owner loss by damaging the property. The remedy here is normally damages.[64] There is a claim in unjustified enrichment against a third party who has interfered with the property. Here the owner will be entitled to compensation for the interference.[65]

Finally, property rights are protected by Article 1 Protocol 1 to the European Convention on Human Rights as implemented by the Human Rights Act 1998.[66]

1.5. Transferability of moveable assets

1.5.1. General

In principle any corporeal moveable asset capable of ownership may be transferred. For there to be voluntary transfer, the transferor must have capacity to do so.

---

[61] See below, para 2.1.1(a).

[62] Carey Miller with Irvine, *Corporeal Moveables*, para 10.06. For a recent example, see *HarperCollins Publishers Ltd v Young* [2007] CSOH 65, discussed in Steven, A J M, 'By the Book: Enrichment by Interference', (2007) 11 Edinburgh Law Review 411.

[63] Carey Miller with Irvine, *Corporeal Moveables*, paras 10.01 and 10.02.

[64] See, for example, Thomson, J, *Delictual Liability* (3rd ed, 2004), pp 23-25.

[65] See Steven, A J M, 'Recompense for Interference in Scots Law', 1996 Juridical Review 51; MacQueen, H L, *Unjustified Enrichment* (2004), pp 43-44 and Hogg, *Obligations*, paras 4.72-4.79.

[66] Carey Miller with Irvine, *Corporeal Moveables*, paras 1.23-1.25; Steven, A J M, 'Property Law and Human Rights', 2005 Juridical Review 293.

1.5.2.   Contractually limiting transferability

It is likely that an outright contractual bar on transfer would not be enforced by the courts. In a famous statement in a case relating to land, Lord Young said: 'You cannot make a man proprietor and yet prohibit him from exercising the rights of proprietorship'.[67] Again, by analogy to land, less absolute prohibitions would be allowed. For example, if John is the owner of a thing, he can confer a right of pre-emption in favour of another person, Julie. This means that if John decides to sell the thing, he must give Julie the right of first refusal. Such an arrangement would be binding *inter partes*. It would also bind a third party who knew about it, under the 'offside goals' rule.[68]

1.5.3.   Accessories

These are discussed below, in chapter 11.[69]

2.   Possession

2.1.   Notion of possession

2.1.1.   Requirements

(a)   General

The fundamental characteristics and requirements of the law of possession were established by the institutional writers, such as Stair and Erskine, who drew heavily from the Roman concept of possession. Since then it has been under-researched.[70] Essentially, possession is established where there is (a) a physical relationship with the property and (b) an intention to hold that property for one's own use or benefit. Both elements must be present for possession proper to exist.[71]

---

[67] *Moir's Trs v McEwan* (1880) 7 R 1141 at 1145.

[68] See below, chapter 6.

[69] See below, para 11.1.

[70] The main modern accounts are Reid, *Property*, paras 114-192 and Carey Miller with Irvine, *Corporeal Moveables*, paras 1.18-1.22. Two recent contributions are Carr, D, *Possession in Scots Law: Selected Themes* (2005) and Donnelly, C, 'From Possession to Ownership: An Analytical Study of the Declining Role of Possession in Scottish Property Law', 2006 Juridical Review 267.

[71] Stair, II.1.18.

(b)   Initial act of detention

The *corpus possidendi*, also known as the act of the body or detention, is relatively easily satisfied. The possessor must make an initial act of detention in respect of the property.[72] It must be held and detained for that person's use, to the extent that use by others is prevented, perhaps by keeping the thing on his or her body or storing it in a secure place.[73] In other words, a person in possession should have exclusive physical control of the property.

(c)   *Animus*

The second mandatory element for the establishment of possession is the *animus possidendi*, or act of the mind. The character of this intention to hold is uncertain. Two elements are said to exist: (a) the intention to exercise exclusive physical control over the thing, that is a mental state which reflects the physical act of detention; and (b) the intention to control the thing for one's own benefit.[74]

It is not considered a difficult task to evidence exercise of control over the thing, but it is awkward to distinguish between the acts of the body and the corresponding acts of the mind. Very often the presence of one confirms the existence of the other. Indeed, a presumption as to *animus* arises from the satisfaction of the *corpus* requirements. The converse is true too: there is greater willingness to infer possession where the act is equivocal, if the necessary *animus* is also present.[75] Thus it is inappropriate to place too much emphasis on the individual requirements of possession at the cost of the greater picture.

The prevailing opinion is that the possessor must intend to hold the property for his or her own use.[76] The test is *animus sibi habendi*. Under this, the possessor need not be owner of the property. This allows those with subordinate real rights to possess to the extent of their own interest and on behalf of the owner. Some commentators support a contrary, and Roman, view, namely that the *animus* element of possession comprises in part an intention to hold as owner,[77] but in general the wider view is accepted.

---

72 Stair, II.1.18.
73 These being two examples offered by Stair, II.1.11.
74 Stair, II.I.17.
75 Reid, *Property*, para 118.
76 Stair, II.1.17 and Reid, *Property*, para 125.
77 Erskine, II.1.20. See further Carey Miller with Irvine, *Corporeal Moveables*, para 1.18.

Both elements of the mental component must be present. Without the intention to control, there is no possession. Without an intention to exercise that control for one's own benefit, one does not have possession but only simple detention. It is the *animus* which distinguishes between possession proper and the other forms of factual possession which are associated with physical control.

(d)   Legal capacity

Whether an *incapax* person can take possession of property is unclear. The Scottish Law Commission Report on the Legal Capacity and Responsibility of Minors and Pupils draws a distinction between active and passive capacity, that is between the capacity to perform civil acts having legal effect and capacity simply to hold rights.[78] There would appear to be no difficulty with a child or insane person having possession of property provided that they are capable of forming the intention necessary to acquire possession. This may depend on the nature of the property and whether one can assume that they have the appropriate intention having regard to their age (as regards children) and the nature of the property.[79]

(e)   Physical control without *animus*/intention

Physical control without *animus* is insufficient to establish true legal possession.[80] Nevertheless, the term 'possession' can be used in a looser sense, one which could cover a relationship created between person and thing, but which lacks any *animus* component. For example, one could describe a *de facto* position, such as where a thief is in the process of taking property from another's premises, as 'possession'.[81] Another case is where property is held precariously subject to the acquiescence of the owner. Also, in contractual situations, the holder's mental element is not based on any proprietary real right but rather on a weaker personal relationship with the possessor. Thus, he or she could be said not to have *animus*. However, these situations amount to possession in the most general terms.

---

[78] Scottish Law Commission, 'Report on the Legal Capacity and Responsibility of Minors and Pupils', (Scot Law Com No 110, 1987), para 3.22.

[79] Compare the position as regards acquisition of ownership. See below, para 5.3.2.

[80] Erskine, II.1.26; Stair, II.1.17; Bankton, II.1.26 and Bell, *Principles*, § 1311.

[81] Carey Miller with Irvine, *Corporeal Moveables*, para 1.18 and *Nacap Ltd v Moffat Plant Ltd* 1987 SLT 221.

Where the mental test for possession is not satisfied, it is nevertheless possible to establish an alternative state of physical control. Scottish law recognizes the existence of 'a conditional and limited possession'[82] established under a contract between the holder and the owner. This relationship, known as 'custody' or 'detention' exists where the possessor holds not for himself or herself but for the owner of the property. Thus his or her intention fails to satisfy the test for true possession: possession with the intention of holding for one's self.[83]

(f)   Decisiveness of physical proximity

Although generally both elements are required to establish possession, there is some flexibility associated with the corpus element. However, this is confined to the means by which physical contact is obtained and the interpretation of equivocal behaviour. Although title to property can be transferred by non-physical methods such as constructive and symbolic delivery, possession cannot come into existence without an initial physical act.[84] Furthermore, the initial act must be positive in character; mere proximity to the thing will not be sufficient.

The Civic Government (Scotland) Act 1982 section 67 requires the finder of lost or abandoned property to deliver it to the police. It has been suggested that the terminology used within the Act, namely the definition of 'finder' as 'any person taking possession of the property' infers that the finder has taken possession of the object by mere seizure.[85] This seems to use the term 'possession' in a looser sense.

Reference should also be made to the so-called 'container' cases.[86] While English, these may well represent the Scottish position too. They address the problem where an object lies concealed within a larger object, the former object being unknown to the possessor of the latter. In *Parker v British Airways Board*, the English Court of Appeal ruled that an occupier of the building could possess property of which he had no knowledge but which lay within his building provided that he had the manifest intention

---

[82]   Bell, *Principles*, § 1311.
[83]   See Erskine, II.1.20: 'Yet detention is not sufficient by itself; the possessor must also hold it as his own right.' See also *Nacap Ltd v Moffat Plant Ltd* 1987 SLT 221 for a discussion of the distinction between a right of possession and a contractual right of use.
[84]   Carey Miller with Irvine, *Corporeal Moveables*, para 1.18.
[85]   Reid, *Property*, para 124, n 4.
[86]   *Bridges v Hawkesworth* (1851) 21 LJQR 75; *Hannah v Peel* [1945] 1 KB 509; [1945] 2 All ER 288; *Kowal v Ellis* (1977) 76 DLR (3d) 546; *Parker v British Airways Board* [1982] 1 QB 1004; [1982] 1 All ER 834.

to exercise control over anything which might be on the premises.[87] The degree of control over the premises, in this case an airport departure terminal, was all-important. *Parker* was relied on in the Scottish sheriff court case of *Harris v Abbey National plc*,[88] but a fuller judicial analysis of this area in Scotland is awaited.[89]

(g)   Possession *animo solo*

Once possession has been established, it is not necessary to remain in the physical proximity of the object at all times. Possession can be maintained by the act of the mind alone: *animo solo*.[90] This retention of possession is assumed from the fact of initial detention. Either an interruption challenging the possessor's holding or positive steps of dissociation by the possessor in relation to the thing is necessary to break the relationship. It is also possible for a person to hold property by civil possession, a position whereby the property is in the physical control of another.[91] This is discussed below.[92]

(h)   Good faith

The distinction between good and bad faith possession plays a significant role in the acquisition of title based on or associated with possession.[93] Good faith was identified by the institutional writers as a relevant qualification to the *animus* of the holder.[94] Its presence or absence also determines which remedies are available to a dispossessed person and his ability to recover fruits of the property.[95]

There are suggestions that true possession can only be acquired if the possessor is in good faith as only a *bona fide* party can believe and have grounds for believing that he is owner. However, this would only be relevant

---

[87] *Parker v British Airways Board* [1982] 1 QB 1004; [1982] 1 All ER 834.

[88] 1997 SCLR 359.

[89] See here Donnelly, 'From Possession to Ownership: An Analytical Study of the Declining Role of Possession in Scottish Property Law' at 270.

[90] Stair, II.1.19; Erskine, II.1.21; and Bankton, II.1.29.

[91] Carey Miller with Irvine, *Corporeal Moveables*, para 1.20.

[92] See below, para 2.1.2(a).

[93] Carey Miller with Irvine, *Corporeal Moveables*, para 1.21.

[94] See Erskine, II.1.25.

[95] Gordon, *Scottish Land Law*, paras 14-43ff. See also the discussion of remedies below, para 2.4.2.

if the stricter definition for possession *i.e.* holding as owner is adopted.[96] If, however, as suggested the test is simply the holding of property for one's own use, then a *mala fide* party is capable of acquiring possession as that weaker intention can be established and maintained irrespective of the circumstances of acquisition.

2.1.2. Types of possession

(a) General

Two forms of possession are recognized in Scottish law, natural possession and civil possession. The distinction is based on the intensity of the relationship of the person to the asset.[97] The property can also be held under custody.

Natural possession refers to cases where the possessor is in actual physical control of the thing. In contrast, civil possession refers to the situation where the thing is in the physical control of another.[98] Where one holds an object for another, that other having civil possession, he or she is the custodian of the property. For example, employees are custodians of their company's property. In relationships such as employment, possession through the holding of an agent or employee comes closer to natural possession than civil possession through an extraneous contractual party.[99] Thus possession appears to operate along a spectrum with degrees of civil possession.[100] This range has been attributed to differences in the intention of the custodian.[101]

(b) Custody

The person who holds the object under civil possession may be entitled to physical control due to the existence of a contract or his or her having a subordinate real right in the property. Therefore that person may not only

---

[96] Carey Miller with Irvine, *Corporeal Moveables*, para 1.20, n 95. See also *Louson v Craik* (1842) 4 D 1452 which suggests that *mala fide* holding of a thing cannot give possession, but states this in light of the understanding that the defender held the goods solely for and on behalf of the owner.

[97] Bankton suggested an alternative use of terminology where the distinction between natural and civil possession was based on whether the possessor held for his own use or for himself as owner: Bankton, II.1.26. This version was never adopted in practice.

[98] Stair, II.1.10 and 14; Erskine, II.1.22 and Bell, *Principles*, § 1312.

[99] Carey Miller with Irvine, *Corporeal Moveables*, para 1.20, n 96.

[100] Stair, II.1.10; Erskine, II.1.22; and Bell, *Principles*, § 1312.

[101] Carey Miller with Irvine, *Corporeal Moveables*, para 1.20, n 96.

be holding the property for another but also for his or her own use. Consequently, he or she may be a custodian and a possessor. However, although that person may be entitled to physical control and natural possession, his or her right is subscribed by the terms of the contract under which he holds the property.[102] In contrast to this limited right, a civil possessor has a controlling position resting on some superior right to possession, usually but not necessarily ownership.[103] The custodian's right to physical control is founded on the possessor's superior right, without which it cannot survive. Nevertheless, in law, there is no inequality between civil and natural possession.[104]

(c)   Examples of types of possession

Example 1: The general view is that an employee is a custodian of the company's property. The company itself is the possessor, having civil possession.[105]

Example 2: A lessee possesses the property, in the form of natural possession, to the extent of his or her right of lease. The owner of the property is also in possession, through civil possession. The lessee is the custodian of the property to the extent of the owner's retained interest.

Example 3: In a custody relationship, the person is holding exclusively for another. That party therefore lacks the intention to hold for his or her own use and accordingly is not in possession.[106] However, where custodians have a right of security, such as pledge or lien, over the property being held, they then have possession of that property.[107]

Example 4: Where a family member or other household member has been allowed to use the property of another, he or she then has only a licence or personal right to possess.[108] The owner of the property, the licensor, will usually hold the real right to natural possession.

---

[102] Carey Miller with Irvine, *Corporeal Moveables*, para 1.20.

[103] Reid, *Property*, para 121; *Clerk v Earl of Home* (1747) Kilk 11. See also Carey Miller with Irvine, para 1.20 and Erskine, II.1.22.

[104] Reid, *Property*, para 121.

[105] Reid, *Property*, para 121 and *Birrell Ltd v City of Edinburgh District Council* 1982 SLT 111. There is some discussion of the position of an employee in Gordon, G H, *Criminal Law* (3rd ed, 2000), para 14-03.

[106] See Stair, II.1.17; Erskine, II.1.20; and Bell, *Principles*, § 1311.

[107] *Hamilton v Western Bank of Scotland* (1856) 19 D 152 at 161. See also *Sim v Grant* (1862) 24 D 1033.

[108] See Reid, *Property*, para 128.

(d) 'Functions of possession' and categories of possession

Generally, natural and civil possession are not distinguished in law in terms of effect. A civil possessor is as entitled to the proprietary consequences of his possession as a person in natural possession. Occupation may be an exception to the general principle, as it requires natural possession.[109]

2.1.3. Intensity of relationship

(a) Keeping possession

As discussed above, possession may be maintained by act of the mind alone – *animo solo*.[110] Providing the possessor retains the appropriate *animus* and no one disturbs his or her physical control over the property, the property remains in his or her possession. If, however, there is positive abandonment of the thing, that is the mental state of the possessor is consciously changed, the property will cease to be possessed as the *animus* necessary for possession is no longer held. Similarly if another person, who does not recognise the possession of the possessor, takes physical control of the property, the original possessor will lose his or her right to possession. An example is where lost property is taken by the finder under a 'finders keepers' attitude.[111]

(b) Examples

Example 1: Where a person has forgotten his or her coat, it nevertheless remains in his or her possession as a result of the notion of possession *animo solo*. Although the person is no longer in physical contact with the property, he or she nevertheless intends to keep it. The ownership of the coat has not been forgotten, merely its location. Unless the possession is challenged, for example, by another person taking the coat as his or her own, the coat will remain in the possession of the original possessor.

Example 2: To acquire possession (and indeed ownership) of a wild animal or fish, the act of appropriation must be complete.[112] It is sufficient to wound the animal fatally so that it cannot escape. Complete capture is not necessary; a person is deemed to have acquired the wild animal if he or

---

[109] See below, para 14.2.
[110] See above, para 2.1.1(g).
[111] Reid, *Property*, para 122.
[112] Bell, *Principles*, § 1289; Reid, *Property*, para 541.

she is in pursuit and the animal has no chance of escaping the pursuer.[113] Acquisition of property by occupation will be considered further below.[114]

Example 3: Civil possession can be transferred by informing the custodian, for example when a warehouseman is told to hold for another, the new person will acquire civil possession without taking physical control of the thing. Transfer of natural possession requires satisfaction of both the physical and mental elements of possession. In both situations, the transfer of possession is instantaneous and does not occur until the conditions are completely satisfied. Transfer of possession is closely linked to transfer of ownership and therefore will be considered in greater detail below.[115]

(c)   'Possession' of rights

As a key component of the acquisition of possession is the initial act of detention, things such as rights, which lack physical presence, generally cannot be possessed.[116] However, in order to permit the operation of positive prescription and registration of title, a fiction is used, whereby some types of incorporeal heritable property are deemed capable of possession.[117] There is no case law in respect of incorporeal moveable property.[118]

2.2.   Functions of possession

The following are the main functions:

(a) Possession is an important feature in the acquisition of title by occupation.[119]
(b) Although the Sale of Goods Act 1979 dispenses with the need for delivery in the transfer of corporeal moveable property,[120] the statute includes provisions for the sale of goods by a seller in possession and a buyer in possession.[121]

---

[113] Bell, *Principles*, § 1289 and Stair, II.1.33.

[114] See below, para 14.2.

[115] See below, para 5.4.

[116] Stair, II.7.1; Erskine, II.9.3 and Bankton, II.1.28.

[117] Reid, *Property*, para 121.

[118] For further discussion of the possibility of possessing rights, see Carr, *Possession in Scots Law*, pp 47-60.

[119] See below, para 14.2.

[120] See below, para 5.1.2.

[121] Sale of Goods Act 1979, ss. 24 and 25. See below, para 5.9.2.

(c) A presumption of ownership arises from a person's possession of a moveable thing.[122]

(d) A possessory interest in a moveable may give a right of action in delict for pure economic loss if this is caused by damage to that property.[123]

The importance of possession in the acquisition of title to property will be discussed in more detail in chapter 5.[124]

2.3. Acquisition of possession

This will be dealt with in chapter 5.[125]

2.4. Protection of possession

2.4.1. General

The *jura possessionis* include the right to protect one's possession, whether or not it has been lawfully acquired or is held as of right.[126] Whether the remedy is available to a person with possession but without title against a party with title to the property is less clear. Case law suggests that it is not,[127] although some commentators disagree[128] and the institutional writers consider possession alone to be sufficient.[129] However, it may be available as an interim measure until the possessory position is clarified.[130] The remedy

---

[122] Reid, *Property*, para 130. See below, para 5.3.1.

[123] Reid, *Property*, para 116.

[124] See below, para 5.4.

[125] *Ibid.*

[126] Reid, *Property*, para 115 and Bankton, I.3.20.

[127] *Watson v Shields* 1996 SCLR 81. But earlier case law is less consistent: *Montgomery v Hamilton* (1548) Mor 14731; *Lady Renton v Her Son* (1629) Mor 14733; and *Gadzeard v Sheriff of Ayr* (1781) Mor 14732 suggest that bare possession is sufficient whereas *Wishart v Arbuthnot* (1573) Mor 3605; *Gib v Hamilton* (1583) Mor 16080; *Mudiall v Frissal* (1628) Mor 14749; and *Strachan v Gordons* (1671) Mor 1819 suggest that some title to the property must be shown. See also the view of Rankine, J, *The Law of Land-ownership in Scotland* (4th ed, 1909), pp 21-22. While these authorities relate to land it is thought that similar principles apply to moveables.

[128] See Reid, *Property*, para 162.

[129] Stair, I.9.17 and IV.28.2; Erskine, IV.1.15; and Bankton, I.10.126.

[130] *Chisholm v Chisholm* (1898) 14 Sh Ct Rep 146; Rankine, *Landownership*, p 9; and Gordon, *Scottish Land Law*, para 14-14.

available on the basis of possession alone is known as *spuilzie* and is discussed in the next paragraph.

2.4.2. Specific remedies

There is no action with a specifically fast procedure. However, the simplest action for any holder of property who has been extrajudicially dispossessed against his or her will is known as *spuilzie*. This term refers to both the dispossession and the action available as a result. Despite its simplicity, spuilzie is virtually unused in modern practice.

Spuilzie is unique in that it is the only remedy available to a possessor who has no right in the property[131] that is a bare possessor. He or she must, however, be a possessor and not a mere custodian of the property or have merely an unexercised right to possession.[132] But natural possession is not required. The party may possess by mind alone[133] or be in civil possession, although in the latter case, he or she is not entitled to violent profits *i.e.* penal damages.[134] Spuilzie targets any one who vitiously dispossesses the possessor and entitles the aggrieved party to redelivery.[135] This repossession may be effective even against good faith purchasers from the dispossessor,[136] although this has been doubted.[137]

The decision, however, will not be deemed conclusive as to the right to possession.[138] The defender will be free to enforce his or her claim to possession in a separate action.[139] Thus where an owner has lost possession he or she can bring an action to establish the right to possess, based on ownership, and be reinstated.

Where the party who has been dispossessed has a *right* to possession, he or she will be able to recover his property from a person who does not have that right and will have access to additional remedies. Owners, lessees and liferenters are examples of those with a *jus possidendi* or right

---

[131] Reid, *Property*, para 146.

[132] Reid, *Property*, para 163 and Rodger, A F 'Spuilzie in the Modern World', 1970 SLT (News) 33.

[133] See also Stair, I.9.25 and IV.28.1 and Erskine, II.7.16.

[134] Reid, *Property*, para 163; Stair, I.9.26 and IV.28.3; Bankton, I.16.146; *Bruce v Bruce* (1628) Mor 3609; *Steill v Hay* (1666) Mor 3611; *Campbell v Glenorchy* (1668) Mor 10604; *Mercantile Credit Co Ltd v Townsley* 1971 SLT (Sh Ct) 37.

[135] See Carey Miller with Irvine, *Corporeal Moveables*, para 10.26 and *Laird of Durie v Duddingston* (1549) Mor 14735.

[136] Stair, I.9.16 and IV.30.3; Reid, *Property*, para 165.

[137] See Carey Miller with Irvine, *Corporeal Moveables*, para 10.28.

[138] Erskine, IV.1.15 and Bankton, I.10.126.

[139] Reid, *Property*, para 162.

to possession. In such cases the available judicial remedy is delivery.[140] As well as return of the property, the wrongfully dispossessed will also be entitled to an accounting of the fruits of possession for the period of possession and either ordinary profits or, if the wrongful possession was vitiously acquired, violent profits.[141]

2.4.3. Defence of possession

An action which is used to protect possession is known as a possessory remedy. It is available to anyone with possession of the property even if they hold for themselves but without title to possess (for example, a thief) as the legal remedy is designed to prevent disturbance of one's possession.[142] This remedy is one of the rights which arise from possession; as lawful possessor, the pursuer is entitled to peaceful and exclusive use of the property.[143] The law is almost entirely concerned with the defence of possession of land. However, it can be assumed that similar principles would apply to corporeal moveables capable of trespass or encroachment. Two suggested examples are (a) property such as a ship which, due to its size, is capable of land-like trespass or encroachment[144] and (b) property which is frequently but temporarily taken into the physical control of the dispossessor, such as when a neighbour who habitually and without permission borrows a lawnmower.[145] Case law confirms that the principles which are used in land cases are applicable to situations involving moveable property.[146]

2.4.4. Remedies based on a 'better right' to possession

Possessory remedies can be divided between those based on the *jus possessionis* and those based on the mere fact of possession.[147] There is no direct equivalent of the *actio Publiciana* for moveables.[148]

---

[140] Reid, *Property*, para 151.
[141] Reid, *Property*, para 151ff.
[142] Gordon, *Scottish Land Law*, para 14-14.
[143] Erskine, II.1.1 and Reid, *Property*, para 174.
[144] See *Phestos Shipping Co Ltd v Kurmiawan* 1983 SC 165, 1983 SLT 388 and *Shell UK Ltd v McGillvray* 1991 SLT 667.
[145] Reid, *Property*, para 191.
[146] *Wilson v Shepherd* 1913 SC 300, 1912 2 SLT 455. See also *William Leitch & Co Ltd v Leydon* 1930 SC 41; 1930 SLT 8; affirmed 1931 SC (HL) 1, 1931 SLT 2.
[147] See the preceding two paragraphs.

2.5.   Self-help

Any possessor is entitled to use self-help to defend against dispossession.[149]
The use of violence, however, should be avoided as this may lead to criminal
or civil liability. By analogy to the rules for trespass on land, force should
only be used as a last resort and kept to minimum. An example of permissible self-help would be to lock a thing away so no-one can take it. There are
no formal time limits for the use of self-help. As the mere fact of possession
gives rise to the right not to be dispossessed, self-help in principle is available against any party seeking to interfere with the possession. Of course, as
against a third party with the right to possess, self-help may be only be of
temporary assistance as that party can recover possession judicially by asserting his or her title. There are no specific statutory rules on self-help in the
context of possession. The general common law rules apply.

3.   Rights to hold, use or acquire moveables

3.1.   Lease of moveables

3.1.1.   Terminology

A lease of corporeal moveable property is usually referred to as a contract
of 'hire'. The word 'lease' tends to be used primarily in relation to the
equivalent contract over land.[150] A contract of 'hire' is a nominate contract in Scottish law.[151] However, as a result of the development of the
modern industry of 'finance leasing'[152] the word 'lease' is used more frequently in the context of hire of corporeal moveables.

3.1.2.   Finance leasing

In finance leasing the party hiring the moveables (the lessee) selects the
moveables from a manufacturer or seller. In contracts of hire the lessee
would be referred to usually as the hirer. The lessee will request a finance

---

[148] But for land, there is the seven year possessory judgment, which is not used in
modern practice. See Reid, *Property*, para 146.

[149] Reid, *Property*, paras 179, 184 and 191-192.

[150] The point is made by Hugo, C and Simpson, P, in 'Lease' in Zimmermann, Visser
& Reid, *Mixed Legal Systems*, p 301 at 302.

[151] Wood, R Bruce, 'Leasing and Hire of Moveables' in *The Laws of Scotland: Stair
Memorial Encyclopaedia* (2001), para 4.

[152] The development of which is described *ibid* at paras 5-7.

house to acquire ownership of the moveables before supplying the assets on a lease. The finance house is the lessor. The lessor will probably not take possession of the asset and will almost certainly never see it. The lessor enters a contractual agreement with the lessee for the hire of the specific asset for a fixed duration. The lessor will retain ownership of the asset, while the lessee will have possession and use of the asset subject to making regular payments for the duration of the contract.[153]

It has been suggested that 'lease' of corporeal moveables where the lessor had no involvement in selection of delivery of the goods may be an innominate contract, not subject to the usual implied terms of hire contracts.[154]

There is little modern Scottish case law, legislation or writing on hire of corporeal moveable property.[155] This dearth of material is despite the fact that in British business today the leasing industry comprises a huge market.[156]

3.1.3. Property rights

(a) The nature of the rights

Professor Sir Roy Goode states in the context of English law that the growth of leasing 'illustrates how little importance is attached by the businessman to the legal concept of ownership. To him what matters is the substance, not the form.'[157] A similar statement can be made in the context of Scottish law.

---

[153] See Goode, R M, *Commercial Law* (3rd ed, 2004), pp 723-730.

[154] See G M *Shepherd Ltd v North West Securities Ltd* 1991 SLT 499.

[155] The most recent legislation is the Sale and Supply of Goods Act 1994 which inserted implied terms as to title and quality into all leases of moveables through insertion of ss. 11G-11S into the Supply of Goods and Services Act 1982. The leading modern treatment is Wood, 'Leasing and the Hire of Moveables'. See too Gow, J J, *The Mercantile and Industrial Law of Scotland* (1964), pp 241-249. There have been very few articles on the general area in recent decades. Important contributions include Sutherland, R, 'The implied term as to fitness in contracts of hiring', 1975 Juridical Review 133 and Forte, A D M, 'Finance leases and implied terms of quality and fitness: a retrospective and prospective review', 1995 Juridical Review 119.

[156] There are no separate statistics for transactions in Scotland but within the UK as a whole the members of the FLA (formerly the Finance Leasing Association) had £85.1 billion of new business. This comprised £27.2 billion in the business sector and UK public services (representing 30.4% of all non-land related fixed capital investment in the UK in 2005) and £57.9 billion in the UK consumer sector (representing 25.6% of all unsecured lending in the UK). Based on statistics released by the FLA. There is information in their press release of 4 July 2006 accessible at http://www.fla.org.uk/downloads/download.asp?ref=3443&hash=8d087c381fd782a8bad950df8222cca.

[157] Goode, *Commercial Law*, p 722.

The hire or lease of corporeal moveable property confers no independent real right in the asset.[158] The supplier/lessor retains ownership of the asset. This is the only real right within the asset. The right of the hirer/lessee is merely a personal right against the supplier/lessor.[159] In Scotland only leases of land confer a real right, and then only by statutory intervention.[160]

The consequence is that irrespective of the duration of the hire agreement, the amount of consideration, or determination of who has physical control of the asset, the hirer of the asset has no proprietary right. Accordingly, if the supplier goes into insolvency the asset is at risk and the hirer will be dispossessed. Similarly, if the supplier sells the asset to a third party the hirer's right to possess is probably terminated.[161]

(b)   Protection of possession

One interesting question is whether the hirer has any protection under property law, irrespective of the lack of a real right in the asset. For example, if a hirer is dispossessed would he or she have title to recover the asset from a third party with whom the hirer has no contractual relationship? Or, if the hired asset is damaged can the hirer sue for the economic loss he or she suffers?

A hirer does not have title to sue a third party for delivery of goods in the third party's possession.[162] However, a hirer would have title to sue for damage to the hired property in his or her own possession. For example, in a case involving hire of a helicopter,[163] where that helicopter was damaged it was held that the hirer had possession and had title and interest to sue, stressing that merely having a contractual obligation to indemnify the lessor did not confer such title. The possessory interest of the hirer was essential to found the action.[164] This case suggests that if the possession of the hirer has the substance of ownership then title to sue for pure economic loss in delict is conferred. Other cases reach a similar conclu-

---

[158] Other than a right not to be vitiously dispossessed.

[159] See Stair, I.15.4.

[160] Leases Act 1449, Registration of Leases (Scotland) Act 1857 and Land Registration (Scotland) Act 1979, s. 3.

[161] Hugo and Simpson, 'Lease' at 306.

[162] *McArthur v O'Donnell* 1969 SLT (Sh Ct) 24 to the contrary inappropriately applies case law on title to sue for damage to property in the context of recovery of property. See Reid, *Property*, para 127, n 9.

[163] *North Scottish Helicopters Ltd v United Technologies Corporation Inc* 1988 SLT 77.

[164] The judge indeed suggests that the hirer has a possessory title (*ibid* at 80) although this expression is not generally known in Scottish law.

sion,[165] although the law is by no means clear.[166] Having analysed the authorities Professor Reid does not reach a concluded view on whether the hirer has a real right to possess.[167]

3.2. Other contractual rights

The position of a hirer having merely a personal right against the owner of the corporeal moveables is no different from that of other parties with contractual rights against the owner. A party holding a right of preemption or option to purchase conferred by the owner has merely a personal right against the owner. The personal right can be defeated by the insolvency of the owner or transfer to a third party. However, as is discussed elsewhere, the 'offside goals' rule in certain cases may enable the party with the personal right to ultimately acquire ownership at the expense of a third party transferee.[168]

The question of the entitlements of a buyer on a retention of title clause will be considered later.[169]

4. Definitions

4.1. Field of application

4.1.1. Immoveable/moveable

Like most legal systems Scotland makes a fundamental distinction between immoveable and moveable property. Immoveable property is normally referred to as 'heritable property' for historic reasons arising out of

---

[165] In *Mull Shellfish Ltd v Golden Sea Produce Ltd* 1992 SLT 703 the claim related to damage to mussels where no claim could be raised in relation to mussels that had not settled on ropes under the control of the pursuer.

[166] In *Nacap Ltd v Moffat Plant Ltd* 1987 SLT 221 there was no title to sue in respect of damage to pipes in the possession of the pursuer. However, Lord Davidson in *North Scottish Helicopters* distinguishes the *Nacap* case because the quality of possession in *Nacap* was restricted with the pursuers not having exclusive use of the pipes. *Nacap* was followed in the most recent case in the area *TCS Holdings Ltd v Ashtead Plant Hire Co Ltd* 2003 SLT 177 which surveys the authorities. This case involves a tenant of land and asserts that exclusive possession is required to raise an action in delict for pure economic loss.

[167] Reid, *Property*, para 127.

[168] See below, chapter 6.

[169] See below, chapter 15.

the law of succession.[170] The rules for the transfer of moveable property, unsurprisingly, do not extend to immoveable property, other than by analogy. However, as has been noted, the underlying principles are generally the same.[171]

As in many western systems of property law, the state interposes itself in transactions relating to land in a manner that is not mirrored when private individuals transfer moveables. This interposal takes the form of requiring registration in a state administered Land Register as a constitutive step for transfers of land, standard securities over land and leases exceeding twenty years.[172] Some moveables, primarily those of a category that may be regarded by the state as of comparable importance to land, do require registration, but as noted below,[173] this is not necessarily a mandatory step for transfer.

Bearing this dichotomy in mind, it is crucial to distinguish between what is moveable and what is not. The test is one that a layman can easily understand. Immoveable objects consist of land and what is physically attached to it, such as plants,[174] buildings or other erections, while moveables consist of everything else. Difficulties, however, can arise in the grey areas at the edges of this outwardly simple definition. For example, previously moveable items that are annexed to land can become classified as immoveable by virtue of the permanence or degree of physical attachment.[175]

Other anomalies also exist, such as the treatment of keys to a building. While these are undoubtedly moveable in the conventional sense of the word (if they were not one would struggle to lock the front-door before work in the morning), Scottish law classifies keys as heritable property.[176] Indeed, conveyancing practice in certain areas involves a physical delivery of house-keys by hand to buying agents, which shows how the transfer

---

[170] See Steven, A J M, 'Transfer of Title in Scottish Law' in Rainer, J M and Filip-Fröschl, J (eds), *Transfer in Title Concerning Movables Part 1 – Eigentumsübertragung an beweglichen Sachen in Europa* (2006), p 155 at 157.

[171] See above, para 1.1.3(a).

[172] See below, para 5.2.3.

[173] See below, para 5.5.

[174] There is a speciality in relation to industrial crops, which are classified as moveable even before they are harvested. This was confirmed in the recent case of *Boskabelle Limited v Donald Black Laird* [2006] CSOH 172; 2006 SLT 1079. See further Carey Miller, D L, 'Right to Annual Crops', (2007) 11 Edinburgh Law Review 274 .

[175] See below, para 11.1.5.

[176] Carey Miller with Irvine, *Corporeal Moveables*, para 3.17, citing *Fisher v Dixon* (1845) 4 Bell's App 286 and Bell, *Principles*, § 1475. Such constructive annexation, the authors submit, can also apply from moveable to moveable, giving the example of a jack supplied with a motor vehicle.

of a small moveable object, while not a constitutive act with regard to transferring title, can be equated with the act of transferring a larger immoveable object. This is perhaps reflective of the system of feudal conveyancing that historically existed in Scotland, which involved an elaborate ceremony culminating with the act of physically delivering clods of earth from transferor to transferee.[177]

4.1.2. Tangible/intangible

Like many legal systems, Scots law treats corporeal and incorporeal things differently.[178] It is easy to see why this is the case as a matter of principle and as a matter of common sense.[179] Thus, Scottish law treats and characterises property like debts or other contractual claims differently to solid, tangible objects. There may be an association between an incorporeal thing and a corporeal thing, such as the stave or other media a tune has been recorded on,[180] but other than this practical crossover a very definite system of separate treatment can be seen in operation. This is evidenced by the importance afforded to the act of intimation of a transfer of an incorporeal thing, a process known as assignation, as compared to the importance placed on party intention or transfer of possession in other circumstances.[181]

4.1.3. Intellectual property

Intellectual property is perhaps best viewed as a subcategory of incorporeal property. This is if one overlooks the very specific rules that apply in relation to certain types of IP rights, such as novelty and innovation in relation to patents,[182] or the delictual rules which forbid the commission of a wrong, like the rules preventing passing off a product to take advantage of someone else's goodwill. Although sometimes difficult to classify

---

[177] For the history of this process, and for an overview of how it was reformed to become relevant to the modern era, see Carey Miller, D L, 'Transfer of Ownership' in Reid and Zimmermann, *History*, vol 1, 269.

[178] See Steven, 'Transfer of Title in Scottish Law' at 157.

[179] Carey Miller with Irvine, *Corporeal Moveables*, para 1.07.

[180] *Ibid*. The example is given of the manuscript of a book.

[181] Reid, *Property*, para 653.

[182] For a recent case Scottish case on the revocation of a patent, see *Arrow Generics Ltd, Petitioners* 2006 SLT 919 and associated discussion by Professor MacQueen in 'Patents Revoked', Scots Law News 598, available at http://www.law.ed.ac.uk/sln/blogentry.aspx?blogentryref=6871.

in terms of traditional property law analysis,[183] IP rights are still capable of 'ownership', or, if that term is unpalatable to those who feel incorporeal rights cannot be owned, 'management'.[184] They can be assigned in much the same way as debts or contractual claims,[185] but there may be certain statutory requirements relative to the assignation of intellectual property rights.[186] Notwithstanding these requirements, it is clear that IP rights are classified as incorporeal property.[187] One area of some controversy relates to whether a right to private information can be properly classed as proprietary, and the development of Scottish case law has been limited, but it seems clear that any right developed in this area would be treated as incorporeal property.[188]

4.1.4. Company shares

Shares, like intellectual property, can be analysed properly as incorporeal moveable property.[189] Again, special company law rules apply in certain situations: the shares of a publicly quoted company can generally be traded without restriction,[190] but private limited companies are prohibited from offering shares to the public directly.[191] Another company law pecu-

---

[183] Reid notes that any attempt to classify IP rights using traditional categories of property law is 'rapidly abandoned' and that they tend to be 'treated on their own' in modern law. See Reid, K G C, 'Obligations and Property: Exploring the Border' in Visser, D, (ed) *The Limits of the Law of Obligations* (1997), p 225 at 229-230.

[184] See Carey Miller, D L and Combe, M M, 'The Boundaries of Property Rights in Scots Law', vol 10.3 EJCL, (December 2006), http://www.ejcl.org/103/art103-4.pdf, at 4 for discussion.

[185] See, for example, the case of *Profile Software Ltd v Becogent Ltd* [2005] ECDR 26; 2005 WL 2996849, which was heard before Lord Kingarth in the Outer House of the Court of Session.

[186] The Patents Act 1977, s. 32 provides for a register of patents, and s. 33(3) details all the transactions that must be registered. This list includes assignation. Failure to register is relevant in the event of competing grants, under s. 33(1). For trade marks, the Trade Marks Act 1994, s. 25(2) has a similar list of registrable transactions, with s. 25(3) detailing the consequences of failing to register.

[187] The Trade Marks Act 1994, s. 22 classifies trade marks as incorporeal moveable property and the Patents Act 1977, s. 31(2) which does the same for patents and states that it is possible to grant licences for, grant securities over and assign a patent.

[188] Carey Miller and Combe, 'The Boundaries of Property Rights in Scots Law' at 18.

[189] Companies Act 1985, s. 182. See now the Companies Act 2006, s. 541.

[190] Subject to the provisions of the UK regulatory regime, which will not be looked at here.

[191] Companies Act 1985, s. 81. See now the Companies Act 2006, s. 755.

liarity to bear in mind, which will apply unless a company's constitution documents[192] amend the default position, is that newly allotted shares are subject to a right of pre-emption in favour of existing members.[193] Failure to comply with this pre-emption could result in personal liability for any directors who knew of this restriction and disregarded it,[194] but any shares alloted in breach of this pre-emption would give the allottee title; provided, of course, that a company's disregard for company law did not also result in an invalid allotment of shares.[195]

Other considerations that must be kept in mind when dealing with company shares include the restriction on a company acquiring its own shares,[196] the historic prohibition on a company giving financial assistance to a person for the purpose of acquiring shares in that company,[197] and the protection that is afforded to minority shareholders in certain circumstances.[198]

4.1.5. Negotiable instruments

Negotiable instruments also fall into the category of incorporeal property. They are regulated by the Bills of Exchange Act 1882, a statute that has continuing relevance even in the modern era.[199] One thing that distinguishes negotiable instruments from other property is that the *nemo plus* rule does not apply when such an instrument is transferred.[200] The acquirer of a negotiable instrument need not be concerned with its prove-

---

[192] These constitution documents are known as the memorandum of association and articles of association.
[193] Companies Act 1985, s. 89. See now the Companies Act 2006, s. 561.
[194] Companies Act 1985, s. 92. See now the Companies Act 2006, ss. 563(2) and 568(4).
[195] Companies Act 1985, s. 80 requires a general meeting to be called prior to the allotment of new shares, so theoretically company members should be on notice that a share allotment is being contemplated.
[196] *General Property etc Co Ltd v Mathieson's Trs* (1888) 16 R 282.
[197] Companies Act 1985, s. 151. The rules in relation to the provision of financial assistance to private companies have been relaxed by Chapter 2 of Part 18 of the Companies Act 2006, but s. 678 of the 2006 Act retains the prohibition in relation to public companies. Section 679 extends this prohibition to structures that could potentially avoid it, by also prohibiting the provision of financial assistance by public companies for the acquisition of shares in its holding company.
[198] Companies Act 1985, s. 459 and Insolvency Act 1986, s. 122(1)(g). See now also the Companies Act 2006, s. 994.
[199] A number of amendments have been made to bring this Act up to speed with modern commerce, such as the Cheques Act 1957 and the Cheques Act 1992.
[200] Bills of Exchange Act 1882, s. 38(2).

nance, and can be sure that the title acquired will be good.[201] This is important, as Scottish bank notes are in fact promissory notes, a form of bill of exchange, rather than legal tender.[202]

4.2.   Corporeal moveables: scope

Where a physical object falls into the concept of a corporeal moveable, as a general proposition the law will allow proprietorial rights to be held in relation to that thing and for the thing to be subject to transactions between private individuals. It is rare to encounter something that is not, or indeed cannot, be subject to the right of ownership,[203] but there are certain objects that are *actually* incapable of ownership, and some things that are *practically* inalienable by their owner, and thus *extra commercium*. The first category includes running water,[204] rain, wind, live human beings[205] and dead bodies.[206] The position in relation to body parts and organs is less clear.[207]

Things in the second category include property which, although owned, cannot be alienated without contravening the terms under which it is held. An example is certain property held by the National Trust for Scotland.[208] These objects, although essentially moveable, cannot be subject to transfer, and thus this report will spend no further time considering them. No special rules exist in relation to artistic property or religious artefacts.[209]

---

[201] This is to be contrasted with the standard position when incorporeal property, or indeed property of any sort, is transferred, which point is discussed further below.

[202] Crerar, L D, 'Banking, Money and Commercial Paper' in *Stair Memorial Encyclopaedia* (2000), para 150.

[203] See Whitty, N R, 'Rights of Personality, Property Rights and the Human Body in Scots Law', (2005) 9 Edinburgh Law Review 194 at 222, discussed further below.

[204] Erskine, II.1.5.

[205] *Knight v Wedderburn* (1778) Mor 14545.

[206] See Whitty, 'Rights of Personality, Property Rights and the Human Body in Scots Law' at 213-231 but compare MacQueen, H L, 'Scots Law News', (2006) 10 Edinburgh Law Review 1 at 9, where it is observed that a Scottish court has held that there can be a proprietary interest in a Peruvian mummy which was available to creditors doing diligence (diligence being the Scottish term for debt enforcement).

[207] See, for example, *Stevens v Yorkhill NHS Trust* [2006] CSOH 143, at paras 54 and 60, a delictual action for the wrong of taking human organs without permission. See now the Human Tissue (Scotland) Act 2006, but this does not provide any clarification on the property law question.

[208] National Trusts for Scotland Order Confirmation Act 1935, Sch, para 22.

[209] Carey Miller with Irvine, *Corporeal Moveables*, para 1.02.

The law has no problem in treating gas, liquids, electricity and animals as corporeal moveables. It has no policy issues with classifying animals as 'things'. This is perhaps illustrated by reference to the specific statutory provision relative to domestic animals used to prevent property disputes on the break up of a marriage or civil partnership, making family pets exempt from the normal presumption of common ownership of matrimonial property.[210] It could be argued that, to a very small degree, a concession is made to the animal kingdom by drawing a distinction between domestic animals and wild, or feral, animals. Wild animals are *res nullius*,[211] but ownership of these can be acquired through occupation.[212] Once ownership is acquired, the owner is free to trade and, subject to criminal law controls to prevent cruelty and to protect endangered species, even kill an animal.

Ownership can even be acquired if the act of acquiring was illegal or a civil wrong, *i.e.* fishing or hunting without permission of the landowner, or otherwise poaching or hunting illegally,[213] but there may be specific statutory rules which compensate for this common law position by requiring forfeiture of any poached creatures.[214]

---

[210] The Family Law (Scotland) Act 1985, s. 25(1) provides that both parties to a marriage or civil partnership are presumed to have a right to an equal share in any household goods obtained in prospect of or during a marriage or civil partnership, but s. 25(3) qualifies the meaning of household goods by stating this does not include money or securities, road vehicles or domestic animals. See also the Family Law (Scotland) Act 2006, s. 26.

[211] Unlike other property, it is not subject to the maxim *quod nullius est fit domini regis*. See Carey Miller with Irvine, *Corporeal Moveables*, para 2.02.

[212] See below, para, 14.2.

[213] Carey Miller with Irvine, *Corporeal Moveables*, para 2.03, citing the unequivocal statement by Erskine, at II.1.33, that 'all game, though it should be caught in breach of these acts, or within another mans property, belongs, by the necessity of law, to him who hath seized it'. Hunting may also be prevented by rules against animal cruelty, as, for example, contained in the Protection of Wild Mammals (Scotland) Act 2002. Once again, these rules do not affect the ownership of any wild animal caught by prohibited means.

[214] For example, the Poaching Prevention Act 1862.

Transfer of ownership from the owner to the transferee ('derivative acquisition')

5. Which system of transfer is used?

5.1. Introduction

5.1.1. A unititular system

Scottish property law, being civilian, is unititular. With the exception of indivisible common or joint ownership by more that one individual,[215] the concept of ownership 'necessarily excludes every other person but the proprietor'.[216] This was recently confirmed in a case regarding the ownership of immoveable property,[217] but this decision applies equally to moveable property.[218] There is no staggered transfer of ownership; ownership passes in one moment in time.[219]

5.1.2. Voluntary transfers: a binary structure

There is a major distinction between transfers under: (a) contracts of sale;[220] and (b) contracts of barter (*i.e.* a reciprocal exchange of moveables) and gift. Only in the latter is delivery essential. This anomaly, brought on by legislative reform at the end of the nineteenth century,[221]

---

[215] See below, chapter 17.

[216] Erskine, II.1.1.

[217] *Burnett's Tr v Grainger* 2004 SC (HL) 19. See Gretton, G L, 'Ownership and Insolvency: *Burnett's Tr v Grainger*', (2004) 8 Edinburgh Law Review 389.

[218] On this unitary system of property law, see above, para 1.1.3(a) and Carey Miller with Irvine, *Corporeal Moveables*, para 1.04 and Reid, *Property*, para 1.

[219] See above, para 1.1.3(g). See also *Accountant in Bankruptcy v Mackay* 2004 SLT 777.

[220] Defined by s. 2 of the Sale of Goods Act 1979 as 'a contract by which the seller transfers or agrees to transfer the property in goods to the buyer for a money consideration, called the price'.

[221] The relevant Act being the Sale of Goods Act 1893, superseded some years later by the Sale of Goods Act 1979.

has arguably stunted the development of the Scottish common law, as sale is undoubtedly the most common commercial transaction entered on a day-to-day basis.[222] In order to keep this account both relevant and of manageable size, sale will therefore be the primary focal point. It must be remembered, however, that a separate and highly developed transfer regime still exists at common law. This body of law applies in relation to more irregular forms of transfer,[223] where a purported sale transaction is void, where the operation of the Sale of Goods Act 1979 has been excluded by contract or where the Act has been disapplied by the operation of section 62(4) of the legislation.[224] Indeed, the very existence of two parallel systems for the transfer of moveables can only be of interest to comparative scholars. Scotland is therefore in the curious, if not unique, position of having two legal regimes for voluntary transfer of ownership operating simultaneously, a fact which adds weight to the description of Scottish law as a mixed legal system.

Contracts of sale, as a result of the reforms which brought Scotland into line with English law, are governed by a totally different set of statutory rules to other contracts. These rules removed the requirement for *traditio* to transfer ownership in the case of sale; now ownership transfers when the parties intend it to.[225]

5.1.3. Transfers on death

Scottish law, like other legal systems, requires an executor to administer the estate of a deceased person. An executor is involved in this process whether the deceased is testate or intestate.[226] When he or she takes office, a process known as confirmation,[227] the executor acquires title to the moveable property of the deceased as trustee.[228] It is then for the executor to distribute the estate to the beneficiaries of the deceased,

---

[222] Carey Miller with Irvine, *Corporeal Moveables*, para 8.02; Goode, *Commercial Law*, p 37.

[223] See, for example, the case of *Balcraig House's Trustee v Roosevelt Property Services Ltd* 1994 SLT 1133 on the issue of what constitutes a 'sale'.

[224] See below, para 15.3.2.

[225] See below, para 5.2.3.

[226] Gretton describes this feature of Scottish law as 'curious' in a European law context: Gretton, G, 'Trusts' in Reid & Zimmermann, *History*, vol 1, p 480 at 515.

[227] The comparative English terminology is 'probate'.

[228] See generally, Scobbie, E M, *Currie on Confirmation of Executors* (8ᵗʰ ed, 1995). Since 1964, by virtue of the Succession (Scotland) Act 1964, s. 14(1) both immoveable and moveable property of a deceased require to be administered by an executor. Prior to this legislative reform, only moveable property vested in an executor on confirmation. See further Macdonald, D R, *Succession* (3ʳᵈ ed, 2001), paras 13.01-13.03.

either following the directions of a will or under the law of intestacy. It is unclear who owns a corporeal moveable after an individual's death but prior to confirmation,[229] but it is settled that an executor cannot administer an estate prior to confirmation. Any such dealings with the estate are classified as 'vitious intromissions' and can make the executor liable for the deceased's debts.[230]

The highly complex issue of vesting can be thought of as ancillary to, or a precursor for, ownership, as the real right of ownership cannot be acquired without the right having first vested in the beneficiary,[231] so no further study of the nature of vesting will be made here. One must remain aware, however, that proprietary consequences can follow where intestate or testate rights of a beneficiary have or have not vested, particularly in the event of his death. This is a difficult issue and may depend on the exact terms of the will[232] and will not be considered here.

5.1.4. Promises and donation

Attention should also be paid to unilateral promises, long recognised as binding.[233] Up until 1995, a promise had to be proved by writ or oath of the person who made the promise (*i.e.* in writing or orally in a court of law) before it could be regarded as enforceable.[234] This rule was abolished and replaced by a statutory regime contained in the Requirements of Writing (Scotland) Act 1995, which provides that a gratuitous unilateral obligation, except an obligation undertaken in the course of business, must be in writing to be legally binding.[235] This rule, however, does not seem to

---

[229] There is similar, and arguably greater, uncertainty over the situation with immoveable property. Before acquiring title to land, an executor must confirm to the estate and complete title. For discussion, see Gretton, G L, 'What is Vesting?', 1986 JLSS 148; Maher, G, 'The Rights and Wrongs of Vesting', 1986 JLSS 396; Gordon, W M, 'The Wrongs and Rights of Vesting', 1987 JLSS 218; and Patrick, H, 'What is a Real Right in Scots Law?', 1988 JLSS 98.

[230] Any such irregular dealings can be cured, or 'purged', if confirmation is obtained within a year and a day. See Scobbie, *Currie on Confirmation of Executors*, paras 1.49-1.53, citing Erskine, III.9.52 and *Stevenson v Ker* (1663) Mor 9873.

[231] See further Gretton, 'What is Vesting?', 148.

[232] See Macdonald, *Succession*, chapter 11.

[233] Stair, I.10.4. See McBryde, W W, 'Promises in Scots Law', (1993) 42 ICLQ 48.

[234] Sellar, W D H, 'Promise' in Reid and Zimmermann, *History*, vol 2, p 252.

[235] Requirements of Writing (Scotland) Act 1995, s. 1(2)(a)(ii). See also s. 1(3), which deals with the issue of personal bar, and forbids a promisor from escaping legal relations if another person has suffered loss as a result of acting, or refraining from acting, when relying on the promise and with the knowledge or acquiescence of the promisor.

apply to gratuitous contracts: a subtle but perhaps important variation. Therefore, it may be possible to escape these formal requirements in certain circumstances.[236]

Once these formal requirements are met or, in the case of gratuitous contracts, avoided, any moveable thing subject to the obligation in question would be transferred in accordance with the common law. As noted above, this, again drawing from its Romanist foundations, requires *traditio* to transfer ownership.[237] But as it is trite law that delivery will transfer ownership, the focus in the case law[238] is on delivery as challenging the strong presumption against donation.[239]

5.1.5. Non-contractual claims and court orders

Claims for damages and some claims under *negotiorum gestio* or unjustified enrichment tend to be for money rather than for specific property, so accordingly the rules relating to transfer of ownership are not as important where currency is concerned.[240] It is possible for a court to make an order for specific implement to transfer property in such a situation, but such a course of action is not common. Other claims of a similar nature would include those implied by maritime law relating to general average or salvage.[241] Finally, in some cases that may appear at first to fall under the heading of unjustified enrichment or *negotiorum gestio* it is possible that the remedy being sought is vindicatory, and therefore the rules relating to transfer of ownership are not entirely relevant, as the remedy being sought is to restore something owned by the pursuer.[242]

---

[236] Reid, K G C, 'Annotations to The Requirements of Writing (Scotland) Act 1995', in *Current Law Statutes*, Vol 1 (1995), para 7.5.

[237] The traditional position of the institutional writers is perhaps best expressed by Erskine, at III.3.90, where it is noted 'though the *pactum donationis* confers on the donee a *jus ad rem*, a right of suing for performance, it gives him no right in the thing itself; the donor continues proprietor till delivery'.

[238] See, for example, *Milne v Grant's Executors* (1884) 11 R 887 and *Thomson v Dunlop* (1884) 11 R 453.

[239] In the words of Lord President Inglis, the law requires 'very strong and unimpeachable evidence' to overcome the presumption against donation. See *Sharp v Paton* (1883) 10 R 1000 at 1006.

[240] Carey Miller with Irvine, *Corporeal Moveables*, para 1.19. See also Reid, K G C 'Unjustified Enrichment and Property Law', 1994 Juridical Review 167.

[241] Gloag and Henderson, *The Law of Scotland* chapter 23. The relevant law on salvage is now contained in the Merchant Shipping Act 1995, which applied the International Convention on Salvage of 1989.

[242] Gloag and Henderson, *The Law of Scotland*, para 25.22.

Obviously, when it comes to protecting an ownership right which already exists transfer rules do not come into play, and the rules and means whereby an owner can recover a thing form a sizeable subject in their own right.[243] Any dispute over a moveable thing may turn on whether ownership has transferred by some means, perhaps by a recognised exception to the *nemo plus* rule or by operation of the doctrine of personal bar.[244] If it has, all the transferee (*i.e.* the previous owner) can realistically claim for is damages.

There are certain situations where the court is empowered to order the transfer of property, a process Professor Reid describes as 'judicial conveyance'.[245] There are, in fact, two identifiable sub-categories of this process, the first directly effecting a transfer of property and the second being an order addressed to an individual to effect the transfer of property. The first category would include certain orders relating to insolvency[246] and orders for forfeiture of property as a criminal penalty.[247] An example of the second category would be a court order to transfer property made under section 8 of the Family Law (Scotland) Act 1985 (as amended) on divorce or on the dissolution of a civil partnership. Here, a court order would not effect transfer directly, but transfer could be compelled if the order was not complied with.[248] This contrasts with the first category, where 'actual transfer occurs at the time when the relevant court interlocutor is pronounced'.[249]

---

[243] Carey Miller with Irvine, *Corporeal Moveables*, chapter 10.

[244] See below for further discussion of the rules of this doctrine.

[245] Reid, *Property*, para 664. Eight examples of judicial conveyance are listed.

[246] See below, chapter 9.

[247] See Carey Miller with Irvine, *Corporeal Moveables*, para 1.25. The relevant legislation dealing with forfeiture as a criminal penalty can be found in Part 2 of the Proceeds of Crime (Scotland) Act 1995, while 'confiscation orders' can be made under Part 3 of the Proceeds of Crime Act 2002. Very few court cases have actually been required under this legislation, as most challenges are in fact dropped prior to reaching court. See 'Victim of its Success', 2007 JLSS July/56.

[248] As noted by Reid, this is a somewhat meaningless distinction, but it is a distinction nonetheless. Reid, *Property*, para 664, n 1.

[249] Reid, *Property*, para 664. In the case of sequestration, the Bankruptcy (Scotland) Act 1985, s. 31 operates to backdate the transfer to the date of sequestration rather than the date on which the act and warrant is issued by the court.

5.1.6. Abstract or causal?

(a) General

As noted above,[250] an abstract system of transfer applies to conveyances of land. In relation to corporeal moveable property, however, the point has not been authoritatively settled and case law on the matter is sparse.[251] It is clear that a mutual intention to transfer and to receive ownership is required before ownership is transferred,[252] but whether or not this intention must be based on a founding obligation – or *justa causa* – or if the transfer can be abstracted and separated from an underlying contract is highly debateable.[253] A Scottish Law Commission Memorandum felt a number of cases, namely *Cuthbertson v Lowes*,[254] *Stuart & Co v Kennedy*[255] and *Wilson v Marquis of Breadalbane*,[256] pointed towards an 'implicit' acceptance of the abstract theory of transfer.[257] Subsequent literature, however, has highlighted that alternative, and equally plausible, readings can be made of these cases without leading to the same conclusion.[258] Other cases also lead to similarly ambiguous results,[259] so a definitive position on this matter is difficult to ascertain.

It has been argued that, insofar as the law 'maintains a strict difference between contract and conveyance',[260] it adopts an abstract approach. This

---

[250] See above, para 1.1.3(h).

[251] Carey Miller with Irvine, *Corporeal Moveables*, para 8.07, notes 'there is a dearth of authority and a relative paucity of comment by way of analysis of the process of derivative acquisition, applicable to corporeal moveables, in Scots law.' See now also van Vliet, L, 'The Transfer of Moveables in Scotland and England' (2008) 12 Edinburgh Law Review 173 at 192-198.

[252] Stair, III.2.3 notes the importance of intention, observing 'for by it, rights are both acquired, relinquished and alienated'.

[253] See further Reid, *Property*, paras 607-612; McBryde, *Contract*, paras 13.01-13.11 and Carey Miller with Irvine, *Corporeal Moveables*, paras 8.07-8.10.

[254] (1870) 8 M 1073.

[255] (1885) 13 R 221.

[256] (1859) 21 D 957.

[257] Scottish Law Commission Consultative Memorandum No 25, 'Corporeal Moveables: Passing of Risk and Ownership' (1976), para 14.

[258] See McBryde, *Contract*, para 13.10 and Carey Miller with Irvine, *Corporeal Moveables*, para 8.10.

[259] *Morrisson v Robertson* 1908 SC 332.

[260] Carey Miller with Irvine, *Corporeal Moveables*, para 8.10.

view has strong support.[261] Indeed, the view has also been expressed that the abstract theory of transfer is the only theory that can logically apply:

'Arguably, this is the only rational conclusion in respect of a system which, in principle, requires a separate legal act of delivery (*traditio*) to effect the passage of property; this is because the criterion of a 'separate' legal act is one motivated by acts of will of the parties specifically associated with the act.'[262]

Despite these convincing contributions to a much neglected debate in recent years, it is entirely possible that this issue will be revisited in the future. With regard to sale, however, the very structure of the system introduced by the Sale of Goods legislation seems to preclude an abstract analysis.[263] While it is possible to analyse a sale transaction as involving a separate contract and conveyance,[264] as the Act provides no framework for transferring property where a contract of sale is void, the Act is thus inherently causal. In contrast, because of the requirement for a deed of conveyance for the transfer of land, the contract/conveyance distrinction is clearly defined.[265]

(b)   Real agreement

In the context of requiring more than simply an underlying obligation to transfer ownership, the law has a certain amount in common with the notion of the '*Verfügungsgeschäft*'. It is clear that a unilateral declaration by a transferor cannot transfer ownership.[266] The settled common law distinction between contract and conveyance is only supportable on the basis of a separate legal act of delivery. This must be justified by the agreement of transferor and transferee that property will pass. This may be seen to amount to a 'real agreement'; not necessarily as a matter of a specific declaration, but inferred from the circumstances or actions.[267]

---

[261] Reid, *Property*, paras 608-609. See also Reid, K G C, 'Unjustified Enrichment and Property Law', 1994 Juridical Review 167 at 175, n 29, which submits that the Scottish approach is abstract.

[262] Carey Miller, D L, 'Scottish Property: a System of Civilian Principle' in MacQueen, H L *et al* (eds), *Regional Private Laws and Codification in Europe* (2003), p 118 at 124.

[263] Carey Miller with Irvine, *Corporeal Moveables*, para 9.17; Reid, *Property*, para 610.

[264] Carey Miller, D L, 'Scottish Property: a System of Civilian Principle' at 130.

[265] See above, para 1.1.3(h).

[266] It could, however, impose a personal obligation on the person making the declaration, by virtue of the Scots law doctrine of promise.

[267] Carey Miller with Irvine, *Corporeal Moveables*, para 8.10.

5.2. General issues

5.2.1. Payment

Scottish law did not receive the Roman law rule requiring payment before transfer, but instead, at common law, had an alternative rule that 'allowed the unpaid seller to recover the goods from the buyer on the basis of presumptive fraud. The developed form of the rule required the seller to act within three days of delivery – the *inter triduum* rule'.[268] In modern law, this rule can be equated with the statutory right of the seller to stop goods in transit where payment has not been received.[269] It is also possible to reserve the transfer of ownership until the price has been paid by the transferee.[270] Such a reservation of title would not necessarily be implied in a contract. Within the terms of the Sale of Goods Act 1979, it is also possible to create 'all sums' reservations of title, allowing title to be retained by the seller until all debts due from the buyer are paid.[271]

5.2.2. Ascertainment

(a) General

Under the common law, the question of ascertainment of goods is, understandably, subordinated to the act of delivery. Thus, historically, 'the problem of a contract in respect of unascertained goods did not assume any proprietary dimension'.[272] As noted above, in the vast majority of commercial transactions, ownership now passes when the parties intend it to pass,[273] regardless of whether payment of the purchase price is made and regardless of whether delivery is effected. This statutory rule, however, can only apply in relation to specific or ascertained goods,[274] so further legislative rules have had to supplement the position and solve

---

[268] Carey Miller with Irvine, *Corporeal Moveables*, para 11.26, citing *Inglis v Royal Bank* (1736) Mor 4936.

[269] Sale of Goods Act 1979, s. 44. See below, para 5.6.3.

[270] See below, chapter 15.

[271] *Armour v Thyssen Edelstahlwerke AG* 1990 SLT 891. See below, para 15.3.2.

[272] Carey Miller with Irvine, *Corporeal Moveables*, para 9.13. The passing of risk at common law, however, is another matter entirely and separate to any proprietorial issues. See *Widenmeyer v Burn Stewart & Co* 1967 SC 85.

[273] Where intention is not clear, a series of rules apply to deem when intention to transfer, and thus transfer of ownership itself, occurs. See below, paras 5.2.2(c) and 5.2.3(b).

[274] Section 17(1). See also Sale of Goods Act 1979, s. 16.

the ascertainment problem that the common law avoids by requiring
traditio. Exactly what is meant by intention will be discussed below.[275]

(b)   Specific goods

Specific goods are defined as 'goods identified and agreed on at the time a
contract of sale is made and includes an unidentified share, specified as a
fraction or percentage, of goods identified and agreed on as aforesaid', and
ordinarily it is fairly easy to apply this test to a given set of facts.[276] The
statute provides no such definition for ascertainment. This is unfortunate
because the answer to this question will have proprietary consequences
for the parties to a sale transaction. What seems clear is that the concept
refers to goods which were not specific or agreed upon at the time of the
contract of sale, but have since become identified as the subject matter of
the contract.[277] With unascertained goods, this is not the case.

Although this leaves us with an unfortunate double negative, ascertained goods are essentially goods that are not unascertained. Since the
reforms of the mid-nineties, there are now essentially three categories of
unascertained goods that are provided for under the 1979 Act. These
include the traditional category involving 'the identification of particular
items',[278] and the newer category of 'a share of bulk goods'.[279] The former
category can be further divided into 'future goods'[280] and 'generic
goods'.[281]

---

[275] See below, para 5.2.3.

[276] Sale of Goods Act 1979, s. 61(1) as amended by the Sale of Goods (Amendment)
Act 1995. For background analysis of these reforms see Carey Miller with Irvine,
Corporeal Moveables, para 9.06, n 63.

[277] See Carey Miller with Irvine, *Corporeal Moveables*, para 9.06 and the references
contained therein.

[278] Carey Miller with Irvine, *Corporeal Moveables*, para 9.13, covered by 1979 Act, s. 18,
rule 5(1) and (2).

[279] *Ibid.*

[280] *Ibid.* The authors clarify this description by describing these goods as 'goods not yet
ascertained in the absolute sense of goods to be manufactured or acquired by the
seller for the purposes of giving effect to the contract'. Even this division can be
subdivided, into the categories of goods to be manufactured and goods to be acquired: See Carey Miller with Irvine, *Corporeal Moveables*, para 9.14.

[281] *Ibid.* This description is elaborated on by describing generic goods as 'goods identified for the purpose of the contract by an accepted description of kind and quantity, but where the particular items to be delivered have not yet been allocated to
the contract'.

(c)   Rule 5(1)

The first situation to consider is rule 5(1) of section 18, and the rule is probably best explained by setting it out in full:

> 'Where there is a contract for the sale of unascertained or future goods by description, and goods of that description and in a deliverable state are unconditionally appropriated to the contract, either by the seller with the assent of the buyer or by the buyer with the assent of the seller, the property in the goods then passes to the buyer; and the assent may be express or implied, and may be given either before or after the appropriation is made.'

Rule 5(2) goes on to provide that goods are presumed to be unconditionally appropriated to the contract if they are delivered to the buyer or to a carrier for the purpose of transmission to the buyer without reservation.

The key concepts of rule 5(1) can thus be identified as 'unconditional appropriation' (as supplemented by rule 5(2)) and 'assent' by the non-appropriating party. Both must be present for the rule to apply.[282] With future goods that the seller is to acquire rather than make, all that the buyer need do is agree to take them on acquisition by the seller for the rule to apply.[283] With manufactured goods, the rule will apply when the goods are completed and when 'set aside for delivery in a manner ... sufficient to justify the objective conclusion that unconditional appropriation has occurred'.[284] With generic goods, the seller will clearly have to have taken some steps to allocate specific goods from the generic class to the contract of sale. Appropriation could be express, implied by mutual conduct, or could be inferred by reference to 'prior conduct, or trade custom or practice.'[285]

(d)   Bulk goods

With regard to the new subclass mentioned above – share of bulk goods – these are now catered for by two sub-rules, which can be described under

---

[282] See Carey Miller with Irvine, *Corporeal Moveables*, para 9.14 for a detailed analysis of this rule and the references to the relevant case law and academic writing therein. See also Reid, *Property*, para 635.

[283] See the discussion of the English case of *Carlos Federspiel & Co SA. v Charles Twigg & Co Ltd* [1957] 1 Lloyd's Rep 240 in Carey Miller with Irvine, *Corporeal Moveables*, para 9.14, n 5.

[284] Carey Miller with Irvine, *Corporeal Moveables*, para 9.14.

[285] *Ibid.*

the heading 'ascertainment by exhaustion'.[286] Prior to 1995, there could be no appropriation of goods from a bulk (for example, a quantity of grain from a silo) until the particular subjects of the sale contract had been isolated from that bulk.[287] If appropriation was precluded, transfer of ownership under rule 5(1) was precluded also.[288] The new sub-rules provide for a process of ascertainment of a bulk that has been reduced to a size equivalent to or less than a buyer's order. If the buyer is the only individual entitled to the goods left in that bulk, those goods will be appropriated to the sale and property will transfer to the buyer.

The reforms of 1995 also made a more fundamental change to the law, which operates as an exception to the general statement contained in section 16. The rule that no property can pass without ascertainment is now prefixed with the statement '[s]ubject to section 20A below'. Section 20A introduced a rule for the transfer of ownership in a *pro indiviso*, or undivided, share of goods forming part of a bulk, prior to ascertainment of particular goods. For the rule to apply, the sale must be for a specified quantity, the bulk must be identified and unlike the section 18 rules which operate independently of payment the buyer must have made payment to the seller for some or all of the goods. Subject to contrary agreement by the parties, the rule will then apply to transfer a *pro indiviso* share to the buyer and make the buyer an owner in common of the bulk.

Section 20A(3) clarifies the position in property law terms, stating that 'the undivided share of a buyer in a bulk at any time shall be such share as the quantity of goods paid for and due to the buyer out of the bulk bears to the quantity of goods in the bulk at that time'. Where there are numerous buyers and the aggregate of their respective shares exceeds what is left of the bulk, section 20A(4) operates to make the buyers co-owners on a *pro rata* basis.[289] This section will thus protect buyers who have paid some or all of the price from the insolvency of the buyer, where they would have previously been left with a personal right only to claim in the insolvent party's estate.

---

[286] *Ibid* at para 9.15.

[287] See further Campbell, N R, 'Case Comment: Passing of Property in Contracts for the Sale of Unascertained Goods', [1996] Journal of Business Law 199, discussing the English case of *Re Stapylton Fletcher Ltd* [1994] 1 WLR 1181, which related to the passing of property in wine which had been appropriated from the seller's trading stock.

[288] See *Hayman & Son v McLintock* 1907 SC 936.

[289] A new s. 20B, also inserted by the reforms, regulates the legal relationship of these co-owners, who will most likely find themselves in such a co-ownership situation unwittingly.

5.2.3. Party autonomy

(a)　General

Party autonomy has traditionally had a limited role with regard to property in Scottish law. The question of what parties may or may not have intended is invariably subordinate to some requirement of a final constitutive step, which publicised the transaction for third parties. With regard to land, this publicity was achieved by registration, in the case of transfer of ownership,[290] or by a tenant entering into possession, following an agreement to lease.[291] Similarly, parties are not free to transfer incorporeal property, like debts, by intention alone either. The process of assignation requires both mutual intention of the transferor and transferee and intimation to the other party, or parties, to the existing contract to be effective.[292]

Security rights in moveables have also traditionally required something more than mutual intention to be created at common law.[293] This extra step corresponds to delivery at common law, requiring a transfer of possession from the owner who is granting the security to the grantee. This allows third parties to equate possession of a moveable with a real right. Again, this has been eroded somewhat by statute and reasons of commercial expediency. Companies can grant floating charges to secure both their immoveable and moveable property without a great degree of publicity,[294] while all-sums reservation of title clauses in relation to moveables are also now acceptable to the Scottish legal system.

---

[290] The Registration Act 1617 introduced a Scottish register of deeds for transactions involving land and since then registration has been a necessary step to obtain ownership of land.

[291] This rule flows from the Leases Act 1449.

[292] The requirement for publicity through intimation stems from a similar era to the rule which makes leases real through possession. See Luig, K, 'Assignation' in Reid & Zimmermann, *History*, vol 1, p 398 at 403 citing *Drummond v Muschet* (1492) Mor 843.

[293] See Steven, A J M, 'Rights in Security over Moveables' in Reid & Zimmermann, *History*, vol 1, p 333.

[294] Compare the Companies Act 1985, s. 410 with the Bankruptcy and Diligence etc (Scotland) Act 2007, s. 37 which is to introduce a register of floating charges. Section 38(3) of this Act provides that failure to register a floating charge will render the charge ineffective as a security over a company's assets. See below, para 18.2.2.

(b)   Sale of goods

As noted, the common law required delivery of a corporeal moveable to transfer ownership to the transferee.[295] This remains the case with regard to barter, but not with regard to sale. Following the 1893 reforms,[296] party autonomy now trumps delivery as a means of transferring ownership; provided, of course, the goods are specific or ascertained.

Intention, like the goods that are subject to the contract of sale, may also have to be ascertained. Section 17(2) of the 1979 Act provides that it is to be inferred from the terms of the contract, party conduct and circumstances.[297] If such inference is impossible, five rules apply to ascertain when property is to pass.[298] These rules, while important in instances when the parties are silent,[299] are totally subordinate to clearly expressed intention.[300] Party autonomy is thus the key factor in this system, and all other subordinate factors serve to supplement intention when it is difficult to ascertain.

The framework of rule 5 has been discussed above[301] and will not be considered again here, but the remaining rules can apply to the following effect where intention is not clear. The important deeming elements of these four rules respectively include:

(a) the time an unconditional contract for the sale of specific goods in a deliverable state is made;
(b) the seller performing an act he was bound to do to make property deliverable and notifying the buyer this act has been done;
(c) the seller weighing, testing, measuring or performing some other act in relation to the goods and notifying the buyer of this; and
(d) the buyer accepting goods delivered for approval, or on a sale and return basis or otherwise, by his conduct or by retaining possession without giving notice of rejection within a reasonable time.

---

[295] See, for example, the statement of Erskine where he notes ownership 'remains with the seller or vendor till the delivery of the subjects'. See Erskine, III.3.2.

[296] See now the Sale of Goods Act 1979, ss. 16-21, 23-25 and 62.

[297] *Scottish Transit Trust v Scottish Land Cultivators* 1955 SC 254.

[298] Sale of Goods Act 1979, s. 18. This rule, discussed above, is concerned more with issues of ascertainment than intention, while the previous four rules operate only in relation to specific goods or, in the case of rule 4, when goods are delivered for approval or on a similar basis.

[299] On the application of these rules, see Carey Miller with Irvine, *Corporeal Moveables*. paras 9.07-9.12.

[300] The rules do not come into play 'if the intention of the parties is quite plain': *Woodburn v Andrew Motherwell Ltd* 1917 SC 533 at 538.

[301] See above, para 5.2.2(c).

Party autonomy can only be taken so far, as there is a *numerus clausus* of real rights.[302] It is not for individuals to create new real rights, nor is it for individuals to create new ways of transferring these existing real rights.[303] Despite this, it is entirely possible to delay transfer to a later moment of time by inserting a time period or condition, or even contract to allow ownership transfer to coincide with delivery. Interestingly, the first rule for ascertaining intention listed in section 18 of the 1979 Act expressly stipulates that ownership of specific goods in a deliverable state passes when the contract is made, and that it is 'immaterial whether the time of payment or the time of delivery, or both, be postponed'. As discussed above, however, this rule will only come into play where the intention of the parties is not clear, so it is perfectly possible for this rule to be avoided by agreement.

5.3. Validity of obligation and defective transfers

5.3.1. General

Any transaction and subsequent conveyance involving a moveable that ostensibly transfers ownership will fall into one of three categories when analysing the validity of the transfer and the status of the transferee's title.[304] Contract and conveyance can be good, void or voidable. While the issue of 'right to dispose' will be considered further below, it may be beneficial to consider the issue of contract and conveyance in tandem to set the scene.

Where the transferor and transferee have *consensus in idem* and are not lacking in capacity, and the transferor has title to the moveable involved in the transaction, the underlying contract is valid and 'good' title will be passed to the transferee. Where the transfer is by a non-owner, Scottish terminology describes the transferee's title as 'void'. The transfer has no effect, unless it falls within one of the recognised exceptions to the *nemo*

---

[302] See further Paisley, R R M, 'Dogmatic rigidity', (2005) 9 Edinburgh Law Review 267.

[303] See further Reid, K G C, 'Obligations and property: Exploring the Border' in Daniel Visser (ed), *The Limits of the Law of Obligations* (1997) at p 225 and Carey Miller, D L and Combe, M M, 'The Boundaries of Property Rights in Scots Law', vol 10.3 EJCL, (December 2006), http://www.ejcl.org/103/art103-4.pdf, for analysis of the rigidity of Scottish property law when faced with attempts to erode it using the law of obligations.

[304] The validity of the underlying transaction and the unimpeachable status of the derivative title occasioned by the transaction will normally coincide, but it is possible for this not to be the case – a point discussed in Reid, *Property*, para 607.

plus principle.[305] This would be the case even if parties were in total agreement as to what they were doing and what they were trying to transfer. The only way such a contract could transfer ownership is if a moveable subsequently came into the ownership of the transferor, thus allowing the doctrine of accretion to apply, which would immediately transfer ownership to the transferee without the need for a further contract.[306]

Where an underlying contract is void, perhaps because of confusion as to the underlying *causa* of the transfer, but a subsequent conveyance is valid, ownership will be transferred.[307] This view sits well with the presumption of ownership that Scottish law affords to the possessor of a moveable.[308] This presumption, which remains of great importance even in the present day,[309] would mean anyone that has delivered property in a way that could feasibly have transferred ownership would be unable to re-acquire possession.[310] With regard to sale, it is clear that the scheme of the Sale of Goods Act 1979 is essentially causal, and thus transfer under the terms of the Act is reliant on the underlying *causa*.[311] That said, while an invalid contract of sale 'necessarily bars transfer under the Act it may not be a complete bar to transfer'.[312] A void sale followed by a form of conveyance valid at common law would still transfer good title to the transferee.

Lastly, in a limited number of scenarios the transferee's title is 'voidable', that is to say it is vulnerable to be set aside with *ex nunc* effect. These situations tend to relate to fraud or misrepresentation when ownership was transferred. Such scenarios could include unfairly inducing an individual to enter a transaction by making representations to them,[313] attempts to unfairly

---

[305] Such as a sale by a seller who has remained in possession of goods or a sale by a buyer that has legitimately obtained possession to goods but prior to completing title thereto, under the Sale of Goods Act 1979, ss. 24 and 25 respectively. See below, para 5.9.2.

[306] See below, para 5.9.4.

[307] This point is not uncontroversial. See Reid, *Property*, paras 608-610 for discussion. In relation to land, it is clear that an underlying invalid contract will not be fatal to the title conferred by a validly registered disposition, but the lack of a clear and separately written act of conveyance has perhaps muddied the situation in relation to moveables: Reid, *Property*, para 611.

[308] Erskine, II.1.24; Reid, *Property*, para 130. See above, para 2.2.

[309] See, for example, *Prangnell-O'Neill v Lady Skiffington* 1984 SLT 282 and *Chief Constable, Strathclyde Police v Sharp* 2002 SLT (Sh Ct) 95, and respective case analyses: PF, 'Case and Comment: In pari causa melior est conditio possidentis?', 1985 Juridical Review 138; and Carey Miller, D L, 'Title to Moveables: Mr Sharp's Porsche', (2003) 7 Edinburgh Law Review 221.

[310] Carey Miller with Irvine, *Corporeal Moveables*, para 1.19.

[311] Reid, *Property*, para 610.

[312] *Ibid.*

[313] As in the famous case of *MacLeod v Kerr* 1965 SC 253.

avoid the insolvency process and ranking procedure set down by law,[314] or being involved in a double sale.[315] An individual defrauded by such a scheme will have a right to set aside, or 'reduce', the contract and thus, from that point onwards, remove ownership from the fraudulent transferee. In such a situation, the transferee's title is subsistent until reduction takes place, so transfers that occur before reduction will transfer ownership, and if this transfer is made in 'good faith and for value', that is the subsequent acquirer was not party to the fraudulent scheme, the good faith acquirer will obtain a good and unimpeachable title.[316]

5.3.2. Lack of capacity

As a matter of general principle, no individual or juristic body can trans-fer ownership of a moveable when they lack capacity, unless such an incapacity is somehow purified by law.[317] For example, a child under the age of sixteen (by virtue of the Age of Legal Capacity (Scotland) Act 1991) can only enter a contract '(a) of a kind commonly entered into by persons of his age and circumstance, and (b) on terms which are not unreasonable'.[318] Thus, an eight year old child would lack capacity to buy a Ferrari motor car, but would have capacity to buy a miniature model Ferrari at a fair price from a toy shop. Scottish law also has special rules for mentally handicapped individuals, now referred to as adults with in-capacity following recent legislative reform,[319] which requires the in-volvement of an adult with incapacity's guardian to validate any transac-tion. Certain juristic bodies may also be restricted in what actions they have capacity to perform by the *ultra vires* doctrine, which has been of

---

[314] Under common law a debtor in a state of insolvency is prevented from making what is known as a gratuitous alienation, and similar statutory rules exist in the Bankruptcy (Scotland) Act 1985, s. 34(1) to challenge alienations within a set period. Similarly, unfair preferences (*i.e.* arrangements which favour one creditor over others) can be challenged under the Bankruptcy (Scotland) Act 1985, s. 36. Similar rules exist for corporate entities under the Insolvency Act 1986. See below, para 9.1.

[315] Although the majority of cases relating to this rule penalising private knowledge of a prior right, now known as the 'offside goals' rule following a sporting analogy in the leading case of *Rodger (Builders) Limited v Fawdry* 1950 SC 483; 1950 SLT 345, relate to land, it is generally accepted that the rule also relates to corporeal move-ables. See below, chapter 6.

[316] Carey Miller with Irvine, *Corporeal Moveables*, para 8.11. The statutory enactment of this rule is found at section 23 of the 1979 Act.

[317] Carey Miller with Irvine, *Corporeal Moveables*, para 8.05.

[318] Age of Legal Capacity (Scotland) Act 1991, s. 2(1).

[319] Adults with Incapacity (Scotland) Act 2000.

great importance for individuals transacting with local authorities and limited companies in the past,[320] and continues to be of importance when transacting with companies not incorporated under the Companies Acts.[321]

5.3.3. Void contract

Any defect in the underlying contract rendering it void would be retroactive. Thus, a contract where the seller believes he is selling one item and the buyer believes he is buying another, or a comparable situation involving a mistake as to identity,[322] with the same belief in existence at the time of conveyance, would not give a 'limping' title. Similarly, if one party were forced to enter a contract because of threats of violence, such a vice of consent would be retroactive.

5.3.4. Voidable contract

This was discussed above.[323]

5.3.5. Mistake as to solvency

There is no way to avoid a contract with retroactive effect in this situation; if a general misrepresentation was made and the contract was later reduced, this would only be classified as an *ex nunc* defect. It could be possible for the parties to a contract to enter an arrangement *inter se* (perhaps in the terms of a sale and leaseback or similar commercial arrangement), but even if such an arrangement was entered into, it would not prohibit an owner from transferring the real right of ownership to a third party.

---

[320] A number of cases relating to local authorities, in both England and Scotland, led the Government to legislate specifically to protect third parties dealing with these entities. See the Local Government (Contracts) Act 1997.

[321] See Reid, *Property*, para 599. Parties dealing in good faith with companies incorporated under the Companies Acts and their directors are protected by the Companies Act 1985, ss. 35, 35A and 35B with the relevant rules now being found in the Companies Act 2006, ss. 39 and 40 (not yet in force).

[322] *Morrisson v Robertson* 1908 SC 332.

[323] See above, para 5.3.1.

5.3.6. Termination of contract

Again, as above, there are no specific rules and thus the drafting of the contract would be crucial. The law would allow a reservation of title arrangement which could, if drafted properly, relate to non-payment and non-conformity,[324] thus preventing ownership from ever transferring to a 'transferee' and protecting the other party to the transaction.

If property had transferred to the transferee, any contractual terms or any arrangement entered into to supplement the transfer of ownership would be purely personal. These would not stop a third party acquiring a right from the owner under private arrangement (provided there were no issues of bad faith, such as private knowledge of an option to purchase). If ownership of the moveable had not transferred, on termination of the contract any remedy would be vindicatory.

In the circumstances of a conditional transaction, any applicable 'resolutive' condition will apply retroactively to the act of delivery in the same way as it would apply to the underlying contract. Such a result would be in accordance with the wishes of the parties. This would also be the case with moveables transferred to a transferee who has the duty to administer the moveable and where the moveable is transferred for security purposes.

5.4. *Traditio* (delivery)

5.4.1. Introduction

Scottish law, having rejected the need for delivery in the late nineteenth century in relation to sale, can arguably be looked on as having moved away from the impracticalities of transferring possession in favour of the more transaction friendly need for consensus alone. To adopt such an analysis of the sale of goods reforms, however, would be slightly misleading. These were not brought on after a consideration of the purposes of the delivery requirement, or of the different policy factors behind the need for delivery.[325] Instead, they were brought into Scottish law after a late amendment to what was previously an English codification extended the reach of the relevant piece of legislation to include the northern part of Great Britain. The reasons behind this amendment, and whether this Act amounted to an imposition of English law on Scotland, were oft-

---

[324] See below, generally, chapter 15.

[325] For such a consideration, see Carey Miller with Irvine, *Corporeal Moveables*, para 8.13.

discussed by legal scholars over the course of the twentieth century,[326] but an explicit policy analysis of whether delivery is a welcome stage of transfer was lacking at the time of the initial legislation.

5.4.2.   Modern relevance of delivery

Derivative acquisition by way of the common law route and the delivery requirement this entails continues to be relevant today, as demonstrated by the extensive coverage given in modern accounts of the law relating to moveable property.[327] It should also be noted that while the 1893 reforms may have removed delivery as a required step entirely, the common law was arguably beginning to reject a strict delivery requirement anyway. While the publicity aspect of delivery can and has been characterised as crucial, it can perhaps be overplayed. As early as the nineteenth century, and prior to the Sale of Goods Act reforms, it was noted that 'an adherence to this plain and simple rule [requiring delivery] is utterly impossible amidst the complicated transactions of modern trade'.[328] This is perhaps reflected in Scottish law's traditional flexibility when it comes to recognising forms of actual delivery, and by virtue of the fact that there is no *numerus clausus* of forms of actual delivery.[329]

5.4.3.   The need for an overt act

The requirement for at least some act over and above intention is, however, clear from common law, especially given the presumption of ownership accorded to the possessor of a thing.[330] The paradigmatic case is, of course, the physical delivery of a moveable by the transferor handing it to

---

[326] The leading text advocating the former imposition analysis is Smith, T B, *Property Problems in Sale* (1978), but compare Rodger, A, 'The Codification of Commercial Law in Britain', 1992 LQR 570. Rodger states '[t]he idea that the bill was imposed on Scotland by English interests could hardly be less true' at 581, and details how Scottish interests were decidedly in favour of Lord Watson's proposed amendments to allow Scotland's law of sale to be essentially aligned with that of England.

[327] Carey Miller with Irvine, *Corporeal Moveables*, paras 8.12-8.27. See also the *dicta* of Lord Rodger of Earlsferry quoted at para 8.12, from the immoveable property case of *Burnett's Trustee v Grainger* 2004 SC (HL) 19 at para 88, which makes eminently clear that the maxim *traditionibus non nudis pactis rerum dominia transferuntur* applies to the passing of title of moveables when the 1979 Act does not apply.

[328] Bell, *Commentaries*, I, 178.

[329] Carey Miller with Irvine, *Corporeal Moveables*, para 8.17.

[330] See above, para 2.2.

the transferee,[331] and this would undoubtedly qualify as delivery. On the other hand, a *constitutum possessorium* brought about by intention alone whereby the transferee holds for the transferor may not be enough to transfer ownership at common law;[332] there would need to be other circumstances to support that ownership had in fact transferred.[333]

5.4.4. Forms of delivery

In between these two extremes, Scottish law recognises that delivery can be effected in a number of ways. For example the delivery of keys to a yard containing moveables was held to be sufficient in one case,[334] while cases relating to the marking of generic goods as for the transferee will very much turn on their own facts.[335] The important factor seems to be that a change of possession must have taken place, and a degree of 'latitude' exists in the circumstances that can evidence such a change of possession.[336]

An extensive body of case law also exists in relation to constructive delivery, which can be split into three categories that essentially mirror the Roman law conceptions of delivery of *brevi manu*, *longa manu* and *constitutum possessorium* but, as noted by Professor Gordon, these categories do not exist in Scotland other than by analogy.[337]

While this comparison is useful to make for present purposes, what matters is whether ownership of a thing has transferred,[338] rather than whether the means of transfer can be characterized as fitting a certain category. As has been noted, 'Scots law has developed a distinctive classification based upon the categories of actual, symbolical and construc-

---

[331] Carey Miller with Irvine, *Corporeal Moveables*, para 8.16.

[332] It would, however, be effective under the 1979 Act, s. 17 but the evidential difficulties of proving such an arrangement are obvious.

[333] See the case of *Eadie v Young* (1815) Hume's Dec 705, where the moveables involved were clearly marked and rent was paid for them and thus title was transferred, despite the fact the moveables remained in the possession of the transferor.

[334] *West Lothian Oil Co Ltd v Mair* (1892) 20 R 64.

[335] See, for example, the contrasting cases of *Gibson v Forbes* (1833) 11 S 916 (where property was transferred by setting aside bottles of wine and making the relevant book entries) and *Boak v Megget* (1844) 6 D 662.

[336] Carey Miller, D L, 'Scottish Property: a System of Civilian Principle' in MacQueen, H L, *et al* (eds), *Regional Private Laws and Codification in Europe* (2003), p 118 at 124, while discussing the *Gibson* case.

[337] Gordon, W M, *Studies in the Transfer of Property by Traditio* (1970), pp 215-222 and Carey Miller with Irvine, *Corporeal Moveables*, para 8.15.

[338] Reid, *Property*, para 619.

tive'.[339] While the scope of symbolical delivery may be somewhat restricted, relating only to bills of lading and bills of exchange, the other
two categories provide a useful and flexible framework to allow delivery
to be recognised in a variety of situations even when delivery may not
have ostensibly taken place.

As noted above, the concept of actual delivery is fairly wide, forming
what may be called 'an extended category'.[340] With this wide scope of
application, it is unsurprising that there is no *numerus clausus* of modes of
delivery.[341] Thus parties are free to create new forms and the law is free to
recognise novel circumstances for delivery, a position which directly
contrasts with the limitations on forming new property rights, discussed
above. Constructive delivery applies to 'accommodate a transmission of
title without the necessity of an actual handing of natural possession to
the transferee',[342] and thus covers situations where it would be tenuous to
extend the already extended category of actual delivery. This can apply
where the delivery process involves a third party,[343] or where circumstances are such to be analogous to the Roman law catgories of *traditio
brevi manu*[344] and delivery by *constitutum possessorium*.[345]

While the role of *traditio* may remain of interest only in limited situations such as barter and pledge, Scotland still has a considerable body of
case law and authority relating to how delivery can be effected. This may
remain instructive from a comparative point of view. For example, pre-
Sale of Goods Act cases like *Boak v Megget*[346] and *Orr's Tr v Tullis*[347] are
instructive as to the role of marking goods in delivery. *London Scottish
Transport Ltd v Tyres (Scotland) Ltd*,[348] decided subsequently on the inability to unilaterally resurrect a right of lien, could point to a definitive
Scottish answer to the problem as to whether a buyer can unilaterally
decide to take, or 'steal', goods from the possession of a seller.

The *Orr's Tr* case also provides a good example of when a *constitutum
possessorium* can be established and recognised by a legal system sceptical

---

[339] Carey Miller with Irvine, *Corporeal Moveables*, para 8.15.

[340] *Ibid.*

[341] *Ibid*, para 8.17.

[342] *Ibid*, para 8.20.

[343] *Anderson v McCall* (1866) 4 M 765.

[344] Carey Miller with Irvine, *Corporeal Moveables*, para 8.21.

[345] *Ibid*, paras 8.23-8.25.

[346] (1844) 6 D 662.

[347] (1870) 8 M 936. Needless to say, from these cases the importance of marking the
goods is inversely proportional to the importance of transferring possession. If possession is completely passed, marking plays a limited role, but where an ostensible
transfer of possession is lacking, marking becomes crucial.

[348] 1957 SLT (Sh Ct) 48.

of rights created without publicity: a number of recent cases relating to land law have not recognised a transfer or a creation of new rights where possession could have been attributed to a right of ownership[349] or a valid lease.[350] By analogy, the law would be equally sceptical of recognising a transaction that affects third parties without any outward publicity.

5.5. Registration

Ordinarily, the transfer of corporeal moveables does not require registration or formal writing.[351] Possession of a moveable has been equated to having a registered deed in relation to immoveable property,[352] and in most transactions, '[f]or obvious practical reasons',[353] no registration will be necessary.

In some specific situations, however, the law imposes controls over moveable property. This may manifest itself in the criminal law or strict regulation, perhaps by making ownership of an unregistered firearm illegal, but such controls do not necessarily affect questions of proprietorship.[354] Motor vehicles provide a case in point, although detailed requirements in relation to vehicle documentation are prescribed by law, questions of ownership are still determined by the general law of property.[355]

---

[349] *Clydesdale Bank plc v Davidson* 1998 SC (HL) 51, where co-owners of land purported to grant a lease to one of their own number, but the 'tenant's' possession was actually attributable to *pro indiviso* ownership rather than the ineffectual lease.

[350] *Bell v Inkersall Investments Ltd* 2006 SLT 626 where possession was attributable to a series of short term grazing licences for animals, rather than a lease which the occupier claimed was impliedly in existence. See Anderson, C, '*Bell v Inkersall Investments Ltd*', 2006 SLT *(News)* 221.

[351] Stair, II.1.42. As noted above, however, writing may be necessary for certain types of obligation.

[352] See *Moore v Gledden* (1869) 7 M 1016, where Lord Neaves compared possession of a moveable to sasine, the old feudal term which is now equated with modern day registration.

[353] Carey Miller with Irvine, *Corporeal Moveables*, para 8.14.

[354] In addition to unregistered firearms, examples include motor vehicles and dangerous animals, and to this ever increasing list one could now add dangerous fireworks or incendiary devices, by virtue of the Police, Public Order and Criminal Justice (Scotland) Act 2006, s. 76. While such prohibitions may not affect the issue of proprietorship, any prohibition can effectively rule out the exercise of proprietary rights. See Carey Miller with Irvine, *Corporeal Moveables*, para 1.12.

[355] Carey Miller with Irvine, *Corporeal Moveables*, para 1.15.

Other more valuable assets may require registration also, such as the specific categories of ships,[356] aircraft[357] or petroleum.[358] Such registration is not necessarily constitutive.[359]

5.6.   Protection of the seller

5.6.1.   General

In addition to a contractual retention of title provision, a seller can protect his or her position in a number of other ways. One such way is by retaining goods due to a transferee who has not performed a reciprocal obligation pursuant to an agreement to transfer. The right to retain goods is provided for at common law, but this retention is obviously tied to the fact that ownership remains with the transferor until delivery.[360] The Sale of Goods reforms in 1893, following on from the earlier commercial reforms introduced by the Mercantile Law Amendment Act Scotland 1856,[361] removed the requirement of delivery to transfer ownership, and title may well have transferred even though the seller is still in possession.

The Sale of Goods Act 1979 provides several rights for an unpaid seller to protect his or her position. The term 'unpaid seller' is defined by section 38 of the Act as a seller of goods where 'the whole of the price has not been paid or tendered', or where a negotiable instrument has been tendered as conditional payment, and the condition has not been ful-

---

[356] Merchant Shipping Act 1995, s. 8.

[357] Air Navigation Order 2005 (SI 2005/1970), part 4.

[358] See Halliday, J M, *Conveyancing Law and Practice in Scotland*, vol 1, (2nd ed, 1995), paras 9.76-9.94.

[359] Carey Miller with Irvine, *Corporeal Moveables*, para 1.15, notes that the mere requirement of registration 'does not ... mean that registration is a prerequisite to title'.

[360] As noted in Carey Miller with Irvine, '[r]etention applies as a basis upon which an owner may withhold the transfer of title ... pending performance of what is due by way of counter obligation': *Corporeal Moveables*, para 11.21. The common law rules on retention remain relevant for contracts of exchange.

[361] See further Sutherland, E, 'Remedying an Evil? Warrandice of Quality at Common Law in Scotland', 1987 Juridical Review 24. These protective measures did not change the underlying common law position – 'the property of goods sold but not delivered remains still with the seller' (per Lord Neaves in *Wyper v Harveys* (1861) 23 D 606 at 615). However, as noted by Brown, the protection afforded by the 1856 Act and the reduction of the Scottish principle it entailed was such to raise the question 'is it worth while to contend for the principle itself?' See Brown, R, 'Assimilation of the Law of Sale', 1891 Juridical Review 297 at 300.

filled.[362] Once within this definition, section 39 clarifies that an unpaid seller has a number of protections, namely:

(a) a lien on the goods or right to retain them for the price while he or she is in possession of them;
(b) a right to stop the goods in transit after he or she has lost possession, in the event of the buyer's insolvency;
(c) a right of re-sale, subject to the terms of the 1979 Act; and
(d) where the ownership has not transferred, he or she has a right to withhold delivery and a right of stoppage in transit, comparable to the rights that exist when title has passed.

The rights of lien, stoppage in transit and re-sale will now be considered in more detail.

5.6.2. Lien

The scope of the lien is clarified by section 41(1) as applying to situations where goods have been sold with no stipulation as to credit, where any credit the goods were sold on has expired, and where the buyer becomes insolvent. A precursor to any of these situations is that the unpaid seller must be in possession, and what constitutes possession will turn on the facts and circumstances of any particular case. Part delivery of some of the goods does not extinguish the right to retain, as section 42 explicitly provides the right of retention will apply over the undelivered goods unless circumstances are such that it seems the part delivery was actually part of a wider agreement to waive the lien.[363]

Three situations that will extinguish the lien, however, include delivery of the goods to a carrier without reserving a right of disposal, where 'the buyer or his agent lawfully obtains possession of the goods',[364] and express waiver.[365] Section 43(1)(b) rules out the possibility of terminating the lien by the buyer obtaining possession unlawfully.[366] In the hypothetical example where a transferee 'steals' goods four days before they were

---

[362] 'Seller' is defined in fairly wide terms for the purposes of this section, but in slightly different terms to the general definition contained in s. 61(1). See Carey Miller with Irvine, *Corporeal Moveables*, para 11.23 for discussion.

[363] Carey Miller with Irvine, *Corporeal Moveables*, para 11.24.

[364] Possession may mean either natural or civil. See Carey Miller with Irvine, *Corporeal Moveables*, para 11.25. See also *Paton's Trs v Finlayson* 1923 SC 872.

[365] Sale of Goods Act, s. 43(1).

[366] See Carey Miller with Irvine, *Corporeal Moveables*, para 11.25, for discussion of what 'lawfully' means.

due to be delivered one may draw an analogy with this section and not recognise the 'theft' as a valid delivery.[367] Alternatively, should the 1979 Act apply, it may be that the 'theft' of the buyer would run contrary to any agreement to transfer, and hence no consensus and reciprocal intention to give and receive would be present.

5.6.3. Stoppage in transit

Where possession has been lost, a seller may still be entitled to resume possession of goods in transit to an insolvent buyer. As discussed above, this rule replaced the common law rule allowing a seller a three day window to recover goods from an insolvent buyer, and is now provided for by section 44 of the 1979 Act. Many of the concepts that relate to the right of retention, such as unpaid seller and insolvent buyer,[368] apply equally to the right of stoppage in transit, but the central concept of 'in transit' is unique to this right of stoppage.[369]

Like the question of whether a party is in possession, whether goods are 'in transit' is a question that will very much turn on the given circumstances. Section 45(1) provides that goods are in transit from 'when they are delivered to a carrier ... for the purpose of transmission to the buyer, until the buyer ... takes delivery of them from the carrier'. From an unpaid seller's perspective, the crucial point is when transit ends, and this is where the right is lost.[370] This is not necessarily at the point when goods reach their appointed destination, as section 45(2) provides that transit finishes when delivery is obtained before the goods reach their appointed destination (subject to the section 45(1) rule that the buyer or his agent takes delivery).[371] Transit does not begin again should the buyer direct that the goods are to be transported somewhere else.[372]

Assuming transit has not come to an end, a seller may exercise the right of stoppage 'either by taking actual possession of the goods or by giving notice of his or her claim to the carrier ... in whose possession the

---

[367] See also *London Scottish Transport Ltd v Tyres (Scotland) Ltd* 1957 SLT (Sh Ct) 48 which relates to an attempt by an unpaid seller (by virtue of the buyer's insolvency) to revive the right of lien by recovering goods which had already been delivered. See Steven, A J M, *Pledge and Lien* (2008), para 13-33.

[368] The definition of insolvency is provided for by s. 61(4), and it is worth noting that one need not be actually sequestrated or, if the buyer is a company, in liquidation to fall within the definition.

[369] Carey Miller with Irvine, *Corporeal Moveables*, para 11.27.

[370] See *Muir v Rankin* (1905) 13 SLT 60.

[371] On the authority point, see *Mechan & Sons Ltd v North Eastern Ry Co* 1911 SC 1348.

[372] 1979 Act, s. 45(3).

goods are'.[373] If the stoppage is effected by notice, the carrier 'must rede-liver the goods to, or according to the directions of, the seller'.[374]

Finally, an unpaid seller is protected from the actions of the buyer and any purported transfer by him or her does not affect a right of retention or a right of stoppage in transit, unless the unpaid seller has assented to the transfer.[375]

5.6.4. Right of re-sale

Under the Sale of Goods Act 1979 a seller in possession who has previ-ously transferred ownership to a buyer has power to confer title to a third party.[376] This provision gives good faith third parties protection when purchasing from possessors. However, while the seller has the *power* to confer title his or her *right* to re-sell the goods is limited. Of course, if the seller has retained ownership he or she retains the right to sell the goods and confer good title on third party acquirers. However, in certain cases the seller will have transferred ownership but exercised his or her lien or right to exercise stoppage in transit. In these cases section 48 of the Sale of Goods Act 1979 applies.

The key provisions are section 48(3), which provides that where a seller has exercised a right of lien, retention, or stoppage in transit, and the goods are perishable, or where the unpaid seller intimates an inten-tion to re-sell then the seller has a right to re-sell the goods if the buyer does not pay the price and section 48(4) where a seller is entitled to pre-serve a right of re-sale. In either case section 48(2) provides that if own-ership has passed to the third party and the right of lien or stoppage in transit has been exercised then the seller can confer good title on any purchaser.

5.7. Real agreement

As noted above,[377] the law recognises that some form of declaration or agreement separate from an underlying obligation to transfer property is in fact necessary to transfer that property.

---

[373] 1979 Act, s. 46(1).

[374] 1979 Act, s. 45(3).

[375] 1979 Act, s. 47(1). See Carey Miller with Irvine, *Corporeal Moveables*, para 11.29, for analysis of what may amount to 'assent'.

[376] Sale of Goods Act 1979, s. 24.

[377] See above, para 5.1.6(b).

5.8.   Payment

Neither the common law nor the Sale of Goods Act 1979 require payment to transfer ownership.[378] As detailed above, a simple reservation of title clause can be used in any contract where the purchase price is not paid. Often parties will expressly provide for ownership to pass upon payment, and, by virtue of section 17, such an agreement would indeed transfer ownership when payment is received. Thus, the problem constellation (where the buyer pays only 50% of the contract price and the seller, after partially terminating the contract, demands 50% of the goods back), could not be solved without reference to the terms of any agreement. If the contract contained a clause requiring the full purchase price to be paid, or indeed all sums due from the buyer to the seller under any separate agreements,[379] the seller could claim all the goods back, leaving the buyer with a personal right to claim back the 50% already paid to the seller(either under a relevant term of the contract or, if no such term was explicit, the law of unjustified enrichment). If the contract was silent as to when title to the goods was to transfer, the section 18 scheme would apply to determine when the parties actually intended to transfer ownership.

5.9.   The right to dispose

5.9.1.   The general rule: *nemo plus*

Over and above the protective measures already mentioned, perhaps the most fundamental protection the law affords to an owner's right of *dominium* is the general rule that only the owner of a moveable can transfer title. The *nemo plus* rule[380] permeates derivative acquisition of land and moveables in Scotland and indeed many other legal systems[381] providing that no transferor can pass any better title than he or she had. However, some exceptions to the rule do exist.[382] For example, a good faith acquirer of a negotiable instrument or money can acquire a good title, regardless of

---

[378] See above, para 5.2.1 and Carey Miller with Irvine, *Corporeal Moveables*, para 9.02, n 36, quoting Stair, I.14.2.

[379] *Armour v Thyssen Edelstahlwerke AG* 1990 SLT 891.

[380] See above, para 1.1.3(i).

[381] See above, para 1.1.3(i); Van Vliet, L P W, *Transfer of movables in German, French, English and Dutch Law* (2000), p 28 and Carey Miller, D L, *The Acquisition and Protection of Ownership* (1986), para 9.2.1.3 for a discussion of the limited exceptions to this rule in South Africa.

[382] See Atiyah, P S, Adams, J N and MacQueen, H, *The Sale of Goods* (11th ed, 2005), chapter 20 and Reid, *Property*, paras 669-683.

the title of the transferor,[383] as may a purchaser buying unclaimed goods or animals from the police.[384] The transferor may also appoint an agent who then acquires power to administer and transfer the assets of the principal.[385]

5.9.2. Statutory exceptions

With regard to transfer of moveables, statute provides a number of exceptions to the rule against non-owner transfer. The Factors Act 1889,[386] allows good faith acquirers of goods from mercantile agents,[387] provided such an agent is 'with the consent of the owner, in possession of the goods or of the documents of title to goods', to acquire title to goods transferred 'as if [the mercantile agent] were expressly authorised by the owner of the goods'.[388] The Sale of Goods Act provides further exceptions to the *nemo plus* rule along similar lines,[389] including sale by a seller in possession[390] and sale by a buyer in possession.[391] The status of these sections as 'exceptions' to the normal situation is perhaps best illustrated with reference to a statement by Lord President Clyde from the case of *Thomas Graham and Sons v Glenrothes Development Corporation*:

> 'Section 25 is a statutory recognition of an exception to the general rule that only an owner of goods can transfer the property in them. The section enables an apparent owner to transfer someone else's goods to a third party in certain specific circumstances.'[392]

---

[383] Bills of Exchange Act 1882, s. 38(2).

[384] Civic Government (Scotland) Act 1982, s. 71.

[385] This is usually done by a formal deed, known as a power of attorney.

[386] This rule was introduced by the Factors (Scotland) Act 1890, which applied the earlier English legislation of the Factors Act 1889.

[387] Defined by s. 1(1) as 'a mercantile agent having in the customary course of his business as such agent authority either to sell goods, or to consign goods for the purposes of sale, or to buy goods, or to raise money on the security of goods'. See Reid, *Property*, para 671 for a detailed analysis of the special position of mercantile agents under the Factors Acts.

[388] Factors Act 1889, s. 2(1).

[389] It is clear that these rules are properly categorised as statutory exceptions to the *nemo plus* rule, rather than an application of the Scottish doctrine of personal bar. See Reid, E C and Blackie, J W G, *Personal Bar* (2006), para 11.25. The impact of personal bar on property law is discussed further below, at para 5.9.3.

[390] Sale of Goods Act 1979, s. 24.

[391] Sale of Goods Act 1979, s. 25.

[392] 1967 SC 284 at 293.

Although this *dictum* relates to the situation of a buyer in possession under the 1893 Act, it remains relevant to both exceptions under the current legislation. The first exception arises when an owner has sold a thing yet retained possession and subsequently sells again to a different party,[393] while the second arises where a buyer has taken possession of goods and has any necessary documents of title with the consent of the seller, but ownership has not yet transferred.[394]

The policy behind the exceptions for sellers and buyers in possession is to allow an individual acting in good faith to take a situation at face value when purchasing from an ostensible owner, and in these exceptional cases appearances are such that penalising an acquirer by not recognising a valid transfer would be grossly unfair.[395] Both these exceptions require delivery to the good faith acquirer, intention alone is not enough.[396] Were this not the case, there would be little point in protecting this acquirer. A rule based solely on intention could lead to an illogical prioritisation of the third party at the expense of either the 'true' owner or a fourth or fifth party buying from a seller or buyer still in possession. These exceptions cover not only transfer. They also apply to the granting of security by way of pledge.[397]

These exceptions can apply in a number of commercially important scenarios. For example, the protection given to an acquirer taking title from a seller in possession could operate to trump the rights of an original 'acquirer' where it has been arranged, perhaps for convenience, that the seller retains possession for a certain period of time.[398] The exception for those acquiring from a buyer in possession is of potentially huge importance when dealing with goods sold subject to a retention of title clause.[399] An example of this very scenario is found in the case of *Archivent Sales and Development Ltd v*

---

[393] On the issue of what constitutes 'possession' of the seller, see the Privy Council decision of *Pacific Motor Auctions Pty Ltd v Motor Credits (Hire Finance) Ltd* [1965] AC 867 and associated discussion in Carey Miller with Irvine, *Corporeal Moveables*, para 10.21.

[394] Ownership could, for example, have been retained by virtue of a contractual reservation of title. The scope of the rule in s. 25 is restricted when the relationship between seller (*i.e.* the original owner) and the buyer in possession is in fact a conditional sale agreement governed by the Consumer Credit Act 1974: See Carey Miller with Irvine, *Corporeal Moveables*, para 10.22.

[395] Carey Miller with Irvine, *Corporeal Moveables*, paras 10.21-10.22.

[396] Delivery, it seems, need not be physical. See the English case of *Michael Gerson (Leasing) Ltd v Wilkinson* [2001] 1 All ER 148 and associated discussion in van Vliet, L P W, 'Michael Gerson (Leasing) Ltd v Wilkinson: A Comparative Analysis', (2001) 5 Edinburgh Law Review 361.

[397] See Reid and Blackie, *Personal Bar*, para 16.05 and Carey Miller with Irvine, *Corporeal Moveables*, para 11.12.

[398] A point discussed below at para 7.1.

[399] See below, paras 7.3 and 15.4.1.

Strathclyde Regional Council,[400] where goods had been sold subject to a valid retention of title clause.[401]

The *Archivent* case proved to be the classic 'tale of two innocents', one of whom had to bear the loss occassioned by the subsequent insolvency of a buyer in possession. For Strathclyde Regional Council to escape this loss, they had to prove that R D Robertson (Builders) Limited (the initial buyer) had complied with all the criteria contained in section 25 of the 1979 Act so as to fall within that section. On the facts of the case it was accepted that possession of the goods had been obtained with the consent of the seller, and, secondly, that the initial buyer had delivered or transferred the goods to them in good faith. As the criteria were met, R D Robertson (Builders) Limited's transfer on to Strathclyde Regional Council had the same effect as a transfer by 'a mercantile agent in possession of the goods ... with the consent of the owner' and thus title to the goods was acquired.

The result in this case would have been different if the defender had been aware of the retention,[402] as this would have meant the defender was not acting in good faith.[403] Good faith is similarly relevant for the seller in possession exception.[404]

Another exception to the *nemo plus* rule can be found in section 48(2) of the 1979 Act, which allows an unpaid seller to grant a good title to a third party as against the non-paying buyer when acting pursuant to a right of lien, retention or stoppage in transit.

The sale of motor vehicles subject to a hire purchase agreement provides yet another potential exception to the rule against non-owner transfer, providing the acquirer is a private purchaser in good faith without notice of the hire purchase contract.[405] Where there is no hire purchase contract this section cannot apply, and any transaction under a purported hire purchase agreement will be void.[406] Similarly, the section

---

[400] 1985 SLT 154.

[401] The validity of the retention of title is considered in Carey Miller with Irvine, *Corporeal Moveables*, para 12.03.

[402] An issue which was never contested: *Archivent Sales and Development Ltd v Strathclyde Regional Council* 1985 SLT 154 at 156-157.

[403] See below, para 6.2.

[404] On the issue of good faith, see the recent English case of *Fairfax Gerrard Holdings Ltd v Capital Bank Plc* [2007] 1 Lloyd's Rep 171, where it was held that the 'purchaser's' notice of the buyer in possession's previous dealings meant it was not in good faith and thus it could not rely on s. 25.

[405] Hire Purchase Act 1964, s. 27(2) as amended by the Consumer Credit Act 1974.

[406] See the English case of *Shogun Finance Ltd v Hudson* [2004] 1 AC 919, and for comment Carey Miller, D L, 'Plausible Rogues: Contract and Property', (2005) 9 Edinburgh Law Review 150.

cannot apply when the acquirer is a 'trade or finance purchaser',[407] as the rule exists to protect private individuals who have no means of checking or ascertaining the exact commercial situation in relation to a moveable, while trading dealers should have access to such information.[408] The rule may still come into play where a private purchaser subsequently acquires from an intervening trade or finance purchaser, and thus it does not penalise a private individual who has the misfortune to appear further down a contractual chain than an individual buying from the original hirer.[409]

5.9.3. Personal bar

(a)   General

While it can be argued that personal rights and an individual's conduct should not impact on property law and third party expectations, with the restriction on party autonomy discussed above being a prime example of this,[410] both the common law and the Sale of Goods Act 1979 recognise the possibility of an owner ratifying the transfer of a moveable by a non-owner. By virtue of the doctrine of personal bar, roughly equivalent to the English rules of estoppel, an owner may be barred from denying that a transfer has taken place by virtue of his or her positive conduct, or perhaps even by his or her negative omission to act.

(b)   Common law

The position in relation to moveable property is not settled at common law,[411] but it has been tentatively suggested that 'there may be a role for personal bar, as a defence against a claim to ownership, by way of an assertion that the right of ownership has in fact passed from claimant to

---

[407] Hire Purchase Act 1964, s. 29(2).

[408] See Carey Miller with Irvine, *Corporeal Moveables*, para 10.23, and the discussion of *North West Securities Ltd v Barrhead Coachworks Ltd* 1976 SC 68.

[409] Hire Purchase Act 1964, s. 27(3).

[410] See further Carey Miller and Combe, 'The Boundaries of Property Rights in Scots Law' at 6-20.

[411] For example, Rankine, J, *Personal Bar* (1921), pp 55-57 and 225-227, suggests that while the doctrine may not apply to the transfer of immoveables (the transfer of which requires more in the way formal steps), it may apply to moveables, but Reid, *Property*, para 672, suggests that no proprietary consequences should follow in a situation of common law personal bar. See Carey Miller with Irvine, *Corporeal Moveables*, para 10.19, n 5.

defender in possession'.[412] This view contrasts with that of Reid and Blackie, who note that '[t]he common law of personal bar may remove an owner's right to assert title, but it does not extinguish it or confer title on the buyer'.[413] Proceeding on the basis that there is a role for personal bar in the circumstances, it must also be borne in mind that the law already provides a degree of protection to a possessor, by virtue of the presumption that the possessor of a thing is the owner. This presumption could subordinate the role of personal bar somewhat, but there is no reason in principle why personal bar could not be pleaded against the original owner if circumstances are such that the 'transferee' does not actually possess the moveable or if the presumption of ownership was successfully rebutted by the claimant.[414]

(c)   The Sale of Goods Act

While the presumption of ownership may relegate the role of common law personal bar, a far more fundamental reason for the common law's limited scope is the statutory rule contained in section 21 of the Sale of Goods Act 1979. The law relating to sale governs the vast majority of commercial transactions, and thus 'recourse to the common law model is likely to be rare'.[415] Furthermore, the existence of this rule has stunted any potential growth of the scope of the common law doctrine, as disputes involving barter and gift with an additional personal bar ingredient are virtually unheard of. While a common law doctrine of personal bar may remain, it would require an unlikely and exact constellation of circumstances before the issue could be litigated in a Scottish court.

The statute restates the *nemo plus* rule, but instantly qualifies this general position. The rule against a non-owner or non-authorised agent transferring applies 'unless the owner of the goods is by his conduct precluded from denying the seller's authority to sell'. This section, applying across the whole UK, adopts neither the English terminology of estoppel nor the Scottish terminology of personal bar,[416] thus giving rise to potential interpretative difficulties on both sides of the border.

---

[412] Carey Miller with Irvine, *Corporeal Moveables*, para 10.19.

[413] Reid and Blackie, *Personal Bar*, para 11.24. While this statement is undeniably clear, it is worth noting that the practical effect of an owner being unable to assert ownership is to all intents and purposes the same as an owner actually losing title.

[414] Carey Miller with Irvine, *Corporeal Moveables*, para 10.19.

[415] *Ibid.*

[416] The reason for the exact wording is discussed in Carey Miller with Irvine, *Corporeal Moveables*, para 10.20.

From a Scottish perspective the drafting of the rule is unfortunate: as noted by Reid and Blackie, 'its scope is by no means clear'.[417] The rule itself does not clarify what is meant by conduct, so one must turn to the Scottish common law and English case law for guidance as to what conduct actually entails.[418] An analogy with Scottish common law is complicated slightly by virtue of the fact that the statutory rule seems to concern itself only with the actions of the seller and places no relevance at all on the situation of the buyer. For personal bar to apply there must be an element of unfairness, which is clearly omitted from the legislation, but Reid and Blackie submit that a Scottish court would be likely to read such a requirement into section 21,[419] so this apparent discrepancy between statute and common law may be unimportant.

It is clear that 'conduct' does not necessarily entail a positive act, rather it may be a 'failure to correct a misleading impression which leads to bar'.[420] It is also clear that the simple act of transferring possession or documents is not enough for bar to operate.[421] Reid and Blackie submit that there 'must be some further conduct which has misled third parties',[422] but in the absence of any judicial analysis of section 21(1) it remains unclear what range of behaviour 'conduct' can cover.[423]

What is the actual effect of section 21(1) where a moveable has been acquired from a non-owner and that owner was 'precluded from denying' this non-owner's power to sell? Reid and Blackie submit that, while the statute does not explicitly state that ownership passes, by implicitly passing something in the face of the restriction on passing 'no better title', some kind of 'better title' must have passed.[424] An alternative view is that '[p]resumably in Scotland the actual conferring of title would be by statutory authority'.[425] In the absence of case law, the exact route by which title is acquired is unclear.

---

[417] Reid and Blackie, *Personal Bar*, para 11.17.

[418] See Reid and Blackie, *Personal Bar*, paras 11.18-11.22 for discussion.

[419] Reid and Blackie, *Personal Bar*, para 11.23, citing *Croan v Vallance* (1881) 8 R 700.

[420] Reid and Blackie, *Personal Bar*, para 11.20, citing the English case of *Moorgate Mercantile Co Ltd v Twitchings* [1977] AC 890.

[421] *Mitchell v Heys and Sons* (1894) 21 R 600. Compare *Bryce v Ehrmann* (1904) 7 F 5.

[422] Reid and Blackie, *Personal Bar*, para 11.22. See also Carey Miller with Irvine, *Corporeal Moveables*, para 8.20, which suggests the rule is 'essentially a statutory form of a concept of inferred agency'.

[423] Reid and Blackie, *Personal Bar*, para 11.24.

[424] *Ibid.*

[425] Reid, *Property*, para 680.

5.9.4. Accretion

Where a person obtains title or authority to dispose a moveable at a time later than an initial 'transfer', the property law doctrine of accretion applies. Although more readily associated with the transfer of land,[426] it is possible for the doctrine to apply with regard to moveables as well.[427] Let us say A transfers C's property to B. C remains the owner. C then transfers to A. The person who 'acquired' the property from A is now the owner, that is B. The interaction of this situation with the presumption of ownership arising from possession may, however, render the above scenario unlikely, but provided A initially acquired C's property in a manner that appeared inconsistent with a transfer of ownership, the doctrine could subsequently apply if C conveyed the property to A.[428]

6. Double / multiple selling

6.1. General

A may agree to sell or otherwise transfer an asset to B and then afterwards to carry out a similar transaction with the property with C. If the *causa* is sale the Sale of Goods Act 1979 will, in principle, apply. In terms of this property passes on the basis of the parties' intention without any necessary delivery requirement.[429] If, for any reason, the 1979 Act does not apply, the Scottish common law will; this requires an act of delivery to transfer ownership.[430]

Both at common law and under the 1979 Act there is a critical distinction between contract and conveyance. Under the latter property may pass on the basis of a concluded contract where this is what the parties intend.[431]

If A sells to B, then subsequently sells to C, at common law in principle delivery to C will make C owner. B has only a personal right to damages from A. However, if C was aware of the prior contract then C's bad

---

426 See Reid, *Property*, paras 677-679.

427 See the discussion in Carey Miller with Irvine, *Corporeal Moveables*, para 8.33. In a 1983 article, Professor W A Wilson submitted that the doctrine applies both to moveable and immoveable property, and the doctrine is also, it is submitted, applicable to incorporeal property. See Wilson, 'Romalpa and Trust', 1983 SLT (News) 108 and Anderson, R G, '*Buchanan v Alba Diagnostics*: Accretion of Title and Assignation of Future Patents', (2005) 9 Edinburgh Law Review 457.

428 Carey Miller with Irvine, *Corporeal Moveables*, para 8.33.

429 Sale of Goods Act 1979, s. 17(1). See above, para 5.4.

430 Carey Miller with Irvine, *Corporeal Moveables*, para 8.12-8.15.

431 Reid, *Property*, para 628; Carey Miller with Irvine, *Corporeal Moveables*, para 9.05.

faith makes his or her acquisition defective and open to reduction (*i.e.* being set aside) at B's instance. But C acquires a subsistent title which can be transferred pending its reduction. B's remedy to reduce the transfer to C on the basis that C was aware of B's prior right (known as the 'off-side goals' rule)[432] is the only remedy open to B.

6.2.   Good faith

There is authority supporting the view that, to sustain a claim of good faith, the circumstances may require proof that reasonable investigations were made by a subsequent purchaser pending his or her taking title.[433] For example, where C was aware that B had made a prior offer it may be that C should have investigated the position as to a possible contract between A and B. Arguably, in this situation, it is not enough for C to rely on A's assurance that B is no longer in the picture because A may well be seeking to secure a higher price from C. At the same time, any duty to investigate could not be an onerous one because this would in-hibit commerce.[434] The better view is that good faith should require in-vestigations only where the buyer has knowledge of some particular fact or facts which suggest that an earlier party may have priority.

Where C has knowledge pointing to another's possible prior right to obtain title no more than reasonable investigations in the circumstances should be required. This is in contrast to the case of *a non domino* transfer by way of an exception to *nemo plus*.[435] In this case a transferee's neces-sary claim to good faith may be unsustainable by reference to the circum-stances – for example, the level of price – regardless of actual knowledge.

B is subject to the same good faith requirement in respect of a transfer to him as C would be. This good faith requirement means that acquisition by a party in bad faith – to the extent of meeting the criterion of being aware of another's prior entitlement – is defective and open to possible reduction by judicial process at the instance of the deprived party. Where A is in negotiations with two or more prospective purchasers it is entirely possible that the situation might arise in which B and C were both aware of possible acquisition by the other.

Section 24 of the Sale of Goods Act 1979 has special rules in relation to double sales where the seller retains possession. This is discussed else-where.[436]

---

[432] See Reid, *Property*, para 695.

[433] *Rodger (Builders) Ltd v Fawdry* 1950 SC 483 at 499.

[434] See, generally, Carey Miller with Irvine, *Corporeal Moveables*, para 8.31.

[435] See Reid, *Property* para 672.

[436] See above, para 5.9.2.

7. Selling in a chain

7.1. General

The question of selling in a chain where A sells to B, who sells to C with delivery from A to C has not been subject of any case law in Scotland. This may be because the Sale of Goods Act 1979 downplays the importance of delivery in the process of transferring ownership in the context of a sale.

The transactions can be analysed as follows: when A sells to B ownership will transfer when the parties intend it to transfer under section 17 of the Sale of Goods Act 1979. If there is no discernible intention this will be (in the case where there are specific ascertainable goods in a deliverable state) on conclusion of the contract. Thus, although A retains possession ownership may already have passed to B. Consequently, when B sells to C the same rules apply. C can acquire ownership from B irrespective of there being no delivery of the goods to C. Throughout the time that A retains possession B and C are at risk, because A can confer good title on a good faith acquirer for value under section 24 of the Sale of Goods Act 1979.[437]

Though there appears to be only one real contract (agreement to transfer and agreement to acquire) in relation to the two underlying sales it is suggested that there are two real contracts in this context: A intends to transfer to B, who intends to acquire; and B intends to transfer to C, who intends to acquire.

7.2. Insolvency

The ostensibly causal system of transfer evident in the Sale of Goods Act 1979 means that resolution of disputes in insolvency are in principle straightforward, although potentially difficult evidentially. Various possibilities are considered.[438] In each case, unless an express aspect of the agreement to transfer, delivery is irrelevant.

First, where A becomes insolvent. If A is made insolvent after ownership transfers to B, B is protected; if A is made insolvent before ownership transfers to B – the moveable can be claimed by A's representative in insolvency who has a choice as to whether or not to adopt the contract.[439]

Second, where B becomes insolvent. If B becomes insolvent before the asset transfers to B from A, A is protected. If B becomes insolvent after

---

[437] See above, para 5.9.2.

[438] Insolvency is considered in more detail, below in chapter 9.

[439] See below, para 9.1.2.

transfer from A, A's creditors have no entitlement to the asset. In this latter case it is necessary to determine if B's insolvency is before or after the transfer to C under section 17 of the Sale of Goods Act 1979. If B is made insolvent before the transfer to C, then B's representative in insolvency is entitled to the asset; if insolvent after the transfer B's representative in insolvency has no entitlement to the asset and C is protected.

Third, where C becomes insolvent. If C becomes insolvent before the asset is transferred then B is protected and can resell the asset. If C becomes insolvent after acquisition then C's representative in bankruptcy is entitled to the asset.

7.3.   Contractual relationships

Having considered insolvency it is necessary to examine the impact of the contractual relationship between B and C on transfer. For example, if B imposed conditions on the transfer to C (for example through the insertion of a retention of title clause) what is the consequence? It is suggested that B would remain owner under the Sale of Goods Act 1979 even after delivery of the asset to C. B would have no intention to transfer until the suspensive condition had been satisfied. However, as is the case generally in retention of title B would be at risk from C's actions. C could use the asset and acquire it through original acquisition (for example, by accession or specification), or C could sell the asset on to a third party in good faith who would acquire good title under section 25 of the Sale of Goods Act 1979 through acquisition from a buyer in possession.[440]

The position under the Sale of Goods Act is dependent on there being a valid contract of sale of goods. If the contract between A and B is invalid B will not acquire ownership. In that case even though there is intention to transfer and intention to acquire B will not acquire ownership unless the asset is delivered to B.[441] If in this case the transaction between B and C is valid ownership will not transfer to C as B is not an owner and by virtue of the *nemo plus* principle enshrined in section 21 of the 1979 Act cannot confer ownership. What though if A delivers to C? There is intention to acquire on the part of C and intention to transfer on the part of A. Although this has not been considered in the cases or academic analyses it appears there are two possible approaches: (a) there is a transfer directly from A to C based on the conveyance from A to C and not dependent on any underlying agreement; or (b) it is arguable that accretion might apply:[442] where the *a non domino* transfer from B to C is validated by a subsequent

---

[440] See above, para 5.9.2.

[441] For the modes of delivery, see above, para 5.4.

[442] See above, para 5.9.4.

transfer from the owner (A) to the *a non domino* transferor (B) assuming that there may be deemed intention to pass to B (meaning that B would hypothetically acquire for a logical second in order to validate the transfer to C). The position differs slightly if the transaction between A and B is valid, but that between B and C is invalid. In this situation ownership may transfer from A to B without delivery. However, if the underlying transaction between B and C is invalid ownership will not transfer to C without delivery (as transfer of ownership is dependent on the common law, not the 1979 Act). If A then delivers the goods to C ownership may transfer: there is again mutual intention to acquire and transfer. However, in this case A cannot transfer because ownership has passed to B. Ownership will only pass to C if A can be treated as B's agent for the purposes of delivery.

If both transactions are invalid, A will retain ownership as without delivery there can be no common law transfer. If A then delivers to C the mutual intention to acquire and transfer between A and C will probably see ownership transfer to C. This analysis in each case is based on the assumption that at common law Scotland adopts an abstract approach to the transfer of ownership.[443]

However, as there is no case law or academic writing on these questions this section is based on an application of principle.

8.   Transfer by indirect representation

8.1.   General

The terminology 'indirect/direct representation' is not known in Scottish law. In respect of transfer or acquisition through another, the law is more in the English common law than the civil law tradition.[444] The critical conceptual difference is that in the Anglo-American development the agent functions as a mere 'conduit pipe' for the transmission of the right. In the less radical civilian form, the result came to be achieved by the model of an intermediate party receiving and passing on rights.[445]

In the common situation of an agent acting in terms of the authorisation of a disclosed and named principal, property will pass directly be-

---

[443] See above, para 5.1.6.
[444] See, generally, Macgregor, L J, 'Agency' in MacQueen, H L, and Zimmermann, R, (eds), *European Contract Law* (2006), p 123.
[445] See Buckland, W W, and McNair, A D, *Roman Law and Common Law* (2nd ed, 1965), pp 217-221; Smith, T B, *A Short Commentary on the Law of Scotland* (1962), pp 776-777; Zimmermann, R, *The Law of Obligations* (1990), pp 45-58; Forte, A D M and van Niekerk, J P, 'Agency' in Zimmermann, Visser and Reid, *Mixed Legal Systems*, pp 240-243.

tween principal and third party. Only where the agent signs a transfer document without qualification, as a party to the transaction, is there any risk of personal liability.[446] In the situation of an agent acting for a disclosed but unnamed principal the law is not well developed.[447] If, however, the agent proceeds with the transaction refusing to identify the principal, there is authority for his or her personal liability.[448]

The position of agency functioning to facilitate normal contractual relations means that the primary question is whether an agency situation exists. This, of course, is an issue of contract rather than property law. In a transfer situation, where agency exists, X ('in the middle') does not acquire on any *pro tem* basis because transfer is received for and on behalf of the principal. Regarding the question of whether the agency is expressly or impliedly authorised, Professor Reid[449] observes that '[p]urported transfers which are not authorised are void even, it is thought, where they lie within the agent's apparent (ostensible) authority although in that case the principal is personally barred from challenging the title of the transferee.' While, in principle, there can be no transfer without the owner's participation in terms of the critical intention to pass property, the intention element may be satisfied on a constructive basis when the owner's conduct precludes denial of an intention to transfer. Statutory provisions[450] associated with the common law concept of personal bar[451] derive from the same policy basis as implied authority.[452]

The law's general receptiveness to agency is in recognition of its important role in commerce. The prevalence of corporate sellers of moveables calls for an approach in which property can pass and rights and duties can be established between remote parties as the norm. The role of agency is accordingly recognised in section 32(1) of the Sale of Goods Act 1979:

'Where, in pursuance of a contract of sale, the seller is authorised or required to send the goods to the buyer, delivery of the goods to a carrier (whether

---

[446] Macgregor, L J, 'Agency and Mandate' in *Stair Memorial Encyclopaedia* (Reissue 2002), paras 128-131.

[447] Macgregor, 'Agency and Mandate', paras 137-146.

[448] *Gibb v Cunningham and Robertson* 1925 SLT 608. See Macgregor, 'Agency and Mandate', para 142.

[449] Reid, *Property*, para 670.

[450] See, for example, the Sale of Goods Act 1979, ss. 24 and 25. See above, para 5.9.2.

[451] See, generally, Reid and Blackie, *Personal Bar*, chapter 11.

[452] See *Bank of Scotland v Brunswick Developments (1987) Ltd (No 2)* 1998 SLT 439 at 443-444 *per* Lord President Rodger: '[T]he law in England and Scotland on apparent or ostensible authority is the same and in particular ... in both systems it is built on the doctrine which is known as estoppel in English law and personal bar in Scots law.' See Macgregor, 'Agency' at 128-129.

named by the buyer or not) for the purpose of transmission to the buyer is prima facie deemed to be delivery of the goods to the buyer.'[453]

A party who leaves goods or documents of title with another in circumstances which give an impression of agency may be subject to the common law doctrine of 'personal bar', or a statutory equivalent, on the basis of which transfer may be inferred.[454]

8.2. Undisclosed principal

Regarding the particular situation of 'indirect representation', Scotland has been influenced by English law in the case in which a party acts for an 'undisclosed principal' by transferring or acquiring in his own name on behalf of another.[455] In this situation the third party believes that the person with whom he or she is transacting is the principal.

Trade practice and custom are relevant to the question of the competence of the transfer or acquisition of property without disclosure of a representation factor.[456] In the present treatment only the relevant general position will be considered.

In the situation of an undisclosed principal, the principal may disclose his or her position and assert rights against the third party on the basis that the agent acted within authority.[457] The third party in this situation may assert rights against either the agent or the principal.[458] A nineteenth century dictum is directly relevant to the property position:

'... if a person really acting for another goes into the market and buys as if for himself, he binds himself, but if the party from whom he buys finds out his true position then he can treat him as an agent only. He cannot have two principals to deal with, and no double remedy is allowed.'[459]

---

[453] For a summary of other relevant provisions see Reid, *Property*, para 671.

[454] See Carey Miller and Irvine, *Corporeal Moveables*, paras 10.19 and 10.20.

[455] See Smith, *A Short Commentary on the Law of Scotland*, pp 776-777.

[456] Gloag and Henderson, *The Law of Scotland* , para 19.30; Macgregor, 'Agency and Mandate', para 132.

[457] The 2003 Principles of European Contract Law (PECL) provide for direct actions between principal and third party in the circumstances of undisclosed principal essentially according to the British model. However, as a Scottish commentator notes, PECL applies the label 'indirect representation' to this in a questionable way; see Macgregor, 'Agency', 139.

[458] See Macgregor, 'Agency and Mandate', para 147.

[459] *Meir & Co v Küchenmeister* (1881) 8 R 642 at 646 *per* Lord Young, as referred to in Macgregor, 'Agency and Mandate', para 147.

In this situation the disclosed principal adopts the transaction as concluded by the agent and is accordingly liable on that basis. The situation
is one in which the third party makes an election between the alternative
liability of the agent, with whom he contracted, and that of the disclosed
principal, now seeking to assert rights in the transaction negotiated between agent and third party. The position is illustrated by a simple early
case involving the sale of a horse by an auctioneer; disclosure by the
principal of his position gave the third party the option to return the
unsound animal to him; by so doing the third party elected to hold the
principal bound.[460] The right of election open to a third party is not exercised by the mere commencement of proceedings[461] but rather through
proceeding to finality by obtaining a decree.[462]

The terms of the contract between agent and third party may, of course,
exclude the possibility of an undisclosed principal.[463] It is probably also the
case that the intervention of an undisclosed principal will be barred on the
basis of bad faith where concealment was intended to deceive.[464]

Analysis of the effect of disclosure by the principal of his or her position is problematic[465] but it is accepted that 'the principal does not become the agent's assignee.'[466]

8.3.   Ancillary issues

In a normal agency situation the agent is not involved in the legal relationship between the parties and his or her insolvency is of no possible
relevance to the transaction. In the undisclosed principal situation in
which the third party has a choice between agent and principal the solvency of either will obviously be a consideration in the exercise of that
choice. In this regard, it is relevant that the bar of election is constituted
only by actual judgment for, as Lord Justice-Clerk Moncreiff observed
'[t]he fact of the pursuer having sued the wrong man will not bar him
from suing the right one.'[467]

The possible implications in terms of interaction between contract and
property law are not affected by the agency factor. Where the principal is
disclosed the issue whether property has passed from or to that principal

---

[460] *Ferrier v Dods* (1865) 3 M 561.

[461] *Meir & Co v Küchenmeister* (1881) 8 R 642 at 644-645.

[462] *Craig & Co v Blackater* 1923 SC 472. See Macgregor, 'Agency and Mandate', para 156.

[463] Macgregor, 'Agency and Mandate', para 153.

[464] *Ibid* at para 154.

[465] *Ibid* at para 148.

[466] *Ibid* at para 150.

[467] *Meir & Co v Küchenmeister* (1881) 8 R 642 at 644-645.

will, of course, be a property law question. The rules controlling the issue of legal relations in the context of an undisclosed principal situation will apply equally concerning the question whether property has passed and to whom. Where the third party is seller/transferor it will be his or her option to effect transfer to the agent or to the now disclosed principal. Where the third party is buyer/transferee it will be his or her option to claim transfer from either the agent or the now disclosed principal.

Although of limited application in the context of moveable property, any requirement of registration would be likely to be a consideration regarding the timing of an undisclosed principal's assertion of his or her position. The final conclusion of any transaction between a third party and the agent of an undisclosed principal will necessarily mean that any subsequent stage is between principal and agent.

In the circumstances of a party transacting competently and voluntarily as if he or she was principal there are no concerns regarding the protection of his or her interests or those of his or her creditors.

Open and flexible rules of agency, including scope for inferred agency, have been recognised for a long time to be a commercial necessity in a sophisticated economy. This interest is the justification for the relevant legal rules.

9. Insolvency

9.1. General

9.1.1. Insolvency administrators

Scotland has a number of types of formal insolvency administrators.[468]

(a) Trustees in sequestration

Where a debtor is not a company incorporated under the Companies Acts the relevant insolvency administrator is known as the trustee in sequestration. The trustee in sequestration is the insolvency administrator for natural persons, firms constituted by a partnership agreement, and other bodies corporate such as local authorities or universities. The powers of the trustee in sequestration are found in common law and the Bankruptcy (Scotland)

---

[468] There are various informal mechanisms, such as the use of a trust deed by a non-corporate debtor.

Act 1985.[469] In summary (detailed aspects of the impact on property rights are considered below) the trustee in sequestration ingathers the debtor's assets and realises them to distribute to the creditors in accordance with creditor rights.[470]

(b) Company insolvency administrators

Where the debtor is a company the relevant insolvency administrators[471] are either: (i) the liquidator; (ii) the administrator; or (iii) the receiver.

(i) Liquidator

The liquidator is the appropriate insolvency practitioner when the company is being wound up under the Insolvency Act 1986. Winding up can be voluntary (where it is initiated by the shareholders of the debtor company) or compulsory (where initiated by application to the courts). In either case a liquidator is appointed who takes control of the company assets and realises them to distribute to the creditors. The liquidator will ultimately wind up the company. This dissolves it.

(ii) Administrator

The administrator is the appointee in company 'administration' under the Insolvency Act 1986, as amended by the Enterprise Act 2002. The administration process involves the debtor company being given time to reorganise its business with a view to trading out of difficulty. If a company goes into administration (as initiated by the company or by the petition of a creditor (including the creditor in a floating charge)) the management is replaced by an administrator who then administers the company assets in the interests of all creditors of the debtor company. A moratorium is placed on the enforcement of debts against the company.

---

[469] As amended. There is substantial reform by the Bankruptcy and Diligence etc (Scotland) Act 2007, in force in relation to bankruptcy matters from 1ˢᵗ April 2008.

[470] General textbooks on sequestration are McBryde, *Bankruptcy* and McKenzie Skene, *Insolvency*.

[471] Textbooks on corporate insolvency processes are McKenzie Skene, *Insolvency*; St Clair, J B and Lord Drummond Young, *The Law of Corporate Insolvency in Scotland* (3ʳᵈ ed, 2004); and (specifically on receivership) Fletcher, I and Roxburgh, R, *The Law and Practice of Receivership in Scotland* (3ʳᵈ ed, 2005).

(iii) Receiver

The final formal instance where an insolvency practitioner may be involved is receivership. Receivership is a mode of enforcing a floating charge. A creditor in a floating charge created before the coming into force of the relevant sections of the Enterprise Act 2002 (or some charges created after) can appoint a receiver. The powers of the receiver are set out in the Insolvency Act 1986. The receiver replaces the management of the company and administers the debtor company assets. Additionally, a company going into receivership can trade out of its difficulties and regain solvency. Although it is possible with both administration and receivership that if the company does not trade out of insolvency then the debtor company will be liquidated in a petition initiated by the administrator or receiver. While administration and receivership have elements in common there is one crucial difference. In receivership the receiver is acting as manager of the company while owing obligations to the floating charge holder who appointed him or her. In administration the administrator is acting for the creditors as a whole.

The differing processes have differing legal consequences. In the following section an attempt will be made to avoid generic non-technical terms.

9.1.2. Rights of insolvency practitioners relative to contracts

(a) No general rule

There is no general rule in any formal insolvency process which automatically terminates contracts. Instead, it is possible in the insolvency processes for contracts to be adopted and performance to continue.[472]

(b) Trustees in sequestration

Despite the general principles that the trustee in sequestration does not by mere appointment as trustee agree to the continued performance of the contractual obligations incurred by the bankrupt, it is possible for the trustee to adopt these contracts. This has long been the position[473] and allows the

---

[472] See McBryde, *Bankruptcy*, paras 9-99–9-126. The leading statement of the law is that of Lord President Inglis in *Myles v City of Glasgow Bank* (1879) 6 R 716 at 725. The City of Glasgow Bank collapsed in the later nineteenth century prompting much litigation. Many of the modern principles of insolvency can be traced to developments in the aftermath of the bank collapse.

[473] The leading case is *Kirkland v Caddell* (1838) 6 S 860, but it merely endorses a line of cases from the introduction of sequestration.

trustee in sequestration to incur personal liability,[474] or liability on behalf of the creditors, and agree to perform the contractual obligations. The rule is now statutory.[475] This is done to prevent the application of general principles of mutuality of contract. Such application would entitle the other contracting party to suspend performance, and consequently prevent the trustee from ensuring performance. Adoption therefore gives flexibility to the trustee. For example, if a bankrupt is a manufacturer holding partly produced assets the trustee may choose to adopt contracts whereby the products required to produce a saleable end product are supplied, and the end product manufactured. This will be the case if the cost of obtaining the supplied goods will be outweighed by the sale costs of the final product.

The statutory rules of adoption provide that the trustee has to adopt the contract within a reasonable time, otherwise he or she will be deemed to have abandoned it. However, it is not possible to adopt a contract which expressly provides for its termination on the occurrence of sequestration. The other contracting party can force the hand of the trustee in sequestration by requesting the trustee to adopt. If the trustee does not so adopt within 28 days (or such later period as provided for by the sheriff) then the contract will be treated as abandoned.[476] If a contract is abandoned what are the consequences? The failure to adopt means that the bankrupt will not have performed the contractual obligations and accordingly the contract will be breached. This entitles the other contracting party to claim damages for the breach of contract in the sequestration and rank as an unsecured creditor.[477]

Adoption of contracts is really about the incurring of obligations by the trustee in sequestration. The provisions on vesting of assets provide that the trustee acquires the right to enforce the various contracts that have been entered into by the company, and can therefore sue for payment of any unpaid debts owed to the bankrupt.[478]

(c)   Company insolvency administrators

The position for other insolvency practitioners is similar.[479]

---

[474] *Dundas v Morrison* (1857) 20 D 225.

[475] Bankruptcy (Scotland) Act 1985, s. 42.

[476] Bankruptcy (Scotland) Act 1985 s. 42(2) and (3).

[477] *Crown Estate Commissioners v Highland Engineering Ltd* 1975 SLT 58.

[478] Bankruptcy (Scotland) Act 1985, s. 31.

[479] See McKenzie Skene, *Insolvency Law*, pp 190-191, 198-199 and 205-206.

(i)   Administration

The principles for administration are identical in Scottish and English law.[480] If a company enters administration this does not of itself terminate contracts, unless there is an express clause to this effect within the contract. The administrator can elect to adopt existing contracts and such costs as are incurred in performing the contracts will rank ahead of unsecured creditors in the administration as an expense in the administration. If the contract is not adopted then the contract may be breached and the other contracting party may claim breach of contract and damages against the debtor company.

(ii)   Receivership

Receivership is similar. Existing contracts continue but the receiver has an option as to whether or not to adopt the existing contracts.[481] Failure so to adopt will render the company potentially liable for breach of contract and damages.

(iii) Liquidation

On liquidation the company is not being preserved as a going concern, as the purpose of liquidation is the dissolution of the company. However, even there the rule is similar. Liquidation does not, of itself, terminate contracts entered into by the debtor company unless the contract makes express provision to the contrary. Again the liquidator has the power to adopt the contract,[482] although Donna McKenzie Skene notes that as the carrying on of business can only be so far as necessary for the winding up[483] the liquidator 'should only adopt contracts for that purpose.'[484] If a contract is not adopted it is abandoned which again leads to breach and the possibility of the other contracting party ranking for damages for breach of contract. Unlike the position for sequestration the contracting party cannot give an ultimatum to the liquidator to adopt the contract. Instead, a power is given to apply to court to seek rescission: termination in response to the debtor company's material or fundamental breach of contract.[485]

---

[480] See Goode, R M, *Principles of Corporate Insolvency* (2005), para 10-94.

[481] Insolvency Act 1986, s. 57.

[482] *Asphaltic Limestone Concrete Co Ltd v Glasgow Corporation* 1907 SC 463 and *Turnbull v Liquidator of Scottish County Investment Co* 1939 SC 5.

[483] Insolvency Act 1986, Sch 4 para 5. See too ss. 165 and 167 of the 1986 Act.

[484] McKenzie Skene, *Insolvency*, p 205.

[485] Insolvency Act 1986, s. 186.

9.2. Rights of insolvency administrators to challenge pre-insolvency transactions

9.2.1. General

Scottish law has long permitted challenges to pre-insolvency transactions. These challenges can be made under common law or under statute. The earliest statutes allowing challenges were passed in the seventeenth century and governed the law in this area until 1985.

In this section there is a discussion of the power to challenge transactions at common law; the power to challenge undervalue transactions under statute; the power to challenge unfair preferences under statute; and other miscellaneous challenges. These transactions have much in common with the *actio Pauliana* although there has been no research to indicate whether or not the *actio* was formally received from Roman law.

9.2.2. Common law

(a) Fraud

A fraudulent transaction made by the insolvent debtor prior to becoming formally insolvent is challengeable. Fraud is a problematic concept.[486] It has a wide definition in private law exemplified by Erskine's definition as 'a machination or contrivance to deceive'.[487] This was similar to the civilian concept of *dolus malus*. However, under the influence of English law, fraud is sometimes treated as being limited only to those instances where there is an intention to deceive.[488] In the context of challengeable transactions in insolvency, though, the wider definition remains applicable. This means that case law from the general law of fraud in Scotland is not necessarily authoritative in the context of challengeable transactions. The case law in this area has been subject to to a detailed review by Professor McBryde.[489]

---

[486] See McBryde, *Contract*, chapter 14.

[487] Erskine, III.1.16.

[488] See MacQueen, H L and Thomson, J, *Contract Law in Scotland* (2nd edn, 2007), para 4.27 for an example.

[489] McBryde, *Bankruptcy*, paras 12.25-12.48. For an important earlier analysis, see Goudy, H, *Bankruptcy* (4th ed, 1914), chapters 3 and 4.

(b) The common law requirements

McBryde's requirements are summarised within his textbook on *Bank-ruptcy*[490] as follows:

'(1) there must be prejudice to creditors …; (2) at the time of the transaction the debtor must be insolvent or about to become insolvent; (3) it is not neces-sary that the transferee should be aware of the debtor's insolvency although that may be a method of proving fraud; (4) if the transferee colludes with the insolvent that is one element in fraud; (5) the debtor must be conscious of his insolvency; (6) the debtor's actions must be voluntary; (7) the debtor can carry on ordinary acts of administration of affairs until the debtor has decided to take steps to hand over the administration of affairs for the benefit of credi-tors; and (8) in general the transaction challenged must be fraudulent.'

(i) Prejudiced creditors

At common law if the debtor transacts in a manner which diminishes the value of the debtor's estate available for distribution to all creditors,[491] for example, by giving up a right to an asset or transferring an asset at under-value, or through the grant of a security to secure a pre-existing debt, then the transaction is potentially, although not necessarily, challengeable. How-ever, where the transactions diminish the estate but are ordinary acts of administration then they are not subject to challenge. For example, payment of debts ordinarily incurred by a business such as utility bills is acceptable. In his analysis Professor McBryde treats *nova debita* as ordinary acts of admini-stration.[492] It is arguable that where a debtor obtains a loan and grants a right in security there is no diminution of the debtor's estate. This is because the increase in value (from receipt of the cash) is balanced with a secured liability which leaves unsecured creditors unaffected.

(ii) Voluntary transactions

To be challengeable it is essential that the transaction is voluntary. If a creditor carries out diligence as ordered by the court (for example, the at-tachment of corporeal moveables in execution of a court order for payment)

---

[490] McBryde, *Bankruptcy*, para 12-29. Later paragraphs explain the analysis.

[491] The leading case is *McCowan v Wright* (1852) 14 D 901 and 968; (1852) 15 D 229 and (1853) 15 D 494. The protracted litigation deals with many differing issues in the law of insolvency.

[492] McBryde, *Bankruptcy*, para 12-45.

which serves to create a real right in security over property, thereby diminishing the estate available for other creditors, then the transaction is involuntary and cannot be challenged. However, if the debtor had granted a right in security over the moveable property in favour of the creditor to secure payment of the debt this would be challengeable as a voluntary transaction.

(iii)   Absolute insolvency

In order to be challengeable it is necessary that at the time of the transaction the debtor is absolutely insolvent in that total liabilities exceed total assets, or as a result of the transaction will become absolutely insolvent,[493] and is aware that he or she is absolutely insolvent or about to become absolutely insolvent.

(c)   Title to challenge the transaction

If a transaction is challengeable as fraudulent the consequence is that the transaction is voidable at the instance of any other creditor of the debtor, the trustee in sequestration, liquidator, or other representative in insolvency. Unlike the statutory rules, discussed below, there is no time limit for challenge, other than the ordinary rules of negative prescription (*praescriptio*) which provide for a twenty year period of challenge.[494] Thus, any third party who acquired from a transferee of the debtor will be protected with an absolutely good title provided he or she was in good faith and gave value. However, if there has been no further transaction the title is capable of challenge. If the transaction was based on a written document the appropriate remedy is reduction of the document. However, typically where the asset subject to the transaction is corporeal moveable it will be in the possession or custody of the debtor's transferee. In these cases the appropriate remedy is delivery.

9.2.3.   Statutory challenges

There are a number of statutory regimes relevant to the challenge of pre-insolvency transactions.

---

[493] See *Whatmough's Tr v British Linen Bank* 1934 SC (HL) 51 and *Abram Steamship Co Ltd v Abram* 1925 SLT 243. An alternative view is expressed by McBryde, *Bankruptcy*, paras 12.32 and 12.33.

[494] Prescription and Limitation (Scotland) Act 1973, s. 8 applies as the short period in s. 6 does not apply to actions to restore property.

(a)   Gratutitous alienations

Section 34 of the Bankruptcy (Scotland) Act 1985 deals with gratuitous alienations and there is a mirror provision in section 242 of the Insolvency Act 1986.

(i)   Title to challenge

Title to challenge lies with any creditor whose debt was incurred before the events of insolvency discussed in the next section,[495] or the relevant office holder (trustee in sequestration, trustee under a protected trust deed, liquidator, or administrator).

(ii)   Transactions that can be challenged as gratuitous alienations

The following paragraphs detail the requirements for transactions that can be challenged as gratuitous alienations.

(aa)   Alienations

There has to be an alienation by the debtor[496] occurring within the requisite time period. Typically, such an alienation will be voluntary, such as a sale or a gift by the debtor. Where the alienation is involuntary, for example, following a court decree[497] the law is not clear.[498] The statute has specific provisions, for example regulating the situation where the debtor has transferred assets from his or her patrimony when implementing an order to make capital payment on divorce.[499] Other types of transaction are sometimes treated as alienations. This includes instances where the debtor has renounced a right to an asset. For example, a debtor may be entitled to inherit an asset through a legacy in a will, or as a result of application of the rules of intestate succession. If the debtor gives up the right to the asset this can be treated as an alienation for the purposes of the statutory rules.

---

[495] See below, para 9.2.3(a)(ii)(bb). Although if the process is administration the creditor cannot challenge the transaction.

[496] 'Debtor' is defined to include deceased debtors: Bankruptcy (Scotland) Act 1985, s. 73.

[497] For example, on divorce a court may order a debtor to transfer assets to his or her former spouse.

[498] At common law a court decree induced by a fraudulent debtor could – in certain cases – be set aside: *Laurie's Tr v Beveridge* (1867) 6 M 85.

[499] Bankruptcy (Scotland) Act 1985, s. 35.

(bb)   The statutory time periods

The requisite time period is based on a trigger event. The time is either a five year or two year period. The shorter period applies where the transferee in the challenged alienation is not an associate of the insolvent debtor. The longer period applies where the alienation is to an associate. The expression 'associate' is defined in section 74 of the Bankruptcy (Scotland) Act 1985. This is applicable both to sequestration and company insolvency processes.[500] An 'associate' includes the spouse or civil partner of the debtor; a firm of which the debtor is a partner; partners in a firm with the debtor (or the spouses of such partners); relatives (including grandparents, grandchildren, aunts, uncles, nephews, and nieces); employers or employees; a company of which the debtor is a director; a company which is the parent or a subsidiary of the debtor company.

The five or two years is the period ending with the date of sequestration,[501] the granting of a trust deed for creditors[502] which has become a protected trust deed,[503] the death of the debtor (if the issue arises in an insolvent executry), liquidation,[504] or administration, whichever insolvency process is applicable.

---

[500] See Bankruptcy (Scotland) Act 1985, s. 34(3); and Insolvency Act 1986, s. 242(3). But for corporate challenges s. 435 of the 1986 Act is also relevant.

[501] The date of sequestration is dependent on whether the sequestration proceedings were initiated by the debtor or a creditor or trustee. Where initiated by the debtor the date of sequestration is the date of the award of sequestration by the court. Where initiated by the creditor or a trustee acting under a trust deed the date of sequestration is the date on which the action of sequestration is initiated – with the court granting a 'warrant to cite' the debtor. The warrant to cite authorises the creditor to serve the petition for sequestration on the debtor and requires the debtor to attend the court. Bankruptcy (Scotland) Act 1985, s. 12(4).

[502] The procedure of granting a trust deed for creditors is an informal insolvency process available to non-company debtors. It allows the debtor to convey assets to a trustee for the benefit of the debtor's creditors. Such an arrangement allows the creditors to be paid and the process to be kept out of court. See McKenzie Skene, *Insolvency*, pp 376-379.

[503] Trust deeds become protected trust deeds (and subject to special treatment under the 1985 Act) when the conditions in Sch 5 to the 1985 Act are satisfied. These conditions require notification of the trust deed to all creditors, and the trust will become a protected deed provided that a majority of the creditors (or the holders of one third of the total indebtedness) have not objected within 5 weeks.

[504] The date of liquidation is dependent on whether the liquidation is a voluntary or compulsory winding up. A voluntary winding up involves the shareholders of the company agreeing by special resolution (with a 75% majority) to wind up a solvent company. The date of liquidation in this case is the date on which the resolution is

In determining whether a transaction takes place within the relevant period it is necessary to determine when the transaction became 'completely effectual'. This is the key point.[505] This matter was not judicially resolved until 2005. The case of *Accountant in Bankruptcy v Orr*[506] confirmed what had been anticipated by academic commentators[507] that the date on which a transaction became completely effectual was the date on which the transferee acquired the real right of ownership. In *Orr*, a transaction involving land, this was the date of registration of the conveyance in the transferee's favour. In relation to corporeal moveables it will be the date of delivery if the transaction is a gift or otherwise effective at common law, or the date on which the parties agree ownership will pass if the transaction is a sale covered by the Sale of Goods Act 1979.

The effect can be demonstrated with the following example. If a transferor enters a contract to sell goods to his wife in April 2002, but agrees with his wife that property in the goods will pass in July 2002 then if the transferor is sequestrated as a result of a petition for sequestration raised by one of the transferor's creditors in June 2007 when warrant to cite is given and where sequestration is awarded in August 2007 the sale can potentially be challenged, provided that the defences discussed below do not apply. This is because (a) the transfer is to an associate and the time period is 5 years; (b) the date of sequestration is the date of the warrant to cite in June 2007; and (c) the transaction which is challenged became completely effectual when the real right of ownership passed in July 2002.

(iii)   Defences to the statutory challenge

The structure of the legislation is to indicate that the transaction will be capable of challenge, if it falls within the requirements set out in the previous section, unless the transferee can establish that one of the defences set out in section 34(4) was applicable. The onus of proof is on the transferee once the challenger has established that there was an alienation within the appropriate time period.

There are three defences: (a) that the debtor was absolutely solvent; (b) that the alienation was a permitted gift; or (c) that the transferee gave adequate consideration for the transfer. Each is considered.

---

passed: Insolvency Act 1986, ss. 86 and 129. However, where the winding up is compulsory (*i.e.* following a court action initiated by a creditor, the administrator, a receiver or others) the date of winding up is the date on which the petition was presented to the court: Insolvency Act 1986, s. 129(2).

[505] See 1985 Act, s. 34(3) and the 1986 Act, s. 243.

[506] 2005 SLT 1019.

[507] McBryde, *Bankruptcy*, para 12-70; McKenzie Skene, *Insolvency*, 235.

(aa)   The debtor was absolutely solvent

Absolute solvency is where an individual's assets exceed his or her liabilities. It is a sufficient defence to a claim that a transaction should be challenged if the transferee can show that subsequent to the challenged transaction the debtor/transferor was absolutely solvent. Professor McBryde notes that, 'When the debtor's business affairs were complex it will be necessary to detail the financial position.'[508]

(bb)   The transaction was a permitted gift

Certain gifts are acceptable (for both company and non-company debtors) including birthday or Christmas gifts. Other gifts are not listed but would include instances where gifts are ordinarily made such as gifts to commemorate religious festivals[509] or other family celebrations.[510] As well as these gifts certain gifts to charities or for charitable purposes are also acceptable. For the purposes of the statutory rules 'charitable purposes' does not have a technical meaning that coincides with other areas of law. In any of these cases the gift is to be reasonable having regard to the debtor's circumstances. For example, if the debtor has total assets worth £100,000 giving his eldest child a new Ferrari motor car will not be reasonable given his assets. However, if the debtor has total assets worth £10,000,000 the gift of the Ferrari may be reasonable.

(cc)   The consideration was adequate

Although the sidenote to the sections in both the Bankruptcy (Scotland) Act 1985 and the Insolvency Act 1986 states that the provisions apply to gratuitous alienations there is no statutory requirement that in order for an alienation to be successfully challenged that it must be gratuitous. Hence, while gratuitous transfers (for example, the debtor giving away his vintage car to a friend) are covered, the provisions equally apply to transactions at undervalue.

For this defence to apply it is necessary that the transaction has a consideration. Consideration is usually taken to mean that there is an ex-

---

[508] McBryde, *Bankruptcy*, para 12-77.

[509] For example Eid gifts in the Islamic faith or Easter gifts.

[510] For example, confirmation within the Roman Catholic faith; Barmitzahs within the Jewish faith; or other family celebrations such as weddings.

change of money or money's worth[511] in return for the asset transferred by the debtor,[512] and that this have some material or patrimonial value. To be consideration for the purpose of the provision it is necessary that the money or money's worth be given by the transferee in exchange for the asset transferred. It is not possible for, for example, a loan by the transferee to the transferor to be later converted into consideration for an asset transferred by transferor to transferee.[513]

Once it has been ascertained that there was a consideration it is necessary to consider if the consideration was adequate. Whether or not the consideration is adequate is ascertained by looking at the consideration at the time of the transaction. While retrospectively a valuation may appear inadequate – at the time of the transaction it may have been acceptable. For example, if raw materials are sold from the transferor to the transferee in year 1 at £100,000 – from the perspective of year 2 (when the raw materials are now worth £1,000,000 as a result of a worldwide shortage of supply due to economic sanctions against the country which supplies most of the raw materials) the original price may appear inadequate. However, in the context of the transaction in year 1, where the general world economic climate did not anticipate a shortage the price is adequate.

Adequacy of consideration does not require the transferee to have paid the best possible price between the parties.[514] However, as St Clair and Drummond Young note,

"Adequate consideration' implies the application of an objective standpoint and while not necessarily equivalent to the best price that could be obtained, it should be what could reasonably be expected in the circumstances as between parties acting in good faith and at arm's length. 'Adequacy' must be tested at the time of the transaction, but the matters of which the valuer might take account include events which affected the value but took place between the transactions and the valuation, particularly the extent to which they were foreseeable at the transaction date.'[515]

This approach is confirmed judicially in the case of *Lafferty Construction Ltd v McCombe*.[516]

---

[511] For example, the transfer of an asset in exchange for the asset transferred by the debtor.

[512] *MacFadyen's Tr v MacFadyen* 1994 SLT 1245.

[513] *Ibid.*

[514] The case of *Short's Trustee v Chung* 1991 SLT 472 which deals with a transfer of land confirms this.

[515] St Clair and Drummond Young, *Corporate Insolvency*, para 10-08.

[516] 1994 SLT 858.

Determining whether or not the consideration is adequate can involve finely balanced questions. A transferee may think that he or she has obtained a bargain, but if the price is not high enough there is a risk that the transaction may be set aside under the statutory rules. The consequences for the transferee are severe because if the transaction is successfully challenged as a gratuitous alienation then the transferee ranks as a postponed creditor in the insolvency – meaning that he or she ranks after the ordinary unsecured creditors, and will receive no payment unless and until all of the ordinary unsecured creditors have been paid in full.[517] In such a case the transferee would lose the property and the price that he or she innocently paid. It has been suggested by St Clair and Drummond Young that this consequence may be contrary to the European Convention of Human Rights.[518]

(iv)   Remedies

Where there is a successful challenge the remedy is 'reduction' (which will apply if the transfer is based on a written conveyance) or 'restoration' of property to the debtor's estate – which will require the transferee to redeliver any corporeal moveable which is subject to a successful challenge to the debtor. Such redelivery will, though, not be possible if the original transferee who acquired the voidable title has transferred the asset on to a third party who acquired the asset for value and in good faith. In such a case the transferee's transferee will acquire an absolutely good title which is exempt from challenge and the challenger's only claim will be for such 'other redress' as the court deems appropriate. It is suggested by Professor McBryde, on the basis of pre-1985 Act cases, that such redress can involve the original transferee being required to hand over the price obtained to the officeholder.[519]

(b)   Unfair preferences

The rules on unfair preferences are found in section 36 of the Bankruptcy (Scotland) Act 1985 and the mirror provision in section 243 of the Insolvency Act 1986. They may apply to transfers of corporeal moveables

---

[517] See Bankruptcy (Scotland) Act 1985, s. 51(3)(c) and r. 4.66(2) of the Insolvency (Scotland) Rules 1986.

[518] St Clair and Drummond Young, *Corporate Insolvency*, para 3-05.

[519] McBryde, *Bankruptcy*, para 12-98. This is based on the decisions in *Dickson v Murray* (1866) 4 M 797 and *Moroney & Co v Mathew Muir and Sons* (1867) 6 M 7.

although more commonly would apply to the grant of securities. The rules can be summarised as requiring the following.[520]

(i) Title to challenge

Title to challenge lies with any creditor whose debt was incurred before the trigger event discussed in the next section,[521] or the relevant office holder (trustee in sequestration, trustee under a protected trust deed, liquidator, or administrator).

(ii) Transactions that can be challenged

The statutory provisions indicate that an unfair preference is a transaction which has 'the effect of creating a preference in favour of a creditor to the prejudice of the general body of creditors', that is to say that as a result of the action of the debtor one creditor benefits and the general body of creditors is disadvantaged. Thus, if a debtor grants a security in favour of creditor X for a pre-existing debt the effect is that X benefits (through having a security over an identified asset allowing creditor X to obtain payment for his or her debt through realisation of the secured asset) and the other creditors are disadvantaged (because the assets available to the general body of creditors have diminished as the asset secured by the security will (subject to the value of the asset and the debt) not be available for distribution to the general body of creditors). The transaction is to take place within a six month time period before a trigger event.

As with gratuitous alienations above the trigger events are sequestration, liquidation, administration and the grant of a trust deed which becomes protected. The six month period runs backwards from the date of the trigger event and the preference will be challenged if the preference becomes completely effectual within the time period.[522]

---

[520] The analysis draws on McBryde, *Bankruptcy*, paras 12-105–12-147 and McKenzie Skene, *Insolvency*, 239-242.

[521] Although if the process is administration the creditor cannot challenge the transaction.

[522] It is thought that the approach of *Accountant in Bankruptcy v Orr* will apply, in that the date the transaction becomes completely effectual is when the grantee in the preference obtains a real right.

(iii)   Defences

If the challenger can establish that a transaction appears to be an unfair preference the grantee in the transaction has defences that are available. There are four main defences: (a) the transaction was made in the ordinary course of business; (b) the transaction was a payment in cash for a debt due; (c) the transaction involved a reciprocal obligation; and (d) the transaction involved the grant of a mandate authorising payment of arrested funds.

The second defence is not really relevant to corporeal moveables other than cash as it involves the debtor paying cash to a creditor for an outstanding debt. The others may have some relevance to corporeal moveables and are considered in the following paragraphs.

(aa) The transaction was made in the ordinary course of business

It is suggested by Professor McBryde that certain sales where the insolvent debtor delivers or returns goods under agreements entered in good faith can be transactions made in the ordinary course of business.[523] There is also case law (both before and after the 1985 Act) on the grant of securities and on sham sales (where there was no actual delivery).[524] In both cases it is suggested that the transaction is not in the ordinary course of business, although clearly the facts will determine whether the transaction is one carried out in the ordinary course of business. The former situation involved the handing over of a bill of lading, which is itself a controversial issue.[525]

(bb)   The transaction involved a reciprocal obligation

The defence available to the grantee of the challenged transaction in this case is based on the principle that a transaction may create a preference to one creditor, but that this is not generally to the prejudice of the general body of creditors. This will arise where the insolvent debtor receives something and grants the preference in return. For example, if a debtor owed £250,000 of debts and had £200,000 of assets (including an oil painting worth £50,000) the debtor could agree to borrow £50,000 from a bank in return for the grant of a pledge of the painting in favour of the bank. The total assets of the debtor would increase to £250,000 (given

---

[523] McBryde, *Bankruptcy*, para 12-123 citing *Anderson's Tr v Fleming* (1871) 9 M 718 and *Loudon Bros v Reid and Lauder's Tr* (1877) 5 R 293.

[524] *Balcraig House's Tr v Roosevelt Property Services Ltd* 1994 SLT 1133.

[525] *McClelland v Rodger & Co* (1842) 4 D 646.

that the proceeds of the loan would be added to the debtor's patrimony) of which £50,000 would not be available to the general creditors – being the painting pledged to the bank. The total liabilities of the debtor would now amount to £300,000 of which £50,000 is the bank's secured indebtedness. Thus, the general body of unsecured creditors have total indebtedness due to them of £250,000 and £200,000 of available assets.

The granting of a preference as a reciprocal obligation for a loan, referred to in the textbooks and cases as *nova debita*, does not serve to prejudice the general body of creditors.[526] Where this is the case the transaction is not objectionable. However, if the transaction is a security for existing indebtedness then it can be challenged. So, if in the example above the bank was an existing creditor and sought a pledge of the painting as security for the existing debt the effect of this would be to prejudice the general body of creditors. The total indebtedness of the unsecured creditors would now amount to £200,000; the total assets available to the unsecured creditors would now be £150,000.[527]

(cc)   The transaction is a mandate to release arrested property

One of the modes of diligence (execution of judgments) in Scotland is arrestment.[528] Ordinarily this remedy is available only against incorporeal property, such as bank accounts. However, where a debtor's goods are held by a third party (for example furniture is held by a storage company while a debtor moves home, or a whisky company has its whisky housed in a warehouse) then a creditor of the debtor can obtain an arrestment of the goods, effectively a judicial right in security over the goods which prevents the debtor from obtaining the goods from the custodier.

If the creditor wishes to sell the asset the creditor has to raise what is called an action of furthcoming. This process, though, involves additional costs. Accordingly, a debtor may be persuaded to grant a mandate – authorising transfer of the asset or a portion of the sale proceeds of the arrested asset – in favour of the creditor. Such a mandate, however, would be a voluntary act of the debtor which benefits one creditor (the arrester) at the expense of the other creditors. The defence provides that where such a mandate is granted, and the arrester holds a decree for payment of the debt, and there was no collusion between arrester and debtor in ob-

---

[526] See, for example, Antonio, D G, 'Some thoughts on *nova debita*', 1957 SLT (News) 13; McKenzie Skene, *Insolvency*, 241; McBryde, *Bankruptcy*, paras 12-130–12-134; and *Nicoll v Steelpress (Supplies) Ltd* 1993 SLT 533.

[527] For example, see the old case of *McCowan v Wright* (1855) 15 D 494.

[528] Gretton, G L, 'Diligence and Enforcement of Judgments', *Stair Memorial Encyclopaedia*, vol 8 (1992), paras 247-321.

taining decree or arrestment, then the mandate is simply an informal mechanism of the arrester obtaining what he or she would otherwise be entitled to through the raising of an action of furthcoming.

(iv)   Remedies

Where there is a successful challenge to an unfair preference the remedies, as is the case for gratuitous alienations, are reduction and restoration. If the preference is a security such as a pledge then the redelivery of the asset to the debtor would serve to extinguish the pledge. Such redelivery will, though, not be possible if the original grantee who acquired the voidable title has transferred the asset on to a third party who acquired the asset for value and in good faith. For example, the creditor in a pledge may have assigned the pledge and the right to payment of the debt to a third party assignee. In such a case the transferee's transferee will acquire an absolutely good title which is exempt from challenge and the challenger's only claim will be for such 'other redress' as the court deems appropriate, such as the payment of the value of the property to the debtor's estate.[529]

(c)   Avoidance of floating charges

In certain cases a company debtor that has granted a floating charge in the period before insolvency can see that grant of floating charge challenged. The rules are in section 245 of the Insolvency Act 1986. This provision only applies to floating charges created after 29 December 1986.[530] Where the charge was created before that date they can only be reduced insofar as the old law applied.[531] The old law was found in section 617 of the Companies Act 1985 which provided for striking down if the charge was created in the 12 months before the commencement of winding up.

The Insolvency Act 1986 repealed section 613(3) of the Companies Act 1985[532] which had provided that floating charges could not be treated as gratuitous alienations or unfair preferences at common law or under statute. The repeal of this rule suggests that floating charges may be caught by the general unfair preference rules under section 243 of the Insolvency Act 1986 or at common law.[533]

---

[529] McBryde, *Bankruptcy*, para 12-142.

[530] St Clair and Drummond Young, *Corporate Insolvency*, para 10-23.

[531] Insolvency Act 1986, sch. 11, para 9.

[532] Which simply repeated the rule from Companies (Floating Charges and Receivers) (Scotland) Act 1972, s. 8.

[533] This is the view of St Clair and Drummond Young, *Corporate Insolvency*, para 10-22.

(i)   Statutory time periods

Floating charges created in a year, or, if the charge has been granted to a person connected with the company,[534] two years prior to the commencement of winding up or administration of a debtor company will be 'rendered invalid' unless one of the defences applies.[535]

(ii)   Defences to the statutory challenge

There are two main defences. The first is where the floating charge was granted to someone not connected with the debtor company, the floating charge cannot be challenged if at the time the floating charge was granted the debtor company was not unable to pay its debts, within the definition of section 123 of the Insolvency Act 1986, or was not rendered unable to pay its debts as a result of granting the floating charge.[536] The second defence applies whether or not a charge is granted to a connected person: the charge will not be rendered invalid to the extent that it was granted in exchange for new debt. The principles applicable to the *nova debita* exception discussed above in the context of unfair preferences are equally applicable here.

(iii)   Remedies

Unlike the provisions and common law rules discussed previously there is no provision for reduction or other restorative remedy. Instead section 245 of the 1986 Act merely provides that the charge is 'rendered invalid'. The meaning of this is not completely clear. It appears to provide that the charge is made void, although the underlying debt which the charge secures will not be avoided. Thus, if the debt has been repaid prior to administration or liquidation the officeholder has no right of recovery of the sums paid to the chargeholder.[537]

---

[534] As defined by the Insolvency Act 1986, s. 249, which includes directors, shadow directors, or associates of the company or directors or shadow directors. Associate is defined by Insolvency Act 1986, s. 435, which takes the definition from the Bankruptcy (Scotland) Act 1985.

[535] McKenzie Skene, *Insolvency*, 243-244.

[536] This defence is not applicable where the charge is created in favour of a connected person.

[537] See McKenzie Skene, *Insolvency*, pp 244-245 and St Clair and Drummond Young, *Corporate Insolvency*, para 10-30.

(d)   Other challengeable transactions

Both the Bankruptcy[538] and Insolvency Acts[539] provide special rules for
the challenge of extortionate credit transactions. If there were grossly
exorbitant repayment rates, or a transaction grossly contravenes the principles of fair dealing the transaction can be set aside.

9.3.   Insolvency of the transferor

9.3.1.   General

There is no general protection given to a transferee under donation,
exchange or sale prior to the transfer of the real right of ownership. The
parties have a certain degree of freedom in determining when ownership
transfers.[540] Under the law of sequestration (personal insolvency) when a
debtor is sequestrated his or her assets vest in the trustee in sequestration
from the date of sequestration.[541]

9.3.2.   Effect of sequestration

The effect of sequestration is to act as a deemed delivery of all corporeal
moveables owned by the bankrupt at the date of sequestration[542] with the
exception of certain assets which are excluded from vesting being: (a)
assets which the bankrupt holds in trust for third parties – where the
titular ownership of the bankrupt is encumbered by a beneficial interest
in favour of the beneficiary or beneficiaries in the trust;[543] (b) assets
which are kept in a dwellinghouse and are (i) exempt from the diligence
of attachment (the seizure of the corporeal moveables in the enforcement
of a decree) under section 11(1) of the Debt Arrangement and Attachment (Scotland) Act 2002;[544] or (ii) are assets which are not non-essential assets under Schedule 2 to the 2002 Act.[545]

---

[538] Bankruptcy (Scotland) Act 1985, s. 61.
[539] Insolvency Act 1986, s. 244.
[540] Although the real right of ownership may not have been transferred given the
effect of a reservation of title clause. See below, chapter 15.
[541] Bankruptcy (Scotland) Act 1985, s. 31(4).
[542] Bankruptcy (Scotland) Act 1985, s. 31(4)(b). For the date of sequestration, see
above, para 9.1.3(c)(i).
[543] Bankruptcy (Scotland) Act 1985, s. 33(1)(b).
[544] See below, Annex C for details.
[545] The list of assets which are not non-essential is given below in Annex C.

9.3.3. Other insolvency processes

The position for other insolvency processes differs slightly because in these processes the assets do not transfer to the officeholder. However, as Donna McKenzie Skene notes[546] the definition of 'property' in section 436 of the Insolvency Act 1986 is relevant to both administration and liquidation processes – although this inclusive definition does not make reference to ownership of assets. The *tantum et tale* principle applies to insolvency processes applicable to companies as it applies to sequestration and the liquidator or administrator of an insolvent transferor will in re-placing the management of the company have power over those assets owned by the company (and can realise those assets to satisfy credi-tors),[547] but will not have power over assets owned by the transferee.

9.3.4. Trusts

Given the exceptions to the general vesting rule, it could be argued that where parties have not made special agreement on transfer of ownership (through, for example, the insertion of a reservation of title clause) the transferee could seek some protection through requiring the transferor to hold the goods in trust for the transferee.[548] However, it has been sug-gested that where a trust is used as a security device in this way that the trust is contrary to public policy and should not be upheld.[549] The ques-tion, though, remains open.

---

[546] McKenzie Skene, *Insolvency*, chapter 21.

[547] See the general discussion on adoption of contracts at para 9.1 above. See also Anderson, R G, 'Fraud on Transfer and on Insolvency: ta...ta...*tantum et tale*', (2007) 11 Edinburgh Law Review 187.

[548] Such an approach is suggested by Lord Hoffmann in the leading case on transfer of land and sequestration, *Burnett's Trustee v Grainger* 2004 SC (HL) 19.

[549] There is debate in the context of land: Steven, A J M and Wortley, S, 'The Perils of a Trusting Disposition', 1996 SLT (News) 365 refers to a case involving move-able property, *Ewart v Hogg* (1893) 1 SLT 63, although this case turned on the wording of an agreement that purported to create a trust and transfer ownership at the same time, a clear repugnancy. Compare Chalmers, J, 'In Defence of the Trust-ing Conveyancer', 2002 SLT (News) 231.

9.3.5.   Sale of Goods Act implications

As discussed above, the transfer of ownership of corporeal moveables by sale is not tied to the delivery of the goods.[550] Due to the fact that the 1979 Act arguably provides for a causal approach to transfers the position where the contract is invalid but the goods have already been delivered to the transferee is not clear. It is suggested that if the causal basis of transfer was sale then avoiding the contract of sale will mean the 1979 Act does not apply, but it is conceivable that the 'seller' may have intended to transfer goods to the 'buyer' who intended to acquire.[551] If there was delivery with the requisite intention and the 'seller' became insolvent subsequent to that, it is suggested that ownership could have transferred to the 'buyer' *i.e.* an abstract approach.[552] Nevertheless, any potential claim in unjustified enrichment held by the 'seller' against the 'buyer' would now vest in the officeholder.

9.4.   Insolvency of the transferee

9.4.1.   General

How Scottish law deals with the interaction between the transfer of corporeal moveables and the insolvency of the transferee is determined by the rules on transfer of ownership. If ownership has passed to the transferee prior to the insolvency of the transferee then generally the transferor will – if he or she has any claim to the goods – have to rely on a personal right of recovery that would entitle the transferor to rank as an unsecured creditor. The transferor does not have a protected right as there is a fixed list of rights in security, and protection for the purchaser is not part of the *numerus clausus*. If, though, ownership has not yet transferred to the transferee then the transferor will be able to vindicate his or her right of ownership. These general principles are not varied by considerations of possession of the moveables (although there is a rebuttable evidential presumption that possession presumes ownership).[553] If the transferor has not delivered the property to the transferee and ownership has not passed the transferor will be entitled to retain the property.

   The situations in which the transferor is entitled to recover the property arise from defects in the underlying obligation and are considered

---

[550] See above, para 5.4.1.

[551] Reid, *Property*, para 610.

[552] See above, para 5.1.6.

[553] See above, para 2.2 and Reid, *Property*, para 609.

above in the analysis of the abstract theory of transfer and Scottish law.[554] In determining if the property revests automatically in the transferor it is necessary to determine if the transfer is void or voidable.[555] If the underlying transaction is void (and the defect similarly taints the transfer) then there will be automatic revesting in the transferor as the transfer never took place. If the underlying contract is voidable as a result of fraud and the transfer is similarly tainted case law suggests that the transferor is entitled to regain the property[556] although one might (on general principles) expect an insolvency administrator to take the property unencumbered.[557] The position for other vices or defects of consent is not clear.

9.4.2. Statutory protection

In some situations within the context of sale transactions the transferor has a degree of protection from the transferee's insolvency. These are statutory instances within the Sale of Goods Act 1979 and are for the benefit of an unpaid seller. The law in Scotland is similar to that in England and Wales.[558] An unpaid seller is defined in section 38 of the 1979 Act.

The remedies are available only for sellers and those in the position of seller. Buyers that have rejected goods and are seeking repayment of the purchase price are not included.[559] The definition in this section is broader than the general definition of 'seller' within the 1979 Act and includes certain agents. Additionally, the definition of an unpaid seller includes the seller that has accepted a tendered conditional payment, for example, payment by cheque by the buyer, so if the condition is not satisfied, for example, the cheque is dishonoured by non-payment, the seller is still an unpaid seller.

The rights of the unpaid seller are summarised in section 39 of the Sale of Goods Act 1979. They are implied by law meaning that the parties to a contract of sale of goods can contract out of them should they so choose.[560] There are three remedies for the unpaid seller, which are available where ownership has transferred to the buyer. They are:

---

[554] See above, para 5.1.6.

[555] *Ibid.*

[556] *Campbell, Robertson & Co v Shepherd & Paterson* (1776) 2 Pat App 399.

[557] See above, para 9.1 on adoption of contracts.

[558] Carey Miller with Irvine, *Corporeal Moveables*, paras 11.23-11.29.

[559] Carey Miller with Irvine, *Corporeal Moveables*, para 11.23. In these cases the buyer is entitled only to a claim for repayment of the unpaid price.

[560] Sale of Goods Act 1979, s. 55.

(a) the unpaid seller's lien;

(b) a limited right of re-sale (available where the seller is in possession of the assets and subject to restrictions); and

(c) where the buyer is insolvent[561] a right to stoppage in transit, preventing delivery of the goods to the buyer.

These remedies are considered in detail in chapter 5.[562]

10.   Risk

10.1.   General

If a party has to bear the accidental loss or damage of corporeal moveables which are being transferred then that party is at risk. Risk is closely related to contractual frustration in Scottish and English law. In certain circumstances the contract may be frustrated – terminating the obligations of the parties. This will occur if moveables are destroyed before ownership passes but subsequent to conclusion of the contract[563] or in other cases. These cases include where a contract cannot be performed as a result of war;[564] or where it is otherwise impossible or impracticable to perform the contract[565] (for example, as a result of the passage of legislation prohibiting transactions).[566] The supervening event not having been the fault of either contracting party, the contract is frustrated meaning that neither transferor nor transferee is required to fulfil his or her obligation.[567]

However, in certain cases the event will occur after transfer of ownership, or the event may affect the value of the moveables although not rendering them destroyed. For example, a purchaser may buy raw materials speculatively anticipating that the materials will appreciate in value as a result of an international shortage of the materials. A new discovery of the raw materials will impact on the value of the materials but does not render the contract frustrated. Risk determines which party bears the patrimonial loss in such a case.

---

[561] As defined by the 1979 Act, s. 61(4): Where the buyer has 'ceased to pay his debts in the ordinary course of business or ... cannot pay his debts as they become due, whether he has committed an act of bankruptcy or not'.

[562] See above, paras 5.6.1-5.6.4.

[563] For sales of goods this rule is statutory: Sale of Goods Act 1979, s. 7. See *Leitch v Edinburgh Ice and Cold Storage Co Ltd* (1900) 2 F 904.

[564] See McBryde, *Contract*, paras 21-22–21-25.

[565] McBryde, *Contract*, paras 21-26–21-30.

[566] See *Caledonian Insurance Co v Matheson's Trs* (1901) 3 F 685.

[567] McBryde, *Contract*, paras 21-37–21-43.

10.2. Common Law

The common law position on risk, which is still applicable to contracts of exchange, follows the Roman law rule. Risk therefore passes on conclusion of the underlying contract, and thus occurs at a point some time before delivery and the transfer of ownership.[568]

10.3. Sale of Goods Act

For sales of moveables the rule is now statutory and found in section 20 of the Sale of Goods Act 1979. The general principle is that risk follows ownership, *res perit suo domino*, and as has been seen from the discussion of transfer in the context of sale ownership does not necessarily follow possession.[569] The consequence of section 20(1) is that where goods are at the buyer's risk he or she will still have to pay the price even if the goods have been damaged or destroyed.[570]

However, the position differs where there is a consumer contract. Under section 20(4)[571] where one party is a consumer (that is, not someone acting in the course of a business) and the other party is acting in the course of business,[572] risk lies with the seller business until delivery to the consumer.[573]

Outwith consumer sales the position in section 20(1) is simply a default position and can be contracted out of by the parties. Indeed in commercial practice, especially where goods are being transported, parties often make special provision for the passing of risk. It is conceivable that the passing of risk can be severed from the passing of ownership to take account of the particular circumstances of a case.

In determining whether there is a contrary intention to pass risk at a time distinct from the passing of ownership there are three possible situations. The parties may make express contractual provision, although it is

---

[568] The leading case on exchange and risk is *Windenmeyer v Burn Stewart & Co Ltd* 1967 SC 85 which follows the common law position in cases involving the sale of moveables in cases such as *Hansen v Craig and Rose* (1859) 21 D 432.

[569] See above, para 5.1.

[570] As s. 7 only allows for frustration of the contract where goods are destroyed before risk passes to the purchaser.

[571] Inserted by the Sale and Supply of Goods to Consumers Regulations 2002 SI 2002/3045, reg. 4.

[572] Sale of Goods Act 1979, s. 61(1) defines consumer contract in accordance with Unfair Contract Terms Act 1977, s. 25.

[573] Atiyah, P S, Adams, J N and MacQueen, H, *The Sale of Goods* (11th ed, 2005), pp 359-360.

not necessary to refer explicitly to risk. It may be implied from the agreement between the parties, for example, an agreement to insure indicates that the parties treat risk as having passed but does not mean necessarily that ownership has passed. It may arise out of trade custom in specific areas. For example, in export sales in a 'c.i.f.' contract ('cost, insurance, and freight' contract) risk passes on shipment[574] and the seller has fulfilled his or her obligations on shipment and delivery of insurance policies and bills of lading; and ownership passes when the documents (insurance and bills of lading) are transferred and paid for.[575] The division of risk and ownership is not uncommon.

Additionally subsections (2) and (3) divorce risk and ownership where there has been fault. In section 20(2) where there is a delay in delivery, the party at fault is liable for any loss which arises and would not have arisen but for the fault.[576] Subsection (3) ensures that the common law duty of care owed by a custodier of property is not replaced by the statutory rule on risk. Thus, where property is damaged while in the custody of the seller, before delivery but after ownership has transferred, the seller/custodier may be liable.[577]

The general position in relation to risk is also varied where the goods are in transit. Section 32 of the Sale of Goods Act 1979 makes special provision. The effect of section 32(2) is that if goods are damaged in transit then although ownership and risk may have passed to the buyer at an earlier stage the seller may be liable for the damage. Alternatively, the buyer may simply reject the moveables.[578]

Section 32(3) imposes an obligation on the seller to notify the buyer to allow the buyer to insure, or risk will remain with the seller even though it may ordinarily pass. This subsection is not consistently interpreted by the courts in England. While theoretically it may apply to export sales (other than c.i.f. contracts) where goods are shipped Atiyah suggests 'in practice it will rarely be of much importance because in most cases the buyer will … have enough information to insure the goods specifically.'[579] These provisions do not apply in consumer sales.[580]

---

[574] *Ibid* at 430.

[575] *Ibid* at 431.

[576] There is no Scottish case law on this, only an English case, *Demby Hamilton & Co Ltd v Barden* [1949] 1 All ER 435.

[577] *Knight v Wilson* 1949 SLT (Sh Ct) 26.

[578] Atiyah, Adams and MacQueen, *Sale of Goods*, pp 422-423 discusses the cases. There appears to be no Scottish case law on the point.

[579] Atiyah, Adams and MacQueen, *Sale of Goods*, pp 425-426 following discussion of the most important English case in the area, *Wimble Sons and Co Ltd v Rosenberg & Sons* [1913] 3 KB 743. Again, there appears to be no Scottish case law on point.

[580] Sale of Goods Act 1979, s. 32(4) inserted by Sale and Supply of Goods to Consumers Regulations 2002, SI 2003/3045.

Part III:
Original acquisition

II. Acquisition by accession, commixture, specification

II.1. Accession of moveables

II.1.1. Definition

Accession takes place when two pieces of corporeal property become joined in such a way that one is considered to have become subsumed by the other. The property which is subsumed is known as the 'accessory'. The property into which it is subsumed is known as the 'principal'. For example, an engine accedes to the car into which it is installed. The result of accession is that the owner of the principal becomes owner of the accessory too. Accession is a mechanical doctrine dependent on objective factors. The policy behind this is that third parties should be able to tell whether it has operated. It follows that it is impossible for parties to contract so as to exclude its operation.[581] Nor is good faith required.[582]

II.1.2. Accession of moveables to moveables

Accession will happen where the items have been attached permanently. In the words of Bell, this is where 'there can be no separation',[583] or perhaps, more accurately no separation without causing serious damage to the property.

II.1.3. Identification of the principal

In the case of accession of moveables to land, there is no difficulty identifying the principal. It is always the land. With moveables to moveables it

---

[581] *Shetland Islands Council v BP Petroleum Development Ltd* 1990 SLT 82 at 94 *per* Lord Cullen.

[582] Stair, II.1.38-39; Erskine, II.1.15.

[583] Bell, *Principles*, § 1298.

is more complicated and the law cannot be regarded as settled. Bell's analysis[584] is as follows. First, if with two substances one can exist separately and the other cannot then the first is the principal. An example would be paint used on a car, which no longer has an independent existence.[585] Secondly, where both things can exist separately, the principal is the one 'which the other is taken to adorn or complete'.[586] For example, a diamond will accede to a ring. This might be expressed in an alternative way, namely that the principal is the item which gives its name to the finished product. Bell's final rule is that if the two foregoing rules are not relevant then 'bulk prevails; next value'. In the absence of case law, however, one cannot be sure if this is correct.

11.1.4. Compensation

Compensation is only available in limited circumstances and here bad faith is relevant. The basis is the law of unjustified enrichment.[587] Where the act was instructed or performed by the owner of the principal, the former owner of the accessory is entitled to the value of the object.[588] If the owner of the principal acted in bad faith, there is an entitlement to a higher level of compensation. This is because there is a duty to make reparation and liability is for 'the greatest value, according to the estimation of the former owner'.[589] The Roman rule that at least twice the value must be paid does not, at least according to Bankton, apply.[590] There is, however, a lack of case authority.

Where the act of accession was performed or instructed by the owner of the accessory, that person is generally not entitled to compensation. An exception to this is if he or she acted in the reasonable but mistaken belief[591] that he or she owned the principal or had a long term right in the property. In this case, there would be a claim for the value by which the owner of the principal was enriched.[592] Where the act of accession was performed or instructed by a third party, the owner of the accessory

---

[584] *Ibid.*

[585] See Carey Miller with Irvine, *Corporeal Moveables*, para 3.19.

[586] Bell, *Principles*, § 1298.

[587] Reid, *Property*, para 577.

[588] Stair, II.1.8 and 39; Bankton, I.9.43 and II.1.17.

[589] Stair, II.1.9. See also Bankton, I.9.43.

[590] Bankton, I.9.43; Reid, *Property*, para 577, n 3. See also Steven, A J M, 'Recompense for Interference', 1996 Juridical Review 51 at 61-62.

[591] *Barbour v Halliday* (1840) 2 D 1279; *Buchanan v Stewart* (1874) 2 R 78; and *Duke of Hamilton v Johnston* (1877) 14 SLR 298.

[592] Stair, I.8.6 and II.1.39-40; and Bankton, I.9.43 and II.1.17.

could recover the value of the accessory from the third party, although this may be limited to cases where the third party has acted in bad faith.[593] Alternatively, there may be a claim against the owner of the principal for the value by which the principal has been enriched.

11.1.5. Accession of moveables to land

Moveable property which accedes to land is known as a 'fixture'. The owner of the land becomes the owner of the whole. Whether accession has taken place depends on the application of three elements.[594] First, there requires to be physical union. Things which are irrevocably attached such as buildings are always fixtures. It is not always necessary for the moveable to be actually attached. A heavy object such as a summer house may accede because of its weight alone.[595] If the accessory cannot be removed without seriously damaging it or the principal, then it will have acceded.[596] Unless the physical union test provides a decisive result, the other two elements must be considered.

The second element is functional subordination. Does the item appear to be attached for the improvement of the land or for the better enjoyment of the item itself? In some cases, the answer is clear. A heating system is clearly installed to improve a house and therefore accedes.[597] In other cases, the attachment may both enhance the moveable and the land. A picture is better viewed if hung, but this also improves the wall in question. Much may depend on the exact circumstances.[598]

The third element is permanency. Only quasi permanency is required to satisfy this. In the leading case of *Brand's Trustees v Brand's Trustee*[599] machinery was installed by a tenant under a mining lease with the full intention of removing it at the expiry. It was held nonetheless to have acceded. It has been suggested judicially that the deemed intention of particular types of annexers such as individuals who hire the item rather than own it should be factored in when assessing whether there has been

---

[593] Reid, *Property*, paras 173 and 577; Stair, I.7.2 and Erskine, III.1.70.

[594] Reid, *Property*, paras 579-582.

[595] *Christie v Smith's Exr* 1949 SC 572.

[596] *Elitestone Ltd v Morris* [1997] 2 All ER 513. This is an English case but law here north and south of the border is very similar, following *Brand's Trustees v Brand's Trustees* (1876) 3 R (HL) 16. For a comparative account of the subject, see van Vliet, L P, 'Accession of Movables to Land' (in 2 parts), (2002) 6 Edinburgh Law Review 67 and 199.

[597] *Assessor for Fife v Hodgson* 1966 SC 30.

[598] *Cochrane v Stevenson* (1891) 18 R 1208.

[599] (1876) 3 R (HL) 16.

accession.[600] However, this seems to ignore House of Lords authority that intention is not relevant.[601] This is the better view. Accession should be decided solely by objective factors.[602]

11.2.   Commixtion (commixture) and confusion

Commixtion arises from the mixing of solids or separate entities and confusion results from the mixing of liquids.[603] If the mixture is incapable of being separated into its constituent parts or if it has been made by mutual consent, then it becomes owned in common by the owners of the contributing materials.[604] Ownership will be in proportion to the quantity contributed or, if the components are of different value, the value of the contributions.[605] The parties can agree otherwise. Where the mixture is capable of separation, for example, sheep which are marked, there is no change in ownership of the respective parts. The owners can reclaim their own property. This area of law is undeveloped. But, it is considered that, like with accession, bad faith is only relevant to the question of compensation. Similarly, the rules on compensation are analogous to those for accession.

11.3.   Specification, processing

Specification takes place where a new kind of thing is manufactured from materials belonging wholly or partly to others. The case always cited by the institutional writers,[606] following Roman law, is grapes being used to make wine. This seems more apposite to the temperate climate of Italy than Scotland. Stair's example of wood being used to build a boat seems more in point.[607] It is essential for specification that a new type of thing is created, *i.e.* a new species. It was held in one case that joining two halves of a car together met this requirement.[608] This, however, is actually acces-

---

[600] *Scottish Discount Co v Blin* 1985 SC 216.

[601] *Brand's Trs v Brand's Trs* (1876) 3 R (HL) 16.

[602] See above, para 1.1.3(d).

[603] Reid, *Property*, para 564.

[604] Stair, II.1.36 and 37; Erksine, II.1.17; Bankton, II.1.14-16; and Bell, *Principles*, § 1298(2).

[605] Stair, III.1.36 and 37; Erskine, II.1.7; and Bell, *Principles*, § 1298.

[606] For example, Erskine, II.1.25.

[607] Stair, II.1.41.

[608] *McDonald v Provan (of Scotland Street) Ltd* 1960 SLT 231.

sion as it merely amounts to joining.[609] Where, however, a vehicle is built from scratch out of raw materials such as metal, this is truly a new species.[610] It was argued unsuccessfully in one case that where baby salmon (smolts) are industrially reared in a fish farm so as they grow to become adults, specification takes place.[611]

The middle view developed in Roman law is accepted as regards ownership of the new species.[612] The manufacturer acquires it if the work carried out is, in a practical sense, irreversible. If this is not the case, title is given to the owner of the materials. An example of practical irreversibility would be a boat, which in theory could be returned to planks of wood, but not in a way which it appears that the boat was never built in the first place. Of course, it may be that the manufacturer is carrying out the process as the agent of the owner of the materials. In that case the latter will naturally acquire ownership. Likewise, the matter in general can be governed by an agreement between the parties.[613]

A difficult question is whether the manufacturer needs to be in good faith to acquire ownership. The better view is that his or her state of mind should be relevant only to the issue of compensation.[614] The rules on recompensing the party who does not acquire title are similar to those for accession. Where ownership has been acquired by the manufacturer he or she must repay the value of the materials to their erstwhile owner. In *International Banking Corporation v Ferguson Shaw & Sons*[615] oil had been used in good faith to make margarine. The value of the oil had then to be paid to the former owner. However, where ownership remains with the owner of the materials the manufacturer has no claim, unless that person reasonably believed that he or she owned them.

11.4. Further general aspects

Co-ownership will normally only arise in commixtion and confusion and the division of ownership is dealt with above.[616]

---

609 This analysis was accepted in the South African case of *Khan v Minister of Law and Order* 1991 (3) SA 439 (T).

610 *Wylie & Lochhead v Mitchell* (1870) 8 M 552.

611 *Kinloch v Damph Ltd v Nordvik Salmon Farms Ltd*, Outer House, 30 June 1999 (unreported, available at www.scotcourts.gov.uk).

612 Reid, *Property*, para 561.

613 *Wylie & Lochhead v Mitchell* (1870) 8 M 552.

614 For discussion, see Reid, *Property*, paras 561 and 562 and Carey Miller with Irvine, *Corporeal Moveables*, para 4.06.

615 1910 SC 182.

616 See above, para 11.2.

The parties can override the rules on commixtion and confusion, and specification by agreement. However, it is impossible to contract out of accession because it is a strictly mechanical doctrine. It is, however, possible to confer a right of removal as regards the accessory and certain removal rights, for example, for trade fixtures, arise by operation of law.[617]

A reservation of title clause will be defeated by accession, commixtion, confusion or specification.[618]

The legal effect on third parties' rights *in rem* on the original things has not been the subject of analysis, but it is thought on general principles that these would be extinguished.

The compensation rules are discussed above.[619] The need for legal capacity has not been analysed, but it is considered that as the processes are mechanical, capacity is not necessary.

12. Good faith acquisition

12.1. Field of application

12.1.1. General

Consider the following scenario: A is the owner of a moveable. The moveable is 'transferred' by non-owner B to the potential 'good faith acquirer' C. Assuming that seller B was never the owner then in principle property does not pass when a non-owner, with no authority from the owner, purports to transfer. The essential position of the law is that title can be transferred by 'the dispositive will of the owner alone'.[620] Accordingly, in the absence of this required starting point for derivative acquisition, 'good faith on the part of the transferee is irrelevant'.[621] There is, however, a limited category of varied exceptions to this position dealt with above,[622] all subject to the requirement that a transferee must have 'obtained the thing in good faith and for value.'[623] The exceptions arise either from common law or legislation.[624]

---

[617] Reid, *Property*, para 586.

[618] *Archivent Sales and Development Ltd v Strathclyde Regional Council* 1985 SLT 154; *Kinloch v Damph Ltd v Nordvik Salmon Farms Ltd*, Outer House, 30 June 1999 (unreported, available at www.scotcourts.gov.uk). See below, para 15.4.2.

[619] See above, paras 11.1-11.3.

[620] Stair, III.2.3.

[621] Reid, *Property*, para 669.

[622] See above, para 5.9.

[623] Carey Miller with Irvine, *Corporeal Moveables*, para 10.15.

[624] Carey Miller with Irvine, *Corporeal Moveables*, paras 10.15-10.23.

In the case where the seller B's right (to dispose) has been terminated then a problem will only arise where B is in a position to effect transfer, typically through continuing possession of the goods. Termination of authority to dispose could only be an issue if communicated to B in advance of his or her disposition to C. Until the changed position is communicated to C, or C's knowledge can be inferred, he or she will be able to rely on the *status quo ante* in terms of being in a position to acquire, whether on the basis of direct disposition from the owner or through one of the exceptions open to a good faith acquirer for value. The common law doctrine of personal bar is potentially applicable.[625]

If B's contract with his or her supplier (seller S) has ended then the approach adopted in the previous paragraph may be applicable to the circumstances of possession of goods, or the relevant documents of title, by a non-owner who purports to transfer. A statutory provision is also potentially relevant to the common situation of supplier and subsequent parties in a commercial chain; in the circumstances of disposition by a buyer who has obtained possession (but, of course, not ownership) of the goods or relevant documents of title; he or she may pass title to one who acts in good faith and gives value.[626]

12.1.2. Double sale

The classic double sale scenario involves a disposition by an owner disregarding an existing obligation to transfer ownership to an earlier entitled purchaser.[627] The circumstances may involve a non-owner intermediate party but, of course, there could only be acquisition by a second good faith purchaser if there would have been acquisition in such circumstances of transfer by a non-owner. This matter is more fully dealt with above.[628]

12.1.3. Other cases

A distinct situation would be where B has possession on the basis of a subsistent but defective title open to reduction (*i.e.* being set aside) by A,

---

[625] Carey Miller with Irvine, *Corporeal Moveables*, para 10.19. See Factors (Scotland) Act 1890, s. 2 re the powers of a mercantile agent regarding the disposition of goods.

[626] Factors (Scotland) Act 1890, s. 9 and Sale of Goods Act 1979, s. 25(1).

[627] See above, chapter 6.

[628] *Ibid.*

typically because of fraud by B on A.[629] C, who acquires in good faith and for value from B, will obtain an unimpeachable title and A will be left with only a claim for compensation from B.[630] This, of course, is not strictly a case in point in an *a non domino* context because, as owner on the basis of a defective but subsistent title, B can effect transfer.

12.1.4. Stolen or lost goods

The good faith transferee who acquires a stolen or lost moveable innocent of the circumstances obtains no better title than his or her transferor had. Stair[631] refers to the *vitium reale* of theft which 'passeth with the thing stolen to all singular successors'.[632] In the case of lost property, legislation[633] supports the common law preservation of an owner's right. In principle the Crown is residual owner of apparently unowned but previously owned moveables.[634] An owner can always recover on the basis of his or her extant title to the thing and by showing that possession terminated in circumstances not consistent with a transfer of ownership. The correlative of this position – the only significant concession to a good faith acquirer – is the rebuttable presumption that the possessor of a moveable is its owner.[635] The law's strong tendency towards protection of the right of ownership is also reflected in the limitation position. A purchaser in good faith is protected by negative prescription (limitation) only on the basis of the claimant having failed to exercise his or her right for 20 years.[636]

12.1.5. Registered moveables

There are no 'registered moveables' in the sense of a register controlling the position as to title. Ships, aircraft and motor vehicles are subject to

---

[629] A defective but subsistent title is also sometimes designated a voidable title in contrast to a void title which, of course, is no title at all; see Reid, *Property*, para 601.

[630] See Carey Miller with Irvine, *Corporeal Moveables*, para 8.30.

[631] Stair, II.12.10.

[632] See Carey Miller with Irvine, *Corporeal Moveables*, para 10.15.

[633] Civic Government (Scotland) Act 1982, s. 73.

[634] See Carey Miller with Irvine, *Corporeal Moveables*, para 2.06. This remains the case despite the recent abolition of feudal tenure: see Abolition of Feudal Tenure etc (Scotland) Act 2000, s. 58(1).

[635] See Carey Miller with Irvine, *Corporeal Moveables*, para 1.19.

[636] See Prescription and Limitation (Scotland) Act 1973, s. 8.

registration requirements[637] but possible 'transfer' by non-owner B to the potential 'good faith acquirer' C would be controlled by the general law stated above. Motor vehicles subject to a hire-purchase or conditional sale agreement are an exception. The controlling legislation provides for possible acquisition by a private purchaser in good faith on disposition by the debtor – who is not yet owner.[638]

12.1.6. Negotiable instruments

In principle C who gives value and acts in good faith may obtain a bearer negotiable instrument free of defects. In certain limited circumstances the loss of a negiotiable instrument by theft or deception may result in a subsequent good faith party obtaining a right to the instument as if he or she had obtained it in a *bona fide* transaction with the drawer. The risk of this can be avoided by simple steps open to the drawer of various forms of negotiable instrument. This, however, is a specialised area of law which cannot be considered in any meaningful detail in the present context.[639] In Scotland banknotes, issued by one of the Scottish issuing banks, are promissory notes and hence bills of exchange rather than legal tender in the technical sense.[640]

12.1.7. Money

Money must be open to free transfer without any possible issue of a defect of title; as such it cannot be open to recovery *in specie* by vindication.[641] A 'money claim' is not a claim for specific notes but one for an amount of money. Even stolen money which can be identified because it has been marked cannot be vindicated from a good faith party who has given value, in the same way as might be possible in the case of an item of corporeal moveable property.

---

[637] Merchant Shipping Act 1995; Air Navigation Order 2005 (SI 2005/1970), Part 4.

[638] See Hire Purchase Act 1974, s. 27; Carey Miller with Irvine, *Corporeal Moveables*, para 10.23.

[639] See Gloag and Henderson, *The Law of Scotland* chapter 20.

[640] Crerar, L D, 'Banking, Money and Commercial Paper' in *Stair Memorial Encyclopaedia* (Reissue, 2000), para 150.

[641] Stair, II.1.34; Carey Miller with Irvine, *Corporeal Moveables*, para 1.19.

12.1.8. Works of art

There are no special private law property rules relating to works of art.[642] However, any claim to good faith possession of a work of art by an art dealer may, in practice, be subject to a possible due diligence standard involving the issue of whether the relevant registers of stolen art were checked. The recognised practice of looking into 'provenance' would be relevant to any issue of possible good faith acquisition by a dealer. Of course, the question would only arise in the scenario under consideration in one of the exceptional situations in which recovery by A was precluded by reason of the circumstances under which A had parted with possession to non-owner B.

12.1.9. 'Universitas rerum'/bulks

The common law and the Sale of Goods Act 1979 provide special rules for the transfer of bulk goods. Property in an undivided share in bulk goods is potentially transferable; the relevant requirements are provided for in sections 16 and 20A of the Sale of Goods Act.[643]

12.2. The need for value

C can only acquire the moveable in good faith if he or she 'acquired' it for value from B. The reason is not clear but is considered by the modern authorities.[644] There appears to be policy justification for the rule but the issue has not been formally addressed and it accordingly seems appropriate to say that the reason is historical.

It is debatable as to what would constitute a sufficient *quid pro quo*. There is no authority on the point of the distinction between a gratuitous acquisition and an acquisition for value. The better view is that consideration would not be sufficient if it was so low that there would be room for an argument that meaningful value was not given (and consequently that the acquirer is not in good faith). There may be decisions from other contexts which could have a possible bearing on this issue, for example, gratuitous dispositions in circumstances of insolvency.[645] There is no author-

---

[642] See Carey Miller, D L, 'Title to art: developments in the USA', (1996) 1 SLPQ 115. European or international treaty or convention provisions directed to unlawful trade in antiquities are beyond present scope.

[643] See above, para 5.2.2(d).

[644] See Reid, *Property*, para 699; Carey Miller with Irvine, *Corporeal Moveables*, para 8.32.

[645] See above, para 9.2.

ity on whether the giving of value requires an actual price to be paid, but it is submitted that the better view is that no more than an obligation involving counterperformance is necessary. To require any more than this would not be consistent with the primary requirement of good faith which is more to do with C's perception of the position than the actual position.

In circumstances in which acquisition was on the basis of an onerous obligation but the promised performance was not in fact made there might be potential for an enrichment claim.

12.3. The need for possession by the transferor

In order to pass title to C, the transferee, it is necessary that B, the 'transferor' has possession or physical control of the asset. At any rate such possession is necessary to the extent that in the circumstances concerned A, the 'true owner', must necessarily have relinquished control and allowed scope for B to assume control, at least to some sufficient degree to make possible good faith acquisition by C. Scottish law puts the emphasis on the protection of the true owner and looks to the circumstances in which possession was lost or parted with. Where the thing was stolen from A it is subject to a *vitium reale*.[646] In this case C cannot acquire even if B had no knowledge of the theft and had him or herself acquired on a basis consistent with acquisition of title.

There is no need to classify the requisite forms of possession and the law does not do so. As indicated, the essential factor is that B holds or controls on a sufficient basis to give scope to the honest belief by C that he or she has acquired title or has a right of disposal.

12.4. The need for possession by the acquirer

In this context the standard requirements of derivative acquisition are applicable. The first question will be whether the Sale of Goods Act 1979 or the common law applies. C can only acquire by way of exception to the *nemo plus* principle if one of the recognised exceptions can be invoked.

Constitutum possessorium is competent at common law but its application is treated with caution by the courts.[647] Under the 1979 Act property can pass on any basis which the parties intend; in principle, provided acquisition is competent, there is no reason why C should not acquire title to the thing in circumstances of B's continuing to hold it. This could only be relevant in terms of possible implications for C's good faith.

---

[646] Stair, II.12.10.
[647] See above, para 5.4.4 and Reid, *Property*, para 623.

12.5.   Circumstances of the 'transfer'

There is no general basis for acquisition *a non domino* by a *bona fide* purchaser in the 'ordinary course of business'. The particular relevant exceptions already referred to are, of course, applicable in an 'ordinary course of business' context. Equally, there is no general concept of a 'consumer purchase' exception to the controlling *nemo plus* position.[648] Scottish law has never recognised a concept of 'market overt'. Prior to its abolition in English law[649] the doctrine's application in Scotland was excluded by the Sale of Goods Act.[650] There is no public auction exception to the *nemo plus* principle.

12.6.   The way the original owner 'lost' the moveable

There has already been consideration of whether it is necessary that the original owner A has 'entrusted' the asset to the 'transferor' B to effect the transfer.[651]

If the original owner A has sold the moveable to the 'transferor' B and this contract suffers from some defect (*i.e.* it is void or voidable for any reason) acquisition by C is only possible if B has acquired a subsistent title, *i.e.* one which is voidable rather than void.[652] Pending reduction, *i.e.* judicial setting aside, of the act of transfer, B can pass a good title to C. But C cannot be in good faith if judicial proceedings have been commenced by A against B. The relevant issue is whether the act of transfer, rather than the contract of sale, is void or voidable because '[a] good conveyance will save a bad contract.'[653] Of course it may be that the standing of the contract and the act of transfer correspond; under the Sale of Goods Act this is particularly likely but the point remains that the relevant inquiry should be directed to the act of transfer.

Lack of capacity has the potential to affect the act of transfer in the same way as it affects the underlying contract. The position as to capacity on the basis of age is governed by legislation[654] which essentially provides that acts by a person under 16 are void while those of someone over 16 but under 18 are voidable.[655]

---

[648] See, generally, Reid, *Property*, para 672.

[649] Sale of Goods (Amendment) Act 1994, s. 1. See Carey Miller with Irvine, *Corporeal Moveables*, para 10.15, n 29.

[650] Sale of Goods Act 1979, s. 22(2).

[651] See above, para 12.1.

[652] As Reid, *Property*, para 610 observes, there is no intermediate position and an ostensible title is either subsistent or no title at all.

[653] Reid, *Property*, para 601, n 3.

[654] Age of Legal Capacity (Scotland) Act 1991.

[655] See Carey Miller with Irvine, *Corporeal Moveables*, para 8.05.

12.7. Good faith

12.7.1. General

If C acquires from B, purporting to be owner, he or she must believe that to be true. If C acquires from B, purporting to have A's authority to dispose of the thing, similarly he or she must believe that scenario to be a true position. The good faith must necessarily match the circumstances.

12.7.2. Standard of good faith

This issue is dealt with above in relation to double sales.[656] There is no direct authority but a possible duty to make enquiries, where circumstances should give cause for concern, is consistent with a definition of good faith encompassing a measure of objectivity. In other property contexts, for example, the acquisition of fruits by a *bona fide* possessor[657] the good faith requirement involves a tension between subjectivity and objectivity.[658]

12.7.3. Time when good faith is required

In the context of the act of transfer being controlling it follows that C must be in good faith at the time of acquisition. Recent authority,[659] regarding a double sale problem in an immoveable property transaction, supports this. In the decision concerned it was held that good faith at the time of contract is irrelevant if prior to the act of registration the acquirer became aware of the true circumstances as to another's prior right.[660]

12.7.4. Burden of proof

There is no formal presumption of good faith, although at the same time it would invariably be for the person seeking to establish that a transac-

---

[656] See above, para 6.2.

[657] See below, para 19.1 and Carey Miller with Irvine, *Corporeal Moveables*, para 6.05.

[658] See, generally, Reid, *Property*, paras 132-135.

[659] *Alex Brewster & Sons v Caughey* 2002 GWD 10-318.

[660] Carey Miller with Irvine, *Corporeal Moveables*, para 8.31 supports this decision; however, other writers question it: See Wortley, S, 'Double Sales and the Offside Trap', 2002 Juridical Review 291, Anderson, R G, 'Offside Goals before *Rodger Builders*', 2005 Juridical Review 277 at 287-289.

tion was not in good faith to raise the circumstances relevant to establishing bad faith. There are no additional special rules.

12.8.   Lost and stolen goods

The term 'lost property' has been defined as 'property the ownership of which is temporarily uncertain'.[661] There is no definition in the Civic Government (Scotland) Act 1982 which regulates the position relating to the finding of 'lost or abandoned' property.[662] However, in respect of lost, or apparently lost, property the statute is directed to owned property in which the ownership position is unknown and, to this extent, the statute reflects the above definition.

'Stolen property' is property taken from the owner, or removed without the consent of the owner, in circumstances which amount to, or would amount to, theft according to the criminal law. As noted,[663] the *vitium reale* of theft passes to subsequent parties regardless of knowledge of the circumstance. This 'real defect' preserves the priority of the owner's right to recover the thing.

The position of the law in respect of lost property and stolen property has been explained;[664] in both cases a strong emphasis on protection of the owner's interests reflects the consistent policy position of the law.

12.9.   No right of original owner to buy back

The exceptional situations allowing *a non domino* acquisition by a *bona fide* party are consistent with an owner's imputed intention – inferred from conduct or circumstances – to transfer ownership. In these circumstances, there can be no rational basis for a right in the original owner to buy back the asset concerned from a good faith acquirer.[665]

12.10.   Encumbrances on ownership

In principle, a subordinate real right will not be affected by the act of disposition which transfers the ownership right in the thing concerned. If a person C buys a moveable from the owner A – or a person A who has

---

[661] Reid, *Property*, para 547.

[662] See Civic Government (Scotland) Act 1982, Part VI (ss. 67-79).

[663] See above, para 12.1.4.

[664] *Ibid.*

[665] See above, para 5.9.2.

the authority to dispose of the moveable – but the moveable is encumbered with a property right of a third party, for example, pledge, C's ownership will remain encumbered by the pre-existing real right.

12.11. Consumer acquirers

There is no special protection for good faith consumer acquirers. The common law and statutory exceptions to the controlling *nemo plus* position could be seen as providing protection to consumer acquirers.[666]

13. Acquisitive and negative prescription

13.1. Functions, justification and criticism of acquisitive prescription

There are clear statutory rules for the acquisitive prescription of land.[667] The period is normally ten years. For moveables, there are some old cases which suggest a forty-year common law period, but their authority is doubtful.[668]

The basis of acquisitive prescription is discussed by a number of the institutional writers, often in the context of land rather than moveables.[669] For example, Stair states that it is justified by 'public utility ... and also because the law accounteth it as a dereliction of the owner's right, if he own it not, neither pursue it within such time.'[670] Erskine writes that the state is correct 'to punish by forfeiture itself the negligence of proprietors when the great purposes of government demand it'.[671] Bell states that acquisitive prescription is required 'for the settling of men's minds and the encouragement of improvement.'[672] In relation to land, the operation of acquisitive prescription is considered to be very helpful as it simplifies the process of checking the validity of a title. In this regard, a recent decision of the European Court of Human Rights, which casts

---

[666] See above, paras 5.9.2 and 5.9.3.

[667] Prescription and Limitation (Scotland) Act 1973, ss. 1-3.

[668] Johnston, D, *Prescription and Limitation* (1999), chapter 14; Reid, *Property*, para 565; Carey Miller with Irvine, *Corporeal Moveables*, chapter 7.

[669] The text here relies on Johnston, *Prescription and Limitation*, chapter 1.

[670] Stair, II.12.1-10.

[671] Erskine, III.7.1.

[672] Bell, *Principles*, § 606.

doubt on the legality of prescription, causedconcern, but the subsequent contrary decision of the Grand Chamber provides some reassurance.[673]

In relation to moveables, the lack of a clear acquisitive prescription regime has not caused significant problems. This may be because of the well recognised presumption of ownership arising from the mere possession of a corporeal moveable.[674]

13.2. Requirements

There is a limited amount of institutional writing and old case law suggesting a forty-year acquisitive period for corporeal movables.[675] This is assessed in the standard text on corporeal moveables as follows:

> 'The case law applicable to a rule of acquisitive prescription based upon forty years' continuous possession of a moveable thing is hardly conclusive. At most it supports the possibility of such a rule. Given the institutional writer authority it would appear that there is support to a sufficient degree to enable a modern court to recognise a 40-year positive prescription rule of the common law. But the likelihood of judicial clarification cannot be high.'[676]

In the 1970s, the Scottish Law Commission proposed a five-year acquisitive period where possession is founded on an apparent title and obtained in good faith. It proposed a ten-year period where there had merely been open, peaceable and uninterrupted possession, adverse to the owner.[677] The proposals have never been implemented.

13.3. Negative prescription of ownership

Ownership of corporeal moveables is subject to a twenty-year period of negative prescription.[678] For prescription to run, the right must be unex-

---

[673] *J A Pye (Oxford) Ltd v United Kingdom* (2006) 43 EHRR 3 (European Court of Human Rights); (2008) 46 EHRR 45 (Grand Chamber). See G L Gretton, 'Private Law and Human Rights' (2008) 12 Edinburgh Law Review 109.

[674] See above, para 2.2.

[675] Notably, Stair, II.12.11; Bankton, II.12.1; Hume, *Lectures*, III, 228; *Parishioners of Aberscherder v Parish of Gemrie* (1633) Mor 10972 and *Ramsay v Wilson* (1666) Mor 9113.

[676] Carey Miller with Irvine, *Corporeal Moveables*, para 7.03.

[677] Scottish Law Commission, Consultative Memorandum No 30, 'Corporeal Moveables: Usucapion or Acquisitive Prescription', (1976).

[678] Prescription and Limitation (Scotland) Act 1973, s. 8.

ercised or unenforced and no relevant claim made in relation to it. However, where property has been stolen, prescription does not operate as against the thief or 'any person privy to the stealing'.[679] The result of negative prescription is that the real right of ownership is lost and the property falls to the Crown (the state) under the rule *quod nullius est fit domini regis*.[680] But in such circumstances, the Crown would require to rebut the presumption of ownership arising from possession.[681]

14. Other forms of original acquisition

14.1. Finding

It is not possible to acquire title to a moveable by merely finding it. If the property is ownerless, then a title can be required if the requirements for occupancy are satisfied. These are discussed below.[682] If the property is owned by another party, then their ownership in principle will be unaffected. Property which has been abandoned belongs to the Crown.[683]

There is, however, a set of statutory rules dealing with lost and abandoned property in the Civic Government (Scotland) Act 1982.[684] The finder has to take reasonable care of the property and must without reasonable delay report the finding or take the property to the police.[685] Normally, the police must keep the property for a minimum of two months.[686] If the property is not claimed within that period by the true owner, there a number of possibilities for its disposal including offering it to the finder or selling it. Where the property is given to the finder, the true owner may claim it back from him or her during the first year thereafter.[687] Where the property has been disposed of for value, the acquirer's title is unchallengeable. If, however, the net proceeds of sale exceed £100 the previous owner can make a compensation claim against the police for an amount no higher than the amount of the net proceeds of sale. This claim must be made within a year of the sale.[688]

---

[679] 1973 Act, Sch 3, para (g).
[680] Reid, *Property*, para 540.
[681] See above, para 2.2.
[682] See below, para 14.2.
[683] See below, para 16.1.
[684] See Reid, *Property*, paras 548-552.
[685] Civic Government (Scotland) Act 1982, s. 67.
[686] 1982 Act, s. 68(4).
[687] 1982 Act, s. 71(2).
[688] 1982 Act, s. 72.

14.2.   Occupatio

Where a piece of corporeal property is not already owned it can be acquired by occupation (*occupatio*). This is achieved by seizing hold of the property with the intention to become owner.[689] There is relatively little ownerless property. The main examples are shells, pearls, gems and pebbles on the sea-shore, running water and wild animals.[690] With an exception, occupation can only take place once. For example, once entered into a container, running water becomes owned. It can never be ownerless again. The exception concerns wild animals. If they regain liberty they become unowned once more.[691] Thus the mouse which escapes from its pursuer, Debbie, who managed to get hold of it temporarily under the cupboard in the kitchen, is no longer Debbie's property. The rule does not apply to farmed fish on the basis that they are not truly wild.[692] Animals which have freedom of movement but return to a particular place, such as bees and pigeons, remain owned provided that they continue to come back. Where game is seized illegitimately by poachers on someone else's land they will acquire a title by occupation, but this can be subsequently forfeited by a court.[693]

14.3.   Separation

In principle, separation of one piece of property from another does not affect the title.[694] For example, someone who removes an antique fireplace from a house does not become its owner. There is an exception for tenants who exercise the right to remove trade fixtures which they have installed.[695] On removal, the tenant reacquires ownership.

---

[689] In the words of the Latin maxim, *quod nullius est fit occupantis* (what belongs to no-one becomes the property of the taker). This right is a prerogative right of the Crown in respect of ownerless or unclaimed property. The right is preserved by Abolition of Feudal Tenure etc (Scotland) Act 2000, s. 58 (1) and (2)(b)(i).

[690] Reid, *Property*, paras 274 and 542.

[691] Erskine, II.1.10.

[692] *Valentine v Kennedy* 1985 SCCR 89.

[693] Reid, *Property*, para 545.

[694] Reid, *Property*, para 574.

[695] *Brand's Trustees v Brand's Trustees* (1876) 3 R (HL) 16.

Part IV:
Additional questions

15. Reservation of title

15.1. General

This chapter considers the position at common law, the position under the Sale of Goods Act, the problem of sham sales, and then the current law.

15.2. Common law

It has long been established that it is competent to insert a suspensive condition into a contract of sale of goods to delay the transfer of owner-ship to the purchaser.[696] Such a condition could relate to the passage of a specific period of time or the occurrence of a specified event, such as the payment of the price for the asset. The suspensive condition found in the contract of sale of corporeal moveables served to postpone the transfer of ownership until fulfilment of the condition. The consequence of this was that if the purchaser became insolvent the seller could reclaim the asset. A consistent line of case law dating back to the eighteenth century con-firms this.[697]

---

[696] Stair, I.14.4. See also Erskine, III.3.11.

[697] See *Macartney v Macredie's Creditors* (1799) Mor App Sale No 1 – the earliest re-ported case we have been able to trace where the sale of cattle was suspensive on a bill of exchange being honoured. The purchaser was sequestrated before the price was paid. See also *Cowan v Spence* (1824) 3 S (NE) 28; *Wright v Forman* (1828) 7 S 175; *Duncanson v Jeffer's Tr* (1881) 8 R 563; *Hogarth v Smart's Tr* (1882) 9 R 964; *Murdoch & Co Ltd v Greig* (1889) 16 R 396. The contrary decision of *Cropper v Donaldson* (1880) 7 R 1008 has been much criticised: see Gloag and Irvine, *Rights in Security*, p 242 and Carey Miller with Irvine, *Corporeal Moveables*, para 12.02, n 20 and text.

15.3.   The Sale of Goods Acts 1893 and 1979

15.3.1. Introduction

When the Sale of Goods Act 1893 was introduced to Scotland it was not
thought that this would have any impact on the law relating to suspensive
conditions – other than in the context of protection for third parties.[698]
    The rule providing that ownership passed when the parties intended it
to pass merely restated the common law position as to suspensive conditions relevant to the transfer of ownership.[699] Indeed this view was treated
as confirmed by Richard Brown due to the enactment of section 19(1) of
the 1893 Act which remains largely unchanged[700] in section 19(1) of the
1979 Act. Brown's analysis of this provision in 1895 was that it gave
'statutory sanction to conditions suspensive of the passing of property.'[701]
However, he identified one potential problem to validity introduced by
the 1893 Act: section 61(4) of the Act (now section 62(4) of the 1979
Act) prohibited sham sales.[702] This is now considered.

15.3.2. Sale of Goods Act 1979 section 62(4)

(a)   General

Section 62(4) applies throughout the United Kingdom,[703] but it is primarily of importance in Scotland as in England sales which are truly attempts
to create securities are regulated by the Bills of Sale Acts 1878 and 1882.
These statutes provided that if transactions that are truly securities are
not registered in England then the transaction is void.[704] Accordingly,
section 62(4) is simply one element in the regulation of security devices.
    This can be contrasted with Scottish law. Here there is no equivalent
to the Bills of Sale Acts. For a period after the passage of the Mercantile
Law Amendment Act Scotland 1856 the strict rules of Scottish law on
rights in security were ameliorated somewhat. That Act provided that

---

[698] Gloag and Irvine, *Rights in Security*, pp 243-244 and Brown, R, *Notes and Commentaries on the Sale of Goods Act 1893* (1895), at pp 83-84.

[699] Gloag and Irvine, *Rights in Security*, p 243 and Brown, *Sale of Goods Act 1893*, pp
83-84.

[700] Subject to minor amendments.

[701] Brown, *Sale of Goods Act 1893*, p 99 (see also pp 99-101 for general discussion).

[702] Brown, *Sale of Goods Act 1893*, p 84.

[703] As is apparent from the terminology used in the subsection as 'mortgage' and
'charge' are technical terms of English law.

[704] *North Central Wagon Finance Co Ltd v Brailsford* [1962] 1 WLR 1288.

where a seller had entered a contract to sell corporeal moveables to a purchaser while ownership of the assets passed only on delivery of the moveables to the purchaser, from the instant of conclusion of the contract the creditors of the seller could not attach the asset remaining in the possession of the seller. Whether this provision applied to sales which were truly securities was not clear until the House of Lords decision in *McBain v Wallace & Co.*[705] The House of Lords held that it was not necessary to consider the motives in entering the transaction and applied the 1856 Act to protect the purchaser.[706] *McBain* was applied to a number of transactions, although the judges[707] were somewhat uncomfortable in its application. In one case, *Allan & Co's Trustee v Gunn & Co*[708] Lord Rutherford Clark noted that,

'I fear great danger to the law in cases where parties resort to apparent transactions of sale in order to obtain a security which is not tolerated by the law of Scotland.'[709]

However, the 1856 Act was repealed by the Sale of Goods Act 1893 (now the 1979 Act). As well as repealing the 1856 Act, the 1893 Act contained section 61(4), now section 62(4) of the 1979 Act, which reversed *McBain v Wallace.*[710] The effect was that attention had to turn to the background common law which, as identified above, is that securities over corporeal moveables require the creditor to have possession of the moveable.[711] This mirrored the common law requirement of delivery as a prerequisite for transfer of ownership.[712] The conflict between the 1979 Act, which allows for transfer of ownership without the delivery of the assets to the purchaser, and the common law means that transaction structured as sales but truly securities may be ineffectual as a result of the combined operation of section 62(4) and the common law.

---

705 (1881) 8 R (HL) 106 affirming (1881) 8 R 360.

706 The Inner House had reached the same result on different grounds, the argument being primarily based on the nature of the asset not allowing practical delivery. A similar result was reached in the case of *Darling v Wilson's Tr* (1887) 15 R 10 where the assets were pipes running under a road.

707 With the notable exception of Lord Young. See Gow, J J, *The Mercantile and Industrial Law of Scotland* (1964), pp 94-95 for an indication of the polarisation of argument on the bench.

708 (1883) 10 R 997.

709 *Ibid* at 1000.

710 Brown, R, *Sale of Goods Act 1893*, (1895)p 282 and *Gavin's Tr v Fraser* 1920 SC 674.

711 Stair, I.13.14; Erskine, III.1.34 and Bell, *Commentaries*, II, 25.

712 See generally Carey Miller with Irvine, *Corporeal Moveables*, paras 8.12-8.27.

This places great importance in commercial transactions, for example, sale and lease-back arrangements and others, in determining when section 62(4) applies.

(b)   Application

There have been a number of cases since the passage of the 1893 Act where a transaction has been characterised as a 'sham' sale.[713] However, there are no clearly established criteria identifying when a transaction in the form of a sale is truly a security. Attempts to propose criteria have been made by Professor Gretton[714] and by Scott Styles.[715] However, these have not been tested judicially, and neither proposed solution fits the variety of cases that have been before the courts.

(c)   Consequences of the application of section 62(4)

Section 62(4) does not, of itself, render a 'sham' sale invalid. Its wording makes clear that the consequence of its application is that the 1979 Act does not apply to contracts of sale which are intended to be securities. Thus, if a transaction would have been valid at common law then it will be effective, irrespective of the application of section 62(4).

Such disputes as there were in the pre-1980s cases related to consideration of whether the common law allowed the creation of securities without possession. The consensus was that the creditor required to take possession.[716] It has been suggested by Professor Gretton that there is a difficulty inherent in the section: 'The subsection preserves the old law in relation to securities. But which old law? Common law? Or the amalgam

---

[713] See *Robertson v Hall's Trustee* (1896) 24 R 120, *Jones & Co's Trs v Allan* (1901) 4 F 374, *Rennet v Mathieson* (1903) 5 F 591, *Hepburn v Lee* 1914 1 SLT 228, *Gavin's Tr v Fraser* 1920 SC 674, *Newbigging v Ritchie's Tr* 1930 SC 273, *Scottish Transit Trust v Scottish Land Cultivators* 1955 SC 254 and *G & C Finance Corporation Ltd v Brown* 1961 SLT 408.

[714] Gretton, G L, 'The Concept of Security' in Cusine, D J (ed), *A Scots Conveyancing Miscellany: Essays in Honour of Professor J M Halliday* (1987), p 126 at 132-134.

[715] Styles, S C, 'Debtor-to-creditor sales and the Sale of Goods Act 1979', 1995 Juridical Review 365.

[716] Carey Miller with Irvine, *Corporeal Moveables*, para 11.14. The contrary view is associated particularly with Lord Young (see his dissenting judgments in *Jones & Co v Allan* (1901) 4 F 374 at 385 and *Rennet v Mathieson* (1903) 5 F 591 at 597-598). Lord Young's view is discussed by Professor Gretton in 'The Concept of Security' at 137.

of common law and statute that existed here in the interval between the Mercantile Law Amendment Act Scotland 1856 and the Sale of Goods Act 1893?'[717]

Professor Gretton suggests that the logical argument is that disapplication of the Sale of Goods Act revived the 1856 Act, which was repealed by the 1893 Act.[718] However, this argument is flawed in that the Interpretation Acts, most recently the Interpretation Act 1978, make clear that when a provision is repealed it is repealed for all purposes, irrespective of what happens to the repealing legislation.[719] The consequence then of the application of section 62(4) is that a contract for sale of corporeal moveables which is truly a security is not covered by the Sale of Goods Act 1979, but is instead covered by the common law.

(d) Common elements of section 62(4) cases before the retention of title cases

In drawing together the cases on section 62(4) it is difficult to discern clear principles which determine when a transaction was to be set aside as an intended security device rather than a sale. However, certain points emerge from the facts of the cases.

First, each sale struck down by section 62(4) or its predecessor involve a purported sale by the debtor to the creditor. The debtor then retained possession of the asset invalidating the transaction at common law if section 62(4) disapplied the Sale of Goods Act.

Secondly, in each case the court has taken the view that the funding for the transaction was a loan. This is the case either where the parties have stated in evidence or in the supporting documentation that the financing is a loan with interest payable; or where the transaction is structured in such a way that there is a *pactum de retrovendendo* where the original 'seller' does not merely have a right to reacquire the asset, but is under a legally enforceable obligation to do so – whatever the state of the asset at the time.

Thirdly, it appears that a sale and hire purchase back is challengeable because the hire purchase element, although not placing the original seller under an obligation to reacquire, gives him or her a right to reacquire that gives the expectation that there will be reacquisition (given

---

[717] Gretton, 'The Concept of Security' at 137.

[718] *Ibid.* This appears to be the import of Lord Young's decisions in the area. See the cases referred to in the note above.

[719] In *Gavin's Tr v Fraser* 1919 2 SLT 301 at 304 Lord Sands suggests 'There is a certain dialectical ingenuity in this argument, but I do not think that it is based upon sound principles of statutory construction.'

that the hire purchase payments will repay the loan element of the trans-action). This can be contrasted with the situation identified by Professor Gretton where there is a sale and lease-back or a sale and lease-back with an option to repurchase. In the former case he[720] and Bruce Wood[721] ar-gue that as there is no obligation to reacquire (and consequently no duty on the part of the creditor to account in the event of selling the goods to a third party) the transaction should be enforceable.[722] In the latter sce-nario Professor Gretton suggests the transaction should be valid given that the option to repurchase will usually require to be exercised at nearer market value than that payable as the final payment in a hire purchase transaction. In this case the hire payments do not serve to amortise the loan.[723]

Against this background it may have been thought unlikely that re-tention of title could test section 62(4). Such a transaction involves the creditor selling to the debtor, with no loan element. Further, as shown above the law had long recognised the idea of suspensive conditions post-poning the transfer of ownership of corporeal moveables. However, fol-lowing the *Romalpa* case in England[724] as retention of title became a common device in commercial transactions the Scottish courts took a surprising approach.

15.3.3. The retention of title cases in the 1980s

(a)   Introduction

Scotland introduced the floating charge in 1961 as a security effective over the entire asset base of a debtor company.[725] The rules of ranking for floating charges provided that where the charge contained a negative pledge clause[726] (as they invariably do) then the charge ranks ahead of any real rights in security created subsequent to the charge.[727] In order to trump the floating charge other creditors of the debtor company could not rely on

---

[720] Gretton, 'The Concept of Security' at 134.

[721] Wood, R B, 'Sale and Leaseback', (1982) 27 JLSS (Workshop) 267 at 286.

[722] The only Scottish case on the topic is a poorly argued Sheriff Court decision which is generally thought to be wrongly decided: *Wood v Gillies* (1904) 20 Sh Ct Rep 141.

[723] Gretton, 'The Concept of Security' at 135.

[724] *Aluminium Industrie Vaasen BV v Romalpa Aluminium Ltd* [1976] 2 All ER 552.

[725] Companies (Floating Charges) (Scotland) Act 1961.

[726] A clause whereby the debtor agrees either (a) not to grant any further securities affecting the same assets; or (b) that the floating charge will rank ahead of any se-curities created subsequent to it.

[727] Companies Act 1985, s. 464(1) and (1A).

making use of a real right in security because typically the debtor company's largest creditor, a bank, had a floating charge granted in its favour at an earlier stage. Accordingly, other creditors would make use of devices whereby ownership did not pass to the debtor company, for the floating charge could not attach assets that did not fall within the company patrimony. The consequence was an increase in use of retention of title clauses, particularly after the use of such clauses had been endorsed by the English courts in the *Romalpa* case.

The Scottish cases fall into two distinct categories: price only retention of title clauses; and all sums retention of title clauses.

(b)   Price only clauses

The courts found no difficulty with simple retention of title clauses where the parties agree that the transfer of ownership is suspended until payment of the purchase price. Such a clause was at issue in *Archivent Sales and Development Ltd v Strathclyde Regional Council*[728] and Lord Mayfield indicated the effect was that 'the goods remained the property of the seller [and] could have been reclaimed for the liquidator or receiver.'[729]

(c)   All sums clauses

The alternative is where the contract provides that ownership does not pass until all debts due from the purchaser to the seller are satisfied. This includes not just the cost of the assets but other sums. Such clauses are particularly useful to the seller where there is ongoing trade between seller and purchaser.

The courts in the 1980s did not view all sums retention of title clauses as suspensive conditions in the transfer of ownership. Instead, they were viewed as attempts to create securities without possession and accordingly affected by section 62(4) of the 1979 Act. The cases were primarily decided by the same judge, Lord Ross, initially as a Lord Ordinary and subsequently the Lord Justice-Clerk.[730] Academic commentary was critical of these decisions.[731]

---

[728] 1985 SLT 154. See above, para 5.9.2.

[729] 1985 SLT 154 at 156.

[730] The second most senior judge in the Scottish courts. The cases are the Outer House decisions of *Emerald Stainless Steel Ltd v South Side Distribution Ltd* 1982 SC 61 (considered in Reid, K G C and Gretton, G L, 'Retention of title in Romalpa clauses', 1983 SLT (News) 77, and 'Retention of title for all sums: a reply' 1983 SLT (News) 165; compare Smith, T B, 'Retention of title: Lord Watson's legacy', 1983 SLT

First, the prior authorities on section 62(4) did not deal with the situation where the transaction was a creditor to debtor sale. This in itself would not determine the question but is indicative that the cases expanded the prior case law.

Secondly, as Professors Reid and Gretton pointed out, where the transaction had elements of both sale and security, but there was discernible intention between the parties that there was a contract of sale then the functional security was incidental and section 62(4) did not apply.[732] The approach of the courts was to target the specific clause, the all sums retention of title clause, to determine if the transaction was a contract of sale or not. This approach, coupled with severing the clause in some cases as contravening section 62(4), did not sit with section 62(4) which required consideration of the transaction as a whole.

Thirdly, the sale does not involve a loan, the indebtedness 'secured' is typically from previous or subsequent transactions between seller and purchaser. There is no formal repayment mechanism or interest rate put in place.

Fourthly, the effect of application of section 62(4) is to disapply the Sales of Goods Act 1979 leaving reliance on the common law. The position under the common law was that ownership passed when there was delivery and the parties intended ownership to pass.[733] The effect of applying section 62(4) is not to assert a transfer of ownership from seller to purchaser unless the court also implied an intention to transfer on the seller. The seller's intention is clearly not to transfer in these cases.[734] Despite this the courts held that ownership had transferred. Such an approach did some violence to general proprietary principles.

(d)   *Armour v Thyssen*

The position, though, was clarified by *Armour v Thyssen* when that case reached the House of Lords.[735] In the Lords, the Court of Session cases on all sums clauses were overturned by a unanimous decision. Referring to the earlier case law Lord Keith noted that the use of suspensive condi-

---

(News) 105); *Deutz Engines Ltd v Terex Ltd* 1984 SLT 273 (considered in Gretton, G L and Reid, K G C, 'Romalpa clauses; the current position', 1985 SLT (News) 329) and the Second Division decision of *Armour v Thyssen* 1989 SLT 182.

[731] See the articles by Gretton and Reid in the previous note.

[732] Reid and Gretton, 'Retention of title for all sums: a reply', 1983 SLT (News) 165 at 166. This view is based on *Gavin's Tr v Fraser*.

[733] See above, para 5.4.

[734] See Carey Miller with Irvine, *Corporeal Moveables*, para 12.06, n 59.

[735] 1990 SLT 891.

tions in relation to transfer of ownership was well established in Scottish law.[736] Further the Lords noted two key elements in support of their decision. First, section 17 of the Sale of Goods Act 1979 expressly provides for the role of the contractual intention of the parties as a determining factor in the passing of ownership. Secondly, the scheme of the 1979 Act envisaged the possibility of retention of title clauses as the express wording of section 19 deals with the situation where there is a reserved right of disposal.

Additionally, the Lords were clear that an all sums retention of title clause was not a transaction struck at by section 62(4). As Lord Keith noted: 'Such a provision does in a sense give the seller security for the unpaid debts of the buyer. But it does so by way of a legitimate reservation of title, not by virtue of any right over his own property conferred by the buyer.'[737]

This blanket approval for all sums clauses is despite the rather unusual terms of the clause at issue which provided:

'(1) All goods delivered by us remain our property (goods remaining in our ownership) until all debts owed to us, including any balances existing at relevant times – due to us on any legal grounds – are settled. This also holds good if payments are made for the purpose of settlement of specially designated claims. *Debts owed to companies, being members of our combine, are deemed to be such debts.*' (emphasis added)

The sums due included debts owed to third parties to the transaction. This element was not commented on by the court.

(e)   Analysis

The effect of retention of title clauses following *Armour*, be they price only, all sums, or based on some other suspensive condition, is relevant to the intention to transfer ownership. Such a clause does not create a right in security, and while functionally it may give the seller a security, it does so through regulating the transfer of ownership. The retention of title clause is effective without any requirements for registration. Further, the specific rules of section 62(4) of the Sale of Goods Act 1979 which target sham sales do not apply to retention of title clauses.

The consequences of retention of title clauses in insolvency processes and debt enforcement proceedings are straightforward. Ordinarily in insolvency processes the insolvency affects all assets owned by the insolvent. If

---

[736] 1990 SLT 891 at 893.
[737] 1990 SLT 891 at 895.

the insolvent purchaser is subject to a retention of title clause the assets subject to the clause are not affected by the insolvency and can be reclaimed and repossessed by the seller.[738] This is the case in sequestrations, liquidations, and receiverships. Similarly diligence, the method of debt enforcement in Scotland, can only be carried out against assets owned by the debtor. If the purchaser owes money to a third party, the third party cannot attach the assets possessed by the purchaser although subject to a retention of title clause.

In the situation where the price has been partly paid and the purchaser becomes insolvent and the seller possesses the assets the seller will be obliged to account to the purchaser and the representatives in insolvency for the difference between the value of the repossessed assets and debt outstanding from purchaser to seller at the instant of insolvency.[739]

While there is protection for the seller in the insolvency of the purchaser the seller's protection is – to a degree – limited by general proprietary rules and the provisions of the Sale of Goods Act itself.

15.4.   Risks to the seller

15.4.1. Sale by buyer in possession

As is discussed elsewhere where in a sale of goods there is a buyer who has acquired possession of the assets from the seller – although ownership has not yet transferred to the buyer – the buyer in possession can in certain cases under section 25 of the Sale of Goods Act 1979 pass a good title to a third party purchaser or create an effective real right in security in favour of certain third parties.[740]

Thus, good faith purchasers from buyers holding assets subject to a retention of title clause acquire good title. This will extinguish the original seller's title – rendering the retention of title clause valueless.[741] Accordingly, in practice, a variety of techniques have been adopted by sellers to extend their protection from the risk of a sub-sale. Sellers have provided that the purchaser can resell as agent for the original seller; some have attempted to use trusts to provide that sale proceeds from any sub-sale by the buyer in possession are held in trust for the original seller.

---

[738] 1990 SLT 891 at 895. See St Clair and Drummond Young, *Corporate Insolvency*, para 14-03.

[739] St Clair and Drummond Young, *Corporate Insolvency*, para 14-03 argue this is based on the *condictio causa data non secuta*.

[740] See above, para 5.9.2. The leading case is *Thomas Graham and Sons v Glenrothes Development Corporation* 1967 SC 284.

[741] *Archivent Sales and Developments Ltd v Strathclyde Regional Council* 1985 SLT 154.

15.4.2. Loss of title by original acquisition

As well as the risk of subsequent sale by the original purchaser there are also risks arising from the application of proprietary principles. A retention of title clause will often be used in the context of sale and supply of goods to manufacturers. In these circumstances the intention is that the goods subject to clause will cease to exist through the application of accession, specification, or commixtion/confusion and that the original seller's right of ownership will be extinguished or otherwise affected. The detailed rules in relation to these doctrines are considered elsewhere.[742] However, in summary: (a) where corporeal moveables are subject to accession their identity may be subsumed into that of another asset – extinguishing the title of the accessory; (b) Where they are subject to specification and the manufacture of a new entity ownership of the original materials the manufacturer can acquire title; and (c) Where they are subject to commixtion/confusion the mixture is a new entity which is co-owned in *pro indiviso* shares by the owners of the constituent parts.

In order to deal with the risks parties occasionally use contractual terms to attempt to disapply or influence the application of the property principles. It is, however, problematic in principle for an expression of intention to influence the allocation of proprietary rights in such a context.

In one case it was suggested that the law of accession could be influenced by express wording of a retention of title clause[743] although this case is affected by considerations of international private law. This decision is contrary to other authorities such as *Shetland Islands Council v BP Petroleum Development*[744] where it was held that an express contractual provision could not influence the mechanical application of accession. A similar view is given in another retention of title case, later overruled on other grounds.[745]

It appears then that the law of accession certainly cannot be circumvented by a retention of title clause. Similarly, specification probably cannot be affected by such a clause, but there is a contrary line of argument. This is because the application of specification is arguably based on the allocation of property rights 'where there has been no prior determination as to how rights are to be allocated'.[746] If the parties have indeed

---

[742] See above, paras 11.1-11.3.

[743] *Zahnrad Fabrik Passau GmbH v Terex Ltd* 1985 SC 364. See North, P M and Fawcett, J J, *Cheshire and North's Private International Law* (13th ed, 1999), pp 947-948.

[744] 1990 SLT 82.

[745] *Deutz Engines Ltd v Terex Ltd* 1984 SLT 273 at 274-275 *per* Lord Ross mentioned by Carey Miller with Irvine, *Corporeal Moveables*, para 12.14.

[746] Carey Miller with Irvine, *Corporeal Moveables*, para 12.15.

made such a determination (or at least purported to do so), it may follow that the law should give effect to this determination. There is no case law on this to date.

15.5. Protections beyond reservation of title

15.5.1. Trusts

(a) Rationale

Where a seller is concerned that the purchaser may sell on the corporeal moveables he or she may attempt to provide within the original contract that the proceeds of any subsequent sale are to be held in trust by the original purchaser for the benefit of the seller. A trust is used because in the insolvency of the original purchaser assets held in trust are protected. Trust property is held in a separate patrimony. While trustee the original purchaser is the owner of the assets held in trust. As the assets, however, are held on account for a third party they are exempt in the original purchaser's insolvency.[747]

(b) Mechanics

As a result of this trusts are occasionally used to circumvent the restrictions on the grant of securities over corporeal moveables and incorporeal moveables. Where they are used as commercial securities the practice tends to involve the debtor declaring that assets they own are now to be held in trust for the creditor. Such a trust is sometimes referred to as a 'truster-as-trustee trust'. They require the truster[748] to make a declaration of trust[749] which is to be in writing.[750] The declaration of trust is to iden-

---

[747] The rule stated here is found in various places: *Heritable Reversionary Co Ltd v Millar* (1892) 19 R (HL) 43 provided that assets held in a latent trust were protected in the personal insolvency of the trustee. A similar result is reached in *Bank of Scotland v Liquidator of Hutchison, Main & Co* 1914 SC (HL) 1 in the context of corporate insolvency. The rule on personal insolvency is now statutory: Bankruptcy (Scotland) Act 1985, s. 33(1)(b).

[748] The person creating the trust.

[749] The formal statement by the truster, the person who establishes the trust, that the trust is created.

[750] Requirements of Writing (Scotland) Act 1995, s. 1(2)(a)(iii).

tify the trustee[751] (in such cases the trustee is also the truster) and the trust purposes.[752] In order to effectively constitute the trust, and to transfer assets into the separate and protected trust patrimony, the truster/trustee requires to intimate the declaration of trust to the beneficiary,[753] in these cases the creditor.[754]

(c) Case law

The courts have been equivocal on trusts as commercial securities[755] with decisions in favour[756] and against,[757] sometimes decisions turning on practical issues within the case[758] rather than on points of principle.

There has only been one reported instance of an express trust in the context of retention of title, and this case is viewed by Wilson and Duncan as the leading decision in the area of trusts as commercial securities:[759] *Clark Taylor & Co Ltd v Quality Site Development (Edinburgh) Ltd.*[760] There was a retention of title clause which was buttressed by a trust clause which provided:

'(b) In the event of the buyer reselling or otherwise disposing of the goods or any part thereof before the property therein has passed to him by virtue of Clause 11 (a) hereof then the buyer will, until payment in full to the seller of the price of goods, hold in trust for the seller all his rights under such contract of resale or any other contract in pursuance of which the goods or any part thereof are disposed of or any contract by which property comprising the said goods or any part thereof is or is to be disposed of and any money or other consideration received by him thereunder.'

---

[751] The person who holds the trust assets and has to administer the assets in accordance with the purposes of the trust.

[752] The basis upon which the assets are to be held in trust.

[753] The person for whom the trust assets are held.

[754] *Allan's Trs v Lord Advocate* 1971 SC (HL) 45.

[755] See Gretton, G L, 'Using Trusts as Commercial Securities', (1988) 33 JLSS 53 and Wilson, W A and Duncan, A G M, *Trusts, Trustees, and Executors* (1995), chapter 4.

[756] *Tay Valley Joinery Ltd v CF Financial Services Ltd* 1987 SLT 207.

[757] *Export Credit Guarantee Department v Turner* 1981 SLT 286.

[758] *Tay Valley* turns on the underlying contract being written under English law justifying – in the view of the court – a liberal view of trust creation; *Export Credits* turned on the practice of intimation of the declaration of trust and trust assets.

[759] Wilson and Duncan, *Trusts, Trustees and Executors*, para 4-06.

[760] 1981 SC 111.

The case went to the First Division of the Court of Session to consider the efficacy of the clause. It was held that it failed for a number of reasons.

The first problem was that the clause did not validly create a trust. The clause was not effective as a declaration of trust as it did not confer beneficial interest in relation to any identifiable fund.[761] Instead at best it could be interpreted as imposing a contractual obligation on the purchaser to create a trust which suggests is not possible to have the declaration of trust as an adjunct to the retention of title clause.[762] The purchaser is truster and trustee and can only be contractually bound to act.[763] If the seller is concerned about protecting his or her position the purchaser's role in establishing the trust is not welcome.

An alternative approach would be to transfer ownership subject to a resolutive condition providing for cancellation of the sale and consequent reversion of ownership to the seller if the purchaser does not create a trust over the goods for the benefit of the seller within a short time period. This, however, runs the risk that the transaction may be challenged as a fraudulent transaction or unfair preference.[764] While the purchaser will be able to confer an absolutely good title on third party purchasers (whether or not they are aware of the trust),[765] the original seller will probably still have a claim on the funds obtained by the original purchaser for any subsequent sale.[766]

---

[761] While the case has been criticised by Professor Reid, 'Trusts and Floating Charges', 1987 SLT (News) 113, and Professor Wilson, 'Romalpa and Trust', 1983 SLT (News) 106 it has not been overruled (although the *Tay Valley Joinery v CF Financial Services Ltd* 1987 SLT 207 case approves the wording of a style drafted by Professor J M Halliday, *Conveyancing Law and Practice*, Vol I (1985), pp 284-294 which is virtually identical to that disapproved in *Clark Taylor*).

[762] Although compare *Tay Valley Joinery Ltd v CF Financial Services Ltd* 1987 SLT 207.

[763] See Carey Miller with Irvine, *Corporeal Moveables*, para 12-10.

[764] See above, para 9.1.

[765] This is the effect of Trusts (Scotland) Act 1961, s. 2 which provides that where a sale is made or security granted by trustees in breach of trust a third party dealing with the trustee obtains an unchallengeable right.

[766] *Jopp v Johnston's Tr* (1904) 6 F 1028 confirms that where assets held in trust are sold, the proceeds when placed in the trustee's account and mixed with the trustee's personal assets can be vindicated by the beneficiary, even to the extent that withdrawals from the funds are attributed to the trustee's personal assets rather than being attributed to the trust property. This is discussed by Carey Miller with Irvine, *Corporeal Moveables*, para 12.13 and Wilson and Duncan, *Trusts, Trustees and Executors*, para 10.10.

Secondly, there is a repugnancy if the contract both reserves title and purports to create a trust. Reservation of title means the seller retains ownership. Declaration of trust implies that ownership has transferred.[767]

Thirdly, in *Clark Taylor* itself while the basis of the decision lay in the lack of beneficial interest the First Division indicated some concern with the use of trusts to circumvent the usual rules applicable in insolvency processes.

The policy concern that trusts circumvent insolvency rules and the general publicity principle has attracted some academic support[768] and recently led to the Scottish Law Commission to consider whether truster as trustee trusts should be permitted at all and if permitted whether they should be registered.[769]

15.5.2. Agency

An alternative approach for the seller is to permit the purchaser to sell the goods on to third parties, but to provide expressly that in any subsequent sale by the original purchaser the purchaser is acting as agent for the original seller. There is no Scottish case law on this as yet, but such an action would arguably serve to protect the seller through the doctrine of constructive trusts.[770] The proceeds of sale, even if intermingled with the personal assets of the original purchaser/agent would still be subject to claim by the original seller/principal.[771]

Where a purchaser owes fiduciary obligations, under the law of trusts or the law of agency, in the event of sale the proceeds are thought to be held in constructive trust for the creditor in the fiduciary obligation (in this case the original seller).[772] It is not clear how the policy considerations which influenced the court in relation to *Clark Taylor* apply in the context of constructive trusts, and it should be noted that generally the Scottish courts are not in favour of constructive trusts.[773]

---

[767] *Glen v Gilbey Vintners Ltd* 1986 SLT 553 suggests as much.

[768] Reid, K G C, 'National Report for Scotland' in Hayton, D J, Kortmann, S C J J and Verhagen, H L E, *Principles of European Trust Law* (1999), p 67 at 79-82, Wilson and Duncan, *Trusts, Trustees and Executors*, chapter 4, and Gretton, 'Using Trusts as Commercial Securities'.

[769] Scottish Law Commission, 'Discussion Paper on the Nature and the Constitution of Trusts', (Scot Law Com Disc Paper No 133, 2006), paras 4.16-4.21.

[770] On which see Gretton, G L, 'Constructive Trusts', (1997) 1 Edinburgh Law Review 281 and 408 for the fullest modern treatment.

[771] *Jopp v Johnston's Tr* (1904) 6 F 1028.

[772] See *Michelin Tyre Co Ltd v Macfarlane (Glasgow) Ltd* 1917 2 SLT 205.

[773] In two cases subsequent to the publication of Professor Gretton's 'Constructive Trusts' senior Court of Session judges expressed discomfort with constructive trusts. See *Bank*

16.   Abandonment; further ways to lose property

16.1.   Abandonment

Ownership of moveables may be lost by abandonment.[774] This requires a specific intention to abandon the property. Merely temporarily mislaying it is not sufficient. Intention will be clear in some cases and not so clear in others. For example, someone discarding property from a boat into the sea obviously intends to abandon it. Someone, however, who has lost a golf ball but intends to come back at some point in the future to look for it, can be regarded differently. The rule is that abandoned property falls to the Crown *i.e.* the state.[775] This includes hidden treasure.[776] Where abandoned property is taken without the Crown's permission, this is theft.[777] The abandonment of dangerous or noxious substances is subject to statutory controls. For example, the disposal of radioactive substances requires an authorisation from the Scottish Environmental Protection Agency,[778] and the discharge of trade effluent requires the consent of Scottish Water.[779] Hazardous waste, known as 'special waste' in Scotland, must be disposed of in a manner prescribed by legislation.[780]

16.2.   Destruction

Where a moveable is physically destroyed, naturally any rights in it are extinguished.[781]

---

of *Scotland v MacLeod Paxton Woolard & Co* 1998 SLT 258 at 274 *per* Lord Coulsfield and *Mortgage Corporation v Mitchells Roberton* 1997 SLT 1305 at 1310 *per* Lord Johnston.

[774] Reid, *Property*, para 568.

[775] Reid, *Property*, para 547. This rule was not altered by the recent abolition of the feudal system. See Carey Miller with Irvine, *Corporeal Moveables*, para 1.06.

[776] Carey Miller with Irvine, *Corporeal Moveables*, para 2.06. See *Lord Advocate v Aberdeen University and Budge* 1963 SC 533.

[777] *Mackenzie v Maclean* 1981 SLT (Sh Ct) 40.

[778] Radioactive Substances Act 1993, s. 13.

[779] Sewerage (Scotland) Act 1968, s. 26.

[780] Special waste equates to anything classified as 'hazardous' under the Hazardous Waste Directive (91/689/EEC), article 1(4). The relevant legislation in Scotland is found in the Special Waste Regulations 1996, the Special Waste Amendment (Scotland) Regulations 2004 and the Special Waste Amendment (Scotland) Amendment Regulations 2004, while guidance on the consignment of special waste can be found at http://www.sepa.org.uk/guidance/waste/amendment_faq.htm.

[781] Reid, *Property*, para 568.

17.   Co-ownership

17.1.   Introduction

Scotland's unified system of property law[782] means that while in many areas there are special rules which apply to corporeal moveables, in the law of co-ownership there is no special regime. There has been very little litigation here. Most case law relates to land, and this focus is shared by academic commentators. Accordingly, in this section many of the cases and writings referred to relate to co-ownership of land.

Ownership is unititular in that there can be only one real right of ownership in any one asset at any one time.[783] However, it is permissible for ownership to be shared by two or more parties. This is co-ownership. The shares can be unequal in size,[784] and are not attributed to specific parts of the asset. Hence, a car held by two parties, A and B, is not held with A having ownership of the front wheels, the doors, and the engine, and B having ownership of the rear wheels and the chassis. The ownership of every part of the car is shared by A and B. As Lord President Dunedin put it: 'The position of [co-ownership] is very peculiar, because all the owners hold together in common, and they have, if I may so express it, a metaphysical right in every minutest atom of which the property is composed.'[785]

17.2.   The division of co-ownership

Co-ownership can be viewed as the generic term (although sometimes the expression '*pro indiviso* ownership' is used)[786] and in holding corporeal moveables there are two categories of co-ownership: common ownership; and joint ownership. The terminology was though only clarified relatively recently,[787] and it is not uncommon for practitioners, and individuals, to refer

---

[782] See above, para 1.1.3(a).

[783] The leading modern judicial statement is found in the judgment of Lord President Hope in *Sharp v Thomson* 1995 SC 455 at 469.

[784] As is implicit in the decision of the House of Lords endorsing a Whole Court decision in *Menzies v Macdonald* (1856) 2 Macq 463, affirming (1854) 16 D 827 which permitted unrestricted subdivision of an individual co-owner's share.

[785] *Grant v Heriot's Trust* (1906) 8 F 647 at 658.

[786] Reid, *Property*, para 17. Historically other terms were used by institutional writers including 'conjunct ownership' by Erskine, III.8.4 and 'part ownership' by Bell, *Commentaries*, II, 54.

[787] *Magistrates of Banff v Ruthin Castle Ltd* 1944 SC 36 at 68-69 (*per* Lord Justice Clerk Cooper) quoting a passage which was (and still is) in a leading textbook: Gloag, W M

to those holding in common ownership as 'joint owners'.[788] Indeed, in various pieces of documentation produced by the Scottish Executive the expression 'joint owners' is used when referring to owners in common.[789]

17.3. Common ownership

Common ownership is the normal instance of co-ownership. In common ownership there are certain fundamental principles:[790] *in re communi melior est conditio prohibentis* (he who vetoes is in the stronger position);[791] *in communionem vel societam nemo compellitur detineri* (no-one can be compelled to remain in a communion of property against his will);[792] and any co-owner can deal with his or her undivided share independently from the others.[793] Each principle has a role in questions of transfer and the grant of subordinate real rights over corporeal moveable assets.

Common to the principles are the ideas of freedom and individualism. Despite common ownership necessarily involving the co-operation of two or more individuals there is protection for the individual common owner through the use of a veto in relation to certain actions. A common owner has an identifiable share of ownership. This individual share in ownership is treated in some respects as severable from the interests of the other co-owners. For example, the common owner is not bound to take account of the other co-owners in actions relating to transfer (which is discussed in more detail later). He or she is free to escape from co-ownership by independent dealing with his or her share; and is free to dissolve the co-ownership through calling for division of the asset.

---

and Henderson, R C, *Introduction to the Law of Scotland* (1939) at pp 489-490. The text is in the most recent (12ᵗʰ) edition (2007) at para 35.43. Lord Cooper's view was not endorsed by the other member of the court but has been adopted by later commentators: Smith, *A Short Commentary on the Law of Scotland* (1962), pp 479-481; Gordon, *Scottish Land Law*, paras 15-10-15-11; Reid, *Property*, paras 19 and 20.

[788] See Reid, *Property*, para 17; Kleyn, D G and Wortley, S, 'Co-ownership' in Zimmermann, Visser & Reid, *Mixed Legal Systems*, pp 708-712.

[789] For example, see a public information booklet on *Housing Grants: An Applicant's Guide to Improvement and Repair Grants for Private Housing* (2003) at 12 and 13 http://www.scotland.gov.uk/Resource/Doc/47176/0028734.pdf.

[790] This follows the discussion by Kleyn and Wortley, 'Co-ownership', 706, nn 14-16 where civilian and *jus commune* derivations are considered.

[791] Bell, *Principles*, § 1075.

[792] *Brock v Hamilton* (1852) 9 D 701 at 703.

[793] *Clydesdale Bank plc v Davidson* 1998 SC (HL) 51 at 60B.

17.4. Joint ownership

This freedom can be contrasted with joint ownership. Joint ownership arises in only limited circumstances: trusts[794] and unincorporated associations (clubs).[795] A reference in the leading judicial statement on the binary nature of Scottish co-ownership, *Magistrates of Banff v Ruthin Castle Ltd*, to property held by a partnership being an instance of joint property[796] is inaccurate as in Scotland a partnership agreement (*societas*) creates a firm, which has a separate juristic personality and so owns property in its own name.[797]

The instances of joint ownership share two principal characteristics: there is an external relationship independent to that of mere co-ownership; and the property is held by the owners for the benefit of others and consequently they do not have independent interests. In a trust the trustees are owners of the property,[798] although their ownership is for the benefit of the beneficiaries of the trust. In an unincorporated association the members hold the property for themselves and for other members.[799] There are no separate severable shares in joint ownership. As Lord Justice-Clerk Hope stated:

---

[794] See *Gracie v Gracie* 1910 SC 899 at 904 (*per* Lord Kinnear) and Wilson, W A and Duncan, A G M, *Trusts, Trustees and Executors* (2nd ed, 1995), para 1-66.

[795] Unlike some jurisdictions there are no formal rules of community of property in marriage although there is a presumption of co-ownership between husband and wife or civil partners (under Family Law (Scotland) Act 1985, s. 25) or cohabitants – be they heterosexual or same-sex cohabitants (under Family Law (Scotland) Act 2006, s. 26) in household goods which are defined in each Act as 'any goods (including decorative or ornamental goods) kept or used at any time during the [relevant relationship's] home for the joint domestic purposes of the parties to the [relationship], other than – (a) money or securities; (b) any motor car, caravan or other road vehicle; (c) any domestic animal.'

[796] *Magistrates of Banff v Ruthin Castle Ltd* 1944 SC 3 at 68 *per* Lord Justice-Clerk Cooper.

[797] Partnership Act 1890, s. 4(2).

[798] *Inland Revenue v Clark's Trustees* 1939 SC 11 is probably the leading case here (see Lord Moncrieff at 26) and the position is confirmed by Lord President Hope in *Sharp v Thomson* 1995 SC 455, at 475. The matter is, though, not fully developed by the Scottish courts. See for example Gretton, G L, 'Trust and Patrimony' in MacQueen, H L (ed), *Scots Law into the 21st Century: Essays in Honour of W A. Wilson* (1996), p 182.

[799] *Murray v Johnstone* (1896) 23 R 981 is the leading case on club property. It is not wholly clear.

'There is no such thing as a separate but *pro indiviso* right ... in each trustee. Each has the full title along with the other ... and if they die, his title carries the whole right, to the exclusion of any others.'[800]

Sometimes the title held by joint owners is described as 'elastic'.[801] The effect is that where moveable property is held on trust or owned by the members of a club then changes in the trustees or in membership of the club do not require conveyances for implementation. If a trustee resigns from a trust, or a club member resigns from a club, he or she does not need to convey the property to the remaining trustees or members. Instead the title contracts automatically.[802] The position is similar if a trustee or club member dies.[803]

It is thought that the rule for new club members joining a club or new trustees being appointed is similar in effect. Thus, when a person joins a club he or she automatically becomes a joint owner of the club property without requiring any conveyance in his or her favour.[804] For trustees the position is thought to be the same for corporeal moveable property[805] although the statutory deed used for the appointment of new trustees and the confirmation of their appointment incorporates an express conveyance of the trust property.[806] Whatever the position regarding moveables it is arguable that for immoveable property registration requirements require satisfaction.[807]

17.5.   Rules on transfer and grant of rights

17.5.1. General

Given the distinction between common and joint property in that the former has discrete severable shares and the latter involves a unified title there is a difference of approach for each.[808] In this section juristic acts affecting the co-owned property are considered. The expression 'juristic

---

[800] *Gordon's Trs v Eglinton* (1851) 13 D 1381 at 1385.

[801] *Dalgleish v Land Feuing Co Ltd* (1885) 13 R 223 at 230 and 231 *per* Lord Shand.

[802] See Trusts (Scotland) Act 1921, s. 20 (although this simply restates the common law position from *Dalgleish, ibid*) and *Murray v Johnstone* (1896) 23 R 981.

[803] See, for example, *Oswald's Trs v City of Glasgow Bank* (1879) 6 R 461 and *Murray v Johnstone* (1896) 23 R 981.

[804] *Murray v Johnstone* (1896) 23 R 981.

[805] See, for example, *Dalgleish v Land Feuing Co Ltd* (1885) 13 R 223 at 228 (*per* Lord Mure) and at 229 (*per* Lord Shand).

[806] Trusts (Scotland) Act 1921, s. 21, Sch B.

[807] See Reid, *Property*, para 35, n 9.

[808] This section is based on Kleyn and Wortley, 'Co-ownership' at 719-723.

acts' is used to encompass both voluntary and involuntary transfers of ownership, and the creation of subordinate or limited real rights voluntarily and involuntarily. Aside from the specialities noted below there are no special rules.

17.5.2. Common property

It has been stated that a common owner is as entitled to deal with his or her *pro indiviso* share as with any other asset.[809] However, co-ownership necessarily restricts the extent of dealing in certain ways. This is apparent when one considers the distinction between those acts which affect a co-owned asset as a whole, and those affecting individual shares. The latter is considered first.

In common property a common owner is entitled to alienate his or her undivided share by *inter vivos* transfer, or *mortis causa* on intestate or testate succession.[810] The generally applicable rules for transfer apply to the common owner's transfer of an individual share.[811] Alienation includes subdivision as well as outright transfer, and case law relating to immoveables suggests that subdivision of the share is permitted without restriction,[812] even where it has an impact on the extent to which any co-owner can use the property.[813] It was suggested by a judge in the minority in the leading case on the topic that to permit subdivision of a share while retaining a share of ownership that permitted use of the co-owned property was inequitable.[814]

While it is clear that unrestricted subdivision is permissible for immoveable property there is no case law for corporeal moveable property. It has been suggested that a practical limit on the number of potential common owners will arise given that co-ownership entitles the common owner to make use of the asset.[815] However, it is also acknowledged that where the co-ownership is for investment with an informal agreement between the parties limiting use then 'a physically small object may be subject to the co-ownership of a large number of parties'.[816] Alienation and subdivision are not the only actions permitted to individual common

---

[809] Reid, *Property*, para 28.

[810] Reid, *Property*, para 28; and Bell, *Principles*, § 1073.

[811] See above, chapter 5.

[812] This point is clarified by the majority in *Menzies v Macdonald* (1854) 16 D 827 aff'd (1856) 2 Macq 463.

[813] *Ibid per* Lord Deas (a judge in the minority).

[814] *Ibid* at 836 *per* Lord Justice Clerk Hope.

[815] Carey Miller with Irvine, *Corporeal Moveables*, para 1-14.

[816] *Ibid*.

owners in respect of their shares. They can create limited real rights provided that there is no immediate entitlement in the holder to use or possess the whole of the property. A share can be encumbered by a non-
possessory security be it created expressly,[817] tacitly,[818] or judicially.[819]

Where a juristic act is intended to affect the whole of commonly
owned property then the consent of each common owner is required. It is
possible to distinguish two situations: where the act relates to a right
which can also be granted in respect of an undivided share (sales and
non-possessory securities); and where the act concerns a right which can
have legal effect only if granted in respect of the whole property (where
the right involves conferring possession on the third party).

In the former case if the grantee in the juristic act does not attain the
consent of all co-owners, the act is still legally effective in relation to
those common owners that have assented to the act. For example, C
wishes to acquire ownership of a racing pigeon co-owned by A and B. If
only A assents to the transfer then it is thought that C will simply acquire
A's share.[820] B's share will not have transferred to C. The position is the
same for non-possessory securities where there is authority in relation to
immoveable property.[821]

In the latter case a common owner cannot act unilaterally. This is because the nature of the juristic act is such that it necessarily affects the
co-owned property as an entity. For example, the grant of a pledge over a
corporeal moveable requires exclusive possession of the asset to be given
to the creditor.[822] It is suggested by Kleyn and Wortley that similarly no
individual co-owner could grant a proper liferent (usufruct).[823]

---

[817] *Schaw v Black* (1889) 16 R 326.

[818] The tacit security would be the landlord's hypothec. There is no case law on the
question.

[819] Judicial securities are created by the court allowing a creditor to enforce a debt
through diligence. For authorities see Bell, *Principles*, § 1073; Debt Arrangement
and Attachment (Scotland) Act 2002, s. 35 (for attachment of corporeal moveables).

[820] Although C's position may be that C does not even acquire a share of ownership,
depending on the view of the abstract theory of transfer. If C is looking to acquire
the whole property, but only A has agreed to the transfer, A is only intending to
transfer A's own share. Does this preclude C from acquiring ownership of that
share, as the intentions of transferor and transferee do not coincide?

[821] See *McLeod v Cedar Holdings Ltd* 1989 SLT 620, although compare *Michael v
Carruthers* 1998 SLT 1179.

[822] Reid, *Property*, para 28.

[823] Kleyn and Wortley, 'Co-ownership' at 723.

17.5.3. Joint property

For joint property there are no severable identifiable shares. It is not possible for an individual joint owner to transfer the property.[824] Instead the joint owners can only transfer the property or grant limited real rights over it by acting as a whole. Generally in joint property the terms of the external relationship set out rules of management. For example, the constitution of a club may establish that a two thirds majority can decide to act in relation to club property. Or a deed of trust may provide that a simple majority of trustees can act in relation to trust assets. Where the provisions of the external relationship are clear they will govern in relation to decision making. However, Professor Reid points out that even where these rules permit for majority rule in decision making 'it does not necessarily follow that a simple majority suffices for the juristic act'.[825]

Further, there are complications if the trustees or club members act in breach of the trust or of the club constitution. In such cases with clubs it is necessary for the third party acquiring the asset or right over the asset to have the assent of all club members.[826] In trusts the position is complicated in that a third party acquiring the property or a limited real right over the property can rely on section 2 of the Trusts (Scotland) Act 1961. This is a peculiar provision the effect of which is that certain grantees, either purchasers or creditors in a security, from trustees can acquire an unchallengeable title (or security) even if in bad faith where the terms of the trust have not been complied with.

However, it is not clear from this provision or from the distinction that Professor Reid draws between decision making and implementation by the juristic act when a third party grantee can be satisfied that trustees or club members are in a position to transfer ownership or to grant a right in security. How does a third party determine which joint owners must assent to the performance of the juristic act?

Section 7 of the Trusts (Scotland) Act 1921 appears to suggest that provided a quorum of trustees, normally a majority, have executed a deed (a written document implementing a juristic act) then it cannot be challenged if a third party is in good faith and unaware of any procedural irregularity. Although as Professor Reid notes, 'The true meaning and effect of section 7 is problematic.'[827] Such cases as there are relate to immoveables and there is no clear position.[828] Given the uncertainty in

---

[824] *Livingstone v Allan* (1900) 3 F 233.

[825] Reid, *Property*, para 36.

[826] *Murray v Johnstone* (1896) 23 R 981 at 990 *per* Lord Moncreiff.

[827] Reid, *Property*, para 36, n 8.

[828] The relevant cases predate s. 7 of the Trusts (Scotland) Act 1921. See Wilson and Duncan, *Trusts, Trustees and Executors*, paras 23-21–23-25. The leading case is *Harland*

the law it appears that in practice advice is to seek the assent of all joint owners for implementation of the juristic act.[829]

17.6. Termination

17.6.1. General

Again the position differs for common and joint property. Each is considered separately.

17.6.2. Common property

(a)   Introduction

Common owners are not obliged to work together where relations between them have broken down. Each is given an escape route either through the transfer of an individual share, although the market is limited and this has little practical utility; or through the entitlement a remedy based on the *actio communi dividundo*.[830] This remedy is the action of division or action of division and[831] sale[832] which provides for physical division of the common property, or, where physical division is not possible, sale of the asset and subsequent division of the proceeds.

(b)   Division

A common owner has an almost absolute entitlement to apply for division.[833] The courts do not allow consideration of equitable factors in determining whether or not to grant an action of division and sale.[834] In certain cases the entitlement to division of common property is qualified. The restrictions relevant to corporeal moveables are where: there is a

---

Engineering Co v Stark's Trs 1913 2 SLT 448, 1914 2 SLT 292. The Lord Ordinary (Ormidale) held that majority rule sufficed. His view was doubted by the Inner House judges, although the appeal related to the question of expenses only.

[829] Reid, *Property*, para 36.

[830] *Brock v Hamilton* (1857) 19 D 701.

[831] Sometimes 'or'.

[832] See Reid, *Property*, paras 32-33.

[833] *Upper Crathes Fishings Ltd v Bailey's Exrs* 1991 SLT 747 and authorities in Reid, *Property*, para 32.

[834] *Upper Crathes Fishings Ltd v Bailey's Exrs* 1991 SLT 747.

temporary[835] contractual agreement between the parties;[836] a co-owner being personally barred by his or her conduct from pursuing an action of division;[837] or where the common property is 'a thing of common and indispensable use'.[838]

When any common owner raises an action of division and sale and the qualifications are not relevant then there are two possible disposals that may be sought: either physical division; or sale and division of the proceeds. In the latter case it appears there are two possibilities: either a public auction[839] or by private agreement. A third possibility, a closed auction involving only the common owners, has proved controversial and is considered below.

The default position is that the appropriate disposal of an action for division and sale will be physical division.[840] This will be appropriate in only limited cases where physical division will not destroy the asset, nor diminish its value. Often physical division is wholly inappropriate. Commonly owned individual assets such as items of furniture or paintings cannot be cut in two or more shares without destroying the essence of the asset. Further even where there is a group of assets (six Chippendale chairs, for example) breaking up the set of assets into three for each common owner will greatly reduce the value of the chairs.

The courts have proposed some rules to determine whether physical division is appropriate. In *Thom v Macbeth*[841] it was suggested that initially the court will consider if physical division is possible in a way that gives each co-owner an appropriate share. If it is, the court then considers if division is reasonably practicable without sacrificing to an appreciable extent the interests of some or all of the parties.[842] The effect is to ask, would physical division of the thing greatly diminish its value? Such a

---

[835] *Grant v Heriot's Trust* (1906) 8 F 647.

[836] *Upper Crathes Fishings Ltd v Bailey's Exrs* 1991 SCLR 151 at 152 *per* Lord President Hope; *Burrows v Burrows* 1996 SLT 1313; and *Bush v Bush* 2000 SLT (Sh Ct) 22 (where it was held that a contract had not been entered into to deprive the pursuer of the entitlement to an action for division and sale). Such a contractual agreement would not bind singular successors of the common owners.

[837] *Upper Crathes Fishings Ltd v Bailey's Exrs* 1991 SCLR 151 and *Bush v Bush* 2000 SLT (Sh Ct) 22. For the requirements of personal bar, see Reid, E, 'Personal bar: case-law in search of analysis', (2003) 7 Edinburgh Law Review 340. Again this would not bind singular successors of the common owners.

[838] Bell, *Principles*, § 1082 discussed in *Rafique v Amin* 1997 SLT 1385 at 1388A. The examples all concern immoveable property.

[839] Called a 'roup' in Scotland.

[840] Reid, *Property*, para 33.

[841] (1875) 3 R 161.

[842] *Ibid* at 164 *per* Lord Justice-Clerk Moncreiff.

test can be applied in varying contexts. Professor Reid suggests that 'in the typical case common property is not divisible'.[843]

If physical division is not possible the court will order sale. This may be by public auction or by private bargain.[844] Once the property is sold, usually to a third party, the proceeds are divided among the co-owners.

(c) Buying out the other common owner

However, an alternative is suggested by the institutional writers[845] in indicating that any one of the common owners may be able to acquire the property by buying the share(s) of the other(s). This approach was approved by the court in the 1780s[846] although was not judicially considered again until the 1980s in two Outer House cases. *Scrimgeour v Scrimgeour*[847] was an undefended action where the pursuer was permitted to acquire the defender's *pro indiviso* share at a price to be fixed by the court. The decision was not followed in *Berry v Berry (No 2)*.[848] The decision in *Scrimgeour* is in line with *Milligan* and the Institutional authorities and has been supported by commentators.[849] However, it is not without difficulties. A private deal between the parties may prejudice the common owners in that any price may be appreciably less than that which could be obtained by exposure of the property on the open market. It is possible that resolution of this difficulty could come through a solution proposed by the Lord McCluskey in *Scrimgeour*,[850] being adopted by permitting the parties to be the sole bidders in a closed auction. However, there is no case law permitting this as yet.

---

[843] Reid, *Property*, para 33.

[844] Whereby the property is marketed and subject to the blind bidding. This has the effect of increasing the likely price to the benefit of all co-owners: see *Campbells v Murray* 1972 SC 310; *Miller Group v Tasker* 1993 SLT 207.

[845] Bankton, I.8.40; Erskine, III.3.56; Hume, *Lectures*, III, p 403, n 3 and accompanying text; and Bell, *Commentaries*, I, p 62.

[846] *Milligan v Barnhill* (1782) Mor 2486. The defender argued that he could not be made to transfer his share to his co-owner – the remedy sought by the pursuer. The defence was repelled.

[847] 1988 SLT 590.

[848] 1989 SLT 292.

[849] Reid, *Property*, para 33, nn 25 and 26 and Kleyn and Wortley, 'Co-ownership' at 732-733.

[850] 1988 SLT 590 at 593.

17.6.3. Joint property

As there are no severable shares in joint co-ownership, a joint owner cannot raise an action of division and sale,[851] except where there is a bare trust[852] with assets held by joint owners the beneficiaries can seek this action.[853]

18.   Further rules applying to unspecified goods

18.1.   Transfer of shares in an identified bulk

There are special rules in the Sale of Goods Act 1979 sections 20A and 20B dealing with this matter.[854] The law here is the same as in England and is briefly discussed above.[855]

18.2.   Floating charges

18.2.1.   Reasons for introduction

The floating charge was not recognised by Scottish common law. In the well-known words of Lord President Cooper, 'It is clear in principle and amply supported by authority that a floating charge is utterly repugnant to the principles of Scots law'.[856] It is in fact a creature of English equity, which was introduced to Scotland by statute in 1961.[857] It was felt then, not unjustifiably, that the common law of security was too restrictive, in particular in relation to the delivery requirement for the pledge of corporeal moveables.[858] As a non-possessory security, the floating charge solved this problem. In 1972, receivership, the special procedure by which a floating charge is enforced, was imported north of the border too,[859] al-

---

[851] Reid, *Property*, para 35, n 12.

[852] A trust with no purposes other than holding the property to the beneficiary's order.

[853] *Bailey v Scott* (1860) 22 D 1105 and *Johnston v Macfarlane* 1987 SLT 593.

[854] For discussion, see Carey Miller with Irvine, *Corporeal Moveables*, para 9.15.

[855] See above, para 5.2.2(d).

[856] *Carse v Coppen* 1951 SC 233 at 239.

[857] Companies (Floating Charges) (Scotland) Act 1961.

[858] Eighth Report of the Law Reform Committee for Scotland, (1960, Cmnd 1017), para 2.

[859] Companies (Floating Charges and Receivers) (Scotland) Act 1972. The current legislation is the Companies Act 1985, ss. 462-487 and the Insolvency Act 1986, ss. 50-71. Future regulation will be by the Bankruptcy and Diligence etc (Scotland) Act 2007, ss. 37-49, which provisions are not yet in force.

though the reforms of the Enterprise Act 2002 mean that it only now normally applies to those charges granted prior to 15 September 2003.

The floating charge sits uneasily with Scottish law. It was introduced without proper consideration of how its English equitable features would fit with civilian Scottish property law. This is compounded by the deficient drafting of the legislation, which has led to many difficulties, most notably as regards the relationship between the floating charge and diligence (execution).[860] Some improvements have been made by the new provisions in the Bankruptcy and Diligence etc (Scotland) Act 2007, which are not yet in force.[861]

18.2.2. Requirements

Floating charges may only be granted by companies and by a few other commercial entities.[862] Writing is required.[863] The security is created[864] merely by signature of the debtor and delivery of the constitutive deed to the creditor. Registration in the Companies Register must follow within 21 days on pain of nullity.[865] Under the 2007 Act, registration in a new Register of Floating Charges will be required to create the security.[866] Usually a floating charge extends to the totality of the company's assets, or, to use the statutory formulation, the company's entire *property and undertaking*.[867] Therefore, both immoveable and moveable property and corporeal and incorporeal property may be encumbered, and the charge is a general security. The fact that a creditor has a security over the entirety of the company's assets makes the floating charge extremely popular with lending institutions such as banks.

The idea of the security is that it *floats* over the company's assets. Assets sold by the company automatically escape the charge with no special formalities required. Assets newly acquired fall within its reach. Only

---

[860] The leading case is *Lord Advocate v Royal Bank of Scotland* 1977 SC 155. See Wortley, S, 'Squaring the Circle: Revisiting the Receiver and 'Effectually Executed Diligence', 2000 Juridical Review 325.

[861] 2007 Act, ss. 37-49.

[862] Companies Act 1985, s. 462(1). See Gordon, *Scottish Land Law*, paras 20-205.

[863] Not by the Requirements of Writing (Scotland) Act 1995, but by the fact that the particulars of the charge must be registered within 21 days of its signature. See Companies Act 1985, s. 410.

[864] The security is not, however, a real right unless or until it attaches on receivership or liquidation. See below.

[865] Companies Act 1985, s. 410.

[866] Bankruptcy and Diligence etc (Scotland) Act 2007, s. 38.

[867] Companies Act 1985, s. 462(1).

when the debtor defaults on the principal obligation and the floating charge holder enforces the security by appointing an administrator (for new charges), or a receiver (for pre-Enterprise Act charges), or where the company is placed into liquidation, does the charge actually attach to the property.[868] At this point the creditor obtains a limited real right or, in the terminology of English law, the floating charge becomes a fixed security.[869]

In a consultation paper published in 1994, the Department of Trade and Industry proposes an extension to the current law in respect of non-possessory security.[870] It wishes to see all businesses being able to create floating charges over their property.[871] Further, it proposes the introduction of a new registered hypothec over moveables, to be known as the 'moveable security'.[872] The consultation paper does not make any alterations to the existing common law securities.[873] Its proposals have not been implemented, probably because of later research commissioned by the Scottish Executive which concluded that there was no compelling case for this.[874]

---

[868] Companies Act 1985, s. 463(1); Insolvency Act 1986, s. 53(7). The Enterprise Act 2002, s. 250 limits severely the power of a floating charge holder to appoint a receiver, and in most cases an administrator must be appointed.

[869] *National Commercial Bank of Scotland Ltd v Telford, Grier Mackay & Co Ltd* 1969 SC 181.

[870] Department of Trade and Industry Consultation Paper, 'Security over Moveable Property in Scotland', November 1994. Discussed by Murray, J 'Reform of Security over Moveable Property', 1995 SLT (News) 31, Patrick, H, 'Reform of Security over Moveable Property: Some General Comments', 1995 SLT (News) 42; Steven, A J M, 'Reform of Security over Moveable Property: Some Further Thoughts', 1995 SLT (News) 120 and O'Donnell, D, and Carey Miller, D L, 'Security over Moveables: A Longstanding Reform Agenda in Scots Law', (1997) 5 ZEuP 807. See also Crerar, L D, *The Law of Banking in Scotland* (2007), pp 536-540.

[871] Consultation paper, para 2.10.

[872] Consultation paper, para 2.11.

[873] Consultation paper, para 2.9.

[874] Scottish Executive Central Research Unit, 'Business Finance and Security over Moveable Property' (2002), pp 99-100.

19. Consequences of restitution of moveable to the owner

19.1. Fruits

19.1.1. Introduction

The fundamental rule is set out by Stair: 'Under restitution doth fall not only the things of others, but their natural birth and fruits extant.'[875] In restitution cases, recovery is not only of the thing itself or its equivalent value but also of its 'fruits and accessions'.[876] Thus, if a cow is the subject of restitution, her calf must also be returned. This rule will apply to most cases of restitution, for example (1) where there has been a transfer based on a void contract; (2) where there has been a void right of use and (3) where the property was stolen. In cases where a right has been avoided, it is submitted that the possessor is entitled to the fruits for the period prior to this. Similarly, in cases where a right to use has ended the possessor will have the right to the fruits (unless agreed otherwise) up until this time.

19.1.2. Natural and civil fruits

A distinction is made between natural and civil fruits, that is, between those fruits resulting directly from the thing being the object of restitution, and those resulting from exploitation of that thing, usually profits. The maxim *accessorium sequitur principale*[877] is recognised in respect of natural fruits. Thus, the leaves and lemons on a tree are owned by the tree owner, and the owner of a cow will become owner of her offspring. In essence, an action of restitution for the fruits of a thing owned by the pursuer is no more than an action of vindication.[878] The same is not true of the profits resulting from exploitation of a thing.

Stair stated that 'industrial fruits and artificial profits, in so far as they arise from the haver's industry and not from the thing, fall not under restitution'.[879] As such, products manufactured by the thing are probably not subject to restitution. The Scottish Law Commission, however, doubts whether such a distinction between natural and civil fruits re-

---

[875] Stair, I.7.10.

[876] Scottish Law Commission, 'Recovery of Benefits Conferred under Error of Law', (Scot Law Com Disc Paper No 95, 1993), vol 2, para 2.156 (vi).

[877] Carey Miller with Irvine, *Corporeal Moveables*, para 3.01.

[878] Reid, K G C, 'Unjustified Enrichment and Property Law', 1994 Juridical Review 167 at 197.

[879] Stair, I.7.10.

mains.[880] What matters is the extent of enrichment extant at the hands of the defender, and equity, including the good or bad faith of the possessor, will play a role in determining the extent of recovery of fruits.

19.1.3. Fruits consumed, spent or destroyed

If the fruits have been consumed, the general position is that a claim lies in *quantum lucratus*. According to Stair, the basis of the action is the extent of enrichment surviving, rather than the enrichment received at the owner's expense. Thus, 'if [the possessor] have increased his spending *bona fide* because of his having, he is free.'[881] In other words, the defender's liability is subject to the defence of change of position.[882]

A separate and important defence available to the good faith possessor is *bona fide* perception and consumption. Stair[883] and Bankton[884] both acknowledged the maxim *bonae fidei possessor facit fructos perceptos et consumptos suos*. This was the Roman rule that a good faith possessor of land belonging to someone else becomes owner of the fruits on separation. In principle, it should also apply to the fruits of moveables. Slightly narrower, the *bona fide* perception and consumption defence operates to make the good faith possessor liable only for the fruits remaining unconsumed by the time of the claim to recover the principal thing, even if he has been enriched. In *Houldsworth v Brand's Trs*,[885] Lord Gifford stated that the defence arises '[f]rom considerations of equity'.

A presumption of consumption can be drawn from gathering the fruits, hence the decision of *Ferguson v Lord Advocate*[886] in which it was held that the good faith possessor need not prove *consumptio*. Such a presumption would not likely operate where the 'fruit' was the young of an animal. Although Erskine[887] claimed that the defence extended to both unconsumed and consumed fruits, the weight of authority limits it to the fruits which have been consumed.

---

[880] Scottish Law Commission, 'Recovery of Benefits Conferred under Error of Law', vol 2, para 2.141.

[881] Stair, I.7.10.

[882] For discussion of this defence, see Borland, G C, 'Change of Position in Scots Law', 1996 SLT (News) 139 and Hellwege, P, 'The Scope of Application of Change of Position in the Law of Unjust Enrichment: A Comparative Study', [1999] RLR 92.

[883] *Ibid.*

[884] Bankton, I.8.29.

[885] (1876) 3 R 304 at 316.

[886] (1906) 14 SLT 52.

[887] Erskine, II.1.25.

19.1.4. Fructification expenses

The Scottish Law Commission has expressed the view that the Roman rule of *deductis impensis* applies.[888] This means that any obligation to restore the fruits is 'less expenses'.[889] The Commission has also suggested that where a possessor has a claim for recompense for improvements, this will be subject to deduction of the fruits consumed, 'except insofar as attributable to the improvements.'[890] In the case of the good faith possessor, the rule does not matter because fruits do not generally have to be restored and in this situation a claim for fructification expenses would probably not be upheld.

19.1.5. Non acquisition

There appears to be no authority on the liability of a possessor who has not acquired the fruits that the moveable could have generated. Any such liability would, however, be restricted to bad faith possessors. This is because good faith possessors, as discussed above, are entitled to the fruits and if they choose not to harvest them that is a matter for them.[891]

19.2.   Loss and deterioration of the moveable

19.2.1. Total loss or destruction

Where the moveable is destroyed, it is clear that specific restitution cannot be made. At most the former possessor and defender in the action can be made liable in restitution for the value of the thing. Loss or destruction might be attributable to the actions of the defender, to nature or to some other event or occurrence. It would appear that, regardless of the good or bad faith of the defender, he or she will not be liable for the value of the thing where its loss has occurred through no fault of his or her own.[892] He or she will only be liable to the extent he or she is enriched. It

---

[888] See D 12.6.65.5.

[889] Scottish Law Commission, 'Recovery of Benefits Conferred under Error of Law', (1993), vol 2, para 2.141.

[890] *Ibid* at para 2.155, citing Bankton, I.8.15.

[891] Carey Miller with Irvine, *Corporeal Moveables*, para 6.07.

[892] Bell, *Principles*, § 537; *Cantiere San Rocco v Clyde Shipbuilding and Engineering Co* 1923 SC (HL) 105 at 110-111 *per* Lord Birkenhead LC and at 119 *per* Lord Shaw; Reid, K G C, 'Unjustified Enrichment and Property Law', 1994 Juridical Review 167 at 179.

is submitted that this is a general rule applicable in a restitution situation. Likewise, if a possessor in good faith consumes, sells or destroys the moveable in his or her possession (thus causing the loss), the general position is that he or she is liable only to the extent of the enrichment.[893] In this case, he or she will be liable in recompense to the extent that he or she is *lucratus*.

Bell appeared to believe that the good faith possessor is liable for the value of the thing '[i]f it have perished by the receiver's fault'.[894] He may not be correct, as his statement lacks authority.[895] A modern writer[896] however, takes a similar stance: 'Good faith is no defence to a deprived owner's action for the value of the property lost ... But bad faith may mean that any profits made through the wrongful act of deprivation can also be claimed.' He uses the surrogate principle (*i.e.* the value of the property is a surrogate for the property itself, prior to destruction or consumption) to explain this.

The case law nonetheless is to the effect that the good faith possessor is not liable. In *Faulds v Townsend*,[897] the Lord Ordinary said (albeit in an *obiter dictum*): 'If the advocator purchased the horse, not merely in good faith, and without knowledge that it was stolen, but with due care and caution under the circumstances, and then disposed of the horse by slaughtering and using it up, also with the due care and caution which the law requires in the prosecution of his business, then he would only be liable in *quantum lucratus*.' This was supported more recently in *North West Securities v Barrhead Coachworks*,[898] Lord McDonald noting the principle that 'liability to make restitution disappears with loss of possession except insofar as the former possessor is *lucratus*.'[899]

A possessor in bad faith will generally be liable for the value of the thing. There is a presumption of good faith possession, but negligence or recklessness will amount to less than good faith, even if there is no proof of dishonesty or malicious intent. In *Walker v Spence and Carfrae*,[900] good faith buyers of sheep which had been sold *a non domino* and slaughtered or sold before the action was raised were held not liable in restitution or recompense because there was no proof that the defenders had been en-

---

[893] Steven, A J M, 'Recompense for Interference in Scots Law', 1996 Juridical Review 51 at 60.

[894] Bell, *Principles*, § 537.

[895] Reid, 'Unjustified Enrichment and Property Law', at 179, n 48.

[896] Carey Miller with Irvine, *Corporeal Moveables*, para 10.10.

[897] (1861) 23 D 437 at 439. See Steven, 'Recompense for Interference in Scots Law' at 60.

[898] 1976 SC 68.

[899] *Ibid* at 70.

[900] (1765) Mor 12802.

riched. In contrast, the defender in *Findlay v Monro*[901] was held liable for
the value of an ox which had been sent erroneously to him and subsequently consumed. Although Monro had not been in bad faith, 'there was
not so much as a title of donation, or any other to sustain his *bona fides*.'
His lack of due care was enough to strip him of his *bona fides* status, thus
rendering him liable in restitution for almost the whole value of the ox.
In *Ferguson v Forrest*,[902] a mare which had been sold *a non domino* to the
defender, who did not take adequate steps to protect himself. The animal
died in his possession (apparently through no fault of his). He was nev-
erthless held liable. This appears to support the conclusion that faultless
loss does not exonerate the bad faith possessor, perhaps qualifying Professor Reid's contention (above) that faultless loss does not attract liability.

19.2.2. Things in the possession of a third party

Stair[903] laid down three rules to cover cases where a possessor has sold the
thing to a third party. First, the owner of the property may claim it directly from the third party (a vindicatory action). Secondly, the owner
generally has no action against the former possessor, other than for any
profits from resale. Thirdly, if the former possessor was in bad faith, he or
she is also liable in restitution for the full value of the property.[904] In
Jarvis v Manson,[905] the profits made on a stolen ring, which had come into
the hands of a jeweller and then sold in good faith, were recoverable. As
the jeweller was in good faith, he was liable in unjustified enrichment
only to the extent of profit made on resale, not to the whole value of the
ring. If, on the other hand, the defender has disposed of the property in
bad faith, then he or she is liable for the full value of the thing based on
the principle *pro possessore habetur qui dolo desiit possidere*.[906]

19.2.3. Deterioration or damage

Just as the moveable might gain value in the hands of the possessor, it also
might lose value. It would appear that, in most cases, changes in value have

---

[901] (1698) Mor 1767.

[902] (1639) Mor 4145.

[903] Stair, I.7.11.

[904] Reid, 'Unjustified Enrichment and Property Law' at 179.

[905] 1954 SLT (Sh Ct) 93.

[906] Evans-Jones, R, *Unjustified Enrichment*, vol 1 (2003), para 9.32; using authority
from Stair, I.7.2 and Hume, *Lectures*, III, p 234.

no effect.[907] Reid's rationalisation of this position is thus: 'The measure of [the defender's] enrichment is his ownership of [the pursuer's] former property, and by restoring ownership to [the pursuer] the enrichment is fully reversed.'[908] This, however, changes where the damage or deterioration has been caused through fault of the possessor. In this case, Reid states that the possessor might be liable in compensation.[909] Rankine likens the responsibility of the possessor to that of a liferenter (usufructuary). This means liability for fault but not accidental loss.[910]

The suggestions of Reid and Rankine infer that greater liability is imposed upon good faith possessors for damage caused by them than for total loss caused by them. In the latter the weight of authority favours the position that the good faith possessor is liable only *quantum lucratus*, but in the former, it is submitted that he or she will be liable to the extent of the reduction in value and also to the extent of the enrichment. Gordon's position is different. He stresses that the good faith possessor, unlike a liferenter, is unaware of the true position, and believes that the object is his or hers to do as he or she pleases with it – consume it, destroy it or damage it.[911] Thus, it is difficult to impute an obligation not to damage what he or she believes is his or her own.

The inconsistency between the redress for damage caused by the possessor and destruction caused by the possessor can probably be explained by the operation of separate legal mechanisms. The liability for damage caused by the possessor will lie in delict,[912] and this action will be equally available where the thing has been totally destroyed.

19.2.4. Defences

Where an action lies in enrichment, the defence of change of position is probably available. Although authority is scarce on this matter, in *Caledonian Railway v Harrison and Co*,[913] the court held that the pursuers were entitled to restitution of the goods 'unless the defenders would be prejudiced thereby,'[914] but in the event, such prejudice was not proved. This

---

[907] Evans-Jones, R and Hellwege, P, 'Taxonomy of Unjustified Enrichment in Scots Law', (1998) 2 Edinburgh Law Review 180 at 214.

[908] Reid, 'Unjustified Enrichment and Property Law' at 178.

[909] *Ibid* at 178.

[910] Rankine, J, *The Law of Land-ownership in Scotland* (1909), 93.

[911] Gordon, *Scottish Land Law*, para 14.59.

[912] Reid, 'Unjustified Enrichment and Property Law' at 178.

[913] (1879) 7 R 151.

[914] *Ibid* at 157.

would suggest that a defence at least akin to the change of position is available where prejudice to the defender is averred and proved.

It is also unclear whether the defence of *bona fide* perception and consumption is available to the defender. The maxim from which the defence is drawn, *bonae fidei possessor facit fructose perceptos et consumptos suos*, refers only to the fruits of the thing possessed. There is, however, authority to suggest that the defence applies also to the subject itself. In *Hunter's Trs v Hunter*,[915] a woman received greater funds into a trust than she was entitled to. Lord Young precluded recovery of the overpayments on the basis of this defence. This decision was later strongly disapproved by Lord President Dunedin in *Darling's Trs v Darling's Trs*.[916] In any event, the defence is not necessary because, as discussed above, recovery of subjects consumed by the good faith possessor is probably limited to the extent of the enrichment.

19.3.   Reimbursement for improvements and expenses

19.3.1. General

In some cases, the improver can simply remove the improvement and therefore does not have any claim to be reimbursed. This depends upon whether the improvement has acceded to the principal. Accession occurs where there is an 'indissoluble union'[917] between the principal thing and the accessory attached by the possessor. Once again these rules can be regarded as generally applicable to restitution actions.

19.3.2. Accession has not occurred

Where accession has not occurred, ownership of the attachment remains with the possessor, even after the 'principal' has returned to its owner. As such, the 'natural' obligation[918] is owed by the owner to restore the attachments to the possessor. Where restitution is sought by the possessor, separation is not only permitted but demanded: 'If restitution be demandable, not of money, but of a thing delivered and received unduly, the thing must be restored in the same condition in which it was received'.[919] For instance, if Alice possessed Ben's car under a void contact, then upon

---

[915] (1894) 21 R 949.

[916] 1909 SC 445.

[917] Reid, *Property*, para 589. For accession, see above, chapter 11.

[918] Stair, I.7.1.

[919] Bell, *Principles*, § 537.

return of the car to Ben Alice can insist upon removing the tyres which she had attached to it. Since accession did not occur (the union of the tyres to the car was not permanent enough), ownership of the tyres was not conferred upon Ben[920] This is a form of vindicatory restitution.[921] According to Professor Reid, the very term 'improvements' necessarily implies that accession has occurred. Thus, more relevant is whether a right of severance exists with respect to an accessory that has acceded to the thing possessed.

19.3.3. Accession has occurred

Where the accessory accedes to the principal, as a matter of property law the existing title to the accessory is extinguished and a new title in favour of the owner of the principal is created.[922] By the Latin maxim *accessorium sequitur principale* (the accessory follows the principal thing) the owner of the principal becomes owner of the accessory also.[923] Thus, if Cathy takes Donna's ring without permission, and adds a ruby to it, then upon attachment the ruby becomes the property of Donna.[924] Cathy's title to the ruby is extinguished; vindication is not possible. Upon restitution of the ring to Donna, does Cathy have the right to separate the ruby from the ring and claim it back? In general, the answer is no. In any event, if Donna decided she did not like the ruby and removed it, the ruby would nonetheless remain her property.[925] The only right of severance arising by operation of law is in the case of the tenant who has attached fixtures for the purposes of his trade.[926] Where a moveable has acceded to a moveable, only through agreement can the right of severance be obtained by the owner of the accessory, and even at that, the right is personal and does not bind a successor in title to the property.

Where there is no *ius tollendi*, the possessor might have a claim in unjustified enrichment for the value of the accessory. In the past, this was the general rule.[927] By the nineteenth century, however, the position had

---

[920] Carey Miller with Irvine, *Corporeal Moveables*, para 3.20.

[921] As opposed to enrichment restitution, in which ownership lies with the defender or a third party, but not the pursuer; see Reid, 'Unjustified Enrichment and Property Law' at 169.

[922] Carey Miller with Irvine, *Corporeal Moveables*, para 3.01.

[923] *Ibid.*

[924] Stair, II.1.39. The stone accedes to the gold 'though more precious than the gold'.

[925] Upon separation, ownership does not revert; Reid, *Property*, para 574.

[926] Reid, *Property*, para 586. See also the Agricultural Holdings (Scotland) Act 1991, s. 18.

[927] Stair, II.1.40.

changed. A possessor who attached his or her property to that of another, allowing accession to occur, had no claim.[928] This is the modern default rule.[929]

There is a vital exception relevant for the good faith improver. If the possessor held the erroneous belief that he or she had greater right to the property (for instance, believing himself to be the owner), to the extent that he or she could make improvements, then the owner of the property will be liable in recompense *quantum lucratus*.[930] It should be emphasised that this is the only remedy available. Restitution is not available with respect to the accessory. Thus the good faith possessor who has installed a fireplace cannot demand is removal and return.

19.3.4. Value of the improvement or the expenses of the possessor?

A good faith possessor has, on relinquishing possession, a claim in recompense for improvements carried out to the property.[931] Often the value of the improvement – that is the extent to which the owner has been enriched by improvements – mirrors the money spent by the possessor; but sometimes large expenditure has little to show for itself in terms of value of the property, and conversely, sometimes a small expenditure produces a significant increase in the property's value.

The seventeenth century case law established that the relevant measure of recovery was the extent of the owner's enrichment, rather than the expenses incurred by the possessor. In *Jack v Pollock*,[932] for example, a widow was refunded the cost of repairing a ruinous tenement and the extent of recovery was 'in so far as he should be a profiter by greater [rent] after the relict's death.'[933] This remains the general rule today. In *Shilliday v Smith*[934] Lord President Rodger said: 'If A is unjustly enriched by having had the benefit of B's services, the enrichment can be reversed by ordering A to pay B a sum representing the value of the benefit which A has enjoyed.'[935] The relevant time at which enrichment is assessed is the time when the owner resumes possession or when good faith ceases, which ever

---

[928] *Barbour v Halliday* (1840) 2 D 1279.

[929] Reid, 'Unjustified Enrichment and Property Law' at 183.

[930] The leading modern case is *Shilliday v Smith* 1998 SC 725. See generally, Wolffe, W J, 'Enrichment by Improvements in Scots law' in Johnston, D and Zimmermann, R (eds), *Unjustified Enrichment: Key Issues in Comparative Perspective* (2002), p 384.

[931] Stair, I.8.6; Reid, *Property*, para 173.

[932] (1665) Mor 13412.

[933] *Ibid.*

[934] 1998 SC 725.

[935] *Ibid* at 728.

is earlier.[936] Thus, a 'value surviving' approach is preferred over a 'value received' approach.[937] It should be emphasised that the measure of recovery is the extent by which the owner has been objectively enriched. If the owner has not been enriched, there will be no recovery, regardless of the possessor's expenditure.

It is unsurprising that the measure of recovery, though based upon the value of enrichment, is limited to the actual expense of the good faith possessor. It was stated by Bell that: 'The recompense due in such cases is measured by the enhanced permanent value of the subjects at the time when the true owner resumes possession, arising (apart from any natural increment of value) from improvements executed during the subsistence of *bona fide* possession; but it cannot exceed the sum originally expended.'[938] This remains the clear position today. Where the enrichment was by way of a service only, rather than expenditure on materials, the enrichment is judged in terms of the service's market value to the owner at the time it was received.[939]

19.3.5. Recoverable expenses

Where the principal claim is for recovery of possession by the owner, the defender's claim for reimbursement for expenses will take the form of a counterclaim for recompense for improvements. Thus, recompense will be awarded to the extent of the owner's enrichment, but limited to the loss suffered by the defender. If there is no enrichment, there will be no recovery of expenses. As Hume says, 'as the one party must substantially be a loser, so must the other be substantially richer, (*locupletior*), by the transaction.'[940] The use of the word 'substantially' is also authority for application of the *de minimus* rule in reimbursing expenses. Reimbursement of expenses will also be set off by any fruits consumed by the possessor, except those fruits attributable to the improvements.[941]

Only certain improvements, however, are deemed to enrich the person who benefits from them.[942] According to Hume,[943] 'T'is essential ... that the improvements are not of a fanciful sort, or such as are suited only to

---

[936] Bell, *Principles*, § 538.

[937] Evans-Jones and Hellwege, 'Taxonomy of Unjustified Enrichment in Scots Law' at 214.

[938] Bell, *Principles*, § 538.

[939] Evans-Jones, *Unjustified Enrichment*, para 9.18.

[940] Hume, *Lectures*, III, 167.

[941] SLC Discussion Paper No 95, vol 2, para 2.155.

[942] Evans-Jones, *Unjustified Enrichment*, para 7.32.

[943] Hume, *Lectures*, III, 172.

the particular taste and humour of the late possessor ... they must be subsisting meliorations, which add to the value of the subject as restored.' 'Fanciful' improvements of this sort are classed as 'luxurious or voluptuary' expenses (*impensae voluptuariae*) which, according to Bankton,[944] are not recoverable in recompense by the improver.

Expenses which are recoverable are those classed as necessary (*impensae necessariae*) and useful or profitable (*impensae utiles*). Necessary expenses are described by Rankine as 'outlay necessary for the upkeep of the subject'[945] and will typically enrich the owner in the form of a saving. These expenses will be recoverable even by a bad faith possessor.[946]

Only good faith improvers can recover useful or profitable expenses, for example repairing a thing which is in a state of neglect, or upgrading the thing. As enrichment is judged objectively,[947] there is nothing the owner can do if the improvements are not to the individual owner's taste (for example, if the walls have been painted cream as opposed to white). The consequences of the objective test are, however, limited by the exclusion of recompense for voluptuary expenses.

19.3.6. Improvers in bad faith

As Stair viewed recompense as an obligation, rather than a right, he considered the obligation to arise even where a person in bad faith makes improvements on the property of another.[948] Erskine, however, doubted Stair's view, proposing that only the good faith possessor was allowed a claim.[949]

The leading case is *Barbour v Halliday*[950] in 1840. There, a distinction was drawn between a direct claim and a counter-claim. The court refused the bad faith improver's claim. It, however, left open the possibility of a counterclaim for the cost of materials and other expenses in an action by the owner to recover possession. Such a counterclaim was allowed in *Paterson v Greig*.[951] Moreover, a direct claim for necessary expenses will probably succeed, even where the improver was in bad faith.[952]

---

[944] Bankton, I.9.42.
[945] Rankine, *Land-ownership*, p 88, n 64.
[946] *Ibid* at 89-90; Reid, *Property*, para 172.
[947] Evans-Jones, *Unjustified Enrichment*, para 9.15.
[948] Stair, I.8.6.
[949] Erskine, III.1.11.
[950] (1840) 2 D 1279.
[951] (1862) 24 D 1370.
[952] Reid, *Property*, para 172.

19.3.7. Can an owner avoid reimbursement for expenses?

The good faith possessor's claim for improvements finds its roots in equity, and there are strong policy foundations to support it. As Rankine has said in the context of land,[953] 'It is obviously fair and equitable that he who has possessed a piece of property in the honest belief that it was his own and has at his own expense, and on that footing, enhanced the value of the subject, should not be compelled to give it up to the true owner, who in the meantime has been ignoring or neglecting his rights, without some remuneration for the improvements.' This is one area in which the law is certain. An owner who wants to avoid reimbursing a good faith possessor for improvements has one option: to ensure that any property which should rightfully remain in his possession does so and does not wander into the hands of some other person.

19.4. Possessor's right to retain the moveable

19.4.1. General

If there is a restitution action by the owner of the moveable against a possessor who has carried out improvements, it is unclear whether the latter may withhold the property until compensated. There are a couple of elderly cases involving land in which a possessor who had carried out improvements was allowed to retain until his expenses had been met.[954] The institutional writer Bankton writes that there is a right of retention in this situation.[955] In some other cases, the courts have refused the right, but for unclear reasons.[956] There has not been any modern case law, or indeed any case law on moveables. It is contended, however, on general principles that such a right of retention, or to give its technical name, lien, is competent.[957] If this is correct, the lien would exist where there is a valid claim under the law of unjustified enrichment. Issues such as good and bad faith and the type of expenses recoverable would properly be issues as regards establishing the claim rather

---

[953] Rankine, *Land-ownership*, p 86.

[954] *Binning v Brotherstones* (1676) Mor 13401; *York Buildings Co v Mackenzie* (1797) 3 Pat 618.

[955] Bankton, *Institute* I.8.15; I.9.42; II.9.68.

[956] *Duke of Gordon v Innes* (1824) 3 S 10; *Agnew v Earl of Stair* (1824) 3 S 229; *Sinclair v Sinclair* (1829) 7 S 242. See also *Barbour v Halliday* (1840) 2 D 1279.

[957] Pienaar, G J and Steven, A J M, 'Rights in Security' in Zimmermann, Visser and Reid, *Mixed Legal Systems*, p 758 at 780-783. See also Whitty, N R and Visser, D, 'Unjustified Enrichment' in the same work at 431-432.

than the lien.[958] If a lien was indeed to be recognised, it should be treated as a real right, as this is the status of liens arising in connection with a contractual obligation.[959] The same rule should apply in relation to liens in an enrichment context.

19.4.2. Garage repair cases

Where property belonging to A has been improved by B at the instruction of C in circumstances where C is not acting as A's agent, there is sheriff court authority that B has no claim in unjustified enrichment against A.[960] For example, C steals A's car and places it in B's garage for repairs. A can recover the car without paying B's bill. There is also Court of Session authority that B does not have a lien here.[961] In that case, however, enrichment law was not considered and the decision has been criticised.[962] As a matter of general principle, there cannot be a lien unless there is an obligation to be secured.[963] Hence for the right to be recognised here, the courts would have to depart from the position that there is no liability in unjustified enrichment.

19.5.   Expenses of the restitution

In accordance with general litigation principles, where the owner is successful in his action for restitution, then the defender in the action will bear the expenses.

---

[958] See above, para 9.3.

[959] Pienaar and Steven, 'Rights in Security' at 783-784.

[960] *Kirklands Garage (Kinross) Ltd v Clark* 1967 SLT (Sh Ct) 60; *Express Coach Finishers v Caulfield* 1968 SLT (Sh Ct) 11. See Whitty, N R, 'Indirect Enrichment in Scots Law', 1994 Juridical Review 200 at 206.

[961] *Lamonby v Arthur G Foulds Ltd* 1928 SC 89.

[962] Wilson, W A, *The Scottish Law of Debt* (1991), para 7.8.

[963] But compare the South African case of *Brooklyn House Purchasers (Pty) Ltd v Knoetze and Sons* 1970 (3) SA 563 (T) discussed in Pienaar and Steven, 'Rights in Security' at 782.

National Report on the Transfer of Movables in Cyprus

Stéphanie Laulhé Shaelou
Stelia Stylianou
Karolina Anastasiou

Table of Contents

Part III:
'Original' acquisition –
no direct transfer of ownership from owner to transferee

Part IV:
Additional questions

Introduction

A. The history of Cyprus

The Republic of Cyprus (hereafter called 'the Republic')[1] is a relatively 'young' Republic, since the island of Cyprus has only gained the status of an independent and sovereign state in 1960 after the Zurich and London Agreements (hereafter called 'the Agreements'). The Agreements, reached between Greece and Turkey, looked on a plan for the establishment of an independent state. They comprised of three treaties on the basis of which the Constitution of the newly created state was drafted. The three treaties were 'The Treaty of Guarantee', 'The Treaty of Alliance' and 'The Treaty of Establishment' which collectively provided, *inter alia*, for Greece, Turkey and Great Britain guaranteeing the independence, territorial integrity and security of the Republic; the establishment of Greek and Turkish military contingents in Cyprus and; the preservation of two British sovereign military bases in Cyprus.[2]

The island of Cyprus holds a 'strategic' position. It is situated at the eastern corner of the Mediterranean Sea at the crossroads of three continents, namely, Europe, Asia and Africa. Its position made it an attractive target for foreign powers who have indeed conquered Cyprus over the years. Up to 1960, Cyprus has been under the rule of foreign conquerors. First were the Achaeans back in 1400 BC who introduced the Greek culture and language on the island. Beside the fact that many other conquerors followed the Achaeans (as it will be seen below) and that Cyprus has developed its own cultural characteristics, the island has never lost the sense of being a centre of Greek character, culture and traditions. The Greek language and culture are preserved by the Greek Cypriots up to this day.[3]

Then came the Phoenicians, Assyrians, Egyptians, Alexander the Great, Persians, Romans, Byzantines, Venetians, Turks and British, the latter two

---

[1]   For a general introduction, see Andreas Neocleous & Co, *The Introduction to Cyprus Law* (2000) (referred in this Report as 'Andreas Neocleous & Co'), Chapters 1 and 2.

[2]   For more information, please refer to James, A, 'The making of the Cyprus settlement 1958-60', (1998) 10(2) Cyprus Review 11; Polyviou, P, *Cyprus: Conflict and Negotiations 1960-1980* (1980); Polyviou, P, *Cyprus: in search of a constitution: negotiations and proposals 1960-1975* (1976).

[3]   Evangelides, P, *The Republic of Cyprus and its Constitution with special regard to the constitutional rights* (1996).

being the most recent foreign rulers. The Turks invaded the island in 1570 and remained there until 1878 when Turkey was persuaded (after an undertaking by Great Britain to protect Turkey against the expansionist aims of Russia) to cede Cyprus to Great Britain, which would occupy, administer and make Laws and Conventions for the island. The island became a British Colony in 1925 after Turkey agreed to give up all its claims to Cyprus under the Treaty of Lausanne in 1923.[4]

B.   The legal system

The history of Cyprus[5] is therefore marked by long periods of foreign occupation and the present legal system, best characterised as a 'mixed legal system', reflects that history. As already noted, Cyprus's most recent foreign rulers were Turkey and the United Kingdom. The Turks brought with them the Ottoman law.[6] A comprehensive criminal code was adopted, namely the Imperial Ottoman Penal Code. The Ottoman Civil Code (*Mejelle*) and the Ottoman Land Code covered most of the land law. Furthermore, there were two kinds of courts established. The *Sheri* courts which were administering Islamic and Ottoman law and the ecclesiastical courts of the Greek Orthodox Church. These courts had supreme authority in family matters, exercising jurisdiction over Muslims and Christians, respectively.

When the British came to Cyprus in 1878, they established Assize Courts, District Courts and a Supreme or High Court.[7] They left the division between Sheri courts and the ecclesiastical courts intact for family matters until 1882 when the judicial system was revised and the jurisdiction of the Sheri courts was transferred to the civil courts. Supreme Court jurisdiction over matrimonial cases of the Greek Orthodox population remained with the ecclesiastical courts, except for guardianship and adoption, which were transferred to the civil courts in 1935 and 1956, respectively. The exceptional treatment of matrimonial cases is retained up to date and is embodied in the 1960 Constitution.

Ottoman law was applicable in all cases in which the defendants or accused were Ottoman subjects. In all other cases, English law and Cypriot statute law applied. This division between Ottoman and non-Ottoman subjects and generally Ottoman Law was preserved until 1935

---

[4]   Articles 16 and 27 of the Treaty of Lausanne.

[5]   For the issues treated in this part of the introduction, see Andreas Neocleous & Co, see note 1 above, pp 11-2.

[6]   *Ibid.*

[7]   High Court of Justice 1878 – An ordinance for the establishment of a High Court of Justice 1878. Cyprus Courts of Justice Order in Council 1882.

when the 'more scientific and workable'[8] British common law and its principles were finally fully introduced in Cyprus.

Since the date when Cyprus gained its independence (16th August 1960) and up until July 2006 (see below), the Constitution of the Republic of Cyprus constituted the supreme law of the Republic and had superior force over any other law.[9] The laws previously applicable were to remain in force in the Republic, until repealed by or amended by its laws.[10] Some branches of the law had been codified in 1959. For example, the Civil Wrongs law (Chapter 148 of the Laws of Cyprus, hereinafter referred to as 'Cap 148') and the Contract law (Cap 149) codified the English common law existing on the island before 1960; the Criminal Code (Cap 154) replaced the Ottoman Penal Code; and the Criminal Procedure Law (Cap 155) and the Sale of Goods Law (Cap 267) were established based on English statutes existing at the time.

Since the 1st of May 2004, Cyprus has become a member of the European Union. Community law, which is based on international treaties, is considered to form a 'distinct legal system which is capable of creating directly effective rights for those subject to it', which must be regarded as 'independent of national laws' but also 'superior to them'.[11] The express reference to EU law supremacy should have been decided by the House of Representatives on the basis of Articles 182(2) and (3) of the Constitution. The House of Representatives however ratified the Treaty of Accession on the basis of Article 169 of the Constitution,[12] following an opinion of the Attorney General confirming that no amendment to the Constitution was necessary prior to the ratification of the Treaty. The potential conflict between EU law and the Constitution in the Cypriot legal order eventually came before the Supreme Court, who could only uphold the supremacy of the Cypriot Constitution over Community law, during the challenge of the constitutionality of the European arrest warrant under Cypriot law.[13] As a result of judicial activism, the Constitution was amended by Law 127(I)/2006, to the effect that Article 1A was created and Articles 2(11), 140, 169 and 170 of the Constitution were amended.

Save as provided in the previous paragraph regarding the supremacy of Community law in the Cypriot national legal order, there are also other sources of law in the Republic which together with the Constitution and

---

8   *Vassiliou v Vassiliou* 16 CLR 69, *per* Crean, CJ, p 72.

9   Article 179(1) of the Constitution; *Malachtou v Armefti* (1987) 1 CLR 207.

10   Article 188 of the Constitution.

11   Emiliou, N, 'Cyprus', in TMC Asser Instituut, *The impact of EU accession on the legal order of new EU member states & (pre-) candidate countries: hopes & fears* (2006), p 305.

12   Ratifying Law No 35(III)/2003, Official Gazette No 3740 of July 2003.

13   *Attorney General of the Republic of Cyprus v Costas Constantinou*, 7th of November 2005, No 294/2005 [2007] 3 CMLR 42.

Community law form the Cypriot 'body' of law. The following constitute, *inter alia*, sources of law:

The laws made under the Constitution;[14] all the laws which were in force before 16th August 1960 and which were saved under Article 188 of the Constitution, except in so far as other amendments have been made or shall be made by a law under the Constitution; the common law and the doctrines of equity, save in so far as other provisions have been or shall be made by any law made or becoming applicable under the Constitution and;[15] the Acts of Parliament of the United Kingdom of Great Britain and Northern Ireland which were applicable in Cyprus immediately before the Independence day (16th August 1960), save in so far as other provisions have been or will be made by any law or becoming applicable under the Constitution and in so far as they are not inconsistent with, or contrary to, the Constitution.[16]

C.   Conclusions on the Cypriot legal system

It can therefore be asserted, that Cyprus has a 'mixed' legal system. Of course as already obvious, Cyprus like many other former British colonies,[17] has inherited most of the elements of the English common law and it can be said that its legal system is *largely* based on that of England and other Commonwealth jurisdictions.[18] For example the Cypriot Contract Law (Cap 149) and the Sale of Goods Law (Cap 267) are based on the Indian pattern; the Criminal Procedure Law (Cap 155) is based on English statutes; and the Civil Wrongs law (Cap 148) is based on English tort law. The adoption of the Anglo-Saxon system of common law has the following consequences on the law of the Republic of Cyprus:[19]

(a) English law is applied in all areas of law in Cyprus which are not expressly regulated by legislation. Furthermore, where the legislators codify common law principles, the resulting codification will not be regarded as exhaustive and other fields of English law that have not been codified will have equal force with the field that has been codified.[20]

---

[14]   Articles 78 and 82 of the Constitution.

[15]   Section 29(1) Courts of Justice Law 14 (I)/1960.

[16]   *Ibid.*

[17]   For example, USA, India, Pakistan, Canada and Australia.

[18]   Cyprus became a member of the British Commonwealth in 1961 after a decision of the Cyprus Parliament.

[19]   Pikis, G M, *The English Common Law, the rules of equity and their application in Cyprus* (1981).

[20]   *Universal Advertising and Publishing Agency v Panagiotis A Vouros* 19 CLR 87, where the judge said characteristically that the codification of the law in question was 'nothing

(b) Codified provisions of English common law are interpreted according to the interpretation given to the corresponding provisions from English courts.[21]

(c) Exceptions to any rule of the common law are applicable even if they are not expressly stated in the main body of the legislation. For example the High Court of Cyprus has decided in *Christos Markou v Gregoria Michael*[22] that the relevant provision of Contract Law is subject to the exceptions of the common law, even though the text of the legislation only embodies the general rule without the exceptions.

(d) The general principles of English law apply as an integral part of the legislation even though they are not mentioned therein.[23]

English cases are therefore allowed to be cited and used as guidelines (with persuasive effect) in Cypriot courts (adhering to the principle of precedence which is followed by Cypriot courts)[24] and English common law principles to be used where there is no Cypriot legislation in force.[25] Courts have held that where Cypriot law has not made provision for a specific legal point, the courts of the island have held that reliance may be placed on the Common law or the law of equity.[26]

However, although it is true to say that Cypriot legal system derived from the English legal system, English law is not the only law on which modern Cypriot law is based. Cyprus has also retained some elements of Ottoman land law[27] and of Roman-Byzantine law. Furthermore, Cyprus's administrative law[28] is based on and reproduces the principles found in the Greek and French administrative law.

---

more than a transitory legislation intended to prepare the soil of Cyprus for the planting of the common law' and that English common law 'must be planted here as a living growth which can be pruned by legislation and judicial decision to suit local conditions; but it cannot flourish if it is chopped up into statutory definitions'.

21   *Georghios Milliotis v The Commercial Firm P Ioannou & Co* 20(2) CLR 75.

22   19 CLR 282.

23   *A G Patiki & Co and Others v Demetra Georghiou Patiki* 20 (2) CLR 77.

24   *Queen v Haralambos Erodotou* 19 CLR 144, p 146.

25   This is supported also by section 29 of the Courts of Justice Law 14 (I)/1960.

26   *Solomos Stylianou v The Police* (1962) CLR 152; *A Mouzouris and Another v Xylophagou Plantations Ltd* (1977) 1 CLR 287.

27   This is because the modern Cypriot land law, namely *The Immovable Property (Tenure, Registration, and Valuation) Law* (Cap 224) enacted in 1946, does not have retrospective effect and therefore cases with factual circumstances dating before the enactment of this law will be decided on the basis of the law which was in force prior to September 1946, *i.e.* the Ottoman Land Code.

28   Law 158(I)/1999, 'A law codifying the General principles of Administrative Law that must govern the actions of the administration'.

Part I:
Basic information on property law

I. Notion of ownership and property rights

I.I. General basics

There is no comprehensive legislation in force in Cyprus dealing exclusively with movable property (or the transfer of movable property), although there are statutes dealing generally with immovable property (land, things built on land etc.).[29] Rules on this area of law are taken out from other statutes and case law. Furthermore, as already mentioned because Cyprus follows the Anglo-Saxon common law system, English cases, common law and equity principles can be used as guidance where there is no legislation in force or case law on a particular legal point.

The most important statutes for our purposes include, *inter alia*, the following (in their current form). Reference to these and to other laws will be made in this report where relevant:

(a) The Sale of Goods Law (Law 10(I)/1994)
(b) The Civil Wrongs Law (Cap 148)
(c) The Companies Law (Cap 113)
(d) The Contract Law (Cap 149)
(e) Statutes on Immovable property
(f) The Merchant Shipping (Registration of Ships, Sales and Mortgages) Law (Law 45/1963)
(g) Right of Intellectual Property Law (Law 59/1976)
(h) Bills of Exchange Law (Cap 262)
(i) Bankruptcy Law (Cap 5)

---

[29] Including, *inter alia*, the Immovable Property (Registration and Valuation) Law of 1907, the Immovable Property (Tenure, Registration and Valuation) Law-Cap 224, the Immovable Property (Transfer and Mortgage) Law of 1965 and the Immovable Property Tax Law of 1980.

1.1.1. Rights in rem / rights in personam

The distinction between *rights in rem* and *rights in personam* exists in Cyprus and derives from internationally agreed principles. Rights *in personam* are personal rights, that is, contractual rights against a counter-contracting party and not rights over property. Therefore a party to a contract of sale is entitled to notice of performance and damages in the event of breach of the contract. By contrast, a right *in rem* is a proprietary right that is a right over property. Normally rights *in personam* exist before rights *in rem* are created. For example a contract for the sale of land does not confer rights *in rem*, but purely personal rights. If the contract is breached, the buyer will not be entitled to the land, but merely to damages for breach of contract. Once the sale is completed, the buyer will obtain rights *in rem* over the land.[30]

The distinction between rights *in rem* and rights *in personam* has always existed in theory in Cyprus. The distinction between the two is however only referred to expressly in the case of land. In the case of land, the term rights *in rem* (estates in land) denotes any right directly connected with the ownership and tenure of any immovable property and capable of being registered at the Land Registry (for example leases for more than 15 years and restrictive contracts). The Cyprus courts have held that a mortgage which burdens immovable property for the security of a debt does not constitute rights *in rem*, but only a contractual right for the benefit of the mortgagor and also a charge on the immovable property.[31] It has also been held that an estate in land cannot be acquired either by abandonment or by estoppel.[32] Therefore, in the case of movable property, the only rights *in rem* over movables available are the actual possession and ownership of the movable object. All other rights created over movable property constitute mere contractual rights.

In *Attorney General of Cyprus v Thanos Hotels Suppliers Ltd*[33] Pikis J said that the **Immovable property (Tenure, registration and valuation) Law**[34] has introduced the capitulary of rights *in rem*, something that was previously unknown in Cypriot Law, allowing the acquisition of such ownership rights over immovable property for a limited period of time by the lessee of the property. The law provides that lease of land for a long period of time,

---

30 *Despina Markidou v Kyriacos Kiliaris and another*, Civil Appeal No 6357.

31 *Spyros Michaelides v Chrysses Demetriades etc* (1968) I CLR 211.

32 *Ayios Andronikos Development Co Ltd v The Republic of Cyprus and Other* (1985) 1 CLR 2362.

33 Civil Appeal No 11297.

34 Cap 224.

meaning a lease for 15 years or more[35] can be registered in the Land Registry, under the terms and conditions of the Law, creating in this way a right
in rem for the benefit of the lessee. The right *in rem* coexists with the land
and constitutes a kind of ownership, capable of being transferred.[36] There
is no such principle applying by analogy in the case of movable property in
Cyprus. A lease of a movable object, for example a car, would never constitute a right *in rem* no matter how long the life of the lease is.

1.1.2. Numerus clausus of property rights

Numerus Clausus is the latin phrase meaning closed or otherwise restricted number. The question of whether there is a *numerus clausus* of
property rights under Cypriot law is not an easy one to answer. There is
no literature by Cypriot academics and/or practitioners on this matter.
Although it seems (as in many other common law countries) that there is
no express *numerus clausus* of property rights under Cypriot law (this can
also be inferred from the fact that the principle of the freedom of contract
constitutes the cardinal principle of Cypriot Contract law, established
and safeguarded by the Constitution),[37] courts seem reluctant to accept
that there are other possible property rights other than the 'traditional'
ones, meaning those that have been established and used over the time.
So it can be said that although there is no fixed list of property rights
expressly recognised by statute or case law, a list of 'traditional' property
rights can exist in usage.

1.1.3. General principles / rules on Cypriot property law / field of application and definitions

As already mentioned, there is no comprehensive legislation in force in
Cyprus dealing in general with the general principles and rules on 'movable property'. Rules on movable property are to be found in bits and
pieces, here and there, in different statutes and case law. As there is no
such thing under Cypriot law as a single piece of legislation where 'the
rules on movable property' can be found, but rather a body of rules and
principles applicable to movable property under Cypriot law, one may
proceed with the description of movable property in Cyprus *a contrario* on

---

[35] Section 65B and 65C of the Immovable Property (Tenure, Registration and valuation) Law, Cap 224.
[36] See also *Nikos Rolandis and others v The Republic of Cyprus* Case No 203/90.
[37] Article 26(1) of the Constitution.

the basis of the general principles and rules applying to other areas of law ancillary or associated in any manner whatsoever to movable property.

(a) Real property (immovable property/estates in land)

As such, there are different pieces of legislation applying to different types of property which owed to be referred to as follows. Immovable property issues are dealt with by a series of statutes referring *exclusively* to immovable property and by other general legislation which regulate matters relating to immovable property. All these laws collectively constitute the Cypriot land law. Under **section 4** of the **Immovable property (Tenure, registration and valuation) Law-Cap 224**[38] which forms the basic enactment governing most issues related to immovable property, no estate, interest, right, privilege, liberty, easement or any other advantage whatsoever in, on or over any immovable property shall subsist or shall be created, acquired or transferred, except under the provisions of Cap 224.

The term 'immovable property' is defined in **section 2** of Cap 224 to include:

(a) land;
(b) buildings or other erections, structures, or fixtures permanently affixed to any land or to any building or other erection or structure;
(c) trees, vines and any other thing whatsoever planted or growing on any land and any produce thereof before severance;
(d) springs, wells, water and water rights, whether held together with or independently of any land;
(e) privileges, liberties, easements and any other rights and advantages whatsoever appertaining or reputed to appertain to any land or to any building or other erection or structure;
(f) an undivided share in any property hereinbefore set out,

It has been argued, *a contrario*, that movable property is any other form of property not falling within the definition of immovable property as this is found in the Immovable property (Tenure, Registration and Valuation) Law. Therefore, all the above are excluded *per se* from the terminology of 'movable property' in Cyprus.

---

[38] Cap 224.

(b)   Personal property (movable property / rights in movables)

Personal property is any other form of property which does not constitute real property. Movable property is divided in principle into two categories, namely tangible movable property (choses in possession) and intangible movable property (choses in action).[39] Intangible movable property is further divided into intangibles represented by documents of title (*e.g.* negotiable instruments, these being capable of being transferred by transfer of the document itself) and 'pure'[40] intangibles not represented by any document. There are different rules/regulations depending on the type of movable in question. Before going on to consider the distinguishing characteristics of tangible and intangible movable property, it is important to see how the term 'movable property' has been defined in Cypriot law.

As already mentioned, movable property is any other form of property not falling within the definition of immovable property as this is found in Cap 224. On the other hand, however, the term 'movable property' has normally been equated with the term 'goods'. Definitions of 'goods' can be found in many statutes dealing with particular matters. The most important definition is that contained in **The Sale of Goods Law of 1994** which defines goods in the following way:

> 'Goods means *any kind of movable property* other than actionable claims and money, and includes stock and shares, growing crops, grass and things attached or forming part of the land which were agreed to be severed before sale or under a contract of sale'.[41]

Apart from the definition provided in the Sale of Goods Law, there are references and definitions of the term 'goods' and/or 'movable property' in many other pieces of legislation. For example the **Trustees Law-Cap 193** provides that movable property means any property of every description which is not immovable property.[42] Furthermore there is a definition provided in the **Civil Wrongs Law-Cap 148** for the purposes of various torts committed on movable property. The definition is the following:

> 'Movable property means all lifeless things and animals, and includes money, the produces of trees and vines, cereals, vegetables and other crops and water, whether or not these have been removed from the land or not'.[43]

---

[39] *Despina Markidou v Kyriacos Kiliaris and another*, Civil Appeal No 6357; *World Tide Shipping Corporation v Vassiliko Cement Works Ltd*, Admiralty Action 64/75.

[40] Goode, R, *Commercial Law* (2004) (hereinafter cited as 'Goode').

[41] Section 2(1) Law 10(1)/1994.

[42] Section 3 Trustees Law, Cap 193.

[43] Section 2(2) Civil Wrongs Law, Cap 148.

The **Contract Law** defines goods as follows:

> 'Goods means *movable property* of any kind and it includes bills of exchange, promissory notes, ordinary or non-ordinary notes, other than those which are secured by mortgage over immovable property, shares certificate or shares certificates to the bearer of the company'.[44]

Furthermore, various other definitions exist in other statutes which include, *inter alia*, The Restrictive Trade Practices Law of 1956, the Trading Stamps Law of 1964, the Harbours Law of 1957 and the Trade Descriptions Law of 1968.[45] Nevertheless, the classification between movable property as in personal property is usually as follows:

(i) Tangible movable property (choses in possession)

Choses in possession means 'things in possession' as the word 'chose' is the French word signifying the word 'thing'. Choses in possession are therefore goods, chattels, objects and generally personal corporeal items whose physical possession can be transferred by one person to another by delivery. Choses in possession can therefore be physically possessed and actually enjoyed.

The transfer of tangible movable property is governed by the Sale of Goods Law of 1994. According to the definition provided above, goods are all kinds of movable property *other than actionable claims and money* and *includes stock and shares*. It is important to note that weirdly, shares are included in the definition of goods. Weirdly because one thinks of shares as a chose in action and indeed **section 2** of the **1994 law** is in sharp contrast with **section 61** of the English **Sale of Goods Act of 1979** which excludes shares from the definition of goods. In this respect it is not clear either when the Sale of Goods Law applies in relation to the transfer of shares nor what the term 'shares' means. It could be argued with sufficient certainty that the term 'shares' in the Sale of Goods Law refers to the 'certificates representing the shares'. But in such case, the shares could best be described as falling under the category of intangible movable property represented by documents.

This line of argumentation is confirmed by the fact that there has been no case where the Sale of Goods Law was applied in relation to the

---

[44] Section 106 Contract Law, Cap 149.

[45] Reference to the definitions provided in all these Laws was made in *Kouloumbis Panayiotis and others v The Ship Maria* where the court was trying to ascertain whether a ship is 'goods or chattels' subject to seizure in execution of a judgment. After a consideration of all these definitions, it was held by the court that a ship constitutes goods or chattels.

transfer of the certificates representing the shares. Instead the transfer of shares is generally governed by the provisions of the **Companies Law, Cap 113** and the Articles of Association of each company. In particular, **section 71** of the Companies Law provides that the shares or any other interest of any member in the relevant company constitute personal property which can only be transferred in the way prescribed by the Articles of Association of the relevant company. The rules on the transfer of shares will be discussed below in more detail.

There is also a separate category of registered tangible movables, where the transfer of ownership of the movables is affected by registration. This category includes: ships,[46] animals,[47] firearms,[48] cars and motorcycles.[49] The rules for the transfer of ownership of these assets will be discussed below under the heading 'Registration'.

(ii)   Intangible movable property (choses in action)

In *Despina Markidou v Kyriacos Kiliaris and another*, Pikis J said that a chose in action is a term of art that imported different meanings at different stages in the evolution of English law. Literally, it means 'a thing recoverable by action'.[50] Presently, it signifies an actionable right of a personal character as contrasted to a right *in rem*. A more accurate definition has been given in *Torkington v Magee*[51] by Channell J where it was said that a chose in action is 'a legal expression used to describe all personal rights of property which can only be claimed or enforced by action and not by taking physical possession'.

Choses in action therefore provide their owner a right of action for their possession and not possession as such. They are intangible personal property rights recognised by the law which cannot be enforced without action and which do not confer present possession of a tangible object. It is common to refer to the transfer of choses in action as 'assignments' and not transfers. This is because choses in action involve valuable intangible personal property rights, interests or claims such as the benefit of a contract or otherwise a contractual claim, which are not transferable in their physical form as choses in possession. The term 'transfer' seems to embody not only the transfer of ownership but also the physical transfer of

---

[46] Merchant Shipping (Registration of Ships, Sales and Mortgages) Law 45 (I)/1963.

[47] Animal's Certificates Law, Cap 29.

[48] Law for the Acquisition, Possession, Transfer and Import of firearms and for other relevant matters, Law 113(I)/2004.

[49] Motor Vehicles and Road Traffic Law, Law 86 (I)/172 as amended.

[50] Citing *Halsbury's Laws of England*, 3rd ed, Vol 4 para 991.

[51] *Torkington v Magee* [1902] 2 KB 427, p 430.

the object in question. It is more accurate to say that a person holding a contractual claim *assigns* his personal claim to another since the object of an assignment is to sell these claims to a person who, in turn, steps into the shoes of the seller or vendor, as the case may be.

The position in England under the old common law was that no chose in action could be assigned except by or to the King, unless the debtor assented to the assignment. Equity found this inconvenient and therefore it recognised the assignment of legal choses of action as a valid disposition of personal property.[52] General statutory provision for the assignment of choses in action was first made by s. 25 (6) of the Judicature Act 1873, which is repeated and substantially re-enacted by s. 136 of the Law of Property Act 1925. An assignment which fails to comply with the statutory requirements is not necessarily invalid, as it can perfectly operate as a good equitable assignment.[53] A valid assignment of choses in action today may take place either by statutory (legal) assignment, by equitable assignment or by assignment by the operation of law as follows:

- Section 136 of the Law of Property Act 1925 provides that in order for an assignment to derive validly from the statute the following conditions must be satisfied:
  a) it must be in writing
  b) it must be absolute
  c) it must be signed by the assignor
  d) written notice must be given to the debtor
- A valid equitable assignment, requires a clear intention to assign. Writing and consideration may also be required, whereas notice is not essential even if desirable in some circumstances.
- Assignment by operation of law is relevant in cases where the party to the contract has died or where the debtor is adjudicated bankrupt and his property vests in his trustee in bankruptcy.

In Cyprus the law on the question of the assignments of contracts is to be found in **sections 37, 40 and 41** of the **Contract Law, Cap 149** even though there are no express provisions on this point.[54] In *Andreas Chrysostomou v G S Halkousi and Sons*[55] it was held that there exists no express provision regarding assignment of debt under the Cypriot Contract Law. **Sections 37 and 40** of Cap 149, which correspond to sections 37 and 40 of the Indian Contract Act 1872, can only be regarded as provisions which do

---

[52] *Wright v Wright* (1750) 1 Ves Sen 409, p 411.
[53] Eliades, T, 'Assignments of Choses in Action', (1978) 4/6 Kypriako Nomiko Bima 6-14.
[54] See generally the article by Eliades, T, *ibid*.
[55] (1978) 1 CLR 10.

not relate directly to the matter of the assignment of a debt and which, in circumstances such as those of the present case, do not operate, in any way, so as to exclude the assignment of a debt.

In *Despina Markidou v Kyriacos Kiliaris and Another*[56] (which involved assignment of rights created under a contract for the sale of land)[57] it was held that there is no statutory assignment under Cyprus law. This is because in England, as already noted above, statutory assignment is the offspring of statute, namely the Property Act of 1925 and not part of the common law of the country which is made applicable in Cyprus by **section 29 of the Courts of Justice Law.**[58]

However, it is already clear that statutory assignment is not the only species of assignment known to English law. Equitable assignment has been recognised as part of Cypriot law in *Chrysostomou v Chalkousi & Sons*.[59] The decision followed the provisions of s. 29 (1)(c) of the Courts of Justice Law which provides for the application of the doctrines of equity in so far as no other provision is made in Cyprus statutory law.

In the case of equitable assignment, no specific form is required to effect an assignment.[60] Form is never significant in equity. Equity looks to the intent. So long the intent to assign is disclosed, equity will give effect to it. Assignment will be effective the moment it is communicated to the assignee; however an equitable assignment made between an assignor and an assignee is complete even if no notice has been given to the debtor concerned.[61] Public policy prohibits the assignment of certain rights, such as salaries and pensions of public officers, as well as awards of alimony and maintenance. However, as we may summarise, the judicial trend is towards extending the class of rights assignable in equity.[62]

So generally it can be seen that the general principle arising from case law is that rights qualified as choses in action could be assigned in equity without any legal impediment, provided always there was an intention to assign. Whether a particular transaction amounts to an equitable assignment, is a matter to be gathered from the contents of the document relied upon as setting up an assignment.[63]

---

[56] *Ibid.*

[57] See also *Butler Estates v Bean* [1941] 2 All ER 893 where it was held that a contract of lease is equally assignable.

[58] Law 14 (I)/1960.

[59] (1978) 1 CLR 10.

[60] *Inland Revenue Commissioners v Electric and Musical Industries, Ltd* [1949] 1 All ER 120, p 126.

[61] *Gorringe v Irwell India Rubber and Gutta Percha Works* [1886] 34 ChD 128.

[62] *Trendtex Trading Corpn v Credit Suisse* [1980] 3 All ER 721.

[63] *IRC v Electric Industries* [1949] 1 All ER 120-6.

Although shares are included in the definition of goods in the Sale of Goods Law of 1994, other intangible movables are excluded from the wording of the definition. For example intellectual property items (patents, trade marks *etc.*) are choses in action[64] not included in the definition of goods. These are therefore clearly not regulated by the 1994 Law. The assignment of intellectual property rights is governed by the **Right to Intellectual Property Law**.[65] There is also a separate category of intangible movables represented by documents whose assignment is governed by specific laws. An example of these is the **Bills of Exchange Law-Cap 262**, which governs the assignment of bills of exchange.

1.2. Ownership

1.2.1. The notion of ownership

The ownership and possession of personal/movable property constitute proprietary rights (rights *in rem*). Definition of the terms 'ownership' and 'possession' is hard to find. The word ownership in Greek is 'ιδιοκτησία' and comes from the combination of two other words, namely 'ίδιος' which means 'self' and 'κτώμαι' which means 'own' (self owning). The right of ownership is safeguarded by **Article 23** of the **Constitution** which provides that every person has the right to acquire, own, possess, enjoy or dispose of any movable or immovable property. As strange as this seems, it must be said, that it is hard to find an express and clear definition of the term 'ownership' in the court's case law. This is probably because the term 'ownership' is so widely used, both legally and in every day life, that the courts might have found it unnecessary to define it. The only attempt to define ownership was made in *Christou Orfanides v The Republic of Cyprus*,[66] where Pikis J said that 'conceptually the term ownership denotes proprietorship over an immovable or movable asset and indicates the possibility of that asset being transferred / sold / disposed of'.

(a) Legal and equitable ownership

In Cyprus, as well as in other common law jurisdictions, the concept of trust is recognised.[67] For the sake of clarity it is important to state in brief terms what a trust is. The general idea of a trust is that two persons own the same

---

[64] Section 13, Right to Intellectual Property Law, Law 59 (I)/76 as amended.

[65] *Ibid.*

[66] *Christou Orfanides v The Republic of Cyprus*, No 585/93.

[67] The Trustee Law, Cap 193.

property at the same time. The first person in whom property, real or personal, is vested is compelled in equity to hold the property for the benefit of another person, or otherwise for some purposes other than his own (*e.g.* charitable purposes).[68] The person in whom the property is vested is called the legal owner of the property (the trustee) and the person for the benefit of whom property is being held is called the equitable or otherwise the beneficial owner of the property (the beneficiary). The ownership of property can therefore be divided in legal and equitable ownership. Both legal and equitable ownership of the property are considered to be rights *in rem* and they can be transferred from one person to another.

There are different types of trusts. One way of classification of trusts is the way in which they were created. For example, there are express trusts (*i.e.* trusts expressly created by the person imposing them) and implied trusts. Implied trusts can be further divided into resulting and constructive trusts. The former arises from the implied *intention* of the creator of the trust and the latter is imposed by the law in certain cases *independently* of anyone's intention.

(b)   Rights and duties of the trustees (the legal owners of property)

Trustees are usually entrusted with the administration/management of the trust property and they act as representatives of the trust at all times. Trustees have more duties than rights. Their rights basically depend on the instrument, if any, creating the trust. In essence they have such rights and powers as the trust instrument allows for. The beneficiaries can also give the power/authorise the trustees to deal with the trust property in any manner desired.[69] Further, the Trustee Law-Cap 193, confers powers on the trustees which are in addition to the powers conferred by the instrument (if any) creating the trust.[70] However the law expressly provides that those powers should only be enforceable if a contrary intention is not expressed in the instrument creating the trust and should have effect and be subject to the terms of that instrument.

One power conferred to trustees by Cap 193 is that a trustee may invest any trust funds in his hands in one of four ways. For example it can invest the trust funds in any securities which trustees in England are for the time being authorised by the law of England to invest trust funds or in any securities the interest on which is guaranteed by government. This is so provided that such property shall be situated within the limits of a municipal corporation and the sum to be invested is not more than two-

---

[68]   *Snell's Principles of Equity* (1973), p 97.

[69]   Provided the beneficiaries are of full age and capacity to do so.

[70]   Section 2, Trustee Law, Cap 193.

thirds of the value of such property. The law therefore gives powers to the trustees but at the same time limits those powers in order to make sure that they are not contrary to the trust instrument.

Trustees on the other hand have two pivotal duties. The first is that they must administer the trust property prudently and the second is that they must comply strictly with the terms of the trust. Furthermore trustees are considered to owe fiduciary duties to the beneficiaries to the trust. This means that they are under a duty not to place themselves in a position where their private interests may conflict with the trust and are also prevented from obtaining any profit for their fiduciary relationship unless duly authorised.

(c)   Rights of the beneficiaries (the beneficial owners of the property)

The beneficiaries on the other hand have more rights than duties. Their principal rights are the following:

(a) to enjoy interest in the trust property;
(b) to bring a personal action against the trustees for breach of trust or to force them to administer the trust property according to the terms of the trust;
(c) to follow the trust property itself or to claim anything into which it has been converted, and;
(d) to institute criminal proceedings against the trustees.

Cap 193 imposes certain restrictions (instead of 'duties') on the beneficiaries' rights in certain circumstances. For example it provides that where the trust instrument empowers the trustee to sell the property and such sale occurs, the sale shall not be impeached by any beneficiary upon the ground that any of the conditions subject to which the sale was made may have been unnecessarily depreciatory, unless it also appears that the consideration for the sale was thereby rendered inadequate.[71]

1.2.2.   Restrictions on the exercise of the right of ownership

The precise interests linked to the right of ownership depend firstly on the kind of property in question and secondly on whether there are any restrictions on the exercise of the right of ownership to the property in question. As already mentioned a lot of times, the ownership of property constitutes a right *in rem*. The most important interest linked to the right

---

[71]   Sections 12 and 13 of Trustee Law, Cap 193.

of ownership, which is the most significant characteristic of rights *in rem* in general, is that it can survive the insolvency of a third party holder of the property. Other interests, such as the right to use, destroy or right to fruits *etc.* depend on whether the right of ownership is absolute.

It is questionable whether there can ever be 'absolute ownership' of property (whether this is movable or immovable) in its strict sense. This is because there will always be restrictions on the ownership of property by the general laws of each State, however 'absolute' the ownership of property might seem at a first glance. For example restrictions on the right to absolute ownership might derive from:

(a) Constitutional Law (restrictions deriving from the Constitution of Cyprus, for example restrictions for public security, public health and morality and the protection of the rights of third persons – see below).
(b) Private Law (for example Contract Law restrictions relating to someone's incapacity to contract, either because of his age[72] or of his/her state of mind,[73] or restrictions relating to the types of goods involved – see below).

As such, we can assert that the term absolute ownership simply refers to the situation where a person has the most 'complete' form of ownership known and recognised by the law of the State, excluding any restrictions to such ownership based on either Constitutional or Private Law.

The term 'absolute ownership' in this sense can be used in two circumstances. Firstly it might refer to property not being subject to a trust. For example it can be said that a person holds both the legal and equitable title in the property or that he/she holds the property for his/her own benefit and as such he/she has the 'absolute ownership' in that property. Secondly it might refer to property not being subject to more than one right *in rem*. For example, it can be said that a person has absolute ownership if he has both the right of ownership (legal and equitable) and the right of possession of the property. In the case of land, it can be said that a person has the absolute ownership of immovable property if the property is not subject to any other estate in land such as a lease for more than 15 years.[74] Therefore it can be said that absolute ownership of property whether this is movable or immovable exists where the property is at the free disposal of only one person who has the right to use that property according to his/her desire provided of course that he/she complies with the general laws of the State.

---

[72] Section 11(1) of Contract Law, Cap 149.

[73] Section 11(2), Cap 149.

[74] *Attorney General of Cyprus v Thanos Hotels Suppliers Ltd*, Civil Appeal No 11297, per Pikis J.

(a) Restrictions on the exercise of the right to ownership deriving from constitutional law

In the case of immovable property, it has been said that the right of abso-lute ownership of a person in immovable property comprises the following elements:

- the right to have or to claim such property as his own
- the right to possess
- the right to use
- the right to tenure, enjoyment and collection of fruit, and;
- the right to dispose of which includes the partial or total alienation, the charge, the change or the destruction of the subject of ownership.[75]

Where one or more of these elements is missing, it can be said that the exercise of the absolute right of ownership is restricted. The provisions by which the absolute ownership of immovable property is variably restricted are contained in various laws. For example, restrictions might derive from the text of Article 23 of the Constitution of Cyprus and the laws made pur-suant to this Article. Although Article 23 is the relevant provision provid-ing for the constitutional protection of the right to property, it allows for restrictions and even deprivations of such right in the cases which are set out in the text of this Article and which refer to the interest of public secu-rity or health or public morality or town planning purposes of the public utility or the protection of rights of third persons. Article 23 also allows the compulsory acquisition or requisition by the Republic or the municipalities of immovable property for educational, religious, social, or athletic institu-tions for the community of the owner of the property.

Various laws made pursuant to Article 23 provide restrictions on the right to ownership. These include, *inter alia*, Compulsory Acquisition of Property Law[76] (for compulsory acquisition), Town and Country Planning Law[77] (for town planning zones and restrictions connected with town plan-ning imposed by the government or the appropriate authorities), Municipal Corporations Law[78] (laws and regulations defining the nature or extent of the buildings which the owner is allowed to erect on his property, the per-centage of coverage, the number of floors *etc.*) and Buildings Preservation Law[79] (for orders declaring some buildings as 'preserved buildings').[80]

---

[75] John Boyadjis, *Published lectures on the law in rem*, made for the Council of Legal Studies (1985), p 81 (cited in Andreas Neocleous & Co, see note 1 above, p 593).

[76] Law 15 (I)/1962.

[77] Law 90 (I)/1972.

[78] Law 64 (I)/1964 and corresponding Regulations.

[79] Law 68(I)/1992.

In a nutshell, Article 23 of the Constitution of the Republic of Cyprus gives the general right to ownership and co-ownership and provides exhaustively for any permissible restrictions upon such right.

The right under Article 23 was considered in the case of *Andreas Constandinou*.[81] In this case it was said in relation to dogs that:

'Dogs, which are included in the category of domestic, animals are the subject of property, which is subject to certain restrictions and the provisions for their licensing. One view may be that the principle is that there is a qualified property in a dog [...] and that unless a person is licensed to keep a dog he may not be considered to have the property of it and the rights and protections which flow from the absolute right of property'.[82]

Thus the right to *ownership* of a dog is *qualified* by obtaining a license and it is not merely the case where the ownership remains unaffected but the owner is only subject to sanctions for not having complied with his lawful duty of obtaining a license.

A further derogation may be found in the **Sheeps and Goats (License and Controls) Law**.[83] This law applies to any sheep or goat but does not apply to their unweaned offspring.[84] A person must have a license in order to be able to keep sheep[85] which he must carry with him at all times.[86] No person under the age of sixteen may have such a license. Persons who are in breach of the requirements as to licensing, may be subject to a fine of CYP 150 or a three month imprisonment or both,[87] and the flock may be impounded.[88]

(b)   Restrictions on the exercise of the right to ownership deriving from private law

Another category of legal restrictions on the absolute ownership of property is the category where, by the operation of certain laws, the owner of property is restricted from acting in certain ways because his property is for example

---

[80] For other examples of restrictions on the absolute ownership of immovable property please refer to Andreas Neocleous & Co, see note 1 above, Chapter 14.

[81] *The Improvement Board of Eylenja v Andreas Constandinou* (Civil Appeal Case No 4575).

[82] Reliance was placed on the case *Sentell v New Orleans and Carrollton Railroad Co*, 166 US 698, p 702 (41 Law ed 1169, p 1171).

[83] Cap 91 as amended by Laws 61 (I)/65, 63 (I)/70 and 64 (I)/89.

[84] Section 2, Cap 91.

[85] Section 3 *ibid*.

[86] Section 7.

[87] Section 13.

[88] Section 15.

subject to a charge. In the case of land, property can be subject to a charge by virtue of the existence of an estate in land (real charge) over it for the benefit of another person. Such real charges are a mortgage, the registration of a court judgment known as Memorandum or Memo, a writ of sale of immovables and the deposit of a sale agreement with the Land Registry for specific performance purposes. In the case of movable property, a charge on movable property might exist by virtue of a pledge, mortgage or lien over the property in question for the benefit of a third person.

Many other restrictions on the exercise of the right of ownership can be imposed by contract.[89] As already mentioned, the Cypriot **Contract Law, Cap 149** also provides for restrictions on the exercise of the right of ownership.

An important right linked to the ownership of property is the right to dispose of/sell the property in question. A valid and enforceable contract for the sale of property must exist before the sale occurs. According to **section 11(2) of Cypriot Contract Law** the rights of persons below the age of eighteen to enter into contracts are governed by the law in force in England for the time being. There is a limited right of persons under the age of eighteen to contract. Persons below the age of eighteen years may enter into contracts but only for the bare necessities,[90] or contracts which operate for the benefit of the minor. If the contract does not fall within this exception, the contract is voidable at the instance of the minor either while he is still underage or within a reasonable time as soon as he becomes eighteen. This section can sometimes constitute a restriction of the right of ownership for both the seller (in this case the minor) and the buyer, who might find themselves unable to deal with their property in the desired manner.

Furthermore **section 11(1) of the Contract Law** provides that the persons who are not able to contract are those who are of unsound mind or who are disqualified from contracting by any law.[91] Such contracts will be valid unless the party with sound mind knew that he/she was contracting with a person who by reason of unsoundness mind could not understand the nature of the contract. In such circumstances the contract is voidable at the option of the insane person.[92]

Other restrictions to the exercise of the right of ownership can exist depending on the type of goods concerned. In the case of shares for instance, the **Companies Law, Cap 113** provides for various kinds restrictions. For example:

(a) Section 47 of Cap 113 provides for restrictions on the company to make an allotment of any share capital offered to the public for subscription.

---

[89] For example in the case of land, a covenant.
[90] For example: food, clothing and medical care.
[91] For example persons who are bankrupt under Bankruptcy Law, Cap 5.
[92] Andreas Neocleous & Co, see note 1 above, p 381.

(b) Section 47A provides that public companies may not take up their own shares.

(c) Section 48 prohibits the allotment of shares in certain cases unless a statement in lieu of the prospectus is delivered to the Registrar.

(d) Section 71 provides that the shares or other interest of any person in a company shall be personal estate, transferable in the manner provided by the Articles of the company. Thus this section expressly allows limitations in transferability (and thus ownership) where these are provided for by the Articles of Association.

A final common restriction to the right to absolute ownership of property which merits mentioning here, is the interim order (issued according to **section 5 of the Civil Procedure Law, Cap 6**) by which a defendant in a court case is not allowed to dispose of or alienate his property until the determination of the action against him.

1.3. Other property rights in movables

It has already been noted that there seems to be no formal *numerus clausus* of property rights under Cypriot Law. This can somehow be inferred from the fact that the freedom of contract is established and safeguarded by the **Constitution** of the Republic and in particular **Article 26(1)** which provides that all the citizens have the right to contract freely.[93] As such, it can be argued that there could be unlimited types of property rights, all created by contractual instruments. It has also been mentioned however, that Cypriot courts seem reluctant to accept that there are possible property rights other than the 'traditional' ones. Therefore, for the purposes of this report we should only refer to those traditional property rights that have been established and used over the course of time. The most important property rights are:

(a) ownership and possession of property;
(b) property rights arising from the creation of a lease over property;
(c) property rights of a trustee and a beneficiary under a trust; and
(d) property rights arising by virtue of the existence of a mortgage, a lien, a pledge or charge.

---

[93] This is subject to any contrary provisions of any law or legal principle.

1.4. Protection of property rights

This section introduces Chapter 19 which deals with the consequences of restitution of the movable to the owner.

1.4.1. Criminal law

As a means of safeguarding the rights of a person over his property, which also forms part of his constitutional rights, the Criminal Code contains provisions aimed at safeguarding such rights.[94] For the purposes of the **Criminal Code, Cap 154**, property can take the form of anything animate or inanimate capable of being the subject of ownership.[95]

Section 255(1) of the Criminal code provides that 'A person who, without the consent of the owner, fraudulently and without a claim of right made in good faith, takes and carries away anything capable of being stolen with intent, at the time of such taking, permanently to deprive the owner thereof' commits the act of stealing.

According to **section 306** of the Criminal Code, the offence of receiving entails receiving or retaining stolen property knowing the same to have been stolen or obtained in any way whatsoever under circumstances which amount to a felony or misdemeanour.[96] The offence is punishable by a term of imprisonment of up to two or five years depending on whether the stolen property resulted from the commission of a felony or misdemeanour.[97]

The offence of obtaining goods by false pretences is codified by **section 298** of the Criminal Code. The offence of arson is codified under sections **315(a)** and **319** of the Criminal Code.[98]

1.4.2. Constitutional law

Article **23.1** of the Constitution provides that every person has the right to acquire, own, possess, enjoy or dispose of any movable or immovable property. This right is not however unconditional. It is balanced against certain other considerations where necessary.

---

[94] Andreas Neocleous & Co, see note 1 above, p 499.
[95] *Ibid*, p 509. Section 4 of the Criminal Code offers a very wide meaning which arguably includes any kind of movable property for our purposes.
[96] Andreas Neocleous & Co, see note 1 above, p 508.
[97] *Ibid*.
[98] See case *Yiannakis Papas v The Republic* (Criminal Appeal No 3176).

1.4.3. Contract law

There are a number of remedies available for the protection of the right to property under Cypriot **Contract Law, Cap 149**. The remedies available are different depending on whether property has passed or not (detailed rules on the passing of property can be found below).

(a)   Damages for breach of contract

Section 73 (1) Cap 149 provides that a party to a contract who has suffered a loss as a result of a breach of the contract by the other party, has a right to recover damages from the party who is in breach. Where the breach is of a *condition*[99] of the contract, the contract may be terminated and damages may be claimed. Where the breach is only a breach of *warranty*, there will be a right to claim damages or the buyer may require reduction or extinction of the price, but there will be no right to terminate the contract.[100] He may recover for damages flowing naturally in the ordinary course of matters from the breach **or** loss the parties had in their contemplation at the time of contracting as a possible result of the breach.[101] It is further provided that no damages should be recovered for remote or indirect loss or damage as a result of the breach.

Section 73(3) Cap 149 provides that for the purpose of calculating the damages resulting from the breach, the means available for the remedy of the breach must be taken into account.

It is provided in the **Sale of Goods Act 1994** that where the *seller* wrongfully neglects or refuses to accept and pay for the goods, the buyer may bring against him an action for damages for non-delivery.[102] Where the *buyer* wrongfully neglects or refuses to accept and pay for the goods, the seller has an action in damages for non-acceptance.[103] As will be seen below, in cases where the property in the goods has passed to the buyer, the action is instead an action for the payment of the price.

---

[99] A term which is of the essence of the contract in such a way as it can be seen as going to the 'root' of the contract.

[100] Section 60 Sale of Goods Act 1994.

[101] This section reflects the two limbs of the decision on *Hadley v Baxendale* (1849) 9 Exch 341, which makes the distinction between damages flowing directly from the breach and special damages on the basis of what was in the contemplation of the parties at the time of contracting.

[102] Section 58 Sale of Goods Act.

[103] Section 57.

(b) Action for the price

In cases where the property in goods has passed or payment falls due on a certain date but the buyer refuses to pay the price, there will lie an action for payment of the price.[104] It is provided that where under the contract of sale the property in the goods passes to the buyer and the buyer wrongfully neglects or refuses to pay for the goods in accordance with the terms of the contract, the seller may bring an action for payment of the price.[105] Where under the contract of sale the price is payable on a set day regardless of delivery and the buyer wrongfully neglects or refuses to pay such price, the seller may sue for the price even though the property in the goods has not passed and the goods have not been 'appropriated' to the contract.[106]

1.4.4. Equity

Both specific performance and an injunction are equitable remedies and are not available as of right but remain in the discretion of the court.[107]

(a) Specific performance

Specific performance is available in cases where damages would not be adequate to compensate the aggrieved party.[108] A court will only order specific performance if there is a valid contract, the identity of the parties to it is clear, and the property is sufficiently defined therein.[109] The court will be deterred from granting specific performance if the plaintiff delayed in bringing the claim or showed acquiescence.[110]

Section 76 Cap 149 provides that for specific performance to be available, the contract must be valid under the law, must be written and signed at the end of it by the person who bears the obligation, and the Court must judge that in view of all the circumstances; an order for specific performance is not unreasonable or otherwise inequitable or practically unenforceable. **Section 59** of the **Sale of Goods Act** provides that in any action for breach of contract for the delivery of ascertained goods, the Court

---

[104] Section 56.

[105] Section 56(1).

[106] Section 56(2).

[107] Andreas Neocleous & Co, see note 1 above, p 399.

[108] *Ibid*, p 400.

[109] *Ibid*.

[110] *Ibid*.

has power to make an order, if it finds that it would be correct to do so, at the request of the plaintiff, requiring specific performance of the contract without giving the defendant the option of keeping the goods and paying damages instead. The decision may be with or without terms regarding damages, payment of the price or otherwise as the court finds just.

(b)   Injunction

This is an order of the court requiring an individual to refrain from committing the act complained of in the action, and will only be granted where it would be unjust to confine a plaintiff to an action for damages.[111]

(c)   The right to trace

Tracing is the process by which the law allows the original owner of property to identify assets in the hands of a third party which represent it because they are its exchange product or proceeds.[112] Tracing is available both in common law and in equity. The common law allows tracing where the property in question has not been mixed with other property, whereas equity allows the tracing of property to a wider extent even if that property is then in a different form. If however the identity of the property is lost, then not even equity can trace.

Tracing in equity required a fiduciary relationship to exist prior to the creation of an equitable interest but if this happens, then the beneficiary will be able to trace the property into the hands of anyone even if he is the *bona fide* purchaser for value.[113]

(d)   Restitution – unjust enrichment

In *Minerva Finance and Investment Ltd v Georgio Georgiadi* it was held that unjust enrichment is not in itself a cause of action under English law but is part and parcel with the doctrine of restitution. *Chitty on Contracts* (27th edition) and Goff & Jones *The Law of Restitution* (2nd edition) were cited in support of this. This is the position which Cyprus law adopts. The case of *Ismini Kyriakou Hji Loizi and Others v Irini Iona*[114] is concerned with the

---

[111] Andreas Neocleous & Co, see note 1 above, p 400.

[112] Robert Pearce and John Stevens, *The Law of Trusts and Equitable Obligations* (2002), p 822.

[113] See note 1 above, Andreas Neocleous & Co, p 404.

[114] Civil Appeal No 4366, 17 January 1963.

construction of **section 70 of the Contract Law Cap 149** which provides that 'where a person lawfully does anything for another person, or delivers to him anything, not intended to do so gratuitously, such that the person enjoys the benefit thereof, the latter is bound to make compensation to the former in respect of, or to restore, the thing so done or delivered'. It was established that the fulfilment of the four conditions[115] is a question of construction in each case.

(e) Constructive trust

In a constructive trust, the rules of equity (irrelevant of the intentions of the parties) determine that the property is in the wrong hands and compel the 'trustee' to convey the property to the 'beneficiary'.[116]

1.4.5. Tort / civil wrongs

The Cyprus Tort law or otherwise **Civil Wrongs law** is codified in **Cap 148** of the Laws of Cyprus. The three offences which may be committed against property under this statute are unlawful detention, conversion, and unlawful interference with movable property.

(a) Unlawful interference

Section 37(1) provides that this offence is committed where movable[117] property is unlawfully kept from any person who is legally entitled to immediate possession.

Section 37(2) provides that the burden of proof must be borne by the respondent.

Section 38 gives the court power to order the return of property unlawfully detained in addition to or instead of any other remedy which is provided for by this Act (Cap 148).

---

[115] The four requirements of the case were that (*a*) the act must be done lawfully (*b*) for another person (*c*) it must be done by a person not intending to act gratuitously and (*d*) the person for whom the act is done must enjoy the benefit of it.

[116] Andreas Neocleous & Co, see note 1 above, p 403.

[117] Emphasis added.

(b)   Conversion

Section 39 provides that the tort of conversion is committed when an act is committed regarding movable property which allows the tortfeasor to act in a manner which is inconsistent with the rights of any person who is entitled to immediate possession. **Section 40** provides a defence in certain cases for the *bona fide* purchaser. **Section 41** provides that the rights of possession of such property of any third person are not to be used by the respondent as a defence to an action of conversion. **Section 42** gives the court power to order the return of such property in addition to or instead of any other remedy which is provided for by this Act (Cap 148).

(c)   Unlawful intrusion on movable property

Section 44 provides that the tort of unlawful interference is committed where there is illegal interference with or intervention on the property or where there is any other unlawful act which directly causes damage to the property, caused by an action committed by a person.[118] The burden of proof that the act in question was not illegal is borne by the defendant.[119]

(d)   Damaging falsehood

This tort is codified by **section 25** which provides *inter alia* that the tort is committed by the malicious declaration of a false statement relating to the title of ownership of another person.

1.5.   Transferability of movable assets

1.5.1.   Movable assets that are not transferable

The **Sale of Goods Act 1994** itself does not contain any restrictions on the transferability of assets. *Prima facie*, there are no rules making property inalienable. It is important to note however that there are rules in relation to certain types of assets, which may have the effect of making the transfer unlawful or void. As will be analysed in further sections of this Report, possession of ownership of certain types of property is prohibited in absence of certain licensing or registration requirements. Further, in cases of insolvency of legal persons or bankruptcy of natural persons,

---

[118] Section 44(1).
[119] Section 44(2).

certain transactions may be void or voidable. In such cases, transfers of property within a certain time period before the commencement of the bankruptcy or insolvency may be void or voidable.

1.5.2. Hypothetical scenario

The hypothetical scenario envisaged here is that where two parties (one of them being the owner) agree that a certain asset may not be transferred or otherwise contractually limit transferability in some way. The issue which arises is what effect(s) would such a stipulation have *inter partes* and against a third party.

In view of this, the default position is that general principles of contract law apply. This would mean that *inter partes* there would lie an action for breach of contract.

As against the third party, if he is the *bona fide* purchaser for value without notice he would not be affected by the agreement restricting the alienation of property (he does not commit the tort of procuring breach of contract). If he were aware he would be faced with an action in tort for procuring breach of contract. In Civil Wrongs Law, Cap 148, **section 34** provides that in cases other than industrial action, where a person with knowledge and without just cause causes another to breach a legally binding contract with a third person, then the first person commits a tort against the third person. The requirement is that the breach must be made by C 'knowingly and without sufficient justification'. It appears that such knowledge must be actual knowledge, and that 'constructive' knowledge is not sufficient.[120]

Although the legislation frequently makes reference to the '*bona fide* purchaser' there is no clear set of guidelines in the case law as to what constitutes the *mens rea bona fide* purchaser.

1.5.3. Accessories

There appears to be no such provision under Cypriot law, however the issue of accessories, could fall within the consideration of what constitutes 'contract goods'. The question of whether or not accessories constitute part of the 'contract goods' or the 'contract goods' themselves, would, in any case, constitute an interpretation issue.

---

[120] *Swiss Bank Corporation v Lloyds Bank Ltd* [1979] Ch 548; see McKnight, A, 'Restrictions on Dealing with Assets in Financing Documents: Their Role, Meaning and Effect', [2002] JIBL 193.

The case *Epco (Cyprus) Ltd v Lartico Synthetic Detergents Co and others*[121] concerned a contract giving exclusive rights of sale and distribution of the respondent's products. A construction issue had arisen, namely whether the clause in question could be construed as referring to the products belonging to the respondents and not the products of another person manufactured by the respondents on that other person's behalf. It was said in the above case that the meaning of a document or of a particular part of it has to be sought in the document itself and that the intention of the parties must be discovered if possible, from the expressions used by the parties. In that respect, clear and unambiguous words prevail over any intention, but if the words used are not clear and unambiguous, then the intention will prevail. The case *Lloyd v Lloyd*[122] was referred to in the judgment.

2. Possession

2.1. Notion of possession

As regards possession, there is no clear definition provided in the case law either. It can be said that the meaning of possession depends on the context in which it is used.[123] In *Antrikkos Nikou Christou v Georgios Georgiou*,[124] the court said that possession of immovable property means the occupation or physical control of land. Therefore it can be argued that the general rule is that the degree of physical control necessary to constitute possession may vary from one case to another, for 'by possession is meant possession of that character of which the thing is capable'.[125]

Furthermore, in *Margarita Ikosi v Andreas Karayiannis and others*[126] Josephides J said that it is quite possible to have *de facto* possession of a 'thing'[127] without any bodily contact with it. Possession in law is also known as legal possession. Possession in fact is *prima facie* evidence of possession in law but it is not conclusive evidence of it, for possession in law is something more. The distinction between possession in fact and possession in law lies in the presence of a certain mental element. Whether this intent exists or not must generally be a question of fact. For possession in law there must be a manifest intent not merely to exclude the world at large from interfering with the thing in question, but to do so on one's own account and in one's own

---

[121] Civil Appeal No 5072.

[122] [1837] 2 My & Cr 192, p 202.

[123] *Margarita Ikosi v Andreas Karayiannis and others*, Civil appeal No 4716.

[124] Civil Appeal No 9807.

[125] Citing *Lord Advocate v Young* (1887) 12 App Cas 544.

[126] Civil Appeal No 4716.

[127] The term 'thing' means any kind of property, including movable property.

name.[128] He also went on to say the terms 'possession', 'right of possession', 'legal possession', and 'possession in law' generally mean the same thing, which is full legal possession. Even the 'right to possess' has been equated with 'possession'.[129]

2.2. Functions of possession

So therefore, it can be said that possession can be divided into two categories: possession in law and possession in fact. Possession in law can be further divided into two sub-categories namely actual possession and constructive possession. Bailment is treated as giving both the bailor and the bailee possession in law, constructive possession for the former and actual possession for the latter. Possession in law constitutes a right *in rem*. Any other kind of possession which is not possession in law constitutes possession in fact (for example a mere custodian of a thing will only have possession in fact – see below)

2.3. Acquisition of possession

2.3.1. Possession in law

(a) Description

As stated in *Margarita Ikosi*,[130] the distinction between possession in fact and possession in law generally lies in the presence of a certain mental element. For possession in law there must be a manifest intent not merely to exclude the world at large from interfering with the thing in question, but to do so on one's own account and in one's own name. The phrase 'to do so on one's own account and in one's own name' shows that for there to be possession in law, the person in possession of the property needs to have the intention of holding the property as its owner or bailee under a contract of bailment. The element of intention must be present for both actual and constructive possession.

Actual possession refers to the situation where the person asserting the right to possession actually has physical/direct control over the property in question. As provided in *Antrikkos Nikou Christou v Georgios Georgiou*,[131] the

---

[128] Pollok & Wright, *Essay on Possession in the Common Law* (1888), p 17.

[129] *USA and Republic of France v Dollfus Mieg et Cie SA and Bank of England* [1952] AC 582, p 605.

[130] See note 123 above.

[131] See note 124 above.

degree of physical control necessary to constitute possession may vary from one case to another, for 'by possession is meant possession of that character of which the thing is capable'. Constructive possession on the other hand refers to all other cases where simply the element of physical/direct control over the property is missing. A person who has the right of possession in law will be regarded as having constructive possession of the property if the property in question is actually in the hands of a third person. As such, a person with constructive possession is entitled to protection by the law.

Constructive possession exists for example in bailment cases where the bailor of the goods is regarded as having constructive possession of the goods (the case of bailment is further analysed below). Furthermore, a beneficiary under a trust is also considered to have constructive possession of the goods held on trust for his benefit, if it is the trustee who has physical control over the goods. Constructive possession over movable property can also be asserted where a person holds a lien over some type of movable property which is currently under the direct physical control of another person, *i.e.* the lienee (the owner of the property who grants the lien). Finally another case where constructive possession exists is where a person holds a document (for example a Bill of Lading) which represents the goods. It has been held many times that a Bill of lading represents the goods and that possession of it is equivalent to a physical possession of them.[132]

(b)   Bailment

The law on bailment[133] is complex and deserves a separate section for the purposes of this discussion. Possession of movable property is an inherent feature of a contract of bailment. The first question to consider is what constitutes bailment of movable property? Bailment is defined in **section 106(1)(b) of the Contract Law** as:

> 'the delivery of goods by one person to another for some purpose on a contract that they shall when the purpose is accomplished, be returned or otherwise disposed of according to the directions of the person delivering them'.

The person delivering the goods is called the bailor. The person to whom they are delivered is called the bailee. As already noted, both the bailor and the bailee are considered to have the right to possession in law (subject always to the terms of the contract between them). The bailor will have constructive possession of the goods bailed and the bailee will have

---

[132] *Standard Fruit Company (Bermuda) Ltd v Gold Seal Shipping Company Ltd*, Admiralty Jurisdiction Case 77/90, 22 April 1997.

[133] See generally Andreas Neocleous & Co, note 1 above, Chapter 10.

the actual possession of the goods. Their legal right to possession is evidenced from **section 140 of the Contract Law** which provides that if a third person wrongfully deprives the bailee of the use or possession of the goods bailed, or *does* them any injury, the bailee is entitled to use such remedies as the owner might have used in the like case if no bailment had been made; and either the bailor or the bailee may bring legal proceedings against a third person for deprivation or injury to the goods. Furthermore it was said by Hadjianastassiou J in *Odysseas Patsalides v Kiki Yiapani and Another*[134] that no proposition can be clearer than that either a bailor or the bailee of a chattel may maintain an action in respect of it against a wrongdoer, 'the latter by virtue of his possession and the former by reason of his property'.

The definition of bailment provided in the Contract law allows for a wide interpretation and for many transactions in every day life to be seen as types of bailment. It was once said that a deposit, a pledge, a lease and a mandate constitute, *inter alia*, different types of bailment.[135] For example, the hiring of a car from a car hiring company was treated in many cases as a situation where a contract of bailment can be said to exist.[136] Furthermore in *Pitri Brothers and others v Theodoros M Shiamptanis*,[137] the court of first instance said that the garage owners were guilty of breach of the contract of bailment when a car in their possession caught fire and was destroyed. The judge said 'the facts of the present case support the argument of the plaintiff which I accept and hold that this is a clear-cut case of bailment. All the features of bailment and in particular that of possession are apparent in the present case'. On appeal, counsel for the defendants argued that the trial judge wrongly concluded that the present case was one of bailment. However, during the course of the hearing they abandoned this ground of appeal and limited their appeal on other grounds. The appeal was allowed but the finding of the court of first instance that there was a contract of bailment was essentially left intact.

In *Kourris v Alpo Ltd and Others*,[138] it was held that when the plaintiff delivered his car to the defendant company for service and the car was damaged while it was in the possession of a servant of the defendant (who

---

[134] Civil Appeal No 4632.

[135] In *Georgios Ioannou v Georgios Kounnides*, the judge said that these types of relationships constitute types of bailment according to the English common law (citing in this respect *Halsbury's Laws of England*, 4th ed., Vol. 2, p 832 *et seq*, paras 1801 and 1802; and *Words and Phrases Legally Defined*, Vol I, p 147 *et seq*).

[136] *Vaso Manousou Pontikopoulou v Lakis Christis*, Civil Appeal No 5976; *Costas Skoulias v Takis Philippides*, Civil Appeal No 4026.

[137] Civil Appeal No 7265.

[138] (1981) 1 CLR 217.

was himself defendant no 2), the plaintiff was entitled to damages for breach of the contract of bailment against:

(a) defendants no 1 as bailees and;
(b) defendants no 2 as sub-bailees of his car.

The High Court decided that there was nothing in the relevant provisions of Cypriot Contract Law governing the question of bailments to exclude this part of the British common law, namely the sub-bailment. It then went on to say that in order to decide whether or not sub-bailment exists, the court should take into account, *inter alia*, the existence of authorisation or approval by the bailor that bailment of the relevant property could be sub-bailed to a third person. In *Georgios Ioannou v Georgios Kounnides*,[139] it was held that the authorisation for sub-bailment can be either express or implied. However, it was said in the same case that a sub-bailee can only be said for these purposes to have voluntarily taken into his possession the goods of another, if he has sufficient notice that a person other than the bailee is interested in the goods so that it can properly be said that (in addition to his duties to the bailee) he has, by taking the goods into his custody, assumed towards that other person the responsibility for the goods which is characteristic of a bailee.[140]

The wide interpretation of bailment contracts can also be seen by the statement of Hadjianastassiou J in *Frixos Constantinou v The Firm S Mamas & Co*:

'The contract of hire purchase is one of the variation of the contract of bailment, but it is a modern development of commercial life and the rules with regard to bailments, which were laid down before any contract of hire purchase was contemplated, cannot be applied simpliciter, because such contract has in it, not only the element of bailment, but also an element of sale'.[141]

It can therefore be seen from all of the above cases that bailment is a very wide concept and includes a wide range of circumstances arising in everyday life. Generally, the bailee's responsibility is to take such care of the goods bailed to him as a man of ordinary prudence would take of his own goods of the same bulk, quality, and value as the goods bailed to him. If there is no special contract, the bailee is not responsible for any loss, destruction, or deterioration of the thing involved if he has taken care of it in accordance with the above standard.[142] The standard of care required

---

[139] See note 135 above.

[140] *The Pioneer Container KH Enterprise (cargo owners) v Pioneer Container (owners)* (1994) 2 All ER 250.

[141] Civil Appeal No 4992.

[142] *Lamides v Antoniou* (1982) 2 JSC 369.

to be exercised by a bailee depends on the type of bailment and in particular on whether the bailment is gratuitous (in which case the standard required is higher) or a bailment for reward. In both cases, any breach of duty should arise from the contract of bailment and the bailee must show that any loss of the goods was not due to his fault. The burden of proof in bailment cases rests on the defendant, who must prove that he took the amount of care described above.[143]

2.3.2. Possession in fact

Possession in fact does not require the presence of any mental element. It involves cases of pure physical control over some type of property or in other words cases of pure custody. Being in custody of some type of movable property means the mere act of holding an asset or otherwise of having direct physical control over some type of movable property whose possession in law belongs to another. This is the category under which all cases which do not satisfy the requirements for the existence of a contract of bailment fall. For example it could be said an employee using a company car can sometimes be held to be a bailee of the car and under other circumstances to be a pure custodian of the company car. Furthermore, it can be said that the situation of a family member being allowed to use an asset can sometimes fall under the category of pure custody.

In *Odysseas Patsalides v Kiki Yiapani and another*[144] the wife of a man was found driving her husband's car while he was abroad. She was involved in an accident and she was claiming that she was entitled to damages for the damage caused to her husband's car because at the time she was a bailee of her husband and she was under an obligation to return it to him. She was therefore claiming to be entitled to rely on section 140 of the Contract Law (see above). It was held that the mere fact that she was driving the said vehicle does not lead, safely, even on the balance of probabilities, to the conclusion that she was doing so as a bailee. The plaintiff failed to provide sufficient evidence that a contract of bailment existed between herself and her husband.

Although it is possible to refer to these people (custodians) as being 'in possession' of the object, in reality this simply refers to the mere act of presently holding/having direct physical control over the property in question (*i.e.* mere possession in fact).

---

[143] *Charalambous v Nicola* (1976) 12 JSC 1920.
[144] Civil Appeal No 4632.

2.4.   Protection of possession

In the case of bailment, section 140 of the Contract Law provides that if
a third person wrongfully deprives the bailee of the use or possession of
the goods bailed, or does them any injury, the bailee is entitled to use
such remedies as the owner might have used in the like case if no bailment has been made and either the bailor or the bailee may bring legal
proceedings against a third person for deprivation or injury.

Therefore the protection of possession can be achieved in the first
place by an action for the award of damages under section 140 of the
Contract Law. However, an action can also be brought under tort law.

Under section 37 of the Civil Wrongs Law, Cap 148, the illegal possession of goods (or 'trespass to goods' as the term is generally known in
the common law systems) means the withholding of movable property
belonging to a person who possesses the right to immediate possession
(*i.e.* the owner or bailee of property). Section 38 of the same law provides
that an action can be brought under section 37 for the return of the movable property in question. In addition the court can award any other
remedy in addition or instead of the return of the property (such as the
award of damages to the person with the right to immediate possession).

2.5.   Self-help

The authors are not aware of any case-law whereby the Courts of the
Republic of Cyprus have dealt with the issue of self-help. It seems to us
that even the term 'self-help' is not used in the Cypriot legal language.
What can be found however is a number of criminal law cases on 'self-
defence'.

Self-defence is not expressly mentioned in the **Criminal Code** even
though it has been applied in many cases which came before the court.[145]
What the Criminal Code provides for is the defence of necessity under
section 17 of the Code.[146] Self-defence seems to derive from what is usually referred to as 'natural justice'. The following extract from the Privy
Council in *Palmer*[147] seems to have been embraced by Cypriot courts:

'It is a straightforward concept. It involves no abstruse legal thought. It requires no set words by way of explanation. No formula need be employed in
reference to it. Only common sense is needed for its understanding. It is both
good law and good sense that a man may defend himself. It is both good law

---

[145] *Miliotis v The Police* (1971) 2 CLR 292; *Christou v The Police* (1972) 2 CLR 38.
[146] See generally, Andreas Neocleous & Co, note 1 above, Chapter 12.
[147] [1971] AC 814.

and good sense that he may do, but may only do, what is reasonably necessary. However, everything will depend on the particular facts and circumstances'.

It seems therefore that generally, acts (which are under the circumstances reasonable) done by a person in self-defence are deemed to be justified and therefore not liable to any criminal sanctions. On the basis of all the above it can be said that in the case of property, any person in possession of a movable object who has himself property rights in that movable object (including the rights of possession of a bailee) can defend his rights if these are being under attack. This is so, provided that the immediate defensive action is considered reasonable and necessary under the circumstances. The question of what kind of defensive actions are acceptable is matter to be decided by the court under the specific factual circumstances of any given case.

3. Nature of rights to hold: obligatory rights or rights in rem

See section 1.1.1. above.

4. Field of application and definitions

See section 1.1.3. above.

5. System(s) of transfer used

5.1. Basic overview

5.1.1. The concept of transfer of ownership

The transfer of ownership is a 'unitary' concept in Cyprus law. The owner of goods having the best possible interest in the property may of course contractually or otherwise grant lesser rights in the goods. The owner of goods having an absolute interest can carve out lesser interests and bestow upon, transfer or grant such lesser interest to other parties. However when one refers to the 'passing of property' in Cyprus law, this is understood as referring to the best possible interest and not some lesser interest.[148] Such property passes in its entirety at one moment in time. What may be different from case to case however are the rules by which property is to pass. The issue of the rules governing the passing of property depend on how the right to ownership arises. This will be explained in the following section.

5.1.2. The mode of transfer

Freedom of contract is established by the Constitution of the Republic of Cyprus, and in particular by **Article 26(1)** which provides that all the citizens have the right to contract freely. This right is subject to any contrary provisions of any law or legal principle. Where the right to property accrues under a contract between two parties, there will be a requirement that the contract underlying such an obligation is valid and that it operates so as to give the party in question a right to ownership. The require-

---

[148] Section 2 of the Sale of Goods Act specifically defines 'property' as the entire ownership in the goods and not merely special property in them. It is noteworthy that in the case of *Re Bond Worth Ltd* [1980] Ch 228, Slade J emphasised the point that 'property' in the Sale of Goods Act 1893 (which is largely similar to the Cyprus Sale of Goods Act 1994) refers to the general property in the goods and not merely special property such as that possessed by the bailee.

ments for any contract to be both valid and enforceable will be explained below.

Given that the contract is in fact both valid and enforceable, the mode of transfer of the property will be governed by the contract itself. Thus the contract may expressly govern *inter alia* the issue of whether property is to pass on the payment of the price or whether the vendor retains title until the payment of the price, and whether property is to pass upon delivery or some prior or subsequent time. In absence of such express stipulations by the parties, the issues which may arise as to the mode of the passing of property will be governed by any terms which can be implied[149] as a matter of general contract law. In absence of both express and implied terms, the **Sale of Goods Act 1994** provides a set of default rules which govern the mode of passing of property[150] which depend on the intention of the parties.

Further to the general law of contract, **section 5(1)** of the **Sale of Goods Act 1994** provides that a contract for the sale of goods is made when there is an offer for the sale of good for consideration and such an offer is accepted. **Section 5** of the 1994 Act goes on to provide that the contract may provide for immediate delivery of the goods of the immediate payment of the price or may provide for the above to take place at a later stage, or may provide for partial delivery or payment in instalments.

Section 5(2) of the 1994 Act provides that the contract may be oral or written or partially oral and partially written or may arise from the conduct of the parties. **Section 33** of the **Companies Law, Cap 113** provides for the form of contracts to be made on behalf of the company. It provides that a contract which, if made between private persons, would be required by law to be in writing, and, if made according to English law, to be under seal, may be made on behalf of the company under the common seal of the Company.[151] It is further provided that a contract which, if made between private persons, would be required by law to be in writing, signed by the parties to be charged therewith, may be made on behalf of the company in writing and signed by any person acting under its authority, expressly or impliedly.

Also the nature of the movable should be taken into account. For example if the underlying contract gives rise to a right to the transfer of ownership of shares, the mode of transfer will also be subject to the **Companies Law, Cap 113** and the **Stock Exchange Law**.[152] In certain cases, registration is a prerequisite for one to be deemed the owner of the mov-

---

[149] As a matter of general contract law, implied terms may arise as a matter of fact, as a matter of law or through custom.

[150] Section 19(3) provides that unless a contrary intention appears, property passes when it is intended to pass.

[151] Section 33(1).

[152] No 14(I)/93.

ables in question, although this is not the case with all types of registrable movable property. Also, where a license is required for the holding of certain types of movables, such a license may sometimes be a *prerequisite* for ownership in the sense that one cannot be considered the owner of such property unless one has obtained such a license.[153]

Alternatively the transfer may not be effected by virtue of an underlying contractual obligation but by some other means such as for example by operation of law or by way of a will or testament.[154]

5.2. General issues – 'specific'/'generic' goods

This is not meant to be elaborated as a separate part; issues are dealt with in the relevant parts of the report as appropriate, in particular section 5.3.4.

5.3. Requirement of a valid obligation

5.3.1. Validity and enforceability of the obligation where the underlying obligation is a contract

In order for the right of ownership to accrue, as was explained above, the underlying obligation to transfer ownership must be both valid and enforceable.[155] The distinction is important because in certain cases a contract may be valid but not enforceable.

For a contract to be valid under Cypriot contract law, there must be a valid offer[156] and an acceptance[157] which mirrors that offer, consideration,[158] and an intention to create legal relations.[159] For an agreement to constitute a valid contract the parties must enter into the contract with free consent and must have the capacity under the law to enter into the contract.[160] Further both the consideration and the purpose must be legitimate.[161]

---

[153] *The Improvement Board of Eylenja v Andreas Constandinou* (1971) 1 CLR 167.

[154] For example section 4 of the Wills and Succession Law, Cap 195, provides that succession to an estate may be either by will or by the operation of law or by will and by the operation of law.

[155] *NTTS OV MNPO 'DALVENT' v F/V 0758 ZOLOTETS (CALL LETTERS (UHZT))* (1993) 1 Apofasis Anotatou Dikastiriou (Supreme Court) 877.

[156] *Irini Georgiou v Cyprus Airways*, Civil Appeal No 8957.

[157] *Xenopoulos v Thomas Nelson* (1982) 1 CLR 674.

[158] Section 10(1) of the Contract Law, Cap 149.

[159] *Evripidou v Demosthenous* (1971) 1 CLR 112.

[160] Section 10(1) of the Contract Law, Cap 149.

[161] *Ibid.*

(a)   Capacity to contract

The *capacity* of the parties to enter into a contract is the so-called '*ikano-tita pros to simvalleste*'. It should be noted that issues of *authority* of the agent to bind the principal are not relevant here. This situation must be distinguished. A party may have the *capacity* to enter into a contract, but may legally not have any *authority* from his principal to do so. There are certain cases in which an agreement entered into by someone who lacks the *authority* to enter into an agreement may be binding on the principal.[162] In certain cases where the party entering into the contract does not have the authority of the principal, the contract is binding unless it falls within the cases where the principal can avoid the contract. Even in such cases, it must be noted that the contract is voidable not void *ab initio* and the principal may in certain cases lose his right to avoid the contract. This must be contrasted to cases where there is no *capacity* to contract. In such cases the agreement does not become an enforceable contract at all.

According to **section 11(1)** of the **Contract Law, Cap 149** persons who are not able to contract are those who are not of sound mind or who are disqualified from contracting by any law. Contracts made by persons of unsound mind are valid but if the other party knew that he was contracting with a person who by reason of the unsoundness of his mind did not understand the nature of the contract, then the contract is voidable at the option of the insane person.[163]

Section 11(2) provides that the rights of persons below the age of eighteen to enter into contracts are governed by the law in force in England for the time being. There is a limited right of persons under the age of eighteen to contract. It is expressly provided that a person is not to be deemed incompetent to contract merely because he has not attained the age of eighteen years.[164] Accordingly, persons below the age of eighteen years may enter into contracts for the bare necessities,[165] or contracts which operate for the benefit of the person. If the contract does not fall within this exception, the contract is voidable at the instance of the person either while he is still underage or within a reasonable time as soon as he becomes eighteen.

---

[162] For example section 33A of the Companies Law, Cap 113, provides that the company will be bound against a third party by the acts of its agents which are contrary to the purpose clause of the company, provided that the third party did not have knowledge of the fact that the act of the agent was *ultra vires* and that the act was not contrary to any provision of the law.

[163] Andreas Neocleous & Co, see note 1 above, p 381.

[164] Section 11(2), Cap 149.

[165] Such as food, clothing and medical care for example.

(b)   Free consent

'Consent' is defined as an agreement by two or more persons upon the same thing and in the same sense.[166] 'Free consent' is defined as consent which is not caused by coercion, undue influence, fraud, misrepresentation, or mistake.[167] Agreements where there is no free consent are in certain cases void and in other cases voidable. This will be expanded on below.

(c)   The consideration and purpose must be legitimate

It is provided that the consideration or object of an agreement is lawful unless it is forbidden by law, or is of such nature that if permitted would defeat the provisions of any law; or is fraudulent; or involves or implies injury to a person or property of another; or the Court regards it as immoral or opposed to public policy.[168] Agreements where the object or consideration is unlawful are void.[169] It should be noted that if any part of a single consideration for one or more objects, or any part of any one or several considerations for a single object is unlawful, the agreement is void.[170]

(d)   Where the contract is void or voidable

In Cyprus law when a defect has 'retroactive' effect of such nature whereby ownership is deemed never to have passed, the contract is deemed to be void.

When the defect is such that it gives rise to an 'ex nunc' effect in the sense that the ownership may be terminated from that point onwards then the contract is deemed to be voidable (*'ipo eresi'*). The case *Anthoulla Melaisi v M&M Georghiki Eteria Ltd*[171] is a case regarding the sale of immovable property. Nevertheless it considers the interpretation of **section 55** of the **Contract Law, Cap 149.** It was held that because of the failure to perform at the specified time, the contract was voidable at the option of the seller who took no steps to avoid it on such grounds. In this case therefore, the right to terminate had been waived. The case of *Demetrios Stylianou v Andreas*

---

166 Section 13, Cap 149.

167 Section 24 *ibid.*

168 Section 23.

169 *Ibid.* See also *Glamour Development v Christodoulou* (1984) 1 CLR 444 (Government employee who was not allowed to have a separate profession was not paid for work done).

170 Section 24, Cap 149.

171 (1979) 1 CLR 748.

Photiades[172] establishes clearly that the plaintiff who wishes to rescind a voidable contract does not need to prove damage in order to be able to succeed.[173]

According to **section 10 of Cap 149**, all agreements are contracts if they are made with the 'free consent' of parties competent to contract, for lawful consideration and with a lawful object and are not expressly declared void by this law.

(i)   Voidable agreements

According to **section 19 of Cap 149**, when consent to an agreement is caused by coercion, fraud[174] or misrepresentation, the agreement is said to be voidable at the option of the party whose consent was so caused. According to section 20, when consent to an agreement is caused by undue influence, the agreement is voidable at the option of the party whose consent was so caused.

A contract is also voidable in the case where what is known in English law as 'the doctrine of frustration' comes into play. The doctrine of frustration is encoded in **section 56(2) of Cap 149**.[175]

(ii)   Void agreements

According to **section 21 of Cap 149**, where *both parties* to the agreement are under a mistake of *fact* essential to the agreement, the agreement is *void*. It is however expressly provided that an erroneous opinion as to the value of the thing which forms the subject matter of the agreement is not to be deemed a mistake as to a matter of fact. It is further provided in **section 21(2)** that a contract is not voidable because it was caused by a mistake as to any *law* in force in Cyprus; but a mistake as to a law not in force in Cyprus has the same effect as a mistake of fact. On the issue of avoiding the contract with retroactive effect on account of a mistake as to the solvency of the other party, there appears to be no Cypriot case law. It is however expressly provided that a contract is not void or voidable because it was caused by one of the parties to it being under a mis-

---

172 (1957) CLR 60.

173 See para 77 of judgment '… we have not been able to find any authority for the proposition that such plaintiff cannot succeed unless he proves damage'.

174 See *Demetrios Stylianou v Andreas Photiades* (1957) CLR 60.

175 S. 56(2) 'A contract to do an act which, after the contract is made, becomes impossible, or, by reason of some event which the promisor could not prevent, unlawful, becomes void when the act becomes impossible or unlawful'.

take as to a matter of fact.[176] Thus in the hypothetical case where one of the parties is under a mistaken belief as to the solvency of the other party, this would not be deemed a mistake in this section since the section requires that *both* parties must be mistaken in order for it to come into operation. If the party who is bankrupt is not aware that in his current state he is deemed by the law to be bankrupt (so that it appears that both parties believed that the bankrupt party is in fact solvent) the section again does not apply because this would be considered a mistake of *law*.

As explained above, an agreement which is made in the absence of consideration is void (section 25). Further, agreements will be void if they restrain legal proceedings (section 28), if their meaning is not certain or capable of being made certain (section 29) or if they are agreements by way of wager (section 30).

This is by no means an exhaustive list. An agreement may be void or voidable for other reasons such as for example the infringement of the provisions of the **Fraudulent Transfers Avoidance Law, Cap 62.**

(e)   Consequences on the ownership of the transferee/ transferor of the passing of property

Where a contract is void under the law (as opposed to voidable) any transfer of property is also void. This was established clearly in the case *Anthoulla Papadopoulou v Xenophon Polykarpou*.[177] This was a case of transfer of immovable property by an infant. The appellant-plaintiff was at the time of the transfer fifteen years of age. Following the pre-Independence Supreme Court of Cyprus in *Myrianthousis v Petrou*[178] which followed the Privy Council decision in *Mohori Bibee v Dhurmondas Ghose*[179] it was held that the agreement in question was void.[180] Hence the transfer of ownership was also void.

There is however one important point to note about this judgment. It was held by Stavrinides J that 'as the respondent had improved the property in the meantime, it would be contrary to *natural justice*[181] that the

---

[176] Section 22, Cap 149.

[177] (1968) 1 CLR 352.

[178] 21 CLR 23.

[179] (1930) 30 IA 114; 30 Cal 539.

[180] The case is based on section 11 of the Contract Law, Cap 192 (1949 edition) as it stood prior to its amendment by Law No 7 of 1956, however the part of the judgment which refers to the effect of a declaration that a contract is void is not affected.

[181] P 356 (Emphasis added). It should be noted that natural justice is primarily an administrative law concept and it appears rather odd that this concept was introduced in this area of the law. Usually the courts resort to the aid of restitution to deal with such cases.

judgment should be unconditional'. It was thus held that the judgment must be subject to the condition for the payment of compensation in respect of the improvements. On this point, Hadjianastasiou J arrived at the same conclusion but relied instead on **section 65 of the Contract Law Cap 149** as opposed to the rules of natural justice. He stated that 'in setting aside the transfer at the instance of the appellant, I would order the appellant, in the exercise of my discretion under section 65 of the Contract Law, to pay compensation to the respondent, because she has received an advantage under the agreement discovered to be void'.[182] In arriving at this conclusion, he relied on the judgment of *Ali Selim v The Heirs of Emete Filio Ali*.[183]

It is worth noting that apart from the above principle that a person who succeeds in having a contract declared void may have to pay compensation to the other person who has improved the property, another principle established is that of the argument of hardship.[184]

In the case of *Kier (Cyprus) Ltd v Trenco Constructions Ltd*[185] – which was a case in which the doctrine of frustration had rendered the contract void – it was held that the contract having become void, restitution could be claimed under section 65 of Contract Law Cap 149. The judgment cites Pollock and Mulla, *Indian Contract and Specific Relief Acts* (9th ed N M Tripathi, Bombay 1972), p 461:

'The basis of the section is the doctrine of restitio in integrum. It does not make a new contract between the parties but only provides for restitution of the advantage taken by a party under the contract. Unless the Court can having regard to circumstances of the case restore the parties to their original position section 65 would not be applicable. The section is not wider in scope than the English doctrine of restitution. The obligation to pay compensation under section 65 is quite different from a claim under the contract itself and the two cannot co-exist. Restitutionary remedies, as quasi-contractual, only arise where the original contract is put an end to or contracts become ineffective due to mistake or impossibility or lack of writing or lack of capacity'.

---

[182] Section 65 provides that if a contract is void *ab initio*, or a contract which was voidable has been avoided, then any person who has received such an advantage under such agreement contract is bound to restore such benefit or to compensate the person from whom he has obtained the benefit.

[183] (1946) 17 CLR 143.

[184] See *Munro v Butt* (1858) 8E & B 756; Maxwell, P B, *On the Interpretation of Statutes* (1962), p 199 (cited in the judgment) where it was said that the argument of hardship was always a dangerous one to listen to and is apt to introduce dangerous bad law and has occasionally led to the erroneous interpretation of statutes.

[185] (1981) 1 CLR 30.

Thus it appears that the issue is one of restitution although again it should be noted that in the judgment of the lower Court in this case the trial judge stated[186] that it was considered only 'fair and just'[187] that the money should be returned to the plaintiffs.

5.3.2. Transfer of ownership in cases other than where there is an underlying contractual obligation

(a)   Gift / donation

Cyprus like the UK is one of the few countries which have adopted the doctrine of consideration. The general rule is provided by section 25(1) which provides that a contract which is not supported by consideration is void. This is subject to three exceptions provided by subsections (a), (b), and (c). Section 25 1(a) provides that a contract not supported by consideration is valid if it is in writing and signed by the party who bears the burden of the obligation and is entered into due to natural love and affection between the parties who have a strong family link (this has included brothers but not cousins).

One of the peculiarities of this doctrine however is that *consideration must be adequate but need not be sufficient*.[188] The law is not concerned with amending men's bargains. Thus even so-called 'peppercorn consideration' may be valid consideration. That is even the smallest amount can constitute valid consideration. Indeed in *Chappell & Co Ltd v Nestle Co Ltd*[189] chocolate wrappers were held to be valid consideration. Thus even, though strictly speaking unless a contract falls within the exceptions of section 25, a donation cannot be a valid contract at all; due to its nature, the doctrine can easily be evaded.

Thus a donation can be a contract within the narrow confines of section 25 or if it is supported by 'pseudo-consideration' for the purposes of satisfying the doctrine. Of course however in cases of such pseudo-consideration, one could in such a case argue that it ceases to be a gift.

Perhaps the best way of making a gift in Cyprus law is the declaration of oneself as a trustee of the movable in question such that one holds the legal title for the benefit of the recipient. This would be an express trust. The requirements of the valid creation of a trust must of course be re-

---

[186] *Ibid*, p 44.

[187] Which appears to come close to the administrative law notions.

[188] This is codified in section 25(c), although it is provided that the inadequacy of consideration may be taken into account by the Court in determining the question of whether the consent of the promisor was given freely.

[189] [1960] AC 87.

spected for a trust to validly exist and there must be no contravention of any rule of equity.

A person may make a gift by way of will or testament but he may only make a disposition out of the *disposable portion* of his estate (*i.e.* the portion which remains after the legal portions of certain classes of successors are removed from the estate).[190]

(b)   Court orders

It is of course also possible for property to vest as a result of an order of the Court.

5.3.3.   The cornerstone principle of intention

The most basic principle which arises from the rules on the transfer of ownership is that property passes when it is intended to pass. The intention of the parties may in certain cases appear from the express or implied terms of the contract. In absence of such intention arising from the contract, the **Sale of Goods Act 1994** provides a set of default rules for inferring such an intention.

It is seen that the intention of the parties is the governing principle both on the larger scale and in more particular ways. By this we mean that, not only does intention govern the more general default rules of the Sale of Goods Act such that for example property usually passes on the occurrence of delivery, but also in the sense that what 'delivery' means for the purposes of the particular contract in question is also a matter to be inferred from the intentions of the parties to that contact. Thus we see the principle of the intention of the parties being the cornerstone principle and the other concepts such as the 'identification' of the goods, 'delivery', retention of title, role of payment and passing of risk being concepts which are inextricably linked to the basic rule that property passes when it is intended to pass.

---

[190] Section 21 Wills of Testament and Succession Law, Cap 195.

5.3.4. The concepts of 'identification' of the goods, of delivery, of passing of risk and the role of other factors

(a) 'Specific' and 'generic' goods

Property in goods cannot pass unless the goods have come into existence and have been identified as the contract goods. This is a rule of general application regardless of the intentions of the parties. This identification of the goods may (and usually does) require actual or constructive delivery. Once there is such identification property *can* pass but it does not necessarily pass. Where there is a passing of risk, unless the parties otherwise provide, the passing of property can be inferred under the default rule that risk passes with property.

(b) 'Identification' ('Εξακρίβωση') –
The problem of unascertained goods

When goods are identified as goods corresponding to the contract description, they are said to have become 'ascertained' or 'εξακριβωθούν'.

Section **6(1)** of the **Sale of Goods Act 1994** provides that goods which are the subject matter of an agreement to sell may be goods which are in existence at the time of contracting, which belong to or are in the possession of the seller, or may be goods which will come into existence at some future time. Section **6(2)** provides that a contract of sale may be validly made in relation to goods whose acquisition by the seller depends on an event which may or may not occur. Section **6(3)** provides that when by means of contract a seller undertakes to perform a present sale of future goods, the contract operates as an agreement for the sale of goods.

While there can be an *agreement to sell* unascertained or future goods there can be no *sale* of unascertained (unidentified) or future goods. *Property in goods cannot pass unless the goods are identified.* This appears to be the case even if the goods form part of an identified bulk. Section **18** provides that where there is an agreement for the sale of unascertained goods, the property in such goods does not pass to the buyer unless the goods have been ascertained. It should be noted that the provisions of **section 18** of the 1994 Law, are reproduced in **section 16 of the English Sale of Goods Act 1979** which is expressly made subject to **section 20A of the Sale of Goods Act 1979.** This section provides that where the buyer has paid the price for some or all of the goods which are the subject of the contract which form part of the bulk which is identified, the property in an undivided share in the bulk is transferred to the buyer and the buyer becomes owner in common of the bulk to the extent to which he has made payment. In view of the absence of such an additional provision in Cyprus law, the restriction in relation to goods which have not been ascertained is not qualified in cases where the unascertained goods form part of an identified bulk in the manner in which the restriction is qualified in English law. This complicates matters in relation to issues of commixture and confusion and appears to leave a *lacuna* in the law as will be seen further below.

(c) Unconditional appropriation of goods to the contract ('Υπαχθούν χωρίς όρους')

In relation to the passing of property it must be said that Cypriot law follows English law (see the *Carlos Federspiel* case below) which provides that not only the goods must be ascertained, but they must also be *unconditionally appropriated to the contract*. As explained above, **section 18** requires that property in goods may not pass unless the goods have been ascertained ('εξακριβωθούν'). **Section 23** goes on to provide that they must also be unconditionally appropriated to the contract ('Υπαχθούν χωρίς όρους'). Specifically section 23 provides that when there is a contract for the sale of unascertained or future goods sold by description and goods of such description in deliverable state are unconditionally appropriated to the contract either by the seller with the consent of the buyer or by the buyer with the consent of the seller, then property in the goods passes to the seller. Such consent may be express or implied and can be given before or after appropriation of the goods to the contract.

Unconditional appropriation may in certain cases be implied by law. **Section 23(2)** provides that when, under the contract, the seller delivers the goods to the buyer or a carrier or a bailee of the buyer (whether such bailee is named by the buyer or not) for the purpose of delivering such goods to the buyer and does not reserve the right to sell to someone else the goods in question, then the seller is deemed to have unconditionally appropriated the goods to the contract.

The following case summarises the position under Cyprus law on the matter of ascertainment and unconditional appropriation.

In *Ouzounian, M Soulanian & Co Ltd v Chr Hjiprordomou Estates Ltd*[191] unascertained goods by description were ordered in advance of the anticipated time of delivery and were paid for by the buyers. The sellers kept the goods in their store pending the date in future when the buyers would take delivery of them. The store came under Turkish occupation and delivery of the goods to the buyers was impossible. Property in the goods and therefore risk had never passed from the sellers to the buyers so that the sellers were not bailees for the buyers. The amount paid by the buyers was returned since

---

[191] (1979) 1 CLR 726.

consideration had failed. The goods had been sent from Nicosia to Famagusta (where the buyer was) but they were not delivered to the buyer.

Triandafillides J first referred to the fact that as pointed out in *Demetriades v Caxton Publishing Co Ltd*[192] our Cap 267 re-enacts with small variations the Sale of Goods Act 1893 in England and that it was therefore quite useful and proper to rely on the relevant case law in England.

The judge referred to *Ross T Smyth & Co v T D Bailey Son & Co*,[193] where Lord Wright said that where the sale is of unascertained goods by description, there are at that stage no goods to which the contract can attach. The seller is free to appropriate to the contract any goods which answer the contract description. The judgment then continues by saying that this he does by notice of appropriation which specifies and defines the goods to which the contract attaches. These thereupon he is bound to deliver and the buyer is bound to accept subject to the terms of the contract. That does not however involve the passing of property. The property cannot pass under a contract of sale until the goods are ascertained, but once they are ascertained, the property passes at the time when the parties intend that it shall. As the parties seldom express such intention, the intention will generally be inferred from the terms of the contract, the conduct of the parties and in general the circumstances of the case. Section 18 gives some general rules unless a contrary intention appears.

The judge then referred to *Carlos Federspiel & Co, SA v Charles Twigg & Co*[194] which considers what constitutes appropriation in the sense of the statute. In that judgment it was stated that the element of common intention has always to be born in mind and that a mere setting apart or selection by the seller of the goods which he expects to use in the performance of his contract is not enough. If that is all, he can change his mind and use those goods in performance of some other contract and use some other goods in the performance of this contract.

The following five rules of the case have been approved:

1. To constitute an appropriation of the goods to the contract, the parties must have had, or be reasonably supposed to have had, an intention to attach to the contract irrevocably those goods so that those goods and no others are the subject of the sale and become the property of the buyer.
2. It is by agreement of the parties that appropriation, involving change of ownership is made although in some cases the buyer's assent to an appropriation by the seller is conferred in advance by the contract itself or otherwise.

---

[192] (1973) 1 CLR 35.
[193] [1940] All ER 60.
[194] [1957] 1 Lloyd's Law Reports 240.

3. An appropriation by the seller, with the assent of the buyer is said always to involve actual or constructive delivery. If the seller retains possession he does so as bailee for the buyer.
4. The passing of risk is an indication of whether property has passed.
5. Usually but not necessarily, appropriation is the last act performed by the seller. For instance if delivery is to be taken by the buyer at the seller's premises and the seller has completed his part of the contract and has appropriated the goods when he has made the goods ready and has identified them and placed them in a position to be taken by the buyer and has so informed the buyer, if the buyer agrees to come and take delivery, that is the assent to appropriation. But if there is a further act, an important and decisive act to be done by the seller, then there is prima facie evidence that probably the property does not pass until the final act is done.

Then the judge concluded that on the facts of the case before him, the trial judge was correct to find that the goods had only been provisionally (as opposed to unconditionally) appropriated to the contract and there was nothing to prevent the sellers from selling to other customers of theirs such goods and it was noted that the sellers had at the same time orders for similar cookers and the manager remembered delivering similar goods to other customers.

(d) Further examination of the concepts of 'identification' and 'appropriation'

The problem of identification arises in cases of an agreement to sell future goods by description or goods in bulk which have not been ascertained at the time of contracting. As explained above, such 'identification' is at least a prerequisite for the passing of property. Once such 'identification' has been made, property may pass. It is usually the case that 'appropriation' will be the final act required for the property to pass but this is not necessarily the case. Whether property passes depends on the fulfilment of all the requirements of **section 23** and the position is as explained in *Ouzunian* above which expressly adopts the principles of *Carlos Federspiel*.

One of the important issues arising here relates to whether the unilateral act of one party may constitute appropriation or whether the assent of the other party is required and in which form this assent must be (whether it must be expressed or whether it can be implied and if so, the circumstances in which it may be implied). As explained above, the statute provides that assent to appropriation may be express or implied and may be given before or after appropriation. The following case sheds some light on the concept of implied assent.

Pignataro v Gilroy[195] was a case of implied assent. In this case the defendants contracted to sell to the plaintiffs 140 bags of rice which were at the time unascertained. In due course the defendant notified the plaintiff that 125 bags were available at one address and 15 at another address. Despite two reminders, the plaintiff did not collect the remaining 15 bags. The bags were stolen and the question was whether the property had passed (since in absence of a contrary stipulation, property passes with risk as will be seen below).

It was held by Rowlatt J that property had passed. It was held that by placing the goods at the premises in question there had been an appropriation which the buyers had impliedly assented to in advance by asking for the delivery order. The judge said that 'As he chose to say nothing for a whole month in response to an appropriation made in consequence of his own letter, we think it comes to exactly the same thing as if he had written saying he would remove them and did not'. 'As assent may be implied we think that not only was there evidence of it but that it is the only inference possible on the facts'.

Another issue is whether identification must be irrevocable and whether goods can be replaced after they have been ascertained.

In *Mucklow v Mangles*[196] even the act of printing the buyer's name on the stern of the barge was not held sufficient to appropriate the property to the contract since even so it was open to the seller to remove the name from the stern and sell the barge to someone else. As Heath J put it 'a tradesman often finishes goods which he makes in the pursuance of an order given by one person and sells them to another. If the first customer has other goods made for him within the stipulated time, he has no right to complain; he could not bring it over against the purchaser for the goods sold. The painting of the name on the stern in this case makes no difference.'

Whether the goods have been irrevocably appropriated to the contract however is always ultimately dependent upon the facts of the case. As will be illustrated below, similar cases may yield different results.

In *Langton v Higgins*[197] there was a contract for the sale of the whole of the vendor's crop of oil of peppermint grown in a certain year. The buyer had sent the seller the bottles in which to put the oil. The seller filled the bottles and then sold them to someone else. It was held that the property in the peppermint oil had passed when the bottles were filled. Bramwell B stated in this case 'Can there be more complete evidence of intention to

---

[195] [1919] 1 KB 459; see LS Sealy & RJA Hooley, *Commercial Law Text, Cases and Materials* (2004) (hereinafter cited as 'Sealy & Hooley'), p 320.

[196] (1808) 1 Taunt 318, Court of Common Press; see Sealy & Hooley, *ibid*, p 318.

[197] (1859) 4 H & N 402, Court of Exchequer; see Sealy & Hooley, see note 195 above, p 318.

pass property than when the vendee sends her bottles to be filled with the article purchased and the vendor puts it into the bottles?'

Thus we see that in one case, writing the name of the purchaser on the article to be sold was not held to be unconditional appropriation to the contract but in another putting the liquid into bottles sent by the purchaser, was held to be sufficient to appropriate the goods to the contract and constituted evidence of intention to pass property in the liquid to the buyer at the time the bottles were filled. Thus there must always be a *caveat* about what constitutes appropriation of goods to a particular contract.

5.4. Form of delivery and delivery equivalents

5.4.1. The law

Delivery or '*paradosi*' is defined in **section 2(1) of the Sale of Goods Act** as the voluntary transfer of possession from one person to the other. **Section 107 of the Contract Law, Cap 149** provides that delivery to the bailee may be made by doing anything which has the effect of putting the goods in the possession of the intended bailee or of any person authorised to hold them on his behalf.

It is provided in **section 33 of the Sale of Goods Act 1994** that delivery may be effected in any way in which the parties agree *or* which results in the goods being placed in the possession of the buyer or any person authorised to hold them on the account of the buyer. The first limb of **section 33** is open-ended. It does not necessarily require possession. Section 33 provides clearly that what constitutes delivery for the purposes of each contract may be defined by the parties to the contract. The second limb of section 33 requires possession. It is provided that when the goods come into the possession of the buyer or a person authorised to hold them on account of the buyer, then this will constitute delivery.[198] It is the position of the authors that neither of the two forms of delivery provided by section 33 is in any way 'subsidiary' to each other. They are *alternative* to each other. It is not the case, if for example physical delivery is impossible, that one must then look to other means of effecting delivery. Even where physical delivery is possible, the parties are free to agree that delivery will be effected by means other than physical delivery *e.g.* that delivery by the seller to the buyer will be deemed to occur upon a declaration by the seller that he now holds the goods for the buyer.

---

[198] Although this does not always mean passing of property. Property passes when it is intended to pass so even if there is delivery, if for example there is a reservation of title clause, property will not be deemed to have passed.

Section 36 provides certain default rules in cases where the parties do not make certain important provisions. In making these provisions, both limbs of section 33 are contemplated. It is provided that the issue of whether the buyer is under an obligation to take delivery of the goods or the seller is under an obligation to dispatch such goods to the buyer is a matter which depends in each case on the express or implied terms of the agreement.[199] The section then goes on to provide certain default rules in case certain important matters are not provided for by the parties in their contract.

- **Place of delivery in the absence of agreement on the matter**: In the absence of such an agreement, the goods are delivered at the place found at the time of sale or if the goods were not in existence at the time of contracting, then the place of delivery is the place of manufacture of such goods.[200]
- **Time of delivery in the absence of agreement on the matter**: When under the contract the seller is bound to dispatch the goods to the buyer but no time is set for their dispatch, the seller is bound to dispatch the goods within a reasonable time.[201]
- **Party who must bear the cost in the absence of agreement on the matter**: The cost of putting the goods in a deliverable state is unless otherwise agreed to be born by the seller.[202]

Section 33 above, provides for the alternative that an act which results in the goods being placed in the possession of the buyer or any person authorised to hold them on the account of the buyer will constitute delivery. **Section 36** makes a default provision in respect to this alternative. It is provided that when at the time of sale the goods are in the possession of a third party, there is no delivery from the seller to the buyer unless and until such time as the third person notifies the buyer that he is holding them on his behalf.[203] It is provided that this section does not affect the issue or transfer of any document of title to the goods.[204]

Crucially it is also provided that a request or offer for delivery if made within reasonable time will not allow for any of the legal remedies.[205] What constitutes reasonable time is dependent upon the practical circumstances.[206]

---

[199] Section 36(1).
[200] *Ibid.*
[201] Section 36(2).
[202] Section 36(5).
[203] Section 36(3).
[204] *Ibid.*
[205] Section 36(4).
[206] *Ibid.*

5.4.2. Policy

Insurance appears to be one of the factors which underlie the legal provisions in relation to delivery. This however only concerns the parties to the contract not the community as a whole.

5.4.3. Forms of delivery and delivery equivalents

(a) Description of a delivery

There is no exhaustive mandatory list of what constitutes delivery. The definition given in **section 2** (as above) is a very general one and it requires any delivery to be voluntary. This definition is expanded on in **section 33** and by case law appropriately. Section 33 consists of two limbs. The first limb defines delivery according to the intentions of the parties. The second limb provides a default rule which is linked to 'possession'.

It is provided that when at the time of sale the goods are in the possession of a third party, there is no delivery from the seller to the buyer unless and until such time as the third person notifies the buyer that he is holding them on his behalf.[207] Thus delivery can be effected by what is known in English law as 'novation' and does not require that the buyer obtains physical possession.[208] It is provided that this section does not affect the issue or transfer of any document of title to the goods.[209]

Physical delivery is not necessary for the first limb of section 33 and it does not appear to be necessary that there is physical delivery *to the buyer* under the second limb either since delivery can effectively be made to someone who is authorised to hold the goods on behalf of the buyer.

That the delivery takes place voluntarily is in fact a necessary prerequisite as explained above.

It is the seller or an agent of the seller who can deliver to the buyer[210] but when the goods are in the possession of a third party, then the third party may deliver to the buyer by notifying him that he holds the goods on his behalf.

Delivery *can be* by means of handing over a certain instrument or by handing over complete or partial control regardless of whether physical

---

[207] Section 36(3).

[208] There is an underlying issue of insurance in the requirement of notification. One must know that the goods have been delivered to oneself so that one can insure them.

[209] *Ibid.*

[210] Section 31 provides that it is the obligation on the seller to deliver the goods to the buyer.

delivery is also possible or not, if the contract provides that delivery shall be effected in this way.

An example is the case of *J M Zachariades & Co v Houloussi Bey Mufti-zade ex parte Ibrahim Ali*. (I) purchased certain sheep from the defendant and paid the purchase money. The sheep were allowed to remain in the defendant's possession under an agreement entered into between him and (I). It was held that the property in the sheep had vested in (I) even if no delivery had been effected and the facts proved delivery of the sheep to (I)'s agent.

The claimant sent his nephew to take formal possession of the sheep which was effected by his touching and counting them. They were handed back to the defendant under a written agreement made between him and the claimant that he should have the custody of the sheep in consideration of receiving half the profits derived from the flock. It was not denied that the transaction was *bona fide*.

It had been argued that there had been no delivery of the sheep to the claimant and the sale to him was consequently not complete. The case was decided under the articles of the *Mejelle* regulating the contract of sale (under which the property had passed on the payment of the price) but the following statement must be noted 'If it were necessary to decide the point, we think that there had been **sufficient delivery**[211] of these sheep to the agent of the claimant. Under Article 263, delivery is completed by the vendor giving permission to the vendee to take possession in such a way that there is no obstacle in his doing so. In the present case the claimant's agent went to the farm where the sheep were. The animals were brought out and touched and counted by him, and then put back again. He had gone to the farm for the express purpose of taking delivery of them, and we think that there was a sufficient delivery of them under the law'.

Although this was a case interpreting delivery before 1960 and before the enactment of the Sale of Goods Act in 1994, in view of the wide formulation of the first limb of article 33, it would probably still be considered good law as to the interpretation of 'delivery' as there is nothing to indicate the contrary. It must be stressed however that the case only provides guidance as to the interpretation of delivery.

The question of making a transfer by marking an object for the transferee or affixing a sign on it is intertwined with the question of unconditional appropriation which is discussed in relation to the passing of property in certain cases. For example in relation to goods which come into existence after the time of contracting, if the affixing of the sign or the marking is such as to constitute unconditional appropriation, and the buyer is to pick up the goods from the premises of the seller for example, then the act of affixing the sign or of marking the object may constitute delivery and will

---

[211] Emphasis added.

simultaneously have the effect of passing the property in the goods to the buyer if it cannot be successfully argued by the seller that he could sell such goods to another customer (and therefore evidence that he has not unconditionally appropriated the goods to the contract). In *Carlos Federspiel* the link between delivery and the passing of property was explained. It was said that unless a contrary intention appears, delivery being usually the final act to be performed by the seller will have the effect of passing the property in the goods to the buyer.

So to conclude, the affixing of a sign or the marking of an object *may* constitute delivery if this was the intention of the parties according to the express or implied terms of the contract that this act should constitute delivery, and such delivery *may* have the effect of passing the property in the goods to the buyer. What must be clear however is that affixing a sign or marking will constitute delivery in cases where there is no stipulation as to the place of delivery so that delivery is deemed to be at the premises of the seller (as explained above) or in cases where it is expressly provided that the buyer will take delivery from the premises of the seller. By putting the goods in a deliverable state, affixing a sign and leaving them at his premises for collection, the seller has effected delivery. If there remains a further act to be done by the seller, such as for example delivering to the premises of the buyer or to the buyer's agent, then affixing a sign does not constitute delivery.

(b)   Documents of title – the bill of lading

The Sale of Goods Act 1994 provides that 'documents of title' includes *inter alia* any bill of lading, dock warrant, warehouse-keeper's certificate and any other documents used in the ordinary course of business as proof of the possession or control of the goods, or authorising or purporting to authorise, either by endorsement or by delivery, the possessor of the document to transfer or receive goods thereby represented.[212]

The bill of lading is a document of title. It is a negotiable instrument which can be transferred to other beneficiaries provided the correct procedure is followed. One point that must be clarified at the outset is that this does not mean that title to the underlying goods passes with the transfer of the bill of lading. When there is a contract for the sale of goods, the passing of property is governed by that contract and the principle that property passes when it is intended to pass,[213] and a transfer of the bill of lading indicates nothing more than a delivery of the goods

---

[212] Section 2.
[213] Goode, see note 40 above, p 886.

would do.[214] It is of course possible that the parties agree that the property should pass upon the transfer of the bill of lading but this is the result of the contract provisions and is not the result of the handing over of the bill of lading *per se*.[215] The bill of lading therefore is best seen as a control document by which constructive possession is transferred rather than as a document by which title is passed.[216] This position was recently affirmed in Cyprus law in the case of *Standard Fruit Company (Bermuda) Limited v Gold Seal Shipping Company Ltd*.[217] G Papadopoulou in this case quoted Lord Bramwell in *Sewell v Burdick*[218] where it was said that the property does not pass upon endorsement but by the contract in pursuance of which the endorsement is made; so property passes by the contract. As is explained in the decisions however, whether the rights under the contract of carriage pass with the transfer of the bill of lading is a separate matter. Under the English Bills of Lading Act 1855 the endorsee acquires the right to sue under the contract of carriage for breaches committed both before and after he became owner of the goods. The endorsement need not be special.[219] Simple delivery of the bill of Lading endorsed in blank is sufficient.[220]

---

[214] *Carver Carriage by Sea* (1971), p 913. The point was illustrated also in *Sanders Brothers v Maclean & Co*, [1883] 11 QBD 327, *per* LJ Bowen, p 341: '... A cargo at sea while in the hands of the carrier is necessarily incapable of physical delivery. During this period of transit and voyage, the bill of lading by the law merchant is universally recognized as its symbol, and the endorsement and delivery of the bill of lading operates as a symbolical delivery of the cargo. Property in the goods passes by such endorsement and delivery of the bill of lading, whenever it is the intention of the parties that the property should pass, just as under similar circumstances the property would pass by an actual delivery of the goods. And for the purpose of passing such property in the goods and completing the title of the endorsee to full possession thereof, the bill of lading, until complete delivery of the cargo has been made on shore to someone rightfully claiming under it, remains in force as a symbol, and carries with it not only the full ownership of the goods, but also all rights created by the contract of carriage between the shipper and the shipowner. It is a key which in the hands of a rightful owner is intended to unlock the door of the warehouse, floating or fixed, in which the goods may chance to be.' (cited with approval in *Archangelos Domain Limited v Adriatica Societa per Azione di Navigatione*, Admiralty Action No 41/71).

[215] *Ibid*.

[216] Goode, see note 40 above, p 890; see *The Delfini* [1990] 1 Lloyd's Rep 252, *per* Mustill LJ, p 268.

[217] Admiralty Jurisdiction Case 77/90, 22 April 1997.

[218] 10 App Case 74 p 105.

[219] See note 217 above.

[220] *Ibid*.

In England, the Bolero bill of lading is in use.[221] This is a system which is confined only to members and is not insignificantly expensive so it has not been taken up widely.[222] Whether Cyprus law would accept an electronic bill of lading is a matter which is not yet clear.

(c) The rules for cases where the object is to be carried from the transferor to the transferee by a third party carrier

(i) The law

Section 39(1) of the **Sale of Goods Act** provides that when under the contract the seller is authorised or under an obligation to dispatch the goods to the purchaser, then delivery of the goods to the carrier, whether such carrier is named by the seller or not, for the purpose of their transfer to the buyer or delivery of them at a peer to a person responsible for their safe keeping, *prima facie* constitutes delivery to the buyer.

Section 39(2) provides that unless otherwise authorised by the buyer, the seller is under an obligation to enter into a reasonable contract for the account of the seller with the carrier or the person responsible at the peer, bearing in mind the nature of the goods in question and all the circumstances of the case. If the seller omits to act in this way, and the goods are lost or suffer damage during the transfer or their keeping by the person responsible at the peer, then the buyer may refuse to consider delivery of the goods to the person responsible at the peer as delivery to himself or he may hold the seller responsible for compensating him.

Section 39(3) Unless it is otherwise agreed, when the goods are dispatched from the seller to the buyer by sea under such circumstances in which it would be usual to insure such goods, then the seller is under an obligation to give such notice to the buyer in order to enable him to insure the goods during the sea voyage, and if the seller omits to give such a notification, then the seller will bear the risk in relation to the goods during the voyage.

Section 40 provides that even where the seller agrees to deliver the goods at his own risk at a place other than that where they are found at the time of sale, unless otherwise agreed, it is the buyer who bears the risk of deterioration which necessarily follows from the carriage of the goods.

---

[221] See Goode, note 40 above, pp 895-6.
[222] *Ibid.*

(ii)   Issues arising out of the passing of property

As explained above delivery to the buyer or to the carrier which may also constitute delivery to the buyer *may* but does not necessarily have the effect of passing the property in the goods. Nor is there any rule that says that ownership must necessarily pass upon the goods reaching the place of delivery. **Section 25** of the Sale of Goods Act expressly provides that the seller may retain ownership even after delivery and he may do so expressly or impliedly in certain cases. The basic rule is that property passes when it is intended to pass. If there are terms which expressly provide that property is to pass when the goods are delivered or that property should not pass until a later stage (*e.g.* payment of the price) then this is to be respected. Otherwise, in the absence of express intention, property may pass under the rules of the Sale of Goods Act as these are explained in the *Ouzounian* case.

The carrier in such cases has possession of the goods and as such he is bailee for the buyer or seller (accordingly). As such he has certain rights which arise from the possession of the goods such as the right to an action in conversion in case the goods are damaged. The rights, duties and liabilities which arise from bailment are explained in another section.

The issues of who is to conclude the contract with the carrier and who is to pay the transport are matters to be determined by the contract. If however the contract is to be concluded by the seller, then he is subject to the tortuous duty of care to the buyer and must accordingly enter into 'any reasonable contract' with the carrier.

(d)   Further possibilities

Brevi manu tradition: It is possible where the asset is already in the possession of the buyer for ownership to be subsequently transferred to him by agreement.

Consitutum possessorium: It is possible to transfer the ownership by mere agreement while the asset continues to be in the possession of the transferor after the passing of property. In such a case the transferor holds the asset as bailee (it is possible for the bailment to be gratuitous or otherwise) for the buyer.

Movable is under the control of a third party: It is provided that when at the time of sale the goods are in the possession of a third party, there is no delivery from the seller to the buyer unless and until such time as the third person notifies the buyer that he is holding them on his behalf.[223]

---

[223] Section 36(3) of the Sale of Goods Act 1994.

(e)   Link between revindication and delivery

Let us consider the theoretical case where a number of goods have been delivered under a reservation of title and the buyer pays only 50% of the contract price to the seller and the seller after partially terminating the contract demands some of the goods back.

The cornerstone of the Cyprus law on the sale of goods (as is the case with English law) is the *intention* of the parties. Property according to **section 19 of the Sale of Goods Act 1994** passes when it is intended to pass. The Act then lays down some rules for inferring such intention in the absence of such intention being made expressly clear by the parties.

The delivery of goods under a retention of title is expressly contrary to an intention that property in the goods passes to the buyer. Thus in the example given above, the seller would be entitled to claim back the entire amount of goods (not only the portion of the goods not paid for) and the remedy of the buyer would then lie in restitution or a claim for total failure of consideration.[224]

(f)   The link between delivery and the passing of property

It was explained above that according to the *Ouzounian* case, property usually passes on delivery unless a contrary intention appears. The *Algazera* case is an example of a case where there was evidence of an intention that the property was not to pass upon delivery but upon payment. In the case *Scheepswerf Bodewes-Gruno and The Ship 'Algazera', now lying at the port of Limassol* there was an agreement in writing with the plaintiffs whereby the plaintiffs undertook to build for the purchasers a ship in accordance with certain terms and specifications. The purchasers signed a document to the effect that the ship would not become their property until full payment of the contract price including eventual extra costs. The purchasers delivered two cheques which were never honoured. It was held that, from the authorities on the issue of the transfer of the property in goods from the seller, manufacturer *etc.* to the buyer, it appears that the mere handing of the goods by the seller to the buyer passes the property immediately unless a different intention appears from the terms of the contract of sale. In this case the document which provided that property would not pass until the full amount was paid was evidence of such contrary intention. The handing over therefore of the 'Builder's certificate' could not in any way affect the intention of the parties which expressed that property in the ship would not pass without the consent of

---

[224] See case *Al Karpasitis & Sons* (1989) 1C Apofasis Anotatou Dikastiriou (Supreme Court) 1980.

the plaintiffs. This means that the purchaser could not transfer any share of ownership in the ship, because the ownership had not vested in him.

5.5. Registration

The Sale of Goods Act makes no reference to registration. There is no single provision regarding the registration requirement in relation to all types of movables in general. As will be seen below, specific registration requirements are set forth in relation to certain particular movables.

5.5.1. Registration of ships

(a) The law

Registration of ships under the Cypriot flag is governed mainly by the Merchant Shipping (Registration of Ships, Sales and Mortgages) Laws, 1963 to 2005. These are based on the British Merchant Shipping Acts, 1894 to 1954.

(b) The relevant authority

It is provided that the Director of the Department of Merchant Shipping of the Ministry of Communications and Works shall carry out the duties of the Shipping Registrar of Cyprus.[225]

The department of Merchant Shipping was established and started functioning as a distinct entity in the Ministry of Communications and Works, in 1977.[226] The service had existed, however since 1963 and functioned under the Department of Ports.[227] The Department's activities include: registration of ships, administration and enforcement of the merchant shipping legislation, control of shipping and enforcement of international conventions, investigation of marine casualties, resolving labour disputes on board Cypriot ships, and training and certification of seafarers.[228]

---

[225] Section 3 Law 45 of 1963.

[226] http://www.mcw.gov.cy/mcw/mcw.nsf/dmlshipping_en/dmlshipping_en?OpenDocu ment as at 7/12/2006.

[227] http://www.shipping.gov.cy/ as at 7/12/2006.

[228] http://www.mcw.gov.cy/mcw/mcw.nsf/dmlshipping_en/dmlshipping_en?OpenDocu ment as at 7/12/2006.

(c)   Who can register a Cypriot ship

Part III of the Merchant Shipping Law[229] provides the requirements for registering a ship as a Cypriot ship. A ship may be registered as a Cypriot ship if more than fifty percent (50%) of the shares in the ship are owned by Cypriot citizens or by citizens of other Member States who in the instance of not being permanent residents of the Republic will have appointed an authorised representative in the Republic of Cyprus.[230]

It is also possible to register a ship as a Cyprus ship where the total (100%) of the shares in the ship are owned by one or more corporations, which have been established and operate in accordance with the Laws of the Republic of Cyprus and have their registered office in the Republic, or in accordance with the Laws of any other Member State and have their registered office, central administration or principal place of business within the European Economic Area and which will have either appointed an authorised representative in Cyprus or the management of the ship is entrusted in full to a Cypriot or a Community ship management company in Cyprus, or outside Cyprus or any other Member State but controlled by Cypriot citizens or citizens of Member States and have either appointed an authorised representative in Cyprus or the management of the ship is entrusted in full to a Cypriot or a Community ship management company in Cyprus. The company is deemed to be controlled by Cypriots or citizens of any other Member States when more than fifty percent of the shares belong to Cypriots or citizens of any other Member States or when the majority of the Directors of the corporation are Cypriots or citizens of any other Member State.[231]

(d)   Ownership of the ship

There cannot be more than one hundred shares of ownership in a ship[232] and a ship cannot be owned by more than one hundred natural persons (but the beneficial interest is not affected by this provision or the provisions on co-ownership).[233] Further, there can be no co-ownership of a

---

[229] And more particularly section 5.

[230] http://www.shipping.gov.cy/ as at 7/12/2006, section 5(a) of the Merchant Shipping Act.

[231] http://www.shipping.gov.cy/ as at 7/12/2006, section 5(b) of the Merchant Shipping Act.

[232] Section 4(3)(a).

[233] Section 4(3)(b).

fraction of a share in a ship, but five or less persons may be co-owners of a share, part of or the ship.[234]

Before a ship may be registered as a Cypriot ship, it must be inspected,[235] the relevant Minister must be satisfied that the ship itself is duly marked.[236]

(e) The process of registration

Cyprus law allows for 'provisional registration' followed by a 'permanent registration'. Provisional registration is possible if the vessel is not found at a Cyprus port. According to the Ministry of Communication and Works most foreigners opt for provisional registration first as it gives them time to complete the administrative formalities for permanent registration.[237] It is important for our purposes to note that among the documents which are required are the Bill of Sale or Builder's Certificate, a Certificate of Ownership, which shows that the vessel is free from encumbrances, from the previous registry a 'certificate of de-registration' of the vessel and a declaration of ownership.

Provisional registration lasts for six months but may be extended by another three months so the maximum period is nine months after which time the ship must be permanently registered.[238] Permanent registration is complete once the Registrar, upon receipt of the Carving and Marking Note, issues a Certificate of Registration.[239]

Cyprus law also allows for parallel-in registration such that a foreign flag vessel chartered to a Cyprus company can be registered in the Cyprus Register for a renewable period of two years and parallel-out registration for a period of up to three years.[240]

Cargo vessels older than 23 years, passenger vessels older than 35 years and fishing vessels older than 20 years are not accepted for registration.

It is worth noting that small fishing vessels are governed instead by the **Fishing Vessels (Registration, Sale, Transfer and Mortgage) Law of 1971** (Law 77/71) and their registration is thereby effected by the Fisheries Department of the Ministry of Agriculture, Natural resources and Environment.

---

[234] Section 4(3)(c).

[235] Section 7 makes reference *inter alia* to the place on the ship where the name and registration number should appear.

[236] Section 8 of the Merchant Shipping Act.

[237] http://www.shipping.gov.cy/guide_to_shipreg/provisional_reg.htm as at 8/12/2006.

[238] Andreas Neocleous & Co, see note 1 above, p 277.

[239] *Ibid*, p 279; see also section 15 Merchant Shipping Act 1963.

[240] http://www.shipping.gov.cy/guide_to_shipreg/parallel_reg.htm as at 8/12/2006.

(f)   Effect of registration

The registration of the ship constitutes *prima facie* evidence as to the ownership of the ship.[241] Such evidence can therefore be rebutted. However a *bona fide* purchaser who receives a duly executed and certified bill of sale by or on behalf of the previous registered owner of the ship will obtain good title if he has purchased for value and without notice of the fact that the registered owner is not the true owner.[242] Any dispute as to the ownership of the ship will be resolved by proceedings before the Admiralty Courts of Cyprus.[243] The fact that a vessel is registered under the flag of Cyprus allows a Court of Cyprus to issue a declaratory judgment in respect of the status of the said ship, notwithstanding that the same is under arrest in another country.[244]

(g)   How a sale may be effected

A registered owner who wishes to dispose of a ship must apply to the Registrar of Cyprus Ships who will enable him to do so by granting a certificate of mortgage or a certificate of sale.[245] A certificate of sale may not be granted except for the sale of the entire ship, and a transfer made to a person qualified to be the owner of a Cypriot ship must be by way of Bill of Sale.[246]

5.5.2.   Registration of vehicles

(a)   The law

The relevant legal provisions in relation to the registration of motor vehicles are to be found in the **Motor Vehicles and Road Traffic Act of 1972**.[247] Under this Act the Council of Ministers may issue regulations governing *inter alia* the registration of vehicles governed by this Act and the passing of property in such vehicles.[248] Regulations enacted in pursu-

---

[241] Andreas Neocleous & Co, see note 1 above, p 279.

[242] *Ibid.*

[243] *Ibid.*

[244] *Sotiris Papadopoulos and others v Blue Emblem Shipping Co Ltd* (Admiralty Action No 255/85).

[245] Andreas Neocleous & Co, see note 1 above, p 285.

[246] *Ibid*, p 286.

[247] Law 86 (I)/1972.

[248] Section 5 *ibid.*

ance of this power which are relevant for our purposes are the Automobiles and Motor Traffic Regulations (1984).

(b)   The relevant authority

Under the **Road Traffic Act of 1972**,[249] the Council of Ministers is given power to appoint a Registrar of Motor Vehicles, who is responsible for implementing this law and any Regulations made in furtherance of the law. His duties include ensuring that the law in relation to the registration of motor vehicles is applied.

(c)   The significance of registration

It is provided[250] that the 'owner' for the purposes of this law is the person in whose name the vehicle is registered, and where the vehicle is the subject of an agreement of hire purchase or lease, then the owner is the person in whose possession the vehicle can be found by virtue of that agreement.

The *certificate of registration*, however, is only *prima facie* evidence of ownership.[251]

(d)   Fraudulently achieving registration

A person who obtains a licence or certificate by oral or written misrepresentation, and it is not proven before a Court that he did not act fraudulently (*anef dolias protheseos*), is criminally liable.[252] The crime is punishable by a prison sentence of up to three years or a fine of up to three hundred Cyprus pounds or both.[253] Generally as a matter of law fraud is very difficult to prove, but it is noteworthy that under this section the burden of proof is on the person who has achieved the registration.

---

[249] Section 3.

[250] Section 2.

[251] Regulation 8 of Automobiles and Motor Traffic Regulations (1984); see also *Cleopas Demetriou v South African Eagle Insurance Company Limited*, Civil Appeal No 9617.

[252] Section 15, Law 86 (I)/1972.

[253] *Ibid.*

(e) Fraud with respect to the certificate

A person who forges or alters or allows such forgery or alteration of a certificate of registration is guilty of a crime which is punishable by a prison sentence of up to three years or a fine of up to three hundred Cyprus pounds or both.[254]

(f) Nullification of registration

Registration is nullified where the owner makes an application for such nullification or the vehicle is destroyed and this is evidenced by the relevant 'certificate of destruction'.[255]

5.5.3. Registration of animals

(a) The law

The legal provisions governing the registration of animals include the **Animals Certificates Law**[256] and more particular provisions may be found in the **Dogs Act 2002**.[257] The Animal Certificates Law applies to any horse, mule, donkey, camel, goat, sheep, or oxen or any other thorough breed but does not include any newborn animal still fed by its mother.[258]

(b) Authority responsible for registration

The '*muktar*' of each village is responsible for the registration of animals under Cap 29.[259] A certificate of ownership shall be issued at the request of a person residing in the area for which the '*muktar*' is responsible upon payment of the relevant fees if he is satisfied that the animal belongs to him.[260] He may rely on his knowledge or appearances as to the ownership of the animal.[261]

---

[254] Section 16, Law 86 (I)/1972.
[255] Section 23.
[256] Cap 29.
[257] Law 184(I)/2002.
[258] Section 2, Cap 29.
[259] Section 3.
[260] *Ibid.*
[261] *Ibid.*

(c)   The significance of registration and effect on transfer of ownership

No person can have possession of an animal without a certificate of title.[262] Further no person may purchase an animal unless the seller presents
to him a certificate of title, and if the seller is not the owner, the purchaser must be satisfied that the seller has authority to sell the animal.[263]
Upon sale, the '*muktar*', at the place of sale, shall issue a certificate of
ownership in the name of the purchaser and the name and address of the
seller, and the number and place of issue of the previous certificate must
be recorded on the new certificate.[264] If all the animals to which the certificate of the seller relates have been sold, then the certificate of the
seller must be destroyed and in the alternative case where only some of
the animals on the old certificate of the seller have been sold, the seller's
certificate shall be amended accordingly.[265]

Any sale in breach of these provisions is void.[266] The case of *Achilleas
D Achilleos v Andreas Mavrou, Georgios Mavrou* considers the issue of
section 7 of Cap 29. As the trial judge accepted, what is prohibited by
the provisions of section 7 is the *sale* without certificates of ownership; as
opposed to an *agreement to sell* which does not pass the property in the
movables to the buyer. In view of evidence that the payment of the balance was in this case a condition for the finalisation of the agreement
(failing which the plaintiffs were entitled to have the animals back) and
that the respondents assumed possession as bailees subject to finalisation,
this was a case of an agreement to sell not an outright sale.

The Animals Certification Law Cap 29 does not apply to animals, the
possession and ownership of which are governed by the Contagious Dis-
eases of Animals Laws of 1987 and 1983.

(d)   Particular provisions in relation to dogs

The Director of Veterinary Services or a person authorised to act on his
behalf is responsible for keeping a Register for Dogs in which all dogs
more than six months old must be registered.[267] All registered dogs must
be marked in a permanent way indicating the registration number of the
dog.[268] The medical health record of the dog is required for registration.

---

[262] Section 4(a).

[263] Section 4(b).

[264] Section 5(1).

[265] Section 5(2), Cap 29.

[266] Section 7.

[267] Section 8, Law 184(I)/2002.

[268] Section 9 *ibid*.

Persons who have not duly registered their dogs are deemed to have committed an offence and may be subject to imprisonment for a period of up to twelve months or a fine of up to one thousand Cyprus pounds.[269]

5.5.4. Registration of aircrafts

(a)   The law

The law which governs the registration of aircrafts is the **Civil Aviation Law of 2002.**[270] The Cyprus Register of Aircrafts is kept by the relevant authority under the supervision of the Minister of Communication and Works.[271] Any registration, re-registration and de-registration of an aircraft or rights *in rem* in an aircraft must be recorded in the register, and certificates shall be issued in pursuance of any such act.[272]

(b)   Requirements for registration

An aircraft may only be registered as a Cyprus aircraft if it is not registered in any other register, they have a certificate which shows that they are fit for flying, and they are compatible with certain environmental law requirements.[273] Further the owner of a share greater than 50% or a person having a right to purchase the aircraft or leaseholder for more than six months or other person with rights of this type must be:

- In the case of a natural person a citizen of the Republic of Cyprus or a citizen of an EU country or a country of the Common European Aeronautical Area, even if this person is not residing in the Republic of Cyprus.
- In the case of a legal person, such person must be established in the Republic of Cyprus or in a Member State of the European Union or a state belonging to the Common European Aeronautical Area, or have its 'seat' in such states, or 50% of its property and capital belong to citizens of such states, or those having the power to represent such legal person are citizens of such states as aforementioned.[274]

---

[269] Section 18, N 184(I)/ 2002.
[270] Law 213(I)/2002.
[271] Article 10 section 1, Civil Aviation Law of 2002.
[272] Article 10 section 2, *ibid.*
[273] Article 11 section 1, Civil Aviation Law of 2002.
[274] Article 11 section 1, *ibid.*

Exceptionally, the minister may if he gives appropriate justification register an aircraft which is not in compliance with the above requirements.[275]

5.5.5. Intellectual property

The relevant legal provisions can be found in **The Trademarks Law**,[276] and **The Patents Law**.[277]

In relation to trademarks, where a person becomes entitled, by assignment or transmission, to a registered trademark, he shall make application to the Registrar to register his title and once the Registrar is satisfied on the basis of proof of title that the person is the proprietor of the trademark, he shall cause the particulars of the transmission or assignment to be entered in the Register.[278] It is specifically provided that a document or instrument in respect of which no entry has been made in the register is not admissible in Court in proof of title to a trademark unless the Court otherwise directs.[279] This, in the context of trademarks, registration is crucial to the proprietary right itself.

Under the **Patents Law**, all certificates of patents shall be recorded in the Register of Patents Certificates.[280]

5.5.6. Shares

For the issues surrounding registration of shares see below the additional section in relation to the passing of property in shares.

5.5.7. Miscellaneous

The above considers the main classes of registrable movables. Other property may also be subject to registration by virtue of specific provisions. One such example is certain types of guns which are made registrable by virtue of **Law N 113(I)/2004**[281] within two days of arrival of the weapon in the Republic of Cyprus or within two days after the day of purchase. Application for registration must be made to the Chief of the

---

[275] Section 11(3).
[276] Cap 286.
[277] Law 16(I)/98.
[278] Cap 286, section 27(1).
[279] Cap 286, section 27(2).
[280] Law 16(I)/98 section 3.
[281] Section 33.

Police Department of the area in which the owner resides, and he may register the weapon and issue a licence to hold such weapon and a certificate of registration.[282] It is provided that if the certificate of registration is repealed, by written notice to the holder on the basis of public interest, then the weapon must be returned to the Chief of Police.[283]

5.6. Consensual system

For the passing of ownership or of some aspects thereof upon the conclusion of the contract, see *inter alia* section 5.3.

5.7. Real agreement

No declaration or agreement separate from the underlying obligation is necessary under Cypriot law to effect the transfer of ownership, since what matters is the intention of the parties. See *inter alia* section 5.3.3.

5.8. Payment

The **Sale of Goods Act 1994** provides that the contract may stipulate for immediate payment, or payment by instalments or payment at a later stage.[284]

There is no general rule that title is reserved until payment of the price in full. The general rule that property passes when it is intended to pass applies here also. In the absence of contrary stipulation, payment is not deemed to be a prerequisite for the passing of property. This is illustrated by the following case. In *Alexandros Pilakouri v Georghios Savva Samouti*,[285] under a contract of sale with the appellant, a walnut tree was to be severed by the appellant and the price was to be paid on a set date. The appellant severed the walnut tree and took delivery of it but he failed to pay its value. An action was brought for the recovery of the value of the tree. It was held that there was an agreement to sell and a sale and delivery were effected such that the sale and delivery took place at the same time.

It is of course possible for the seller to stipulate expressly that he reserves the right to dispose of such goods until certain terms (such as pay-

---

[282] Law 113(I)/2004 section 33(1).
[283] Law 113(I)/2004 section 33(2).
[284] Section 5(1).
[285] (1965) 1 CLR 83.

ment)[286] are fulfilled. In such a case property will not pass even if there is delivery of the goods.[287] It is however necessary that this be in the written terms of the agreement.

It would be possible as a matter of construction of the particular contract that such a term could be implied on the basis of the general rules on implied terms but it should be noted that the scope of implied terms is not wide.[288]

The only case in which there is an exception to the rule of an implied reservation of title as a matter of law is in cases falling within **section 25(3) of the Sale of Goods Act 1994**. This section provides that where the seller of goods draws on the buyer for the price, and transmits the bill of exchange and bill of lading to the buyer together to secure acceptance or payment of the bill of exchange, the buyer is bound to return the bill of lading if he does not honour the bill of exchange, and if he wrongfully retains the bill of lading the property in the goods does not pass to him.

Retention of title is dealt with more extensively in **Part IV** of the Report.

5.9. Right to dispose

Often there may be a disposition by a person who is not the owner and who is not authorised by the owner to make such a disposition.[289] The question then becomes whether such a disposition is valid and whether the third party has obtained a better right than the owner in such a case. This requires balancing the rights of the true owner against those of the (often) *bona fide* purchaser for value without notice.

In such cases the traditional default position of the law is encapsulated in the Latin maxim *Nemo dat quod non habet*. This means that nobody can confer a better title than he himself has. This rule however is not absolute. Certain exceptions have been carved out of this rule in response to the

---

[286] See case 'The Algazera' in section 5.4.2. above.

[287] Section 25(1) Sale of Goods Act 1994.

[288] Implication here would be as a matter of *fact*. Implication as a matter of *law* is possible under the statutory provisions of section 25(2) and 25(3) Sale of Goods Act 1994 (see Part IV of the Report).

[289] It should be noted that it is possible that the owner may lose his rights over the property by virtue of the operation of law as opposed to a disposition by some other party. This is the case for example under the Aliens and Immigrants Law, Cap 105 where it is provided in section 16 which allows the seizure and sale of the movable property in certain cases and under The Bankruptcy Law, Cap 5 and The Companies, Cap 113 which vest property rights in the trustee in bankruptcy or administrator who may sell property of the bankrupt or of the insolvent company respectively.

needs of the fast pace of the commercial world today. These exceptions operate to protect the purchaser in certain cases. Different legal systems draw the line at different places. Because of the substantial overlap of the issues arising under this section with the issues in Chapter 12 below (the rules on good faith acquisition) the reader is referred to the broader analysis of the *nemo dat quod non habet* rule and its exceptions in Chapter 12.

It suffices to say here that the exceptions to the *nemo dat* rule may be found in the **Contract Law, Cap 149,**[290] and in **The Sale of Goods Act.**[291] The discussion here should be restricted to the agency exceptions.

5.9.1. Principles of agency

The rules of the law of agency are found in the **Contract Law Cap 149.** Under these rules it will be seen that in certain cases an agent who was not *authorised* by his principal to make a certain disposition may nevertheless be able to make such a disposition validly. The rationale is that the principal has in some way made some representation to the world at large that the agent had such authority to make the disposition as between himself and the *bona fide* purchaser; the *bona fide* purchaser should prevail.[292]

The law of agency provides exceptions to the *nemo dat* rule in cases where the agent even though exceeding the authority which the principal has actually given to him, acts under what is called apparent or ostensible authority. **Part XIII** of the **Contract Law, Cap 149** essentially codifies the English law of agency.

It is important here to make the distinction between *power* and *authority*. The distinction must be made again in order to clarify the difference between actual and apparent authority. It is often said that an agent is limited by the scope of his authority. What this means is that as between himself and his principal, he can only act within the limits of his agreement with the principal. If he does so he is acting within the scope of his actual *authority*. If the principal puts him in a position from which he can perform further acts which are outside this authority, then it can be said that the agent has the *power* to do those further acts albeit without authority. The principal is considered to be bound by an act of his agent outside his *actual* authority[293]

---

[290] Sections 142-198.

[291] Sections 27-30.

[292] Of course the principal will often have an action against the agent in such cases.

[293] Actual authority of an agent can be express or implied (section 146, Cap 149). Authority is express where it is given by words spoken or in writing and it is said to be implied where it is to be inferred from the circumstances of the case, and things said, spoken or written or in the ordinary course of dealing may be accounted circumstances of the case (section 147, Cap 149).

but within his *apparent* authority in the cases where it can be considered that
the principal has in some way made some *representation* to the outside world
that his agent had actual authority to act in the way in which he did.[294] This
rationale is readily comparable to that which underlies the exceptions under
the Sale of Goods Act as will be explained below. As we will see the principal has a cause of action against his agent if the agent has exceeded his actual authority and the principal elects not to ratify[295] the unauthorised act of
the agent, thereby giving him a subsequent right to dispose.

In case of *Liopetri Transport Co v Loucas Constandinou*[296] it was held
that a bus driver who had actual authority to collect ordinary fares but no
actual authority to collect seasonal tickets nevertheless had apparent or
ostensible authority to collect season tickets. Thus payment made to the
bus driver was good payment in discharge of the debt due on the season
tickets. In the following extract of this judgment L Loizou J[297] cites with
approval English case law and gives valuable guidance as to the distinction between actual and apparent authority and as to what may constitute
a representation:

'One of the more recent cases on the subject is the case of *Hely-Hutchinson v.
Brayhead, Ltd. and Another* [1967] 3 All E.R. p. 98, in which the earlier case of
Freeman and Lockyer v. Buckhurst Pak Properties (Mangal) Ltd. [1964] 1 All E.R.
p. 630 is cited with approval and followed.

Lord Denning, M.R., in the course of his judgment in the first case after referring to the Freeman case had this to say on the question of an agent's authority:" It is there shown that actual authority may be express or implied. It is express when it is given by express words, such as when a Board of Directors pass
a resolution which authorises two of their number to sign cheques. It is implied
when it is inferred from the conduct of the parties and the circumstances of the
case, such as when the board of directors appoint one of their number to be
managing director. They thereby impliedly authorise him to do all such things
as fall within the usual scope of that office. Actual authority, express or implied,
is binding as between the company and the agent, and also as between the
company and others, whether they are within the company or outside it.

Ostensible or apparent authority is the authority of an agent as it appears
to others. It often coincides with actual authority. Thus, when the board appoint one of their number to be managing director, they invest him not only

with implied authority, but also with ostensible authority to do all such things as fall within the usual scope of that office. Other people who see him acting as managing director are entitled to assume that he has the actual authority of a managing director. But sometimes ostensible authority exceeds actual authority. For instance, when the board appoint the managing director, they may expressly limit his authority by saying he is not to order goods worth more than £500 without the sanction of the board. In that case his actual authority is subject to the £500 limitation, but his ostensible authority includes all the usual authority of a managing director. The company is bound by his ostensible authority in his dealings with those who do not know of the limitation he may himself do the 'holding-out'. Thus, if he orders goods worth £1,000 and signs himself 'Managing Director for and on behalf of the company', the company is bound to the other party who does not know of the £500 limitation ...'

5.9.2. Revocation

The termination of the authority of an agent does not affect the position of third parties as against the principal if they do not have knowledge of the termination.[298]

5.9.3. Ratification – subsequent entitlement to dispose

As explained above, the principal may elect to ratify the unauthorised acts of his agent. Such ratification operates retrospectively.[299] Ratification may be express or implied[300] in the conduct of the person on whose behalf the acts are done.[301] No ratification can be done by a person whose knowledge of the facts is materially defective,[302] and where a person ratifies an unauthorised act done on his behalf[303] he must ratify the whole of the transaction of which such act formed a part.[304]

---

[298] Section 168, Cap 149; see also *AD Hotel & Catering v Takis Pliava* (1982) 1 CLR 81.

[299] Section 156, Cap 149; see also *Koenigsblatt v Sweet* [1923] 2 Ch 314.

[300] Mere silence cannot constitute ratification, see *Crampsey v Deveney* (1969) 2 DLR (3d) 161, although the position may be different if it is in conjunction with other factors.

[301] Section 157, Cap 149.

[302] Section 158, Cap 149; see also *The Bonita; The Charlotte* (1861) 1 Lush 252.

[303] *Keighley, Maxtead & Co v Durant* [1901] AC 240, The House of Lords supports the position that the act must be done on behalf of the principal in order for the agent to be able to ratify.

[304] Section 159, Cap 149.

6.   Multiple selling

The hypothetical scenario where A sells the same asset to B and afterwards also to C, is governed by **section 30(1) of the Sale of Goods Act**. It
is provided that – this being one of the exceptions to the *nemo dat* rule –
in such a case C aquires ownership, provided that C acts in good faith and
without knowledge of the previous sale to B and that the seller (A) was in
possession of the goods and the goods have been delivered or transferred
from A to C. Where this is the case, then according to the statute, the
effect is the same as if A was expressly authorised by B to act in this way. It
should be clear that delivery is crucial for this to happen. The requirements of delivery and good faith are set out clearly in the express words of
the statute.

In the hypothetical scenario where C knows that the movable has been
previously sold to B, are there any other remedies (*e.g.* in the law of tort)
that enable B to claim the property, and if so, what are the requirements?

There is in fact the tort of procuring breach of contract which in fact
may assist B in the sense that it gives him a cause of action in tort against
whom he does not have an action in contract (the contract is between B
and the original seller). The tort of procuring breach of contract is codified in **section 34 of the Civil Wrongs Law, Cap 148**. The requirement
is that the breach must be made by C 'knowingly and without sufficient
justification'. It appears that such knowledge must be actual knowledge,
and that 'constructive' knowledge is not sufficient.[305]

Although the legislation frequently makes reference to the '*bona fide*
purchaser' there is no clear set of guidelines in the case law as to what
constitutes the *mens rea bona fide* purchaser.

Issues of insolvency are dealt with in **Chapter 9** below.

7.   Selling chains

The discussion in this part of the report will revolve around the theoretical
example where A sells to B and B sells to C. Then A delivers directly to C.
The issues which will be considered will be if B acquires ownership before
ownership passes to C or whether it is possible by some means for ownership
to pass directly from A to C or for C to have recourse against A.

---

[305] *Swiss Bank Corporation v Lloyds Bank Ltd* [1979] Ch 548; see also McKnight, A,
      'Restrictions on Dealing with Assets in Financing Documents: Their Role, Mean-
      ing and Effect', [2002] JIBL 193.

7.1.   General rules: two independent contracts A – B and B – C

The ordinary case where A has entered into an agreement with B or has concluded a sale with B and then, on the basis of this sale or the agreement to sell, B enters into a contract with C for the sale of the same goods to C, is the case of two independent contracts, one involving only A and B and one involving only B and C. In the ordinary course of things, property must pass from A to B and then once B has this property, he may pass it on to C in fulfilment of his contractual obligations.

Of course it is open to B to agree in his contract with A that *delivery* will be made by A directly to C. This however is a matter of what constitutes delivery under the contract between A and B. Just as it is open for A and B to agree that, making the goods available at the premises of A or delivery of the goods by A at a warehouse or by means of a carrier, would in all three cases constitute good delivery by A to B, it is possible in the same way for A and B to agree that good delivery from A to B will be delivery to C. It does not operate so as to pass the *property* directly from A to C. Thus if the contract between A and B fails for some reason, then the property cannot be passed to C.

Under the *nemo dat* rule explained above, B cannot pass to C property unless and until he obtains such property unless it is a case falling within one of the exceptions to the *nemo dat* rule such as the exception provided in section 30 of the Sale of Goods Act 1994 under which the buyer in possession of the goods or document of title, with the permission of the seller, may pass title in the goods even though he does not himself have title.[306]

Therefore in the case of two independent contracts between A and B and B and C property must first pass to B for *at least* the 'logical second' before it passes to C. By virtue of this course of things it is open to B to agree with C in their contract that the title which C is to receive will be in some way restricted compared to the title which A has given to B. It is even possible for B to retain ownership under a retention of title clause in his agreement with C and for property to pass as and when the contract between B and C provides. If there is some defect in the contract between A and B or indeed no contract at all, then no property can pass to C. In such a case, each party has recourse to the party with whom he contracted. C has a cause of action for breach of contract against B and B has a cause of action for breach of contract against A.

---

[306] So in this sense as an exception to the rule, property may pass directly from A to C by virtue of A's loss of title.

7.2.   The possibility of a direct link between A and C

Having considered the ordinary case, we may now consider if there are any circumstances under which it would be possible for some link to exist between A and C giving C a cause of action directly against A.

There are two potential problems in relation to a party in the position of C claiming against A. The first problem is the rule on privity of contract. The second problem is the need for consideration. The two are often linked[307] but it is important to remember that they are strictly speaking separate concepts.[308]

Under the rule of privity of contract, only a party to the contract can enforce the contract. In the example in question here, C not being party to the contract cannot enforce the contract between A and B even if the contract expressly provided rights for C.

There is also the issue of consideration. There is the rule that *consideration must move from the promisee but need not move to the promisor*.[309] Thus if A and B agree that property will be passed directly by A to C and A has received consideration from B, property will pass directly to C because consideration has been provided on his behalf but C would not be able to sue A, not only because he is not party to the contract but also because he has provided no consideration. Even if he is named in the contract as the person to whom the property should pass and is party to the contract (which would solve the problem of privity) C would not be able to enforce the contract against A because he as promisee has not provided consideration. He would thus depend on B enforcing the contract against A.[310]

Although C pays consideration, he does not pay it to A. He pays it to B and this cannot constitute good consideration for A's promise to transfer property to C. There is no benefit to A if C pays B.[311] If C could bring himself under the exception of **section 25(1) (b)**[312] because by paying an amount to B, C has compensated A for something which A would be legally under an obligation to do (namely pay B an amount for a debt already due outside the agreement in question), or under the exception of

---

[307] See *Tweedle v Atkinson* (1861) 1 B&S 393.

[308] *Kepong Prospecting Ltd v Schmidt* [1968] AC 810.

[309] *Bolton v Madden* (1873) LR 9 QB 55.

[310] Note that the same problem arises in cases of trusts which is another way in which the problems of privity and consideration can be approached.

[311] Unless there is deemed to be a collateral contract as will be explained below.

[312] An agreement made without consideration is void unless it is a is a promise to compensate wholly or in part, a person who has already voluntarily done something for the promisor or something which the promisor was legally compelled to do.

section 25(1) (c)[313] then this would satisfy the requirement for consideration on the part of C, but this is a separate matter.

Thus, even if privity can by some means be established, the problem of
lack of consideration subsists.

7.3. Evasion of the problems arising from lack of privity and consideration

The problems arising from the privity of contract rule and the requirement for consideration have been subject to severe criticism in England.
This led to the development of ways of going around these provisions.
The major exception to these rules came with the enactment of the **Contracts (Rights of Third Parties) Act 1999** which allows a third party not
privy to the contract and not having provided consideration under the
contract to obtain benefits under it if the requirements of the Act are
satisfied. Unfortunately there is no equivalent to the Contracts (Rights of
Third Parties) Act 1999 in Cyprus law. But exceptions had existed in
England prior to the enactment of this Act. It is these exceptions which
can be used in order to achieve transfer of property directly from A to C
and to give direct rights against A to C.

7.3.1. Collateral contract

One way in which an action would be available to C directly against A
would be the existence of a collateral contract. In order to have such a
collateral contract there would have to be consideration and an intention
to create legal relations.

In cases of collateral contracts, the consideration for the collateral
contract is the entry into the main contract. Thus by entering into a
contract with B, C has provided consideration to A. Such a collateral
contract was found to exist in the case of a hire-purchase agreement.[314] In
the scenario where a customer buys goods on hire purchase from a dealer,
the main contract is that between the customer and the finance house.[315]
The finance house buys the goods from the dealer and eventually may
give title to the customer. The customer has no direct contract with the
dealer but may sue the dealer on the basis of a representation made by the

---

[313] Being a promise made in writing and signed to pay wholly or in part a debt which
might have been enforced against the promisor but for any law relating to prescription or a limitation action.

[314] *Brown v Sheen & Richmond Car Sales* [1950] 1 All ER 1102.

[315] See Treitel, *The Law of Contract* (2003), p 583.

dealer on the basis of a collateral contract between the customer and the dealer. It could be inferred under the circumstances however that the customer has a collateral contract with the dealer and that the consideration for this collateral contract was the entry by the customer into the contract with the finance house. In this case A steps into the shoes of the dealer, B steps into the shoes of the finance house and C steps into the shoes of the customer. In this example, the finance house obtains title which it passes on to the customer once it is paid in full. Thus again property would not pass directly from A to C but C would acquire an action against A.

If it is also held that A and C *intended* to enter into such a contract such that there is *animus contrahendi*,[316] then all the requirements would be deemed to have been satisfied.

The conclusion to be drawn here is that in the absence of the equivalent of the English Contracts (Rights of Third Parties) Act 1999, there can be no passing of property directly from A to C *and* a right of action of C against A.

7.3.2. Trusts

A classical way in which the problem of privity of contract and the consideration requirement was overcome in England in the years before the enactment of the Contracts (Rights of Third Parties) Act 1999 was the use of the trust. It has been recognised that in Cyprus law also, the trust concept overcomes the weakness of the contract concept.[317] The use of the trust is perhaps the most ideal way to acquire an asset in one's own name and hold it for the benefit of the other party. One *caveat* however is that the property must first be acquired before a trust can be imposed on it. The insolvency of the trustee would not affect the beneficiary.[318]

8. Transfer or acquisition by means of indirect representation

8.1. Modalities

Such transfer by indirect representation can be effected by means of trust (as explained in Chapter 7 above). Under the rules of equity, the trustee may acquire property on behalf of the beneficiary. In such a case, the legal

---

[316] *Ibid*, p 584.

[317] Andreas Neocleous & Co, see note 1 above, p 851.

[318] Section 42 Bankruptcy Law, Cap 5.

title vests in the trustee, and the beneficiary is the holder of the 'beneficial interest'. In such a case, the legal title does not pass to the beneficiary (not even for the 'logical second') and the beneficiary is not in a position to dispose of the goods. The insolvency of the trustee does not affect the property held on trust.[319]

For cases where the indirect holding is the result of a relationship of agency, then the situation is that described in section 5.9.

8.2. The particular issue of shares as movable property

8.2.1. Why the problem arises

As has been explained in the introduction to this Part of the Report, in cases of particular classes of movable property, the passing of property does not depend solely on the general rules for the passing of property under the Sale of Goods Act 1994. The passing of property in shares is subject to the more specific provisions of the Companies Act. It will be seen that in relation to shares, the general rule that property passes when it is intended to pass is displaced by the rule that provides that only he whose name appears in the Register of the company is considered the owner of the shares.

The Sale of Goods Act 1994 includes shares[320] in the definition of 'goods'. It is the position of the authors that this does not clash with the more specific provisions of Cap 113. The Sale of Goods Act 1994 provides for the rules on the passing of property to be governed by the contract between the parties and provides a set of default rules for cases where the parties have not expressly or impliedly made any provisions. When someone acquires shares in a company he is considered a 'member' of the company and he is deemed to have entered into a *contract* with the company on the terms of its articles.[321] Thus the provision in the Companies Cap 113 which provides that shares are transferable in the manner provided by the articles of the company does not contradict the provisions of the Sale of Goods Act.

---

[319] Section 42 Bankruptcy Law, Cap 5.

[320] There is no definition in the Sale of Goods Act as to what constitutes shares for the purposes of that Act.

[321] Section 21(1) Cap 113; see also *Hickman v Kent or Romney Marsh Sheep-Breeders' Association* [1915] 1 Ch 881.

8.2.2. What is meant by 'share'

Cap 113 provides that 'the shares *or any other interest*[322] of any member in
a company shall be personal property transferable in the manner provided
by the articles of the company and shall not be of the nature of real estate'.[323] It is important to emphasise the fact that it is the *interest* in the
property which the section refers to. The distinction should be made
between the interest of a member in a company which is intangible property and the share certificate itself which is in the nature of a chattel.[324]
The distinction is important since in most jurisdictions, shares (as opposed to the certificates) are considered rights and are not classed as
movable property subject to the general provisions for the sale of goods as
is the case under the provisions of the Sale of Goods Act 1994.

8.2.3. When does property pass?

Property in shares only passes once an entry is made in the Register of the
Company.[325] It should be noted that more complex issues of property in
relation to dematerialised[326] and immobilised securities arise in Cyprus
law since there is now an indirect holding system such as CREST which
exists in England.[327] In Cyprus Law matters may be even more complicated by the lack of clear rules in cases of commixture and confusion.
Share certificates do not represent the shares in the same way that for
example the bill of lading represents the underlying goods. The certificate
under the common seal of the company, specifying any shares held by any
member, constitutes merely *prima facie* evidence of title of the member to
the shares.[328] In other words it is not a document of title. As Cyprus law

---

[322] Emphasis added.

[323] Section 71.

[324] See Barak, A, 'The Nature of the Negotiable Instrument' (1983) 18 Israel LR 49,
cited in Sealy & Hooley, see note 195 above, p 488.

[325] *Nicol's case* (1885) 29 ChD 421 CA.

[326] This is known as '*apoilopiisi*'.

[327] See Pretto, A, 'Comparative Personal Property: The Case of Shares', (2001) 1(1)
Global Jurist Advances, Article 2 cited at http://www.bepress.com/gj/advances/
voll/iss1/art2/on 14/12/2006.

[328] Section 79 of Cap 113. Section 77(1) provides that the certification by a company
of any instrument of transfer of shares in or debentures of the company shall be
taken as a representation by the company to any person acting on the faith of the
certification that there have been produced to the company such documents as on
the face of them show a *prima facie* title to the shares or debentures in the transferor named in the instrument of transfer, *but not as a representation that the trans-*

does not permit bearer shares, delivery of the share certificate can never be enough to pass title in the underlying shares.

8.2.4. Other issues

Further there is a specific requirement for a proper instrument of transfer. It is provided that notwithstanding anything in the articles of the company, it shall not be lawful for the company to register a transfer of shares in or debentures of the company unless a proper instrument of transfer has been delivered to the company.[329] The right to transfer shares is unlimited in the case of public companies, but must be limited in the case of private companies.[330]

Provisions relevant to securities listed in the Cyprus Stock Exchange may be found in the **Stock Exchange Law**[331] which prohibits the transfer or registration in the relevant Registers of securities which have been admitted to the Cyprus Stock Exchange if the transaction in question does not bear the necessary seal of the Cyprus Stock Exchange (CSE) which proves that the transaction was made through the CSE or at least is to the knowledge of the CSE.[332]

It should be born in mind that a company may refuse such registration altogether, but in such a case it shall give notice of such refusal within two months.[333]

Crucially, it is provided that any power of the company to register as shareholder or debenture holder any person to whom the right to any shares or debentures in the company has been transmitted by operation of Law shall not be affected. **Section 74 of Cap 113** provides that the transfer of the share or other interest of a deceased member of the company made by his personal representative shall be valid and **section 75 of Cap 113** provides for the registration of the transfer at the request of the transferor.

---

feror has any title to the shares or debentures (emphasis added). Section 77(2) provides that where any person acts on the faith of a false certification by the company, the company shall be under the same liability to him as if the certification had not been made fraudulently.

[329] Section 73, Cap 113.
[330] Andreas Neocleous & Co, see note 1 above, p 330.
[331] Law 14(I)/93, as amended.
[332] Section 24 *ibid.*
[333] Section 76, Cap 113.

9.   Consequences of insolvency of the transferee or
       transferor at different stages of the transfer

9.1.   General issues

This section will primarily set out the legislation governing the issues of
this chapter. It will then go on to consider what is meant by insolvency in
Cyprus Law, will introduce the alternative concept of bankruptcy for
individuals and consider what is meant by 'property' for the purposes of
the particular legislation where this is expressly defined as well as the
relevant time at which bankruptcy and insolvency are deemed to occur.

9.1.1. The bankruptcy-insolvency dichotomy

It should be clear from the outset that in Cyprus there are separate provisions for natural and legal persons in relation to 'insolvency'. In particular
the term 'insolvency' in Cyprus law relates only to legal persons[334] and
the term 'bankruptcy' refers to natural persons.

(a)   Sources of law

Bankruptcy of individuals is governed by **The Bankruptcy Law, Cap 5**[335]
(*Ο Περί Πτώχευσης Νόμος*) and **The Bankruptcy Rules, Cap 6**. Insolvency of legal persons is governed by **The Companies Act, Cap 113**. The
Fraudulent Transfers Avoidance Law, Cap 62 will also be relevant for
the purposes of this section of the Report.

(b)   What constitutes an act of bankruptcy

Section 3 of The Bankruptcy Law provides the cases in which a person
(debtor) commits an act of bankruptcy. In broad terms the gist of this section is that any person who is unable to pay his debts or makes a fraudulent
gift, conveyance, delivery or transfer of his property, or with intent to delay
his creditors departs from the Republic of Cyprus or his dwelling or, makes a
conveyance or creates a charge which would constitute a fraudulent preference if he were adjudged bankrupt, commits an act of bankruptcy.

---

[334] The term here refers mainly to companies. Organisations such as *inter alia* banks and
       insurance companies are governed by particular legislation and so the following provi-
       sions referred to in relation to 'insolvency' of legal persons are limited by this *caveat*.
[335] Cap 5.

(i)   On bankruptcy the property shall vest in the trustee

It is provided that immediately on a debtor being adjudged bankrupt the property of the bankrupt shall vest in the trustee, and until a trustee is appointed, the official receiver shall be the trustee for these purposes.[336]

(ii)   What constitutes the property of the bankrupt

For the purposes of this Law, 'goods' includes all chattels, these being personal and movable property, and 'property' includes *inter alia* goods, and every description of property whether movable or immovable, and whether situated in Cyprus or elsewhere, as well as every description of estate, interest and profit, present or future, whether vested or contingent, arising out of or incident to property as above defined.[337]

The Law subsequently explains in more detail which property is and which property is not to be considered property of the bankrupt available for distribution amongst creditors.[338] All such property as may belong to or be vested in the bankrupt at the commencement of the bankruptcy *or may be acquired or devolve on him before his discharge*[339] shall be available for distribution to the creditors.[340] Also falling within what constitutes divisible property is the capacity to exercise powers and to take proceedings for exercising all such powers in and over or in respect of property as may have been exercised by the bankrupt.[341]

While the above definition of what constitutes property available for distribution may have been expected, what is peculiar to this definition[342] is the inclusion into the definition of goods in the possession, order or disposition of the bankrupt[343] and the interplay between this provision and the provision which protects property held on trust by the bankrupt on behalf of another.[344]

Section 41(c) provides that 'all goods being, at the commencement of the bankruptcy, in the possession, order or disposition of the bankrupt, in

---

[336] Section 49, Cap 5.

[337] Section 2.

[338] Sections 41 and 42.

[339] Emphasis added.

[340] Section 41(a).

[341] Section 41(b).

[342] And in sharp contrast to English law which otherwise Cyprus law generally follows.

[343] Section 41(c), although this section does go on to provide that things in action other than debts due to or growing due to the bankrupt in the course of his trade or business shall not be included within the section.

[344] Section 42, Cap 5.

his trade or business, by the consent and permission of the true owner, under such circumstances that he is the reputed owner thereof' shall be included in the definition.

The saving grace of this rather harsh provision is probably found in what constitutes a *possession order or disposition* and what constitutes *such circumstances that he is the reputed owner thereof*. Alternatively one must fall back on **section 42** of this Law which exempts from the above provision property held on trust by the bankrupt for another and property which would be exempt from execution, and matters may depend on how wide the concept of a 'trust' can be in Cyprus law.

(iii)   Time at which the bankruptcy is deemed to occur

It is provided that the bankruptcy of the creditor shall be deemed to have relation back to, and to commence at, the time of the act of bankruptcy being committed, upon which a receiving order is made against him.[345]

(iv)   Power of the court to adjudicate on questions of ownership

It is provided that the Court shall have jurisdiction to try and adjudicate upon all questions of ownership relating to goods claimed by or from the trustee, whether such property be in the possession of the trustee or not and to decide and adjudicate on any debt or claim due to or from the bankrupt.[346]

(v)   Effective enforcement of the provisions

When considering the position of the bankrupt whether in his capacity as transferor or transferee, it will be important to remember the obligations imposed by the **Bankruptcy Law, Cap 5** which requires such person to give an inventory of his property and creditors, to aid 'to the utmost of his power' in the realisation of his property[347] and to attend the first meeting of creditors and give to them such information as the meeting may require.[348] Also, the Court may summon before it the debtor or his wife, or any other person known or suspected to have in his possession any of the estate or effects belonging to the debtor, and the Court may

---

[345] Section 40 *ibid.*
[346] Section 90(2).
[347] Section 23(3).
[348] Section 23.

examine on oath any such person.[349] These two provisions are potentially powerful weapons. Not only is it possible to investigate into the assets of the bankrupt available for distribution, but it is also possible to obtain the information required in relation to previous dispositions which may be vulnerable if they can be considered to be 'fraudulent' or as intended to give an unlawful preference. There are also criminal sanctions against the debtor where *inter alia* he effectively attempts to mislead the trustee in bankruptcy or prevents the production of books and documents.[350]

(c)   When winding up of a company occurs

The **Companies Law, Cap 113** provides that the winding up of a company may be either by the Court, or voluntary or subject to the supervision of the Court.[351] It is provided that *inter alia* a company may be wound up by the Court if it is 'unable to pay its debts'.[352] A company is considered unable to pay it's debts if a creditor by assignment or otherwise to whom the company is indebted in a sum exceeding £500 CY has served on the company a demand under his hand requiring that the sum is paid and the company for three weeks thereafter neglects to pay the sum or to secure or compound it to the reasonable satisfaction of the creditor.[353] Alternatively a company will be deemed unable to pay its debts if an execution or other process issued on a judgment, decree or other order of the Court remains unsatisfied in whole or in part or if it is provided to the satisfaction of the Court that the company is unable to pay its debts taking into account the contingent and prospective liabilities of the company.[354] In this respect the definition of the inability to pay a debt can be likened to the English provisions which provide for a cash flow test or the alternative 'balance sheet insolvency'.

Section 261 of the Cap 113 makes provisions for the voluntary winding up of the company, and **section 293** provides that when a company has passed a resolution for voluntary winding up, the Court may make an order that the voluntary winding up shall continue but subject to the supervision of the Court.

---

[349] Section 26.
[350] Section 116, Cap 5.
[351] Section 203, Cap 113.
[352] Section 211 *ibid*.
[353] Section 212(a).
[354] Sections 212(b), 212(c).

(d)   Corresponding provisions in relation to insolvency

According to **section 224** a statement of the company's affairs is to be submitted to the official receiver and this will show *inter alia* particulars of the assets, debts and liabilities of the company.

According to **section 233(1)**, the liquidator may with the sanction either of the Court or the committee of inspection make compromises with creditors or compromise debts relating to any claim whether present or future, certain or contingent, ascertained or sounding only in damages. **Section 233(2)**, provides that the liquidator shall *inter alia* have power to sell the real and personal property of the company and things in action and to prove, rank and claim in the bankruptcy insolvency or sequestration of any balance against his estate and to receive dividends in the bankruptcy, insolvency or sequestration in respect of that balance.

Section 234 provides that in exercising his powers, the liquidator shall have regard to any directions given by resolution of the creditors or contributories,[355] that the liquidator may apply to the court for directions[356] and that if any person is aggrieved by an act or decision of a liquidator, he may apply to the Court which will have power to reverse or modify the decision if it thinks just to do so.[357]

According to section 245, the Court may, at any time after the making of a winding up order require any contributory, for the time being on the list of contributories and any trustee, receiver, banker, agent or officer of the company to pay, deliver, convey, surrender or transfer forthwith, or within such time as the Court decides, to the liquidator any money, property or books and papers in his hands to which the company is *prima facie* entitled.

9.2.   Insolvency of the transferor

9.2.1.   Insolvency before the goods are delivered or property passes

When it is the transferor who becomes bankrupt or insolvent, the issue which arises is that of the means available for the protection of the transferee.

The scenario which is likely to give rise to the problem is that in which the transferee has paid a part of or the entire purchase price[358] to the transferor and the transferor has in the mean time become bankrupt or insolvent before the property and/or possession has passed to the transferee.

---

[355] Section 234(1).

[356] Section 324(3), Cap 113.

[357] Section 234(5).

[358] As was explained, payment does not necessarily mean the passing of property.

In cases of the bankruptcy of individuals, where the property in goods, which are existing at the time of the agreement, passes before the relevant time after which the property of the debtor shall form part of the pool of assets available for distribution and the goods are in the possession of the transferee, then provided that the transaction is not intended to defraud the other creditors of the debtor, the property will not be subject to seizure and sale.

Where in relation to existing goods, the property has passed to the transferee[359] but the goods remain in the possession of the transferor with the consent and permission of the true owner, under such circumstances that he is the reputed owner thereof, the goods will form part of the pool of assets of the bankrupt debtor. In such a case he can only prove in the insolvency as an unsecured creditor.

Where the existing goods are in the possession of the transferor and property has not passed to the transferee,[360] then the assets will form part of the pool of assets available for distribution to the creditors and the transferee may prove for any loss in the bankruptcy of the debtor.

In relation to future goods, it is clear from the provisions of the Sale of Goods Act that property in future goods cannot pass before the goods come into existence.[361] Thus it is impossible that property in any future goods to be obtained or manufactured by the transferor shall have passed to the transferee.

In cases where the movables do form part of the pool of assets available for distribution to the creditors of the transferor, the transferee may prove in the bankruptcy or insolvency of the transferor for damages for breach of contract.[362] Subject to the following, all debts and liabilities, present or future, certain or contingent, to which the debtor is subject at the date of the receiving order, or to which he may become subject before his discharge by reason of any obligation incurred before the date of the receiving order, shall be deemed to be debts provable in bankruptcy.[363] In

---

[359] By reference to the general rule that property passes when it is intended to pass; such intention according to the express terms of the agreement between the parties or the default rules provided in the Sale of Goods Act as set out in Chapter 5 of this report.

[360] As was the case for example in *Mucklow v Mangles* (1808) 1 Taunt 318, Court of Common Press, which as was explained above concerned precisely the matter of the insolvency of the transferor.

[361] See Chapter 5 of the Report.

[362] Although usually, unless special damage can be shown, damages for breach of contract in markets where the transferee could have easily entered into an alternative contract for the same goods are subject to the general requirement for mitigation of the loss.

[363] Section 34 (3), Cap 5.

cases of bankruptcy, demands in the nature of unliquidated damages arising otherwise than by reason of contract, promise or breach of trust shall
not be provable in bankruptcy.[364] Further a person having notice of any
act of bankruptcy available against the debtor shall not prove under the
order for any debt or liability contracted by the debtor subsequently to
the date of his so having notice.[365]

The right to set off may potentially be available to the transferee who
has paid an amount to the now bankrupt transferor in cases where the
movables in question now form part of the pool of assets. Where there
have been mutual credits, mutual debts or other mutual dealings between
a debtor against whom a receiving order is made, and any person proving
or claiming to prove a debt under the receiving order, an account shall be
taken of what is due from one party to the other in respect of such mutual
dealings, and the sum due from one party shall be set off against the sum
due by the other party, and the balance of the account and no more shall
be claimed or paid on either side respectively.[366] However, set-off may not
be claimed by a person who had notice of an act of bankruptcy at the
time of giving the credit to the debtor.[367]

Where the transferor has issued execution against the movables it will
be important to determine the time of the execution in order to determine if the transferee will be able to retain the benefit of the execution
where the transferor is bankrupt. According to **section 44 Cap 5**, the
transferee shall not be entitled to retain the benefit of execution or attachment 'unless he has completed the execution or attachment before
the date of the receiving order, and before notice of the presentation of
any bankruptcy petition by or against the debtor, or of the commission of
any available act of bankruptcy by the debtor'.

It is important to note what is meant by 'completion of execution or attachment'. Execution or attachment with respect to goods, chattels or other
movable property to which the debtor is entitled subject to a lien or right of
some person to the immediate possession thereof is deemed to be completed
by attachment, by prohibition of order and sale.[368] With respect to shares in
any public company or corporation, attachment is deemed to be completed
by prohibition order;[369] and with respect to property in the custody or under
the control of any public officer in his official capacity or Court, execution is
deemed to be completed by a prohibition order duly obtained and served.[370]

---

[364] Section 34(1) *ibid.*
[365] Section 34(2).
[366] Section 35.
[367] *Ibid.*
[368] Section 44(2)(b), Cap 5.
[369] Section 44(2)(e) *ibid.*
[370] Section 44(2)(f).

Section 265 of Cap 113 provides that in a voluntary winding up, any transfer of shares, not being a transfer made to or with the sanction of the liquidator, and any alteration in the status of the members of the company made after the commencement of a voluntary winding up shall be void.

9.2.2. Insolvency after the transfer is made

(a)   Fraud

The position where the transfer is considered 'fraudulent' under the **Fraudulent Transfers Avoidance Law, Cap 62** must be distinguished.

Section 3(1) of this Act provides that every gift, sale, pledge, mortgage or other transfer or disposal of any *movable*[371] or immovable property made by any person with the intent to hinder or delay his creditors or any of them in recovering from him, his or their debts shall be deemed to be fraudulent and shall be invalid against any such creditor or creditors; and notwithstanding any such gift or pledge, mortgage or other transfer or disposal, the property purported to be transferred or otherwise dealt with may be seized and sold in satisfaction of any judgment debt due from the person making such gift, sale, pledge, mortgage or any other transfer or disposal.

Section 3(2) further provides that in any application under the provisions of this Law to set aside a transfer or assignment of any property made by any parent, spouse, child, brother or sister of the transferor or assignor otherwise than in exchange for money or for other property of equivalent consideration the onus of proving that such a transfer or assignment is *bona fide* and not made with intent to hinder or delay his creditors shall rest upon the transferor or assignor and upon the person to whom such transfer or assignment has been made.

Section 3(3) provides that no sale, mortgage, transfer or assignment made in exchange for money or other property of equivalent value shall be voidable under the provisions of this Law, unless the purchaser, mortgagee, transferee, or assignee shall be shown to have accepted it with knowledge that such sale, mortgage, transfer, or assignment, was made by the vendor, mortgagor, transferor, or assignor with the intent to delay or defraud his creditors.

There is an important clarification to be made concerning the person who is entitled to apply for the avoidance of such a transfer. It was held in *Ekaterini Limperopoulou v Michalakis Christodoulou and others*[372] that a fraudulent transfer under the provisions of section 3 above, could only be avoided if the creditor who applied for such avoidance was one who was intended at

---

[371] Emphasis added.

[372] (1958) 22 CLR 184 and this was confirmed on appeal.

the time of the transfer to be delayed or hindered from recovering his debt from the transferor. That is, the creditor[373] must be in the contemplation of the debtor at the time the fraudulent transfer is effected. The judge after reading **section 3(1)** stated that 'It is clear from this section that a fraudulent disposition is invalid against a creditor or creditors whom the transferor or transferee intended to hinder or delay. A fraudulent transfer therefore can only be avoided under this section if the creditor who applies for such avoidance was one who was intended at the time of the transfer to be delayed or hindered in recovering his debt from the transferor'.

Section 4 of **Fraudulent Transfers Avoidance Law, Cap 62** provides for the procedure of setting aside any such transfer, and section 5 provides for rectification of the register.

(b)   Transactions void in cases of bankruptcy

Certain transfers or conveyances made prior to bankruptcy of the transferor are avoided as against the trustee in bankruptcy. Where there is a conveyance or transfer of property[374] and the transferor becomes bankrupt within two years after the date of the conveyance or transfer, the transfer shall be void against the trustee in bankruptcy.[375] If the transferor becomes bankrupt at any subsequent time within ten years after the date of such transfer or conveyance, then this will be void as against the trustee in bankruptcy unless the transferee or other party claiming under the transfer is able to show that the transferor was at the time of the transfer able to pay his debts without the aid of the property transferred, and that the interest of the transferor in the property has been passed.[376]

The Bankruptcy law makes a separate provision in relation to cases where a conveyance or transfer of property or charge created thereon is

---

[373] As defined in section 2 of the Fraudulent Transfers Avoidance Law, which provides that 'creditors of a debtor' means not only the persons to whom he is actually indebted, but also every sheriff, and every person acting for a sheriff, who shall lawfully put into execution any judgment given against the debtor, and also every person (if any) in whom the property of the debtor or the right to sell or dispose of it shall either by his own act or by operation of law become vested for the common benefit of all the persons to whom he is indebted.

[374] In cases other than those where such transfer or conveyance was made in favour of a purchaser for value and in good faith, or conveyance was made before and in consideration of marriage, or a settlement made for wife and children of property which has accrued to the settlor after marriage in right of his wife, or in good faith for valuable consideration.

[375] Section 46(1), Cap 5 (emphasis added).

[376] *Ibid.*

made by a person unable to pay his debts as they become due from his own money in favour of any creditor, or of any person in trust for any creditor, with a view of giving such a creditor a preference over other creditors. In such a case, where the transferor is adjudged bankrupt on a petition presented within three months of the making of the transfer or conveyance, then this will be deemed to be fraudulent and void as against the trustee in bankruptcy.[377]

The *bona fide* purchaser for value is however specifically protected from the effect of the two above provisions, so that any conveyance or assignment for value by the now bankrupt transferee shall not be void by virtue of the above provisions, provided that the conveyance or assignment has taken place before the date of the receiving order and that the transferee had no notice of any act of bankruptcy committed before the time of assignment or delivery.[378]

(c)   Transfers void in cases of insolvency

Section 265 provides that in cases of voluntary winding up, any transfer of shares, not being a transfer made to or with the sanction of the liquidator, made after the commencement of a voluntary winding up shall be void.

According to section 216, in a winding up by the Court, any disposition of the property of the company including the things in action, and any transfer of shares or alteration in the status of the members of the company, made after the commencement of the winding up, shall, unless the Court otherwise orders, be void.

Section 305 provides that where a creditor has issued execution against the goods or immovable property of a company or has attached any debt due to the company, and the company is subsequently wound up, he shall not be entitled to retain the benefit of the execution or attachment against the liquidator in the winding up of the company unless he has completed execution or attachment before the commencement of the winding up.

It is further provided **in section 305(a)** that where a creditor has notice of a meeting for a resolution for the voluntary winding up of a company, then the date on which the creditor had such notice is substituted for the date of the commencement of the winding up.

Further **section 305(c) (2)** provides that for the purposes of this section an execution against goods[379] shall be taken to have been completed by seizure and sale.

---

[377] Section 47(1), Cap 5.
[378] Section 48, Cap 5.
[379] As opposed to movable property.

According to **section 301 of Cap 113**, any conveyance, mortgage, delivery of goods, payment, execution, or other act relating to property made or done by or against a company within six months before the commencement of its winding up which, had it been made or done by or against an individual within six months before the presentation of a bankruptcy petition on which he is adjudged bankrupt, would be deemed in his bankruptcy a fraudulent preference, shall in the event of the company being wound up, be deemed a fraudulent preference of its creditors and be invalid accordingly. Section 301 applies to every mode of winding up. It is further provided that any conveyance or assignment by a company of all its property to trustees for the benefit of all its creditors shall be void to all intents.[380]

In such a case, liabilities arise against certain fraudulently preferred persons. Where anything made or done is void as a fraudulent preference under section 301 above, then the person preferred shall be subject to the same liabilities and have the same rights as if he had undertaken to be personally liable as surety for the debt to the extent of the charge on the property or the value of his interest, which ever is less.[381]

9.3. Insolvency of the transferee

9.3.1. Security and quasi-security

If the transferor is in the position of the holder of a charge over the property in question or other property belonging to the transferee, or in the even stronger position of someone who has managed to effectively retain title to the property held by the transferee he will in the first case be able to prove in the bankruptcy of the debtor. It would appear that someone in the second case who has retained title is not required to prove in the bankruptcy of the transferee and will have open to him the remedies of the owner who may demand the return of his property.[382] The Bankruptcy Law Cap 5 defines 'secured creditor' as 'any person holding a mortgage, pledge, charge or lien on the property of the debtor, or any part thereof, as a security for a debt due to him from the debtor'.[383] It becomes immediately clear that quasi-security in the form of retention of title is not included in this definition. It thus warrants consideration in isolation.

---

[380] Section 301(2), Cap 113.

[381] Section 302(1), Cap 113.

[382] Subject to the *caveat* explained above in relation to bankruptcy where the bankrupt was in possession of the property with the consent of the owner such that it appeared to the outside world that he was the owner of the property.

[383] Section 2, Cap 5.

9.3.2. The right to prove

Both secured[384] and unsecured creditors may prove their debts in the bankruptcy of the transferee. If a secured creditor realises his security, he may prove for the balance due to him after deducting the net amount realised, and if he surrenders his security to the official receiver or trustee for the general benefit of creditors, he may prove for his whole debt.[385] If a secured creditor does not either realise or surrender his security, he should before the ranking for dividend, state in his proof the particulars of his security, the date when this was given and the value at which he assesses it. He shall be entitled to receive a dividend only in respect of the balance due to him after deducting the value so assessed.[386]

A secured creditor is entitled to sell the charged property of the bankrupt debtor despite the fact that there is an existing receiving order, but all the proceedings pending against the bankrupt/debtor cannot continue without the necessary leave of the competent court (*Demos Timvakis v Stavrou Kyriakou Kyraikoudi* (1995) 5 CLR 473).[387]

Section 299 of Cap 113 provides that in the winding up of an insolvent company, the same rules shall prevail and be observed with regard to the respective rights of secured and unsecured creditors and debts provable, and to the valuation of annuities and future and contingent liabilities as are in force for the time being under the law of bankruptcy with respect to the estates of the persons adjudged bankrupt.

9.3.3. The security must be valid

(a) General

The above provisions are subject to the *caveat* that the security may in certain cases be invalidated as an unlawful preference as explained above. The charge must not only be valid as to its substance[388] but it must also satisfy the requirements of due form and process.[389]

---

[384] Security may be security over the movables themselves or over any other property of the bankrupt.

[385] Section 37, Schedule 2, paras 9 and 10, Cap 5.

[386] *Ibid*, para 11.

[387] Andreas Neocleous & Co, see note 1 above, p 761.

[388] In the sense that it does not constitute an unlawful preference (see the discussion in section 9.2. which refers to creation of charges as well as transfers).

[389] In the sense that it must be validly registered or otherwise perfected within the specified time.

Section 303 Cap 113 provides that a floating charge on the property of a company created within twelve months of the commencement of the winding up shall, unless it is provided that the company immediately after the creation of the charge was solvent, be invalid, except to the amount of any cash paid to the company at the time or subsequently to the creation of, and in consideration for the charge together with interest on that amount at the rate of five per cent per annum or such other rate as may for the time being be prescribed by order of the Accountant-General.

**(b)   The issue of 'springing security' –
           security cannot *arise* after insolvency / bankruptcy**

If the transferor has not taken security from the transferee prior to the bankruptcy or notice of an act of bankruptcy it is unlikely that any Court in Cyprus will allow a clause which will bring security into existence at the time when bankruptcy occurs. In other words, a so-called 'springing security' clause which provides that security over an asset (whether this is the movable transferred to the transferee or some other asset) is to arise in favour of the transferor upon the occurrence of insolvency. While freedom of contract is the constitutional right of all the citizens of the Republic of Cyprus[390] this right is limited in the sense that any contract term may not be consistent with legislation or general principles of Cyprus law. Such a term allowing for 'springing security' would be inconsistent with the priorities set by statute when a person becomes bankrupt or a company becomes insolvent and infringes the rule which requires *pari passu* distribution of equally ranking claims.[391] In fact, such a springing security clause may fail even if it stipulates for the security to arise before the bankruptcy or notice of act of bankruptcy if it is within a certain amount of time before the bankruptcy or insolvency that renders it an unlawful preference.

---

[390] Article 26 (1) of the Constitution of the Republic of Cyprus.

[391] See Andrew McKnight, 'A Review of the Developments in English Case Law During 2004 – Part 2', [2005] JIBLR 154. According to Andrew McKnight, the 'British Eagle principle' (*British Eagle International Airlines Ltd v Cie Nationale Air France* [1975] 1 WLR 758) requires that the available assets of the insolvent debtor should be used to meet the claims of the unsecured creditors on a *pari passu* basis. See also Andrew McKnight, 'A Review of the Developments in English Case Law During 2003 – Part 1', [2004] JIBLR 119. According to *Money Markets International Stockbrokers Ltd v London Stock Exchange Ltd* [2002] 1 WLR 1150, English public policy provides that a provision in a contract or other instrument by which the property of a person shall pass to another or be confiscated upon the person's insolvency is void. Although the later article refers to English public policy, it could be expected that the courts in Cyprus would take a similar stance.

9.3.4. Rights of proof and the issue of priority

(a) General principles

If property has passed and one is unsecured, one can prove one's debt in the bankruptcy or insolvency subject to the rules of priority.[392] It is provided in the Bankruptcy Law Cap 5 that every creditor shall prove his debt as soon as may be after the making of a receiving order by delivering or sending to the official receiver an affidavit verifying the debt, and that one must bear the cost of proving one's debt unless the Court otherwise specially orders.[393]

It is worth noting that the creditor may prove for a debt not payable when the debtor committed the act of bankruptcy as if it were payable presently.[394]

Section 285 of Cap 113 provides that in a voluntary winding up the distribution of company property will be on the basis of a *pari passu* ranking.

Section 298 provides that in every winding up all debts payable on a contingency, and all claims against the company, present or future, certain or contingent, ascertained or sounding only in damages, shall be admissible as proof against the company, a just estimate being made, so far as possible, of the value of such debts or claims as may be subject to any contingency or sounding only in damages, or which for some other reason do not bear a certain value.

(b) Limitations of proof

A 'debt provable in bankruptcy' or 'provable debt' for the purposes of the Bankruptcy Law Cap 5 includes any debt or liability made provable in bankruptcy by Cap 5.[395] Subject to the following, all debts and liabilities, present or future, certain or contingent, to which the debtor is subject at the date of the receiving order, or to which he may become subject before his discharge by reason of any obligation incurred before the date of the receiving order, shall be deemed to be debts provable in bankruptcy.[396] In cases of bankruptcy, demands in the nature of unliquidated damages aris-

---

[392] Section 38, Cap 5 (Priorities include government taxes and wages; in cases not falling within the priorities there shall be *pari passu* distribution of claims ranking equal amongst themselves); section 39 (Postponement of husband's and wife's claims); section 90 (the Court shall have full power to decide all questions of priorities).

[393] Schedule 2, paras 1,2, and 6, Cap 5.

[394] Schedule 2, para 22 *ibid.*

[395] Section 2.

[396] Section 34(3).

ing otherwise than by reason of contract, promise or breach of trust shall not be provable in bankruptcy.[397] Further a person having notice of any act of bankruptcy available against the debtor shall not prove under the order for any debt or liability contracted by the debtor subsequently to the date of his so having notice.[398]

(c)   Corresponding provisions in insolvency

Section 251 of Cap 113 gives the Court the power to fix a time or times within which creditors are to prove their debts or claims or to be excluded from the benefit of any such distribution made before those debs are proved.

(d)   Disclaimer of onerous property

Section 304 of Cap 113 allows the company to disclaim onerous property. It is provided that where any part of the property of a company which is being wound up consists of immovable property burdened with onerous covenants, of shares or stock in companies, of unprofitable contracts, or of any other property that is unsaleable, or not readily saleable, by reason of its binding the possessor thereof to the performance of any onerous act or to the payment of any sum of money, the liquidator of the company, notwithstanding that he has endeavoured to sell or has taken possession of the property or exercised any act of ownership in relation thereto, may with the leave of the Court and subject to the provisions of this section, by writing signed by him, at any time within twelve months after the commencement of the winding up or such extended period as may be allowed by the Court disclaim property.

However section 304 (4) provides that the liquidator shall not be entitled to disclaim any property under this section in any case where an application in writing has been made to him by any persons interested in the property requiring him to decide whether he will or will not disclaim and the liquidator has not, within a period of twenty-eight days after the receipt of the application or of such further period as may be allowed by the Court, given notice to the applicant that he intends to apply to the Court for leave to disclaim, and, in the case of a contract, if the liquidator, after such application as aforesaid, does not within the said period or further period disclaim the contract, the company shall be deemed to have adopted it.

---

[397] Section 34(1), Cap 5.
[398] Section 34(2).

Section 304 (5) provides that the court may on the application of any person who is against the liquidator, entitled to the benefit or subject to the burden of a contract made with the company, make an order rescinding the contract on such terms as to payment by or to either party of damages for the non-performance of the contract, or otherwise as the Court thinks just, and any damages payable under the order to any such person may be proved by him as a debt against the company.

Section 304 (6) provides that a person who claims an interest in any disclaimed property may apply to the court for an order for the vesting of the property in or the delivery of the property to any person entitled thereto, and the court may grant such an order if it seems just that the property may be delivered by way of compensation on such terms as the Court thinks just, and the property shall vest accordingly without any conveyance or assignment for such purpose.

(e) Set-off as an alternative or in conjunction with proof

Where the transferee of movable property has become bankrupt, it may be possible for the transferor to set off any amount owed by the transferee to him in respect of property which has passed to the transferee provided that there are mutual debts. It is provided in the Bankruptcy Law Cap 5 that where there have been mutual credits, mutual debts or other mutual dealings between a debtor against whom a receiving order is made, and any person proving or claiming to prove a debt under the receiving order, an account shall be taken of what is due from one party to the other in respect of such mutual dealings, and the sum due from one party shall be set off against the sum due by the other party, and the balance of the account and no more shall be claimed or paid on either side respectively.[399] However, set-off may not be claimed by a person who had notice of an act of bankruptcy at the time of giving the credit to the debtor.[400]

If after set-off there remains a balance in favour of the transferor, the transferor can prove the remainder of that amount in the bankruptcy of the transferee.

---

[399] Section 35, Cap 5.
[400] *Ibid.*

9.3.5. The right to stop the goods in transit
'Ανακοπή εν Διακομίσει'

Subject to the other provisions of the Sale of Goods Act 1994, where the buyer of the goods becomes 'bankrupt'[401] the unpaid seller who has parted with possession of the goods has the right of stopping them in transit, that is to say, he may resume possession of the goods so long as they are in the course of transit, and he may retain them until payment or the tender of the price.[402]

The Act then goes on to explain when the goods are deemed to be 'in transit'. Goods are deemed to be in transit from the time when they are delivered to the carrier or other custodian for the purpose of transmission to the buyer, until the buyer or his agent in that behalf takes delivery of them from the carrier or bailee.[403] If the buyer or his agent on that behalf obtains delivery of the goods before their arrival at the appointed destination, the transit is at an end.[404] If after the arrival of the goods at the appointed destination, the carrier or other bailee informs the buyer or his agent that he holds the goods on his behalf and continues in possession of them as bailee of the buyer or his agent, the transit is at an end, and it is immaterial that a further destination for the goods may have been indicated by the buyer.[405] If the goods are rejected by the buyer and the carrier or other bailee continues to be in their possession, the transit is not deemed at an end even if the seller has refused to receive them back.[406] Where the goods are delivered to a ship chartered by the buyer, it is a question depending on the circumstances of the particular case whether they are in the possession of the master as a carrier or as agent to the buyer.[407] Where the carrier or the bailee wrongfully refuses to deliver the goods to the buyer or his agent in that be-

---

[401] It is interesting to note that the word 'bankrupt' is specifically used and the alternative of 'insolvent' for companies does not appear in the relevant section of the Cypriot Act. In the corresponding section 44 of the English Sale of Goods Act 1979 (which is in all other respects the same as section 51 of the Cypriot Sale of Goods Act 1994) uses the word 'insolvent' without providing for the alternative of bankruptcy. Section 2 of the Sale of Goods Act 1994 provides that 'bankrupt', for the purposes of this Act, means the person who ceases to pay his debts in the ordinary course of his business, or who is unable to pay his debts when these become due, whether having committed the act of bankruptcy or not.

[402] Section 51 Sale of Goods Act 1994.

[403] Section 52(1) *ibid.*

[404] Section 52(2).

[405] Section 52(3).

[406] Section 52(4).

[407] Section 52(5).

half, the transit is deemed to be at an end.[408] Where part delivery of the goods has been made to the buyer or his agent in that behalf, the remainder of the goods may be stopped in transit, unless such part delivery has been made under such circumstances as to show an agreement to give up possession of the whole of the goods.[409]

The Act then considers the issue of how stoppage in transit may be effected. It is provided that the unpaid seller may exercise his right of stoppage in transit either by taking actual possession of the goods or by giving notice of his claim to the carrier or other bailee in whose possession the goods are.[410] Such notice may be given either to the person in actual possession of the goods or to his principal.[411] If given to the principal, the notice is ineffective unless given at such time and under such circumstances that the principal, by the exercise of reasonable diligence may communicate it to his agent or servant in time to prevent delivery to the buyer.[412] When notice of stoppage in transit is given by seller to the carrier or other bailee in possession of the goods, he must redeliver the goods to, or according to the directions of, the seller and the expenses of the redelivery must be born by the seller.[413]

10. The passing of risk

According to **section 26 of the Sale of Goods Act 1994**, unless otherwise agreed, the risk[414] remains with the seller up to the time the property passes to the buyer, but, when the property passes to the buyer, the risk lies with the buyer whether there is delivery or not. Then, section 26 goes on to explain that when delivery is delayed either through fault of the buyer or the seller, then the risk will lie with the party responsible for the delay in relation to any damage which would not have occurred in the absence of such delay. It is stated finally that the provisions of this section do not affect in any way the duties and responsibilities of either the seller or the buyer as bailee of the goods for the other party.

As explained above in the *Ouzounian* case property in the goods and therefore risk had never passed from the sellers to the buyers so that the sellers were not bailees for the buyers. The case supports the provision of the legislation that property passes with risk.

---

[408] Section 52(6) Sale of Goods Act 1994.

[409] Section 52(7).

[410] Section 53(1).

[411] *Ibid.*

[412] Section 53(1).

[413] Section 53(2).

[414] Reference to issues of risk have also been made in other parts of the Report.

Part III:
'Original' acquisition –
no direct transfer of ownership
from owner to transferee

II. Accession, specification, commixture and confusion

This area of Cypriot law remains largely unexplored and this leaves much room for assumptions. Much of the following discussion is speculative and it transpires that there is need for legislation to fill in certain gaps in this area of the law.

II.I. Accession

Accession derives from the Latin word *accessio*. It involves a subsidiary item of property being irreversibly attached to another item which is termed the principal such that the principal is changed (and usually improved).[415] Accession has been defined as a procedure whereby property belonging to X becomes property of Y because it has been affixed or annexed to that which belongs to Y.[416] This definition proposes that where the subsidiary accedes to the principal in such a way that the principal prevails, the property in the subsidiary is lost and all that remains is property in Y. Although there is no case directly on this point in Cyprus law, it would appear that this would be the position followed by the courts on the basis that the right to property cannot exist in a vacuum. If the subject matter is lost then there can be no proprietary right. Nor can there be a right to trace in law if the subject matter can no longer be identified. What must remain however could *in certain cases* be some claim against the owner of the (possibly) improved goods.

Such remedy would perhaps lie in a claim in restitution for unjust enrichment. For such a remedy to be available, the owner of property X must

---

[415] Birks, P, 'Mixtures' in Palmer, N & McKendrick, E (eds), *Interests in Goods* (1998) (hereinafter cited as 'Palmer & McKendrick').

[416] Curzon, *Dictionary of Law* (2002) (hereinafter cited as 'Curzon'), p 4.

bring himself within **section 70 of The Contract Law, Cap 149**[417] and the four conditions provided in the case of *Ismini Kyriakou Hjiloizou and others v Irini Iona*[418] which sets out four requirements which must be fulfilled in order for the remedy to be available. The four requirements of the case were that (*a*) the act must be done lawfully (*b*) for another person (*c*) it must be done by a person not intending to act gratuitously and (*d*) the person for whom the act is done must enjoy the benefit of it. It was held that whether the four conditions are fulfilled is a matter of fact in each case.

The granting of additional remedies under tort law *instead of* or *in addition* to the remedy of restitution for unjust enrichment as *per* **section 38 Cap 148** or **section 42 Cap 148** (see **section 19.2.2.** below) could also be envisaged in the event that the compensation rules of accession, specification or commixture for the possibly improved goods gave a right to the market value, but:

(a) the owner of the material already concluded a contract for sale regarding the material under which he had achieved a higher price; or

(b) the owner of the material intended to use the property for his own production purposes and now has to buy substitute goods, which causes at least transportation costs and/or also agent costs or an increase in the price.

11.2. Specification

The difference between specification and accession is that while in accession one of the original assets (the principal) is still identifiable, in cases of specification, the result of the merger is a new thing altogether. *Specificatio* is defined as the making of a new article from the chattel of one person by the work of another.[419] If the Cypriot courts decide to follow the English courts on the interpretation of the line of cases concerning retention of title,[420] the right to trace into the new product will be lost and the property in the new product will vest entirely in the owner of the new product. Again as in cases of accession, it could be possible that a remedy lies in restitution and/or in tort within the parameters set out above.

---

[417] 'Where a person lawfully does anything for another person, or delivers to him anything, not intended to do so gratuitously, such that the person enjoys the benefit thereof, the latter is bound to make compensation to the former in respect of, or to restore, the thing so done or delivered'.

[418] Civil Appeal No 4366.

[419] Curzon, see note 442 above, p 396.

[420] See Part IV.

11.3. Commixture and confusion

This category is by far the most complex. First the distinction between three possible cases should be made.

1. Cases where the mixture is separable and the parts are identifiable;
2. Cases where the mixture is separable but the parts are not identifiable;[421]
3. Cases where the mixture[422] is not separable at all.

Under the first scenario where the mixture is separable and the parts are identifiable, each owner should remain the owner of their own part, with the right to have it separated from the whole. In the case of the second and third scenario, the position is unclear under Cyprus law and it can be safely assumed that the principles of English common law will be applicable (see section 9.4. of the English Report in this Volume).

As has been explained above in this report with respect to mixtures in contractual situations, the first part of **section 26 of the Sale of Goods Act 1994** mirrors section 20 of the English Sale of Goods Act 1979. Unfortunately the additional section 20A of the English Act has not been codified in the equivalent Cypriot Act. This additional section applies unless the parties expressly disapply it and provides that where there is a sale of a specified quantity of unascertained goods which form part of an identified bulk and the buyer has paid the price of the contract goods, then property in an undivided share in the bulk is transferred to the buyer and the buyer becomes owner in common of the bulk to the extent to which he has made payment. Where the aggregate of the undivided shares of the buyers in bulk exceed the whole of the bulk, then the undivided share of each buyer shall be reduced proportionally so that the aggregate of the undivided share is equal to the whole of the bulk. Thus although the position in England has become clear at least in cases where the goods although unascertained form part of an identified bulk, this is at least for the time being not the case in Cyprus.

---

[421] What is known as a 'granular mixture'; see Birks, P, 'Mixtures' in Palmer and McKendrick, note 441 above.

[422] What is known as a 'liquid mixture', *ibid.*

12. Rules on good faith acquisition

12.1. Description of the concept

Cyprus law, like English law differs from the Continental legal systems in that there is no separate doctrine of good faith. There are certainly instances where the law requires a party to have acted *bona fide*[423] before he may assert certain rights especially if those rights are to be asserted against innocent third parties. This is arguably not enough to constitute a free-standing doctrine in the sense known to the Continental systems.

Other instances of notions similar to good faith may be seen in cases where a party seeks the assistance of equity. In order to be able to enjoy the benefit of an equitable remedy, certain requirements must first be met. The maxim '*he who comes to equity must come with clean hands*' is certainly such an instance where the obligation to have acted 'equitably' is imposed on such party. Further in cases of trusts, the trustee is under an obligation to act in the best interests of the beneficiary and this is true more generally in cases where there is a *fiduciary relationship*.

The term 'good faith' is neither defined in the Sale of Goods Law of 1994 nor in the Contract Law (Cap 149). However reference to the term 'good faith' is made several times in the **Sale of Goods Law 1994**. In particular, good faith has a pivotal role to play in relation to the 'transfer of title' sections. The relevant sections of the Sale of Goods Act are set out below. The reader is also referred to the introduction to the *nemo dat quod non habet* rule above in section 5.9. as well as to the Sale of Goods Act exceptions and the Contract law agency exceptions to this rule.

The exceptions to the *nemo dat quod non habet* rule provided by The Sale of Goods Act, require that the person making the disposition be in possession of the goods or of the documents of title to the goods with the *consent* of the lawful owner.[424] Thus, as will be seen in the following cases, it is not possible for a *thief* to rely on these statutory exceptions.

Another element which appears from the exceptions in the Sale of Goods Act is the element of estoppel. If the owner has acted in a way which will prevent him from denying the authority of the seller to sell, then the purchaser's title will prevail over that of the owner. The rationale is somewhat the same as that underlying the rules of agency. In a sense the rule is that as between the true owner and the purchaser where neither of them are at fault, the rightful owner will prevail, but if the owner is somehow at fault either because he has made some sort of representa-

---

[423] There have been some references made in the course of discussion in this report to the '*bona fide* purchaser'.

[424] It should be noted that section 30(1) is drafted in terms of implied *authorisation* rather than *consent*.

tion (whether by allowing the seller to be in possession or by putting his agent in such a position that it would appear to the outside world that he has power to make the disposition) or because he has acted in such a way that an *estoppel* will arise against him, then the rights of the *bona fide* purchaser for value without notice will prevail.

12.2.   The transfer of title sections of the Sale of Goods Act

The provisions on the transfer of title can be regarded as exceptions to the *Nemo dat quod non habet* rule. It should be noted that the following exceptions mirror the corresponding exceptions of the English Sale of Goods Act 1979.[425]

Section 27 sets out the general rules. It provides that when goods are sold by any person who is not the owner of such goods and does not sell them under the authority or with the consent of the owner, then the buyer acquires no better title to the goods than that of the seller unless the owner of the goods is precluded by his conduct from denying the authority of the seller to sell. Thus the law here provides for an *estoppel* to arise against the owner in such cases.[426]

It is then provided that, when the commercial agent with the assent of the owner has possession of the goods or documents of title to the goods, any sale made by such agent in the usual course of business carried out by commercial agents, is valid as if he was expressly authorised by the owner of the goods to act in this way, so long as the buyer acted in good faith and at the time of the contract of sale he had no knowledge that the seller did not have authority to sell. This part of section 27 preserves the validity of the provisions of the Contract Law in relation to the law of agency.

Section 28 provides that when goods belonging to different co-owners are with the assent of all co-owners to be found in the exclusive possession of one of them, then the property in the goods passes to any person who in goods faith purchases these from the co-owner without knowing that at the time of the contract of sale the seller was not authorised to sell.

Section 29 provides that if the goods came into the possession of the seller by virtue of a contract which is voidable under **section 18 or 19 of the Contract Law**, but the contract has not been avoided by the time of sale, then the buyer obtains good title to the goods provided that he buys them in good faith without knowledge of the defect in the seller's title. This section therefore preserves the validity of the general rules preventing rescission of a contract *inter alia* after there has been a disposition to a third party. Thus if there is misrepresentation, coercion or fraud as pro-

---

[425] Sections 21, 23, 25, 26.
[426] The natural home of the doctrine of *estoppel* is in equity.

vided by sections 18 and 19 of the Contract Law Cap, the owner loses his right to rescind the contract when the goods are acquired by a third party. The key to this section is that there is title to the goods to be conveyed albeit voidable. Thus as Goode has noted in relation to the corresponding English section, this is strictly speaking not an exception to the *nemo dat* rule although in effect it does constitute such an exception because the owner loses his right to avoid the contract once the disposition has been made.[427] If on the other hand there is no title at all (*i.e.* not even a voidable title) for example because they were stolen or there was an effective reservation of title,[428] then this section will have no application because there was no title in the first place.

Section 30(1) provides that when a person who has sold goods, has or continues to have possession of the goods or documents of title to the goods, then delivery or transfer of the goods or documents of title, by that person or by a mercantile agent acting for him, under any sale, pledge or other disposition thereof to any person who receives the same in good faith and without knowledge of the previous sale,[429] has the effect it would have if the person making the delivery or transfer was expressly authorised by the owner of the goods to make the same.

Section 30(2) provides that when a person who has bought or has entered into an agreement to buy goods obtains with the consent of the seller possession of the goods or documents of title to the goods, the delivery or the transfer by such person or a mercantile agent who acts on his account, of the goods or the documents of title by virtue of sale, pledge or other disposition thereof to any person who receives the same in good faith and without the knowledge of any lien or other right of the original seller in respect of the goods, has the same effect as it would have if there had been no such right of lien or other right.

The case of *Cleopas Demetriou v South African Eagle Insurance Company Limited*,[430] considers the issue of good faith and the application of **sections 27 and 30** above. In this case, the appellant had purchased a car from the seller who was not the rightful owner of the car. The car had been stolen so it was held that the statutory exceptions to the *nemo dat* rule had no application here, therefore neither **section 27** nor **section 30** above could be relied upon. Further no estoppel arose against the insurers for failure to set in motion the investigation in a timely manner as was argued by the appellant.

---

[427] Goode, see note 40 above, p 425.

[428] Although someone who has effectively reserved title may lose such title by virtue of some other exception to the *nemo dat* rule.

[429] It is important to note that here only the term 'sale' is included as opposed to the corresponding English section and the other limb of this section (s. 30(2)) which includes other dispositions.

[430] Civil Appeal No 9617.

This is important to note because it clarifies the distinction between estoppel under section 27 and good faith under section 30. According to the evidence which was adduced in the case, he was not a *bona fide* purchaser acting in good faith. Hence the provisions of section 30 had not been satisfied in this case since *inter alia* there has been no good faith on the part of the purchaser. Crucially the certificate of registration of the vehicle was considered to constitute only *prima facie* evidence of title which is rebuttable on contrary evidence.[431] Thus the fact that the vehicle was registered in the name of the seller did not prevent the finding of the Court.

As was explained above, the essence of **sections 28, 29 and 30** are that the goods or documents of title are in the possession of the seller with the consent[432] of the owner. According to case law on the corresponding section to section 30, consent is effective even if it is obtained by fraud.[433]

The above sections refer to 'documents of title'. The previous section on possession discusses what is meant by 'documents of title'. It is useful to note that a certificate of registration of a vehicle[434] and share certificates[435] are not considered documents of title, nor was registration in a shipping register considered conclusive evidence of title.[436]

It should be noted that good faith is a pre-requisite for the application of **section 30**. This is in contrast with **section 27 of the Sale of Goods Act** which instead provides protection in the form of an estoppel[437] in the sense that the owner must be estopped from denying that the seller was authorised by him to make the sale.

---

[431] The court here relied on case *Central Newbury Car Auctions Ltd v Unity Finance Ltd and Another* [1956] 3 All ER 905.

[432] Although it should be noted that while sections 27 and 30 are drafted in terms of *'singatathesi'* (consent), section 28 uses the term 'adia' which strictly speaking means permission.

[433] Goode, see note 40 above, p 433-4; see case *Cahn v Pockett's Bristol Channel Steam Packet Co* [1899] 1 QB 1 159.

[434] Regulation 8 of Automobiles and Motor Traffic Regulations (1984); see *Cleopas Demetriou v South African Eagle Insurance Company Limited*, Civil Appeal No 9617.

[435] Section 77, Cap 113.

[436] In *NTTS OV MNPO 'DALVENT' v F/V 0758 ZOLOTETS (CALL LETTERS (UHZT)*, Civil Appeal No 9011, it was considered that subsequent registration in a separate shipping register was not conclusive evidence of title. The fact that there was no evidence of a transfer and that the ship was originally registered in another register were relied upon in reaching the conclusion that the ship had not in fact been transferred. The subsequent registration did not affect this finding.

[437] Which is an equitable doctrine and requires 'clean hands' (on the basis of the equitable maxim that he who comes to equity must come with clean hands) on the part of the person who seeks to rely on it (here the purchaser) so the requirement of good faith is indirectly imposed on the person who seeks to rely on section 27.

12.3. The implied term of the right to sell

It should be noted that the **Sale of Goods Act 1994** imposes an implied term that the seller has the right to sell and that the buyer will take free from any encumbrances which may burden the goods. **Section 14 (1)** of the Sale of Goods Act provides that in a contract for the sale of goods, unless the surrounding circumstances of the contract are such that a contrary intention appears, it is an implied term (*condition* which is of the essence to the contract) on the part of the seller that in the case of a sale he has the right to sell the goods, and in the case of an agreement to sell he will have the right to sell at the time at which the sale is to be made. Section 14(2) provides that it is an implied *warranty* that the buyer will be able to enjoy quiet possession of the goods. **Section 14(3)** provides that it is an implied *warranty* that, before or at the time of contracting, goods are free of any encumbrance or charge in favour of any third party which was not made known to the buyer or which the buyer did not have knowledge of.

12.4. Other references to good faith

References to good faith are also made sporadically in many other laws including the **Companies Law (Cap 113)** and the **Bills of Exchange Law (Cap 262)**. References to good faith in the latter are of particular importance for the purposes of this discussion. In *Ioannis Patsalis v Karabet Afsharian*[438] Triantafyllides J dealt with the issue of whether or not the respondent was a holder in due course in the sense of **section 29** of the Bills of Exchange Law.

For a person to be a holder in due course he must be a holder who has taken a bill, complete and regular on the face of it, (*a*) before it was overdue, and without notice that it has been previously dishonoured, if such is the fact, and (*b*) in good faith and for value and without notice at the time, when the bill was negotiated to him, of any defect in the title of a person, who negotiates a bill; illegal consideration is expressly enumerated in sub-section (2) of section 29.

By **section 30 (2)** of the same Law, every holder of a bill is *prima facie* deemed to be a holder in due course but if in an action on a bill it is admitted or proved that the acceptance, issue, or subsequent negotiation of the bill is affected with, *inter alia*, illegality the burden of proof is shifted, unless and until the holder proves that, subsequent to the alleged illegality, value has in *good faith* been given for the bill. The term 'good faith' is then defined in **section 90** of the same Law (and in fact it is the only statutory definition of 'good faith' that can be found in Cypriot law). It is

---

[438] Civil Appeal No 4497.

provided that a thing is deemed to be done in good faith, within the meaning of the Law, where it is in fact done honestly, whether it is done negligently or not.

Therefore, section 90 of the Bills of Exchange Law provides the definition of good faith missing from the Cypriot Contract Law and the Sale of Goods Law of 1994. Whether or not something was done in 'good faith', the courts accept that it is a matter to be decided on the facts of each case.

13.   Rules for 'acquisitive' prescription of movables

There are no formal rules providing for the acquisitive prescription (or 'adverse possession' as the term is known under Cypriot law) of movable property under Cypriot Law. By adverse possession is meant the acquisition of ownership by possession of the property for a substantial period of time. However, as is the case under English law, one can suggest that there can be other rules, such as the limitations of actions rules which can lead to the same result – *i.e.* acquiring ownership by possession.

The Cypriot Act corresponding to the English Limitation Act of 1980 is the Limitation of Actions Law of 1959, Cap 15 of the Laws of Cyprus; this has been recently amended by a 2007 Act.

Section 3(1)(f) of Cap 15 provides that no action shall be brought upon, for or in respect of any goods sold and delivered, shop bill, hotel bill, book debt, work and labour done, wages of artisans, labourers or servants, after the expiration of 3 years from the date on which the cause of action accrued.

In addition **section 5** provides that no action shall be brought upon, for or in respect of any cause of action not expressly provided for in the Law or expressly exempted from the operation of the Law, after the expiration of 6 years from the date when such cause of action accrued.

The above provisions can have the effect of vesting ownership in a person who wrongfully acquired possession of goods in the first place. This is not as unfair as it seems since Cap 15, makes provision for cases of fraud and/or mistake. **Section 7** provides that where in the case of any cause of action for which a limitation period exists:

(a) the right of action has been concealed by the fraud of the defendant
   or his agent or any person through whom he claims as his agent or;
(b) the action is for the relief from the consequences of a mistake,

the period of limitation shall not begin to run until the plaintiff has discovered the fraud or the mistake as the case may be, or could have discovered it with reasonable diligence.

Section 7 goes on to provide that the above shall not enable any action to be brought to recover or enforce any charge against, or set aside any transaction affecting any property which:

(a) in the case of fraud has been purchased for valuable consideration by a person who was not a party to the fraud and did not at the time of purchase know or have reason to believe that any fraud had been committed;

(b) in the case of a mistake, has been purchased for valuable consideration subsequently to the transaction in which the mistake was made by a person who did not know or had no reason to believe that the mistake had been made.

In the case of immovable property, it used to be the case that adverse possession was allowed (the prescriptive period was 10-15 years depending on the type of immovable property involved). Today, **section 9 of the Immovable property (Tenure, Registration and Valuation) Law (Cap 224)** provides that no title to immovable property will be acquired by any person by adverse possession as against the Republic of Cyprus or a registered owner. However section 9 has no retrospective effect and therefore any rights acquired by adverse possession under the provisions of the law prevailing before 1st September 1946 will continue to be valid, notwithstanding the prohibitions of section 9.[439]

14. Other forms of original acquisition / finding & abandonment

It has already been noted that under Cypriot law, acquisitive prescription is not recognised as a way of obtaining ownership of a movable or immovable (as is the case today) property. An ancillary matter to the 'concept' of acquisitive prescription is the case of 'finding' of abandoned property. Would the person finding property whose owners are unknown ever have the right to obtain ownership of that property?

We would firstly like to point out a maritime law case in which the Cypriot Courts dealt with the issue of abandonment of a ship (a 'derelict' ship), which clearly shows the position under Cypriot law. In *Petros Petrou v The Ship Submet*[440] the applicants found an abandoned boat in the sea. The boat was in obvious danger and the applicants managed to salvage the boat after 9 hours. The boat was abandoned under unknown

---

[439] For more details on the rules of adverse possession of immovable property, see Andreas Neocleous & Co, note 1 above, Chapter 14.

[440] Admiralty Action No 33/99.

circumstances and its owners were never traced. The judge said that there was no authority under Cypriot law whereby the right of the finder – of a boat abandoned in the sea – to obtain ownership of a boat is recognised.

Counsel for the applicants based their claim on two old English cases. The judge said that those cases simply referred to the right of the finder of the boat to have absolute possession and control over the boat as against third parties but not as against the true owner. He also cited the following passage from one of those cases in support of his finding:

'In the case of salvors there is a distinction between a derelict and a vessel which, though in great danger, has not been abandoned by the master and crew. In the case of a derelict, the salvors who first take possession have not only a maritime lien on the ship for salvage services, but they have the entire and absolute possession and control of the vessel, and no one can interfere with them except in the case of manifest incompetence'.[441]

He went on to approve a passage from Kennedy's *Law of Salvage*[442] which says that where a vessel is in fact derelict, the first salvors taking possession of her *prima facie* have a right of exclusive possession. Their rights may be protected by an injunction and/or an award of damages and possibly by a declaration.

The claim of the applicants for obtainment of ownership of the salvaged boat was therefore rejected. The court said however that the finders were entitled under **section 24** of the **Wreckage Law (Cap 298)** to reasonable reward for saving the boat. **Section 34** of the same law lists the different factors to be taken into account for the determination of the amount of the reward (which includes the extent of damage, the danger involved, the value of the property and the time required for its rescue). The court cited and approved in this regard the Cypriot case *Branco Salvage Limited v The Ship 'Dimitrios' and her cargo and freight.*[443] The court said further that the right to reward is based on the appreciation that one who exposes himself and his property to danger for the rescuing of naval property is entitled to a reward as a matter of natural justice.

The authors of this report are not aware of any similar case involving any other kind of movable property (*i.e.* other than naval property). Therefore, the issue lies open and is free of any court authority in relation to other kinds of movable property.

However, the authors assume that the aforementioned case can be used as an authority, in subsequent cases, for the principle that finding abandoned property does not give someone the right under Cypriot law to claim ownership of that property. The finder of abandoned property has

---

[441] *Cossman v West* (1886-1890) All ER, p 957.

[442] (1985), p 518.

[443] (1968) 1 CLR 252.

the right of absolute possession of and control over the property as against third parties but not as against the true owner. The above principle can be justified by the fact that 'abandonment' is hard to establish. Abandonment can only be established if there is a clear and unequivocal testimony by the true owner of the property that he/she *intended* for all practical purposes to abandon the property in question. If property was intended to be abandoned then the best way for the courts to justify the existence of the new owner is to treat the original owners as makers of a gift to the subsequent taker of the property.[444] Without this testimony however, it can never be established that the property was in fact abandoned.

A further issue for discussion in relation to abandonment is the following. At which stage, or otherwise what is the crucial act after which the owner of the property is considered to have abandoned the property? There are three possibilities:

1. When the thought is made that he wants to abandon the property in question.
2. When he disposes of the property in question and walks away.
3. When the finder takes the property into his/her possession.

With most kinds of choses in possession, we assume that property can be abandoned unilaterally when the owner of the property decides to leave his property aside by walking away from it – by 'deserting' his property. A watch, a bicycle, or any other kind of object can be abandoned by its owner by a unilateral act. But what about shares in a company (if these are considered as choses in possession at all) and choses in action? Could these be abandoned unilaterally?

The ownership of shares in a company is entered into the relevant register of members of the company. Likewise, other kinds of property (motorvehicles and animals for example) are entered in publicly available registers. It seems that these kinds of movable property cannot be disposed of unilaterally by mere abandonment. Further acts are required, for example deregistration, before such property can be said to have been abandoned.

A final issue to consider is the question in whom property vests in the case where it is rendered ownerless after the occurrence of a certain event. This is not strictly speaking 'abandoned' property, but can be mentioned here for the sake of completeness. There are various provisions in the Laws of Cyprus which provide that such property is deemed *bona vacantia* and belongs to the Republic of Cyprus. For example, **section 308**

---

[444] *Moorhouse v Angus & Robertson* [1981] 1 NSWLR 790, in this case trial judge McClelland treated abandonment as analogous to a gift (cited in Birks, P, 'Abandonment', in Palmer and McKendrick, see note 441 above).

of the Cypriot **Companies Law, Cap 113,** provides that where a company is dissolved, all property and rights whatsoever vested in or held on trust for the company immediately before its dissolution (not including property held by the company on trust for any other person) shall be deemed to be *bona vacantia* and shall accordingly belong to the Republic, and shall vest and may be dealt with in the same manner as other *bona vacantia* accruing to the Republic. An analogous provision is made in the **Wills and Succession Law, Cap 195,** for property belonging to a deceased person with no successors. In such a case, the property of the deceased devolves on the Republic.

The meaning of the term *bona vacantia* was considered in *Armando Nassar Marine Services Ltd v The Central Bank of Cyprus.*[445] The judge cited **Halsbury's Laws of England** and said that this principle is applicable only when there is no claim for the ownership of the property in question. The justification for this principle is that the property in *bona vacantia* is vested in the Crown 'to prevent the strife and contention to which title by occupancy might otherwise give rise'.

---

[445] Case No 897/88.

15. Rules on the reservation of title

15.1. Description

The Cypriot rules on the reservation of title can be found in the **Sale of Goods Law of 1994**. In particular, **section 25** of the Law is entitled 'reservation of the right of disposal' and provides that where there is a contract for the sale of specific goods or where goods are subsequently appropriated to the contract, the seller may, by the terms of the contract or appropriation, reserve the right of disposal of the goods until certain conditions are fulfilled (for example payment of the price); and in such a case, notwithstanding the delivery of the goods to the buyer, or to the carrier or other bailee or custodier for the purpose of transmission to the buyer, the property in the goods does not pass to the buyer until the conditions imposed by the seller are fulfilled.[446]

Section 25(2) provides that where goods are shipped and by the bill of lading the goods are deliverable to the order of the seller or his agent, the seller is *prima facie* to be taken to reserve the right of disposal. Where the seller of goods draws on the buyer for the price and transmits the bill of exchange and bill of lading to the buyer together to secure acceptance or payment of the bill of exchange, the buyer is bound to return the bill of lading if he does not honour the bill of exchange, and if he wrongfully retains the bill of lading the property in the goods does not pass to him.[447]

So therefore, what is retained under Cypriot Law is not a mere security right but the property in the goods involved, *i.e.* the ownership of the property. This rule exists mainly for the protection of the unpaid seller in case where the buyer becomes bankrupt. So therefore where the buyer becomes bankrupt and has not previously paid for the property in question, the unpaid seller is protected by virtue of section 25(1) of the Sale of Goods Law 1994 despite the fact that the property in question was in the buyer's possession. Provided that payment of the price was by the terms of the contract a condition precedent for the passing of property in

---

[446] Section 25(1) of the Sale of Goods Law 1994.
[447] Section 25(2) *ibid.*

the goods, the seller is protected and the reservation of the right of disposal is effective as against both the buyer and third parties.

15.2.   Consideration of English law and cases

As has been explained in Part II of this report, property passes when it is intended to pass.[448] Regardless of the default rules[449] for determining the passing of property where no such intention appears from the contract, the conduct of the parties or the surrounding circumstances. **Section 19** of the English **Sale of Goods Act 1972** very clearly provides that when there is such intention property does not pass until the term which must be fulfilled is in fact fulfilled. The parties are therefore on the basis of section 19, free to stipulate that property should not pass even after delivery[450] of the goods until the occurrence of a certain contingency such as for example (as is usually the case) payment of the price.

Indeed the courts in Cyprus have ruled favourably on the matter, recognising retention of title clauses in certain cases. In *'The Algazera'*[451] there was an agreement in writing with the plaintiffs whereby the plaintiffs undertook to build for them a ship in accordance with certain terms and specifications. The purchasers signed a document to the effect that the ship would not become their property until full payment of the contract price including eventual extra costs. The purchasers delivered two cheques which were never honoured. It was held that from the authorities on the subject of the transfer of the property in goods from the seller, manufacturer *etc.*, to the buyer, it appears that the mere handing of the goods by the seller to the buyer passes the property immediately unless a different intention appears from the terms of the contract of sale. In this case the document which provided that property would not pass until the full amount was paid was evidence of such contrary intention. The handing over therefore of the 'Builder's certificate' could not in any way affect the intention of the parties which expressed that property in the ship would not pass without the consent of the plaintiffs. This means that the purchaser could not transfer any share of ownership in the ship, because the ownership had not vested in him.

---

[448] Section 19 of the Sale of Goods Law 1994.

[449] Sections 20-24 *ibid.*

[450] Which under the default rules would be *prima facie* evidence of an intention to pass the property in the goods unless a contrary intention appears.

[451] *Scheepswerf Bodewes-Gruno and The Ship 'Algazera', now lying at the port of Limassol* (1980) (Civil) 1 CLR 404.

In an earlier case,[452] the same result was reached on the basis that the contract was an *executory contract*. In this case, the parties entered into an oral agreement whereby the respondent agreed to sell to the appellant a cart and mule for a set price. Although the cart and mule were delivered to the appellant, it was agreed that they were not to become the appellant's property until the full price had been paid. The full price was to be paid within one year. The Court of Appeal upheld the judgment of the lower court that since the price had not been paid within one year, the cart and mule should have been returned or the price should have been paid. The respondent had regained possession of the cart and mule and sold them to somebody else. The Court of Appeal held that he was entitled to do so since *the cart and mule had been held to have been his own property*.

15.3. Cases where the subject matter has been altered

In the two cases above, the underlying goods were not altered in any way. If the Cyprus courts follow the English court decisions on the interpretation of the corresponding section then this will be as far as it goes. In a line of cases following the landmark *Romalpa*[453] case in which the subject matter had been altered in some way, the retention of title failed to cover the new product. In *Re Bond Worth*,[454] where 'acrilan' fibre was supplied for the purpose of the manufacture of carpets, the clause attempting to achieve retention of 'equitable and beneficial' ownership of the carpets produced by the use of the fibre failed, and gave rise only to a 'floating charge' which failed for lack of registration. In *Borden*[455] a clause which attempted to retain title in resin which was used to make chipboards and the chipboards themselves failed on the ground that once the resin was irreversibly incorporated into the chipboard it ceased to be resin and the judge, Buckley LJ, found it impossible for the plaintiffs to have reserved any property in the chipboard because they never had any property in it in the first place. Similarly in *Re Peachdart*,[456] property could not be retained in leather which was used to make handbags, but a different result was seen in *Hendy Lennox*.[457] In the latter case, Staughton J held that the proprietary rights of the sellers in engines sold were not

---

452 *George Michael of Nicosia v Costas Georgiou of Aglanja* (Civil Appeal No 3654).

453 *Aluminium Industrie Vaaseen BV v Romalpa Aluminium Ltd* [1976] 1 WLR 676, Queen's Bench Division and Court of Appeal, which in fact lends its name to retention of title clauses which are sometimes referred to as 'Romalpa Clauses'.

454 *Re Bond Worth Ltd* [1980] Ch 228, Chancery Division.

455 *Borden (UK) v Scottish Timber Products Ltd* [1981] Ch 25, CA.

456 *Re Peachdart Ltd* [1984] Ch 131, Ch D.

457 *Hendy Lennox (Industrial Engines) Ltd v Grahame Puttick Ltd* [1984] 1 WLR 485, Queen's Bench Division.

affected when the engines where wholly or partially incorporated into gen-
erator sets.[458] This case was distinguished from the previous cases on the
basis that here the goods had not lost their identity merely because they
became attached to other things.

Thus while in cases such as *Romalpa* the title in the aluminium foil was
retained and the seller could 'trace'[459] into the proceeds of the sale of the
foil, in cases where the subject matter loses its identity, title to the goods is
lost. The rationale underlying the above cases is very likely to be followed by
the Cyprus courts should the matter of the effectiveness of the retention of
title clause in relation to goods ever come before the courts.

16.   Abandonment; further way to lose property

Please refer to **Chapter 14** where the issue of abandonment is addressed.

17.   Transfer rules for 'co-ownership'

The **principles of co-ownership and of severance of movables** follow the
English common law, as described in Chapter 14 of the English Report in
this Volume. There are no express statutory rules on the transfer of goods
owned in common under Cypriot law. Such rules exist for immovable
property and are contained in **sections 24 to 35 of the Immovable Property Law, Cap 224.** But they do not appear to be directly relevant to the
transfer or partition of movables to the extent that the Land Registry is
involved in all transactions (registration, transfer and partition).

It can be said with certainty that a co-owner is in a position to pass a
good title to a third party without giving notice of the fact that he is a co-
owner, provided that the goods were in his possession with the other
owner's permission. This should amount to the severance of the movables
if held in joint tenancy, leading to tenancy in common. For more details
on the **liability among co-owners**, see **section 19.3.3.** below.

18.   Further rules applying to unspecified goods

18.1.   Transfer of shares in an identified bulk

See *inter alia* **sections 5.3.4. and 11.3.** of this Report.

---

[458] It is crucial to note that the engines remained identifiable by virtue of a serial
number.

[459] Tracing is an equitable remedy, see *Re Hallett's Estate* (1880) 13 ChD 696, CA.

18.2. Floating charge

Cyprus law is one of the countries which recognise the floating charge.[460] The classical definition of the floating charge which is most frequently cited is that of Romer LJ in *Re Yorkshire Woolcombers Association* and *often* has three characteristics.[461] The assets may be used in the course of business, and they comprise a mass which fluctuates from time to time. The charge may cover present and future assets of the company giving the charge. It is said to 'hover' over the pool of assets and is said to 'crystallise' on the occurrence of insolvency or any other event named by the parties at which time it turns into a fixed charge. The floating charge must be registered at the Registrar of Companies within twenty-one days.[462]

The benefit of the floating charge is that it allows the holder of such charge some security and simultaneously it allows the business giving the charge the power to deal with assets in the ordinary course of business without inhibiting the smooth operation of the business.

The distinction between the fixed and the floating charge is important. The matter has recently been clarified by the English House of Lords in a landmark decision with the participation of seven (as opposed to five) members of the House of Lords. According to Lord Scott in *National Westminster Bank Plc v Spectrum Plus Ltd*,[463] the difference between a fixed and a floating chare is the liberty to deal with the assets. Whether the charge covers both present and future assets and whether the assets change from time to time are not factors determinative of whether the charge is a floating charge. That is even if the assets are certain and do not change from time to time, the charge may still be considered a floating charge as opposed to a fixed charge if there is liberty on the part of the company giving the charge to deal with the assets.

It gives the secured creditor two remedies in the event of default.[464] The holder of such a charge may crystallise the charge over the assets caught by the charge at the time of crystallisation, and may in certain occasions where the charge encompasses substantially all of the assets of the company give the creditor the right to appoint a receiver to take control over the business as a whole.[465]

---

[460] Reference to the position of the holder of a floating charge in insolvency situations and the cases where it will be avoided has been made in the Insolvency section above.

[461] Although as will be seen below only one of the three characteristics is determinative of the existence of a floating as opposed to a fixed charge.

[462] Section 90(2)(d) of the Companies Law, Cap 113.

[463] [2005] UKHL 41.

[464] http://www.neocleous.com/assets/mainmenu/744/editor/Cyprus.pdf.

[465] http://www.neocleous.com/assets/mainmenu/744/editor/Cyprus.pdf, see section 89(1), Cap 113 which provides for the appointment of a receiver (who acts for the benefit of

19.   Consequences of restitution of the movable to the owner

This Chapter draws on **section 1.4. of this Report** and must be read in conjunction with it. The doctrine of restitution was described in section 1.4. as including unjust enrichment being 'part and parcel' of the doctrine. In *Ismini Kyriakou Hji Loizi and Others v Irini Iona*, the Cypriot courts constructed **section 70 of Cap 149** as allowing restitution provided, however, that 'the person for whom the act is done enjoys the benefit of it', thereby excluding *prima facie* the possibility of restitution under this section when the acquisition takes place with or from another possessor. The requirement of a *bona fide* owner or possessor was not set out as a condition of restitution in this case.

Reference must be made to the wider concept of acquisition at common law and in equity, in particular to assess the good faith of the possessor. Viscount Dilhorne in *Lawrence* stated that the term 'belonging to another' signifies no more than that at the time of the appropriation or of the obtaining of the property, it belonged to another person.[466] The receiving of the goods therefore need not be exclusive but might be shared with the person who stole the property (in case of theft) or with another receiver/possessor (in case of co-ownership or transfer to a third party).[467]

19.1.   Acquisition of possession based on a void / avoided / otherwise ineffective contract

19.1.1.   Quasi-contracts and restitution

Quasi-contract and restitution are considered to be a category of the common law which provides remedies for cases in respect of money had and received, unjust enrichment or unjust benefit, to prevent an individual from retaining money given to him, *e.g.* by mistake so that the innocent party will avoid suffering a loss because the standard contractual remedies are not available to him due to the non-existence of a contractual relationship between the parties. This will be because the parties' efforts to make a binding agreement failed or because their negotiations never reached the stage of an acceptable contract. These remedies involve situations where the parties have some relationship relating to, but falling

---

the holder of the charge as opposed to the company) to take over and pay the holder of the charge in the absence of insolvency.

[466] [1972] AC 626, p 633; see also Andreas Neocleous & Co, note 1 above, p 500.

[467] See Andreas Neocleous & Co, *ibid*, p 509.

outside, contract. Restitution provides a set of rules which provide for the recovery of money or property, aiming to prevent unjust enrichment.[468]

Equity also provides a remedy for cases of unjust enrichment and, to achieve this, two methods are followed, being:

- The doctrine of a constructive trust: An individual who receives money and/or property is considered to be the trustee of it for the plaintiff so that all the trust remedies are available to the plaintiff as the beneficiary; and
- A tracing order, so that the property can be traced by the true owner, even if changes have occurred or the property has been mixed with other property.[469]

Under the principle of quasi-contract, in an action for money had and received, the money sought to be recovered must have been received by the defendant under such circumstances as would create a privity between himself and the plaintiff. There are three situations in which money paid to the defendant can be recovered by the plaintiff as follows:

- There is a total failure of consideration;
- The money was transferred under a mistake of fact; and
- The money has been paid to a third party for the benefit of the defendant.[470]

These three situations will now be briefly analysed.

In the first case, a party can recover all his money deposited or paid under a contract if he receives nothing in return (where there is a total failure of consideration), in an action for money had and received.

An aggrieved party can recover all his money in a case where a contract is frustrated even though there has only been a partial failure of consideration. However, with the exception of the doctrine of frustration, a claim for money had and received cannot be maintained if the contract has been partly performed and the plaintiff has obtained some benefit from it.[471]

In the second instance, money paid under a mistake of fact will be recoverable provided that the mistake made relates to a material fact and under normal circumstances, if the mistake was true, the payment would have been legal or the plaintiff would be obliged to pay the money. In cases where the contract is void due to a mistake of fact, recovery will be

---

468 Andreas Neocleous & Co, see note 1 above, p 401.
469 *Ibid*, 402.
470 *Ibid*.
471 *Ibid*.

possible but the plaintiff in such a case would have to show that the defendant would be obliged to pay the money. No issue of entitlement to benefits arises here.

If, however, the mistake relates to a mistake of law and a person has paid money with complete knowledge of the facts, he cannot recover the money at common law, even if the payment was made as a consequence of a threat of legal proceedings.[472]

In the last and final situation mentioned above, *i.e.* if money has been paid to a third party, the plaintiff will be in a position to claim his money only if he was not acting as a volunteer in paying the money and he was under constraint. This means that if the plaintiff was acting wilfully and was doing this because he wished to do so, he will not be able to recover; if he was acting because he was forced to do so to save a situation, he will be able to recover.

The plaintiff must show that he paid the money to the defendant for his use on his express or implied request to him. It will be insufficient to prove only that the defendant was liable to pay the money to the third party and that the plaintiff discharged such liability. Furthermore, it must be proved that the defendant paid the money under a legal obligation to the third party.

An additional remedy is available, that of *quantum meruit* basis calculation. The plaintiff under this heading will not have paid the defendant money, but may have done some work or provided some benefit to him. The plaintiff's compensation is not defined by any agreement between the parties so he will seek to be compensated on a *quantum meruit* basis, relying on the benefit he has provided.[473]

Money paid on a *quantum meruit* basis can be recovered where the contract is void if the work was equally performed.[474]

19.1.2. Constructive trust

The constructive trust is used in cases where an innocent party gives money or property to the defendant under circumstances which provide grounds for recovery. In such a situation, the plaintiff may pursue an action requesting an order of the court that the defendant is holding the money or the property as a constructive trustee for him as the beneficiary.

In a constructive trust, the rules of equity, irrelevant to the intentions of the parties, determine that the money or the property is in the wrong

---

[472] *Ibid.*

[473] Andreas Neocleous & Co, see note 1 above, 403.

[474] *Associated Levant Lines v N Anastasiou* (1972) 5 JSC 504; *Kyriakou v Petrou* (1961) 1 CLR 300.

hands and compel the 'trustee' (the defendant) to convey the property to the beneficiary (the plaintiff). Under these circumstances, the trust is used as a remedial institution and, to distinguish it from the pure equitable constructive trust, it is called 'a constructive quasi-trust'.

In cases where the property of the plaintiff can be identified in the hands of the defendant, the plaintiff, being the true owner of that property, can pursue a claim requesting the remedy of tracing, to 'follow' the property and seek its recovery. This remedy may lie against an innocent recipient of the property even though there is no personal claim against him whether in tort, in quasi-contract or in equity. If the recipient is insolvent, the true owner may claim specific performance and obtain priority over the claims of the other creditors.[475]

19.1.3. Tracing at common law and in equity

The remedy of tracing is available both at common law and in equity. The common law permits a plaintiff to trace and claim his property if it has not been mixed with other property and can be identified as it was before its delivery to the defendant. If the property is money and the money is mixed with other money of the defendant in his bank account, it cannot be identified. A remedy could lie in the tort of conversion or an action in quasi-contract for money had and received under common law.

Tracing in equity requires a fiduciary relationship to exist prior to the creation of an equitable interest; once an equitable interest in the property is established, the beneficiary will be in a position to trace the property into the hands of anyone irrespective of the fact that he is a *bona fide* purchaser for value or the property is no longer identifiable.

Equity allows the tracing of property to a wide extent even if that property is then in a different form. If a trustee mixes trust money with his own in his bank account, a beneficiary can claim a first charge on the mixed fund or any asset purchased with the mixed fund. If trust funds of two separate trusts are mixed, there is an equal equity in each beneficiary and each can claim, trace, and share on a *pari passu* basis or enjoy, *pari passu*, an equitable lien or charge on an asset purchased with the mixed fund. But if the identity of the property is lost, then not even equity can trace it.

---

[475] Andreas Neocleous & Co, see note 1 above, 403.

19.1.4. Bailment

The principle on which a party can rely and claim damages for breach of a contract of bailment is that of *restitutio ad integrum*. This principle provides that a plaintiff can recover and be compensated for possible future losses, but he still must establish such a possibility.

19.2. Theft

19.2.1. The offence of stealing

In accordance with **section 255(1) of the Criminal Code (Cap 154)**, in order for goods to be considered as stolen, the court must determine as part of the *actus reus* that the subject matter was something capable of being stolen and that it was taken and carried away by the offender.[476] In *Police v Chrysomilis and Others*,[477] the Supreme Court held that sand severed from the land became a movable thing capable of being stolen and subsequently adopted a quite flexible approach to movables.[478]

The expression 'fraudulently and without a claim of right', 'in good faith', and 'with the intent to permanently deprive the owner' as set out in section 255(1) describe the mental element (*mens rea*) of the offence and must be proved in order for a conviction to be obtained.[479] In this respect, the offender must act in a fraudulent manner, regardless of any intent he must subsequently return the stolen property to its rightful owner; the intention to deprive the owner from his property must be permanent. Whether there are reasonable grounds for believing that there was an intention to return the property is determined on the facts of each case.[480]

The formation of the intent to permanently deprive need not necessarily take place at the exact moment of the taking and carrying away of the property. The act of taking or carrying away is considered to be a continuous act and the intent to deprive will be formed through the synergy of 'time' and 'appropriation'; the appropriation of the stolen property continues in time up to the point where the intention to permanently deprive is formed in the mind of the offender. It is possible therefore for someone who has taken property belonging to another with the intent to

---

[476] Andreas Neocleous & Co, *ibid*, p 500.
[477] (1975) 1 JSC 124.
[478] *Police v Protopapas* (1973) 10 JSC 1382.
[479] See *Platritis v Police* (1976) 2 CLR 174.
[480] Andreas Neocleous & Co, see note 1 above, p 501.

return it to be found guilty of stealing when he subsequently changes his mind and decides to keep the property.[481]

19.2.2. Receiving stolen goods

According to **section 306 of the Criminal Code**, the offence of receiving entails receiving or retaining stolen property knowing the same to have been stolen or obtained in any way whatsoever under circumstances which amount to felony or misdemeanour. After having established that the property in question has been stolen or has been obtained under circumstances which amount to a felony or a misdemeanour, the prosecution must establish that the accused received or retained the property. The terms 'receiving' or 'retaining' do not imply that the offender must have physical contact with the property. Common law authorities suggest that to establish receiving, it is necessary to establish possession in the sense of control by the defendant.[482] It is also possible that an offender may physically receive or retain the property but nevertheless may not exert any control over it. This may occur in a situation where the master orders the servant to receive certain goods and keep them in a certain place.[483] Receipt of the goods need not be exclusive but might be shared with the person who stole the property[484] or with another receiver.[485]

In the case of theft or receiving of stolen goods, the possessor has no good title to the goods and will be requested to restitute the goods to the owner, without however any entitlement to benefits on the part of the owner in this criminal law setting. The situation may vary at tort under the tort of unlawful interference (see section 38 Cap 148) and/or under the tort of conversion (see section 42 Cap 148), where the court can order the return of the property unlawfully detained instead of or *in addition to* any other remedy provided in Cap 148. In the absence of further relevant authority on this matter, the question remains open as to what kind of additional remedies could be granted by the court in addition to the general principles of restitution at common law justified by the unjust enrichment of the possessor (see also section 11.2. of this Report).

---

[481] *Ibid.*
[482] *Wiley* (1850) 2 Den 37; *Watson* [1916] 2 KB 385.
[483] *Cavendish*, 45 Cr App R 374.
[484] *Smith* (1855) Dears 494; *R v Seiga*, 45 Cr App R 25.
[485] *Payne*, 3 Cr App R 259; see Andreas Neocleous & Co, see note 1 above, p 509.

19.3.   Acquisition from a non-owner

19.3.1.   Estoppel

The doctrine of estoppel referred to herein prohibits the true owner of goods from denying his ownership. As a result, the buyer would then acquire a good title to the goods by estoppel and no restitution would take place. This kind of estoppel may arise by reason of a representation made by the true owner that the seller is the owner of the goods.

Where the true owner of the goods, either by his words or conduct, represents or allows the representation of another that the other is the owner of the goods, any sale made by that person will be valid against the true owner as if the seller was the true owner, provided that reliance was placed by the buyer on such a representation. The representation must be clear and unequivocal.[486]

19.3.2.   Mercantile agents

If a mercantile agent is in possession of goods or the title to them with the owner's consent, and he proceeds with a sale of the goods during the course of his business, any sale carried out under these circumstances will be valid and a good title will pass to the buyer as if the agent had the authorisation of the owner to act in that way. The buyer must have been acting in good faith and not have been aware of the fact that the agent did not have an authorisation to sell. In that case, the **remedies available will be ordinary** (see below).

19.3.3.   Co-owner

In the case of *Ismini Kyriacou* previously mentioned, the High Court in allowing the appeal held that at common law, one tenant in common of a house who expends money on ordinary repairs had no right of action against his co-tenant for contribution. Moreover, as there was no express statutory provision in Cyprus with regard to the liability of a co-owner to contribute to the cost of repairs carried out by another co-owner, the plaintiff could only succeed in her claim for contribution if she could bring it within **section 70 of the Contract law**.[487]

While constructing section 70 Cap 149 in four conditions (see above), the court noted that a co-owner cannot be bound to contribute to the

---

[486] Andreas Neocleous & Co, see note 1 above, p 412.
[487] See sections 1.4.4. para (d) and 19 above.

cost of repairs of the well 'where (a) the repairs were done against his will, *i.e.* he refused consent to the repairs being carried out, and (b) he had no option but to enjoy the benefit, *i.e.* to benefit out of the increase of the water in the well'.[488]

This however remains a case limited to wells being immovable property owned in common not falling under the same category as watercourses and channels used in common. Under **section 15 of Cap 224 (Immovable Property Law)**, the co-owners are liable to contribute to the cost of cleaning and repairing of watercourses and channels owned in common.

19.4. Remedies

19.4.1. Ordinary remedies

Section 47 of the Sale of Goods Act provides that an unpaid seller of goods has the following remedies against the goods:

- A lien on the goods for their price while they are still in his possession;
- In case of insolvency of the buyer, a right of stoppage of the goods in transit after the goods ceased to be in his possession; and
- A right to resell the goods in accordance with the provisions of the Act.

These remedies are available to the seller in addition to his right to sue the buyer for the price and for damages for non-acceptance as a form of security for payment of the price and as a form of preference of the seller over the general creditors of a bankrupt buyer.[489]

The above ordinary remedies do not appear to be applicable in a **three-party relationship** since the possession is either with the seller or with the buyer, unless the goods have been **duly deposited** with a third party on behalf of the seller or of the buyer (the case of the mercantile agent in particular).

There could also exist a lien over the property to secure the expenses of repair in the 'garage cases', which must be satisfied before the owner can regain possession.

---

[488] *Ibid*, para (6). The defendants had previously been adjudged to pay £7.250 each, being their share in the cost of repairs carried out by the plaintiff who is one of the co-owners.

[489] Andreas Neocleous & Co, see note 1 above, p 417-8.

19.4.2. Extraordinary remedies

Section 62 of the Sale of Goods Act specifically provides for a right of restitution in cases of failure of consideration and for a right to recover interest or special damages. Unless the contract otherwise provides, the Court may order the payment of interest on the price at such rate as it deems appropriate in favour of the seller as from the date the goods were offered or payment fell due, and in favour of the buyer claiming the return of the price as from the date at which payment was made.

In any case, it would appear that such interests or special damages would be calculated at the date of the award by the court and could reflect any **loss or deterioration of the movables.**

Table of Literature

I. Books

Atiyah, P S, Adams, J N and MacQueen, H, *The Sale of Goods*
(11th ed Pearson/Longman, New York/London 2005)
Lord Bankton, *An Institute of the Laws of Scotland*
(1751-1753, Stair Soc vols 41-43, Edinburgh 1993-1995)
Bell, G J, Commentaries on the Law of Scotland (7th ed, ed Lord McLaren, 1870)
Bell, G J, *Principles of the Law of Scotland* (10th ed, ed Sheriff Guthrie, 1899)
Bell, A P, *Modern Law of Personal Property in England and Ireland*
(Butterworths, Dublin 1989)
Bennett, H and Armour, J (eds), *Vulnerable Transactions in Corporate Insolvency*
(Hart Publishing, Oxford 2002)
Birks, P, *An Introduction to the Law of Restitution* (Clarendon Press, Oxford 1989)
Birks, P (ed), *English Private Law* (Oxford 2000)
Birks, P (ed), *Laundering and Tracing* (OUP, Oxford 1995)
Blackstone, Sir W, *Commentaries on the Laws of England*, Volume II
(Of the Rights of Things) (Oxford, 1766)
Bradgate, R, *Commercial Law* (Butterworths, London 2000)
Bridge, M, *Personal Property Law* (2nd ed Blackstone, London 1996)
Bridge, M, *Personal Property* Law (3rd ed OUP, Oxford 2002)
Bridge, M, *Sale of Goods* (OUP, Oxford 1997)
Brown, R, *Notes and Commentaries on the Sale of Goods Act 1893*
(W Green, Edinburgh 1895)
Buckland, W W and McNair, A D, *Roman Law and Common Law*
(2nd ed, by F H Lawson, CUP, Cambridge 1965)
Burn, E H, *Cheshire & Burn's Modern Law of Real Property*
(16th ed Butterworths, London 2000)
Burrows, A (ed), *English Private Law* (2nd ed OUP, Oxford 2007)
Burrows, *The Law of Restitution* (2nd ed Butterworths, London 2002)
Byrne, R and Binchy, W (eds), *Annual Review of Irish Law*
(Roundhall Ltd, Dublin 1996-2006)
Byrne, R & McCutcheon, P, *The Irish Legal System*
(4th ed Butterworths, Dublin 2001)

Carey Miller, D L, *The Acquisition and Protection of Ownership*
(Juta, Cape Town 1986)

Carey Miller, D L with Irvine, D, *Corporeal Moveables in Scots Law*
(2nd ed W Green, Edinburgh 2005)
Carver, T G & Colinvaux, R P, *Carver's Carriage by Sea*, Vol II
(12th ed Stevens & Sons, London 1971)
Clarke, A and Kohler, P, *Property Law* (CUP, Cambridge 2005)
Clerk, J F and Lindsell, W H B, *Clerk and Lindsell on Torts*
(19th ed Sweet & Maxwell, London 2006)
Cornish, W R, Nolan, R, O'Sullivan, J, and Virgo, G, (eds),
Restitution: Past, Present and Future (Hart Publishing, Oxford 1998)
Courtney, M, *The Law of Private Companies* (2nd ed Butterworths, Dublin 2002)
Crerar, L D, *The Law of Banking in Scotland* (2nd ed Tottel, Haywards Heath 2007)
Curzon, L B, *Dictionary of Law* (6th ed Pearson Education Limited, Harlow 2002)
Cusine, D J (ed), *A Scots Conveyancing Miscellany:*
Essays in Honour of Professor J M Halliday (W Green, Edinburgh 1987)
Cusine, D J and Paisley, R R M, *Servitudes and Rights of Way*
(W Green, Edinburgh 1998)

Davies, P L, *Gower and Davies' Principles of Modern Company Law*
(7th ed Sweet & Maxwell, London 2003)

Emiliou, N, 'Cyprus' in TMC Asser Instituut, *The impact of EU accession*
on the legal order of new EU member states & (pre-) candidate countries:
hopes & fears (TMC Asser Press, The Hague 2006)
Erskine, Sir J, *An Institute of the Law of Scotland* (8th ed, ed J B Nicholson,
Edinburgh 1870)
Evangelides, P, *The Republic of Cyprus and its Constitution with special regard to*
the constitutional rights (Difo-Druck, Bamberg 1996)
Evans-Jones, R, *Unjustified Enrichment*, vol 1 (W Green, Edinburgh 2003)

Fletcher, I and Roxburgh, R (eds), *Greene and Fletcher: The Law and Practice of*
Receivership in Scotland (3rd ed Tottel, Haywards Heath 2005)
Forde, M, *Bankruptcy Law in Ireland* (Butterworths, Dublin 1990)
Forte, A D M (ed), *Good Faith in Contract and Property Law* (Hart, Oxford 1999)

Getzler, J and Payne, J, *Company Charges: Spectrum and Beyond*
(OUP, Oxford 2006)
Gloag, W M and Henderson, R C, *Introduction to the Law of Scotland*
(3rd ed, 1939)
Gloag, W M and Henderson, R C, *The Law of Scotland*
(12th ed, by Lord Coulsfield and H L MacQueen, W Green, Edinburgh 2007)
Gloag, W M and Irvine, J M, *Law of Rights in Security*
(W Green, Edinburgh 1897)
Goode, Sir R M, *Commercial Law* (2nd ed Penguin Books, Harmondsworth 1995)
Goode, Sir R M, *Commercial Law* (3rd ed Penguin, London 2004)

Goode, Sir R M, *Principles of Corporate Insolvency Law*
  (3rd ed Sweet & Maxwell, London 2004)
Goode, Sir R M, *Proprietary Rights and Insolvency in Sales Transactions*
  (Sweet & Maxwell, London 1989)
Gordon, Sir G H, *Criminal Law*
  (3rd ed, by M G A Christie, W Green, Edinburgh 2000)
Gordon, W M, *Studies in the Transfer of Property by Traditio*
  (Aberdeen University Press, Aberdeen 1970)
Gordon, W M, *Scottish Land Law* (2nd ed W Green, Edinburgh 1999)
Goudy, H, *Bankruptcy* (4th ed, ed TA Fyfe, W Green, Edinburgh 1914)
Gow, J J, *The Mercantile and Industrial Law of Scotland*
  (W Green, Edinburgh 1964)
Gravells, N P, *Land Law: Text and Materials*
  (3rd ed Sweet & Maxwell, London 2004)
Gray, K J and Gray, S F, *Elements of Land Law*
  (3rd ed OUP, Oxford 2004, 4th ed OUP, Oxford 2005)
Gretton, G L, 'Diligence and Enforcement of Judgments' in *The Laws of Scotland:
  Stair Memorial Encyclopaedia*, vol 8 (Butterworths, Edinburgh 1992)
Guest, A G, Benjamin, J P, *Benjamin's Sale of Goods*
  (6th ed Sweet & Maxwell, London 2006)
Guest, A G, *Oxford Essays in Jurisprudence* (OUP, Oxford 1961)

Halliday, J M, *Conveyancing Law and Practice*, vol 1 (W Green, Edinburgh 1985)
Halliday, J M, *Conveyancing Law and Practice in Scotland*
  (2nd ed, by I J S Talman, 2 vols, W Green, Edinburgh 1995 and 1996)
Halsbury's Laws of England, Vol II (4th ed London Butterworths, London), Vol IV
  (3rd ed London Butterworths, London)
Hamel, J, *Le Contrat de Commission* (Paris 1942)
Harpum, C, *Megarry and Wade, The Law of Real Property*
  (6th ed Sweet & Maxwell, London 2000)
Hayton, D J, Kortmann, S C J J and Verhagen, H L E, *Principles of European
  Trust Law* (Kluwer and Tjennk Willink, The Hague and Deventer 1999)
Hogg, M, *Obligations* (2nd ed Avizandum, Edinburgh 2006)
Hume, D, *Lectures*, vols I-VI (Stair Soc vols 5 (1939), 13 (1949), 15 (1952),
  17 (1955), 18 (1957) and 19 (1958), ed G C H Paton, Edinburgh)

Johnston, D, *Prescription and Limitation* (W Green, Edinburgh 1999)
Johnston, D and Zimmermann, R (eds), *Unjustified Enrichment:
  Key Issues in Comparative Perspective* (CUP, Cambridge 2002)

Keane, R, *Company Law* (3rd ed Butterworths, Dublin 2000)
Kennedy, W R, *Kennedy's Law of Salvage* (5th ed Stevens & Sons, London 1985)

Lynch, I, Marshall, J and O'Farrell, R, *Corporate Insolvency and Rescue: Law and Practice* (Butterworths, Dublin 1996)

MacCormick, Sir N, *Institutions of Law: An Essay in Legal Theory* (OUP, Oxford 2007)

Macdonald, D R, *Succession* (3rd ed W Green, Edinburgh 2001)

MacQueen, H L (ed), *Scots Law into the Twenty First Century: Essays in Honour of W A Wilson* (W Green, Edinburgh 1996)

MacQueen, H L, *Unjustified Enrichment* (W Green, Edinburgh 2004)

MacQueen, H L and Thomson, J, *Contract Law in Scotland* (2nd ed, Tottel, Edinburgh 2007)

MacQueen, H L, Vaquer, A and Espiau, S E (eds), *Regional Private Laws and Codification in Europe* (CUP, Cambridge 2003)

MacQueen, H L and Zimmermann, R (eds), *European Contract Law* (Edinburgh Studies in Law, Edinburgh University Press, Edinburgh 2006)

Maitland, F W, *Equity: A Course of Lectures* (Chaytor and Whittaker (eds), Brunyate (rev)) (2nd ed CUP, Cambridge 1969)

Markesinis, B S and Munday, R J C, *An Outline of the Law of Agency* (4th ed Butterworths, London 1998)

Maxwell, P B, *On the Interpretation of Statutes* (11th ed Blackwell Publishing on behalf of the Modern Law Review, 1962)

Meagher, R P, Heydon J D and Leeming, M J, *Meagher, Gummow and Lehane's Equity: Doctrines and Remedies* (4th ed Butterworths, Australia 2002)

McBryde, W W, *The Law of Contract in Scotland* (3rd ed W Green, Edinburgh 2007)

McBryde, WW, *The Law of Bankruptcy in Scotland* (2nd ed W Green, Edinburgh 1995)

McCormack, G, *Reservation of Title Clauses* (2nd ed Sweet & Maxwell, London 1995)

McGhee, J (ed), *Snell's Equity* (31st ed Sweet & Maxwell, London 2005)

McKenzie Skene, D W, *Insolvency Law in Scotland* (T & T Clark, Edinburgh 1999)

McMahon, B & Binchy, W, *Irish Law of Torts* (2nd ed Butterworths, Dublin 1990)

Miles, R, *Blackstone's Sale & Supply of Goods & Services* (Blackstone Press, London 2001)

Neocleous, A & Co, *The Introduction to Cyprus Law* (Yorkhill Law Publishing, Salzburg 2000)

Nicholas, B, *An Introduction to Roman Law* (Clarendon, Oxford 1962)

North, Sir P M and Fawcett, J J, *Cheshire and North's Private International Law* (13th ed LexisNexis UK, London 1999)

Palmer, V V (ed), *Mixed Jurisdictions Worldwide: The Third Legal Family*
(CUP, Cambridge 2001)

Palmer, N E, *Palmer on Bailment* (Law Book Company, Sydney 1979)

Palmer, N E, *Palmer on Bailment* (2nd ed Sweet & Maxwell, London 1991)

Palmer, N E, and McKendrick, E, (eds), *Interests in Goods*
(2nd ed LLP, London and Hong Kong 1998)

Pearce, R A and Stevens, J, *The Law of Trusts and Equitable Obligations*
(3rd ed Lexis Nexis Butterworths, London 2002)

Pikis, G M, *The English Common Law, the rules of equity and
their application in Cyprus* (1981)

Pollock, F & Mulla, D F, *Indian Contract and Specific Relief Acts*
(9th ed N M Tripathi, Bombay 1972)

Pollock, F & Wright, R S, *Essay on Possession in the Common Law*
(Clarendon Press, Oxford 1888)

Polyviou, P, *Cyprus: Conflict and Negotiations 1960-1980* (Holmes & Heir, 1980)

Polyviou, P, *Cyprus: in search of a constitution:
negotiations and proposals 1960-1975* (Holmes & Heir, 1976)

Pretto-Sakmann, A, *The Boundaries of Personal Property:
Shares and Sub-shares* (Hart Publishing, Oxford 2005)

Rankine, Sir J, *Personal Bar* (W Green, Edinburgh 1921)

Rankine, Sir J, *The Law of Land-ownership in Scotland*
(4th ed W Green, Edinburgh 1909)

Rainer, J M and Filip-Fröschl, J (eds), *Transfer of Title Concerning
Movables Part 1 – Eigentumsübertragung an beweglichen Sachen in Europa*
(Peter Lang, Frankfurt 2006)

Reid, E C and Blackie, J W G, *Personal Bar* (W Green, Edinburgh 2006)

Reid, K G C (with Gretton, G L, Duncan, A G M, Gordon,
W M and Gamble, A J), *The Law of Property in Scotland*
(Butterworths/Law Society of Scotland, Edinburgh 1996)

Reid, K and Zimmermann, R (eds), *A History of Private Law in Scotland*, vols 1
(Introduction and Property) and 2 (Obligations) (OUP, Oxford 2000)

Reynolds, F M B and Bowstead, W, *Bowstead and Reynolds on Agency*
(17th ed Sweet & Maxwell, London 2001)

Rogers, W V H, *Winfield & Jolowicz on Tort*
(16th ed Sweet & Maxwell, London 2002)

Rogers, W V H, *Winfield & Jolowicz on Tort*
(17th ed Sweet & Maxwell, London 2006)

Rotherham, C, *Proprietary Remedies in Context*
(Hart Publishing, Oxford 2002)

Scobbie, E M, *Currie on Confirmation of Executors*
(8th ed W Green, Edinburgh 1995)

Sealy, L S and Hooley, R, *Commercial Law Text, Cases and Materials* (3rd ed Lexis Nexis, London 2004)

Sealy, L S and Milman, D, *Annotated Guide to the Insolvency Legislation 2006/2007* (9th ed Sweet & Maxwell, 2006)

St Clair, J B and the Hon Lord Drummond Young, *The Law of Corporate Insolvency in Scotland* (3rd ed W Green, Edinburgh 2004)

St German, C, *Doctor and Student* (91 Seldon Society, 1551)

Smith, Sir T B, *A Short Commentary on the Law of Scotland* (W Green, Edinburgh 1962)

Smith, Sir T B, *Property Problems in Sale* (Sweet & Maxwell, London 1978)

Smith, L D, *The Law of Tracing* (Clarendon Press, London 1997)

Smits, J (ed), *The Contribution of Mixed Legal Systems to European Private Law* (Intersentia, Antwerp 2001)

Snell, E H T, *Snell's Principles of Equity* (26th ed Sweet & Maxwell, London 1973)

Stair, Viscount J D, *Institutions of the Laws of Scotland* (2nd ed, ed D M Walker, University Presses of Edinburgh and Glasgow, 1693 republished Edinburgh 1981)

Steven, A J M, *Pledge and Lien* (Edinburgh Legal Education Trust, Edinburgh 2008)

Stone, R, *Law of Agency* (Cavendish Publishing, 1997)

Thomson, J M, *Delictual Liability* (3rd ed LexisNexis UK, Edinburgh 2004)

Thompson, M P, *Modern Land Law* (3rd ed OUP, Oxford 2006)

TMC Asser Instituut *The impact of EU accession on the legal order of new EU member states & (pre-) candidate countries: hopes & fears* (TMC Asser Press, The Hague 2006)

Treitel, G H, *The Law of Contract* (11th ed Sweet & Maxwell, London 2003)

Tyler, E L G and Palmer, N E, *Crossley Vaines on Personal Property* (5th ed Butterworths, London 1973)

van Maanen, G E and van der Walt, A J (eds), *Property Law on the Threshhold of the 21st Century* (Maklu, Antwerp 1996)

van Vliet, L P W, *Transfer of movables in German, French, English and Dutch law* (Ars Aequi Libri, Nijmegen 2000)

Virgo, G, *The Principles of the Law of Restitution* (Clarendon Press, Oxford 1999)

Virgo, G, *The Principles of the Law of Restitution* (2nd ed OUP, 2006)

Visser, D (ed), *The Limits of the Law of Obligations* (Juta, Kenwyn 1997)

White, F, *Commercial Law* (Thomson Roundhall, Dublin 2002)

Wilson, W A, *The Scottish Law of Debt* (2nd ed W Green, Edinburgh 1991)

Wilson, W A and Duncan, A G M, *Trusts, Trustees, and Executors* (2nd ed W Green, Edinburgh 1995)

Wood, R B, 'Leasing and Hire of Moveables' in *The Laws of Scotland:*
Stair Memorial Encyclopaedia (Lexis-Nexis Butterworths Scotland, ed N R
Whitty *et al*, Reissue Edinburgh 2001)
Worthington, S, *Personal Property Law: Text and Materials*
(Hart Publishing, Oxford 2000)
Worthington, S, *Proprietary Interests in Commercial Transactions*
(Clarendon Press, Oxford 1996)
Wylie, J M, *Irish Land Law* (3rd ed Butterworths, Dublin 1997)
Zimmermann, R, *The Law of Obligations* (Juta, Cape Town 1990)
Zimmermann, R, Visser, D and Reid, K (eds), *Mixed Legal Systems in*
Comparative Perspective: Property and Obligations in Scotland and South Africa
(OUP, Oxford 2004)

2. Articles

Ali, N, 'Developments in Fixed and Floating Charges: Legal Principles, Policy
Issues and Implications for Structured Financing', (2006) 13 (2) CLP 46
Anonymous, 'Victim of Its Success', 2007 JLSS July/56
Anderson, C, '*Bell v Inkersall Investments Ltd*', 2006 SLT (News) 221
Anderson, R G, '*Buchanan v Alba Diagnostics*: Accretion of Title and
Assignation of Future Patents', (2005) 9 Edinburgh Law Review 457
Anderson, R G, 'Offside Goals before Rodger Builders', 2005 Juridical Review 277
Anderson, R G, 'Fraud on Transfer and on Insolvency:
ta...ta...*tantum et tale*,' (2007) 11 Edinburgh Law Review 187
Antonio, D G, 'Some thoughts on *nova debita*', 1957 SLT (News) 13

Barak, A, 'The Nature of the Negotiable Instrument', (1983)
18 Israel Law Review 49
Battersby, G, 'A Reconsideration of "Property" and
"Title" in the Sale of Goods Act', [2001] JBL 1
Bell, J, 'The Place of Bailment in the Modern Law of Obligations', in:
Palmer and McKendrick (eds), *Interests in Goods* (2nd ed LLP, London 1998)
Bennett, H N, 'Attachment of Chattels to Land', in: Palmer and McKendrick
(eds), *Interests in Goods*, (2nd ed LLP, London 1998)
Birks, P, 'Mixtures', in: Palmer and McKendrick (eds), *Interests in Goods*
(2nd ed LLP, London 1998)
Borland, G C, 'Change of Position in Scots Law', 1996 SLT (News) 139
Bowes-Smith, E, and Hill, J, 'Joint Ownership of Chattels', in:
Palmer & McKendrick (eds), *Interests in Goods* (2nd ed LLP, London 1998)
Bradgate, R and White, F, 'Sale of Goods Forming Part of a Bulk: Proposals for
Reform', [1994] Lloyd's Maritime and Commercial Law Quarterly 315
Bradgate, R, 'Retention of Title in the House of Lords:
Unanswered Questions', (1991) 54 Modern Law Review 726

Breslin, J, 'Brumark Investments Ltd: Charges Over Book Debts,
    Divisibility of Assets, and the Role of Conduct in Interpretation of
    Contracts', (2001) 8 (9) CLP 207
Breslin, J and Smith, K, 'The House of Lords Decision in Spectrum Plus –
    the Implications for Irish Banking Law', (2005) 12 (9) CLP 228
Brown, R, 'Assimilation of the Law of Sale', 1891 Juridical Review 297
Burns, T, 'Better Late than Never: the Reform of the Law on the Sale of Goods
    Forming Part of a Bulk', (1996) 59 MLR 260

Calnan, R, 'Property, Security and Possession in Insolvency Law',
    (1997) 11 JIBFL 530
Campbell, N R, 'Case Comment: Passing of Property in Contracts for the
    Sale of Unascertained Goods', [1996] Journal of Business Law 199
Carey Miller, D L, 'Plausible Rogues: Contract and Property',
    (2005) 9 Edinburgh Law Review 150
Carey Miller, D L, 'Right to Annual Crops', (2007)
    11 Edinburgh Law Review 274
Carey Miller, D L, 'Title to Art: Developments in the USA', (1996)
    1 Scottish Law and Practice Quarterly 115
Carey Miller, D L, 'Title to Moveables: Mr Sharp's Porsche', (2003)
    7 Edinburgh Law Review 221
Carey Miller, D L and Combe, M M, 'The Boundaries of Property Rights in
    Scots Law', vol 10.3 EJCL, (December 2006)
Chalmers, J, 'In Defence of the Trusting Conveyancer',
    2002 SLT (News) 231
Crilley, D, 'A Case of Proprietary Overkill', [1994] RLR 57

De Lacy, J, 'The Anglocisation of Irish Retention of Title',
    [1990] Irish Law Times 279
Donnelly, C, 'From Possession to Ownership:
    An Analytical Study of the Declining Role of Possession in
    Scottish Property Law', 2006 Juridical Review 267
Donnelly, C, 'Reforming Personal Property Securities Law;
    Is there a Case for a Single Securities Register?', (2000) 7 (1) DULJ 50
du Plessis, J, 'The promises and pitfalls of mixed legal systems: the South African
    and Scottish experiences', (1998) 3 Stellenbosch Law Review 338

Eliades, T, 'Assignments of Choses in Action', (1978)
    4/6 Kypriako Nomiko Bima 6-14
Evans-Jones, R and Hellwege, P, 'Taxonomy of Unjustified Enrichment in
    Scots Law', (1998) 2 Edinburgh Law Review 180

Farran, S and Cabrelli, D, 'Exploring the Interfaces between
    Contract Law and Property Law: A UK Comparative Approach', (2006)
    13 Maastricht Journal of European and Comparative Law 403
Farrar, J H and Chai, C K, 'Romalpa Revisited Again', [1985]
    Journal of Business Law 160
Forte, A D M, 'Finance leases and implied terms of quality and fitness:
    a retrospective and prospective review', 1995 Juridical Review 119
Fox, D, 'Bona Fide Purchase and the Currency of Money', [1996] CLJ 547
Fox, D, 'Relativity of Title at Law and Equity', [2006] CLJ 330

Goode, Sir R M, 'Ownership and Obligation in Commercial Transactions',
    103 [1987] LQR 433
Goode, Sir R M, 'The Modernization of Personal Security Law',
    (1984) 100 LQR 234
Goodhart, H L and Hamson, C J, 'Undisclosed principles in contracts',
    (1932) 4 CLJ 320
Goodhart, W and Jones, G, 'The Infiltration of Equitable Doctrine
    into English Commercial Law', (1980) 43 MLR 489
Gordon, W M, 'The Wrongs and Rights of Vesting', 1987 JLSS 218
Gray, K, 'Property in Thin Air', [1991] CLJ 252
Gregory, R, 'Romalpa Clauses as Unregistered Charges –
    A Fundamental Shift?', (1990) 106 LQR 551
Gretton, G L, 'Constructive Trusts', (1997)
    1 Edinburgh Law Review 281 and 408
Gretton, G L, 'Ownership and Insolvency: *Burnett's Tr v Grainger*',
    (2004) 8 Edinburgh Law Review 389
Gretton, G L, 'Private Law and Human Rights' (2008)
    12 Edinburgh Law Review 109
Gretton, G L, 'Trusts Without Equity', 1999 ICLQ 599
Gretton, G L, 'Using Trusts as Commercial Securities', 1988 JLSS 53
Gretton, G L, 'What is Vesting?', 1986 JLSS 148
Gretton, G L and Reid, K G C, 'Romalpa clauses; the current position',
    1985 SLT (News) 329

Haley, M, 'The Law of Fixtures: an Unprincipled Metamorphosis',
    [1998] Conv 137
Halson, R, 'Rescission for Misrepresentation', [1997] RLR 89
Hanbury, H G, 'The Future of Equity', (1987) 93 LQR 529
Hansmann, H, and Kraakman, R, 'Property, Contract and Verification:
    The Numerus Clausus Problem and the Divisibility of Rights', Harvard Law
    School Public Law Research Paper 037, at http://www.ssrn.com/lsn/index.html
Harris, D R, 'The Concept of Possession in English Law', in: Guest (ed),
    Oxford Essays in Jurisprudence (OUP, Oxford 1961)

Hellwege, P, 'The Scope of Application of Change of Position in the
    Law of Unjust Enrichment: A Comparative Study', [1999] RLR 92
Honoré, A M, 'Ownership', in: Guest (ed),
    Oxford Essays in Jurisprudence (OUP, Oxford 1961)
Hudson, A H, 'Abandonment', in: Palmer & McKendrick (eds),
    Interests in Goods (2nd ed LLP, London 1998)
Hudson, A H, 'Is Divesting Abandonment Possible at Common Law?',
    (1984) 100 LQR 110
James, A, 'The making of the Cyprus settlement 1958-60',
    (1998) 10(2) Cyprus Review 11
Jones, G, 'Retention of Title Clauses: Ten Years from Romalpa',
    (1986) 7 Co. Law. 233

Keay, A, 'Preferences in Liquidation Law: Time for a Change', [1998]
    Company Financial and Insolvency Law Review 198

MacFarlane, B, 'Identifying Property Rights: A Reply to Mr Watt', [2003]
    Conveyancer and Property Lawyer 473
MacQueen, H L, 'Mixture or Muddle? – Teaching and Research in
    Scottish Legal History', (1997) 5 Zeitschrift für Europäisches Privatrecht 369
MacQueen, H L, 'Scots Law News', (2006) 10 Edinburgh Law Review 1
MacQueen, H L, 'Patents Revoked', Scots Law News 598, available at
    http://www.law.ed.ac.uk/sln/blogentry.aspx?blogentryref=6871
Maher, G, 'The Rights and Wrongs of Vesting', (1986) 31 JLSS 396
Mance, J, 'The Operation of an 'All Debts' Reservation of Title Clause',
    [1992] LMCLQ 35
McBryde, W W, 'Promises in Scots Law', (1993) 42 ICLQ 48
McKendrick, E, 'Restitution and the Misuse of Chattels –
    The Need for a Principled Approach', in: Palmer & McKendrick (eds),
    Interests in Goods (2nd ed LLP, London 1998)
McKendrick, E, 'The Passing of Property in Part of a Bulk, in Interests in Goods',
    in: Palmer & McKendrick (eds), *Interests in Goods* (2nd ed LLP, London 1998)
McKnight, A, 'A Review of the Developments in English Case
    Law During 2003 – Part 1', [2004] Journal of International
    Banking Law and Regulations 97
McKnight, A, 'A Review of the Developments in English Case Law
    During 2004 – Part 2', [2005] Journal of International Banking Law
    and Regulations 154
McKnight, A, 'Restrictions on Dealing with Assets in
    Financing Documents: Their Role, Meaning and Effect',
    [2002] Journal of International Banking Law 193
McMeel, G, 'The Redundancy of Bailment', [2003] LMCLQ 169
Merrill, T and Smith, H, 'Optimal Standardisation in the Law of Property:
    The Numerus Clausus Principle', 110 Yale Law Journal (2000)

Murray, J, 'Reform of Security over Moveable Property', 1995 SLT (News) 31

Nolan, R C, 'Equitable Property', (2006) 122 LQR 232

O'Donnell, D and Carey Miller, D L, 'Security over Moveables:
    A Longstanding Reform Agenda in Scots Law', (1997) 5 ZEuP 807
Ogowewo, T, 'When is a Cow not a Cow? Loss of Title and Retention of
    Title Clauses', [1996] ICCLR (No. 12) Analysis Section
P F, 'Case and Comment: In pari causa melior est conditio possidentis?',
    1985 Juridical Review 138
Paisley, R R M, 'Dogmatic rigidity', (2005) 9 Edinburgh Law Review 267
Patrick, H, 'Reform of Security over Moveable Property:
    Some General Comments', 1995 SLT (News) 42
Patrick, H, 'What is a Real Right in Scots Law?', 1988 JLSS 98
Pawlowski, M, 'The Forfeiture of Possessory Rights in Land and Chattels',
    (1999) 21 Liverpool Law Review 77
Pretto, A, 'Comparative Personal Property: The Case of Shares',
    (2001) 1(1) Global Jurist Advances, Article 2 cited at
    http://www.bepress.com/gj/advances/vol1/iss1/art2/ accessed on 14/12/2006

Reid, E, 'Personal bar: case-law in search of analysis',
    (2003) 7 Edinburgh Law Review 340
Reid, K G C, 'Obligations and property: exploring the border',
    1997 Acta Juridica 225
Reid, K G C, 'The Idea of Mixed Legal Systems', (2003) 78 Tulane Law Review 5
Reid, K G C, 'Trusts and Floating Charges', 1987 SLT (News) 113
Reid, K G C, 'Unjustified Enrichment and Property Law',
    1994 Juridical Review 167
Reid, K G C and Gretton, G L, 'Retention of title in Romalpa clauses',
    1983 Scots Law Times (News) 77
Reid, K G C and Gretton, G L, 'Retention of title for all sums: a reply',
    1983 Scots Law Times (News) 165
Reynolds, F M B, 'Practical Problems of the Undisclosed Principal Doctrine',
    [1983] CLP 119
Lord Rodger of Earlsferry, 'Spuilzie in the Modern World', 1970 SLT (News) 33
Lord Rodger of Earlsferry, 'The Codification of Commercial Law in Britain',
    (1992) 108 LQR 570

Sealy, L, '"Risk" In the Law of Sale', [1972] CLJ 225
Smith, Sir T B, 'Retention of title: Lord Watson's legacy',
    1983 Scots Law Times (News) 105
Steven, A J M, 'By the Book: Enrichment by Interference',
    (2007) 11 Edinburgh Law Review 411
Steven, A J M, 'Property Law and Human Rights', 2005 Juridical Review 293

Steven, A J M, 'Recompense for Interference in Scots Law',
    1996 Juridical Review 51
Steven, A J M, 'Reform of Security over Moveable Property:
    Some Further Thoughts', 1995 SLT (News) 120
Steven, A J M and Wortley, S, 'The Perils of a Trusting Disposition',
    1996 SLT (News) 365
Styles, S C, 'Debtor-to-creditor sales and the Sale of Goods Act 1979',
    1995 Juridical Review 365
Sutherland, E E, 'Remedying an Evil? Warrandice of Quality at
    Common Law in Scotland', 1987 Juridical Review 24
Sutherland, R, 'The implied term as to fitness in contracts of hiring',
    1975 Juridical Review 133
Swadling, W J, 'Rescission, Property and the Common Law', (2005) 121 LQR 123
Swadling, W J, 'The Proprietary Effect of a Hire of Goods', in:
    Palmer & McKendrick, *Interests in Goods* (2nd ed LLP, London 1998)

Ulph, J, 'The Sale of Goods (Amendment) Act 1995: Co-ownership and the
    Rogue Seller', [1996] Lloyd's Maritime and Commercial Law Quarterly 93

van Erp, S, 'A Numerus Quasi-Clausus of Property Rights as a Constitutive
    Element of a Future European Property Law?', EJCL, Vol 7.2 (June 2003)
van Vliet, L P W, '*Michael Gerson (Leasing) Ltd v Wilkinson*:
    A Comparative Analysis', (2001) 5 Edinburgh Law Review 361
van Vliet, L P W, 'Accession of Movables to Land: I and II',
    (2002) 6 Edinburgh Law Review 67 and 199
van Vliet, L P W, 'The Transfer of Moveables in England and Scotland'
    (2008) 12 Edinburgh Law Review 173

Watt, G, 'The Proprietary Effect of a Chattel Lease',
    [2003] Conveyancer and Property Lawyer 61
Webb, D, 'Title and Transformation: Who Owns Manufactured Goods?',
    [2000] Journal of Business Law 513
Whitty, N R, 'Indirect Enrichment in Scots Law', 1994 Juridical Review 200
Whitty, N R, 'Rights of Personality, Property Rights and the Human Body in
    Scots Law', (2005) 9 Edinburgh Law Review 194
Whitty, N R, 'The Civilian Tradition and Debates on Scots Law',
    1996 Tydskryf vir die Suid-Afrikaanse Reg 227 and 442
Wortley, S, 'Squaring the Circle: Revisiting the Receiver and
    'Effectually Executed Diligence', 2000 Juridical Review 325
Wilson, W A, 'Romalpa and Trust', 1983 Scots Law Times (News) 106
Wood, R B, 'Sale and lease-back', (1982) 27 Journal of the
    Law Society of Scotland (Workshop) 267

3. Other papers

Carr, D, *Possession in Scots Law: Selected Themes*
(Unpublished University of Edinburgh MSc Thesis, 2005)

Company Law Review Group First Report (2000-2001) available at
http://www.clrg.org/_fileupload/1streport/clrg_master.pdf

Cork, Sir K, 'Insolvency Law and Practice: Report of the Review Committee'
(Cmnd 8558, 1982 HMSO)

Department of Trade and Industry Consultation Paper,
'Security over Moveable Property in Scotland', November 1994

Diamond, A L, Review of Security Interests in Property (HMSO, London 1989)

Eighth Report of the Law Reform Committee for Scotland, (1960, Cmnd 1017)

Law Commission Consultation Paper 164, 'Registration of
Security Interests: Company Charges and Property Other than Land'
(The Stationery Office, 2002)

Law Commission Report, 'Sale of Goods Forming Part of a Bulk',
(Law Com No 215; Scot Law Com No 145, HC 807, 1993)

Law Reform Commission, 'Report on Debt Collection (2)
Retention of Title' (LRC 28, Dublin 1989)

Law Reform Commission, 'Report on Aggravated,
Exemplary and Restitutionary Damages'(LRC 60, Dublin, 2000)

Report of the Crowther Committee on Consumer Credit (Cmnd 4596, 1971)

Scottish Executive Central Research Unit,
'Business Finance and Security over Moveable Property' (2002)

Scottish Law Commission, Consultative Memorandum No 30,
'Corporeal Moveables: Usucapion or Acquisitive Prescription', (1976)

Scottish Law Commission, 'Report on the Legal Capacity and
Responsibility of Minors and Pupils', (Scot Law Com No 110, 1987)

Scottish Law Commission, 'Recovery of Benefits Conferred under
Error of Law', (Scot Law Com Discussion Paper No 95, 1993)

Scottish Law Commission, 'Discussion Paper on the Nature and the
Constitution of Trusts', (Scot Law Com Disc Paper No 133, 2006)

Twelfth Report of the Law Reform Committee,
'Transfer of Title to Chattels', Cmnd 2958 (1966)

4.   Internet sources

http://www.mcw.gov.cy/mcw/mcw.nsf/dmlshipping_en/dmlshipping_en?
OpenDocument accessed on 7/12/2006

http://www.shipping.gov.cy/ accessed on 7/12/2006

http://www.shipping.gov.cy/guide_to_shipreg/provisional_reg.htm
accessed on 8/12/2006

http://www.shipping.gov.cy/guide_to_shipreg/parallel_reg.htm
accessed on 8/12/2006

http://www.neocleous.com/assets/mainmenu/744/editor/Cyprus.pdf
accessed on 15/12/2006

Table of Abbreviations

AC	Appeal Cases – Law Reports
ACLC	Australian Company Law Cases (CCH) 1982-
affd	affirmed
ALJ	Australian Law Journal
ALJR	Australian Law Journal Reports (LBC)
All ER	All England Law Reports
ALR	Australian Law Reports 1973-
App Cas	Appeal Cases 1875-90
art	article
B & Ad	Barnewall and Adolphus' King's Bench Reports 1830-1834
B & Ald	Barnewall and Alderson's King's Bench Reports 1817-1822
B & S	Best & Smith's Queen's Bench Law Reports 1861-1865
BCC	British Company Law Cases 1983-
BCLC	Butterworths Company Law Cases 1983-
Beav	Beavan's Rolls Court Reports 1838-1866
Bell's App	Bell's House of Lords Appeal Cases (Scot) (1842-50)
Bing	Bingham's Common Pleas Reports 1822-1834
Bing NC	Bingham, New Cases, English Common Pleas 1834-1840
Burr	Burrow's King's Bench Reports tempore Mansfield 1757-1771
CA	Court of Appeal Reports, by Johnston (NZ) 1867-1877
Cal	Calthrop's Customs and Liberties of London
Camp	Campbell's Nisi Prius Reports 1808-1816
Cap	Chapter of the Laws of Cyprus
CB	Common Bench Reports by Manning, Granger & Scott, 1845-1856
CB(NS)	Common Bench Reports by Manning Granger & Scott, New Series 1856-1865
CC	County Council
cf	compare
Ch	English Law Reports, Chancery Division 1891-
Ch App	Law Reports, Chancery Appeals 1865-1875
ChD	Law Reports, Chancery Division 1876-1890
CJ	Chief Justice
CL	Current Law
CLJ	Cambridge Law Journal

CLP	Current Legal Problems
CLR	Commonwealth Law Reports (Australia);
	Cyprus Law Reports
Cmnd	Command Paper
Co Law	Company lawyer
Co Rep	Coke's King's Bench Reports 1572-1616
Comp L	The Company Lawyer
Conv	Conveyancer and Property Lawyer
Corn LR	Cornell Law Review
CP	Law Reports, Common Pleas 1865-1875
CPD	Law Reports, Common Pleas Division 1875-1880
Cr & Ph	Craig and Phillips' Chancery Reports 1840-1841
Cr App R	Criminal Appeal Reports 1908-
Cr M & R	Crompton, Meeson and Roscoe's
CSOH	Outer House of the Court of Session (a single judge)
CUP	Cambridge University Press
D	Digesta; Dunlop Bell & Murray's Reports, Session Cases, Second Series (Scotland) 1838-1862
Dears & B	Dearsly and Bell's Crown Cases Reserved 1856-1858
Dears CC	Dearsly's Crown Cases Reserved 1856-1858
De G & J	De Gex and Jones' Chancery Reports 1857-1859
Den	Denison and Pearce's Crown Cases Reserved 1844-1852
Dick	Dicken's Chancery Reports 1599-1798
DLR	Directors Law Reporter
DULJ	Dublin University Law Journal
E & B	Ellis & Blackburn's Queen's Bench Reports 1851-1858
EB & E	Ellis, Blackburn & Ellis' Queen's Bench reports [ER 120]
EC	European Community
ECDR	European Copyright and Design Reports
e.g.	exempli gratia (for example)
EGLR	Estates Gazette Law Reports
EJCL	Electronic Journal of Comparative Law
El & B	Ellis & Blackburn's Queen's Bench Reports 1851-1858
Eq Ca Abr	Equity Cases Abridged 1667-1744
ER	English Reports 1210-1865
et seq.	et sequens/et sequentia (and the following one/ones)
etc.	et cetera
EWCA Civ	Court of Appeal (Civil Division)
EWHC	High Court
Ex	Law Reports, Exchequer Reports 1847-1880
Ex D	Law Reports, Exchequer Division 1875-1880
Exch	Exchequer Reports

F	Fraser, Session Cases, 5th Series (Scotland) 1898-1906
F & F	Foster and Finlason's Nisi Prius Reports 1858-1867
GWD	Green's Weekly Digest
H & C	Hurlstone and Coltman's Exchequer Reports 1862-1866
H & N	Hurlstone & Norman's Exchequer Reports 1856-1862
HC	House of Commons
High Ct	High Court
HL Cas	Clark's House of Lords Cases 1847-1866
HLC	Clark's House of Lords Cases 1847-1866
HMSO	Her Majesty's Stationery Office
Hume's Dec	Hume's Decisions, Court of Session (Scotland) 1781-1822
IA	Law Reports, Indian Appeals
i.a.	inter alia (among other things)
i.e.	id est (that is)
ibid.	ibidem (in the same place)
ICCLR	International Company and Commercial Law Review
ICLQ	International and Comparative Law Quarterly
ILT Jo	Irish Law Times Journal
ILRM	Irish Law Reports Monthly 1981-
ILTR	Irish Law Times Reports (Ireland) 1867-
IR	Irish Reports 1894-
Ir Ch R	Irish Chancery Reports, 2nd Series 1850-1866
Ir CLR	Irish Reports Common Law Series, 2nd Series 1850-1866
Ir Jur Rep	Irish Jurist Reports
Israel L Rev	Israel Law Review
J	Justice
JBL	Journal of Business Law
JIBFL	Butterworths Journal of International Banking and Financial Law
JLSS	Journal of the Law Society of Scotland
JIBL	Journal of International Banking Law
Johns & Hem	Johnson & Hemming
JSC	Judgments of the Supreme Court
KB	King's Bench
Kilk	Kilkerran's Court of Session Decisions (Scotland) 1738-1752
Law Com	Law Commission
Law ed	United States Supreme Court Reports Annotated
LC	Lord Chancellor

LCJ	Lord Chief Justice
Ld Raym	Lord Raymond's King's Bench Reports 1694-1732
LJ	Law Journal
LJ	Lord Justice
LJKB	Law Journal Reports, King's Bench, New Series 1831-1946
LJQB	Law Journal Reports, New Series, Queen's Bench 1831-1946
Lloyd's Rep	Lloyd's Law Reports 1968-
LLP	Lloyd's of London Press
LLR	Liberian Law Reports
LMCLQ	Lloyd's Maritime and Commercial Law Quarterly
LQR	Law Quarterly Review
LR	Law Reports 1865-
LR Ir	Law Reports (Ireland) 1878-1893
LRC	Law Reports of the Commonwealth
LS	Legal Studies
LT	Law Times Reports 1859-1947
Lush	Lushington's Admiralty Reports 1859-1862
M	Macpherson's Session Cases, 3rd Series (Scotland) 1862-1873
M & G	Maddock & Geldart's Reports
M & W	Meeson and Welsby's Exchequer Reports 1836-1847
Macq	Macqueen's Scotch Appeal Cases 1851-1865
MLR	Modern Law Review
Mod Rep	Modern Reports 1669-1755
Mor	Morison's Dictionary of Decisions (Scotland) 1540-1808
MR	Master of the Rolls
My & Cr	Mylne & Craig's Chancery Reports
My & K	Mylne & Keen's Chancery Reports 1832-5
n	note
No	Number
NSWLR	New South Wales Law Reports (LBC) 1971-
NZLR	New Zealand Law Review (continues NZRL Rev)
op cit	opus citatum / opere citato
OUP	Oxford University Press
P	Law Reports, Probate, Divorce and Admiralty Division 1891-
p	page
para	paragraph
paras	paragraphs
Pat	Paton's Scotch Appeals, House of Lords 1726-1821
Peake Add Cas	Peake's Additional Cases 1795-1812
PC	Privy Council

Ph	Phillips' Chancery Reports 1841-1849
pp	pages
Prec Ch	Precedents in Chancery 1689-1722
QB	Law Reports, Queen's Bench 1891-1901 1952-
QBD	Law Reports, Queen's Bench Division 1875-1890
R	Rettie's Session Cases, 4th Series (Scotland) 1873-1898
r	rule
reg	regulation
RLR	Restitution Law Review
S	Shaw's Session Cases (Scotland) 1st series 1821-1838
s.	section
SA	South African Law Reports
SC	Court of Session Cases (Scotland) 1907-
SC (HL)	Court of Session Cases, House of Lords (Scotland) 1907-
SCCR	Scottish Criminal Case Reports
Sch	Schedule
SCLR	Scottish Civil Law Reports
Scot Law Com	Scottish Law Commission
Scot Law Com Disc Paper	Scottish Law Commission Discussion Paper
Sh Ct	Sheriff Court
Sh Ct Rep	Sheriff Court Reports (Scotland) 1885-1963
SI	Statutory Instrument
Sid	Siderfin's King's Bench Reports 1657-1670
SJ	Solicitors' Journal
SLC	Scottish Law Commission
SLPQ	Scottish Law and Practice Quarterly
SLT	Scots Law Times
SLT (News)	Scots Law Times (News Section)
ss.	sections
Stair Soc	Stair Society Publications
Stra	Strange's King's Bench Reports 1716-1749
Str Ev Cas	Strange's Cases of Evidence 1698-1752
Taunt	Taunton's Common Pleas Reports 1809-1819
TLR	The Times Law Reports 1884-1952
TR	Durnford & East's Term Reports 1785-1800
UKHL	United Kingdom House of Lords
US	United States Supreme Court Reports (Official Series)

VC	Vice-Chancellor
Ves Jr	Vesey Junior 1789-1817
Ves Sen	Vesey Senior's Chancery Reports 1747-1756
Vol	volume

| WL | Wellington District Law Society Library |
| WLR | Weekly Law Reports 1953- |

| ZEuP | Zeitschrift für Europäisches Privatrecht |

Schriften zur Europäischen Rechtswissenschaft /
European Legal Studies / Etudes juridiques européenes

Band / Volume 1:
Andreas Fötschl, Hilfeleistungsabreden und contrat d'assistance.
Eine rechtsvergleichende Untersuchung zum französischen, deutschen,
österreichischen und englischen Recht. 2005. ISBN 978-3-935808-56-9

Band / Volume 2:
Hanna Sivesand, The Buyer's Remedies For Non-Conforming Goods.
Should there be Free Choice or are Restrictions Necessary? 2005.
ISBN 978-3-935808-75-0

Band / Volume 3:
Christoph Jeloschek, Examination and Notification Duties in Consumer
Sales Law. How far should we go in protecting the consumer? 2006.
ISBN 978-3-935808-88-0

Band / Volume 4:
Matthias Ruffert, The Transformation of Administrative Law in Europe –
La mutation du droit administratif en Europe. 2007.
ISBN 978-3-935808-91-0

Band / Volume 5:
Olha Cherednychenko, Fundamental Rights, Contract Law and the
Protection of the Weaker Party. A Comparative Analysis of the
Constitutionalisation of Contract Law, with Emphasis on Risky
Financial Transactions. 2007. ISBN 978-3-86653-043-0

Band / Volume 6:
Wolfgang Faber / Brigitta Lurger (Eds.), Rules for the Transfer of Movables.
A Candidate for European Harmonisation or National Reforms? 2008.
ISBN 978-3-86653-060-7

Band / Volume 7:
Wolfgang Faber / Brigitta Lurger (Eds.), National Reports on the Transfer of
Movables in Europe. Volume 1: Austria, Estonia, Italy, Slovenia. 2008.
ISBN 978-3-86653-073-7

Band / Volume 8:
Odavia Bueno Díaz, Franchising in European Contract Law. A comparison between the main obligations of the contracting parties in the Principles of European Law on Commercial Agency, Franchise and Distribution Contracts (PEL CAFDC), French and Spanish law. 2008. ISBN 978-3-86653-075-1

Band / Volume 9:
Paraskevi Paparseniou, Griechisches Verbrauchervertragsrecht. Eine Untersuchung vor dem Hintergrund des Gemeinschaftsprivatrechts. 2008. ISBN 978-3-86653-049-2

Band / Volume 10:
Carsten Stölting, Vertragsergänzung und implied terms. Eine rechtsvergleichende Untersuchung des deutschen und englischen Rechts. 2009. ISBN 978-3-86653-093-5

Band / Volume 11:
Wolfgang Faber / Brigitta Lurger (Eds.), National Reports on the Transfer of Movables in Europe. Volume 2: England and Wales, Ireland, Scotland, Cyprus. 2009. ISBN 978-3-86653-096-6